ILLUMINATING SOCIAL LIFE

FIFTH EDITION

Titles of Related Interest From Pine Forge Press

Key Ideas in Sociology, Third Edition, by Peter Kivisto

Sociological Theory in the Classical Era: Text and Readings, Second Edition, by Laura D. Edles and Scott A. Appelrouth

The Social Theory of W.E.B. DuBois, edited by Phil Zuckerman

Sociological Theory, by Bert N. Adams and R. A. Sydie

Classical Sociological Theory, by Bert N. Adams and R. A. Sydie

Contemporary Sociological Theory, by Bert N. Adams and R. A. Sydie

The Globalization of Nothing, Second Edition, by George Ritzer

Enchanting a Disenchanted World, Third Edition, by George Ritzer

McDonaldization: The Reader, Third Edition, edited by George Ritzer

Second Thoughts: Seeing Conventional Wisdom Through the Sociological Eye, Fourth Edition, by Janet M. Ruane and Karen A. Cerulo

Development and Social Change, Fourth Edition, by Phillip McMichael

Investigating the Social World, Fourth Edition, by Russell K. Schutt

Race, Ethnicity, Gender, and Class: The Sociology of Group Conflict and Change, Fifth Edition, by Joseph F. Healey

Diversity and Society: Race, Ethnicity, and Gender, Third Edition, by Joseph F. Healey

Race, Ethnicity, and Gender: Selected Readings, Second Edition, edited by Joseph F. Healey and Eileen O'Brien

The Production of Reality: Essays and Readings on Social Interaction, Fifth Edition, by Jodi O'Brien

Sociology: Exploring the Architecture of Everyday Life, Readings, Eighth Edition, edited by David M. Newman and Jodi O'Brien

ILLUMINATING SOCIAL LIFE

Classical and Contemporary Theory Revisited

FIFTH EDITION

PETER KIVISTO

Augustana College
University of Turku

⑤SAGE | PINE FORGE

Los Angeles | London | New Delhi
Singapore | Washington DC

For information:

Pine Forge Press
An Imprint of SAGE Publications, Inc.
2455 Teller Road
Thousand Oaks, California 91320
E-mail: order@sagepub.com

SAGE Publications Ltd.
1 Oliver's Yard
55 City Road
London EC1Y 1SP
United Kingdom

SAGE Publications India Pvt. Ltd.
B 1/I 1 Mohan Cooperative
 Industrial Area
Mathura Road, New Delhi 110 044
India

SAGE Publications
 Asia-Pacific Pte Ltd
33 Pekin Street #02-01
Far East Square
Singapore 048763

Printed in the United States of America

Library of Congress Cataloging-in-Publication Data

Illuminating social life : classical and contemporary theory revisited / editor, Peter Kivisto. — 5th ed.
    p. cm.
Includes bibliographical references and index.
ISBN 978-1-4129-7815-6 (pbk.)
    1. Sociology—Philosophy. 2. Sociology—History. 3. Social history—1970- I. Kivisto, Peter, 1948-

HM585.I44 2011
301.01—dc22   2010031674

This book is printed on acid-free paper.

10   11   12   13   14   10 9   8   7   6   5   4   3   2   1

Acquisitions Editor:	David Repetto
Editorial Assistant:	Maggie Stanley
Production Editor:	Catherine M. Chilton
Copy Editor:	Liann Lech
Typesetter:	C&M Digitals (P) Ltd.
Proofreader:	Eleni-Maria Georgiou
Indexer:	Julie Grayson
Cover Designer:	Gail Buschman
Marketing Manager:	Erica DeLuca

Contents

About the Editor

Peter Kivisto, PhD (New School for Social Research), is the Richard A. Swanson Professor of Social Thought and Chair of Sociology at Augustana College and Finland Distinguished Professor at the University of Turku, Finland. Among his recent books are *Key Ideas in Sociology* (3rd ed., 2011); *Social Theory: Roots and Branches* (4th ed., 2011); *Beyond a Border* (2010, with Thomas Faist); *Citizenship: Discourse, Theory, and Transnational Prospects* (2007, with Thomas Faist); *Intersecting Inequalities* (2007, with Elizabeth Hartung); and *Incorporating Diversity: Rethinking Assimilation in a Multicultural Age* (2005). His primary scholarly and teaching interests revolve around social theory and ethnic and immigration studies. He has served as secretary-treasurer of the American Sociological Association's Theory and International Migration Sections and is the immediate Past-Editor of *The Sociological Quarterly.* In 2010–2011, he served as the President of the Midwest Sociological Society.

Preface to the Fifth Edition

Since the first edition of *Illuminating Social Life* appeared in 1998, I have received many messages from students and professors alike, either telling me how much they appreciated the book or offering suggestions for new chapters in subsequent editions. The favorable assessments have been most gratifying, and all of the recommendations I have received have been taken very seriously in developing each subsequent edition. The current edition is no exception. The target audience for the book is as it always was intended: American undergraduates taking a required theory course as part of their sociology major or minor. All of the contributors to this collection and I have what we consider to be a good sense of that target audience, and we realize keenly how varied it actually is. Given the fact that the book continues to be widely used throughout the country, the evidence would seem to bear out our belief that we know our intended readers.

That being said, in recent years, I have become aware of the fact that *Illuminating Social Life* is also being read by sociologists and sociology students in other nations. Although it perhaps isn't so surprising that one can find the book in academic bookshops in Britain—where, in contrast to the United States, sociology sections continue to thrive—I have discovered that the book is also read in other places in Europe. Indeed, when I was invited not long ago to teach a theory course at Åbo Akademi University in Turku, Finland, my students—who included not only Finns, but also students from Germany and Italy—were already familiar with the book. A couple of years later, when I taught a similar course at Bielefeld University in Germany, I had a similar experience.

Given that many of the topics contained in the book can easily resonate with students from other advanced industrial nations, this interest is perhaps not particularly surprising. However, what was rather unexpected is the fact that this interest extends to students in developing nations as well. Paralleling my experience in Finland and Germany, when I was invited to be a Visiting Scholar at Huazhong University in Wuhan, China, several of the students in my class had read all or parts of an early edition of the book. Reinforcing the central themes raised by Anne Hornsby's chapter on the Internet, students from around the world have discovered how to find me. Some of them have been unable to afford

Illuminating Social Life, and their university libraries are operating with severely limited budgets. For that reason, they have contacted me and requested that I send them complimentary copies of either the current or earlier editions. In all instances, I have been more than willing to send a copy of the current version of *Illuminating* as a gift. During this past year, for example, students in Ethiopia, Ghana, Nigeria, China, and most recently Iran have been in touch with me. They have remained in contact with me after having read the book, offering their own commentaries and insights on or asking questions about the collection's various chapters. When this book was first planned a decade ago, I never envisioned that a global dialogue like this would have emerged. But I am pleased that it has, and have found these exchanges to be most rewarding.

Indeed, if any current student readers would like to contact me, I'll save you the trouble of Googling me and simply let you know that my email address is peterkivisto@augustana.edu. I can, of course, only afford to give away a limited number of books. For that reason, I would encourage students in the wealthier nations who have used the book to consider one of two possibilities: The first is that you can simply keep the book for your personal library. However, if you don't want to do so, the second choice is that you think about donating the book to a university library in a developing nation. There are several organizations that help to make this possible. I'll suggest one here: Book Aid International. Their Web site, www.bookaid.org, provides information about how to donate books through them and identifies a number of direct links to universities in various developing nations.

The fifth edition contains two new chapters—on race-based critical theory and on symbolic interaction. In the first of these, authors Douglas Hartmann and Joyce M. Bell provide an overview of new approaches to race that focus on the dominant and often invisible white race, leading to a critical analysis of the way white Americans talk about diversity. In the second, authors David Schweingruber and Nancy Berns explore the world of door-to-door sales from a long-established theoretical perspective that encourages ethnographic research. Other chapters have been updated where appropriate. Nowhere is this more evident than in Anne Hornsby's chapter on the Internet. Her substantive revision is intended to take account of changes in computer-mediated communication that have occurred during the past few years. Christopher Prendergast has produced a sustained new postscript that updates the earlier findings while encouraging readers to explore recent events in the troubled American automotive industry. Revision work is also evident in the chapters by William Staudenmeier, Steven Dandaneau, Judith Lorber and Patricia Yancey Martin, Anne Eisenberg, and William Swatos, Jr.

The Rationale for Illuminating Social Life

The purpose of this book is to illustrate the importance of sociological theory to students attempting to make sense of the world they inhabit. By applying various social theories from the past and the present to selected facets of modern life, the authors who have contributed to this collection of essays share a common purpose: to illustrate how different social theories are capable of providing significant understanding that would not be grasped without theory.

I have taught social theory for more than 25 years and am very aware of the trepidation with which many students approach this seemingly mysterious or irrelevant subject. Indeed, this book is a direct response to the ways that students react to theory. All the contributors are equally aware of this anxiety. Indeed, aside from our one coauthor who is now a lawyer, we have collectively amassed hundreds of years of experience teaching theory to thousands of undergraduates. Over the years, we have worked hard to get students at our respective home institutions to become comfortable with theorizing while at the same time attempting to convince them of the value of theory. From experience, we have learned that one especially effective way to accomplish these goals is by the application of particular theories to concrete examples from everyday life.

Undergraduate students frequently have a difficult time appreciating the relevance of sociological theory. They all too often fail to see the connection of their theory courses to the "substantive" courses in the departmental offerings. Instead, theory courses are seen either as excursions into the history of ideas or as exercises in overly abstract and arcane discourses that, they believe, can only be of interest to sociologists specializing in social theory. In short, students harbor suspicions about the value of social theory for them.

Although we can sympathize with this suspicion, all the contributors to this book are convinced that theory is essential for anybody trying to make sense of the swirling events and perplexing circumstances all of us encounter in our daily lives. In fact, it is fair to say that without realizing it, everyone is a social theorist. The philosopher of science N. R. Hanson (1958) thought that this was the case when he wrote that "all observation is a theory-laden activity" (p. 3). By this, he meant that everyone, not merely social theorists, looks at the world through a variety of implicit theoretical lenses. These lenses afford angles of vision that allow us to see and interpret, in novel ways, aspects of the social world.

There are, however, major differences between everyday uses of theory and the sociological uses of theory. By pointing out that in the former case, theories are generally implicit, whereas in the latter they are explicit, I mean to indicate that sociological theories are subjected to examination to determine whether they are coherent, logically consistent, and empirically supported. Everyday theories are simply taken-for-granted assumptions about aspects of the social world that can prove to be more or less helpful in going about the business of our daily lives. They are generally not scrutinized in a critical and reflective way. In contrast, sociological theories are constantly tested to determine if they are actually applicable in any inquiry into aspects of the social world. If they prove to be inapplicable—if they do not further our understanding of whatever it is we are studying—they are discarded. Numerous theories in sociology have proven themselves, over time, to be invaluable tools for advancing the sociological imagination and for helping us to make sense of the social conditions that frame our lives. The chapters assembled in this collection testify to this fact.

This book contains 14 chapters devoted to different theories. Part I contains four chapters that address aspects of the theories of the four scholars who are seen today as the most influential figures from the formative period in the history of sociology: Karl Marx, Max Weber, Émile Durkheim, and Georg Simmel. Part II examines 10 contemporary theoretical orientations or mixes that have had a profound impact on sociology in recent years. We make no claim to have included all the most influential contemporary theories; this would require a multivolume book. The theories on which we do focus include neofunctionalism, exchange theory and rational choice, critical theory, feminism, symbolic interactionism, dramaturgy, postmodernism, and globalization theory. Both parts of the book begin with a brief introduction that can serve to outline the general contours of the approaches taken by particular theorists and theory schools.

I stress that this book is not necessarily meant to be a substitute either for reading theorists in their own words or for more conventional social theory texts that survey the discipline in much greater detail. Rather, it is also meant to function as a supplemental text that can be profitably used in conjunction with other readings. All the authors hope that by provoking and stimulating readers with engaging illustrative cases, many students will want to delve more deeply into social theory—and that they will do so without suffering from theory anxiety.

In preparing the manuscript for publication, I benefited from the input of a variety of people. First and foremost, I thank all the scholars who wrote chapters for the book. We have gotten to know one another rather well, despite the fact that a few of us have never met face-to-face. I suppose it might be said that we are an example of the cyberspace communities that Anne Hornsby writes about in her chapter on surfing the Net. George Ritzer needs to be singled out for thanks because his earlier work on McDonaldization served as a model for the rest of us. Moreover, I thank him for allowing me to pick up a project that he, in fact, had initiated. I owe a debt of gratitude to Bill Staudenmeier for long ago proposing the book's title.

Thanks to the following reviewers of earlier editions:

Stephen Adair, Central Connecticut State University

David Brown, Illinois State University

Ione Y. DeOllos, Ball State University

Patricia Fanning, Bridgewater State College

Thomas J. Fararo, University of Pittsburgh

Glenn A. Goodwin, Pitzer University

Jim Gramlich, University of Illinois at Chicago

John Hamlin, University of Minnesota, Duluth

Jay Howard, Indiana University–Purdue University, Columbus

Chien Ju Huang, North Carolina Central University

Lutz Kaelber, University of Vermont

Neil McLaughlin, McMaster University

Donald Nielsen, University of Wisconsin–Eau Claire

William I. Robinson, New Mexico State University

Andrew Perrin, University of North Carolina, Chapel Hill

Stuart Schoenfeld, York University

Ralph Pyle, Michigan State University

David Williamson, University of North Texas

Sally Raskoff, University of Southern California

Stephen Zehr, University of Southern Indiana

The following readers provided valuable commentary and suggestions that inform this edition:

Sarah Jane Brubaker, Virginia Commonwealth University

Diane Kayongo-Male, South Dakota State University

David K. Brown, Illinois State University

Patricia Leavy, Stonehill College

Ione Y. DeOllos, Ball State University

Gerhard Schutte, University of Wisconsin–Parkside

Rebecca Kim, Pepperdine University

Daniel Egan, University of Massachusetts, Lowell

Kara Ann Zugman, California State University, Bakersfield

Close to home, I thank my secretary, Jean Sottos, for all the work she put into the preparation of several chapters. I also express my delight in having had the opportunity to coauthor a chapter with one of my former students, and a person with a bright future, Dan Pittman. At home, Sarah, Aaron, and Susan read and commented on one or more of the chapters and in other ways encouraged me along the way.

For the first two editions, Steve Rutter proved to be a creative and perceptive publisher. For the third edition, I extend a huge debt of gratitude to Jerry Westby. Jerry is a consummate pro who knows books and the publishing industry extremely well. I learned a lot working with him. He turned the fourth edition over to Ben Penner, a young but gifted editor. More recently, I have had the pleasure to get to know and work with Dave Repetto. He is a creative and energetic editor who has the savvy that comes from years of experience. During the past 2 years, I have worked on three book projects with Dave and have come to appreciate his always constructive, always supportive input. Other folks at Pine Forge assisted me in many ways, large and small, and to them I want to express my heartfelt appreciation.

Reference

Hanson, N. R. (1958). *Patterns of discovery.* Cambridge, UK: Cambridge University Press.

PART I

Classical Sociological Theory

Introduction

Peter Kivisto

Of all the many early figures in the history of sociology, four stand out as the most enduringly important: Karl Marx, Max Weber, Émile Durkheim, and Georg Simmel. In different ways, the members of this quartet both shaped the discipline during its formative period and continue to influence sociological thinking today. Although their respective understandings of modern society overlapped in many ways, each of these scholars nonetheless emphasized certain features of contemporary life at the expense of others. Each developed a distinctive theoretical approach that served to provide a novel way of interpreting facets of social life. The course of events since their deaths has proven time and time again that this foursome possessed remarkable insight into the nature and the dynamics of the modern age. Indeed, their insights are crucial to understanding recent social changes associated with the economic transformations brought about by advanced industrial capitalism, the cultural dynamics of modernity and postmodernity, and the political transformations under way as a result of globalization. None of the essays in Part I pretends to capture the fullness of any of the theorists under consideration. Rather, the authors have attempted to extract from the work important elements that can be treated on their own terms but manage at the same time to reveal something of the overall thrust of the particular theorist's intellectual legacy.

Chapter 1, by John P. Walsh and Anne Zacharias-Walsh, explores the contemporary relevance of a person who historically preceded the other three scholars:

Karl Marx (1818–1883). Unlike the others, Marx never held an academic appointment but instead lived his life as a revolutionary outsider. His ideas—or at least particular interpretations of his ideas—had a profound impact on the history of the 20th century, from the success of the Russian Revolution to the collapse of communism in the late 1980s.

Marx, in a unique synthesis of German philosophy, French political ideas, and British economics, sought to understand the dynamics of capitalism. Key to understanding Marx is a realization that he was not concerned with understanding industrial society in general, but rather with revealing the unique dynamics of capitalist industrialization. Indeed, the major sociological question he sought to answer was, How does capitalism work? In addressing this question, Marx also addressed three corollaries: (a) Is capitalism an economic system that necessarily exploits some classes in the interests of another class? (b) If it is exploitative, is a nonexploitative industrial system possible? and (c) If a nonexploitative system is possible, how can it come about?

Marx thought that capitalism, being driven by the quest for profits, necessarily placed that quest above the quest for a just, humane, and equitable society. His writings are an attempt not only to claim that capitalism inevitably exploits the working class, but also to show why and how this is so. These questions were the ones that most preoccupied him. Marx wrote far less about the alternatives, in part because he had a decided aversion to utopian dreamers. Thus, although Marx thought that a nonexploitative system—which he called socialism or communism—was possible, he had far less to say about what this type of economy would look like and how it would be established than he did about the character of existing capitalism.

What the chapter by Walsh and Zacharias-Walsh illustrates is that today, during a major transformation in the economy, key elements from the core of Marx's analysis of the dynamics of capitalism are as relevant as they were in the 19th century. Specifically, the authors seek to illustrate by using concrete examples of recent labor struggles that contemporary capitalism does not differ from its earlier manifestations insofar as it continues to be based on the systematic exploitation of workers.

In Chapter 2, George Ritzer explores and updates one of the central theoretical concerns of the great German social thinker Max Weber (1864–1920): his theory of the rationalization of modern life. Weber was one of the most important academics responsible for the development of sociology in Germany. The scope of topics he studied was encyclopedic. Thus, he wrote about economics, politics, culture, and religion. Within these arenas, his interests were equally far ranging. In economics, for example, he wrote about the agrarian economies of the ancient world as well as about current events, such as the emergence of a socialist economy in revolutionary Russia after World War I. In perhaps his most famous and provocative thesis, on the relationship between what he called the "Protestant ethic" and the "spirit of capitalism," Weber argued that there was an "elective affinity" between Protestant theology and the worldview of capitalism, and this affinity served to account for the fact that capitalism arose in countries where the Protestant Reformation had proven to be successful.

No matter how controversial this thesis would subsequently prove itself to be, what is clear from his argument is that Weber thought that the various institutional spheres that make up society are interconnected. This is certainly the case in his discussion of the topic of central concern to Ritzer: rationalization. Weber thought that a rational, scientific worldview increasingly came to characterize the modern age, with its emphasis on reason. When applied to a capitalist economy, rationalization entailed, as Ritzer notes, such features as predictability, calculability, efficiency, and control. All of these are employed by capitalist managers intent on increasing profitability and control over the market.

Weber was one of the great pessimists of his day, and he felt that the progressive advance of rationalization (and its subsidiary, bureaucratization) threatened our freedom. In perhaps the most widely quoted passage from his writings, he contended that our futures would come to resemble an "iron cage." Ritzer's article is an attempt to use this insight by analyzing what is to all of us an altogether familiar and taken-for-granted feature of our social landscape: the fast-food restaurant. The concept of McDonaldization is designed to update and specifically apply the Weberian idea of rationalization to this phenomenon. In the spirit of Weber, Ritzer seeks to explore the darker side of this pervasive phenomenon.

Regarding the third classic theorist, Émile Durkheim (1858–1917), we discover someone with a far more optimistic view of what the modern world holds in store for us. Insofar as he was a pivotal figure in the establishment of sociology in the French university system, Durkheim was the contemporary counterpart of Weber. His ideas had a profound impact on sociology, not only in France but also internationally. Indeed, it is fair to say that in the long run, Durkheim's ideas played a larger role in shaping American sociology than did the ideas of the three other people discussed in Part I.

Durkheim was concerned with understanding differing forms of human community and the distinctive bases of solidarity that undergirded them. In a rather sweeping fashion, he sought to illustrate how preindustrial, premodern communities were, in significant ways, different from industrial, modern ones. He described earlier societies as being based on mechanical solidarity, whereas contemporary society was predicated on organic solidarity. Central to Durkheim in his attempt to distinguish mechanical from organic societies is the division of labor. In earlier societies, this division was rather minimal because people—or kin units—performed a wide array of tasks necessary to sustain their lives. In stark contrast, in modern industrial society, the division of labor is highly developed. The size and complexity of such societies necessitates the specialization of work. Because people are unable to perform all the tasks associated with sustaining their lives, they are highly dependent on others. Modern society thus fosters interdependency.

Reviewing these ideas and building on them in Chapter 3, Anne M. Hornsby examines the novel phenomenon of "Net communities." She is interested in seeing whether these cyberspace communities are merely extensions of modern organic communities or can be seen—because of the lack of physical proximity and the disembodied character of Internet social interactions—as a new form of community. In other words, she questions whether Durkheim's ideas can adequately grasp the world of the Internet or whether we need to build on, but go beyond, his original contributions to social theory.

The final person discussed in Part I is the German sociologist Georg Simmel (1858–1918). During his lifetime, Simmel's career was consistently stymied because of his Jewish background. Anti-Semitism was chiefly responsible for preventing him from rising to the heights of the German academic world. Nonetheless, his body of thought was held in high regard by his contemporaries in both Europe and America. Weber was especially impressed by his intellectual achievements. Disturbed by the injustice that befell his colleague, Weber used his considerable influence to try to advance Simmel's career. This proved in the long term to be helpful because Simmel eventually was able to obtain a professorship that he richly deserved.

Simmel had a substantial impact on what was known as the Chicago School of sociology, the most influential center for the development of sociology in the United States during the early part of the 20th century. After his death, Simmel's reputation grew, albeit slowly and somewhat fitfully. Today, his ideas are not only seen as key to sociologists of modernity, but also embraced by theorists who describe themselves as postmodernists.

As a student of contemporary social and cultural life, Simmel's thinking frequently appeared to reflect what he described as a central trait of the modern world: its fragmentary nature. Known as a fine essayist, Simmel provided finely textured descriptions, or snapshots, of social relations and individual types. He was interested in conflict, which he saw as potentially both destructive and creative. Simmel was not a systematic social theorist, but his ideas do reflect a carefully articulated and coherent theoretical framework.

William J. Staudenmeier, Jr., an expert in alcohol studies, reveals the varied ways that Simmel's ideas can be employed to examine the role of alcohol in society. In the spirit of Simmel, Staudenmeier approaches his topic from several different perspectives, showing in the process the many ways that Simmel's ideas can be employed to shed light on various facets of it.

Together, these four chapters reveal the ongoing relevance to us, as we move into the second decade of the 21st century, of ideas first formulated during the 19th and early 20th centuries. It is for this reason that sociologists continually return to the ideas of their forebears. They do so not simply to understand something about the history of the discipline, but also because these ideas still have much to say to us about contemporary society.

CHAPTER 1

Working Longer, Living Less

Understanding Marx Through the Workplace Today

John P. Walsh and Anne Zacharias-Walsh

John P. Walsh *is Professor of Public Policy at the Georgia Institute of Technology. His research and teaching interests focus on work, organizations, and science and technology policy. His recent work compares innovation systems in Japan and the United States, and he has spent several years working in Japanese universities. He has published in journals such as* Science, Research Policy, Work and Occupations, *and* Social Studies of Science. *He has been teaching Marx to undergraduates for almost two decades and hopes that the taste of Marx presented here will encourage readers to read* Capital *(Marx, 1867/1977). He encourages students who have questions about Marx or the chapter to email him at john.walsh@pubpolicy.gatech.edu. Also, he hopes to someday be able to limit his working day to 8 hours.*

Anne Zacharias-Walsh *is an independent writer and activist specializing in labor issues. She recently completed a highly successful multiyear project that brought together American and Japanese female workers in an effort to help Japanese activists develop grassroots organizations that can fight effectively for working women's rights. She is especially happy to report that, through the project, the once isolated working women's organizations have now formed a national network in Japan and are working jointly to win rights for women on the job and in society at large. Zacharias-Walsh began studying Marxist theory as an undergraduate in connection with her work in the movement for peace and justice in Central America. She began writing about labor while earning a master's degree in cultural theory at Carnegie Mellon University in Pittsburgh.*

We want to feel the sunshine

We want to smell the flowers

We're sure that God has willed it

And we mean to have eight hours.

We're summoning our forces

From shipyard, shop and mill

Eight hours for work, eight hours for rest,

Eight hours for what we will.

—Hymn of the Eight-Hour Movement (1886)

In all its handouts, capitalism promises that everyone will benefit from a prosperous economy: What's good for General Motors (GM) is good for the country; a rising tide lifts all boats. Yet neither the robust business climate of the 1990s nor the period of economic growth in the United States in the early years of this century has led to increases in workers' standard of living. Instead, soaring corporate profits and business-friendly government have resulted in stagnant wages, deteriorating working conditions, loss of job security, union busting, and the worst income disparity since the 1930s. Corporate America increased productivity by decreasing the number of employees, increased profits by holding down workers' wages, and increased working hours while keeping unemployment high. In other words, contrary to "trickle-down" predictions, the corporate world has consolidated power, and workers are, by all indicators, worse off for it.

In 1991, the highly profitable A. E. Staley Company, a corn-processing plant based in Decatur, Illinois, offered its employees a contract that called for increasing the regular workday to 12 hours, mandatory overtime, pay cuts, and benefit takebacks. At the same time, Staley reportedly turned a 22% profit, while its parent company, the British conglomerate Tate and Lyle, reaped $400 million in profits on $5.5 billion in sales.

The employees resisted the proposed contract at the bargaining table and in public protests. In June 1993, the company locked out its regular employees and brought in replacement workers to run the plant. Although that move launched a 2-year battle that became the rallying point in the struggle to revitalize the American labor movement, in the end the company won out, forcing the workers to accept draconian concessions in the midst of booming business.[1] With its vast financial resources and ever-growing supply of replacement workers, and with state power (in the form of state and local police) stepping in whenever "necessary" to contain the dispute, the company was able to hold out longer than 760 workers who had not received regular paychecks in more than 2 years. In other words, instead of passing along some of its good fortune to workers, Staley used its beefed-up resources as a whip against the employees, taking more and more away from workers merely because it had become strong enough to get away with it.

In recent decades, Americans have seen increased polarization as the benefits of a strong economy flow disproportionately into the hands of the already wealthy. Longer hours are by no means the only setback to which workers are subjected in the face of corporate prosperity. While worker productivity rose 16.6% from 2000 to 2005, total compensation for the median worker rose only 7.2% (Greenhouse & Leonhardt, 2006). Even the conservative business press acknowledged the trend. The *Wall Street Journal* reported in 2006 that while the overall economy grew by nearly 12% since 2001, median income dropped 0.5%. The *Journal* also quoted new Commerce Department data that showed that corporate profits hit a 40-year high, accounting for 12.2% of the nation's gross domestic product in the second quarter of 2006, while the average wages measured as a percentage of GDP declined to 2.8% in the same period, the lowest on record. "Many of the benefits from the five-year economic expansion have gone to the nation's highest earners, while the average worker has struggled to stay in place," the *Journal* noted with apparent surprise (Etter, 2006, p. A7).

Proponents of capitalism are hard-pressed to explain this pattern of growing inequality and polarization in the face of an expanding economy and increasing productivity. Pundits often fall back on "psychologizing" the problems (people are poor or unemployed because of some personal failing: lack of motivation, drug problem, reliance on welfare, etc.) or on "naturalizing" these ills by pronouncing them intransigent facts of human existence. The writings of Karl Marx, however, offer a different interpretation.

More than 125 years ago, Marx (1867/1977) argued that under capitalism, workers must, by definition, lose economic ground as productivity and profits increase. Far from an anomaly or accidental by-product, this pattern is inherent in a capitalist mode of production.

Our point is not to suggest that Marx was a visionary. His writings and theories remain viable today because of the nature of his project: Marx's analysis of capitalism is designed to uncover the dynamics and contradictions inherent in a system that converts all human relations into economic relations. His central work, *Capital*, is a detailed explication of the logic of capitalism (and given that logic, the necessary, albeit often counterintuitive, implications of it). By revealing that logic, Marx is able to write about actual conditions in his time while also giving future readers tools for analyzing capitalism and its workings in other historical moments. The purpose of this chapter, then, is to take Marx out of 19th-century industrial England and, by analyzing current workplace conditions in Marxist terms, enable the reader to begin to understand Marxism and the cogency of Marxist theory today.

Capital's three volumes contain a multifaceted theory, even a summary of which is beyond the scope of this chapter. We therefore focus our discussion on the cornerstone of Marx's argument: the production of value and surplus value. Following Marx, we argue that the logic of value production mandates the continuous push to extend the working day. We then examine labor trends from the early 1990s through 2006, particularly the reemergence of the 12-hour day and rotating shifts, to demonstrate one of the central claims of Marxism: Capitalism, by its very nature, generates a ceaseless drive to lengthen the working day, with absolute indifference to human needs, abilities, or limitations.

A note before delving into Marxism proper: As is the case with other legendary (if you will) theorists, such as Freud or Einstein, many readers begin to study the material with certain preconceived, "common knowledge" notions about that theorist's work. Unfortunately, these notions are often stereotyped sketches, oversimplified to the point that they bear no useful resemblance to the original. Worse yet, they can, we fear, constrain the way in which a reader approaches the material by setting forth from the outset a frame that is inadequate to the concept. (For example, it is often difficult to convince students to take Freud seriously at first because he is popularly presented as something of a nut who cannot think about anything but penises.) To circumvent this problem, we begin by noting what Marxism is not: Marxism is not the mere conclusion that capitalism is exploitative. That is a critique of capitalism, and it is one with which Marx agrees, but it is not "Marxism." Many theorists before and after Marx have argued that capitalism is exploitative, and modes of production prior to capitalism (slavery and feudalism) were exploitative as well. Marx's contribution is in explaining how, why, and in precisely what ways capitalism, by its own logic, must be so. In other words, the idea that capitalism is exploitative is the beginning, not the end, of Marx's theorizing.

Contemporary Marxist theory contains many strains, some of which dispute the importance of value as a central concept in Marx. In particular, the so-called analytic Marxists (see Mayer, 1994) emphasize exploitation as the central concept and argue that the concepts of value and surplus value are not analytically useful. In contrast to the analytic Marxists, the Marxist humanists (see Dunayevskaya, 1988) argue that alienation is the central concept of Marx and that production of surplus value is the central form of alienation under capitalism. Marx's writings contain much of value and much that can be debated. Our goal in this chapter is to present what Marx wrote in *Capital* and what he emphasized in his writings: that production of value and surplus value is key to understanding capitalism. This presentation, we hope, will help readers form the basis for sifting through contemporary debates (in this book and elsewhere) on how best to develop Marx's theories.

Marx's Theory of Capital

The Concept of Value

According to Marx, the main function of capitalism is not the production of goods (use value), but rather the production of exchange value or, more simply, value.[2] The goal of the capitalist is the production of surplus value. Unlike other modes of production (such as those of hunter and gatherer societies, slave societies, or agrarian feudalism), in which the primary significance of a particular good is its usefulness (use value), the goods produced under capitalism—commodities—are important to capitalists only as bearers of (exchange) value.[3] Marx defines value as the total amount of (socially necessary, abstract) labor time expended in the production of a given commodity.[4]

Value and Commodity Exchange

Because value (as abstract labor time) is the common denominator among all commodities, it allows diverse commodities, such as cotton, steel, hamburgers, and college educations, to be exchanged for each other—or for their objectified equivalent form, money—in the market. When capitalists exchange certain amounts of seemingly diverse types of commodities in the market (one wool coat for two pairs of shoes), they are actually exchanging definite quantities of value that have been objectified, or embedded, in those diverse commodity forms. Capitalists do not care which commodities they have, or which ones they get, so long as they are able to exchange them in sufficient quantities. This indifference to the kinds of goods that are being produced in turn transforms the entire concept of work. The purpose of working used to be to produce particular goods that have some particular use to people—in other words, to produce use value. Under capitalism, the purpose of work is the production of exchange value.

The shift in focus from use value to exchange value underlies many of the dynamics of capitalism, including the drive toward an endless working day.[5] Also, it is this transformation that fundamentally inverts, or subverts, the notion of a mode of production. No longer a system designed to meet human needs, capitalism becomes a system driven by the desire to generate value, and human concerns are replaced by concerns about maximizing surplus value.

It is important to note that Marx's critique of capitalism does not rest on an assumption of anyone "cheating the system." Instead, he begins with the assumption that all goods are exchanged in the market for their full value. Thus, any exploitation would be inherent to capitalism, independent of any capitalist's will or guile.[6]

Labor as Commodity

The capitalist, then, has a difficult task: Selling a commodity above its value does not count as "capitalism" (i.e., does not create new value); the capitalist must find a way to make the value of his or her commodity greater than the sum of the value of its parts. Labor power is the only commodity that fills that bill because it is the only commodity that can create value.

Labor power, or the ability to do a day's labor, is a commodity. It shares the following basic properties with any commodity:

- A day's labor power has a particular amount of value embedded in it.
- A day's labor power is purchased with an equivalent amount of value—in this case, in the form of wages.
- The value of a day's labor power is the quantity of labor time embedded in it.
- The value of a day's labor power is equal to the total amount of socially necessary labor time used to produce the average bundle of (socially necessary) goods a worker must consume each day to be able to come to work again the next day (i.e., the labor embedded in food, clothes, housing, health care, etc.).

Labor: The Secret Behind Surplus Value

Again, it is important to note what Marx is *not* saying. Marx is not merely saying that capitalists are always trying to make workers work longer so they will have more goods to sell and therefore be richer. Rather, Marx argues that by maximizing the amount of time an individual works in a day, the capitalist will be able to maximize the rate of return he or she gets for the wage he or she has paid to that individual. In other words, the capitalist will have maximized the rate of surplus value.

To illustrate the role of labor in the production of surplus value, we arbitrarily assume that 5 hours is the amount of labor time needed to produce a worker's daily subsistence. This means that the value of (or the amount of past labor embedded in) a day's labor is equal to 5 hours. Furthermore, we assume that the quantity of value represented by 5 hours of socially necessary abstract labor time is equal to $100.[7] The capitalist pays the worker $100 for his or her day's labor. Equal values have been exchanged, and everything has been exchanged at its full value. An amazing transformation takes place, however, once we leave the market and enter the realm of production. It is in the realm of production, Marx argues, that the secrets of surplus value, and therefore capitalism, are revealed.

Production of Commodities and Surplus Value

In the market, labor power appears the same as any other commodity. When we enter the sphere of production, however, the crucial difference emerges: labor creates value. All other commodities used in the production process add to the new commodity only the set amount of value already embedded in them as a result of their own production. Assume, for example, that 3 pounds of cotton have 3 hours of labor time embedded in them. No matter how the capitalist uses that cotton, the maximum amount of value it can bestow on another commodity in the process of production is 3 hours' worth. That is, it can transfer only the value it has in it. Labor, however, creates value. Therefore, not only can it transfer the value already embedded in it (its current value) but also, by continuing to work, labor can create and add new value. When the capitalist hires a worker, he or she is buying not merely past labor (i.e., labor that has already been expended in the production process) but also the capacity to labor, or labor power. There is no reason to suppose that the amount of value a worker can create (i.e., the amount of labor time the worker can expend in a day) is necessarily the same as the amount of labor time that was necessary to produce his or her daily means of subsistence. Marx (1867/1977) notes,

> But the past labour embodied in the labour-power and the living labour it can perform; the daily cost of maintaining labour-power and its daily expenditure in work, are two totally different things. The former determines the exchange-value of the labour-power, the latter is its use-value. The fact that half a day's labour is necessary to keep the worker alive during 24 hours does not in any way prevent him from working a whole day. (p. 300)

If the worker is hired but left idle all day, that worker produces no value. If the worker works longer (at the socially necessary rate) than the amount of labor time required to reproduce his or her efforts, the worker creates more value than the capitalist paid, thus producing surplus value.

Marx shows us that to understand the secrets of capitalism, it is important to peer into the details of the production process (details that are hidden from us when we go to the store to buy commodities). We will lay out an extended example of the details of linen production (using hypothetical numbers for simplicity) to illustrate the nature of the production process under capitalism. This section, although somewhat arid, provides the basis for understanding the more dramatic, real-world examples we discuss elsewhere in the chapter. Table 1.1 summarizes all the transactions discussed in this section.

Our capitalist has decided to produce linen. (Because he is a capitalist, his interest is in linen for its exchange value, not its use value.) We make the following assumptions and trace out the first day of production:

- Ten spools of thread are needed to produce 10 yards of linen. The capitalist buys 50 spools of thread (Table 1.1, line 1, column 5) for $50 (column 6), an amount equal to the value of the labor power embodied in that thread.
- In producing 50 yards of linen, the wear and tear on the loom and all other equipment costs (including rent, light, heat, etc.) equal $50 (Table 1.1, column 7).
- The value of a day's labor (i.e., the cost of reproducing a day's labor) is $100 (Table 1.1, column 3), and this $100 represents 5 hours of socially necessary labor time.
- As you can see, in making the purchases necessary to produce linen, our capitalist has exchanged $200 (Table 1.1, column 2) for commodities valued at $200—an even exchange.

We now assume that, working at a normal pace, using the average skill and typical equipment, a worker can turn 10 spools of thread into 10 yards of linen in 1 hour. In 5 hours, the worker will have woven 50 yards of linen (Table 1.1, column 9). The following equation summarizes the day's activities:

Labor		Thread		Equipment		Linen
1 day (5 hours)	+	50 spools	+	loom, etc.	=	50 yards
$100		$50		$50		$200

Thus, the linen contains $200 of total labor: $100 of new labor from our worker and $100 worth of dead labor contained in the thread and the equipment. Therefore, the 50 yards of linen have a value of $4 per yard (Table 1.1, column 10).

The capitalist now takes the cloth to the market and exchanges his linen at full value—$200. He now has the same $200 he started with—not a very fruitful day (compare Table 1.1, columns 2 and 11). After all his transactions, the capitalist is no better off than before. No surplus value was created (column 12).

Production of Surplus Value

Despite this early setback, our capitalist quickly sees his mistake and vows to rectify it. The capitalist recognizes that surplus value can be created only by extending

Table 1.1 The Working Day and the Creation of Surplus Value

					Inputs					Outputs			
(1) Day	(2) Money ($) (3+6+7)	(3) Wage ($)	(4) Hours	(5) Thread (Spools)	(6) Raw Material Costs ($)	(7) Equipment Costs ($)	(8) Labor Power ($)	(9) Cloth (Yards)	(10) Price (per yard) ($)	(11) Value ($) ($9 \times 10$)	(12) Surplus ($) ($11 - 2$)	(13) Profit Rate (%)
1	200	100	5	50	50	50	100	50	4.00	200	0	0
2	300	100	10	100	100	100	200	100	4.00	400	100	33
3	340	100	12	120	120	120	240	120	4.00	480	140	41
4	400	100	15	150	150	150	300	150	4.00	600	200	50

the working day beyond the amount of time necessary to produce the means of subsistence for the worker (5 hours in the example). With this insight, the capitalist goes to the market again.

The following day (see Table 1.1, line 2), the capitalist buys 100 spools of thread (column 5) for $100 (column 6), $100 worth of looms and lights and such (column 7), and hires the worker for another day at $100 (column 3). The capitalist has exchanged $300 (column 2) for commodities valued at $300—again, an even exchange. But this time, he makes the worker work 10 hours (column 4). During this longer day, the worker weaves the 100 spools of thread into 100 yards of linen (column 9). We now have the following equation:

Labor		Thread		Equipment		Linen
1 day (10 hours)	+	100 spools	+	loom, etc.	=	100 yards
$200		$100		$100		$400

Given that the linen was produced using the same technology and conditions and skill (i.e., it contains the same amount of socially necessary labor), it has the same value as yesterday, namely, $4 per yard (Table 1.1, column 10). The value of the linen is therefore $400 (column 11). The cost of the commodities that went into the linen, however, was only $300 (column 2). The capitalist has generated surplus value of $100 (column 12) and a rate of profit (column 13) of 33% ($100/$300). In other words, money has been used to purchase commodities that were then used to create a new commodity whose value is greater than the original capital outlay, and this new commodity is turned back into an equivalent amount of money. This is the essence of capitalism.

Surplus Value and the Extension of the Working Day

We have seen that surplus value is generated only if the worker works longer than the time required to reproduce his or her labor power for another day.[8] It is therefore in the interest of the capitalist to extend the working day as far as possible beyond the point where the worker is simply reproducing his own labor power.

By following the same process and extending the working day to 12 hours, our capitalist can reap $140 of surplus value, with a profit rate of 41% (see Table 1.1, line 3, columns 12 and 13).

By extending it to a 15-hour day, the capitalist can reap $200 in surplus value, with a profit rate of 50% (see Table 1.1, line 4, columns 12 and 13).

By extending the working day beyond what is necessary for reproducing labor power, the capitalist generates surplus labor, and the more he extends it, the greater his rate of profit.

Surplus Labor

Far from a fixed entity, what constitutes a "working day" is a variable thing, limited by some "natural" boundaries but largely defined through social and political struggle. The minimum length of the working day is the amount of time required to produce the average worker's means of subsistence. If labor as a whole works less than this, society is not reproducing itself and will eventually collapse from starvation. Note that the converse is not true: Even if a society as a whole is extracting surplus value, it may still suffer mass starvation. As Nobel Prize–winning economist Amartya Sen (1999) has shown, in capitalist societies, famines are generally a problem not of too little food but of a lack of buying power among the starving.

Theoretically, the maximum length of the working day is 24 hours. In practice, however, it has to be somewhat less because reproducing the labor power requires some time for sleeping, eating, and procreating.

The history of capitalism has been the history of the struggle to define the length of the working day. Capitalists have often attempted to impose working days of 12, 14, 18, and, if possible, 24 hours to maximize their surplus. Marx (1867/1977, p. 353n) describes a public meeting in Nottingham (home of Robin Hood) to *debate* whether the working day should be *reduced* to 18 hours. Against the insatiable demand of capital, workers seek to limit the extension of the working day so that they may be able to sell their labor at the same level of intensity the next day and continue to do so over the course of their lives. This leads to the struggle in the workplace over the definition of a fair day's work.

Politics of the Working Day

Although there is constant pressure to increase the working day (and the workweek and weeks worked per year), the length of the working day is a political question:

> The capitalist maintains his rights as a purchaser when he tries to make the working day as long as possible, and where possible, to make two working days out of one. On the other hand, the peculiar nature of the commodity sold implies a limit to its consumption by the purchaser, and the worker maintains his right as a seller when he wishes to reduce the working day to a particular normal length. There is here therefore an antinomy, of right against right, both equally bearing the seal of the law of exchange. *Between equal rights, force decides.* Hence, in the history of capitalist production, the establishment of a norm for the working day presents itself as a struggle over the limits of that day, a struggle between collective capital, i.e., the class of capitalists, and collective labour, i.e., the working class. (Marx, 1867/1977, p. 344, italics added)

Because the length of the working day is in part a political struggle, labor has some ability to enforce its definition of the "normal" working day. At various points, workers have been successful in their demands for a shorter working day. For example, during the 1990s, workers at Volkswagen in Germany negotiated a reduction in their workweek as a way of spreading work to more people. Similarly, workers in France pushed for a reduction of the workweek from 39 hours to 35 hours (Lardner, 1999). As the collective power of workers declines, however, capital increasingly has its way, and the working day is extended. Union contracts, for example, traditionally have been one of workers' primary tools for defining and limiting the length of the working day. Union membership in the United States, however, has declined from 23.6% of the labor force in 1960 to 12.5% in 2005. During the same period, the length of the working day has steadily increased. In other words, as union membership has declined, workers have been increasingly unable to enforce their definition of a working day.

Increasing the Working Day

In *The Overworked American,* Juliet Schor (1991) documents the increase in the American working day during the prior two decades. As unions have declined, fixed capital has increased, and global competition has increased, capital is increasingly attempting to prop up rates of surplus by extending the working day. Schor estimates that the typical American was working approximately 160 hours more per year in 1987 than in 1969 (Table 1.2). This is the equivalent of working 13 months out of every year.[9] The trend has continued into this century. According to an International Labor Organization (ILO) study, the average American's work hours increased in one decade by almost a full week over the course of a year (Anderson, 2001). The average American worker in 2001 put in 1,978 work hours, up 36 hours from 1990. This is occurring at the same time work hours in other industrial countries are declining and efficiency in many of those countries is increasing. The ILO also found that the average American worker works 100 more hours (nearly 2½ workweeks) annually than average Australian, Canadian, Japanese, and Mexican workers. Americans work 250 hours more than British and Brazilian workers, and 500 hours more than German workers. Within the developing world, only South Korean and Czech workers put in more hours than American workers.

The Return of the 12-Hour Day

One way companies ratchet up the number of hours worked per year is by turning back the clock to the days of 12-hour (or longer) shifts. Although the Staley case

Table 1.2 Annual Hours Paid Employment for Labor Force Participants

Labor Force	Year		Increase
	1969	1987	
All	1786	1949	163
Men	2054	2152	98
Women	1406	1711	305

Source: Schor (1991).

came to symbolize this trend, it was by no means unique in its demands or tactics, as the following examples demonstrate:

- Workers at Caterpillar went on strike in June 1994 after the company—widely reported in the business press to be enjoying robust profits—demanded concessions including 12-hour shifts. During the strike, the company posted record profits while operating with replacement workers who received no benefits.
- In 1994, Uniroyal Goodrich threatened to shut down if workers did not go with 12-hour shifts and 24-hour continuous production. Employees capitulated, fearing layoffs.
- The pulp and paper mill Simpson Tacoma Kraft adopted a 12-hour shift schedule in 2004.
- Even universities are getting into the act, with University of Massachusetts Amherst putting its power plant workers on 12-hour rotating shifts in 2000, eliminating the overtime provision for over 8 hours in a day, and providing compensatory time in lieu of overtime pay for the weeks with 48-hour-long schedules.

Workday acceleration has not been limited to jobs in the traditional blue-collar sphere. The Economic Policy Institute found that middle-class parents, taken together, work 3,335 hours per year, up from just over 3,000 hours per year in 1979, an increase of 8 workweeks per year in just 20 years (Greenhouse, 1999). A comptroller in a company called ClickAction, for example, reports working a 6-week period without a day off. During that period, the employee said, she had to leave for work at 5 a.m. and didn't return home until 10 p.m., at which time she had to wash dishes and make her family's dinner for the next night (Lardner, 1999).

Although aggregate figures show a relatively gradual but steady increase, workweeks and shift lengths in some companies reached hyperbolic levels in the 1990s. Machine operators at Chrysler's Trenton, Michigan, engine plant reportedly work 72-hour weeks. An electrician at the same plant reported working 12-hour shifts, 7 days a week ("GM Pact Fallout," 1994). He also reported working 84 consecutive days. Workers in a GM Buick plant clocked in approximately 57 hours per week. Nearly half of the unionized workers at the Dunlop Tire plant in Tonawanda, New York, worked 50 weekends a year and two night shifts during the regular week ("Union Rejects," 1994).

Overwork and Underwork

The flip side of a longer working day for some people is underemployment, or unemployment for others. In an era of globalization, many American companies have lengthened the working day (and decreased wages) by taking their production offshore to countries with weaker labor laws or enforcement, often developing countries with little or no organized labor movement. The story is painfully familiar: American manufacturing companies move their factories to China, Indonesia, South Korea, Myanmar, and so forth, in search of cheaper labor and more "business-friendly" labor laws and working conditions. As a result, American plants are closed, Americans are thrown out of work, and the communities around the plants suffer.

Workers at Goodyear Tire went on strike in October 2006 after rejecting a contract that would have included two plant closures and other concessions ("Goodyear Workers," 2006). In 2003, the workers accepted one plant closing and concessions on wages, pensions, and health care to save the company. Goodyear, the third-largest tire company in the world with $19.5 billion in sales, turned a profit in 2005 for the first time since 2000. But instead of rewarding the employees for their earlier sacrifices, the company came back asking for more. Although the company was profitable again, executives said more closures and cuts were necessary to keep their advantage over foreign competition. "We simply cannot accept a contract that knowingly creates a competitive disadvantage versus our foreign-owned competition and increases our cost disadvantage versus imports," said Goodyear's chief negotiator, Jim Allen, according to the Reuters report ("Goodyear Workers," 2006).

Thus, one outcome of this increase in the working day and the accompanying increase in productivity (in the sense of getting more surplus value) is the creation of surplus labor. Firms are in a constant search for ways to reduce the number of workers while still increasing output. The popularity of downsizing in the past two decades is a reflection of this desire by capital to increase productivity. Downsizing has the added benefit of increasing what Marx termed the *surplus army*—the set of workers available at any time to be pulled into the production process to supplement, or replace, the existing workforce. An additional 59,000 people would have jobs if the auto industry put a moratorium on overtime, according to the United Auto Workers Union ("Overtime Pressures," 1994). This surplus army of labor keeps pressure on workers to increase their output and be cautious in their demands for an increased share of the output (e.g., through wage increases). Capital is constantly reminding workers that "You can be replaced." News spots of thousands of workers lining up for a few job openings at a factory or hotel or fire department are paraded before the public, reminding them of the surplus army always on call to replace lazy or militant workers.

With the ever-present threat of shutdown, the message from corporate America is that Americans have to be willing to settle for less, despite the company's profitability, or get nothing at all. In his book *Slaves to Fashion*, sociologist Robert Ross (2004) argues that American workers are increasingly driven to do just that. For example, in the first half of the 20th century, the American apparel industry was notorious for operating almost exclusively with sweatshops, which were located in the United States. A number of factors in mid-century, including full employment during World War II, passage of new labor laws, and an increase in unionization rates in the industry, led to a radical reduction in the number of sweatshops operating in the United States. Beginning in the 1970s, however, sweatshops began to reappear and have become increasingly common since then. By 1979, reports of sweatshops in the New York garment district became so prevalent that the government formed a task force to investigate. At that time, the task force found that 35% of the small shops in New York's Chinatown had violated the Fair Standards Labor Act. By 1997, that number had risen to 90% according to a Department of Labor survey (Ross, 2004). Ross attributes the reemergence of domestic sweatshops to the "race to the bottom" that results from global competition. Garment workers in the United States are working for significantly lower wages and under worsening conditions rather than risk losing their jobs to competitors overseas. As capital and commodity markets globalize, the poverty living standards of the developing world become the socially necessary level of subsistence against which American workers are measured. And, capital will fight anywhere in the world to ensure that this socially necessary level stays as low as possible. Currently, China is considering changing its labor laws to crack down on sweatshops and strengthen unions. The American Chamber of Commerce came out against the proposed changes and said that increasing worker protections would result in American companies pulling out of China in search of more favorable environments for their capital (Barboza, 2006).

Competition and Surplus Value

We have shown that the struggle to increase the working day is driven by a need to produce surplus value. The production of surplus value alone, however, is not enough. Capitalists are driven by competition to produce as much surplus value as possible with a given amount of capital. In other words, firms must, under threat of ruin from their competitors (domestic or foreign), maximize the ratio of surplus labor to necessary labor. Capital (in the form of investment capital) is constantly on the lookout for a capitalist who is producing surplus value at a greater rate, quickly switching from the laggard capitalist to the capitalist who is most successful at generating surplus value. In a world of global, round-the-clock stock markets and e-trading, capital is more nimble than ever, putting increasing pressure on firms to increase surplus value.

Competition, particularly for investment dollars, is also behind capital's continual demands for an increase in the length of the working day. Prior to implementing its 12-hour rotating shifts, Staley was pulling in substantial profits (one estimate put them at 22% of sales). Those returns were, however, in the words of Staley executive J.P. Mohan, "inadequate" because Archer Daniels Midland, Staley's major competitor in the region, reportedly posted profits of approximately 26%, making it the more attractive site for investment dollars. Mohan said he needed to implement rotating 12-hour shifts for "Staley in Decatur to be competitive" ("Union Stays," 1992).[10]

The fact that all three of the companies in the Decatur "war zone" (Caterpillar, Staley, and Bridgestone/Firestone) were willing to wage a battle to the death with long-term employees—in an international media spotlight, while profits for each were robust—reveals the importance of the role of competition. Indeed, few of the companies that we looked at used anemic profits to justify moving to longer shifts. As the following examples show, companies routinely pinned the blame on competition:

- Management at GM's Buick City plant in Flint, Michigan, chose to ride out a strike rather than back off on its demands for 12-hour shifts. "Wall Street is telling GM it must cut payroll before investors will line up behind the company. The possibility that this strike could close the automaker just as the 1995 model year opens is of secondary concern to stock analysts" ("GM Pact Fallout," 1994, p. A1). The fact that GM was profitable did not absolve it of its obligation to decrease the workforce.

- In Baltimore, Poly-Seal Corporation, despite its $60 million to $70 million in annual sales, also withstood a strike rather than concede on 12-hour shifts. Poly-Seal Chief Executive Officer Robert Gillman said the company "remains prosperous" but has suffered a decline in the rate of growth of profits, and because its competitors have gone to longer shifts, it must follow suit or its operations will become "economically unfeasible" ("12-Hour Day," 1994).

- Even the venerable *Encyclopædia Britannica* bowed to the demands of competition when management announced it was extending employees' work-week by 2 hours without increasing pay. In a memo to less-than-pleased employees, management wrote, "We compete with some of the most aggressive companies in the business. Their employees work hard, and we must match their efforts to compete with them and maintain Britannica's edge" ("Middle-Class Labor," 1995, p. 1).

Companies are not lying or making excuses when they invoke competition to justify cuts and speed-ups. The laws of competition demand them. Contrary to popular notions like "individual will" and "entrepreneurial talent," capitalists recognize that their decisions are often forced by external factors and occasionally call for state power to regulate competition (usually as a response to worker agitation). Marx (1867/1977) quotes a petition by the potteries (including Wedgwood) in 1863:

Much as we deplore the evils before mentioned [extensive workdays for children], it would not be possible to prevent them by any scheme of agreement between the manufacturers. . . . Taking all these points into consideration, we have come to the conviction that some legislative enactment is wanted. (p. 381n)

Similarly, the pressure on the working day is generated by the logic of capital and does not depend on the wishes of individual capitalists.[11] As such, imposing inhuman shifts is not merely a case of management being anti-worker. During the strike, Caterpillar ran its plants with office workers and other replacements. These friends of management were not exempt from the mandates of capital. Instead, they were forced to put in long hours without recourse to a union contract for protection. One worker, normally a business analyst, spent 12 hours each day assembling tractors and then 2 or more hours at his old desk job, thereby giving his employer two jobs each day. A welder brought from Alabama to be a scab was working 72 hours a week ("Bitter Caterpillar Strike," 1994).

Thus, it is not capitalists as individuals but rather capitalism that demands that all firms excel at the exploitation of labor power, the production of surplus value. Although individual capitalists may deplore the impact of such logic, they act upon these tender feelings under the threat of ruin. All decisions in the workplace are seen through the filter of value production. Even attempts at softening working conditions (such as the Human Relations School, Quality of Work Life programs, and similar management strategies designed to improve working conditions) are promoted and implemented with arguments that they will increase the productivity of labor and hence increase surplus value.

Mechanisms for Increasing Surplus Labor

Lengthening the working day is only one of many ways firms seek to increase surplus value. In their never-ending search for sources of surplus labor, firms have developed a variety of strategies for increasing the length of the working day and squeezing unpaid labor time from employees. Such tactics include so-called flexible scheduling; shaving time; innovation; converting to a part-time/contingent labor force; and, as we saw above, global mobility of production. These tactics are described below.

Flexible Scheduling

The Relay System. Infiltrating and usurping the whole of a worker's day is nothing new in the annals of labor history. In its attempt to get the most value from its labor power, capital is pressed to take over the entire life of the worker. Arguably the most blatant example is what Marx (1867/1977) described as the relay system:

> During the 15 hours of the factory day, capital dragged in the worker now for 30 minutes, now for an hour, and then pushed him out again, to drag him into the factory and thrust him out afresh, hounding him hither and thither, in scattered shreds of time, without ever letting go until the full 10 hours of work was done. As on the stage, the same person had to appear in turn in the different scenes of the different acts. And just as an actor is committed to the stage throughout the whole course of the play, so the workers were committed to the factory for the whole 15 hours, without reckoning the time taken in coming and going. Thus the hours of rest were turned into hours of enforced idleness, which drove the young men to the taverns and the young girls to the brothels. (p. 403)

Through the use of the relay system, the capitalist can extend the working day to 12 or 15 hours while maintaining the fiction of only using (and therefore only paying for) 10 hours of the worker's time. This practice of extending control over the worker's unpaid time and using workers in scattered fragments has continued in various forms. In an unusually simple and direct example of the relay system, a Burger King employee in Glasgow, Scotland, was paid the equivalent of $1.55 for a 5-hour shift because he was only "on the clock" for the moments he was serving customers.

Another example of the relay system comes from one of the United States' largest chains of suburban weekly newspapers. By the nature of their work, reporters tend to work long hours. Morning deadlines, staff meetings, and editors' work ethics often require reporters to come in during the morning, even though their beats may require them to be present to cover events late at night. The union at this company won a contract that called for overtime pay after 37.5 hours per week or 10 hours in a day. To avoid paying overtime, the company put the reporters on a self-regulated relay system. The reporters had to juggle their time so that all meetings would be covered without going over the 10 hours. If a reporter had a morning deadline and a night meeting on the same day, she might have to come in at 10 a.m. to meet deadline, work until 5 p.m., leave for a few hours, then return to work at 7 p.m. to cover the meeting that lasts until 10 p.m.. This reporter would be paid for 10 hours, but 12 hours were dominated by work. Like the actor waiting backstage until his cue, the reporter's off time was really just a holding pattern while waiting to come back to work.

Part Time. Another way that capital can increase surplus value is by not paying the full cost of socially necessary means of subsistence. One technique for accomplishing this is to buy only a small fraction of the worker's day (week, year, work life), but in such a way that the worker is forced to make him- or herself available to the capitalist for the whole of the day.

Walmart, the United States' largest employer, has become famous, or notorious, for its ability to squeeze its workers (and its suppliers' workers) for the maximum amount of surplus value by keeping wages and benefits low, while still maintaining control over the whole of the workers' time. The retail giant is routinely criticized for offering such low wages that many employees rely on food stamps, Medicaid, and other government aid to make ends meet, in effect shifting part of its payroll onto taxpayers.[12] Still, the company recently launched new initiatives to create an even cheaper, more "flexible" workforce. The plan calls for wage caps, more part-time workers, and more workers scheduled on nights and weekends (Greenhouse & Barbaro, 2006). Employees also report being pressured to make themselves available around the clock. Walmart denies that it has such a policy, but in March 2006, workers held a protest rally after managers demanded 24-hour availability and cut the hours of workers who objected. According to the *New York Times,* workers in other stores throughout the country also said they face similar demands (Greenhouse & Barbaro, 2006). Again, such moves are not the work of particularly misanthropic minds; they are merely the rational responses to the demands of capitalism.

To some extent, Walmart is simply doing what business strategists recommend: deploying workers more efficiently to meet the peaks and valleys of business in their stores. Wall Street, which has put pressure on Walmart to raise its stock prices, has endorsed the strategy, with analysts praising the new approach to managing its workers (Greenhouse & Barbaro, 2006).

Demanding round-the-clock availability not only taps into the "benefits" of the relay system, but many Walmart employees say it is also a way to pressure and harass higher-wage, higher-seniority workers into quitting to make room for lower-wage part-timers. Executives deny such intentions, but their protestations look dubious in light of a widely circulated internal memo that was leaked to the *New York Times* in October 2005 (Greenhouse & Barbaro, 2006). In a section on "the most significant benefits-related challenges" to the company, the memo states that "growth in benefits costs is unacceptable (15% per year) and driven by fundamental and persistent root causes (e.g., aging workforce, increasing average tenure)" (Chambers, 2006). In the carefully worded recommendations section, the memo suggests that the company "*redesign benefits and other aspects of the Associate experience,* such as job design, to attract a healthier, more productive workforce" [italics added]. One proposed strategy was gratuitously making the jobs more physically strenuous, such as forcing cashiers to gather carts from the parking lot.

Within a year of that memo's release, several Florida stores' older employees with back and leg problems were suddenly forbidden to sit on stools while performing jobs like cashier, store greeters, and fitting room attendants, even though they had previously been allowed to use them (Greenhouse & Barbaro, 2006).

Contingent Labor. "Contingent labor" is a corollary to the relay system. By relying on temporary, contract, or "consulting" workers, the company can replace full-time employees with a set of workers (often the same workers they used to employ full time) whose labor power is used in small fragments, with the downtime inherent in most work processes pushed onto the worker's ledger. This is the new "flexibility" that firms are pushing for in their attempt to stay competitive. By reducing the actual "work" time, firms can reduce the amount of paid labor while still getting the same amount of total labor power, thereby increasing surplus value (or, in business jargon, "increasing the productivity of labor").

Contingent workers provide their labor as temporaries, consultants, freelancers, and stringers, or in similar positions, and as such, their paid work time is reduced to the minimum required by capital, and many of the fixed costs of work are borne by the worker. For example, many workers now must have a home office with computer, phone, fax, printer, and so on to be able to offer their labor power to capital on an as-needed basis. At the same time, contingent workers, most of whom have no union representation, take home on average $100 less per week than permanent employees, and few receive health benefits (20%) or employer pension plans (25%) ("Contingent Workforce," 2003).

Although they can expect little in the way of reward, contingent workers must also have a multitude of skills to enable them to meet the constantly changing demands of a production system that itself is constantly innovating to take advantage of new techniques for increasing surplus value. Although capital is constantly looking for ways to replace skilled workers with cheaper, less-skilled workers (Braverman, 1974), it also demands that workers are able to be highly productive in any of a number of production processes. This is especially true of contingent workers, who must be able to quickly plug into a wide variety of work settings to meet the ebb and flow of demand in various companies.

How prevalent is the practice? Approximately 33% of American workers are temporary or contingent employees, according to a 1998–1999 study by the Economic Policy Institute (Cook, 2000). Moreover, surveys indicated that between 80% and 90% of firms use contingent workers, and 60% expect to increase their use of contingent labor in the future ("Contingent Workforce," 2003).

A Note on "Flexibility." Not all "flexibility" plans are as nefarious as Walmart's. Indeed, although all such plans are undertaken with the company's best interest in mind, some are genuinely driven by the added goal of helping employees achieve an acceptable work-life balance. For example, many companies have begun offering "flexible scheduling" in the form of compressed workweeks, job sharing, or the option to go part-time as a way to retain high-skilled or professional female employees, because the cost of training a new employee is so high. But although such schedules might be attractive to some high-skilled employees, lower-income employees aren't usually offered "family-friendly" scheduling because they are less costly to replace. For lower-income workers, particularly those without the protection of a union contract, "flexible scheduling" opens the door to longer work hours for some and layoffs for others down the line. For example, some workers are attracted by the idea of a "compressed workweek" (for example, four 10-hour shifts instead of five 8-hour shifts) because it gives them an extra day off each week. Employers usually argue that compressed schedules actually give employees more time with their families because, in theory, it gives them more days off. In practice, however, those off days get eaten up by mandatory overtime. Employees often end up working five 12-hour shifts instead of five 8-hour shifts. Employees at the Formica plant in Evendale, Ohio, for example, routinely work five 12-hour shifts and 7-day weeks, and even 20-day stretches are not unheard of ("Factory OT Shoots Up," 1994). Managers at Griffin Environmental Company in New York admit that they went to a 4-day week with longer shifts because they rely on overtime to meet demand, and they wanted to leave Friday open for overtime hours ("Griffin Environmental," 1995).

Shaving Time

Firms try to increase surplus value in both large and small ways. Extending the working day to 10 or 12 hours is one of the more blatant methods, but firms try other means as well. In an op-ed piece in the *New York Times*, Chicago labor lawyer and author Tom Geoghegan (1999) reported on common ways companies routinely steal time, forcing employees to work for free. Fast-food restaurants often make employees clock out when the restaurant closes, even though the employees have to stay to clean up. The more blatant firms make the employees clock out whenever there are no customers. Hotel employees often work through their breaks, but the break time was still deducted from their paychecks.

Shaving a few minutes of time here and there can really add up for capital's benefit. For example, in 2006, a judge ruled that over the course of 8 years, Walmart was found to have cheated its workers in Pennsylvania out of $78 million in pay by forcing them to work through their unpaid breaks. A woman working as a cake decorator said she worked 8 to 12 unpaid hours each month. Two cashiers said that they were sometimes locked in the store and ordered to restock the shelves, off the clock, before they could leave (Greenhouse, 2006). The prior year, a judge found that Walmart's California stores regularly failed to provide workers with meal breaks, resulting in 8 million violations of labor law in a 5-year period. The company was ordered to pay $172 million to cover the missing meal breaks (Klug, 2005). A 1996 Employer Policy Foundation study estimated "conservatively" that illegally denied overtime pay amounts to at least $19 billion every year (Geoghegan, 1999).

By having workers work off the clock, the capitalist is able to increase unpaid labor and thereby increase the rate of surplus value. Managers are under tremendous pressure to get as much surplus labor as possible from employees and will frequently coerce employees into working off the clock, having them come early, stay late, work through breaks, come in on weekends, take work home—anything that will extend the working day without increasing workers' pay. Workers who accede to such demands are often rewarded with praise and promotions. Those who refuse are badgered, threatened, and occasionally dismissed for not performing up to par.

Innovation

Firms also try to increase surplus labor by innovating to reduce the amount of necessary labor time. Assume our capitalist figures out how to double the productivity of labor (perhaps based on a worker's suggestion during a quality circle meeting). As Table 1.3 illustrates, however, there is an interesting twist to the effects of increased productivity, and it is this twist that accounts for the ceaselessness of capitalism's demands on human labor, without reference to human or humane limitations. Assume the same 10-hour working day posited in Table 1.1 (see Table 1.3, line 1). The worker works 10 hours (Table 1.3, column 4), consuming his own labor (worth $100) plus raw materials and tools worth an additional $200, and produces $400 worth of cloth (column 11), generating a surplus of $100 (column 12) and a 33% profit rate (column 13). Now suppose, however, that our capitalist figures out how to get twice as much work from his worker during that same 10 hours (line 2). The wage ($100) is unchanged (column 3) because the cost of the means of subsistence is unchanged. Working twice as fast, the worker will use up twice as much thread and put twice as much wear on the loom, so the material costs will double to $400, for a total expenditure of $500 (column 2). The worker will produce twice as much cloth (column 9), however, which still has a value of $4 per yard.[13] This 200 yards of cloth is worth $800 (column 11), yielding a surplus of $300 (column 12) and a 60% profit rate (column 13). Because this capitalist is getting twice as much work out of his workers as is typical in his industry, he has generated a substantial surplus. Whether this faster rate of productivity is due to new equipment, new techniques, or sweating workers makes no difference. As long as the capitalist can get cloth produced at a pace above that of his competitors—above the socially necessary rate—he can increase the surplus he generates.

After a while, however, other firms will copy his techniques or come up with others of their own, making the pace of 20 yards per hour the new socially necessary rate. As illustrated in Table 1.3 (line 3), our capitalist still buys $100 worth of labor (column 3) and $400 worth of thread and loom, and the worker produces 20 yards of cloth per hour. Now, however, 20 yards per hour has become the standard rate. All the capitalists are now producing at this rate or have been driven out of business. The value of a yard of cloth has now declined (column 10) to $3 per hour (reflecting the increased "efficiency" with which firms are producing cloth) because there is only $600 of socially necessary labor time (column 11) in the 200 yards of cloth. The surplus has declined to the previous level of $100 (column 12) for a 10-hour day. A greater amount of capital was used to generate this surplus, however; thus, the profit rate (column 13) has declined to 20%.

As a result of what at first appeared to be a profit-enhancing innovation, there is less money to be made in cloth than there was before. Our capitalist, in his search for higher profits and greater markets, and acting from fear of being put out of business in the same way he put others out of business, has in the long run decreased

Table 1.3 Innovation, the Changing Organic Composition of Capital, and the Declining Rate of Profit

				Inputs					Outputs			
(1) Day	(2) Money ($) (3+6+7)	(3) Wage ($)	(4) Hours	(5) Thread (Spools)	(6) Raw Material Costs ($)	(7) Equipment Costs ($)	(8) Labor Power ($)	(9) Cloth (Yards)	(10) Price (per yard) ($)	(11) Value ($) (9 × 10)	(12) Surplus ($) (11 − 2)	(13) Profit Rate (%)
1	300	100	10	10	100	100	200	100	4.00	400	100	33
2	500	100	10	20	200	200	400	200	4.00	800	300	60
3	500	100	10	20	200	200	200	200	3.00	600	100	20
4	700	100	10	30	300	300	300	300	3.00	900	200	29
5	700	100	10	30	300	300	200	300	2.67	800	100	14

his profit rate. Now, he must find a new technique that makes the worker produce even faster.

The capitalist, constantly on the prowl for new sources of surplus, develops another scheme: a new machine that runs 50% faster than the current model. Table 1.3 (line 4) depicts the result. For his $100 wage (column 3), the worker uses up $300 worth of thread (column 6) and $300 worth of this fancy new machine (column 7) and produces 300 yards of cloth (50% more; see column 9). Because our capitalist has a jump on his competitors (so the socially necessary rate has not yet been affected), the cloth still has a value of $3 per yard (Table 1.3, column 10), and he can exchange his cloth for $900 (column 11). He has generated a $200 surplus (column 12) and raised his profit rate (column 13) to 29%. Unfortunately, competition again catches up with him. Soon, everyone has this new machine, everyone is producing 30 yards per hour, and the value of cloth drops to $2.67 per yard (column 10). Thus, he now generates only $800 worth of cloth per day (column 11) for a surplus of only $100 (column 12) and a profit rate of 14% (column 13). Hence, the contradiction with which we began: The capitalist's quest for ever-increasing rates of surplus value is the secret behind increasing demands on workers in the face of rising profits.

The chase for escalating surplus has other effects as well. The capitalist's need to constantly innovate to find new sources of surplus and to stay competitive with other firms means that any particular job or set of skills is likely to become quickly outmoded. Laid-off workers are told to retrain: Capital no longer needs their particular skills, they learn, but might need a different set if only the worker could transform him- or herself. Today's students are training for jobs that are likely to be obsolete within a few years after they graduate. This is all the more true in high-tech fields, in which high levels of skill are demanded and, at the same time, the technology of production is changing so quickly that those skill demands are constantly changing.[14]

This is another of the fundamental contradictions of capitalism, and it plays itself out in the paradox of unemployment coupled with claims that there are jobs going unfilled for lack of qualified workers. It also appears in quality circles and Total Quality Management programs. In these management innovations, workers are driven to constantly find ways of improving productivity to improve the competitive position of the firm. The goal is "continuous improvement," a never-ending stream of innovations that will keep this firm ahead of its competitors. Such programs, however, have the effect of increasing the pace of work for many workers (Banks & Metzgar, 1989). In addition, a very clever worker may uncover an innovation that will eliminate his or her role entirely, and the worker may be rewarded by a layoff, if not of him- or herself, then of a fellow worker. Workers soon recognize this fundamental contradiction and often withhold their contribution by either fighting the introduction of such methods or by giving only token suggestions. Of course, under the conditions of competitive capitalism, such strategies are often doomed by the pressures of competitors who can wheedle or coerce more cooperation from their employees.

Furthermore, in the never-ending search for new sources of surplus, the scale of production is constantly increasing. In the previous example (Table 1.3), at the start, a capitalist could produce at the socially necessary rate by expending only $300 per day (line 1, column 2). After a series of innovations that temporarily increased the surplus (until they were copied by the competition), however, the capitalist now has to invest $700 per day (line 5, column 2) to produce at the socially necessary rate. The scale of production has more than doubled. The capitalist now has twice as much equipment and twice the raw materials invested in producing the same amount of surplus (and a substantially smaller profit rate). In other words, the inorganic composition of capital has grown. Using a census of manufacturing data, we can see the growing inorganic composition of capital: Assets per worker in the American manufacturing sector have grown from $9,000 in 1963 to almost $46,000 by 1987. After controlling for inflation (1983 dollars), these numbers go from $29,000 per worker in 1963 to $40,000 per worker in 1987 (U.S. Census Bureau, 1991, p. 183). By 2002, assets per worker had grown to $115,000 ($64,000 in 1983 dollars) (U.S. Census Bureau, 2005, p. 39). Thus, the inorganic composition of capital grew 38% during the first 24-year period (1963 to 1987), and this growth accelerated to 60% over the next 15 years. In the search for surplus value, capital has expanded to ever-greater proportions. With capital's expansion comes a ballooning of its demands.

Demands of Capital

In addition to the demands of competition are the demands of capital itself. Capital, for Marx (1867/1977), is the objectified embodiment of past labor—dead labor—and its value can be brought to life only when living labor is applied to it. At the Harley-Davidson plant outside Milwaukee (often hailed as one of the success stories of American manufacturing in recent decades), the company labeled the factory's giant, hulking machine tools with their purchase price (often well over the $115,000 average) to remind workers of the value embedded in the equipment, so that workers would be aware of what was lost if the machines were down. An idle factory (idle capital) produces no surplus. Whenever capital sits idle, it represents a loss to the capitalist (what the economist calls "opportunity cost"): "Capital is dead labour which, vampire like, lives only by sucking living labour, and lives the more, the more labour it sucks" (Marx, 1867/1977, p. 342). As the size of the capital outlay increases over time, the size of the vampire demanding living labor becomes increasingly enormous. Its cries to be fed become increasingly irresistible.[15] The demands on workers to be more productive become more incessant and insistent because the stakes are higher: "Capitalist production therefore drives, by its inherent nature, toward the appropriation of labour throughout the whole of the 24 hours in the day" (Marx, 1867/1977, p. 366). Capitalists have been very candid about what is driving the trend toward 12-hour days: "Employers like compressed workweeks and continuous production because it is cost-efficient to keep machinery running all the time. [Twelve-hour shifts are more productive because there is] less downtime in two shifts versus three. Overtime or other added labor costs can also be scheduled away" ("Illinois Jobs," 1995, p. 1). Even more succinctly, to justify a move to 12-hour shifts, managers at Imperial Wallcoverings told the union that "machines aren't making money when they are down" ("Four on, Four off," 1996, p. G1).

Again, the business press provides countless stories of corporations moving to elongated shifts or so-called compressed workweeks in the name of competition and the need to keep their equipment running. It would be impossible to list all U.S.

companies that were on or pushing to adopt 12-hour shifts, but the following partial list serves as an example of how widespread the practice had become in the 1990s: Ford, GM, Chrysler, Fisher-Price, Sorrento, Caterpillar, A. E. Staley, Bridgestone/ Firestone, Goodrich, Sony, Siltec, Hewlett-Packard, Heinz-Starkist, Formica, Gates Rubber, Imperial Wallcoverings, and Poly-Seal. In virtually every case, workers have protested the longer workday, and in virtually every case, management has cited the need for continuous production as the reason for the exorbitant shift lengths.

To facilitate running their plants 24 hours a day, 7 days a week, Caterpillar demanded its employees work 12-hour shifts without overtime for weekend work. In justifying the move to angry workers, an executive at Caterpillar said, "This is about utilization of our multimillion-dollar assets" ("Caterpillar Turns up Pressure," 1992, p. 2). At Gates Rubber Company, management threatened to shut down the Galesburg, Illinois, plant if employees would not agree to 12-hour shifts—not because the company had to struggle to survive, but because business was so good it could not keep pace with demand ("Gates, Union OK Contract," 1996). In other words, even though this is not a case of a company on the verge of collapse, human needs and hardships are eclipsed by the fact that there are even greater profits out there to be made. Because these actions are demanded by the logic of capital, no one is exempt from being called on to work extraordinary hours if the company is "in need." When Allied-Signal's blue-collar workers in Virginia struck in 1993, top management essentially imprisoned white-collar employees inside the plant, forcing them to work 12-hour shifts for 35 straight days. Nearly 1,000 managers-turned-workers were forced to operate dangerous machinery with very little training and to eat, sleep, bathe, and so on in the plant between shifts. The company said it was willing to "take the risk" that some managers would be killed or injured because they had to keep the plant running to keep their customers supplied ("Strike Troops," 1993).[16]

Marx (1867/1977) argues that it was capitalism's need for continuous production that gave rise to the shift system in production, under which some portion of the populace is forced to live on a schedule that effectively cuts them out of participation in most aspects of society. Despite the fact that workers in the 1990s were already protesting the move to 12-hour shifts, 12 hours was often the minimum amount of time they were required to work. In Decatur, as well as in many other parts of the United States, workers currently are required to work 12-hour shifts with mandatory overtime on no notice whenever someone is late or absent or when production demands extra hands.

Again, a look at the garment industry reveals that the only limits on shift lengths are those that workers are able to impose through social and political pressure. In the Mandarin textile plant in El Salvador's San Marcos Free Trade Zone, employees (earning approximately 60¢ an hour) were routinely forced to work 18-hour shifts and 7-day workweeks. Once publicized, the plight of these workers sparked international outrage and demands for justice for the Salvadoran workers. Conditions and shift lengths for garment workers in the United States are also deteriorating. In a particularly dramatic case, a group of Thai workers in El Monte, California, were held in servitude for years, forced to sew garments for up to 22 hours per day for 59¢ per hour ("It's Blood," 1996). According to an investigation of the case by the U.S. Department of Labor (Rizvi, 1995), the shop was a supplier to some of the largest retailers in the nation, including Neiman Marcus, Filene's, J.C. Penney, Macy's West, and Sears. This case represents the extreme, but the U.S. Department of Labor estimated at that time that 70% of all manufacturers in the United States routinely violated overtime regulations.

Capital's solution to this problem of overtime law violations? Change the law. Various proposals have been introduced at the state and federal levels to "revise" the 1938 Fair Labor Standards Act. Their goal has been to eliminate overtime pay for working more than 40 hours in a week to allow employers to impose longer work-weeks without penalty. One proposal would require employers to pay overtime only after a worker worked more than 160 hours in a month, even if those hours were all worked within 2 weeks. Moreover, in 2003, the Bush administration pushed through "overtime reform" despite staunch opposition, even within the Republican-controlled Congress. The Bush administration claimed it was a "worker-friendly" revision because it added a small category of workers to the list of people who are eligible to receive overtime. But, at the same time, the revision recategorizes a significantly larger group of workers as exempt from the law, making it likely that millions of workers will be working longer hours without overtime pay (Eisenbrey & Bernstein, 2003).

Machines and Continuous Production

Despite the obvious toll continuous production takes on human lives, several factors make it the only "logical" practice under the laws of capitalism. First, machinery must be valorized quickly because it quickly becomes obsolete (no longer producing at the socially necessary rate), which results in a loss of value for the capitalist. Fear of obsolescence then drives the capitalist to run his or her factories 24 hours a day to get as much use as possible from his or her machines before they no longer produce at the socially necessary rate. Also, continuous production allows the capitalist to take advantage of super-surplus that comes from innovation and to overcome the declining rate of profit that comes from an increase in constant capital (see Table 1.3). Mechanization provides not only the rationale for continuous production but also a built-in defense mechanism against worker opposition. Replacing employees with machines creates a "surplus army" of unemployed workers who stand at the ready to take the jobs of those who resist the capitalist's increasing demands. The mere threat of this shadowy presence is often enough to silence dissatisfied workers.[17] This is one reason why we have the strange contradiction of increasing work hours and mass layoffs, a contradiction that Marx notes is one of the fundamental characteristics of capitalism and its drive for increasing surplus value.

When the unemployment rate "becomes too low," it generates a frantic search for new sources for the surplus army, including students; housewives; retirees; and, of course, foreign workers. For example, the U.S. government increased the number of visas granted for temporary employment in high-skill jobs, allowing firms to import computer programmers from India, China, and the Philippines. One op-ed commentator from the *New York Times* even called for the repeal of laws preventing firms from using children under age 14, on the grounds that the discipline of work is good for children as young as 9 years old (Brady, 2000).

Marx (1867/1977) argues that the insatiable drive to extend the working day is significant beyond the fact of its inhumanity. It reveals a fundamental transformation that takes place under capitalism:

> Hence that remarkable phenomenon in the history of modern industry, that machinery sweeps away every moral and natural restriction on the length of the working day. Hence too the economic paradox that the most powerful instrument for reducing labour-time suffers a dialectical inversion and becomes the most unfailing means for turning the whole lifetime of the worker and his family into labour-time at capital's disposal for its own valorization. (p. 532)

Mechanization and technological advances both liberate and enslave workers. Although new production technology might reduce the burden of labor, it also increasingly demands longer days and a faster work pace. Similarly, many recent technological advances designed to make life easier for office workers have had the opposite effect. The cellular phone and the portable computer allow workers to escape the office and work where it might be more convenient. This same technology (often provided by the employer) also can be used to require the worker to be available to work any time of the day or night. For example, one computer programmer for a retail chain was given a cellular phone and a portable computer with a cellular modem. He was on call day and night, and when he got a call, he was expected to be logged on to the company's mainframe within 20 minutes. If he went out to dinner, he brought his equipment with him. The company was able to contact him at any time and convert his leisure time to work hours.

The promise of technological liberation is a common theme in advertising, but one can easily imagine alternate, less idyllic scenarios. An advertisement for one consumer electronics manufacturer shows an office worker jogging serenely on a scenic beach. We hear a mysterious ringing from his pocket, and he pulls out a device that is a cellular phone, handheld computer, and fax machine in one. He answers: It's his boss asking for a document. With the flick of a finger, he cheerfully forwards the report, averting crisis (and a trip to the office) through the wonders of technology. The boss tells him he needs to get out of the office more, and the worker smiles, signifying that he has played a fast one on his boss. The implication is that this new technology will allow one to go to the beach when one is supposed to be in the office. It is just as likely, however, that the call came while the man was on his vacation, on Sunday, or during his regular off hours.

Early in the cellular phone boom, researchers conducted experiments to see how this new technology would facilitate geographically dispersed work groups. In one experimental trial, 100 workers in a university, from janitors to high-level administrators, were given cellular phones with free unlimited airtime. Several subjects returned the phones and dropped out of the experiment in disgust, saying the phones robbed them of all sense of "off time." They were at the beck and call of their bosses 24 hours a day, and their leisure time was constantly interrupted by demands from the office. Thus, the same technology that let them wander freely and stay in touch with friends and family also allowed their office to reach out and touch them at any and all times. In other words, the whole world becomes an office, and the whole day one shift.

Capital as Logic

Following Marx (1867/1977), we have argued that the production process, once intended to serve humans' needs, has become entirely indifferent to them under capitalism. Human beings now serve the needs of capital. Indeed, to think otherwise—to argue that an expensive factory should be left idle because workers are tired or that production should be organized using a less efficient but more comfortable process—is considered absurd. Saying that work is taking over our lives and that we should reorganize the economy to put limits on work and reemphasize family and community—while given much lip service—is rarely acknowledged as an argument that should seriously be followed. Indeed, as we have shown, the amount of time Americans spend on the job has increased steadily, and laws limiting the working day have come under attack at the same time "family values" has emerged as the mantra for politicians hoping to take or hold office.

Capital Versus Family

Despite politicians' rhetoric, human and family needs are, in practice, treated as "idealistic goals," whereas the needs of capital—of machines and raw materials—are considered "real-world" issues. The primacy of such issues is so obvious as to transcend the need for justification: hence, such discussion-ending clichés as "We have to look at the bottom line" and "This is business." Once capital invokes the "bottom line" argument, the rest of us are supposed to utter "'nough said" and walk away completely satisfied that the only reasonable course has been followed. To the extent that we do, Marx (1867/1977) argues, the dialectical inversion of objects holding mastery over human beings is revealed.

When one Staley worker said he could not work overtime one night because of family considerations, his supervisor told him, "I don't care what your outside responsibilities are. Once you come here, I own you and you'll stay as long as I want you to." Another worker, a single mother of two school-aged children, pointed out the antimony of family and capital. She routinely works 50 hours or more a week managing a convenience store (with many of those hours coming between 4 p.m. and 8 a.m.). During those same hours, she needs to be home rearing her children. She voiced her despair as follows: "This is the only job I could get that paid enough for me to take care of them, but it never lets me be home when they need me. I can either feed them or be with them, never both." A worker at Dunlop complained that the longer shifts, although leading to higher pay, did not make up for the loss of family time: "We never see our families because we're working every weekend. It's insulting that Dunlop thinks an extra $7 a day is going to compensate for not seeing your kids grow up" ("Union Rejects," 1994, p. C1).

The comptroller at the dot.com that worked 17-hour days for 6 weeks without a day off tells the following story: One night in the middle of this streak, she came home early (9 p.m.) to help her daughter with some homework. After the mom and daughter worked out the problem together, the daughter burst into tears, saying, "Now that I don't have a homework problem, I won't see you again" (Lardner, 1999). Another woman was upset that her children were not able to join family dinners on holidays because they had to be at their jobs in supermarkets, gas stations, restaurants, and so on. Although family gatherings are important, capital is much more concerned with maximizing surplus value and cannot risk the loss that would occur by letting the shops close. This is exacerbated by the ever-present threat from other, less sympathetic capitalists whose businesses will be open and will take sales away from the family-friendly capitalists. Laws mandating that stores close on Sundays or preventing 24-hour retailers have become quaint relics of the adolescence of capitalism. In today's unfettered capitalism, it is the more ruthless capitalist who succeeds in the market. Twenty-four-hour groceries, gas stations, and convenience stores provide opportunities for consumers to engage in commodity exchange day and night. This also means that capital demands access to labor power day and night, weekends and holidays included. Although having the grocery open on Thanksgiving to allow you to buy that extra bag of stuffing or case of beer might make your holiday more enjoyable (and the grocer a little richer), it also means that other people have to spend their holiday staffing all those shops instead of relaxing with their families or friends.

Extended and rotating shifts not only decrease the amount of time a worker can spend with family but also diminish the quality of the time families have together. To research her book *The Time Bind*, sociologist Arlie Hochschild spent 3 years observing and interviewing employees at every level of one Fortune 500 company about how they balance work and family life. Her findings include the surprising fact that some employees, while complaining of not having enough family time due to heavy workloads, did not, in fact, take all of the time off for which they are technically eligible, such as paid vacation and sick time and unpaid maternity/paternity leave. Nor did many avail themselves of company-offered "family-friendly" work schedules, such as job sharing, flextime, or similar programs. Employees' reasons for not taking time off differed. Professional and highly skilled women who were struggling to gain credibility in previously all-male echelons, for example, feared they would lose ground if they took time off for family reasons. In other cases, employees were discouraged from taking time off by hostile or uncooperative supervisors, pressure from coworkers, and the prevailing corporate culture that regarded time spent at work (rather than productivity) as a sign of dedication and commitment to the company.

But Hochschild (2001) also argues that some employees choose to stay at work longer than they have to because the time demands of their jobs have made it literally impossible to build and maintain a successful home life. Parenting has to be squeezed into impossibly small and tightly scheduled fragments of time, leaving the children feeling angry, neglected, and stressed. Couples are torn between wanting to spend time together to nurture their marriage and feeling guilty about taking any more time away from their children. No one is ever satisfied because our jobs simply do not leave

Figure 1.1

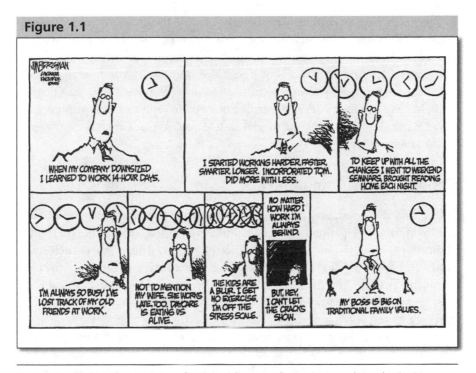

Source: Reprinted with permission of Universal Press Syndicate. Cartoon drawn by Jim Borgman.

us enough time to perform our "second shift" (child and home care) adequately. Hochschild suggests that in our current "job culture," the social spheres of "work" and "home" have changed places. Home, previously a place of comfort, acceptance, and personal support, now has become the site of stress, routinization, and irresolvable conflicts. Meanwhile, by offering the possibilities of success, rewards, and adult friendship, the workplace has taken on more of the positive aspects of home.

In this new model of family and work life, a tired parent flees a world of unresolved quarrels and unwashed laundry for the reliable orderliness, harmony, and managed cheer of work. The emotional magnets beneath home and workplace are in the process of being reversed (Hochschild, 2001).

Although one might seriously question her highly romanticized notions about family life in the past and workplaces in the present, Hochschild's empirical observations of the toll our job culture takes on our families and the way it shapes and defines our personal interactions are compelling. Taken together, they suggest that overlong work hours are eating away at some of the fundamental structures of society and, in the process, engendering a host of social ills.

Even when employees are paid extra for long shifts or for night work, many say the compensation does not make up for the human costs. Depression, divorce, heart disease, hypertension, drug and alcohol abuse, ulcers, and stress are all common side effects of working long or rotating shifts. A study published in *Science* found that among couples with children, night-shift workers' marriages are more likely to end in divorce than marriages of day shifters. In the case of male night-shift workers who have been married less than 5 years, the chance of separation or divorce is six times higher than that for men on days (Presser, 1999). One Michelin worker put it this way: "You work swing shifts to make more money for your family, but you end up losing it all anyway. If you lose your family, you lose all that you worked for to begin with" ("Swing Shifts," 1993, p. 3). Workers at the Buick plant in Flint, Michigan, agreed. Although earning twice their 40-hour pay, hourly employees at Buick City went on strike to protest GM's exorbitant demand for overtime ("GM Hunkers Down," 1994).

Capital Versus Community

A common theme among workers who oppose the longer working day is that it destroys their participation in community life. Workers in Decatur, Illinois, told us about a city festival (Founders Day) that took place during the height of their struggles over the working day. The workers boycotted the festival in protest of the city's complicity with the companies in this labor dispute. In the end, the festival was a bust because of the central role that working people play in such events, both as participants and as organizers.

As the working day gets longer, workers are increasingly cut off from participation in community life. The increased time spent at work—and the increased time required to recover from a longer working day—constrains participation in activities and voluntary associations such as reading groups, political organizations, social clubs, sports leagues, and churches. One Staley worker stated, "We are the ones who coach the Little League. We organize the town picnics. We are the ones that do all the things that keep this town going. We can't do that now." As workers increasingly become abstract labor power on 24-hour call to the whims of capital, they are no longer able to participate in the intermediate institutions that fill out the structure of society. According to Marx (1867/1977),

> It is self-evident that the worker is nothing other than labour-power for the duration of his whole life, and that therefore all his disposable time is by nature and by right labour-time, to be devoted to the self-valorization of capital. Time for education, for intellectual development, for the fulfillment of social functions, for social intercourse, for the free play of the vital forces of his body and his mind, even the rest time of Sunday . . . what foolishness! (p. 375)

That is how capital views workers—as portable labor power. A rubber worker in Decatur, Illinois, echoes this sentiment. Reacting to the 12-hour shifts and 7-day workweeks offered by Bridgestone/Firestone, he said, "You won't have a life. You're not supposed to have any life except work" ("Middle-Class Labor," 1995, p. 1).

Political philosophers such as Robert Putnam have noted this declining participation in community life. In his article, "Bowling Alone: America's Declining Social Capital" (Putnam, 1995), he argues that American society has become more isolated and alienated, with people increasingly forgoing participation in community life. He cites statistics such as the nearly 50% drop in Parent-Teacher Association (PTA) participation during the past 30 years, a significant drop in volunteer work in the past 15 years, and 10% to 50% drops in fraternal organization memberships during the past two decades. The title of his article is derived from the observation that, although bowling participation per se has increased approximately 10% from 1980 to 1993, participation in bowling leagues (a more communal activity) has dropped 40% during that period. Many pundits have long bemoaned the loss of community, blaming it on the selfishness of recent generations or on the alienating effects of television and modern culture. Marx's (1867/1977) analysis more explicitly links the decay of community life with changes in the economic structure. As the data on increasing work hours and more uncertain work shifts show, there has been an increase in time pressure on American workers during the past two decades. Also, as the previous quotes from workers point out (and as the quote from Marx also makes clear), participation in community life suffers as capital extends its reach over ever more of the workers' waking hours. Rotating shifts, unpredictable mandatory overtime, 24-hour on-call responsibilities, weekend and evening work, and elimination of vacation time all remove the space in workers' lives that was used to coach Little League, hang out at the Elks club, attend the PTA, supervise a scout troop, or commit to a Monday night bowling league.

Conclusion

Marx is often (and incorrectly) associated with the political philosophies of countries such as China and the former Soviet Union. The strength of Marx's writings, however, is not in heuristics about a future society; it is in his penetrating analysis of capitalism itself. Marx notes that capitalism is the source of unprecedented wealth and the engine of fantastic innovations, and yet it is also a system that hinges on exploitation, inequality, and misery. Although the demise of so-called communist governments is used by some to discredit Marx, nowhere can the viability of his theories be seen more clearly than in the strongholds of capitalism. Although hourly workers are working more, and under increasingly difficult conditions, the number of households earning below $25,000 a year is growing. At the same time, the share of the national income going to the richest 5% of households has increased approximately 25% ("Middle-Class Labor," 1995). What keeps Marx viable nearly a century and a half after the publication of *Capital* is that his writings offer a structural analysis of why these things must be so.

Unlike many who examine the social landscape, Marx does not attribute these outcomes to the greed or lack of feeling of the capitalist or to the laziness or intemperance of the workers. Instead, he demonstrates how the very nature of a capitalist economy demands such behavior on the part of the owners of capital. Marx also notes that these contradictions lead to both economic and political struggles, and that the two cannot be separated. At times, workers have been able to gain some political power, through mechanisms such as unions or political parties or in times of labor shortages (brought on by wars, for example), and have been able to increase wages, reduce working hours, or put limits on firms' behavior.

The working day is a significant locus of worker resistance throughout the history of capitalism. As Marx notes, the capitalist has bought a full day's labor power from the worker and has the right to the full use of his purchase. The worker has sold the amount of labor that is equivalent to what can be reproduced in a day (so he or she will be able to sell it again tomorrow) and has the right to limit consumption to this amount and no more. "Between equal rights, force decides," Marx wrote, hence, the political struggle over the terms of labor. Marx traces much of the 19th-century struggles in England and the other capitalist countries in Chapter 10 of *Capital*. The struggles in Decatur, Illinois, and elsewhere in the United States echo the themes of Marx's day. The immorality of the overlong workday becomes a rallying cry for worker struggle and worker solidarity. Even in a period of weak unions and little direct action by workers, 12-hour shifts can still get workers to strike and to fight. The dynamics of capital, however, are difficult to resist, and most of such struggles have been losing battles for the workers.

Capitalism is more than a long workday, however. It is also a constant search for new ways of generating surplus. Firms push to increase the speed of work. They are constantly innovating to find new ways to beat the competition (or to keep up with innovating competitors). The increased scale of production such innovations produce puts pressure on firms to keep their machines running day and night, 7 days a week, 365 days a year, pushing workers for still more hours.

Finally, capitalism is a production system based on value production. It is this insight that is central to understanding the dynamics of capitalism. Firms exist to produce surplus value. Producing goods and services is an incidental by-product of that search. Workers exist to provide labor power for the machines and to contribute value and surplus value to the products. Workers serve the firms; firms do not serve the workers. Society exists as a source of workers to produce commodities and consumers to buy commodities. Needs such as time with family, participation in community life, and time for contemplation and self-development are at best incidental to, and often seen as impediments to, the demands of capital for constant production.

The Bible asks, "What does it profit a man to gain the world and lose his soul?" Capital replies, "The profit is the ability to compete another day in the hopes of still more profit." Under capitalism, this is sufficient answer to all questions of the purpose of the economy and all the related institutions of society. On the basis of the analysis presented in this chapter, we can see that, although such a system is driven by the impersonal demands of capital, it is, at its roots, still a social system, a system of people. Given that, we can then ask, Is this the kind of society we want to reproduce? This is the question that underlies Marx's analyses. It is a question that we should continue to ask.

Notes

1. In the 1990s, Decatur, once an anonymous Midwestern industrial town, became known in labor circles throughout the world as the "war zone" after workers at the region's three largest employers, A. E. Staley, Caterpillar, and Bridgestone/Firestone, either went on strike or were locked out of their jobs. The videos *Deadly Corn* and *Struggle in the Heartland* document these fights.

2. Throughout the text, we follow Marx's usage and use the term *value* to refer to exchange value, not use value.

3. Marx contrasts the terms *use value* and *exchange value*. The *use value* of a good refers to the benefits derived from its consumption. The use value of bread is that it serves as food; the use value of a coat is that it keeps one warm. *Exchange value* refers to the ability of a particular quantity of a good to be traded for some quantity of another good. The exchange value of one coat, for example, may be 100 loaves of bread or two pairs of shoes. Capitalism is characterized by its emphasis on exchange value over use value. Ancient slave societies (Egypt, Greece, and Rome) and feudal societies (medieval Europe and feudal Japan), although still based on class exploitation, utilized modes of production based on use value rather than exchange value.

4. The amount of labor time embedded in a given commodity includes the amount of labor time expended in gathering or producing the materials, tools, or machines used in the production process. When comparing the amount of value in given quantities of two commodities (e.g., 20 yards of linen and 100 loaves of bread), what is being compared is the amount of socially necessary abstract labor required to produce that amount of each commodity. By socially necessary, Marx (1867/1977) means "the labour-time required to produce any use-value under the conditions of production normal for a given society and with the average degree of skill and intensity of labour prevalent in that society" (p. 129). A given worker (or workers in a given factory) may work above or below the socially necessary rate and hence contribute more or less socially necessary labor within the same time frame. Abstract labor means undifferentiated labor, abstracted from the particular skills or activities of actual, concrete labor: "working" as opposed to "weaving" or "baking."

5. Marx's theory, which is sometimes referred to incorrectly as the "labor theory of value," can be summarized more properly as the value theory of labor. By converting labor into value production, capitalism fundamentally transforms human activity into a new form—capitalist work.

6. It is certainly the case that individual exchanges can involve one party besting the other, whether through force or through guile. One capitalist may be able to exchange $100 worth of shoes for $110 worth of bread, thereby gaining a $10 "profit." This profit, however, is simply the transfer of value from one person (the dim capitalist) to another (the clever capitalist). No value is created by such exchanges.

7. These numbers are arbitrary. What is key is that some time is needed for what Marx calls "necessary labor" (labor needed to produce a value equal to the value of the means of subsistence).

8. By stating the problem in these terms, we can see that this result is not due to the worker getting paid by the "day" instead of, for example, by the hour. Even if paid by the hour, the worker could potentially produce more in each hour than an hour's share of socially necessary labor time (Marx, 1867/1977, pp. 333–338).

9. Table 1.2 also shows that the increase has affected women substantially more than men.

10. Staley even had the gall to invoke the specter of "foreign competition," despite the fact that it is a British-owned company.

11. Marx (1867/1977) stated, "This does not depend on the will, either good or bad, of the individual capitalist. Under free competition, the immanent laws of capitalist production confront the individual capitalist as a coercive force external to him" (p. 381).

12. In a widely circulated internal memo that was leaked to the *New York Times* in October 2005, Susan Chambers, later named Walmart's executive vice president in charge of human resources, noted that Walmart's wage and benefits policies had come under criticism from labor activists and government officials (who were paying for Walmart's below-subsistence wage policies through Medicare, food stamps, and other public assistance programs). Chambers noted the difficulties Walmart has in defending itself against such

critics: "Wal-Mart's critics can also easily exploit some aspects of our benefits offering to make their case; *in other words, our critics are correct in some of their observations*. Specifically, our coverage is expensive for low-income families, and Wal-Mart has a *significant percentage of Associates and their children on public assistance*" [italics added]. In other words, Walmart is cheating even by the rules of capitalism, because it is not paying the full share of the cost of replacing a day's labor power. (The full memo is available at http://www.nytimes.com/packages/pdf/business/26walmart.pdf.)

13. As in the first example, the cloth's value is $4 per yard, representing the amount of socially necessary labor embedded in the cloth—where socially necessary labor is defined as the labor required to produce the cloth in the usual way, at the usual pace, which was 10 yards per hour.

14. In his chapter on machinery and large-scale industry, Marx (1867/1977) discusses the implications of the constant need for innovation: "Modern industry never views or treats the existing form of a production process as the definitive one. Its technical basis is therefore revolutionary, whereas all earlier modes of production were essentially conservative. By means of machinery, chemical processes and other methods, it is constantly transforming not only the technical basis of production but also the functions of the worker and the social combinations of the labour process. At the same time, it thereby also revolutionizes the division of labour within society, and incessantly throws masses of capital and of workers from one branch of production to another. Thus large-scale industry, by its very nature, necessitates variation of labour, fluidity of functions, and mobility of the worker in all directions" (p. 617).

15. Marx (1867/1977) stated, "Constant capital, the means of production, only exist, considered from the standpoint of the process of valorization, in order to absorb labour and, with every drop of labour, a proportional quantity of surplus labour. In so far as the means of production fail to do this, their mere existence forms a loss for the capitalist, in a negative sense, for while they lie fallow they represent a useless advance of capital. This loss becomes a positive one as soon as the interruption of employment necessitates an additional outlay when the work begins again" (p. 366).

16. Interestingly, one of the reasons the company gave for "sequestering" these managers-turned-workers was that the long shifts would leave them so exhausted they would find it easier just to sleep at the plant. These are the same shifts, however, the company expects the blue-collar employees to work regularly, while also raising their families, participating in the community, and so on.

17. It is hard to imagine a worker who has not heard a variation of, "If you don't like it, there are 10 people out there who would be glad to take your job right now." As effective as that threat usually is (because how many of us can afford to take the chance?), however, it is not always true. Toy industry giant Fisher-Price converted one of its production lines to manufacture new outdoor play equipment. Conditions on that line, however, are so atrocious—12-hour shifts lifting up to 70-pound loads in high heat and bad air—management cannot find enough people to fully staff the line. Regular workers at the plant have agreed to be laid off rather than work under those conditions, so management has had to scramble to keep the line open using temporary workers ("Fisher-Pricers," 1995).

References

Anderson, P. (2001, August 31). Study: U.S. employees put in most hours [Online]. Retrieved from http://archives.cnn.com/2001/CAREER/trends/08/30/ilo.study

Banks, A., & Metzgar, J. (1989). Participating in management: Union organizing on a new terrain. *Labor Research Review, 8*(2), 1–55.

Barboza, D. (2006, October 13). China drafts law to boost unions and end abuse [Online]. Retrieved from http://www.nytimes.com/2006/10/13/business/worldbusiness/13sweat .html

Bitter Caterpillar strike grows more corrosive, costly. (1994, September 26). *Chicago Tribune*, p. 4.

Brady, M. H. (2000, April 13). Growing in the job. *New York Times*, p. 1.

Braverman, H. (1974). *Labor and monopoly capital*. New York: Monthly Review Press.

Caterpillar turns up pressure on UAW. (1992, November 21). *Chicago Tribune*, p. 2.

Chambers, S. (2006). *Reviewing and revising Wal-Mart's benefits strategy* (Wal-Mart internal memo) [Online]. Retrieved from http://www.nytimes.com/packages/pdf/business/ 26walmart.pdf

Contingent workforce. (2003, May). *Business for Social Responsibility* [Online]. Retrieved from http://www.bsr.org/CSRResources/IssueBriefDetail.cfm?Document ID=48981

Cook, C. D. (2000, March 27). Temps demand a new deal [Online]. *The Nation*. Retrieved from http://www.thenation.com/article/temps-demand-new-deal

Dunayevskaya, R. (1988). *Marxism and freedom*. New York: Columbia University Press.

Eisenbrey, R., & Bernstein, J. (2003). *Eliminating the right to overtime pay: Department of Labor proposal means lower pay, longer hours for millions of workers* (EPI Briefing Paper #139) [Online]. Retrieved from http://www.cpi.org/publications/entry/briefing papers_flsa_jun03

Etter, L. (2006, September 2–3). Labor Day: A report card for American workers. *Wall Street Journal*, p. A7.

Factory OT shoots up. (1994, December 2). *Cincinnati Enquirer*, p. A1.

Fisher-Pricers rejecting roto-molding jobs. (1995, May 7). *Buffalo News*, p. B13.

Four on, four off. (1996, March 14). *Providence Journal-Bulletin*, p. G1.

Gates, union OK contract. (1996, March 28). *Galesburg* (IL) *Register-Mail*, p. A1.

Geoghegan, T. (1999, January 24). Tampering with the time clock. *New York Times*, Weekend section, p. 15.

GM hunkers down to control costs. (1994, September 28). *Detroit News*, p. B1.

GM pact fallout: Wall Street wary; workers who like OT will get less. (1994, October 2). *Detroit News*, p. A1.

Goodyear workers go on strike. (2006, October 6). *Reuters-New York Times* [Online]. Retrieved from http://www.nytimes.com/2006/10/06/business/06tire.html

Greenhouse, S. (1999, September 5). Ideas & trends: Running on empty; So much work, so little time [Online]. *New York Times*. Retrieved from http://www.nytimes.com/1999/ 09/05/weekinreview/ideas-trends-running-on-empty-so-much-work-so-little-time .html?scp=460&sq=tuscany&st=nyt&pagewanted=all

Greenhouse, S. (2006, October 14). Wal-Mart told to pay $78 million [Online]. *New York Times*. Retrieved from http://www.nytimes.com/2006/10/14/business/14walmart .html

Greenhouse, S., & Barbaro, M. (2006, October 2). Wal-Mart to add wage caps and part-timers [Online]. *New York Times*. Retrieved from http://www.nytimes.com/2006/10/ 02/business/02walmart.html

Greenhouse, S., & Leonhardt, D. (2006, August 28). Real wages fail to match a rise in productivity [Online]. *New York Times*. Retrieved from http://www.nytimes.com/2006/ 08/28/business/28wages.html

Griffin Environmental uses a four-day week to build overtime into the system. (1995, June). *Syracuse Business*, p. 1.

Hochschild, A. R. (2001). *The time bind: When work becomes home and home becomes work.* New York: Owl Books.

Illinois jobs grow scarce, pay less. (1995, September 4). *Chicago Tribune,* Business section, p. 1.

It's blood, sweatshops and tears: Legitimate garment makers are being squeezed from both sides. (1996, August 23). *Los Angeles Times,* p. A1.

Klug, L. A. (2005, December 23). Jury rules Wal-Mart must pay $172 million over meal breaks [Online]. *New York Times.* Retrieved from http://www.nytimes.com/2005/12/23/business/23nwalmart.html

Lardner, J. (1999, December 12). World-class workaholics: Are crazy hours and takeout dinner the elixir of America's success? *U.S. News Online.* Retrieved from http://www.usnews.com/usnews/biztech/articles/991220/archive_004401.htm

Marx, K. (1977). *Capital: A critique of political economy* (B. Fowkes, Trans.). New York: Vintage. (Original work published 1867)

Mayer, T. (1994). *Analytic Marxism.* Thousand Oaks, CA: Sage.

Middle-class labor in US feels the squeeze as wages decline. (1995, November 29). *Christian Science Monitor,* p. 1.

Overtime pressures GM to hire more. (1994, August 21). *Fort Wayne* (IN) *Journal Gazette,* p. F1.

Presser, H. B. (1999, June 11). Toward a 24-hour economy. *Science, 284,* 1778–1779.

Putnam, R. D. (1995). Bowling alone: America's declining social capital. *Journal of Democracy, 6*(1), 65–78.

Rizvi, H. (1995, October). Slaves to fashion. *Multinational Monitor, 16*(10), 6–7.

Ross, R. (2004). *Slaves to fashion.* Ann Arbor: University of Michigan Press.

Schor, J. (1991). *The overworked American.* New York: Basic Books.

Sen, A. (1999). *Development as freedom.* Oxford, UK: Oxford University Press.

Strike troops: 35-day occupation at Allied-Signal. (1993, August 2). *Richmond Times-Dispatch,* p. B1.

Swing shifts may push employees too far: Companies examine employee options. (1993, September 26). *Spartanburg Herald-Journal,* Business section, p. 3.

12-hour day sparks strike at Poly-Seal. (1994, March 3). *Baltimore Sun,* Business section, p. 1.

Union rejects proposed contract with Dunlop. (1994, November 7). *Buffalo News,* p. C1.

Union stays on job, but strikes out at Staley. (1992, December 12). *Chicago Tribune,* p. 1.

U.S. Census Bureau. (1991). *Census of manufactures, 1987.* Washington, DC: U.S. Government Printing Office.

U.S. Census Bureau. (2005, October). *2002 Economic Census: Manufacturing, Subject Series* [Online]. Washington, DC: U.S. Government Printing Office. Retrieved from http://www.census.gov/prod/ec02/ec0231sg1.pdf

DISCUSSION QUESTIONS

1. Give examples from your own work experience or recent news reports of the company trying to get you to work "off the clock" or trying to make leisure time (or study time) available to the company. How are such requests justified by your boss? How does Marx explain such requests?

2. It has been said recently that "The era of lifetime careers is over. Today's workers should expect a multitude of jobs and must constantly be learning new skills." Use Marx to explain the demise of

the "company man" and the rise of the free agent, flexible worker. Discuss your own education strategy in light of this analysis.

3. Discuss how technological innovations both solve and cause the problem of declining profits and how these innovations put pressure on firms to increase the length of the working day.

4. Marx notes, "Between equal rights, force decides." How does this observation help explain the stagnating wages during this recent period of rising profits, and also the wage growth during the post-World War II expansion in the United States?

5. How does globalization factor into the problems confronting workers in the United States today? What types of social policies would be necessary to advance the economic interests of workers?

CHAPTER 2

The Weberian Theory of Rationalization and the McDonaldization of Contemporary Society

George Ritzer

George Ritzer is Distinguished Professor of Sociology at the University of Maryland. His major areas of interest are sociological theory, globalization, and the sociology of consumption. He has served as chair of the American Sociological Association's sections on theory (1989–1990) and organizations and occupations (1980–1981). He has been a distinguished scholar-teacher at the University of Maryland and has been awarded a teaching excellence award. He has held the UNESCO chair in social theory at the Russian Academy of Sciences and has received a Fulbright-Hays Fellowship. He has been a scholar-in-residence at the Netherlands Institute for Advanced Study and the Swedish Collegium for Advanced Study in the Social Sciences. A revised New Century edition of The McDonaldization of Society *was published by Pine Forge in 2004, and the fifth edition appeared in 2007. The book has been translated into 16 different languages, including German, French, Spanish, Italian, Japanese, and Chinese. Several books have been published that are devoted to analyzing the McDonaldization thesis. His most recent books include* The Globalization of Nothing *(Sage, 2004) and* The Blackwell Companion to Globalization *(2007), as well as the 11-volume* Encyclopedia of Sociology *(2007).*

I n this chapter, I apply one of the most famous and important theories in the history of sociology, Max Weber's (1864–1920) theory of rationalization, to contemporary society.

In Weber's view, modern society, especially the Western world, is growing increasingly rationalized. As the reader will see, Weber regarded bureaucracy as the ultimate example of rationalization. Thus, Weber can be seen as being focally concerned with the rationalization of society in general and, more specifically, its bureaucratization.

This chapter is premised on the idea that, whereas the processes of rationalization and bureaucratization described by Weber have continued, if not accelerated, the bureaucracy has been supplanted by the fast-food restaurant as the best exemplification of this process. Furthermore, we will see that the rational principles that lie at the base of the fast-food restaurant are spreading throughout American society as well as the rest of the world. On the basis of Weber's ideas on the rationalization process, in this chapter I describe the continuation and even acceleration of this process, or what I have termed the "McDonaldization" of society (Ritzer, 1983, 2004).

Four types of rationality lie at the heart of Weber's theory of rationalization (Brubaker, 1984; Habermas, 1984; Kalberg, 1980; Levine, 1981). Practical rationality is to be found in people's mundane, day-to-day activities and reflects their worldly interests (Weber, 1904–1905/1958). In Weber's (1958) terms, through practical rationality, people seek the "methodical attainment of a definitely given and practical end by means of an increasingly precise calculation of adequate means" (p. 293). Therefore, actors calculate all possible means available to them, choose the alternative that best allows them to reach their ultimate end, and then follow that line of action. "All human beings engage in practical rationality in attempting to solve the routine and daily problems of life" (Levine, 1981, p. 12).

Theoretical rationality involves "an increasingly theoretical mastery of reality by means of increasingly precise and abstract concepts" (Weber, 1958, p. 293). Among other things, it involves logical deduction, the attribution of causality, and the arrangement of symbolic meanings. It is derived from the inherent need of actors to give some logical meaning to a world that appears haphazard (Kalberg, 1980). Whereas practical rationality involves action, theoretical rationality is a cognitive process and has tended to be the province of intellectuals.

Substantive rationality involves value postulates, or clusters of values, that guide people in their daily lives, especially in their choice of means to ends. These clusters of values are rational when they are consistent with specific value postulates preferred by actors (Kalberg, 1980). Substantive rationality can be linked more specifically to economic action. To Weber (1921/1968), economic action is substantively rational to "the degree to which the provisioning of given groups of persons with goods is shaped by economically oriented social action under some criterion (past, present, or potential) of ultimate values, regardless of the nature of these ends." Thus, substantive rationality involves a choice of means to ends guided by some larger system of human values.

Formal rationality involves the rational calculation of means to ends based on universally applied rules, regulations, and laws (Kalberg, 1980). Formal rationality is institutionalized in such large-scale structures as the bureaucracy, modern law, and the capitalist economy. The choice of means to ends is determined by these larger structures and their rules and laws.

In looking for the best means of attaining a given objective under formal rationality, we are not left to our own devices, but rather we use existing rules, regulations, and structures that either predetermine the optimum methods or help us discover them. This, clearly, is a major development in the history of the world. In the past, people had to discover such mechanisms on their own or with only vague and general guidance from larger value systems. Now, we no longer have to discover for ourselves the optimum means to some given end, because that optimum means has already been discovered: It is incorporated into the rules, regulations, and structures of our social institutions.

Formal rationality often leads to decisions that disregard the needs and values of actors, implying that substantive rationality is unimportant. One example is a formally rational economic system. The needs that come to be emphasized and realized are those for which actors are able to outbid others because they have an abundance of money, not because those needs are of greater importance or have more human value. Profits are the primary focus rather than issues of humanity. Weber (1921/1968) stresses this disregard for humanity in a formally rational economic system when he writes, "Decisive are the need for competitive survival and the conditions of the labor, money and commodity markets; hence matter-of-fact considerations that are simply nonethical determine individual behavior and interpose impersonal forces between the persons involved" (p. 1186). The primary concern of the entrepreneur within a formally rational economic system that is capitalist is such nonethical objectives as continuous profit making. The workers, in turn, are dominated by the entrepreneurs, who subject the workers to "masterless slavery" in the formal rational economic system (Weber, 1903–1906/1975). In other words, the formally economic system robs the workers of their basic humanity by enslaving them in a world denuded of human values.

Unlike the first three types of rationality, formal rationality has not existed at all times and in all places. Rather, it was created in, and came to dominate, the modern, Western, industrialized world. Weber believed that formal rationality was coming to overwhelm and to supplant the other types of rationality within the Western world. He saw a titanic struggle taking place in his time between formal and substantive rationality. Weber anticipated, however, that this struggle would end with the erosion of substantive rationality in the face of the forward march of formal rationality. The fading away of substantive rationality was regretted by Weber because it "embodied Western civilization's highest ideals: the autonomous and free individual whose actions were given continuity by their reference to ultimate values" (quoted in Kalberg, 1980, p. 1176). Instead of people whose actions were guided by these high ideals, we were to be left in the modern world with people who simply followed the rules without regard to larger human values.

Weber saw bureaucracy as the epitome of formally rational domination. Weber (1921/1968) links bureaucracies and rationalization as follows:

> Bureaucratic rationalization . . . revolutionizes with technical means, in principle, as does every economic reorganization, "from without": It first changes the material and social orders, and through them the people, by changing the

conditions of adaptation, and perhaps the opportunities for adaptation, through a rational determination of means to ends. (p. 1116)

The bureaucracy "strongly furthers the development of 'rational matter-of-factness' and the personality type of the professional expert" (Weber, 1946, p. 240). These "experts" possess a "spirit of formalistic impersonality . . . without hatred or passion, and hence without affection or enthusiasms" (Brubaker, 1984, p. 21). The top officials of the bureaucracy develop rules and regulations that lead lower-level officials to choose the best means to ends already chosen at the highest levels. The rules and regulations represent the bureaucracy's institutional memory, which contemporaries need only to use (and not invent and continually reinvent) to attain some end.

The bureaucracies themselves are structured in such a way as to guide or even to force people to choose certain means to ends. Each task is broken up into a number of components, and each office is responsible for a separate portion of the larger task. Employees in each office handle only their own part of the task, usually by following rules and regulations in a predetermined sequence. The goal is attained when each incumbent has completed his or her required task in proper order. The bureaucracy thereby utilizes what its past history has shown to be optimum means to the end in question.

Weber's overall theoretical perspective was that it was largely the unique development of formal rationality that accounted for the distinctive development of the West. Weber suggests that it was key to the development of the Western world; that it came into conflict with the other types of rationality, especially substantive rationality; and that it acted to reduce them in importance and ultimately to subordinate, if not totally eliminate, them in terms of their importance to Western society.

For Weber, the bureaucracy was the height of (formal) rationality, which he defined in terms of the five elements of efficiency, predictability, quantifiability (or calculability), control through substituting nonhuman technology for human judgment, and the irrationality of rationality.

Bureaucracies operate in a highly predictable manner. Incumbents in one office understand very well how the incumbents of other offices will behave. They know what they will be provided with and when they will receive it. Recipients of the service provided by bureaucracies know with a high degree of assurance what they will receive and when they will receive it. Because bureaucracies quantify as many activities as possible, employees perform their duties as a series of specified steps at quantifiable rates of speed. As with all rationalized systems that focus exclusively on quantity, however, the handling of large numbers of things is equated with excellence, and little or no evaluation is made of the actual quality of what is done in each case. Bureaucracies control people by replacing human judgment with nonhuman technology. Indeed, bureaucracy itself may be seen as one huge nonhuman technology that functions more or less automatically. The adaptability of human decisions vanishes into the dictates of rules, regulations, and institutional structures. The work to be done is divided up so that each office is allocated a limited number of well-defined tasks. Incumbents must do those tasks and no others.

The tasks must be done in the manner prescribed by the organization; idiosyncratic performance will get one demoted or even fired. The idea is to get the job done in a certain way by a certain time without mistakes. The bureaucracy's clients are also controlled. The organization provides only certain services and not others; one must apply for the services on a specific form by a specific date, and one will receive those services only in a certain way.

Weber praised bureaucracies for their advantages over other mechanisms for discovering and implementing optimum means to ends, but at the same time, he was painfully aware of the irrationalities of formally rational systems. Instead of being efficient systems, bureaucracies often become inefficient as the regulations that are used to make them rational degenerate into "red tape." Bureaucracies often become unpredictable as employees grow unclear about what they are supposed to do and clients do not get the services they expect. The emphasis on quantifiability often leads to large amounts of poor quality work. Anger at the nonhuman technologies that are replacing them often leads employees to undercut or sabotage the operation of these technologies. By then, bureaucracies have begun to lose control over their workers as well as their constituents, and what was designed to be a highly rational operation often ends up irrational and quite out of control.

Although Weber was concerned about the irrationalities of formally rational systems, he was even more deeply disturbed by what he called the "iron cage of rationality." Weber saw the bureaucracy as a rationalized cage that encased increasing numbers of human beings. He described bureaucracies as "escape proof," "practically unshatterable," and among the hardest institutions to destroy once they are created. The individual bureaucrat is seen as "harnessed" into this bureaucratic cage and unable to "squirm out" of it. Given its strength, and our inability to escape, Weber concludes resignedly and with considerable unease, to put it mildly, that "the future belongs to bureaucratization" (Weber, 1921/1968, p. 1401). He feared that more sectors of society would come to be dominated by rationalized principles so that people would be locked into a series of rationalized workplaces, rationalized recreational settings, and rationalized homes. Society would become nothing more than a seamless web of rationalized structures.

Weber has a highly pessimistic view of the future. He saw no hope in the socialistic movements of his day, which he felt (and time has borne him out) would only succeed in increasing the spread of bureaucratization and formal rationality.

There is little question that the process of rationalization has spread further and become even more firmly entrenched than it was in Weber's day. The fast-food restaurant, of which McDonald's is the best-known chain, has employed all the rational principles pioneered by the bureaucracy and is part of the bureaucratic system because huge conglomerates now own many of the fast-food chains. McDonald's utilized bureaucratic principles and combined them with others, and the outcome is the process of McDonaldization.

More than 25 years ago, I wrote an essay titled "The McDonaldization of Society." The main thesis of that essay was that Max Weber was right about the inexorable march of formal rationality, but that his paradigm case of that type of rationality and the spearhead in its expansion, the bureaucracy, have been superseded in contemporary American society by the fast-food restaurant. It is the fast-food restaurant that today best represents and leads the process of formal rationalization and its basic components efficiency, predictability, quantification, control through the substitution of nonhuman for human technology,[1] and the ultimate irrationality of formal rationality. A decade after the original essay, as we had begun progressing through the 1990s, I once again examined the process of McDonaldization. I was astounded by the forward progress of McDonaldization during the previous decade and the degree to which it has spread its tentacles ever farther into contemporary society.

The most obvious, and perhaps least important, extension is that fast-food restaurants themselves have grown and expanded. The McDonald's chain, which began operation in 1955, now operates more than 32,000 restaurants in 117 countries serving more than 60 million people a day (see http://www.aboutmcdonalds.com/mcd/our_company.html); the largest 500 U.S. restaurant chains did $199.9 billion in sales in 2005 alone (Ramirez, 1990).[2] No longer restricted to the good old American hamburger, fast-food chains now traffic in pizza and Italian, Mexican, Chinese, and Cajun food, among others. Nor are the fast-food chains limited any longer to low-priced restaurants—now there are "upscale" chains, such as Sizzler (steaks), Red Lobster (seafood), Starbucks (coffee), and Fuddruckers (gourmet burgers), as well as trendy saloons such as Bennigan's and T.G.I. Friday's. While America expands its chains, many other countries are developing their own, most notably the fast-food croissanteries spreading throughout one of the most unlikely of locations for such a phenomenon, the center of gourmet dining: Paris.

Instead of being content to surround college campuses, fast-food chains are increasingly found *on* those campuses. There is also more involvement by the chains in the food served at the nation's high schools and grade schools (Farhi, 1990). Once characterized by an odd and unpredictable mix of restaurants, the nation's interstate highways are coming to be increasingly populated by fast-food chains. A similar thing has happened at the nation's airports. The military has been forced to serve fast food at its bases and on its ships. Fast-food outlets are turning up increasingly in hospitals, despite the innumerable attacks on the nutritional value of the food. Yet another incursion of the fast-food chains is into the nation's baseball parks and other sports venues.

Still another element involves the degree to which a wide array of other kinds of businesses are coming to be operated on the basis of the principles pioneered by the fast-food chains. For example, the vice chairman of one of these chains, Toys "R" Us, said, "We want to be thought of as a sort of McDonald's of toys" (Egan, 1990, p. 29). Other chains with a similar model and similar ambitions include Jiffy Lube, AAMCO Transmissions, Midas Muffler, Hair Plus, H&R Block, Pearle Vision Centers, Kampgrounds of America (KOA), KinderCare (dubbed "Kentucky Fried Children"), NutriSystem, Jenny Craig, Curves, and many more.

McDonald's influence is also felt in the number of social phenomena that have come to be prefaced by "Mc." Examples include McDentists, McDoctors, McChild care centers, McStables (for the nationwide racehorse training operation of Wayne Lucas), and McPaper (for *USA Today*; its short news articles are sometimes called

"News McNuggets") (Prichard, 1987). When *USA Today* began a (later aborted) television program modeled after the newspaper, it was immediately dubbed "News McRather" (Zoglin, 1988). With the latter kinds of extensions, we get to the real core of the expansion of McDonaldization and the real reason for revisiting the process. In the past half-century, McDonaldization has extended its reach into more and more regions of society, and those areas are increasingly remote from the heart of the process in the fast-food business. As the previous examples make clear, dentistry, medicine, child care, the training of racehorses, newspapers, and television news have come to be modeled after food chains. Thus, McDonaldization is the process by which the principles of the fast-food restaurant are coming to dominate more and more sectors of society.

Even the derivatives of McDonald's are, in turn, having their own influence. The success of *USA Today* ("McPaper") has led to changes (shorter stories and color weather maps) in many newspapers across the nation. One *USA Today* editor stated, "The same newspaper editors who call us McPaper have been stealing our McNuggets" (Zoglin, 1988). The influence of *USA Today* is manifested most blatantly in the *Boca Raton News*, a Knight-Ridder newspaper. This newspaper is described as "a sort of smorgasbord of snippets, a newspaper that slices and dices the news into even smaller portions than does *USA Today*, spicing it with color graphics and fun facts and cute features like 'Today's Hero' and 'Critter Watch'" (Zoglin, 1988). As in *USA Today*, stories in the *Boca Raton News* do not usually "jump" from one page to another; they start and finish on the same page. To meet this need, long and complex stories often have to be reduced to a few paragraphs. Much of a story's context, and much of what the principals have to say, are severely cut back or omitted entirely. The main function of the newspaper seems to be to entertain, with its emphasis on light and celebrity news, color maps, and graphics.

The objective of the remainder of this chapter is to demonstrate the continued relevance of Weberian theory by attempting to get at the full reach of McDonald's influence throughout society. I will do this by breaking McDonaldization down into its key elements (Weber's five dimensions of rationalization) and then demonstrating how each of these elements is being manifested in more and more sectors of society.

Efficiency

The first element of McDonaldization is efficiency, or the choice of the optimum means to an end. Many aspects of the fast-food restaurant illustrate efficiency, especially from the viewpoint of the restaurant, but none better than the degree to which the customer is turned into an unpaid laborer. The fast-food restaurant did not create the idea of imposing work on the consumer—getting the consumer to be what is, in effect, an unpaid employee—but it institutionalized and expedited this development. Customers are expected to stand in line and order their own food (rather than having a waiter do it) and to "bus" their own paper and plastic (rather than having it done by a busperson). Fast-food chains have also pioneered the movement toward handing the consumer little more than the basics of the meal. The consumer is expected to take the naked burger to the "fixin's bar" and there turn it into the desired sandwich by adding such things as lettuce, tomatoes, and onions. We all are expected to log a few minutes a week as sandwich makers. We are also now handed an empty cup and expected to go to the fountain and fill our glasses with ice and a soft drink, thereby spending a few moments as what used to be called a "soda jerk." In some ultramodern fast-food restaurants, customers are met by a computer screen when they enter and they must punch in their own order. In these and other ways, the fast-food restaurant has grown more efficient.

The salad bar, also popularized if not pioneered by the fast-food restaurant, is a classic example of putting the consumer to work. The customer buys an empty plate and then loads up on the array of vegetables (and other foods) available. Quickly seeing the merit in all this, many supermarkets have now instituted their own salad bars with a more elaborate array of alternative foods available to the consumer. The salad lover can now work as a salad chef at the lunch hour in the fast-food restaurant and then do it all over again in the evening at the supermarket by making the salad for the evening meal. All this is very efficient from the perspective of the fast-food restaurant and the supermarket because only a very small number of employees are needed to keep the various compartments well stocked.

There are many other examples of this process of imposing work on the consumer. Virtually gone are gas station attendants who filled gas tanks, checked oil, and cleaned windows. We now put in a few minutes a week as unpaid gas station attendants pumping gas, checking oil, and cleaning windows. Instead of having a readily available attendant to pay for gasoline, we must trek into the station to pay for our gas. Or, for customers who do not want to make that trek, they can simply put their own credit cards in a slot, pump the gas, and their account is automatically charged the correct (we hope) amount for the gas pumped, and finally the receipt and the card are retrieved with no contact with, or work done by, anyone working in the gas station.

The latter development was pioneered in the banking industry with the advent of the cash machine, which allows us all to work for at least a few moments as unpaid bank tellers.

When calling many businesses these days, instead of dealing with a human operator who makes the desired connection for us, we must deal with "voice mail" and follow a series of instructions from a computer voice by pushing a bewildering array of numbers and codes before we get, it is hoped, to the desired extension (Barron, 1989).

Efficiency has been extended to the booming diet industry, which encompasses diet drugs, diet books, exercise DVDs, diet meals, diet drinks, weight loss clinics, and "fat farms" (Kleinfeld, 1986, p. 1). Diet books promising all kinds of efficient shortcuts to weight loss are often at the top of the best-seller lists. Losing weight is normally difficult and time-consuming; hence, the lure of various diet books that promise to make weight loss easier and quicker, that is, more efficient. For those on a diet—and many people are on more or less perpetual diets—the preparation of low-calorie food has been made more efficient. Instead of cooking diet foods from scratch, an array of pre-prepared diet foods is available in frozen or microwavable form. For those who do not wish to go through the inefficient process of eating these diet meals, there are diet shakes such as Slim-Fast that can be consumed in a matter of seconds.

In addition, there is the growth of diet centers such as NutriSystem and Jenny Craig ("Big People, Big Business," 1988). Dieters at NutriSystem are provided (at substantial cost) with prepackaged freeze-dried food. The dieter needs only to add water when it is time for the next meal. Freeze-dried foods are efficient not only for the dieter but also for NutriSystem because they can be efficiently packaged, transported, and stored. Furthermore, the company no longer even operates any brick-and-mortar stores. Instead, clients can speak to counselors only through the Web or on the telephone.[3]

Calculability

The second dimension of McDonaldization is calculability. McDonaldization involves an emphasis on things that can be calculated, counted, and quantified. In terms of the latter, it means a tendency to emphasize quantity rather than quality. This leads to a sense that quality is equal to certain, usually large, quantities of things.

As in many other aspects of its operation, the emphasis of McDonald's on quantity (as reflected in the Big Mac) is mirrored by the other fast-food restaurants. The most notable is Burger King, which stresses the quantity of the meat in its hamburger, called the "Whopper" or even the "Triple Whopper," and of the fish in its sandwich called the "BK Big Fish." At Wendy's, we are offered a variety of "Biggies." Similarly, 7-Eleven offers its customers a hot dog called the "Big Bite" and a large soft drink called the "Big Gulp," and now, the even larger "Super Big Gulp." This emphasis on quantity in a McDonaldized society is not restricted to fast-food restaurants. American Airlines boasts that it serves more cities than any other U.S. airline.

What is particularly interesting about all this emphasis on quantity is the seeming absence of interest in communicating anything about quality. Thus, United Airlines does not tell us anything about the quality (passenger comfort) of its numerous flights. The result is a growing concern among critics about the decline or even the absence of quality in society as a whole (Tuchman, 1980).

As with efficiency, calculability has been extended from eating in food chains to many settings, including dieting. Given its very nature, the diet industry is obsessed with things that can be quantified. Weight, weight loss (or gain), and time periods are measured precisely. Food intake is carefully measured and monitored. Labels on diet foods detail number of ounces of food, number of calories, and many other things necessary for clients to be informed dieters.

Another interesting extension of the emphasis on quantity rather than quality is found in *USA Today*. This newspaper is noted for its "junk-food journalism"—the lack of substance in its stories (Prichard, 1987, p. 8). Instead of offering detailed stories, *USA Today* offers a large number of short, easily and quickly read stories. One executive stated, "*USA Today* must sell news/info at a fast, hard pace" (p. 113). One observer underscored the newspaper's corresponding lack of concern for quality and, in the process, its relationship to the fast-food restaurant: "Like parents who take their children to a different fast-food restaurant every night and keep the refrigerator stocked with ice cream, *USA Today* gives its readers only what they want, no spinach, no bran, no liver" (p. 196).

There is also a growing emphasis on the number of credentials one possesses. For example, people in various occupations are increasingly using long lists of initials after their names to convince prospective clients of their competence. Said one insurance appraiser with ASA, FSVA, FAS, CRA, and CRE after his name, "the more [initials] you tend to put after your name, the more impressed they [potential clients] become" (Gervasi, 1990, p. D5). The sheer number of credentials, however, tells us little about the competence of the person sporting them.

The emphasis on quantity rather than quality of publications among academics led to an announcement by then-president of Stanford University, Donald Kennedy, that there would be a change in the university's emphasis on the quantity of an individual's publications in the decision to hire, promote, or grant tenure to faculty members. He was disturbed by a report that indicated "nearly half of faculty members believe that their scholarly writings are merely counted not evaluated when personnel decisions are made" (quoted in Cooper, 1991, p. A12). Kennedy stated,

> First, I hope we can agree that the quantitative use of research output as a criterion for appointment or promotion is a bankrupt idea. . . . The overproduction of routine scholarship is one of the most egregious aspects of contemporary academic life: It tends to conceal really important work by sheer volume; it wastes time and valuable resources. (p. A12)

To deal with this problem, Kennedy proposed to limit the number of publications used in making personnel decisions. He hoped that the proposed limits would "reverse the appalling belief that counting and weighing are the important means of evaluating faculty research" (Cooper, 1991, p. A12). It remains to be seen whether Stanford, to say nothing of the rest of American academia, will be able to limit the emphasis on quantity rather than quality.

Predictability

Rationalization involves the increasing effort to ensure predictability from one time or place to another. In a rational society, people want to know what to expect in all settings and at all times. They neither want nor expect surprises. They want to know that when they order their Big Mac today, it is going to be identical to the one they ate yesterday and the one they will eat tomorrow.

The movie industry is increasingly characterized by predictability. One manifestation of this is the growing reliance on sequels to successful movies rather than producing completely new movies based on new concepts, ideas, and characters. The Hitchcock classic *Psycho,* for example, was followed by several sequels (of course, not made by Hitchcock), as were other less artistically successful horror films such as

Halloween and *Nightmare on Elm Street.* Outside of the horror movie genre, a range of other movies have been succeeded by one or more sequels, including *X-Men, Harry Potter, Pirates of the Caribbean,* and many more. Some, such as *The Lord of the Rings,* are being released premised on the idea that one must watch a number of sequels in order to get the full story. Most recently, some movies have even been released as "prequels," as with the very successful release of the *Star Wars* prequel trilogy.

The routine use of sequels is a relatively new phenomenon in Hollywood. Its development parallels, and is part of, the McDonaldization of society. The attraction of sequels is their predictability. From the point of view of the studios, the same characters, actors, and basic plot lines can be used over and over. Furthermore, there seems to be a greater likelihood that sequels will be successful at the box office than completely original movies; profit levels are more predictable. From the viewers' perspective, there is great comfort in knowing that they will once again encounter favorite characters played by familiar actors who find themselves in accustomed settings. Moviegoers seem more willing to shell out money for a safe and familiar movie than for a movie that is completely new to them. Like a McDonald's meal, these sequels are typically not as high quality as the originals, but at least the consumers know what they are getting.

One of the early manifestations of predictability, the TV dinner, has now been joined, and in some cases superseded, by even more rational meals eaten at home. The microwavable dinner is more efficient to store and cook. To this list of advances, we can now add the freeze-dried foods that blossom into predictable dishes merely through the addition of water and the ready-to-eat, prepackaged Lunchables by Kraft Foods.

A similar process can be seen in the way people go camping. Although some people still "rough it," many others have sought to eliminate most, if not all, of the unpredictability from camping. We have witnessed the development of "country-club campgrounds," spearheaded by such franchises as KOA (Johnson, 1986, p. B1). Instead of simple tents, modern campers might venture forth in an RV to protect them from the unexpected thunderstorms, tick bites, and snakes. Of course, "camping" in an RV also tends to reduce the likelihood of catching sight of the wandering deer or bear ("Country-Club Campgrounds," 1984, p. 90). Furthermore, the Winnebago carries within it the predictable DVD player, VCR, computer, and so on. One camper, relaxing in his air-conditioned 32-foot trailer, stated, "We've got everything right here. . . . It doesn't matter how hard it rains or how the wind blows" (Johnson, 1986, p. B1).

Much of the attraction of the shopping mall is traceable to its predictability. The unpredictabilities of weather are eliminated:

> One kid who works here told me why he likes the mall. . . . It's because no matter what the weather is outside, it's always the same in here. He likes that. He doesn't want to know it's raining—it would depress him. (Kowinski, 1985, p. 27)

The malls, like fast-food restaurants, are virtually the same from one place or time to another. One finds the same chains represented in malls throughout the country.

Finally, those who spend their days wandering through malls are relatively free from the unpredictabilities of crime that beset them when they wander through city streets.

Part of the success of *USA Today* is traceable to its predictability. Because it is a national newspaper, travelers are reassured by the fact that the familiar masthead and contents will be available wherever they go. The structure and makeup of the newspaper is highly predictable from one day to another. The stories are all predictably short and easily digestible. There are as few surprises in one's daily *USA Today* as in one's daily Big Mac; in fact, they are best consumed together.

I close this discussion of predictability in a McDonaldized society with the example of modern, suburban housing. Many of Steven Spielberg's early movies took place in these rationalized and highly predictable suburbs. Spielberg's strategy is to lure the viewer into this highly predictable world and then to have a highly unpredictable event occur. For example, in *ET,* the extraterrestrial wanders into a suburban development of tract houses and is discovered by a child who lives in one of those houses and who, up to that point, has lived a highly predictable suburban existence. The unpredictable ET eventually disrupts not only the lives of the child and his family but also those of the entire community. Similarly, *Poltergeist* takes place in a suburban household, and the evil spirits ultimately disrupt its predictable tranquility. The great success of Spielberg's movies may be traceable to our longing for some *un*predictability, even if it is frightening and menacing, in our increasingly predictable lives.

Replacing People With Nonhuman Technologies

I combine the discussion of two elements of McDonaldization—increased control and the replacement of human with nonhuman technology. The reason for the combination is that these two elements are closely linked. Specifically, replacement of human with nonhuman technology is often oriented toward greater control. The great sources of uncertainty and unpredictability in any rationalizing system are people—either the people who work within those systems or the people who are served by them. McDonald's seeks to exert increasing control over both its employees and its customers. It is most likely to do this by steadily replacing people with nonhuman technologies. After all, technologies like robots and computers are far easier to control than humans. In addition to eliminating some people by replacing them with technologies, those who continue to labor within McDonald's are better controlled by these new technologies. These nonhuman technologies also exert increasing control over people served by the system.

As in the production and consumption of food in the fast-food restaurant, the production of some of the raw materials required by such restaurants—bread, fish, meat, and eggs—has also come to be characterized by increasing control through replacing people with nonhuman technologies. In the case of raising animals for food, relatively small, family-run farms are being rapidly replaced by "factory farms," in which people and animals are controlled by nonhuman technologies (Singer, 1975). One of the first animals to find its way into the factory farm was the chicken. Among its other advantages, chicken farms allow one person to manage more than 50,000 chickens. Raising chickens in this way involves a series of highly predictable steps. The chickens themselves will be far more predictable in size and weight than free-ranging chickens. It is also obviously far more efficient to "harvest" chickens confined in this way than it is to catch chickens that are free to roam over large areas.

Confining chickens in such crowded quarters, however, creates such unpredictabilities as violence and even cannibalism among the animals. These irrational "vices" are dealt with in a variety of ways, such as dimming of the light as the chickens approach full size and the "debeaking" of chickens so that they cannot harm one another.

The replacement of people with nonhuman technology, and the consequent increase in control, is found not only in food production and the fast-food restaurant but also in home cooking. Technologies such as the microwave or conventional oven with a temperature probe "decide" when food is done rather than leaving that judgment to the cook. Ovens, coffee makers, and other appliances are now able to turn themselves on and off. The instructions on all kinds of packaged foods dictate precisely how the food is to be prepared and cooked. Even the now old-fashioned cookbook was designed to take creativity away from the cook, who would be inclined to flavor to taste, and put it in the hands of the rigid guidelines laid down by the book.

A very similar development has taken place in supermarkets. In the past, prices were marked on food products, and the supermarket checker had to read the price and enter it into the cash register. As with all human activities, there was a chance for human error. To counter this problem, most supermarkets have installed optical scanners. Instead of the human checker reading the price, the mechanical scanner "reads" the code and the price for a given code number that has been entered into the computer, which is the heart of the modern "cash register." This nonhuman technology has eliminated some of the human uncertainty from the job of supermarket checker. It has also reduced the number and level of sophistication of the tasks performed by the checker. The checker no longer needs to read the amount and enter it in the cash register. Left are less skilled tasks such as scanning the food and bagging it. In other words, the supermarket checker has undergone "deskilling"—a decline in the amount of skill required on the job.

The next step in this development was to have the customer do the scanning, thereby eliminating the need for a checkout person. The next "advance" was a technology that permits the insertion of the customer's credit card into the scanning system, thereby avoiding the need to move on to a human cashier and pay for the food.

The supermarket scanners permit other kinds of control over customers as well. Prior to the scanner, customers could examine their purchases and see how much each cost; they could also check to be sure that they were not being overcharged at the cash register. With the advent of the scanner, goods no longer have prices listed on them, only bar codes. This change gave the supermarket greater control over customers; it is almost impossible for the consumer to keep tabs on the checkers. When the scanners were instituted at my local market, management announced that it was issuing marking pens to customers who were interested in writing the price on each item. This, again, is consistent with the trend toward getting the consumer to do work historically done by others, in this case by grocery clerks who worked deep into the night to mark each item. In any case, the supermarkets did not keep the markers very long because few hurried shoppers had the desire to spend several additional minutes a day as grocery clerks.

Telemarketing is increasingly ubiquitous in modern society. Many of us are called several times a day in efforts to get us to buy something. Those who work in these telemarketing "factories" are rigidly controlled. They often have scripts that they must follow mindlessly. Furthermore, there are a range of alternative scripts designed to handle most foreseeable contingencies. Those doing the phoning are often listened in on by supervisors to be sure the correct procedures are followed. There are rigid demands for number of calls and sales required in a given time period. If employees fail to meet the quotas, they are summarily fired. Following the usual progression of technological advances, instead of having people solicit us over the phone, some companies are now using computer calls. Computer voices are far more predictable than even the most rigidly controlled human operator. Not only do we have computer calls, but we are also now seeing the utilization of computers that respond to the human voice. A person receiving a long-distance collect call might be asked whether he or she will accept the charges. The computer voice demands, "Say yes or no" or "Press one for no, zero for yes." Although efficient and cost saving, such a system is anonymous and dehumanizing:

> The person senses that he cannot use free-flowing speech. He's being constrained. The computer is controlling him. It can be simply frustrating. . . . People adapt to it, but only by filing it away subconsciously as another annoyance of living in our technological world. (Langer, 1990, p. H3)

An even more extreme version of this is found in the educational variant of the fast-food restaurant, KinderCare. KinderCare tends to hire short-term employees with little or no training in education. What these employees do in the "classroom" is determined by a uniform "instruction book" that includes a preset, ready-made curriculum. All that is required is that the staff member open up the manual to the appropriate place where all activities are spelled out in detail on a day-by-day basis. Clearly, a skilled, experienced, and creative teacher is not the kind of person McChild care centers seek to hire. Rather, relatively untrained employees are more easily controlled by the nonhuman technology of the omnipresent instruction book.

The modern, computerized airplane, such as Boeing's 777, represents an interesting case of substituting nonhuman for human control. Instead of flying "by the seat of their pants" or using old-fashioned autopilots for simple maneuvers, modern pilots "can push a few buttons and lean back while the plane flies to its destination and lands on a predetermined runway." Said one Federal Aviation Administration official, "We're taking more and more of these functions out of human control and giving them to machines." The new, automated airplanes are in many ways safer and more reliable than older, less technologically advanced models. There is a fear, however, that pilots dependent on these technologies will lose the ability to find creative ways of handling emergency situations. An airline manager stated, "If we have human operators subordinated to technology, then we're going to lose that creativity. I don't have computers that will do that [be creative]; I just don't" (Lavin, 1989, p. 1).

The Irrationality of Rationality

There are great gains involved in increasing rationalization, resulting from increases in efficiency, predictability, calculability, and control through the substitution of nonhuman for human technology. I enumerate some of the advantages of the fast-food restaurant and, more generally, other elements of McDonaldized society. The fast-food restaurant has expanded the alternatives available to consumers: More people now have ready access to Italian, Mexican, Chinese, and Cajun foods; the salad bar enables people to make salads exactly the way they want them; microwave ovens and microwavable foods allow us to have dinner in minutes or even seconds; for those with a wide range of shopping needs, supermarkets and shopping malls are efficient sites, and home shopping networks allow us to shop even more efficiently without ever leaving home; today's high-tech, for-profit hospitals are likely to provide higher quality medical care than their predecessors; we can get almost instantaneous medical attention at our local, drive-in McDoctors; computerized phone systems allow people to do things (like getting a bank balance in the middle of the night) that were impossible before, and automated bank teller machines allow people to obtain money any time of the day or night; package tours permit large numbers of people to visit countries that they would otherwise be unlikely to see because of apprehensions about undertaking an individual travel experience; diet centers such as NutriSystem allow people to lose weight in a carefully regulated and controlled system; Winnebagos let the modern camper avoid excessive heat, rain, insects, and the like; and suburban tract houses allow large numbers of people to afford single-family homes.

The rational systems also allow us to avoid the problems created by nonrational systems in other societies. The following is a description of a recent visit by an American journalist to a pizzeria in Havana, Cuba:

> The pizza's not much to rave about; they skimp on tomato sauce, and the dough is mushy.
>
> It was about 7:30 p.m., and as usual the place was standing-room only, with people two deep jostling for a stool to come open and a waiting line spilling out onto the sidewalk.
>
> The menu is similarly Spartan. . . . To drink, there is tap water. That's it— no toppings, no soda, no beer, no coffee, no salt, no pepper. And no special orders. The waiter wears a watch around his belt loop, but he hardly needs it; time is evidently not his chief concern. After a while, tempers begin to fray.
>
> But right now, it's 8:45 p.m. at the pizzeria, I've been waiting an hour and a quarter for two small pies. (Hockstader, 1991, p. A12. Reprinted with permission)

Few would prefer such irrational systems to the rationalized elements of U.S. society.

Although there are many advantages to a McDonaldized society, there are also great costs associated with McDonaldization that can be dealt with largely under the heading of the "irrationality of rationality." In other words, it is my thesis, following Weber, that rational systems inevitably spawn a series of irrationalities that serve to limit, ultimately compromise, and perhaps even defeat, their rationality.

We can conceive of the irrationality of rationality in several ways. At the most general level, it is simply the overarching label for all the negative aspects and effects of McDonaldization. More specifically, it can be seen as the opposite of rationality and its several dimensions. That is, McDonaldization can be viewed as leading to inefficiency, unpredictability, incalculability, and loss of control. Most specifically, irrationality means that rational systems are unreasonable systems. By that I mean they serve to deny the basic humanity, the human reason, of the people who work within or are served by them. Rational systems are dehumanizing systems. Although in other contexts, rationality and reason are often used interchangeably, here they are employed to mean antithetical phenomena.

The most obvious manifestation of the inefficiency of the fast-food restaurant is the long lines of people that are often found at the counters or at the drive-through windows. What is purported to be an efficient way of obtaining a meal turns out to be quite inefficient. The fast-food restaurant is far from the only aspect of the McDonaldized society that operates inefficiently. Columnist Richard Cohen (1990) described the inefficiencies of the automated teller machines (ATMs) as follows:

> Oh Lord, with each advance of the computer age, I was told I would benefit. But with each "benefit," I wind up doing more work. This is the ATM rule of life. . . . I was told—nay promised—that I could avoid lines at the bank and make deposits or withdrawals any time of the day. Now, there are lines at the ATMs, the bank seems to take a percentage of whatever I withdraw or deposit, and of course, I'm doing what tellers (remember them?) used to do. Probably, with the new phone, I'll have to climb telephone poles in the suburbs during ice storms. (p. 5)

At least three different irrationalities are being underscored in the previous quotation: Rational systems are not less expensive; they force us to do a range of unpaid work; and, most important from the point of view of this discussion, they are often inefficient. It might be more efficient to deal with a human teller, either in the bank or at the drive-through window, than to wait in line at an ATM machine, perhaps on a cold, snowy night. For many, it would be far more efficient to prepare a meal at home than to load the family in the car, drive to McDonald's, fill up on food, and then drive home again. This may not be true of some meals cooked at home from scratch, but it is certainly true of TV dinners, microwave meals, or full-course meals brought in from the supermarket. Many people, however, persist in the belief, fueled by endless propaganda from the fast-food restaurants, that it is more efficient to eat there than to eat at home.

The main reason McDonaldization can be seen as irrational, and ultimately unreasonable, is that it tends to become a dehumanizing system that may become antihuman or even destructive of human beings. In terms of the latter, there are a number of ways in which the health, and perhaps the lives, of people have been threatened by progressive rationalization (Spencer, 1983). One example is the high-calorie, fat, cholesterol, salt, and sugar content of the food served at fast-food restaurants. Such meals are the last things the vast majority of Americans need.

Many suffer from being overweight or have high cholesterol levels, high blood pressure, and perhaps diabetes. The kinds of meals typically served at fast-food restaurants only tend to make these health problems much worse. Even more worrisome, they help to create eating habits in children that contribute to the development of these and other health problems later in life. It can be argued that, with their appeal to children, fast-food restaurants are creating not only lifelong devotees of fast food but also people who will grow addicted to diets high in salt, sugar, and fat.

The fast-food industry has run afoul of not only nutritionists but also environmentalists. It produces an enormous amount of trash, some of which is non-biodegradable. Many people have been critical of the public eyesore created by litter from innumerable fast-food meals strewn across the countryside. McDonaldized institutions have a negative effect not only on our health and on the environment but also on some of our most cherished institutions, most notably the family. A key technology in the destruction of the family meal is the microwave oven and the vast array of microwavable foods it helped generate (Visser, 1989). A *Wall Street Journal* poll in the late 1980s indicated that Americans consider the microwave their favorite household product. In fact, the microwave in a McDonaldizing society is seen as an advance over the fast-food restaurant. One consumer researcher stated, "It has made even fast-food restaurants not seem fast because at home you don't have to wait in line." Consumers are demanding meals that take no more than 10 minutes to microwave, whereas previously people were more willing to spend a half hour or even an hour cooking dinner. This emphasis on speed has, of course, brought with it poorer taste and lower quality, but people do not seem to mind this loss: "We're just not as critical of food as we used to be" ("The Microwave Cooks," 1989, p. B1).

The speed of microwave cooking, as well as the wide variety of foods available in that form, makes it possible for family members to eat at different times and places. To give even children independence, companies are marketing products such as Kid Cuisine and My Own Meals. As a result, "Those qualities of the family meal, the ones that imparted feelings of security and well-being, might be lost forever where food is 'zapped' or 'nuked' instead of cooked" (Visser, 1989, p. 40).

The advances in microwave cooking continue. There are already plastic strips on some foods that turn blue when the food is done. The industry is promising strips in the future that communicate cooking information directly to the microwave oven:

> With cooking reduced to pushing a button, the kitchen may wind up as a sort of filling station. Family members will pull in, push a few buttons, fill up and leave. To clean up, all we need do is throw away plastic plates. (Visser, 1989, p. 42)

What is lost, of course, is the family meal, and we must decide whether we can afford the loss:

> The communal meal is our primary ritual for encouraging the family to gather together every day. If it is lost to us, we shall have to invent new ways to be a family. It is worth considering whether the shared joy that food can provide is worth giving up. (Visser, 1989, p. 42)

Thus, it is my argument that, contrary to McDonald's propaganda and the widespread belief in it, fast-food restaurants, as well as the innumerable other McDonaldized institutions, are not truly rational systems. They spawn all kinds of problems for the health of their customers and the well-being of the environment, they tend to be dehumanizing and therefore unreasonable in various ways, and they often lead to the opposite of what they are supposed to create—for example, they lead to inefficiency rather than increased efficiency. All this is not to deny the many advantages of McDonaldization mentioned previously, but rather to point to the fact that there are counterbalancing and perhaps even overwhelming problems associated with the fast-food society.

Perhaps the ultimate irrationality of McDonaldization is the possibility that people could ultimately lose control over the system, and it would come to control us. Already, many aspects of our lives are controlled by these rational systems. It at least appears, however, that these systems are ultimately controlled by people. These rational systems, however, can spin beyond the control of even the people who occupy the highest-level positions within those systems. This is one of the senses in which we can, following Weber, talk of an "iron cage of McDonaldization." It can become a system that comes to control all of us.

There is another fear: that these interlocking rational systems can fall into the hands of a small number of leaders who, through them, can exercise enormous control over all society. Thus, there are authoritarian and totalitarian possibilities associated with the process of McDonaldization. We may come to be increasingly controlled by the rational systems themselves or by a few leaders who master those systems.

This kind of fear has animated many science fiction writers and is manifest in such sci-fi classics as *1984, Brave New World, Fahrenheit 451,* and *The Matrix.* The problem is that these stories describe a feared and fearsome future world, whereas McDonaldization is with us now, has been with us for a while, and is extending its reach throughout society.

Conclusion

The objective in this chapter has been to show the continued, if not increasing, relevance of Max Weber's theory of rationalization to the modern world. Although the bureaucracy may have been replaced by the fast-food restaurant as the ultimate example of a rational structure and bureaucratization by McDonaldization as the heart of the process, the rationalization that undergirds both sets of structures and processes remains at least as powerful a force today as it was in Weber's day. In fact, the old sites remain rationalized while new ones are coming under the sway of the rationalization process. In this sense, we seem even closer to the iron cage of rationalization today than was the case in Weber's day.

Notes

1. In this essay, I combine control and using nonhuman for human technology, whereas in the previous essay they were differentiated.
2. See also http://www.technomic.com/pressroom/top500_left_5_31_06.html.
3. I thank Dora Giemza for these and other insights into NutriSystem.

References

Barron, J. (1989, February 17). Please press 2 for service; press ? for an actual human. *New York Times*, pp. A1, B2.

Big people, big business: The overweight numbers rising, try NutriSystem. (1988, October 10). *Washington Post*, Health section, p. 8.

Brubaker, R. (1984). *The limits of rationality: An essay on the social and moral thought of Max Weber*. London: Allen & Unwin.

Cohen, R. (1990, August 5). Take a message please! *Washington Post Magazine*, p. 5.

Cooper, K. J. (1991, March 3). Stanford president sets initiative on teaching. *Washington Post*, p. A12.

Country-club campgrounds. (1984, September 24). *Newsweek*, p. 90.

Egan, T. (1990, December 8). Big chains are joining Manhattan's toy wars. *New York Times*, p. 29.

Farhi, P. (1990, September 21). Domino's is going to school. *Washington Post*, p. F3.

Gervasi, S. (1990, August 30). The credentials epidemic. *Washington Post*, p. D5.

Habermas, J. (1984). *The theory of communicative action, Vol. 1: Reason and rationalization of society*. Boston: Beacon.

Hockstader, L. (1991, August 5). No service, no smile, little sauce. *Washington Post*, p. A12.

Johnson, D. (1986, August 28). Vacationing at campgrounds is now hardly roughing it. *New York Times*, p. B1.

Kalberg, S. (1980). Max Weber's types of rationality: Cornerstones for the analysis of rationalization processes in history. *American Journal of Sociology, 85*, 1145–1179.

Kleinfeld, N. R. (1986, September 7). The ever-fatter business of thinness. *New York Times*, p. 1.

Kowinski, W. S. (1985). *The malling of America: An inside look at the great consumer paradise*. New York: William Morrow.

Langer, G. (1990, February 11). Computers reach out, respond to human voice. *Washington Post*, p. H3.

Lavin, C. H. (1989, August 12). Automated planes raising concerns. *New York Times*, p. 1.

Levine, D. (1981). Rationality and freedom: Weber and beyond. *Sociological Inquiry, 51*, 5–25.

The microwave cooks up a new way of life. (1989, September 19). *Wall Street Journal*, p. B1.

Prichard, P. (1987). *The making of McPaper: The inside story of USA Today*. Kansas City, MO: Andrews McMeel & Parker.

Ramirez, A. (1990, October 30). In the orchid room . . . Big Macs. *New York Times,* pp. D1, D5.

Ritzer, G. (1983). The McDonaldization of society. *Journal of American Culture,* 6, 100–107.

Ritzer, G. (2004). *The McDonaldization of society* (revised New Century ed.). Thousand Oaks, CA: Pine Forge Press.

Singer, P. (1975). *Animal liberation: A new ethics for our treatment of animals.* New York: Avon.

Spencer, M. (1983). Can Mama Mac get them to eat spinach? In M. Fishwick (Ed.), *Ronald revisited: The world of Ronald McDonald* (pp. 85–93). Bowling Green, OH: Bowling Green University Press.

Tuchman, B. W. (1980, November 2). The decline of quality. *New York Times Magazine,* pp. 38–41.

Visser, M. (1989, December). A meditation on the microwave. *Psychology Today,* pp. 38–42.

Weber, M. (1946). In H. H. Gerth & C. Wright Mills (Eds.), *From Max Weber: Essays in sociology.* New York: Oxford University Press.

Weber, M. (1958). *The Protestant ethic and the spirit of capitalism.* New York: Scribner's. (Original work published 1904–1905)

Weber, M. (1968). *Economy and society* (3 vols.). Totwa, NJ: Bedminster Press. (Original work published 1921)

Weber, M. (1975). *Roscher and Knies: The logical problems of historical economics.* New York: Free Press. (Original work published 1903–1906)

Zoglin, R. (1988, April 11). Get ready for McRather. *Time,* pp. 32–33.

DISCUSSION QUESTIONS

1. Weber thought that the overly bureaucratized, overrationalized world was, to use his image, a huge "iron cage" from which it appeared we could not escape. In what ways do you see yourself and your peers trapped in a McDonaldized world? Do young people perceive such a world to be something like a prison? What are the chances of resisting this trend of escaping from the new iron cage?

2. One of the key elements of McDonaldization is predictability. Why do consumers place such a high premium on predictability? What are some of the social consequences of an increasingly predictable world?

3. This chapter identifies some of the negative consequences of McDonaldization. What do you think the main positive consequences of such a process are? Do the positives outweigh the negatives, or is the reverse the case? Defend your argument.

4. One of the arguments of this essay is that McDonaldization is coming to dominate an increasing number of sectors in our society. Can you think of parts of society that are not McDonaldized? How have they resisted the process? Are they likely to be McDonaldized in the future?

5. Given that McDonaldized systems operate, at least in theory, more efficiently, predictably, and calculably, and are more controllable, than non-McDonaldized systems, is it possible to resist or transform such systems without also using a McDonaldized approach? In order to succeed, must any resistance to McDonaldization be McDonaldized itself?

CHAPTER 3

Surfing the Net for Community

A Durkheimian Analysis of Electronic Gatherings

Anne M. Hornsby

Anne M. Hornsby has turned to sociological theory for a critical lens on understanding and changing society for 20 years. She has found theory both inspirational and useful, not only as a professor teaching theory but as a sociologist in other work settings. Her first realization of the practical power of sociological theory occurred while working for Boston's public health department. She was assigned to investigate organizational dysfunction in neighborhood health clinics, and while searching for a framework that made sense of her findings, she remembered Max Weber's argument about the tension between bureaucracy and democracy. Drawing on Weber's ideas, she effectively communicated her findings to decision makers. She has also served as a consultant on health care reform in Latin America. In 1991, she received a PhD in sociology from Harvard University. She has taught at Tulane University and Loyola University in New Orleans. Currently, she is employed as a senior health policy analyst on Medicare payment policy at the Centers for Medicare and Medicaid Services, U.S. Department of Health and Human Services.

The global and multilayered network of electronic networks known as the Net offers access to an astonishing diversity of information, relationships, and social rituals. Through connections among computers around the world, friends in Egypt and Japan can send each other birthday messages; scholars in the United States can retrieve a new book manuscript in seconds from a university in Australia; a public health worker in Fiji can receive the latest World Bank memo on clean water projects by fax from a laptop in the airspace over South Africa; rock music fans in India can listen to selections from the latest CD of their favorite American group; and a Chilean journalist can listen to replays of U.S. National Public Radio broadcasts.

In addition to retrieving and sending information and messages, there also has emerged an astonishing range of social activities in Net gatherings. Online participants carry out virtual sex, weddings, funerals, and the online equivalent of murder (deleting someone's persona from an online milieu through programming wizardry, clever but unacceptable to most participants). Through social networking sites such as Facebook, chat channels, and discussion groups, people pursue hobbies, seek friends and romance, compose music, and conduct political activism electronically. For example, student activism coordinated through sites such as Meetup.com, MoveOn.org, and RocktheVote.com is associated with the increased youth vote in the 2004 and 2008 U.S. presidential elections.

We can also enter online communities located in virtual worlds, where dozens or thousands of people can simultaneously play adventure games or hang out in cities, farms, or castles they have created just for the purpose of being sociable. Often labeled massively multiplayer online role-playing games (MMORPGs for short) or massively multiplayer online worlds (MMOWs), these virtual worlds have emerged globally as a popular form of virtual activity. In some role-playing worlds, we can engage in conversation with someone we think is another person, when in fact we are talking with a "bot" (derived from robot), a computer program that presents itself as a person by generating conversation (including humorous retorts) and physical self-description when asked.

An excerpt from a transcript of a chat between Julia (a bot residing in a computer in Pittsburgh) and Ace (a human) provides a flavor of how our social boundaries between human and machine are being reworked in life online (Turkle, 1995):

Ace: So why won't you kiss me, Julia?

Julia: Sorry, I'm not into geeks, Ace.

Ace: Julia, I'm not a geek.

Julia: Then lose the pocket protector, Ace. (p. 89)

What do these new developments mean for the social organization of human societies? The emergence of computer-mediated communications has raised a set of entirely new questions about the phenomenon of virtual relationships and the nature of their connections to community life offline. Universities around the world have developed research centers and multidisciplinary degree programs on human-computer interaction (e.g., http://hci.stanford.edu/).

We know that the Net is not just a cyberplace where people create fantasy worlds and pursue information through solitary browsing. Thousands of people also seek conversation, affiliation, support, and affirmation as social beings (Sproull & Faraj, 1995). Almost as soon as the distinction between real life and life online emerged, when the Net became familiar to larger numbers of people in the 1980s and 1990s, the boundaries between real and virtual became oddly blurred. In the following, Turkle (1995) quotes Doug, a Midwestern college junior, who describes a typical evening of life in four windows:

> I'm in some kind of argument in one window and trying to come on to a girl in a MUD [multi-user domain] in another, and another window might be running a spreadsheet program or some other technical thing for school. . . . And then I'll get a real-time message, and I guess that is RL [real life]. . . . RL is just one more window . . . *and it's not usually my best one* [italics added]. (p. 13)

How many others like Doug think life online can be an equivalent experience to real-life interactions? For the first time in human history, many people seriously pose the question of whether we can have intimate relationships of emotional depth and substance with people we know only through a computer-mediated social tie, without face-to-face contact. What impact will there be on our sense of social order and connectedness to other people? What happens online to make people feel they are part of an online community? Are new forms of social solidarity emerging in online communities, or do online communities form and maintain themselves in the way that communities offline do (Cavanagh, 2009)? If almost two billion people around the world access the Net today, what impact will such large-scale attachment to computer terminals and mobile computing devices have on our understandings of what is community?

Chapter Organization

This chapter will analyze virtual social organization on the Net by applying the ideas of French sociologist Émile Durkheim, one of the founders of sociology in the late 19th century. The largely anecdotal and descriptive research on the Net available in the 1990s is now complemented by systematic research studies on the social organization and social uses of the Net (e.g., Dimaggio, Hargittai, Neuman, & Robinson, 2001; Herring, Scheidt, Kouper, & Wright, 2006; Lee, 2005; Wellman & Haythornthwait, 2002). The goal of this chapter, however, is not to review sociological research on the Net. Instead, this chapter has three goals. The first is to offer an overview of the history and organization of the Net. I describe types of Net services (such as e-mail and the Web) and types of electronic gatherings, including social networking sites, wikis, blogs, discussion groups, fantasy worlds, and civic networks. Second, the core of the chapter educates readers about the sociological theories of a great thinker. To do this, I analyze the ways in which electronic gatherings are similar to Durkheimian societies. I present Durkheim's argument about the ingredients that are necessary for stable and cohesive societies, which he calls regulation and integration. Next, I apply Durkheim's ideas on regulation and integration to analyze electronic gatherings as Durkheimian "Net societies."

The third goal of the chapter is to demonstrate how Durkheim's ideas can be applied to understand how experiences in virtual reality are affecting human societies. I discuss Durkheim's ideas about two different ways in which societies can be organized, which he calls mechanical and organic societies. Next, I draw on his ideas to develop a hypothesis about the emergence of a third, new type of society in the 21st century, which I call "cyborg society." This section attempts to illustrate how sociological theory can be used to better understand our rapidly changing world.

I present Durkheim's arguments in some depth to acquaint the reader with the original ideas of a great sociologist and also to demonstrate how an argument can be presented as a sequence of concepts and reasoning. I also quote him throughout the chapter. Too often, people believe that the classic works of a discipline are stuffy, out of date, and incomprehensible. By letting Durkheim speak for himself, I hope to show that his ideas are clear, are still fresh and exciting, and can help us better understand our world today.

Background on the Net and Electronic Gatherings

What Is the Internet?

The Internet is a global electronic network of networks, where computers and other digital devices are connected by standardized technical rules (protocols) for exchanging data, resulting in person-to-person communication and information retrieval (Dimaggio et al., 2001; Internet Activities Board, Network Working Group [IAB/NWG], 1992). The technical protocols underlying the Net, which have been collaboratively established by scientists and engineers over the past 40 years, allow international interoperability among computer networks, just as the federal regulations for the U.S. Interstate Highway System make travel predictable and easy to navigate with standardized networks of roads (same design rules for lane sizes, green signs, and the entrance/exit ramps that serve as nodes linking networks of state and county roads) and standardized flows of vehicles (required minimum and maximum speeds).

Originally, the term *Internet* referred to the experimental system that was designed and built in the 1970s under the auspices of a U.S. Department of Defense agency, the Advanced Research Projects Agency (ARPA). By 1982, the initial version of the Internet (ARPANET) was in operation at a few academic and industrial research locations and included approximately 200 computers. By 1983, the U.S. military had selected the ARPANET as its main computer communication system, which doubled the number of interconnected computers (Batty & Barr, 1994; Comer, 1995; Kahin, 1995).

Today, the Internet's computer networks are linked by dedicated, special-purpose computers called routers or gateways. Gateways can link networks run on different types of computers because of the mid-1970s invention of a special suite of software protocols called TCP/IP. The IP protocols break information (whether an e-mail message, a Web page, or a research paper) into small packets and select paths for routing each packet to its destination ("packet switching"), where all packets are reassembled into the original. The TCP protocols check to make sure all packets arrive and are reassembled without error (Galloway, 2004). To users, the Internet appears as a single huge network because of the TCP/IP suite and other protocols, when in reality, it consists of multiple layers of many different types of computer networks scattered across the United States and throughout the world (Comer, 1995).

Many types of service are available through the Internet today, including e-mail (electronic mail), IM (instant messaging), and the Web (the World Wide Web); and new services appear continually. The Internet's packet-switching technology has been applied to stream television programs and other multimedia services over networks (Internet Protocol Television, or IPTV). The Voice over Internet Protocol (VoIP) has been developed to transmit voice communications using Internet packet-switching technology (instead of or in combination with traditional phone circuit technology), so we can make phone calls over the Internet.

The Internet can be a telephone: literally or through real-time, text-based communication between individuals. It can serve as a library: Specialized Web sites "narrowcast" information to users interested enough to use search engines to find them. It can act as a soapbox for individuals expressing themselves to weblogs and other discussion forums. It can be a medium within which people plan and/or carry out activities. Or, it can operate as a conventional mass medium: Internet Service Providers such as AOL and services such as RealMedia let providers broadcast information to huge user publics simultaneously.

Probably the most familiar Net service is e-mail. Originally, e-mail was designed for communication between two people. Today, we can use e-mail to communicate with large groups of friends and colleagues by creating personally tailored public or private e-mail mailing lists. With the emergence of Wi-Fi (wireless fidelity) services and smart phones (which can access both cellular networks and the Net using a variety of applications, or "apps"), someone walking down the street can use her phone to take a photo of a new restaurant, send it seconds later to a friend just getting out of class, along with an invitation for lunch, and then post the photo to her blog or Facebook page while waiting for her friend. If her phone has a mobile app for Instant Messaging and her friend is online, she may communicate the invitation in real time by IM. Or, she may choose one of several options for immediate but not simultaneous connection: an email, a text message using Short Messaging Service (SMS) and the friend's phone number, or a Tweet (a message of up to 140 characters) through the Net or through a Twitter mobile phone app. (As Net access has become possible anytime, anywhere via hand-held mobile devices, we increasingly experience it as just another service consumed in the course of daily life.)

People often speak of the Net and the World Wide Web as if they are the same. However, the Web is a global system of text and multimedia files (and services for displaying and retrieving these files) that are transported on the Internet "highway system." Web pages are Net sites created using three protocols (Gillies & Cailliau, 2000): (a) Hypertext Markup Language (HTML) is a formatting standard that allows Web resources (e.g., document files) to be read and displayed across many different computers connected to the Net; (b) HyperText Transfer Protocol (HTTP) tells computers how to deliver Web resources around the Net; and (c) Uniform

Resource Locators (URLs) provide a universal address system for identifying (locating) a Web resource (e.g., the URL for the YouTube video site is www.youtube .com). Web browsers such as Mozilla Safari and Internet Explorer read HTML files to translate them into graphical Web pages. The Web is developed and maintained by the World Wide Web Consortium (W3C at http://www.w3.org/), headed by Tim Berners-Lee, an Englishman who invented the Web in 1989 (Berners-Lee, 1989/1990; Gillies & Cailliau, 2000).

An important development in the past decade was the diffusion of RSS (Really Simple Syndication) as a standard for organizing Web site content. RSS is a file format that allows people to subscribe to content feeds (offered by various firms, with content pulled from multiple Web sites) on topics they have selected. With reader software ("feed reader" or "feed aggregator"), users do not have to make repeated visits to Web sites to find new content; the reader can identify what is new and notify the user. Another option is to subscribe to an online content manager to manage the feeds.

Not only can "Netizens" (citizens of the Net) consume content feeds of their design, they also can produce and upload their own feeds to be retrieved by others. For example, the wildly popular YouTube site, founded in 2005, states that every minute, individuals and organizations upload 24 hours of video to its servers (YouTube, 2010). Moreover, as user-generated content for the Web grows in popularity, so do RSS feeds. One blogger writes,

> Bloggers have since adapted it [RSS] to serve up articles they write so they can reach their audience more easily. If I make this article machine readable, then you don't need to check [my blog] . . . every day to see if we've written anything new. Since we use RSS . . . your computer will do that for you. It can distinguish one article from another even if they're on the same page, and tell if a new one appears. Your computer can deliver it as a message to your email inbox, or create a page of all the interesting articles on the web that day. This has since extended to news sites (like MSNBC and CNN). Now other creative services on the web like Netflix are creatively using RSS to deliver new release information and recommendations. (Laws, 2005, p. 1)

One popular use of RSS formats is to transmit podcasts (a neologism combining Apple's iPod with "broadcasting") using "podcatchers" to receive the content feeds. Podcasting, a term that emerged in 2004, means downloading digital audio files (such as a rock song or news broadcast file) from the Web to a computer, then transferring the file to a digital audio player, such as an iPod, for listening at a convenient time. In a 2005 survey, only 12% of 18- to 29-year-olds "had a good idea" of what the terms RSS and podcasting meant, even though about 19% of those ages 18–28 had iPods/MP3 players. In contrast, only 5% of people 65 and older were familiar with these two Internet trends (Rainie, 2005; Rainie & Madden, 2005).

A December 2009 survey by the Pew Research Center (Rainie, 2010) reported a high level of Internet usage in the United States—about 74% of adults ages 18 and older reported using the Net. The 15-year trend is remarkable: In March 1995, only about 15% of U.S. adults accessed the Net, but by 2006, this had risen to three-quarters of American adults, where it remained in 2009. Although there was no gender difference, there was a marked generational difference: 93% of adults ages 19 to 29 reported using the Net.

The most dramatic change in the United States in the past 5 years has been the rise in wireless connection to the Net. In March 2009, about 56% of adults reported accessing the Internet wirelessly using at least one tool (e.g., desktop, laptop, cell phone, smart phone, game console, iPod/MP3 player, or e-book reader). Again, young adults led the way, with 80% of those ages 19-29 using at least one tool for a wireless link to the Net (Horrigan, 2009).

This 2009 survey reveals an important trend in equality of access to the Net in the United States: African Americans and Hispanics report being more active users of the "mobile Internet" than whites. Cell phone ownership is equally distributed by race: 84% of whites, 83% of African Americans, and 89% of English-speaking Hispanics. However, 17% of whites reported going online on a typical day using a handheld device, compared to 29% of African Americans and 29% of Hispanics. "The high level of activity among African Americans on mobile devices helps offset lower levels of access [to] tools that have been traditional onramps to the internet, namely desktop computers, laptops, and home broadband connections" (Horrigan, 2009, p. 4).

In 2009, there were about 1.8 billion Internet users worldwide (about 26% of the world's population), compared to about 400 million in 2000 (International Telecommunication Union, 2010; Miniwatts Marketing Group, 2009). In 2009, the United States and Canada had about 17% of the world's population and 38% of Internet users. This exemplifies what Pippa Norris (2001) refers to as the "digital divide," a divide that differentiates wealthy nations from poor ones in terms of Internet access, and likewise, within nations, it distinguishes the ease of access by the wealthy from the lack of access by the poor. However, the size and shape of the digital divide are changing. In 2000, the United States, Canada, and Europe accounted for 59% of Internet users, but the enormous growth of Internet use in Asia has attenuated this dominance (from 32% to 42% of global users). In addition, other regions increased their share of global usage over the decade, from 1% to 5% (Africa), 1% to 3% (Middle East), and 5% to 10% (Latin America and the Caribbean).

These trends have led a number of Net researchers to argue that the Internet is no longer an exotic space for the wealthy or technologically hip. Accessing the Net has become an activity integrated with daily life for a large number of ordinary people around the world, whose online activities complement but do not supplant real life (Dimaggio et al., 2001; Wellman, 2004; Wellman & Haythornthwait, 2002).

Types of Electronic Gatherings on the Net

Electronic gathering is a name that highlights the core social activity on the Net—conversation about shared interests for the sheer pleasure of it (Sproull & Faraj, 1995).

Table 3.1 Global Internet Usage

World Regions	Population (2009 Est.)	Internet Users (Dec. 2000)	Internet Users (Dec. 2009)	Growth in Usage 2000–2009	2009 Penetration by Region	Region's Share of 2009 Global Usage
Africa	991,002,342	4,514,400	86,217,900	1809.8%	8.7%	4.8%
Asia	3,808,070,503	114,304,000	764,435,900	568.8%	20.1%	42.4%
Europe	803,850,858	105,096,093	425,773,571	305.1%	53.0%	23.6%
Middle East	202,687,005	3,284,800	58,309,546	1675.1%	28.8%	3.2%
North America	340,831,831	108,096,800	259,561,000	140.1%	76.2%	14.4%
Latin America/ Caribbean	586,662,468	18,068,919	186,922,050	934.5%	31.9%	10.4%
Oceania/ Australia	34,700,201	7,620,480	21,110,490	177.0%	60.8%	1.2%
WORLD TOTAL	6,767,805,208	360,985,492	1,802,330,457	399.3%	26.6%	100%

Source: Miniwatts Marketing Group (2009). World Internet usage and population statistic, December 31, 2009, available online at http://www.internetworldstats.com, with author's additional calculations.

The Net literature suggests, however, that people can have a wide range of needs met (to varying degrees) by online groups, including the following:

- Feelings of affiliation and emotional support
- Contact with others who share similar interests
- Access to information, technical advice, and expert opinion
- Access to educational opportunities and job leads
- Entertainment, role-playing, and identity experiments
- Opportunities for political and social activism
- Access to the informal economy, such as swap shops and auctions

Informal Net histories invariably remark on the pleasure and emotional support people get just from the sheer sociability of gathering and chatting online. Computer system administrators and government officials are often described as surprised at the depth of people's interest in all kinds of conversations with all types of people all over the world (Rheingold, 1993).

It is helpful to think of social life on the Net as consisting of three main types of electronic gatherings: (a) social networking and discussion through social networking communities (SNCs), blogs, wikis, and other types of online discussion groups (described further below); (b) fantasy worlds; and (c) civic networks for citizen-government communications and political activism. My typology is based on the main activity that occurs in a gathering, because in reality, activities can overlap. Civic network sites may include blogs or other forms of discussion group, and fantasy worlds may also sponsor discussion groups where members talk about events in the games. Moreover, a range of Net services can be found in all types of electronic gatherings, such as e-mail and podcasting in social networks, civic networks, and massively multi-user online games (MMOGs) via a Wi-Fi connection in a cafe.

Social Networking and Discussion: SNCs, Blogs, and Wikis

The current generation of Web-based applications is increasingly interactive, allowing many-to-many links for creating collaborative works and building social networks for friendships, career advancement, dating, collaborative learning, or all of the above. The phrases "social Web" and "Web 2.0" are used to describe software applications that facilitate user-generated content. On the social Web, people can collaboratively create a digital art piece online; jointly edit an entry in Wikipedia at www.wikipedia.org; invite new contacts into a private network of friends on Facebook.com; or have a debate on a political blog (or Weblog, a Web site where entries have the feel of journal entries, usually posted in reverse chronological order).

SNCs

Facebook, MySpace, Bebo, and Hi5 are four of several hundred social networking sites around the world where members post personal profiles, photos, or favorite music; meet and chat with others; and develop new relationships through friend-of-friend links. Also called social networking communities, SNCs are networks where large numbers of people can be connected to each other by a relatively small number of intermediaries. Facebook began as a social networking site for college students, but opened to organizations and the general public in 2006. Originally created by a Harvard undergraduate in 2004 as an online extension of campus life, Facebook spread rapidly across campuses. For example, a study at University of North Carolina–Chapel Hill found that in 2005, a total of 88% of first-year undergraduates had active accounts on Facebook in their first semester (Stutzman, 2006). In April 2006, the 10 largest social networking sites had reached a combined unique audience of 68.8 million users, drawing in 45% of active Web users (Nielsen/NetRatings, 2006).

Blogs

Weblogs, or simply blogs, have emerged in the 2000s as an important way to publish information, engage in discussions, and form networks with people who share interests. Blogs are frequently modified Web pages containing dated entries, with the newest entries at the top of the page. Ranging from personal journals to analyses of international politics by traditional and nontraditional journalists, "Blogs are popular in part because they enable easy, inexpensive self-publication of content for a potentially vast audience on the World Wide Web, and because they are more flexible and interactive than previous publication formats, print or digital" (Herring et al., 2006, p. 3).

In 1999, two software programs that automated blog creation became widely available (Blogger and Pitas), and by January 2001, Blogger had registered 117,970 users. By May 3, 2010, the Nielsen tracking service BlogPulse identified a total of 126,861,574 blogs around the world, and 918,400 blog posts had been indexed in the past 24 hours (http://www.blogpulse.com/). Herring et al. (2006) found that most blogs are still single-authored personal diaries, although much of the media attention about the blogosphere (the global network of blogs) has been on "citizen journalists" with popular sites commenting on war, the economy, and local or national politics. A 2010 online international survey found that self-expression and sharing expertise remain the dominant motivations for blogging, with 70% of respondents saying that personal satisfaction is how they measure the success of their blog (Sussman, 2009). About 35% of bloggers described themselves as blogging professionally.

There is growing interest in "bridge bloggers"—bloggers who write/talk about their country or region to a global audience. One interesting project from the Berkman Center for Internet and Society at Harvard Law School is Global Voices, a Web site that aggregates ideas and conversations from bridge bloggers around the world, culling from the diverse range of participatory citizens' media—weblogs, wikis, podcasts, RSS aggregators, and online chats (www.globalvoicesonline.org).

Wikis

A wiki is a Web application that allows participants to create and post content to a Web page without having to know HTML code. WikiWikiWeb, the original wiki designed to let programmers collaborate, was launched in 1994 by Ward Cunningham and can still be found at c2.com/cgi/wiki. ("Wiki" comes from a Hawaiian word meaning "quick.") Participants not only can add content, but they can also edit (add to, remove) what anyone else has entered. Wikis can be used within a restricted workgroup as a collaborative work tool (enterprise wikis), or they can be open to anyone on the public Net. Typically, wiki software will let everyone see what has been recently changed, and histories of pages are stored. Collaboration through a wiki site means that no one person is on the hook to write an entire wiki page; instead, everyone adds information at different times, and the product improves over time. Although a pure wiki does not have anyone in charge, generally wikis are not completely anarchic; there are administrators and rules for collaborative processes.

One of the earliest and best-known global wikis is Wikipedia (www.wikipedia .org), where multiple writers have collectively built a free encyclopedia; indeed, there are many Wikipedias in multiple languages. Although the accuracy of the content varies, many observers have been surprised by the quality of collectively generated content. Does collaboration without financial incentive produce quality?

A special report published by the respected science journal *Nature* found that, for the entries sampled from Wikipedia and Encyclopaedia Britannica on a range of science topics, there was a similar level of errors in both encylopedias (in part due to a surprising level of error in Britannica entries), although generally Wikipedia entries were seen as less scholarly (Giles, 2005).

President Obama has been described as the first "wiki candidate" (Cohen, 2008). For example, his precinct captains in several states used a wiki-based site to collaborate and share information rapidly, without going through a webmaster. Many see the interactive protocols built into wikis as signaling new potentials for participatory communities based on textual/audio/visual collaborations. To date, however, evidence of virtual communities organized around wikis is largely anecdotal.

Other Net Discussion Forums

Until recent years, Usenet was the most well-known type of discussion group in the United States and internationally. Launched in 1979, many people equated the Net with Usenet newsgroups ("netnews").

> Usenet is . . . like a giant coffeehouse with a thousand rooms; it is also a world-wide digital version of the Speaker's Corner in London's Hyde Park, an unedited collection of letters to the editor, a floating flea market, a huge vanity publisher, and a coalition of every odd special-interest group in the world. (Rheingold, 1993, p. 130)

Before the Web emerged in the mid-1990s and became the way most people experience the Net, Usenet newsgroups were posted to an estimated 90,000 sites on five continents, constituting the largest system of interconnected message centers on the Net (Baym, 1995). Usenet Archive and the Online Community were purchased by Google in 2001 and folded into the Google.com discussion groups.

Today, the typical discussion group is an Internet forum, where participants can enter content into a Web site to join in a discussion. An asynchronous forum discussion might be supplemented on some Web sites by the option of synchronous chat using a service such as IRC (Internet Relay Chat). Web-based Internet forums live on computer servers around the Net, whether tied to individuals' Web sites and blogs, to gateway services ("Yahoo Groups" or "Google Groups"), or to the increasing number of "gated" online communities that charge subscriptions and require non-anonymous participation (e.g., The WELL, launched in 1985, is one of the oldest online gatherings on the Net).

Fantasy Worlds

With the 2009 release of James Cameron's film *Avatar*, millions of people around the world who do not participate in online fantasy worlds learned about avatars—three-dimensional virtual bodies that are controlled by the players/creators, including customizing shape, size, color, dress, hair, facial expressions, and so on. Avatars exist in fantasy worlds, often called virtual worlds, which are real-time interactive programs that allow people to create one or many alternative identities, build computational objects representing these identities (avatars), and then move as avatars through the worlds, interacting with others for the purpose of achieving goals (often through combat) and/or socializing. Avatar-based experiences will likely be a key chapter in the story of human-computer interaction in the 21st century.

This section discusses two types of fantasy worlds where people interact using their imaginations and digital tools: MUDs/MMOGs and chat rooms. Originally, all fantasy world experiences were text-based, and took place in MUDs or chat rooms. The 1990s and 2000s saw the emergence of graphically rich, three-dimensional virtual worlds that were able to accommodate hundreds, then thousands, of players around the world. These fantasy worlds are called massively multiplayer online games (MMOGs) or MMORPGs (massively multiplayer online role-playing games). Typically, the terms MMOG and MMORPG refer to goal-oriented, combat-based fantasy worlds, whereas the term massively multiplayer online world (MMOW) is often used to refer to fantasy worlds emphasizing noncombat sociability, such as Second Life. However, the term MUD is still used and can refer to both the original text-based fantasy worlds and today's graphics-based worlds. (See The MUD Connector [http://www.mudconnect.com] for a list of MUDs operating around the world.) For this reason, in this chapter, I use the terms MUD and MMOG interchangeably to refer to online fantasy worlds.

MUDs and MMOGs

There are several distinctive features of MUDs and MMOGs that draw millions of people to participate. Doom, a MMOG launched in 1993, pioneered the use of user-created content and immersive graphics that provided participants with a first-person perspective in the virtual world. These two characteristics, in combination with the feature that online worlds continue to evolve while any single player is offline, make fantasy worlds an intriguing setting for human sociability. A defining element of fantasy worlds, however, is that participants can simply "look around" while feeling the simultaneous presence of multiple others due to the increased sophistication of three-dimensional graphics in the past decade. Being able to look around distinguishes online fantasy worlds from blogs or other Web sites. Boellstorff (2008) argues that this immersive, visual embodiment is why MMOGs are experienced as places. Does the experience of place with others increase the likelihood that people develop online communities in fantasy worlds?

Typically, the focus in MUDs and MMOGs is on adventure and quests, although some worlds are designed for pure sociability (e.g., Second Life) and/or educational purposes (e.g., SimEarth: the Living Planet from the Sims series). Virtual worlds are populated by characters that create kinship groupings, affinity networks, polities, and economies while engaging in building palaces, slaying monsters, or simply hanging out in virtual nightclubs and coffee bars. Internationally, one of the most popular MMOGs is World of Warcraft. In the first few months after its 2004 release, World of Warcraft gained a million subscribers (Au, 2008), had approximately 10 million subscribers in 2008, and remains the top-ranking MMOG in 2010. Boellstorff (2008) lists

35 fantasy worlds in operation during his 2004 to 2007 participant observational research on Second Life, another virtual world launched in 2003.

Reflecting the commercialization of the Net during the 1990s, most MMOGs have game moderators and require subscriptions. In 2007, MMOGs generated more than $5 billion in revenue, and by 2008, there were an estimated 17 million active subscribers (Ducheneaut & Yee, 2008; http://www.mmogchart.com/charts/). Virtual economies have spilled over into the real economy, with entrepreneurs selling virtual currency earned in MMOGs to other players, using real currency for the exchange (Castronova, 2006). In gold farm "sweat shops" (in Shanghai, China, and other locations), people have been paid around the clock to play a MMOG to accumulate virtual gold; gold farm owners sell the virtual gold through Web sites for real cash to Western payers short on game-playing time. In 2005 and 2006, the company running World of Warcraft took repeated actions to stop gold farming by suspending thousands of player accounts to protect the virtual economy (Hoyle, 2006; Jade, 2005).

People join fantasy worlds for different reasons (Turkle, 1995), including the following:

- Simple escape
- A psychological adjunct to real life (e.g., picking a fight in a MUD or chat room as an escape valve for anxiety and anger)
- Experimenting with real-life roles (e.g., parenting)
- Having experiences you can only imagine for yourself (e.g., pretending to be a rock star, a professional athlete, or the opposite gender)

Although the main activity in fantasy worlds may be slaying dragons or launching a military invasion of another galaxy, there are MUDs and MMOGs with a focus on creating and displaying an identity for the sole purpose of being sociable (e.g., presenting as a bear who is trying to kiss another online persona, such as an elf). MMOGs also exist where the focus is not only on sociability but also on giving players the experience of constructing and inhabiting virtual social worlds from scratch. Historically, LambdaMoo in the United States and Habitat in Japan were virtual worlds where players designed innovative legal systems and economies.

A fascinating example of this third type of MMOG is Second Life (SL), a 3-D virtual world entirely constructed (i.e. programmed) and "owned" by its residents. SL is a "Web 2.0" world, with all content user-generated. Created by Linden Labs in 2000 and opened to the public in 2003, the idea is that not only techno-geeks and artists but also regular folks are able to create and animate 3-D objects using the technological platform provided by SL. Avatars can "hear" typed chat of other residents within a virtual 30-meter radius around the avatar, which facilitates meeting new friends and developing networks (Boellstorff, 2008).

SL members build multiple worlds, from forest glens and islands to cities and college campuses. SL has skyrocketed in popularity, with the Web site (http://secondlife.com) reporting more than 1 million participants from around the globe in the fall of 2006. Participating in events is one of the main ways participants interact. When I logged on to SL on a Sunday night in May 2010, the featured event was "Runaround Sue's '50s & '60s Sock Hop—Throw on your leather jacket and poodle skirt and dance to the timeless classics of yesteryear . . ." (http://secondlife.com/destinations/events). That night, SL also listed 62 "role-playing communities": 11 fantasy, 8 goth/vampire, 11 historical, 6 pirate/nautical, 9 sci-fi, 4 steampunk, and 13 urban/noir. Joining with a first basic account is free; new arrivals are given a standard avatar design of jeans and T-shirt and $L250 (the SL currency). Socioeconomic stratification emerges from the fee structure: If you want to build a structure, own land, or dress your avatar in different attire, you pay a fee.

Linden Labs and SL are key players in the new field of digital media and learning. On October 19, 2006, the MacArthur Foundation held a press conference to announce digital media and learning grants, and two audiences participated—one in the real-life Museum of Natural History in New York City, and the other in the virtual amphitheater of SL's New Media Consortium (NMC) virtual campus. After announcing a 5-year, $50 million initiative for research on how digital media affect young people's lives, the foundation took questions from both the real-life audience and SL avatars from around the world, who could be seen and heard from a large screen behind the podium.

Education in the future may take place increasingly on virtual campuses like SL's NMC. Imagine members of a science club in St. Paul, Minnesota, holding a competition with members from a sister club in Bangalore, India, to see who can design the best wearable computer in 3 hours, where the competition is performed "on site" and then judged by professor-avatars.

Chat Rooms

Chat rooms are interactive services that can support both discussion groups and fantasy worlds. I discuss chat rooms in the section on fantasy worlds because of what they have in common with MMOGs: People can experiment with alternate identities in real time. Moreover, some chat rooms are two-dimensional, where participants create avatars and move them around to interact. However, most chat rooms are text-based, using Internet Relay Chat (IRC), a popular service offering multi-user chat rooms. Chat rooms allow people to communicate in real time about any subject. On IRC, anyone can review the list of rooms currently open, join one of these, or choose to open his or her own. A room creator selects a topic name and indicates whether the room is public or restricted to people identified by the operator. Commercial companies also offer chat services. Users join IRC rooms by entering a nickname, and people typically choose names that disguise their identity (e.g., a woman chooses "wildman" or people choose animal names). Because of this feature, chat rooms are very popular for carrying on Tinysex (also known as netsex and cybersex), that is, text-based erotic encounters among two, three, or many people. In CyWorld of South Korea, the Web-based chat rooms have transformed a social networking site into a simulated space, and an astonishing 90% of all South Koreans under age 30 have a CyWorld account (Au, 2008).

Unlike MUDs and MMOGs, most chat room communication does not occur in the context of a collectively experienced virtual background, such as cities, mansions, or enchanted forests. Whereas most MUDs and MMOGs are organized around fantasy identities, no one can know whether identities presented in chat rooms are real or fictional. In the early years of chat rooms, many participants assumed that when you entered the private talk mode, people were exchanging real information about themselves. In the mid-1980s, however, aficionados of CompuServe's CB chat service were outraged to discover that a prominent New York psychiatrist in his early 50s had been carrying on intimate friendships with many women using the false persona of Joan, a neuropsychologist in her late 20s who was mute and confined to a wheelchair. This betrayal was one of the first such scandals to shake up cyberculture. One woman described his deceit as "mind rape" (Van Gelder, 1996, p. 534). Debates emerged about the ethical and legal status of hidden role-play and virtual rape.

Many participants feel that role-play in real time gives a special intensity to social experiences in fantasy worlds, whether a MUD, MMOG, or chat room. Of course, people may also join discussion groups using a false identity; this can be accomplished by using a pseudonym to log on remotely via one of the anonymous servers throughout the world (Shade, 1996). However, such behavior is highly discouraged in many discussion groups, and protocols are now available to prevent anonymous participation in Web-based discussion groups. For this reason, I categorize discussion groups and fantasy worlds as separate types of electronic gatherings.

Civic Networks and Net Activism

Civic networks are electronic gatherings for promoting citizen participation in the activities of governance (Schuler, 1996), such as registering voters, recruiting participants for a citywide cleanup campaign, or promoting a regional environmental conference. Net activism using computer-mediated communication to mobilize people for civic activities and political protest was envisioned as a central purpose of the Net by many of the early programmers. They designed computer networking systems to support the development of communities oriented to social justice and democracy. It was hoped that networked computers would offer "a rich array of options to alternative political movements and grass-roots groups concerned with labor, ecology, feminism, peace, civil rights, [and] homelessness" (Downing, 1989, p. 154).

I've noticed two basic types of civic networks: those linked to place (especially local governments) and those focused on sociopolitical issues not specific to a locale. Perhaps the most common example of the first type of civic network is the municipal Web site, which, in addition to information, also typically offers discussion groups, e-mail systems, and perhaps blogs. Two of the early adopters of online civic networking were the Public Electronic Network in Santa Monica and the Seattle Community Network. Residents can log on to these networks to chat and to learn about garage sales, local political issues, and community events. Another long-standing civic net is the Blacksburg Electronic Village (BEV). Home of Virginia Tech University, Blacksburg launched its electronic village in 1993, and it continues to provide a Virtual Town Hall offering town council minutes, rosters of volunteer opportunities, and information on how to get city services. As announced on www.bev.net, BEV also hosts Web pages for more than 150 civic nonprofit groups, with basic service available for no cost and enhanced Web services available for modest annual fees. This is a key function of civic networks—affordable access to the Net for individuals and nonprofit organizations.

One of the oldest examples of the issue-focused type of civic network is the Institute for Global Communications (IGC), formed in 1987 (Schuler, 1996). With subscribers in more than 70 countries, IGC (www.igc.org) supports PeaceNet, EcoNet, WomensNet, and AntiRacismNet. A more recent issue-focused civic network is SourceWatch.org, a wiki sponsored by the Center for Media and Democracy that produces collaborative cataloguing of the activities of public relations firms, activist groups, and government agencies. For example, SourceWatch documents deceptive public relations campaigns during elections.

In addition to routine civic activities, the Net is also a medium for organizing episodes of protest, ongoing social movement activities, and even antigovernment activities. For example, students at Taiwanese universities who had Usenet access and telephone links to relatives in China formed a network of correspondents during the 1989 Tiananmen Square pro-democracy movement, forwarding the latest information from Peking to the rest of the world (Rheingold, 1993). Ten years later, organizers of the 1999 protest in Seattle against the World Trade Organization used the Net to mobilize activists. Mobilizing people for political activism can be done with very different goals in mind. For example, extreme right-wing groups such as Hammerskin Nation and Stormfront have Web pages on the Net offering discussion groups. Extremist groups may also have private computer networks for recruiting and organizing members.

In the 2004 U.S. presidential election, two relative newcomers to the Net activism scene were MoveOn.org and Meetup.com, both of which proved important in assisting campaign field operatives to organize themselves and mobilize volunteers, including many young adults. (Meetup.com has also been described as a social networking site.) Involvement in these virtual networks may have stimulated voter turnout; the rate among young people ages 18–24 jumped 11 percentage points between the 2000 and 2004 elections (Lopez, Kirby, & Sagoff, 2005). Both Dr. Ron Paul's and President Barack Obama's 2008 presidential campaigns leveraged the Net in innovative ways. For example, visitors to Paul's Web site could link to sites such as Meetup, Digg, Twitter, and SMS to communicate with current and potential supporters. The Obama "net-roots" campaign used wikis to train and coordinate precinct captains, and developed YouTube videos and bulk messaging (both e-mail lists and text messaging software) to keep in touch with supporters, organize events, and raise funds, including viral e-mail campaigns to counter disinformation in the media (Gronbeck, 2009; Stirland, 2008).

Net activism internationally is also harnessing cell phone technology, both formally organized by groups and informally emergent clusters of texting. For example, MobileActive is an organization that uses mobile technology for social change by providing assistance to activists around the globe in establishing texting systems as a support infrastructure for a range of projects, from advocacy for civil rights and democratic participation to health, disaster relief, and environmental protection activities. An example of emergent activism is the widespread use of texting in Iran. In 2008, Iranians were exchanging about 20 million text messages each day, not only to send alerts, but to share information, political criticism, and humor (Ramey, 2008); this widespread practice facilitated the collective use of messaging to communicate during the uprisings after their contested 2009 presidential election. Both the Iranian insurgence and the 2008 U.S. presidential campaign provide evidence that "text messaging, cell phone images, Facebook, Twitter, YouTube, and the Internet have given rise to a reservoir of political energy that posits a new relationship between the new media technologies, politics and public" (Giroux, 2009).

Finally, an example of "ubicomp" (ubiquitous computing) by Net activists was the 2006 Debt Hits Hard campaign against pending federal reduction in student aid: The virtual network Campus Progress asked people to text message the word "Debt" to a short code of five digits; the reply was a request for the respondent's e-mail address and zip code. When this information was received by the campaign, the respondent received an e-mail with information on how to contact congressional representatives in that zip code. In addition, the Debt Hits Hard campaign Web page offers three short videos dramatizing the problem that could be accessed on YouTube.com.

The astonishing growth of the Net in the past 40 years has been encouraged, in part, by the decision of North American and European governments to make the Internet an open system (unlike the closed-network systems in many private corporations, which define their technical specifications as private property not to be disclosed). Thus, from the 1960s to the 1980s, when scientists developed new software programs, they uploaded their creations onto the Internet, making them publicly available to the few hundred computers that were linked at the time.

Sharing software (shareware) not only increased the speed of invention and development but also became an important feature of the emerging Net culture, a feature receiving considerable attention in both the social scientific and popular literatures. In a society dominated by an ethos of individualism, analysts are endlessly fascinated by why people online are so helpful to strangers. Keller (1995) stated, "The question of what has promoted the cooperative nature of the Internet is an important one for planners and policy-makers. . . . [T]here may be a potential model for community development or organizational design" (p. 41). This early, and some would say utopian, view of the Net is challenged by many analysts who instead argue that the way people are using the Net undermines community and thus democracy. For example, Sunstein (2009) argues that it is important that citizens of a diverse nation have common experiences, and the power offered by the Net to filter what media content we consume will make it harder for people to understand others with different views and experiences, leading to social fragmentation. In contrast, their research on player participation in World of Warcraft guilds led Ducheneaut and Yee (2008) to conclude that

> idealized social networks are based on tight links, closest in spirit to the bonds seen in a family or kinship group. There is a tendency to associate "social" environments with such characteristics and dismiss anything less as "asocial" or "failed" social spaces. But this mythical conception has not kept pace with the changes introduced by technology in the past decade. The ubiquity of electronic communication means (from IM to cell phones, or even IM on cell phones) has enabled an entire generation of users to pay "continuous partial attention" (Friedman, 2001) to a larger and looser social circle than was previously possible. (p. 97)

Given conflicting research findings and opposing views on the extent to which the Net is a source of community or the end of community, we now turn to Durkheim's ideas on solidarity in society for an analytical framework that can help us think about the communal character of the Net.

Electronic Gatherings as Durkheimian Societies

What Is a Society for Durkheim?

When we ask someone with an accent what society he or she comes from, the person might say, "China," "Argentina," or "Here, the United States." In everyday language, we tend to use the word *society* to refer to nations. However, Durkheim means something different by the concept of society. He uses the term to refer to any form of ongoing and patterned interactions in groups: "Every aggregate of individuals who are in continuous contact form a society" (Durkheim, 1893/1933, p. 276).

Why is regular and continuous contact the crucial ingredient defining a society? Through interacting with others and forming patterns of regular social relationships, we are reminded again and again that there is some purpose to life larger than just our individual self-interests. This larger purpose is society or life in groups. The more we interact with others, the greater emotional arousal we have and the greater draw we feel to group life. Durkheim says that our recurrent social relationships with others remind us about the collective interests of the groups in which we live, group goals, and shared ways of acting to reach these goals. This is a challenge, however, because Durkheim (1957) assumes that our basic animal nature is forever in a struggle against the collective interests of the group in which we live:

> The interests of the individual are not those of the group he belongs to and, indeed, there is often a real antagonism between one and the other. . . . [T]here should be . . . a code of rules that lays down for the individual what he should do so as not to damage collective interests and so as not to disorganize the society of which he forms a part. (p. 14)

Durkheim has a very concrete concept of society. It refers to the groups in which we live our lives and also to larger collectivities such as nations. We cannot interact directly with the United States. Instead, we interact "only with its concrete manifestations, its groups, communities, and associations" (Nisbett, 1974, p. 201). For this reason, society and group will be used interchangeably in this chapter.

What Is Social Solidarity?

Having defined the concept of society, Durkheim turns to his central question, which is one of the great questions of sociology: How are societies created and sustained over time? In other words, where does social order come from? Durkheim uses the term *social solidarity* instead of social order, and by solidarity, he means a state of unity, cohesion, or social harmony that exists when members of a group or society at large share the same moral rules and practices. For social solidarity to exist, all the parts (individuals, groups, or institutions) somehow must be "glued together." Durkheim wants to discover what it is that glues together the parts of society into a cohesive, solidaristic whole.

Social solidarity is not an abstract essence. It takes different forms in different historical periods and varies in strength from group to group in the same society. "It [social solidarity] is not the same in the family and in political societies; we are not attached to our country in the same fashion as the Roman was to his city or the German to his tribe" (Durkheim, 1893/1933, p. 66). Only through empirical research can we discover the nature and strength of social solidarity in any group or society at large.

Because the United States is a society that celebrates individualism, many of us would approach Durkheim's question about the sources of social solidarity from the viewpoint of the individual. We would ask, why and how do individuals choose to get involved in group life in all its different forms—from marriages, neighborhoods, and networks of friends and coworkers to municipal or state voluntary associations, national political parties, and international religious organizations?

Durkheim establishes a different approach. Instead of asking how individuals choose different forms of social interaction and group life, he frames the question from the opposite point of view. He asks, how do societies create and sustain social solidarity by attracting people to the pleasures of group life and by controlling them to conform with societal ways of acting, thinking, and feeling?

Durkheim does not start from the viewpoint that individual choices create and sustain society. Rather, society "creates" people. Societal "ways of acting, thinking, and feeling . . . are not only external to the individual, but are, moreover, endowed with coercive power, by virtue of which they impose themselves upon him, independent of his individual will" (Durkheim, 1895/1938, p. 2). He points out the following two ways in which society exists prior to the individual (Giddens, 1971, pp. 65–71; Lukes, 1973, pp. 19–22):

1. We are all born into preexisting societies. To get along with others in their daily lives, individuals must learn how to consistently act, think, and feel in ways that support societal values (desired ideal states and goals for what "ought" to be) and norms (guidelines for how to behave that help them realize values and attain these social goals).

2. At any one moment in time, a society's ways of acting, thinking, and feeling exist independently of any one person. A pattern of behavior that expresses values and norms will continue if some or even many members of a society are ignorant about how to act or are rebelling by purposely acting in a deviant way.

For example, if a society or group shares the value that democracy is the best form of government, plus the norm that voting is a very important means of upholding democracy, the fact that many people do not vote does not erase the existence of this value and norm. It means instead that the people have been weakly socialized into this behavioral pattern. (If everyone ceases to vote over a long period of time, however, the norm can disappear from lack of use, and the value of democracy can be threatened if other norms do not support it adequately.)

The process of learning how to act, think, and feel in ways that support the shared rules and practices of a group or society at large is called *socialization*. Socialization will not happen unless individuals come into regular contact with others. Ongoing interaction with other group members helps individuals learn and remember the moral rules of their societies.

We can learn what "glues together" societies by analyzing socialization. There are two levels of socialization, which Durkheim calls "regulation" and "integration" (Lehmann, 1993). Socialization is a lifelong process, not just something that children must undergo. *Regulation* refers to the institutional level of socialization: Society controls our animal appetites by giving us a sense of duty and clear guidance about what goals to seek and the proper means to follow in seeking our goals.

Individuals experience regulation as knowing their duties to the group and having feelings of obligation. This guidance provided by society takes a variety of forms, from the informal constraints of public opinion to formally institutionalized rules such as laws. The more numerous and more effective that rules are in constraining individual behavior, the more regulated is a society.

Different institutions in modern societies regulate individuals through one or more of the following mechanisms: (a) defining moral rules, (b) communicating and clarifying them, and (c) enforcing them. Legislatures and parliaments define new laws. Governmental agencies must communicate, clarify, and enforce rules. Families also instill sentiments of duty and obligation to parental authority and that of other relatives by defining, communicating, and enforcing rules of conduct. All societal institutions are involved in regulation in some way. Durkheim is especially interested in how educational institutions can reinforce democracy by teaching civic morals to children.

Integration refers to the level of socialization that occurs in the everyday life experience of interacting in groups. All societies offer individuals opportunities for collective activity. The more regular these opportunities for group activity and the more intense the experiences of acting together in a group, the more integrated and thus solidaristic is the group. Collective activity reinforces over and over again strong social ties, shared beliefs, values and norms, and shared emotions that let members feel duty and attachment to the group.

Unlike many sociological theorists, Durkheim pays attention to the importance of emotions in human life. Knowing your duty and having respect for authority are not enough for social solidarity. Individuals must also desire regular participation in groups, so they must feel that collective life is pleasurable and that it provides a sense of goodness and reward (Durkheim, 1893/1933):

> When individuals who are found to have common interests associate, it is not only to defend these interests, it is . . . to have the pleasure of communing, to make one out of many, which is to say, finally, to lead the same moral life together. (p. 15)

Hence, Durkheim emphasizes the importance of being regularly moved by feelings of excitement and warmth just from the sheer energy generated by doing things with other people. Durkheim (1912/1995) uses phrases such as "rush of energy" (p. 213) to describe the pleasurable feelings that keep us coming back for more connections to group life. He emphasizes that only at the level of everyday group life can society generate a feeling of "warmth which animates its members, making them intensely human, destroying their egotisms" (Durkheim, 1893/1933, p. 26). Integration cannot happen if groups are not "close" enough to individuals to awaken strong feelings and "drag them" like a magnet into social life.

For example, Durkheim is critical of societies that have strong national governments without also having a well-developed sector of secondary associations, such as interest groups and voluntary associations. Durkheim fears that a strong state that is not counterbalanced by a strong civil society of voluntary associations could result in unstable government or even dictatorship (Durkheim, 1893/1933):

> The State is too remote from individuals; its relations with them too external and intermittent to penetrate deeply into individual consciences and socialize them within. . . . A nation can be maintained only if . . . there is a series of secondary groups *near enough* to the individuals to attract them strongly in their sphere of action and *drag them, in this way, into the general torrent of social life* [italics added]. (p. 28)

Integration is best reinforced through interpersonal contact in face-to-face gatherings. When there is "active interchange of views and impressions . . . [and] the circulation of these views and impressions from one person to another" (p. 28), an intensely vital collective life emerges that makes groups solidaristic. In *The Elementary Forms of the Religious Life* (1912/1995), Durkheim states,

> There can be no society that does not experience the need at regular intervals to maintain and strengthen the collective feelings and ideas that provide its coherence and its distinct individuality. *This moral remaking can be achieved only through meetings, assemblies, and congregations in which the individuals, pressing close to one another* [italics added], reaffirm in common their common sentiments. (p. 429)

Vital and solidaristic group life is especially enhanced by participation in rituals. Rituals are a special type of collective activity in which people meet face-to-face to carry out nonpractical actions for symbolic ends (Collins, 1994, p. 206). During moments of ritual, we experience thoughts and feelings that remind us of the moral power of society. Durkheim (1912/1995) says we actually feel this power as a type of pressure—we "feel the weight" (p. 214) of "something in us that is other than ourselves" (p. 213). For example, we use the common phrase "carrying the weight of the world on her shoulders" to describe this moral power of society from the viewpoint of someone who has too many duties or has an overdeveloped sense of obligations to others.

Although we often think of rituals as religious, Durkheim argues that social rituals are moments of great emotional intensity that are crucial to all types of non-religious integration of societies. Rituals make it possible to control and attach individuals to groups even when people are not in each other's presence. During the moments of jointly repeating common gestures, ideas and emotions circulate among group members like a kind of mental current flowing through everyone; this current attaches special "moral charges" to these ideas and feelings (Collins, 1994). This current (which we can experience as goose bumps, hair rising on the back of our neck, or a full and aching heart) helps focus individual attention intensely on others and on the life of the group.

Normal Versus Pathological States of Integration and Regulation

What happens when regulation and integration are weak or missing in group life? All societies have different levels of integration and regulation, and they can change with time. Therefore, Durkheim provides another set of concepts for analyzing societies: The absence of integration is egoism, and the absence of regulation is anomie. Table 3.2 summarizes his typology and shows that, for Durkheim, weak

Table 3.2	Durkheim's Typology of Normal Versus Pathological States of Social Groups		
	Pathologically Weak ⟷	*Normal (in equilibrium)* ⟷	*Pathologically Strong*
Integration (first aspect of social solidarity)	Egoism: excessive individuation and withdrawal due to insufficient degree of collective activity in society	High degree of collective activity in a group or society at large → large number of social bonds that keep attracting individuals into group life (especially if the bonds are based on strongly shared values and norms)	Altruism: overidentification with a group to the extent that an individual's will is eclipsed by social values and norms (e.g., Kamikaze pilots in Japan who committed suicide for national honor)
Regulation (second aspect of social solidarity)	Anomie: normlessness due to sudden rupture of society's control over individual passions or unregulated capitalist activity	Well-developed guidelines for action (values about proper desires and ideal goals and norms about the "right" way to attain goals) that are widely spread through a group or society → effective control over individual behavior	Fatalism: extreme oppression of individual action (e.g., slavery or people persecuted under brutal military dictatorships)

Source: Durkheim (1897/1951).

Note: Each of the four pathological states refers to the quality of the individual connection to society. For Durkheim, societies can change states from normal to pathological and back to normal, depending on the conditions that exist in a given historical period.

integration or regulation creates "pathological" states. (However, Durkheim fails to adequately address the question of what constitutes "normal" levels of solidarity.)

Egoism and one of its consequences, egoistic suicide, emerge when the group's collective activities (meetings, ceremonies, projects, etc.) have declined in number and intensity to the point where individual members are isolated from the "stimulating action of society" that gives them a "rush of energy" (Durkheim, 1912/1995, p. 213).

In conditions of isolation, our attachment to social ties and our obligations to others wither away; we can become excessively individualistic and withdraw from group life. This is why later in his life, Durkheim (1912/1995) decided that rituals are fundamental to group integration—the very acts of jointly repeating gestures such as prayers, chants, songs, and dances strongly charge participants' moral batteries because "a sort of electricity is generated from their closeness" (p. 217).

Anomie develops when society fails to instill in its members a sufficient spirit of discipline that regulates our animal appetites. Anomie is a state of normlessness (Lukes, 1973). Durkheim talks of two main sources of anomie: (a) experience of a crisis and (b) the lack of regulation in capitalist economies. First, in crisis situations, the values and norms that used to make sense no longer have meaning because the conditions of life have drastically changed. For example, suicide rates often increase after severe economic shocks such as massive depressions, when people lose the material security they have worked their entire lives to acquire.

Second, the lack of regulation of capitalist economies produces chronic anomie. For Durkheim, the "free market" of late-19th-century capitalism follows only one rule: the endless pursuit of self-interest. Anarchy is the inevitable result, which leads to a chronic state of normlessness or anomie. There are no shared beliefs in who has what rights and duties relative to whom. Instead, there is constant pressure to consume ever-greater quantities of goods to "keep up with the Joneses" and feed insatiable appetites for material well-being. Moreover, there is ruthless competition replete with industrial monopolies, constant bankruptcies, pressures to fire workers and reduce their wages, and consequent pressures for workers to engage in strikes or even industrial sabotage. Constant conflict and anarchy prevail.

For Durkheim, the "ever-recurring conflicts" symptomatic of chronic anomie are a sign of sickness and lack of moral development that will hold back civilization. To redress this sad state of affairs, the capitalist economy should be regulated in two ways: (a) by the development of state regulations (e.g., those set out by the U.S. Food and Drug Administration and the Securities and Exchange Commission) and (b) through the development of intermediary associations in which citizens define systems of rights, duties, and professional ethics that are appropriate to their spheres of economic activity (e.g., the American Bar Association and arbitration councils for labor-management disputes).

We are now ready to examine evidence on the Net to assess whether regulation and integration have emerged in electronic gatherings. Are any solidaristic Durkheimian societies forming, or are regulation and integration absent in electronic gatherings, thus making the Net a new and powerful source of anomie and egoism?

Do Electronic Gatherings Have Any Characteristics of Durkheimian Societies?

The popular and speculative ideas in the 1990s about the impact of the Net on individual and group life have been undermined by recent research showing that the Internet has neither generated utopian liberation nor destroyed local communities. Rather, the Net has become more integrated into social life for many, and virtual realities are more taken-for-granted. For most people in North America, time on the Net replaces time spent watching television; and online communications do not crowd out face-to-face contact. Instead, the total volume of social contact has increased (Wellman, 2004). A 2006 survey found the following:

> Our evidence calls into question fears that social relationships and community are fading away in America. Instead of disappearing, people's communities are transforming: The traditional human orientation to neighborhood- and village-based groups is moving towards communities that are oriented around geographically dispersed social networks. People communicate and maneuver in these networks rather than being bound up in one solitary community. Yet people's networks continue to have substantial numbers of relatives and neighbors—the traditional bases of community as well as friends and workmates. (Rainie, Horrigan, Wellman, & Boase, 2006)

Much recent scholarly research focuses on whether and how use of the Net affects integration into offline communities (Matei & Ball-Rokeach, 2003; Wellman & Haythornthwait, 2002). The focus in this section is different: Do the particular qualities of electronic gatherings, which are widely described in the literature as "rich in social information, prominent personalities, valued relationships, and behavioral norms" (Baym, 1995, p. 141), contribute to solidarity in Durkheim's sense? Have electronic gatherings generated continuous interaction among a regular core of people such that there is evidence of regulation and integration? Research indicates that varying degrees of regulation and integration have developed in many electronic gatherings (Cavanagh, 2009; Ducheneaut & Yee, 2008; Watanabe, 2007; Wellman et al., 2003). I now discuss mechanisms of regulation, followed by integration.

Mechanisms of Regulation in Electronic Gatherings

As mentioned previously, there are three mechanisms of regulation on the Net: (a) defining rules of conduct, (b) communicating and clarifying rules of conduct, and (c) enforcing rules of conduct. Each of these is discussed in the following sections.

Mechanism 1: Defining Rules of Conduct

There are several layers of norms (moral rules) for Net conduct. One type of rule is called Network Etiquette or "netiquette." One of the original netiquette inventories describing appropriate online behavior was presented in a 1995 memo (http://tools.ietf.org/html/rfc1855) by the Internet Engineering Task Force (IETF), an international standards-setting group for the Net. Many items may seem quaint, but a number of them are also taken for granted today, such as "Use mixed case. UPPER CASE LOOKS AS IF YOU'RE SHOUTING."

Other types of precise behavioral norms are widely used on the Net to compensate for the lack of physical and emotional context online. Emoticons (CONventions for expressing EMOTIons) are icons or pictorial expressions to represent emotions in textual communication. For example, when read sideways, :-) is a smile, and ;-) is a winking face that can indicate sarcasm or humor. Members of electronic gatherings often compile lists of emoticons that are easily available to new users on a Web site who are seeking to learn group norms of communication. Abbreviations used as shorthand for texting and tweeting have also emerged as shared practices in recent years. Netlingo.com is one of many sites that presents the most popular text and chat acronyms, including BRB (be right back), J/K (just kidding), IRL (in real life), and FWIW (for what it's worth).

There are also rules of conduct that point to specific behaviors as appropriate or inappropriate. Some of these rules have sanctions attached to them, such as blocking log-on access, which can be applied by system administrators, chanops (channel operators), sysops (system operators), or discussion group moderators. Many rules, of course, have no sanctions for breaking them except verbal reprimands. Those with sanctions usually are communicated in a written form that newcomers encounter upon joining. For example, Omidyar.net has a link to its page called "Help: Etiquette," where the following rules are seen:

- Use your real name in your profile.
- Don't start the same discussion in multiple groups.
- An occasional "me too" or "I agree" comment is OK, but don't become known for your proclivity for "me too" posts.
- Outright business pitches are OK if in context and in the appropriate areas. Hint: don't make your first post a pitch.
- Stay on topic! If you have an off-topic, but burning, issue that comes up during a discussion, start a new discussion topic about that burning issue in the appropriate group. Then, invite others to join the new discussion by posting an invite in the original discussion. (www.omidyar.net/group/help/ws/Etiquette/)

The Web site UseModWiki (www.usemod.com) provides free wiki server software and guidance for development of a wiki. One link on the site sends you to the Principles of SoftSecurity for Wikis, which include the following:

- *Assume Good Faith.* People are almost always trying to be helpful; so, we apply the Principle of First Trust, confident that occasional bad will be overwhelmed by the good.
- *Peer Review.* Your peers can ensure that you don't damage the system.
- *Forgive and Forget.* Even well-intentioned people make mistakes. They don't need to be permanent.

- *Limit Damage.* When unpreventable mistakes are made, keep the damage within tolerable limits.
- *Non Violence.* Do no violence lest violence seek you. (www.usemod.com)

Typically, broader behavioral norms like UseModWiki examples are presented to visitors/users of a Web site as Terms and Conditions, and/or a Privacy Policy, or sometimes through the "About Us" page on the site. For Web sites where people establish accounts to participate—from MMOGs and community blogs to political news aggregators (such as realclearpolitics.com, a news source seeking to present a range of views)—a site's Terms and Conditions often set forth minimum age requirements, participant responsibilities, and the conditions under which a participant may be banned from the site. For example, the site Technorati.com, a major search engine for blogs, places two statements above the text box where people enter and upload their comments on an article or blog post: "Add Your Comment, Speak Your Mind" and "Personal attacks are NOT allowed." Below is a hot link to the Comments Policy, which provides an explicit regulatory framework, including the following:

> Please think of the comments as a conversation between individuals and interact with civility. We will edit/delete spam comments, duplicate comments, unsupported accusations, personal attacks of any kind, and terms offensive to groups when used in a pejorative manner. In addition, we reserve the right to edit/delete comments that are some combination of **pointlessly** vulgar, vile, cruel, without redeeming qualities, and an embarrassment to the site. (http://technorati.com/technorati-comments-policy/)

Thus, group moderators or fantasy world system operators usually establish the netiquette and broader behavioral norms for their Web sites, often in collaboration with active participants. As in real life, some norms for Net conduct are vague and diffuse, and others are crystallized more precisely. Diffuse rules typically are modeled by the moderator, group organizers, and core group members, whereas crystallized rules often take the form of written guidelines.

Mechanism 2: Communicating and Clarifying Rules of Conduct

For many Net veterans, there is a libertarian orientation to the notion of rules of conduct: People believe there should not be any overarching moral framework that covers the Net. Instead, electronic gatherings should be self-policing. In Durkheim's terms, regulation should exist at the level of the individual discussion group, MMOG, or civic network and not at any higher level in the system. For example, discussion groups often post frequently asked questions (FAQs) to socialize newcomers to the community standards that have evolved. FAQs are often edited by a volunteer on non-commercial sites, and newcomers can read them to get a sense of the Net group culture and activities and learn about more practical matters such as common problems newcomers have in using system commands. Often, FAQs are updated regularly, thus communicating any evolution of the normative framework for a Web site or online virtual world.

Acrimonious debate is another form of communicating to participants that norms have been violated or that they need to be changed. For example, members of discussion groups in the Whole Earth 'Lectronic Link (WELL) understand that there is a diffuse rule of "what you post you have a right to scribble." Scribbling (erasing) all your contributions from the community archives is rarely done, however, because it can destroy the threads of conversation. Rheingold (1993) describes an occasion when a core member scribbled his texts, and there were weeks of debate about whether the norm should change to keep any one individual from destroying a collective product. This is a classic conflict between individual rights and group rights, the very stuff of Durkheimian solidarity.

Mechanism 3: Enforcing Rules of Conduct

What authorities exist on the Net to enforce rules? In real life, the authority to enforce rules is vested in organizations such as courts (criminal and civil law) and administrative agencies (regulatory law), such as the Environmental Protection Agency. Although electronic gatherings have developed internal rules for governance, to date there is no organized central authority for Net governance that is analogous to the federal judicial system of a country.

For example, Usenet used to have a type of limited ruling council that was called the "backbone cabal" (Jones, 1995; Kling, 1996; Shields, 1996). Members of the cabal were the system administrators of sites that carried most of the traffic for Usenet and also absorbed the costs (e.g., AT&T, Apple, Digital, and Bell Labs). This changed when Usenet began using the Internet as well as the UUCP net to pass along news, and system administrators from the original set of organizations no longer had control.

"Trolls" who lurk and then "flame" (express strong, hostile emotions) can destroy an online discussion group. This tendency, combined with the prevalence of hackers in the past 20 years whose programs invade sites on the Net and wreak havoc or destroy code and content, have resulted in more extensive use of code (protocols) to control and exclude. The UseMod Web site (www.usemod.com) exemplifies how code can be used to enforce rules when peer pressure and community expectations do not work; security controls include password systems that do not accept anonymous log-ons, gated communities where only the invited have access, hierarchies of access to different parts of a site, audit trails (record tracking of who did what), and exiling visitors who violate behavioral norms.

It is remarkable that the Internet, as the largest of the Net's linked network systems, is neither owned nor managed by any one central authority or administrative hierarchy. Instead, segments of the infrastructure are owned and managed by a variety of firms, governmental units, and universities. Private firms (e.g., AOL) sell gateways to the Net, but they can enforce rules only for their customers.

By the late 1980s, the Internet had surpassed the U.S. government's ability to manage it, and in 1987, the first private-sector contracts were awarded to Merit Network, IBM, and MCI to upgrade and manage the central network (backbone). This first step at privatization has been very unpopular with many Internet veterans. Because the research that created the technologies supporting the Internet had been funded by U.S. tax dollars, policies defining "acceptable use" of the network once excluded commercial activity. It was not until 1990 that any commercial networks were linked to the Internet. Privatization continued throughout the 1990s, such as the 1993 award of an additional $12 million of contracts for Internet management to private-sector firms, including the giant AT&T. For many Net veterans, this has raised the specter of higher prices and thus increased inequality in access to Internet services (Branscomb, 1995). However, Goldsmith and Wu (2006) argue that laws of nations can still exert control over the Net.

Current political battles over the Net include application of "digital rights management" to software used in Net applications (which would undermine innovative modifications of programs through collaborative programming), and the critical issue of "net neutrality," a political struggle involving corporate control over bandwidth. For example, will corporate lobbying and lawsuits prevent other cities from taking Philadelphia's approach of offering Net services using Wi-Fi for modest access fees?

The Search for Integration in Electronic Gatherings

This section presents evidence on Net experiments in creating social integration. Although many observers see life online as a solitary activity in which individuals sit alone in front of computers, for many folks, meeting in cyberspace has generated a strong sense of emotional attachment to electronic groups. According to Durkheim, emotional attachment to a society comes from and is best sustained by high levels of collective activity, which reinforce members' social ties and their sense of shared worldviews and shared commitments to each other. That is, integration depends on the level and quality of group activity.

Just as in real life, the experience of powerful community can wax and wane. Perhaps it is because of this challenge of creating and sustaining the feeling of community that anecdotal studies of Net life reveal a fascinating feature. Many people desire a sense of strong attachment to their electronic gatherings. This desire for integration is manifested in the following ways:

- Participants in electronic gatherings try to ground physically their online relationships by creating a sense of embodiment in cyberspace. People construct and interact with reference to images of physical spaces and bodies in their shared virtual spaces.
- Group members may agree to take their relationships "offline" and meet socially in real life.

One study found that "members of electronic virtual communities act as if the community met in a physical public space" (Stone, 1991, p. 104). For example, members refer to the discussion group as a physical public space when saying (typing) remarks such as "This is a convenient place to meet." Net users also create descriptions—some quite elaborate—of the physical place in which they are meeting. You can hang out at Larry's Bar on The Sierra Net or Roger's Bar on Big Sky Telegraph (Sproull & Faraj, 1995). Finally, members often invest considerable energy developing descriptions of their bodies or the bodies of their online personae.

It appears that cyberspace is more real when participants are embodied. Several researchers of the Second Life fantasy world have found that people who are physically disabled in real life are active participants in virtual life, finding that SL broadens their social networks (Au, 2008; Boellstorff, 2008).

The second manifestation of desire for feelings of attachment is taking Net relationships offline. In 2006, some participants in Second Life organized a Second Life Community Convention in San Francisco, and the annual event continues today. Another well-known example in Net lore is the WELL. The WELL was created in 1985 as one of the first commercial computer-conferencing networks and still exists today at www.thewell.org. The founders envisioned the WELL as a prototype for regionally based electronic communities (Figallo, 1995).

At first, most WELL members lived in the San Francisco Bay Area because access was available only by direct-dial modem, which was much cheaper for local callers. Consequently, many members thought of the WELL as an online community with a geographical base. However, in 1986, the WELL organization began holding monthly face-to-face gatherings open to anyone, not just WELL users. WELL members also have initiated real-life contact among participants through an annual summer picnic and annual December Pickle Family Circus benefit and potluck in the Bay Area (Rheingold, 1993). The WELL offers an example in which the Net is only one of several "places" in which the same networks of people may interact.

During a public, real-life meeting of people interested in the National Capital Freenet in Ottawa, facilitator David Sutherland announced, "We will hold a meeting the first Tuesday of every month, so we can keep in contact with each other." When asked afterward whether he meant a physical meeting, he replied, "People seem to come out for face-to-face things, though we shouldn't need them, given the media" (Argyle & Shields, 1996, p. 68). Meetup.com has taken this model of blending online mobilizing with offline meetings to promote community activism.

Research to date suggests that many instances of Net sociability do not reflect emotional attachments and long-lasting social ties. Will looser forms of sociability common in Net interactions (e.g., "hanging out" in MMOGs, Facebook, or chat rooms) be able to create and sustain Durkheimian integration? An intriguing example where some participants appear to be socialized into community standards through interactions with others is Halavais's (2009) study of commenting patterns on digg.com. The Digg platform includes a ranking and filtering system that provides a regular flow of feedback to people who post site links and comments on Digg. All site links on Digg are user-submitted; participants select links to sites of interest; review content of choice on the site; and can choose to "Digg it," "Bury it," and/or write a comment about the site. At the time of Halavais's data collection in July 2008, Digg had about 2.8 million registered users; he analyzed almost 200,000 comments by 6,468 users (whom he calls Diggers). He argues that "the filtering system that makes Digg so successful as a destination also enforces a process that trains users to behave in ways that conform to community standards and expectations" (p. 457).

Digg does not exemplify a more utopian view of community as social ties based on trust, commitment, and loyalty. However, Digg.com suggests how regulation and integration are two sides of the same coin of Durkheimian solidarity. To enact the Web site's goal of surfacing the best content on the Net as determined by participants, Digg has rules—a regulatory framework—about how participants define what is best. Some of these rules are hard-coded into the Web site application (i.e., the ranking and filtering system). People operate within this regulatory framework, and it is through their regular interactions (acts of linking, digging, and burying) that new Diggers are socialized and active Diggers are integrated.

Mechanisms of Integration in Electronic Gatherings

Having established that a desire for integration within electronic gatherings is often strong, I have identified three mechanisms that help generate and sustain high levels of collective activity: (a) celebrating rituals, (b) engaging in gift exchange, and (c) building what Durkheimian scholars Bellah, Madsen, Sullivan, Swidler, and Tipton (1985) call "communities of memory."

Mechanism 1: Celebrating Rituals

One longtime participant in the WELL remarked, "You aren't a real community until you have a funeral" (Rheingold, 1993, p. 37). Durkheim would agree that rituals help create and sustain moral community. Rituals produce two important outcomes: social ties and symbols. Durkheim's nephew, the anthropologist Marcel Mauss, who collaborated with his uncle for years, suggests that some symbolic objects can be so powerful that they can tie together people who "are far apart and . . . may never actually see each other face to face" (Collins, 1994, p. 232). There is evidence that members of electronic gatherings draw on symbolic objects that are very powerful in our culture to create rituals that can bond people who never physically meet.

In electronic gatherings, several types of rituals are found, especially in fantasy worlds but also in discussion groups, such as rituals of mating (flirting, having Tinysex, dating, and marrying); rituals of death (online funerals); and rites of passage (creating status hierarchies through which members advance, often based on programming skill). Here, I present one example of mating rituals to represent the types of symbols created and the fanciful but realistic flavor of these occasions, which often seem to be taken quite seriously by participants. Although there are no data on how widespread Net rituals are, there are abundant descriptions of mating rituals. (The following descriptions are taken from Turkle, 1995, pp. 194–196.)

For example, Stewart, a 23-year-old physics graduate student in the Boston area interviewed by Turkle (1995), joined a MUD based in Germany, presenting himself as the persona Achilles. There, he met Winterlight and eventually asked her on a first date. Through text-based dialogue and place description, he simulated a romantic evening with various MUD commands, including picking her up in a limousine at the airport and taking her to dinner at an Italian restaurant (which exists in real life), where he described the menu to her and ordered. This first date led to a courtship and a formal engagement ceremony on the MUD.

The following is an excerpt from his speech at the community engagement ceremony (from his log of their online dialogue):

I have traveled far and wide across these lands. . . . I thank the people of Gargoyle for their support. . . . I searched far and near for a maiden of beauty with hair of sunshine gold and lips red as the rose. With intelligence to match her beauty. . . . Winterlight, will you marry me?

Winterlight gives Achilles a rose, and he gives her a thousand paper stars, two symbols that connote thoughts and feelings of love. The ceremony fills 12 single-spaced pages of text!

The wedding was more elaborate: Achilles created a "sacred clearing in cyberspace, a niche carved out of rock, with fifty seats intricately carved with animal motifs." The ceremony, which was conducted by the persona of a priest, Tarniwoof, included wedding vows that followed the traditional ritual format: "Do you promise to take Silver Shimmering Winterlight as your mudly wedded wife, in sickness and in health, through time-outs and updates, for richer or poorer, until linkdeath do you part?" During the wedding rites, Stewart was in the United States alone in his room, but across the Atlantic, 25 wedding guests traveled to a city in Germany from Sweden, Norway, Finland, The Netherlands, and other regions of Germany to be with Winterlight at a real-life celebration that coincided with the online ceremonies. Everyone dressed for a wedding and shared food and champagne.

Mechanism 2: Engaging in Gift Exchange

Electronic gatherings have developed practices that support the Net norms of building community together and advancing the pursuit of knowledge by sharing expertise. Users often talk of reciprocity or gift exchange: If you give something, you will receive something sometime in the future. The exchange is both self-interested and altruistic. Even if only a small proportion of Net group members respond regularly to requests for assistance and information, "a small number of small acts can sustain a large community because each act is seen by the entire community" (Sproull & Faraj, 1995, p. 75).

I have noticed three common practices that support the norm of reciprocal exchange on the Net: helping strangers, sharing tools, and reciprocal blogrolling. Perhaps the Net practice most widely commented on is helping strangers (Wellman & Gulia, 1995)—for example, helping newcomers maneuver through different types of electronic environments and answering requests for information from strangers. Sharing tools means uploading programs you have written that others may find useful. Finally, blogrolling is including links to other blogs, and it is usually found on a sidebar of the front page of a blog. Helping a blogger whom you respect build readership by citing her blog on your home page is a form of gift exchange.

A fascinating example of gift exchange is the Massachusetts Institute of Technology Web site created by the MIT Media lab (http://scratch.mit.edu/). The goal of Scratch is to empower young people to create and share interactive stories, games, animations, and simulations by using the graphical programming language made available on the site. "Since its launch in 2007, the Scratch website has become a vibrant online community, with more than 400,000 registered members sharing, discussing, and remixing one another's projects" (MIT Media Lab, 2010). For Scratch Day 2010 (an annual international event), the Web site listed online events at schools and community centers in a dozen U.S. states and more than 25 countries, including Russia, Nepal, Mexico, Bolivia, Israel, Iran, Japan, Vietnam, South Africa, Portugal, Sweden, Australia, China, Great Britain, Greece, Colombia, Italy, and Turkey.

In his research on Second Life, Boellstorff (2008) notes how often SL "residents" he interviewed were surprised by the level of virtual altruism. People were "struck by the willingness of persons not just to explain how to fly or build a house, but also to listen to personal problems—from frustrations with an actual-world job to troubles with an inworld lover." One resident reflected on the ubiquity of this ethic of generosity by stating that "I don't think the way SL works is exactly like RL. Most of the people I've met here are very considerate and helpful. In RL, often we're so overloaded with what we have to accomplish just to get to the end of the day that we aren't as generous" (p. 187).

Mechanism 3: Building "Communities of Memory"

Sociologists Bellah et al. (1985) take a Durkheimian perspective on requisites for solidaristic community. They emphasize that solidaristic groups have histories that are not forgotten. They have community traditions. That is, to sustain itself as a community, any society must organize ways to retell its story. An important part of retelling the story is adding to a repertoire of community exemplars—people and practices that have given the group a special flavor, examples of the "good and virtuous" member, stories of pain, suffering, threats the group has experienced and inflicted on others, and stories of achievements.

Some members of electronic gatherings are very conscious of the need for tradition. A WELL system administrator believes in the importance, for the quality of WELL life, of the "keeping of a historical record of its environs, its people, their works, and the relationships and organizations that define the direction of the collective entity" (Figallo, 1995, p. 55). The WELL keeps a great deal of past discussion texts archived on tape and placed in the system on disks that users can access.

Many Net sites include statistics about their site in the FAQs, thus creating another form of community of memory. (FAQs thus fill both functions of regulation and integration.) FAQs present a Net group as a coherent society with traditions that newcomers should assimilate. Many Web pages have a tab called "History" or "About Us" that provides background on the group and also serves the practical purpose of keeping newcomers from asking the same questions and repeating discussion threads that have already occurred, thus avoiding social cleavages between newcomers and old-timers. As Durkheim would argue, in the process of jointly acting with others, ideas are created and practices become taken-for-granted about who "we" are, what we are doing, and why we are doing it—ingredients crucial to solidaristic societies.

Of course, practices that regulate and integrate Net users do not emerge in all social networking communities, blogs, wikis, discussion groups, MUDs, chat channels, or civic networks. Nor does solidarity last forever within any group. When the evidence on mechanisms of regulation and integration is considered, however, it supports the conclusion that electronic gatherings can and do develop characteristics of a Durkheimian society. We need further research to learn how often and to what extent this happens.

Do Electronic Gatherings Represent the Emergence of a Third Type of Durkheimian Society?

The previous section presented Durkheim's argument about the ingredients of social solidarity that are necessary for any society (regulation and integration). This section discusses another important issue he analyzes: How are modern Western societies with capitalist economies organized differently from premodern societies with noncapitalist economies? In other words, after establishing what creates a solidaristic society, Durkheim then seeks to discover the different types of solidaristic societies that have emerged historically.

Durkheim reduces the great variety of human societies to two basic types, which he calls mechanical and organic. Today, sociologists recognize that this simple typology presents a problem because the broad contrast between traditional and modern societies covers an extremely wide range of social organization. For example, the category of traditional society includes both the largely rural societies of early modern Europe, dominated by small, isolated farming villages, and the medieval city-states of Italy, which were densely populated and embedded in a complex web of international trade. Thus, before discussing Durkheim's two types of societies, it is important to understand why he simplified his analysis in this way.

Like many intellectuals of his generation, Durkheim was influenced by organicist thinking: He turns to analogies with biological organisms to analyze human societies. In *organicist thinking,* individuals are analogous to the cells of an organism, and societies are analogous to the human body. For example, as the fetus grows and develops, clusters of embryonic cells (which were originally identical in structure and function) change and specialize, such that some become kidney cells, whereas others become blood cells or form the lungs. Durkheim (1893/1933) suggests, for example, that the modern state becomes the "social brain" because it has "directive power" in a society (p. 84).

This process of specialization into distinct functions or roles is called *differentiation.* Sociologists often analyze processes of institutional differentiation. For example, differentiation in educational institutions around the developed world meant that the one-room schoolhouse gradually developed into a complex system of kindergartens, elementary schools, middle schools, and high schools.

Durkheim uses the term *division of labor* to discuss differentiation. Generally speaking, division of labor refers to the system of work specialization that exists in all societies, such as the division of economic production into jobs and occupations and into higher levels of specialization, such as branches of industry or the separation of household production from factory production (Sayer & Walker, 1992). Durkheim (1893/1933) extends the concept, however: "The division of labor is not peculiar to the economic world; we can observe its growing influence" in all institutional realms, including political systems, religious institutions, the arts, science, and educational systems (p. 40).

Durkheim's Two Types of Society

The influence of organicist thinking leads Durkheim to conceptualize only two basic types of societal organisms—mechanical (simple) and organic (complex):

Mechanical societies are small, simple organisms with no specialized parts. For example, traditional villages are composed of households that are all organized in a similar manner; each household fulfills the same wide range of economic, educational, familial, and religious functions as the other households. That is, each "part" of the organism fulfills the same functions as all the other parts.

Organic societies are complex organisms because they are composed of specialized parts, each of which performs distinct functions to support the whole society. In a complex, modern society, no one household, neighborhood, town, or company can produce everything its members need to survive. Moreover, the economy depends on the family and educational institutions to produce dependable workers with a range of needed skills.

In mechanical societies, social relations are based on the fact that everyone is similar to each other because there is little or no division of labor and little diversity in people's ideas. Everyone shares the same values, norms, and beliefs—even the same religion. In contrast, in organic societies, a complex division of labor has developed. Consequently, people and groups become different from each other—with many different occupations, a great diversity in racial and ethnic backgrounds, and a wide range of religious beliefs and political views.

From organicist thinking, Durkheim also takes the idea that in the long term, organisms tend toward stability and harmony. Although he admits that conflict and disharmony do exist, he sees these as temporary social problems. In the long term, societies will reach states of equilibrium and harmony (perfect coordination) among their parts. For example, the educational system may produce more lawyers than the economy can absorb for a number of years, but then these two institutions will adjust themselves into a state of balance.

Basically, Durkheim was more interested in understanding the bases of social order and solidarity than he was in analyzing conflict. For this reason, Durkheim is often depicted as a conservative thinker who fails to emphasize the role of power and inequality in social life and the inevitability of struggles among groups with competing interests, unlike two other founding figures of sociology, Karl Marx and Max Weber.

What Causes the Differences Between Mechanical and Organic Societies?

In his well-known statement, "Social life comes from a double source, the likeness of consciences and the division of social labor," Durkheim (1893/1933, p. 226) identifies the following two factors, important variables in sociology even today, that determine whether a society is mechanical or organic: (a) the extent (degree of complexity) of the division of labor and (b) the extent to which members of a society share a collective consciousness, by which Durkheim means all the ways of thinking, feeling, and acting that are common to a group or society. (The extent of collective consciousness means the number and intensity of the values, beliefs, norms, emotions, and ways of acting that are shared.) Durkheim adds that when the division of labor becomes more complex, the collective conscience changes. Together, both changes produce a different type of society. Table 3.3 summarizes Durkheim's argument.

In societies with complex divisions of labor and great diversity of people, the collective consciousness becomes very "stretched" and abstract in an attempt to include only values and norms that are meaningful to everybody. As a result, the values and norms that are strongly shared are far fewer in number and are more ambiguous. Thus, society is less able to regulate all behavior, and social solidarity is threatened. Durkheim notes that maybe the only value remaining in modern

Table 3.3 Two Types of Societies

Type of Society	Division of Labor	Collective Consciousness	Basis of Social Ties
Mechanical	Absent or weak	Large number of clear, powerful ideas and feelings shared by all members in very homogeneous societies	Likeness; value consensus grounded in religiously based common culture
Organic	Present or complex	Smaller number of more ambiguous and less constraining ideas and feelings shared by all members; great diversity of people and ideas	Difference; functional interdependence and a few abstract values such as individualism and patriotism

Source: Durkheim (1893/1933), Collins (1994), Giddens (1971), and Lukes (1973).

Western societies in which everyone believes very strongly is individualism—protecting the inherent dignity, worth, and freedom of the individual.

Exactly how does the division of labor become more complex? Durkheim's argument goes as follows:

1. Population size increases.

2. There are changes in how the population is physically distributed across a territory. Improvements in transportation and communication link people and villages more easily. Villages and towns grow together and become new entities called cities. Several cities grow together and become a new entity called a metropolis (the central urban area of a country or region, such as a capital).

3. As urbanization increases, each person has social contact with a great many more people. This results in competition for jobs and other resources.

4. From this competition, an increasingly complex division of labor emerges. For example, people find their occupational niches, companies find their market niches, and different zones of a city specialize in different functions (e.g., the warehouse district, the red-light district, the shopping malls, and the residential sections).

Recall from the description of organicist thinking that the division of labor becomes more complex in two stages. First, association occurs, in which separate organisms (e.g., villages or small towns) grow in size and become linked together through improved transportation and communication systems; that is, they combine and form a new whole. Second, differentiation occurs, in which the parts within the new whole specialize by taking on different functions. The more complex division of labor plus a weaker, more ambiguous collective consciousness comprise a new type of society: Social ties are based on difference instead of likeness.

Electronic gatherings can be seen as examples of organic societies. The millions of people engaged in blogs and discussion groups, social networking sites, fantasy worlds, and civic networks attest to a complex division of labor and a wide diversity of beliefs. Could social activities on the Net also represent the emergence of a third type of society? Although he could not have anticipated the development of computer technology, I use Durkheim's ideas to guide creative thinking about the future impact of the Net on how we live. In this chapter, I can only begin the process of developing a hypothesis about a new, third kind of Durkheimian society. I hope to illustrate how great ideas from the past can still be applied to make sense of our world today.

Cyborg Societies: A Third Durkheimian Type?

For Durkheim, it is through sociability with others that humans come to know their world and create meaning (i.e., become human). We imagine who we are by imagining who we are in relationship to others and to nature. Durkheim likely would not be surprised that people have flocked to the Net to experiment with new forms of sociability.

In *The Division of Labor,* Durkheim argued that as specialization and interdependence of function increase, the extent and intensity of collective consciousness recede in importance as a source of social solidarity. Together, both changes produce a different type of society. In subsequent work, however, Durkheim became less convinced that the collective consciousness recedes in importance in modern societies. Over time, his work focused more on the pre-rational basis of solidarity, that is, the moral and emotional effect of social ties, especially how groups produce ideologies through mechanisms such as ritual practices (Collins, 1994, pp. 190, 204). After he published *The Division of Labor,* Durkheim never again focused explicitly on his concepts of mechanical and organic solidarity. Yet over his lifetime, he continued his interest in both manifestations of the structural relations among people—the evolution of institutions and the symbolic and emotional components of social life that unify groups and societies.

Following Durkheim, I should look for evidence of new forms of differentiation in institutions and evidence of changes in the collective consciousness. I believe there is enough evidence to warrant hypothesizing that a third type of Durkheimian society may be emerging.

My hypothesis is that (a) technological advances (such as computer science and telecommunications systems, including the creation of the Net) are contributing to new institutional divisions of labor (e.g., the impact of blogging on blurring the distinction between the professional journalist and "citizen journalist"), and (b) technological advances are contributing to changes in the collective consciousness—in particular, brand-new ways of thinking and feeling about the relationship between humans and computers are emerging. Together, these changes suggest the emergence of a new type of society—a cyborg society.

We usually use the term *cyborg* to refer to an individual who is part human and part machine. Here, I extend the term to refer to human-computer interactions (also see Haraway, 1991). Because our relations with computers are becoming social in many ways, future societies may have to create new mechanisms of regulation and integration—not only for human-human interactions but also for cyborg interactions. What evidence is there that a cyborg society is developing?

We are in the very early stages of changes in the nature of our relationships with machines and technology. In her research, Turkle (1995) finds that some people are developing intense relationships with their computers; moreover, "these relationships are changing the way we think and feel" (p. 22).

Changing Collective Consciousness

Changes in the way online aficionados think, feel, and act are based, in part, on the following two contemporary ideas:

1. The world is composed of coded messages circulating in networks.

2. Computers and humans are made of and generate coded messages, so our centuries-old distinction between humans and machines no longer makes any sense.

In today's digital world, vast quantities of information exist only in the form of bits (the binary digits 0 and 1) that constitute computer code and circulate through computer networks. Computer software exists as bits; every message we send by e-mail travels as bits. People surf the Net and interact in MMOGs, thinking of the Net as a place. At one level, however, the entire social world of the Net is nothing more than code.

Moreover, many scientists today think of both machines and biological organisms—including humans—as essentially complex systems of coded messages (bits of 1s and 0s) that circulate in networks. For example, one of the most ambitious scientific projects of the late 20th century is the Human Genome Project, whose purpose is to identify and map all the genes in human DNA. From the perspective of this project, human beings are DNA code, and the challenge is to decipher that code. Once we unlock the secret of the code, perhaps we can clone humans just as we manufacture machines.

Norbert Weiner, often called the father of cybernetic science, said in 1964 that "it is conceptually possible for a human being to be sent over a telegraph line" (Keller, 1994, p. 315). Fans of *Star Trek* will recognize this image: turning humans and their machines into sparkling particles (of code?) and "beaming them up." At the other end, the particles or code regenerate the humans and machines into the form of embodied organisms. What humans and machines would share is their common basis of existence as code.

Until recent decades, everyone took for granted the absolute distinction between machine and human. Today, research indicates that this element of the collective consciousness is changing due to growing numbers of people who seek to embody an identity in code (avatars, which may or may not be similar to themselves) and due to the proliferation of computers that act like people in some ways. With regard to the bot Julia, which was quoted in the beginning of this chapter in a conversation with the human Ace, Turkle (1995) asks,

> How does one treat machines that perform roles previously reserved for people [like having conversations]? In other words, once you have made a pass at an online robot, it is hard to look at computers in the same old way. (p. 88)

Turkle's (1995) research suggests that we can find evidence of a new collective consciousness by analyzing the beliefs and practices of kids interacting with computers in play and in school. From interviews with children in the United States and England, and from observing these children using computers, she finds that they are comfortable with a new idea that machines do have personalities, intentions, and ideas.

Computers can sing, talk interactively, and do math with children. Also, more children are beginning to see these machine activities as signs of consciousness. At the same time, however, they do not believe that the computer machinery is alive like humans, because being alive means breathing, having blood, being born, and having real skin. Humans have real bodies, whereas the subjects in cyberspace do not.

When this idea that computers are inanimate organisms—with consciousness but not alive—becomes part of the Durkheimian collective consciousness, what new mechanisms of regulation and integration will develop? If a growing portion of daily life is experienced as webcam views through our handheld iPads, what is the effect on the collective consciousness? One consequence of our changing ideas about human-computer relations is already emerging: People are beginning to raise the issue of what rules of conduct to follow with and through computers. Computers do things for us and can do things to us, whether in the form of bots like Julia or in other forms such as self-help programs, which users know are code, but at the same time, they respond as if there is a psychotherapist inside the machine. (For example, you can purchase "technotherapy" software for help with depression, eating disorders, and stress management.)

Turkle (1995) suggests that we increasingly treat our computers as "intimate machines," and we thus seek rules of conduct for dealing with this situation. For example, she finds growing numbers of people who think that if a computer took on the role of judge in the court system, it might be less racist than a human judge. This begs the questions, what rules should we evolve about what, how, and when computers can do things with us and to us? Should there be limits on where bots can appear in the Net and what they can do? Is virtual rape actionable in real-life courts of law?

In a cyborg society, advanced technologies could invert the way that societies create and maintain themselves—the Durkheimian concern with which this chapter began. Neighborhoods, corporations, and governments could become "just another part of an informational network, now machine, now message, always ready for exchange, each for the other" (Keller, 1994, p. 315). If societal organisms are designed and organized as codes and networks, this will change the ways that humans experience social life.

As Durkheim might say, cyborg social solidarity thus would depend on creating (a) effective regulation for human-computer interactions, and (b) new forms of collective activity among humans and computers to ensure integration. Will we create a new species of social rituals whose participants are humans, computers, and other forms of artificial life, such as those seen today by TV viewers on the space station Babylon 5? Will we enter an era in which we talk about the human rights of androids like Data on *Star Trek: The Next Generation?*

Conclusion

Although the scenario of cyborg solidarity may seem far-fetched, some of these changes are already happening. Children are already creating new ideas about human-computer relations. Many people are already cyborgs, given 20th-century advances such as prosthetic limbs and pacemakers for hearts. People born after 1985 conduct a considerable amount of their socializing through digital connections to family and friends using handheld, mobile devices. This raises the important Durkheimian question of what societies should begin to do about regulating human use of the new technologies of telecommunications, artificial life, and biological cloning.

Today, kids play with transformer toys that "morph" (metamorphize) back and forth between machine, animal, and human. Tomorrow, societies will probably have to concern themselves with the legal regulation of morphing and cloning—who and what get to switch states from body to code to body, and under what conditions?

In the early 21st century, SNCs and the blogosphere dominates the Net, and we find ourselves in a world of vogs (video blogs), spogs (spam blogs), TrackBack (mechanism for communicating across blogs), wikis, blikis (wiki + blog), Wi-Fi, RSS, podcasting, and mash-ups (see "MashUpCamp" on www.wikipedia.org). Do these technological changes in the Net shape the structure of social relations that is key to Durkheim's theory? By giving us critical lenses through which to study, understand, and organize our worlds, sociological theory can help us prepare for the changes cascading on us with tremendous velocity at the start of the 21st century. I hope that this chapter illustrates this potential of sociological theory, through the application of Durkheim's theoretical framework to an analysis of the Net as a social phenomenon.

As sociologist C. Wright Mills (1959) notes, the rapid pace of change outstrips our ability to act in accord with our cherished values. Today, we often "sense that older ways of feeling and thinking have collapsed and that newer beginnings are ambiguous to the point of moral stasis" (p. 4). What we need, Mills argues, is a sociological imagination. This is a quality of mind that enables us to use our skills of reasoning plus the vast amounts of information available to discover a central insight about social life—that our personal troubles are often not just personal but are also public issues affecting many people and even an entire society.

Mills and Durkheim share elements of a vision: When individuals develop sociological imaginations, societal anomie and egoism can be transformed into societal regulation and integration through greater citizen involvement in the collective activities of public life. I share the vision and hope that sociological theory can help build a sociological imagination meaningful to ordinary citizens, thus contributing to the invigoration of our communities and democracies.

References

Argyle, K., & Shields, R. (1996). Is there a body in the Net? In R. Shields (Ed.), *Cultures of Internet: Virtual spaces, real histories, living bodies* (pp. 58–69). London: Sage.

Au, W. J. (2008). *The making of Second Life: Notes from the new world.* New York: HarperCollins.

Batty, M., & Barr, B. (1994). The electronic frontier: Exploring and mapping cyberspace. *Futures, 26*(7), 699–712.

Baym, N. (1995). The emergence of community in computer-mediated communication. In S. Jones (Ed.), *Cybersociety: Computer-mediated communication and community.* Thousand Oaks, CA: Sage.

Bellah, R., Madsen, R., Sullivan, W., Swidler, A., & Tipton, S. (1985). *Habits of the heart: Individualism and commitment in American life.* New York: Harper & Row.

Berners-Lee, T. (1989/1990). Information management: A proposal. Retrieved from http://www.w3.org/History/1989/proposal.html

Boellstorff, T. (2008). *Coming of age in Second Life: An anthropologist explores the virtually human*. Princeton, NJ: Princeton University Press.

Branscomb, L. (1995). Balancing the commercial and public interest visions of the NII. In B. Kahin & J. Keller (Eds.), *Public access to the Internet*. Cambridge: MIT Press.

Castronova, E. (2006, January 19). How a gold farm works. Blog post on *Terra Nova*. Retrieved from http://terranova.blogs.com/terra_nova /2006/01/how_a_gold_farm.html

Cavanagh, A. (2009). From culture to connection: Internet community studies. *Sociology Compass, 3*(1), 1–15. Retrieved from http://leeds.academia.edu/AllisonCavanagh/Papers

Cohen, N. (2008, June 8). The Wiki-way to the nomination. *New York Times*. Retrieved from http://www.nytimes.com/2008/06/08/weekinreview/08cohen.html

Collins, R. (1994). *Four sociological traditions*. Oxford, UK: Oxford University Press.

Comer, D. (1995). *The Internet book*. Englewood Cliffs, NJ: Prentice Hall.

Dimaggio, P., Hargittai, E., Neuman, W. R., & Robinson, J. P. (2001). Social implications of the Internet. *Annual Review of Sociology, 27,* 307–336.

Downing, J. (1989). Computers for political change: PeaceNet and public access data. *Journal of Communication, 39*(3), 154–162.

Ducheneaut, N., & Yee, N. (2008). Collective solitude and social networks in World of Warcraft. In C. T. Romm, C. Romm-Livermore, & K. Setzekorn (Eds.), *Social networking communities and e-dating services: Concepts and implications* (pp. 78–100). Hershey, PA: Idea Group. Retrieved from http://www2.parc.com/csl/members/nicolas/documents/Collective_solitude.pdf

Durkheim, É. (1933). *The division of labor in society* (G. Simpson, Trans.). New York: Free Press. (Original work published 1893)

Durkheim, É. (1938). *The rules of sociological method* (S. Solovay & J. Mueller, Trans.). New York: Free Press. (Original work published 1895)

Durkheim, É. (1951). *Suicide: A study in sociology* (J. Spaulding & G. Simpson, Trans.). New York: Free Press. (Original work published 1897)

Durkheim, É. (1957). *Professional ethics and civic morals* (C. Brookfield, Trans.). London: Routledge/Kegan Paul.

Durkheim, É. (1995). *The elementary forms of the religious life* (K. Fields, Trans.). New York: Free Press. (Original work published 1912)

Figallo, C. (1995). The WELL: A regionally based online community on the Internet. In B. Kahin & J. Keller (Eds.), *Public access to the Internet*. Cambridge: MIT Press.

Galloway, A. R. (2004). *Protocol: How control exists after decentralization*. Cambridge: MIT Press.

Giddens, A. (1971). *Capitalism and modern social theory*. Cambridge, UK: Cambridge University Press.

Giles, J. (2005). Special report: Internet encyclopaedias go head to head. *Nature, 438,* 900–901. Available online at http://www.nature.com/nature/journal/v438/n7070/full/438900a.html

Gillies, J., & Cailliau, R. (2000). *How the Web was born: The story of the World Wide Web*. Oxford, UK: Oxford University Press.

Giroux, H. (2009). The Iranian uprisings and the challenge of the new media: Rethinking the politics of representation. *Fast Capitalism, 5*(2). Retrieved from http://www.uta.edu/huma/agger/fastcapitalism/5_2/Giroux5_2.html

Goldsmith, J., & Wu, T. (2006). *Who controls the Internet? Illusions of a borderless world*. London: Oxford University Press.

Gronbeck, B. (2009). The Web, campaign 07-08, and engaged citizens: Political, social, and moral consequences. In R. E. Denton, Jr. (Ed.), *The 2008 presidential campaign: A communication perspective*. Lanham, MD: Rowman & Littlefield.

Halavais, A. (2009). Do dugg diggers digg diligently? *Information, Communication, & Society,* *12*(3), 444-459.

Haraway, D. (1991). *Simians, cyborgs, and women: The reinvention of nature.* New York: Routledge.

Herring, S. C., Scheidt, L. A., Kouper, I., & Wright, E. (2006). Longitudinal content analysis of blogs: 2003–2004. In M. Tremayne (Ed.), *Blogging, citizenship and the future of media.* New York: Routledge.

Horrigan, J. (2009). Wireless Internet use. July 2009 report by the Pew Internet & American Life Project, Pew Research Center. Available online at http://pewinternet.org/Reports/ 2009/12-Wireless-Internet-Use.aspx

Hoyle, B. (2006, September 23). Gamers' lust for virtual power satisfied by sweatshop workers. *The Times Online, UK.* Retrieved from http://technology.timesonline.co.uk/ tol/news/tech_and_web/article648072.ece

International Telecommunication Union (ITU). (2010). *Measuring the information society.* Geneva: Author.

Internet Activities Board, Network Working Group (IAB/NWG). (1992). The Internet Standards Process–RFC 1310. Retrieved from http://www.ietf.org/rfc/rfc1310.txt

Jade, C. (2005, March 15). Blizzard bans a gold rush. Blog post on *Ars Technica.* Retrieved from http://arstechnica.com/old/content/2005/03/4700.ars

Jones, S. (1995). Understanding community in the information age. In S. Jones (Ed.), *Cybersociety: Computer-mediated communication and community.* Thousand Oaks, CA: Sage.

Kahin, B. (1995). The Internet and the national information infrastructure. In B. Kahin & J. Keller (Eds.), *Public access to the Internet.* Cambridge: MIT Press.

Keller, E. F. (1994). The body of a new machine: Situating the organism between telegraphs and computers. *Perspectives on Science, 2*(3), 311–320.

Keller, J. (1995). Public access issues: An introduction. In B. Kahin & J. Keller (Eds.), *Public access to the Internet.* Cambridge: MIT Press.

Kling, R. (1996). Social relationships in electronic forums: Hangouts, salons, workplaces, and communities. In R. Kling (Ed.), *Computerization and controversy: Values conflicts and social choices.* San Diego, CA: Academic Press.

Laws, K. (2005, February 8). RSS—Really Something Special? Blog post on *Venture Blog.* Available online at http://www.ventureblog.com/articles/indiv/2005/001187.html

Lee, H. (2005). Behavioral strategies for dealing with flaming in an online forum. *Sociological Quarterly, 46*(2), 385–403.

Lehmann, J. (1993). *Deconstructing Durkheim.* New York: Routledge.

Lopez, M. H., Kirby, E., & Sagoff, J. (2005). The youth vote 2004. *July 2005 Fact Sheet,* Center for Information & Research on Civic Learning and Engagement, School of Public Policy, University of Maryland. Retrieved from http://www.civicyouth.org/PopUps/ FactSheets/ FS_Youth_Voting_72-04.pdf

Lukes, S. (1973). *Emile Durkheim.* Middlesex, UK: Penguin.

Matei, S., & Ball-Rokeach, S. (2003). The Internet in the communication infrastructure of urban residential communities: Macro- or mesolinkage? *Journal of Communication, 53*(4), 642–657.

Mills, C. W. (1959). *The sociological imagination.* London: Oxford University Press.

Miniwatts Marketing Group. (2009). World Internet usage and population statistics for December 31, 2009. Retrieved May 2, 2010, from http://www.internetworldstats.com/ stats.htm

MIT Media Lab. (2010, April 19). Scratch 2.0 [Web log message]. Retrieved from http://blog.scratch.mit.edu/

Nielsen/NetRatings. (2006, May 11). *Social networking sites grow 47 percent, year over year, reaching 45 percent of web users.* Press release. Retrieved from http://www .nielsen-netratings.com/pr/pr_060511.pdf

Nisbet, R. (1974). *The sociology of Emile Durkheim.* New York: Oxford University Press.

Norris, P. (2001). *Digital divide: Civic engagement, information poverty, and the Internet worldwide.* Cambridge, UK: Cambridge University Press.

Rainie, L. (2005, July 20). Tech term awareness [Data memo]. Retrieved from http://www .pewinternet.org/Reports/2005/Tech-Term-Awareness.aspx?r=1

Rainie, L. (2010, January 5). Internet, broadband, and cell phone statistics [Data memo]. Retrieved from http://www.pewinternet.org/Reports/2010/Internet-broadband-and-cell-phone-statistics.aspx?r=1

Rainie, L., Horrigan, J. B., Wellman, B., & Boase, J. (2006, April). The strength of Internet ties [Data memo]. Retrieved from http://www.pewinternet.org/Reports/2006/The-Strength-of-Internet-Ties.aspx?r=1

Rainie, L., & Madden, M. (2005, April 3). Podcasting catches on [Data memo]. Retrieved from http://www.pewinternet.org/Reports/2005/Podcasting-catches-on.aspx?r=1

Ramey, C. (2008, January 23). Subversive politics via SMS in Iran. Retrieved from http://mobileactive.org/sms-jokes-iran

Rheingold, H. (1993). *The virtual community: Homesteading on the electronic frontier.* New York: HarperCollins.

Sayer, A., & Walker, R. (1992). *The new social economy: Reworking the division of labor.* Cambridge, MA: Basil Blackwell.

Schuler, D. (1996). *New community networks: Wired for change.* Reading, MA: Addison-Wesley.

Shade, L. (1996). Is there free speech on the Net? Censorship in the global information infrastructure. In R. Shields (Ed.), *Cultures of Internet: Virtual spaces, real histories, living bodies.* Thousand Oaks, CA: Sage.

Shields, R. (1996). Introduction: Virtual spaces, real histories, and living bodies. In R. Shields (Ed.), *Cultures of Internet: Virtual spaces, real histories, living bodies.* Thousand Oaks, CA: Sage.

Sproull, L., & Faraj, S. (1995). Atheism, sex, and databases: The Net as a social technology. In B. Kahin & J. Keller (Eds.), *Public access to the Internet.* Cambridge: MIT Press.

Stirland, S. L. (2008, March). Inside Obama's surging net-roots campaign. *Wired.* Retrieved from http://www.wired.com/politics/law/news/2008/03/obama_tools

Stone, A. (1991). Will the real body please stand up: Boundary stories about virtual cultures. In M. Benedikt (Ed.), *Cyberspace: First steps.* Cambridge: MIT Press.

Stutzman, F. (2006, January 8). Student life on the Facebook [Web log message]. Retrieved from http://chimprawk.blogspot.com/2006/01/student-life-on-facebook.html

Sunstein, C. (2009). *Republic.com 2.0.* Princeton, NJ: Princeton University Press.

Sussman, M. (2009, October 20). Day 2: The what and why of blogging [Web log message]. Retrieved from http://technorati.com/blogging/article/day-2-the-what-and-why2/

Turkle, S. (1995). *Life on the screen: Identity in the age of the Internet.* New York: Simon & Schuster.

Van Gelder, L. (1996). The strange case of the electronic lover. In R. Kling (Ed.), *Computerization and controversy: Values conflicts and social choices.* San Diego, CA: Academic Press.

Watanabe, M. M. (2007). Conflict and intolerance in a web community: Effects of a system integrating dialogues and monologues. *Journal of Computer-Mediated Communication,* 13(2), Available online at http://jcmc.indiana.edu/vol12/issue3/watanabe.html.

Wellman, B. (2004, Fall). Connecting communities: On and off line. *Contexts, 3*(4), 22–28. Retrieved from http://homes.chass.utoronto.ca/~wellman/publications/contexts/contexts-3a.htm

Wellman, B., & Gulia, M. (1995, August). *Net surfers don't ride alone: Virtual communities as communities.* Paper presented at the annual meeting of the American Sociological Association, Washington, DC.

Wellman, B., & Haythornthwait, C. (Eds.). (2002). *The Internet in everyday life.* Oxford, UK: Blackwell.

Wellman, B., Quan-Haase, A., Boase, J., & Chen, W. (2003). The social affordances of the Internet for networked individualism. *Journal of Computer-Mediated Communication, 8*(2). Retrieved May 10, 2010, from http://jcmc.indiana.edu/vol8/issue3/wellman.html

YouTube. (2010). YouTube fact sheet. Retrieved from http://www.youtube.com/t/fact_sheet

DISCUSSION QUESTIONS

1. Which of the mechanisms of regulation and integration discussed in the chapter have you noticed in the electronic gatherings you have joined?

2. How would Durkheim say that the collective consciousness is likely to change given the rise of the social Web and ubiquitous mobile computing?

3. Why does Durkheim think that ritual is a key ingredient for integration of the individual into the greater whole? What do you think? Do you see examples of truly integrative Durkheimian rituals on the Net? If not, what elements are hard to create in virtual interactions? If you join a site like Second Life and participate with other avatars in virtual worlds for some period of time, does that reinforce or change your opinion of the possibility for community on the Net?

4. According to Galloway (2004), hackers of the 1980s were more like freedom fighters than terrorists. They unpacked programs and cracked systems for fun but also to ensure that the inner workings were demystified as a form of control, that software was free ("freeware"), and that everyone would have unlimited access to computers and information. What happened to change that? Use Durkheim's ideas about normal and pathological forms of integration and regulation to analyze the commentary on hackers at Wikipedia (for example, hacker ethics at http://en.wikipedia .org/wiki/Hacker_ethic). Today, do you think that all hacking is criminal activity, or are there forms of civil disobedience?

5. In his study of the fantasy world Second Life, James Au (2008) says that "avatars could very well be the e-mail address of the future Internet" (p. 83). How would conducting your Net communications through your avatar change your experience of the Net and your social networks? What would Durkheim think of this possible development?

6. This chapter ends with a provocative question: Are cyborg societies a third Durkheimian type of solidarity? What do you think? Offer evidence that supports the claim and evidence that challenges it, and provide your own critical answer to the question.

CHAPTER 4

Alcohol-Related Windows on Simmel's Social World

William J. Staudenmeier, Jr.

William J. Staudenmeier, Jr. was educated in engineering at West Point, graduating in 1972. Professor Staudenmeier worked in Air Force Social Actions, which emerged from his concern with racial injustice and his volunteer work with heroin addicts while at West Point. Helping to pioneer workplace treatment programs for military addicts and alcoholics, he was also involved with equal opportunity and treatment, race relations education, and promoting cross-cultural understanding at overseas bases. He received a PhD from Washington University in St. Louis, he has taught at Drake University, and he is currently Professor of Sociology at Eureka College, where he has been awarded the college's highest teaching honor. Also recognized for his scholarly work on the social response to alcohol and other drugs, he was a visiting fellow at Cornell University and a visiting scientist at the University of Edinburgh, Scotland.

The German sociologist and philosopher Georg Simmel (1858–1918) was born in Berlin, the son of a successful businessman. Simmel lost his father while still young and became financially independent due to the inheritance of his guardian's estate. At the University of Berlin, he was the student of some of the leading historians, philosophers, anthropologists, and psychologists of his time. This broad education and the lively intellectual interest it showed were reflected across Simmel's career. In 1881, he received his doctorate in philosophy with a somber-sounding thesis on "The Nature of Matter According to Kant's Physical Monadology" after having had his first dissertation, "Psychological and Ethnographic

Studies on Music" (complete with a section on yodeling), rejected the year before (Coser, 1977; Kivisto, 1998; Levine, 1971; Wolff, 1908/1964).

Upon graduation, Simmel became a private lecturer (*Privatdozent*) at the University of Berlin, compensated only by student fees between 1885 and 1900. He remained uncompensated by the university for the next 14 years while teaching under the honorific title of "professor extraordinary" owing to his international reputation, the fame of his entertaining lectures, and his important position in Berlin intellectual life. In the prestige-conscious world of academia, however, Simmel had not made it; he did not have a permanent academic position, and despite his title, he did not get to participate in university governance. The prevalent anti-Semitism of the time (his father had converted to Christianity from Judaism), Simmel's welcome to otherwise unwanted students (e.g., women, dissidents, and Eastern Europeans), and Simmel's intellectual rebelliousness may all have played a role in his rejection despite the patronage of famous senior academics such as Max Weber and Edmund Husserl. Sadly, in 1914, when he finally was named a full professor at the University of Strasbourg, World War I interfered with his ability to fulfill the duties of the position. He died of liver cancer in 1918 before the end of the war (Coser, 1977).

In contrast to some of the other social theorists covered in this book, who left behind comprehensive theories where the conceptual parts were clearly connected and consistent, Simmel seems more like a butterfly or a bee, flitting from subject to subject, pollinating different intellectual blossoms. To read much of Simmel is an intellectual wonder, a dizzying ride as he moves from topic to topic and from one perspective to another within each topic. Simmel crosses time and place, disciplinary boundaries melt away, and the everyday is mixed with the profound as insights follow quickly one after another. For some cautious scholars, all of this is suspect. When confronted with breadth, intellectuals often question depth; when diverse interpretations are made of the same body of work, theoretical critics wonder if the readers are wishfully seeing their own preferred ideas in a shallow, murky reflecting pool. Speaking for the critics of Simmel, Émile Durkheim called his most magisterial work, *The Philosophy of Money*, more ingenious than valuable. But Schmoller, Goldscheid, and Lukács compared the same work to some of the greatest sociological books of the time. Reflecting the difficulty of classifying Simmel, however, each of them compared it to a vastly different work (Frisby, 1907/1990).

But what of Simmel's influence, his legacy beyond his time? Simmel is considered by various people to be a philosopher, a cultural theorist, a social psychologist, or a sociologist. If we include as his students those who traveled to attend his lectures, our list will encompass several major figures who went on to make a mark in diverse fields of study: Georg Lukács, Siegfried Kracauer, Robert E. Park, Richard Kroner, and George Santayana, to name a few (Frisby & Featherstone, 1997). But Peter Kivisto (1998), editor of this volume, notes, "He did not create a school of thought that could be inherited by subsequent generations of sociologists. Thus, there is no Simmelian sociology in the same way that there is a Marxist sociology, a Weberian sociology, or a Durkheimian sociology" (p. 123). Reflecting on his own intellectual estate, Simmel (1900/1990) wrote, "I know that I shall die without spiritual heirs (and this is good). The estate I leave is like cash distributed among many heirs, each of whom puts his share to use in some trade that is compatible with his nature but which can no longer be recognized as coming from that estate" (p. 4).

For much of the rest of the 20th century, Simmel would remain underappreciated by sociologists. Today, however, his early influence on American sociology is generally accepted, and his self-described "cash" can be seen today in conflict theory, exchange theory, symbolic interactionism, and postmodern social theory (Ritzer, 2000).

Simmel argued during his professional life for "the conception that society consists of a web of patterned interactions, and that it is the task of sociology to study the forms of these interactions as they occur and reoccur in diverse historical periods and cultural settings" (Coser, 1977, p. 177). The particular contents—that is, concrete historical cases or examples—were of interest to the sociologist only as a way of determining the more general patterns and forms of interaction or types of interactants. The noted sociologist Lewis Coser described Simmel's focus as follows:

> In his view, society consists of an intricate web of multiple relations between individuals who are in constant interaction with one another. . . . The larger superindividual structures—the state, the clan, the family, the city, or the trade union—are only crystallizations of this interaction, even though they may attain autonomy and permanency and confront the individual as if they were alien powers. The major field of study for the student of society is, therefore, sociation, that is, the particular patterns and forms in which men associate and interact with one another. (p. 178)

His ambition in doing this, according to German sociologist Richard Münch (1994), was to assert "a distinctive place for sociology in the family of sciences" (pp. 95–96).

When we study a particular aspect of society, such as the human use of alcoholic beverages, it provides us a window on a much larger world. This chapter explores some of Simmel's major and minor ideas using examples that are alcohol related. Like Simmel's writings, coverage in this chapter will include examples from different places and times, ranging from the macro to the micro, and it will assuredly be incomplete in its treatment of alcohol-related content and in its coverage of Simmelian forms and ideas. Although we cannot climb the whole mountain, the view from the foothills is inspiring, the fresh air is exhilarating, and the exercise is good for us. Let us start with one of Simmel's best-known areas—conflict and change.

Alcohol, Conflict, and Change in America

Conflict Over Alcoholic Beverages

The history of the United States has been marked by considerable conflict over alcoholic beverages. David Pittman (1967) has gone so far as to say that, relative to alcoholic beverage use, "in America one finds the prototype of the ambivalent culture." For Pittman, the ambivalent culture is one characterized by "conflict between coexisting value structures" (pp. 8–10). Traditionally, in American society, alcoholic beverages were the dietary beverages of choice, integrated with work, home life, and play. However, the Temperance and Prohibition movements of the 19th and 20th centuries, respectively, combined with successive waves of immigrants with their own distinctive beliefs and practices, led to conflict over the nature of alcohol and alcohol problems and the appropriate social response. Was alcohol necessary for health or destructive of health? Did alcohol promote vigorous work or prevent it? Was alcohol the social lubricant that helped facilitate social relations or the addicting drug that destroyed families and friendships? Each contrasting set of beliefs carried vastly different implications for an enlightened social response. This conflict became political as Prohibitionists and their opponents fought over local, state, and then national legislation or constitutional amendments to prohibit the manufacture, sale, and transportation of alcoholic beverages.

For Simmel, such conflict is an intensive form of interaction that at least temporarily binds the two parties together. People and groups that do not normally interact, often separated by culture and social class, are suddenly arguing, debating, paying close attention to each other's words and actions, and trying to counteract the effect of those words and actions.

The political conflict over Prohibition also enhanced the centralization (i.e., solidarity) of the group and the group identity within the competing parties. Simmel (1923/1955) noted the following:

> This need for centralization, for the tight pulling together of all elements, which alone guarantees their use, without loss of energy and time, for whatever the requirements of the moment may be, is obvious in the case of conflict. (p. 88)

He also noted,

> The group as a whole may enter into an antagonistic relation with a power outside of it, and it is because of this that the tightening of the relations among its members and the intensification of its unity, in consciousness and in action, occur.

Conflict related to alcoholic beverages, however, has not always been just two-sided.

The Third Party and Conflict

For Simmel, social interaction could not be explained by merely looking at the attributes of the individuals or groups in the interaction. Rather, he put forward a social geometry in which the numbers, distance, and symmetry of the interactants (to name a few of the geometric influences) created different possibilities for interaction that could not be explained by reductionism (Coser, 1977; Ritzer, 2000). This social geometry can be seen in the example of alcohol-related conflict in which a third party is added.

Often, a third party becomes involved, and this can be viewed using Simmel's concepts of the dyad and triad. Simmel's ideas about the difference between a group of two (a dyad) and a group of three (a triad) are applied to groups, for instance, when two groups (a dyad of groups) are joined by a third group (a triad of groups), as well as to individuals (e.g., a dyad of two individuals). According to Simmel, there are three typical interactional functions of the third added element: the *divide et impera*, the *tertius gaudens*, and the nonpartisan and mediator. The historical examples in the following paragraphs will illustrate each type in situations of alcohol-related group conflict drawn from different periods of American history.

The first example is from the late 1800s and early 1900s and regards the contentious issue of African Americans and alcohol. Reform-oriented blacks and whites came together in the South on issues of alcohol reform in the 1880s and economic reform with the Populist Party of the 1890s. African Americans were divided in their beliefs about drinking and its social control, just as were Southern whites. Although the available evidence indicated a greater sobriety among African Americans, racist stereotypes raised fears about drunken freed slaves terrorizing good people. Elites, however, were concerned that if the white vote split, the black vote would decide major political contests. Denise Herd writes about how major political leaders used the race and alcohol cards to drive a wedge between the Southern white and black farmers and laborers who had united on economic reform (Herd, 1983; Staudenmeier, 1985). African Americans were blamed by politicians for the failure of several anti-alcohol votes throughout the South. Their vote was seen as corruptible, anti-reform, and decidedly wet (pro-alcohol).[1] This was only part of a broader concern about the negative effects of black political power, and taking away the black vote (disfranchisement) was seen as the solution. White laborers and farmers supported these measures even though these politically successful disfranchisement measures also reduced the numbers of lower-class white voters. Herd (1983) writes, "Prohibition played an important role in the wave of repression which stifled political dissent and maintained reactionary economic policies" (p. 86).

This first case study can also be seen as an example of Simmel's concept of *divide et impera* (divide and rule), one of the three typical interactions with a third party. In this case, the third element is the politically conservative major political leaders, who used the Prohibition issue, among others, to divide the coalition of white and black farmers and laborers who had been seeking economic reform and threatening their political power. *Divide et impera* worked, and they removed the threat of a lower-class black and white political coalition.

The second case regards the early 1930s battle to repeal the 18th Amendment to the U.S. Constitution, the amendment passed in 1919 that had outlawed the manufacture, sale, and transportation of alcoholic beverages since 1920. The anti-Prohibitionist movement gained popularity and support by the end of the 1920s, leading historians Mark Lender and James Martin (1982) to conclude that after 1930, "repeal was clearly an idea whose time had come" (p. 167). The rise of organized crime funded by the profits of illegal booze was seen as a threat to the social order and was tied to corruption in law enforcement. The scale of law violation and the ineptitude of some of the enforcers helped make Prohibition enforcement visibly ineffective. The dry leaders, however, who were out of touch with changing popular opinion, called for harsher and harsher enforcement, thus leading to more public opposition to unpopular criminal justice actions and inconsistent, seemingly arbitrary harshness. At the same time that the leadership effectiveness of the drys diminished, so did the number of their active members and supporters. By 1930, the growing unemployment and decrease in tax revenue associated with the Great Depression provided two more economic reasons for repeal: jobs and tax revenue. The Association Against the Prohibition Amendment made effective use of these rationales during its public relations campaigns, and even such prominent dry supporters as John D. Rockefeller, Jr., and the DuPonts switched sides and favored repeal by the 1930s (Lender & Martin, 1982).

The public conflict between the Prohibitionists and the anti-Prohibitionists was very heated. In the 1932 election, both groups were contesting for the support of the Democratic Party. The anti-Prohibitionists wanted the Democratic candidate, Franklin Delano Roosevelt, to come out as a wet candidate in favor of repeal as one of the measures to fight the Depression by creating jobs and gaining new tax revenue. Roosevelt eventually campaigned for repeal (Gusfield, 1976; Lender & Martin, 1982).

This second case is an example of Simmel's concept of *tertius gaudens* (the rejoicing third party). The Democrats, sensing a good issue, were the *tertius gaudens*, the rejoicing third party that benefits from the conflict between the two other parties but does not cause it. By coming out in favor of the wet cause, the Democrats gained the strong support of the anti-Prohibitionists and a popular economic campaign issue during the Great Depression. Also, their candidate, Roosevelt, won the election, and the 21st Amendment to the Constitution of the United States was passed, repealing the 18th Amendment and ending "the Great Experiment"—national Prohibition.

The third case is from the recent past. The dismissal or serious disciplining of an employee in a unionized work organization is often a cause for conflict between management and the union. Management tries to maintain labor discipline, whereas the union tries to protect the right of workers not to be treated unfairly. Two major areas of conflict over the disciplining of employees for alcohol-related offenses have been the following: (a) Under what circumstances can an employee be disciplined for possessing alcohol at the workplace, drinking, or being under the influence of alcohol during working hours if there is no written alcohol policy? and (b) if an employee has a drinking problem, can he or she be dismissed without first attempting voluntary treatment? To prevent or reduce conflict, management and labor use binding arbitration to resolve such questions. The arbitrator hears the case and then renders a decision, which is normally published for other arbitrators to see. Although the arbitrator has the Solomon-like discretion to rule as he or she sees fit, the publishing of cases encourages arbitrators to rule alike, creating a nonbinding, informal type of case law.

Arbitrators have generally ruled that in the absence of a written policy, employers must show that there was just cause to discipline the employee and that other employees in the same circumstances have been disciplined consistently. Clearly, however, case rulings act to encourage employers to develop written alcohol policies. The second area of conflict, dismissing employees with drinking problems, did not yield as uniform a result. In a review of arbitration cases published between 1963 and 1980, Michael Marmo found that in slightly more than half of the cases in which alcohol rehabilitation was considered, arbitrators required employers to offer it as a chance for the employee with a drinking problem to avoid dismissal (Marmo, 1983).

Arbitrators used different rationales for their decisions. Different cultural positions on alcohol in American society partially explain this inconsistent result (Staudenmeier, 1987).

This third example illustrates Simmel's concept of a third party that is nonpartisan and provides a mediating role to avoid or reduce conflict between the two parties in this case, labor and management. When arbitrators are consistent, the results are more predictable, and the two parties can better avoid conflict. Where arbitrators are inconsistent, uncertainty is greater and conflict more difficult to avoid. In some cases, arbitrators stick with custom, but in others, they are moved by the fashions of their time.

Custom and Fashion

To follow custom is to be accepted by your group. Customary behavior provides the security of knowing what is right without the social risk associated with individual choice. Previous to the 20th century, most American drinking behavior was customary and traditional, although because America was heterogeneous, there were different customs and traditions to be followed. New groups would bring new traditions. Italian Americans would drink wine at meals, German Americans would drink beer at urban beer gardens, and Irish American miners would bring whiskey down into the coal mines to make the work easier and prevent "coal consumption" (black lung disease). In the 20th century, however, the disruptive effects of the rise and fall of national Prohibition, the marketing and sale of individually packaged units of alcohol for at-home consumption, and the introduction and commercial promotion of new beverages and drinks at an unprecedented pace were witnessed.

Simmel thought that in his time, fashion was escaping the bounds of mere personal accoutrements to encompass more of social life and that the rise of the middle classes, with their emphasis on fast-paced change, was one of the causes. Although customary group drinking still persists, the rise and fall of fashions in drinking and drinking places have become more pronounced today than in the past. In the past two decades, for example, wine coolers and liquor coolers have emerged as a significant, new category of drink. Although wine coolers had existed as a bar-mixed drink for a long time, the individual-portion packaging and commercial promotion of, for instance, Bartles & Jaymes coolers were remarkably successful. Different flavors of these coolers went in and out of fashion. New mixed drinks became fashionable, such as fuzzy navels, a concoction of orange juice and peach schnapps. Specialty beers and ales brewed in small, regional breweries became fashionable in the 1990s, and large brewers are now imitating these products. Fashion remains unpredictable, however. Simmel (1957) wrote, "There seem to be two tendencies in the individual soul as well as in society." This dualism can be seen as the "adaptation to society and individual departure from its demands" (pp. 542–543). Imitation serves the former, and the effort to change and distinguish oneself from the pack serves the latter. With custom, the emphasis is on the adaptation to society. Fashion, however, combines both tendencies:

> Fashion is the imitation of a given example and satisfies the demand for social adaptation; it leads the individual upon the road which all travel, it furnishes a general condition, which resolves the conduct of every individual into a mere example. At the same time it satisfies in no less degree the need of differentiation, the tendency towards dissimilarity, the desire for change and contrast. (p. 543)

Fashion also has another dualistic aspect to it—it joins us to the group in fashion and separates us from all others. Thus, it both joins us and separates us from others (Simmel, 1957, p. 544). In part, this is possible with fashion because "in its very nature it represents a standard that can never be accepted by all" (p. 549). For instance, the change in fashion in large drinking and dance places in urban areas in the past 40 years includes go-go dancers, light shows, discos, and urban cowboys. Ironically, the success of any fashion signals its death:

> As fashion spreads, it gradually goes to its doom. The distinctiveness that in the early stages of a set fashion assures for it a certain distribution is destroyed as the fashion spreads, and as this element wanes, the fashion also is bound to die. (p. 547)

Therefore, writes Simmel (1957), "From an objective standpoint, life according to fashion consists of a balancing of destruction and upbuilding" (p. 549). Because we will do things in the name of fashion that we would otherwise not do (the group frees us from carrying the burden of choice), we may be happier to see some fashions die than others.

Drinking Places

Both custom and fashion influence the choice of drinking places because people drink in many different settings. Some examples include one's home, a friend's home, a dormitory, a park, a car, a restaurant, a sporting venue, a tavern, and a private club. Whereas drinking alone often occurs in one's own home, it is less common in public places. The need to be with others is a basic human one and motivates much of the interaction that occurs in the commercial drinking establishments called taverns.

Types of Taverns

Different types of taverns both constitute and are constituted by different types of patrons. Marshall Clinard (1962), in his classic work on public drinking houses, divides public taverns into five types: the Skid Row tavern, the downtown bar and cocktail lounge, the drink-and-dine tavern, the night club, and the neighborhood tavern. Mary Ann Campbell (1991), in her review of the literature on tavern types and based on her own fieldwork, found different types of patrons across the various types of taverns. Neighborhood taverns, for instance, tended to have large groups of regulars. Skid Row taverns, however, had many strangers. Nightclubs had many of that special category of dyad: the couple.

Sometimes, the characteristics of different types of taverns can be found in one place. Clinard (1962) describes the three rooms commonly found in the British pub:

The vault has a bar or counter where an exclusively male patronage drink standing. Most men come singly, and some are total strangers. In the taproom, drinking is a male group affair, and they are seated around plain wooden tables and benches. It is like a clubroom and strangers are not welcome. While games are played in both the vault and the taproom, most are in the latter. The lounge . . . is well decorated and comfortably furnished with tables, chairs and a piano; it attracts women and couples. There are no games. (pp. 278–279)

Exchange in Taverns

Clearly, economic exchange is a core element of the interaction in commercial drinking establishments. We pay our money, and in exchange we get a drink. For Simmel (1900/1990), however, "It is the object of exchange to increase the sum of value; each party offers to the other more than he possesses before" (p. 82). This occurs because each person in the exchange desired what the other had more than what he or she had. That, after all, is why they engaged in the economic exchange in the first place. The end result, in Simmel's colorful prose, is "a surplus of satisfaction." The bar owner wanted the customer's money more than the drink he sold, and the customer wanted the drink more than the money! It is also the peculiar characteristic of economic exchange, however, that it "always signifies the sacrifice of an otherwise useful good"—in this case, our money, which is no longer available to us to purchase, for instance, tickets to the theater or soup for supper (pp. 83–84).

Because of the commercial nature of taverns, all drinking in these places has some element of economic exchange governed by formal rules. Individuals in groups, however, also practice another form of exchange in these settings that follows custom: the practice known as treating or buying rounds. In this case, one person buys drinks for all the others in the group, and eventually, everyone will have a chance to reciprocate and buy a round, although the reciprocity is delayed, normally until most people are ready for another drink. As with other forms of delayed reciprocity, it is considered bad manners not to complete the exchange, follow custom, stay, and buy a round. If a member of the group leaves early before buying a

round, the faux pas can be made up in part by insisting on being the first to treat the next time the group gets together. It would not normally be acceptable, however, if the individual departing early gave the others money to compensate for their expenditure. Why? Simmel (1900/1990) sees money as unique in this regard: "The relationship is more completely dissolved and more radically terminated by payment of money than by the gift of a specific object. . . . Money is never an adequate mediator of personal relationships" (p. 376). Treating, then, has to do with personal relationships, and it is not strictly an economic exchange.

Treating has some of the elements of the aforementioned economic exchange in that there is a loss of the purchasing value of the money used to treat, but if we look closer, what is normally exchanged within the group is identical: a drink. Where, then, is the "surplus of satisfaction"? It comes from the value of giving and receiving in a group in which such actions and the thought of such actions make us feel good and make us feel a part of the group. This is outside the narrow cash nexus of economic exchange because what is calculated here is not mere profit and loss.

Simmel (1900/1990), however, never intended the concept of exchange to be limited to economic exchange. For Simmel, exchange is "an original form and function of social life" (p. 100). He writes that "most relationships between people can be interpreted as forms of exchange" (p. 82). Thus, examples of exchange to be found in taverns include buying and selling drinks and treating, as discussed previously, but also include conversation and even love.

Conversation is at the center of what takes place in many traditional taverns. For Ray Oldenburg (1991), a good tavern

> combines drinking with conversation such that each improves the other. . . . Tempered drinking "scatters devouring cares" as Horace observed and dispels "all unkindness" as Shakespeare knew. In a relaxed and socially conducive setting, drinking becomes the servant of those assembled by easing tensions, dissolving inhibitions, and inclining people toward their latent sense of humanity. The art of drinking subordinates that activity to its senior partner in the synergism, that of talking. It is a telling truth that the abuse of the synergism, excessive drinking, is first signaled by impairment of the power of speech. (pp. 167–168)

When we exchange this kind of conversation in a tavern, we gain without loss, unlike the case with economic exchange, which always involves elements of lost utility as well as gain.

What Oldenburg describes is an excellent example of what Simmel termed sociability—"the play-form of association." Simmel (1910/1971a) comments,

> This world of sociability, the only one in which a democracy of equals is possible without friction, is an artificial world made up of beings who have renounced both the objective and the purely personal features of the intensity and extensiveness of life in order to bring about among themselves a pure interaction, free of any disturbing material accent. . . . Sociability creates . . . an ideal sociological world, for in it . . . the pleasure of the individual is always contingent upon the joy of others. (pp. 132–133)[2]

Strangers and Regulars

In contrast to a more sociable view, however, not all people who enter a tavern enter with others, form a group, or join a group already there. Some enter, stay, and leave as strangers. For Simmel (1908/1971b), "being a stranger is . . . a completely positive relation; it is a specific form of interaction." The stranger is not "the wanderer who comes today and goes tomorrow, but rather . . . the man who comes today and stays tomorrow" (p. 143). The stranger is both close to and distant from others in the tavern. By remaining a stranger, and by remaining outside of the personal attachments forged in the tavern, the individual maintains an objectivity and freedom that others do not have.

Unlike the stranger, however, others find that the rewards of group membership in gathering places outweigh the loss of their freedom of coming and going. In *The Great Good Place*, Oldenburg (1991) describes the often unappreciated human need for gathering places. For Oldenburg, the home is our first place, work our second place, and "the core settings of informal public life" our third place—the place that serves "the human need for communion" (p. 16). Beauty parlors, coffee shops, general stores, and taverns are examples of traditional third places in American society. Some of the common characteristics of third places include the following:

> Third places exist on neutral ground and serve to level their guests to a condition of equality. Within these places, conversation is the primary activity. . . . The character of a third place is determined most of all by its regular clientele and is marked by a playful mood. (p. 42)

Oldenburg also notes the "comfort and support" of third places.

Although the social types of strangers and regulars persist as part of society, individuals may leave the stranger type behind and become a regular at third places by establishing trust over time. Oldenburg (1991) writes,

> The third place gang need only know that the newcomer is a decent sort, capable of giving and taking in conversation according to the modes of civility and mutual respect that hold sway among them, and the group needs some assurance that the new face is going to become a familiar one. This kind of trust grows with each visit. (p. 35)

This atmosphere is captured in the theme song for the television show *Cheers;* Cheers is truly a place "where everybody knows your name." Strangers, however, are no longer just a few. Zygmunt Bauman (1990) writes,

> The world we live in seems to be populated mostly by strangers; it looks like the world of universal strangerhood. We live among strangers, among whom we are strangers ourselves. In such a world, strangers cannot be confined or kept at bay. Strangers must be lived with. (p. 63)

The bars inhabited by strangers can be contrasted with the third-place taverns discussed previously. Oldenburg (1991) describes one bar as having small, private groups talking quietly, separated by everything but their common dress (in this case, the dress of "fledgling attorney and career-woman-after-hours") and protecting their privacy (pp. 172–173). These people have dealt with the problems of universal strangerhood by selecting a place where "the uncertainty entailed in being in the presence of persons who can be 'anybody' has been thereby considerably, though only locally and temporarily, reduced" (Bauman, 1990, p. 65). They bring with them the only company they will keep. Their strategy, however, still leaves them among strangers. This is in stark contrast with the third-place tavern (or coffee shop) in which they could have joined a larger community group.

Among strangers, we find ourselves in "the company of people who are physically close yet spiritually distant." Among strangers in a tavern, we have physical proximity but little moral proximity—"the feeling of responsibility for the welfare and well-being" of the others around us (Bauman, 1990, pp. 66, 69). Oldenburg (1991) also describes a type of tavern he calls the deadly place, where everyone is a stranger and thunderous silence prevails (pp. 169–170). Bauman (1990) characterizes our interaction in this world of strangers as follows:

> There is a wall of reserve, perhaps even antipathy, inevitably rising between you and them—a wall which one cannot hope to scale, a distance one has little chance to bridge. People are tantalizingly close physically, and yet spiritually— mentally, morally—they manage to remain infinitely remote from each other. The silence which separates them, and the distance which is used as a clever and indispensable weapon against the danger sensed in the presence of strangers, feel like a threat. Lost in the crowd, one feels abandoned to one's own resources; one feels unimportant, lonely and disposable. (p. 68)

In stark contrast, E. E. LeMasters (1975) describes the situation he found in a working-class tavern he studied as follows:

> One night I stopped in at the tavern and found the people at the bar talking about a man in his forties who had been a regular patron of The Oasis and was reported to be dying of cancer. One of the men brought a glass jar over and asked me to contribute to a fund for the man's family. "Lee," he said, "put something in this jar. That poor sonofabitch is up there in that hospital tonight dying of cancer and his four little kids are sitting down in that damn house crying." (pp. 141–142)

LeMasters concludes that

> in a very real sense the inner core of the tavern's patrons functions as a mutual aid society: Psychological support is provided in times of crisis; material help is available if needed; children are cared for; cars are loaned; and so on. (pp. 141–142)

The number of these places, however, has been shrinking as Americans drink more at home, drink at bars among strangers, live in communities without walking access to a neighborhood tavern (or coffee shop) due to zoning restrictions and developers' ideas about contemporary American living spaces, or all three (Oldenburg, 1991, pp. 167–168).

This decline is an excellent example of what Simmel (1908/1971c) feared: that the rapidly growing objective culture of modern life, although created by people, had taken on an autonomy of its own and would not help and may even hinder subjective culture—that is, the development of people, their improvement, "cultivation," and "heightened existence." Simmel noted that "things become more perfected, more intellectual, and to some degree more controlled by an internal, objective logic tied to their instrumentality; but the supreme cultivation, that of subjects, does not increase proportionately" (pp. 233–234).

Interaction in Taverns

Waitresses: Subordination and Superordination

Within tavern life there is a hierarchy. Simmel begins his discussion of subordination and superordination with the point that domination is a form of interaction, albeit an often unrecognized form; it is not merely the one-sided action of the dominant person giving orders. Simmel (1908/1964d) writes, "Interaction, that is, action which is mutually determined, action which stems exclusively from personal origins, prevails even where it often is not noted," such as in the case of subordination and superordination (pp. 181–183). He emphasizes the personal freedom that we have in such a relationship:

domination

> Within a relationship of subordination, the exclusion of all spontaneity whatever is actually rarer than is suggested by such widely used popular expressions as "coercion," "having no choice," "absolute necessity," etc. Even in the most oppressive and cruel cases of subordination, there is still a considerable measure of personal freedom. We merely do not become aware of it, because its manifestation would entail sacrifices which we usually never think of taking upon ourselves. (pp. 181–183)

A common example of this would be when an employer requires an employee, as a condition of employment, to do something that he or she would prefer not to do. Waitresses and waiters in some bars may be required to engage in deceptive practices with customers. Some examples are serving bar brands when a customer orders and pays for an expensive brand, serving liquor that is diluted or not a full measure, and serving single shots in mixed drinks when a customer has ordered and paid for double shots. Simmel would emphasize, however, that the employees retain their freedom to leave that employment.

In the interaction between superordinate and subordinate, the subordinate also influences the superordinate (Simmel, 1908/1964c, pp. 185–186). In the example mentioned previously, waiters and waitresses who are engaged in such deceptive practices will often pursue hustles that directly benefit themselves, such as saving unconsumed drinks for resale (Prus & Irini, 1988).

Today, it is common for women to wait on customers who order a drink. Following the repeal of national Prohibition in the United States in 1932, however, which brought back the legal service of alcoholic beverages, a campaign was fought to ban women from serving alcoholic beverages. Both state legislative and union bans were sought by waiters' unions with limited success. Many waitresses agreed at the time, however, that women should not work in establishments that only served alcoholic beverages without any food service, and some waitresses' local unions enforced this provision. The broader attempt to prohibit female serving of alcoholic beverages fizzled, however, by the end of the 1930s. Although there had been little success in keeping women from serving alcoholic beverages as waitresses where food was also served, a similar campaign to ban them from bartending met with greater success after World War II. By 1948, a total of 17 states prohibited female bartenders, and that same year, the Supreme Court upheld the constitutionality of the relevant Michigan state law. It was not until the winning of 1970s sex discrimination lawsuits using Title 7 of the 1964 Civil Rights Act that bartending was opened to women (Cobble, 1991).

One way of viewing these historical cases is as an example of the conflict between two strata (levels) that are next to each other—for example, male and female waiters—but are gradated (unequal), with males having the higher position at that time. Simmel found that conflict often occurred between strata that were next to each other in a hierarchical pyramid rather than just between the top (the superordinate) and those below (the subordinates) (Münch, 1994).

Within the tavern setting, bartenders are usually considered superordinate to waitresses, just as cooks are considered superordinate to waitresses in restaurants. Waitresses, being in a service occupation, are also often considered subordinate to their customers. Ann-Mari Sellerberg (1994) was interested in investigating "typical contradictory features in the service jobs done by women, focusing on conditions that entail subordination and superordination." Her study examined Swedish waitresses and alcohol as a clear example of these contradictory features. Clearly, these waitresses were given responsibility for controlling customers' alcohol consumption and alcohol-related behavior. This control "from below . . . produces a particular reciprocity." Customers will use such devices as foul language, crude behavior, sexual innuendo, and antagonistic behavior "to undermine technical/practical superordination" from the subordinate waitress (pp. 25–31). Sellerberg concluded,

> The analyses put forward in this study are based on Simmel's specific understanding of the nature of social relations: they are dialectical, that is, they consist of opposing tendencies. . . . The waitress's control of the guest's liquor consumption gains its particular significance from being practiced by a subordinate. (pp. 30–31)

Just Business

Certain types of taverns can also be sites for another, very different type of relationship—the pairing of a prostitute and her client. Clinard, for example, notes that the Skid Row tavern is often frequented by prostitutes attempting to solicit customers. Furthermore, Robert Prus and Styllianoss Irini (1988) describe the importance of prostitution in some hotel cocktail lounges to the economic well-being of these hotels and their staff. Typically, these taverns have extensive rules and procedures for managing the interaction among the bar staff, hookers, "johns," and other tavern-goers.

Simmel (1900/1990) was interested in the general form the interaction took, and for him the role of money was crucial; in fact, he used prostitution as a clarifying example of the special nature of a monetary relationship. He wrote,

> Money best serves, both objectively and symbolically, that purchasable satisfaction which rejects any relationship that continues beyond the momentary sexual impulse, because it is absolutely detached from the person and completely cuts off from the outset any further consequences. (p. 376)

Money concludes the deal and releases the customer from further obligation. Although some johns will become regular customers of certain prostitutes, this does not usually create the same ties one would expect in a normal extended relationship. The regular john may at any time choose a new prostitute for a variety of reasons, including cost. One prostitute reports, "You know he's not going to go out with you again for 40 when he can get her for 35" (Prus & Irini, 1988, p. 21).

Establishing a time limit for services is an integral part of the arrangement because it releases the prostitute from further obligation. One of the prostitutes in the hotel bar study reported about the interaction with customers in the hotel room:

> Usually they take about fifteen minutes in the room, and if they take longer, well it's more money. Sometimes you have problems with guys not wanting you to leave, but when their time is up, you just tell them, "Well, I've got other customers waiting for me. I have to go do my work, I'm a business girl." (Prus & Irini, 1988, p. 16)

The interaction is reduced to payment for service. Another prostitute commented, "You think of it as work. They're strangers and you're providing a service. . . . You think in terms of the $40 or whatever it is that the trick might be giving you" (Prus & Irini, 1988, p. 19). Such monetary relationships are seen in stark contrast with other relationships that these prostitutes have with hotel staff, friends, family, pimps, and other lovers.

Clearly, there is something disturbing about this. Simmel (1900/1990) wrote,

> Kant's moral imperative never to use human beings as a mere means but to accept and treat them always, at the same time, as ends in themselves is blatantly disregarded by both parties in the case of prostitution. Of all human relationships, prostitution is perhaps the most striking instance of mutual degradation to a mere means. (p. 377)

The means, says Simmel, are virtually interchangeable. A john with money is just a john; a willing prostitute is just another prostitute.

Such interaction may change the boundaries of what is considered personal. For example, the hotel bar prostitutes usually will not kiss their customers. One prostitute explains that sex "becomes regular, that it's not personal anymore, so what's left that is? Kissing. So then they treat kissing as something they really care about. It's the only thing left, right?" (Prus & Irini, 1988, p. 17).

Simmel recognized, however, that there are always other factors, such as individual personality, that influence the content of social life in the real world. Therefore, some prostitutes may become personally involved with clients, and some prostitutes may view kissing in the same impersonal way they view sex. Clearly, it is also the case that a third party, such as a pimp, the police, or hotel staff, may affect the interaction between the prostitute and the client in the hotel bar. As the interaction changes from that of a dyad to a triad, Simmel would have us once again look for the role of the third party in the triad—the influence of group size.

Group Size

Simmel drew attention to the influence of group size on group dynamics in his classic work, *Sociology: Investigations on the Forms of Sociation.* This section will first examine the influence of group size on group control and then return to the structural question of how a change in the specific number in a group influences interaction within it. In this section, a reconsideration of the dyad and the triad will focus on interacting individuals rather than interacting groups.

When we wish to host a group of friends at a tavern, how many do we need to have to make a party? Two or three casual business acquaintances would probably not make a party, but a dozen good friends would. Clearly, the size of the group matters, but we cannot set a specific number and say that, for instance, six always makes a party, but five does not. Although size is the most important factor in determining whether or not there is a party, Simmel (1908/1964b) offers the following factors that also have an influence:

> Three circumstances—the host's relations to each of the guests, the relations among the guests, and the way in which each participant interprets these relations—form the basis upon which the number of members decides whether there occurs a "party" or a mere togetherness of a friendly or of an objective-utilitarian sort. (p. 111)

Furthermore, although small numbers of friends may content themselves with good conversation, larger numbers mean different requirements for food, dress, behavior, and alcoholic beverages. Interestingly, Simmel (1908/1964b) explains this by saying,

> A "party," therefore, merely because of its emphasis on number, which excludes a common interaction of more refined and intellectual moods, must all the more strongly make use of these sensuous joys that are shared by all with incomparably greater certainty. (p. 111)

Thus, to illustrate, comfortable intimacy, honest companionship, and good conversation are replaced by the "sensuous joys" of eating, drinking, and mating behavior—joys that are more likely to be a sure hit with a larger, less intimate group.

Simmel also found that for large groups, it was impossible to determine generally the influence of one more person. For instance, by what logic or evidence could we hope to determine the difference between a group of 50 and a group of 51 at any time in any tavern? By dealing with the simplest groups, however, he attempted to determine the influence of a specific group number. His classic formulation was investigating the smallest group—the dyad, or group of two—and then exploring the difference that adding one, forming a triad or group of three, would make. Simmel thought that the differences between a dyad and a triad were large and significant. Also, because these differences were due to the numerical structure, they were also general rather than situational.

When there are two people sitting together in a tavern having a drink and talking, individuals who walk in and see them may perceive them as a group—that is, as something more than just two individuals. Each of the drinkers in the dyad, however, perceives only the other—another single individual. According to Simmel, the pair of drinkers would not perceive themselves "as an autonomous, super-individual unit." If either of the two drinkers leaves the other, then the dyad is destroyed. Simmel (1908/1964a) wrote,

> This dependence of the dyad upon its two individual members causes the thought of its existence to be accompanied by the thought of its termination much more closely and impressively than in any other group, where every member knows that even after his retirement or death, the group can continue to exist. (pp. 123–124)

The structural change of the addition of a third member to the group, now a triad, alters that sense of mortality and the role of the members in the group.

When there is a group of three friends drinking in a bar, the departure of one does not destroy the group. The three also do not have to agree on a course of action; two can create a coalition against the third and decide what the group will do. The group thus possesses a position above the individual not subject to every individual's will. The result may be paying for drinks we do not want, staying longer than desired, or leaving the group prematurely. The spatial boundaries of the tavern setting, however, also create a group of sorts—a group that includes all those within the tavern. Clinard (1962) stated that all drinking in taverns is group drinking (p. 271). Even the isolated stranger in a tavern is influenced by the social nature of the drinking, aware of and responding to those in the same tavern space.

Some Contemporary Drinking Problems

This discussion ends where most formal public discussions of alcohol begin—with a few examples from the area of drinking problems and the social response to them.

Alcoholism and Its Treatment

Clearly, Simmel was concerned with the identification and description of social types (such as the stranger discussed previously) as part of his effort to understand the general forms of social life. On the basis of empirical observation, Simmel would identify the more general social type in terms of its social relationships (Ritzer, 2000). Over the years, several names have been given to those individuals in society who drink way too much and experience serious problems over time because of this drinking behavior. The reaction to them has varied as well. In America, these labels include habitual drunkards, inebriates, alcoholics, alcohol addicts, alcohol abusers, problem drinkers, alcohol dependents, substance abusers, chemical dependents, and so on. Although there have been some clear distinctions made by practitioners among these labels, for most Americans today, the term *alcoholism* is the operative one, and its definition is often vague. Among clinicians and researchers, there have been a series of attempts to operationally and clinically define these problems under two levels of problem definition: (a) alcohol abuse, the less serious form; and (b) alcohol dependence, the more serious form. With alcohol dependence, the individual has alcohol-related social problems as well as signs of tolerance (can drink more over time), withdrawal ("a maladaptive behavioral change with physiological and cognitive concomitants"), or compulsive alcohol-related behavior. Alcohol abuse is the label used when the individual has not met the criteria for alcohol dependence but shows "a maladaptive pattern of substance [alcohol] use leading to clinically significant impairment or distress" (American Psychiatric Association, 1994). An example of this would be an individual who is doing poorly at work because of patterns of heavy drinking.

The Epidemiologic Catchment Area Study provides some interesting information about "the structure of alcoholism in the general population." In the study, the researchers use the term *alcoholism* to refer to the condition of anyone who has exhibited alcohol abuse or alcohol dependence or both. On the basis of their results, they estimated "4.5% to 7% of the population being actively symptomatic in the past year" for alcoholism. Alcoholism, they found, "is a disorder of youthful onset," with almost 40% of the cases having their first symptom by age 20 and more than 80% by age 30. Fifty-three percent of the people who had ever had symptoms of alcohol abuse or alcohol dependence or both were currently in remission; that is, they had experienced no symptoms in the past 12 months. Some of these, unfortunately, may be expected to relapse and have future problems. More than half of the cases in remission (54%) had alcoholism symptoms for a relatively short duration, with less than 5 years between the dates of their first and last symptom. The authors conclude that "it is those who try [to stop their symptomatic drinking] and fail that appear for treatment" (Helzer, Burnam, & McEvoy, 1991, p. 98).

Historically, there was a significant decline in the help available for the alcoholic by the time national Prohibition was repealed in 1932. This was the milieu in which Alcoholics Anonymous (AA) emerged in 1935 to become "the best known and most popular therapy for alcoholism." At its core, AA "is a voluntary fellowship of problem drinkers, both men and women, who join with one another in an effort to refrain from drinking alcohol" (Trice & Staudenmeier, 1989, p. 11). The now-famous

12 steps are the program that the alcoholic follows in interaction with other alcoholics. The organization has no dues, no hierarchy, and no formal officers. It is also self-supporting and does not accept donations from other sources (Trice & Staudenmeier, 1989).

A key part of AA is the twelfth step—the obligation of its members to help other alcoholics by encouraging them to affiliate with AA and helping them to become and stay sober. William Madsen (1979) describes the experience of becoming a new AA member as follows:

> The alcoholic person finds that he is merely a "normal" member of the group rather than an idiosyncratic misfit in society. . . . One person said, "I'd always been a stranger on earth, yearning to find someone who understood me. When I found AA, it felt like coming home to a loving family I'd never known." (p. 385)

In his classic studies of affiliation with AA, Harry Trice (1966) found that those who joined AA "showed a stronger need to establish and maintain close emotional ties with others than did alcoholics not affiliated with AA" (pp. 106–107). Madsen (1979) talked further about the transformation that group membership wrought:

> The very alcoholism that had alienated him from society becomes the bond linking him to this loving primary group. Thus, his alcoholism is metamorphosed from a destructive force to perhaps the most positive identity he has ever had. (p. 385)

On the basis of his affiliation studies, Trice (1966) concluded that "despite AA's effectiveness, many alcoholics are unable to affiliate" (pp. 106–107). Therefore, in those cases, other approaches might be required.

In 1966, when Trice published his book *Alcoholism in America*, inpatient alcoholism treatment was so infrequent that it received little coverage in his book. The 28-day, inpatient, hospital-based or -affiliated treatment program with aftercare as an outpatient (following completion of the 28 days), however, became widespread during the next two decades. The dominant treatment approach in these centers is "multimodality"—the use of several different approaches together—and using the 12 steps of AA. Group therapy is a core approach in these settings, emphasizing open communication, disclosure, and insight. As described by Randall Collins (1988), the German theorist Jürgen Habermas optimistically sees group therapy as an "example of the 'ideal speech community,' in which everything can be said without inhibition, and dialogue can go on until consensus is finally reached without any coercion" (p. 37). He sees the number of these freed individuals and groups using ideal speech as growing and improving the world. Perhaps this evolution will occur, but the case of alcoholism treatment is an interesting example of the factors influencing the growth and possible decline of this social form as well because money is involved.

Historically, the growth of inpatient treatment in the United States is linked with the growth of employer-based programs to identify and rehabilitate alcoholic employees (often called employee assistance programs) and the increasing percentage of employees' insurance plans that cover alcoholism treatment. The triumvirate looked like this: (a) Employers identify the employees and make the referral, (b) treatment centers treat them, and (c) the insurance pays for the treatment. For a variety of interesting, seemingly rational reasons at the time, a one-size-fits-all approach emerged, with insurance companies commonly providing benefits for inpatient 28-day treatment but not for outpatient treatment.

Because of the rising cost of health care, managed care emerged as a way to control the health care costs of employers and their insurers. The contribution of alcoholism, drug abuse, and mental health treatment to these escalating costs was widely publicized, and managed care organizations started to restrict the use of inpatient facilities for alcoholics. Managed care led to a precipitous decline in the number and percentage of employer referrals to inpatient alcoholism treatment, and treatment centers were closed across the United States in the early 1990s. For example, one of the industry leaders had a decline in treatment beds from 1,876 in 1989 to 385 in 1993 (Staudenmeier, 1994, p. 10). During congressional hearings, Betty Ford testified, "Today, the real money is to be made in setting up systems to deny and prevent treatment" (Schmidt & Weisner, 1993, p. 377). Currently, there is a tendency toward managed care requiring brief therapy, usually six visits or less, to replace the more expensive alternatives of intensive outpatient, day patient, and inpatient treatment. Cost accountants' decisions based on monetary criteria using selected social science findings to legitimize these decisions won the day in lieu of the more flexible matching of patients to treatment that some of the early proponents of more flexible care had hoped would replace the rigid 28-day approach. One key informant who had hoped for this told me that instead, it was "cost, cost, cost," and they are "doing everything they can not to provide good treatment" (Staudenmeier, 1994, p. 10). Money became the ultimate arbiter of value—and treatment became a shadow of its former self.

The Legal Drinking Age and Alcohol-Related Problems

Prevention, rather than treatment, is the goal of minimum legal drinking age (MLDA) laws, but there is renewed controversy over whether our current laws are effective. In 2008, with a wave of publicity, more than 100 college presidents in the United States signed the Amethyst Initiative Statement calling for a national debate over the soundness of the state laws setting the minimum legal drinking age at 21 (Amethyst Initiative, 2008a). Under the heading "TWENTY-ONE IS NOT WORKING," the statement provides the rationale for their call to debate:

A culture of dangerous, clandestine "binge drinking"—often conducted off-campus—has developed. Alcohol education that mandates abstinence as the only legal option has not resulted in significant constructive behavioral change among our students. Adults under 21 are deemed capable of voting, signing contracts, serving on juries and enlisting in the military, but are told they are not mature enough to have a beer. By choosing to use fake IDs, students make ethical compromises that erode respect for the law. (Amethyst Initiative, 2008b, p. 1)

Supporters of maintaining the current drinking age at 21 reacted quickly and strongly to the Amethyst Initiative. The influential organization Mothers Against Drunk Driving (MADD) asked the public to write letters to the college presidents requesting they support the 21 drinking age and that they remove their names from the Amethyst Initiative Statement. Reflecting their position, the MADD press release of August 19, 2008, was titled "Some University Presidents Shirk Responsibility to Protect Students from Dangers of Underage Drinking." In this press release (MADD, 2008), "the science behind the 21 law" is given:

> As one of the most studied public health laws in history, the scientific research from more than 50 high-quality studies all found that the 21 law saves lives. In addition, studies show that the 21 law causes those under the age of 21 to drink less and continue to drink less throughout their 20's. The earlier youth drink. . . , the more likely they will become dependent on alcohol and drive drunk later. (p. 2)

MADD was joined by the American Medical Association, the Governor's Highway Safety Association, the National Transportation Safety Board, and others in supporting the 21 law.

For those of us who came of age during the Vietnam War, there is a sense of déjà vu to much of this debate. In the early 1970s, state after state lowered their minimum legal drinking age (MLDA) below 21 (most commonly to 18), with 29 states lowering it by 1975. Some of the reasons for this trend included the drafting of 18-year-old men to fight in Vietnam, the related lowering of the voting age to 18 by the 26th Amendment to the U.S. Constitution in 1971, and the concern that youth from states with higher MLDAs would travel to neighboring states with lower MLDAs to get their booze and drive back under the influence. But a mere decade later, by the early 1980s, several states were reversing this change to reinstitute a 21-year-old minimum drinking age, citing concern over alcohol-related traffic accidents among youth. The federal government weighed in on the issue in 1984, passing the Uniform Drinking Age Act, which punished states that did not have a 21-year-old legal age for purchase and public possession with reduced federal highway funds. The law was effective in compelling all under-21 MLDA states to change to a 21-year-old threshold by 1988 (Kindelberger, 2005; Wagenaar & Toomey, 2002). Simmel would not be surprised by the repetition of this conflict.

So, who is right today? What is really going on here? Simmel would have us be persistent and move closer (Sellerberg, 1994). Although we can quibble about the numbers, the science seems clear here: Raising the drinking age nationally to 21 is correlated with a reduction in alcohol-related traffic fatalities. Overall, binge drinking is down among young people as well. On the other side, binge drinking among college women has risen significantly, and binge drinking among college men has stayed steady rather than declining (Grucza, Norberg, & Bierut, 2009). That which goes on behind closed doors and its harmful effects worries many on college campuses. We may have to wait many years for the full price of this trend to be clear; current problems may be a mere down payment on higher rates of future abuse and dependence well beyond the college years. If this depressing vision comes true, and if this harm is related to the current higher drinking age, Simmel would recognize the irony. Ann-Mari Sellerberg (1994) writes,

> The interactions of contradictory forces constantly tend toward the ironic and the paradoxical. This, to Simmel, amounts to a virtually inescapable logic. Human beings create various things in accordance with their intentions and their most intense desires. What they have created, however, assumes an objective form and follows an immanent logic of development, becoming alienated from its origin as well as from its purpose. (p. xiv)

Meanwhile, we and our legislators have to decide which argument is more compelling.

Violence and Vandalism

All groups try to control interaction within their group to make group life more predictable. Due to the wide range of human alcohol-related behaviors, special issues of control are always present in drinking groups. The bases for control of unpredictable and undesirable alcohol-related interaction, however, vary with group size. The German social theorist Richard Münch (1994) described Simmel's ideas regarding control:

> A small group can rely on trust in the personal morality of its members, because they know each other completely. A medium-sized group has outgrown that complete knowledge of each other and needs closer control of actions by the group and a binding definition of its group morality in mores and conventions. A large group cannot even rely on such informal standards embedded in group solidarity but needs much more formal establishment of control by positive law and a legal system. The large group will contain all three levels of regulation but with a growing importance attached to positive law. (p. 102)

An example of a small drinking group relying on trust and associated with few problems of violence or vandalism would be a family or group of friends drinking wine with a meal.

An example of a very large drinking group would be the group at a European soccer game, a beer festival, or a campuswide party. Because of predictable problems of control, there is usually a visible presence of police, private security, or bouncers. Positive law, a reliance on formal laws and rules and their enforcement, becomes much more important with the increase in size. Formal alcohol controls, however, are often less effective than informal group controls, and these venues are often associated with riotous behavior and a breakdown of controls. For instance, in 1988, one midwestern university campus party of approximately 1,000 people was closed by the police following neighborhood complaints. Bricks and bottles were thrown at the police, and a fire was started using a stage and other flammable materials. On the second night of the party, a police car was overturned, and on the third night of the party, to which 5,000 people showed up, another bonfire was started using furniture looted from neighborhood houses, telephone poles, and so on. Threats to neighbors and police were made, including one threat to throw a student who was trying to protect her property into the fire; students and one policeman were treated for minor injuries; and 50 arrests occurred during the third night, which lasted from Saturday night to Sunday morning. Pointing to a change in controls, Brent Bruton and Robert Schafer (1989) observed, "The legal drinking age change [from 18 to 21] has resulted in restrictive alcohol policies in college residence units which have in turn shifted drinking from legitimate contexts with adequate control mechanisms to illegitimate contexts without adequate mechanisms of social control."

The size of the party was clearly of major importance in this case as well. The discussion of medium-sized groups that follows will illustrate some of the variation in alcohol-related aggressive behavior.

For medium-sized groups that rely on closer group control and mores and conventions, we return to the setting of the tavern. The first obvious point is that the mores and conventions that a group enforces vary widely among different taverns. In some American bars, the bar fight is normative—a regular part of the weekend entertainment not to be avoided but to be sought, either as a participant or as an entertained bystander. In these bars, drinking is tied inextricably with aggression, which is itself normative.

This situation contrasts sharply with that described by John Honigmann (1979) in his study of village taverns in an Austrian village. What the villagers seek out in their taverns is "an evening filled with wit and laughter," sociability, and what the villagers call *Lustigkeit* (gaiety) (pp. 418–419). Honigmann observes,

> Drunkenness itself earns men no disapproval; in fact moderate intoxication is the very basis for gaiety. . . . Immoderate drunkenness—intoxication that can no longer be called tipsy, in which a man loses his ability to evaluate and control his acts, and wherein he becomes aggressive—arouses annoyance and even repugnance. Drinking to this extreme occurs uncommonly. (pp. 427–428)

A similar contrast can be found in two examples of drinking situations in settings other than taverns.

In his classic study of the drinking patterns of the Bolivian Camba tribe, Dwight Heath (1962) observes, "Both drinking and drunkenness are the norm on these occasions [ritualized social gatherings] and an integral part of their social ritual." He adds, however, that "aggression and sexual license are conspicuously absent on these sole occasions when beverage alcohol is used" (pp. 25–26). What occurs in the Cambas' behavior as they drink and sit in a circle is at first an increase in sociability and then a quiet "retreat inward" as they get more drunk. In stark contrast, Mac Marshall (1979) describes the common drunken battles on the weekends of young men in the streets of the Micronesian island of Truk: "The positively valued personal attributes of bravery, respectfulness, and strong thought are achieved and validated in large part through drunken fighting, which has substituted for the major traditional avenue available for establishing a positive masculine image: warfare" (p. 130).

In a society in which the suppression of aggression is the norm, Marshall (1979) notes, drunkenness allows the young men to be aggressive and demonstrate their masculinity while "they are looked upon as crazy and therefore not responsible for their words and deeds" (p. 130).

In their influential book *Drunken Comportment: A Social Explanation,* Craig MacAndrew and Robert Edgerton (1969) help to explain this wide variation in drunken behavior:

> Rather than viewing drunken comportment as a function of toxically disinhibited brains operating in impulse-driven bodies, we have recommended that what is fundamentally at issue are the learned relations that exist among men living together in a society. More specifically, we have contended that the way people comport themselves when they are drunk is determined not by alcohol's toxic assault upon the seat of moral judgment, conscience, or the like, but by what their society makes of and imparts to them concerning the state of drunkenness. (p. 165)[3]

MacAndrew and Edgerton (1969) conclude, "Since societies, like individuals, get the sorts of drunken comportment that they allow, they deserve what they get" (p. 173).

Conclusion

In G. K. Chesterton's (1925) famous obituary of George Bernard Shaw, he reflected on his impressions of Shaw during their one meeting:

> He did not talk about the books he had written; he was far too much alive for that. He talked about the books he had not written. . . . I went out of that garden with a blurred sensation of the million possibilities of creative literature. (pp. 166–167)

And so it is that Georg Simmel leaves us feeling the same way, with a sense of the "million possibilities" of sociological inquiry. For some, like Jürgen Habermas (1996), Simmel is "a different type" and "a creative although not a systematic thinker" (p. 405). For Habermas, "Simmel's pieces vacillate between essay and scientific treatise; they *roam* around the crystallizing thought" (p. 407). Simmel is criticized for his lack of coherence across his work, his undeveloped ideas, and his lack of unifying theory. But what of Simmel's ambition and intent? Lawrence Scaff (2000) observes,

> Critical synthesis of contradictory viewpoints, system building, or reconciliation between opposing forces in the world was not Simmel's ambition, however. For

again and again he presents himself to us as a man of ideas having an uncommon will to originality, adopting an "experimental" stance, a mode of writing, and a "style" that reveals the unique grammar of his thinking. His emphasis is on maintaining the dualisms, the dyadic tensions, rather than imposing a new synthesis or schematic "master narrative." (p. 253)

And what of us? Can we appreciate and enjoy the original, creative gifts of this "different type"? Can we learn from his view of modern life?[4]

For Simmel, life was full of conflicts, contradictions, and dualisms (Ritzer, 2000), and the case of alcohol-related social phenomena illustrates well the accuracy of his observation. Alcoholic beverages remain a major object of conflict in American society. Conflicts over the drinking age, warning labels, drunk driving, alcohol advertising, the price of alcohol, the nature of alcohol problems, and the appropriate response to alcoholism are just some of the political conflicts of the past decade. In addition, alcohol-related social life is full of contradictions and dualisms (good and bad, permissions and controls, intimate and distant, etc.), which were discovered as we explored this aspect of the social world and illuminated "the general" pointed to by Simmel in forms and types that could be found in our particular alcohol-related cases.

Being a student is part of the quest for improving your subjective culture—your own development—using the material and nonmaterial cultural objects found in society. Part of your challenge may be to find an answer to the social (and individual) quandary posed by Simmel (1908/1971c), a quandary clearly including alcoholic beverages for today's college student but certainly not limited to alcohol-related content: "The dissonance of modern life . . . is caused in large part by the fact that things are becoming more and more cultivated, while men are less able to gain from the perfection of objects a perfection of the subjective life" (p. 234).

How do we create a delightful life in a world of artificial delights? How do we master the material world if we do not keep our distance from it? How do we live a good life in a world full of more and more cultivated goods? Finally, returning to our case, how do we keep good drinks from destroying the good drinker?

Notes

1. Ironically, African Americans were also either blamed or given credit for the passage of local Prohibition in several cases. For example, for a description of their role in passing local option in Alexandria, Virginia, see Women's Christian Temperance Union. (1883). *Temperance and prohibition papers* (Series 3, roll 1, p. xxii) [Microfilm].

2. For an interesting application of Simmel's ideas on sociability to alcohol, see J. Partanen (1991). *Sociability and intoxication, alcohol and drinking in Kenya, Africa, and the modern world.* Helsinki, Finland: The Finnish Foundation for Alcohol Studies. Thanks are due to Robin Room at the University of Stockholm for making me aware of this source.

3. I am not sure, however, that Simmel would agree with this statement because he saw the pernicious, unwanted effects of the realm of objective culture on subjective culture. If

objective culture creates conditions that lead to drunken comportment that is unwanted, can the individual change it or can he or she only at best avoid it?

4.   David Frisby calls Simmel "the first sociologist of modernity." Frisby, D. (1997). Georg Simmel: First sociologist of Modernity. In R. Boudon, M. Cherkaoui, & J. Alexander (Eds.), *The classical tradition in sociology: The European tradition* (Vol. 2, pp. 323–349). Thousand Oaks, CA: Sage.

References

American Psychiatric Association. (1994). *Diagnostic and statistical manual of mental disorders* (4th ed.). Washington, DC: Author.

Amethyst Initiative. (2008a). About. Retrieved August 28, 2009, from http://www.amethystinitiative.org/about/

Amethyst Initiative. (2008b). Statement. Retrieved August 28, 2009, from http://www.amethystinitiative.org/statement/

Bauman, Z. (1990). *Thinking sociologically.* Cambridge, UK: Basil Blackwell.

Bruton, B. T., & Schafer, R. B. (1989, April). *Social control and student drinking behavior: An exploratory case study of an issueless riot.* Paper presented at the annual meeting of the Midwest Sociological Society, St. Louis, MO.

Campbell, M. A. (1991). Public drinking places and society. In D. J. Pittman & H. Raskin White (Eds.), *Society, culture, and drinking patterns reexamined* (pp. 361–380). New Brunswick, NJ: Rutgers Center of Alcohol Studies.

Chesterton, G. K. (1925). *Tremendous Trifles* (pp. 166–167). New York: Dodd, Mead and Company.

Clinard, M. B. (1962). The public drinking house and society. In D. J. Pittman & C. R. Snyder (Eds.), *Society, culture, and drinking patterns* (pp. 270–292). New York: Wiley.

Cobble, D. S. (1991). Drawing the line: The construction of a gendered work force in the food service industry. In A. Baron (Ed.), *Work engendered: Toward a new history of American labor* (pp. 216–242). Ithaca, NY: Cornell University Press.

Collins, R. (1988). *Theoretical sociology.* New York: Harcourt Brace Jovanovich.

Coser, L. (1977). *Masters of sociological thought.* New York: Harcourt Brace Jovanovich.

Frisby, D. (1990). Preface to the second edition. In G. Simmel, *The philosophy of money* (D. Frisby, Ed.; T. Bottomore & D. Frisby, Trans.; 2nd enlarged ed., pp. xvi–xvii). New York: Routledge. (Original work published 1907)

Frisby, D., & Featherstone, M. (1997). Introduction to the texts. In D. Frisby & M. Featherstone (Eds., Trans.), *Simmel on culture* (pp. 2, 23–24). Thousand Oaks, CA: Sage.

Grucza, R. A., Norberg, K. E., & Bierut L. J. (2009). Binge drinking among youths and young adults in the United States: 1979–2006. *Journal of the American Academy of Child and Adolescent Psychiatry, 48,* 692–702.

Gusfield, J. R. (1976). *Symbolic crusade.* Urbana: University of Illinois Press.

Habermas, J. (1996). Georg Simmel on philosophy and culture: Postscript to a collection of essays (M. Deflem, Trans.). *Critical Inquiry, 22*(3), 403–414.

Heath, D. B. (1962). Drinking patterns of the Bolivian Camba. In D. J. Pittman & C. R. Snyder (Eds.), *Society, culture, and drinking patterns* (pp. 25–26). New York: Wiley.

Helzer, J., Burnam, A., & McEvoy, L. (1991). Alcohol abuse and dependence. In L. N. Robins & D. A. Regier (Eds.), *Psychiatric disorders in America* (pp. 81–98). New York: Free Press.

Herd, D. A. (1983). Prohibition, racism, and class politics in the post-Reconstruction South. *Journal of Drug Issues, 13,* 77–94.

Honigmann, J. (1979). Dynamics of drinking in an Austrian village. In M. Marshall (Ed.), *Beliefs, behaviors, & alcoholic beverages* (pp. 414–428). Ann Arbor: University of Michigan Press.

Kindelberger, J. (2005, March). *Calculating lives saved due to minimum drinking age laws* [Traffic Safety Facts, Research Note]. Washington, DC: NHTSA National Center for Statistics and Analysis.

Kivisto, P. (1998). *Key ideas in sociology.* Thousand Oaks, CA: Pine Forge.

LeMasters, E. E. (1975). *Blue-collar aristocrats: Life-styles at a working-class tavern.* Madison: University of Wisconsin Press.

Lender, M., & Martin, J. (1982). *Drinking in America: A history.* New York: Free Press.

Levine, D. N. (Ed. & Trans.). (1971). *Georg Simmel on individuality and social forms.* Chicago: University of Chicago Press.

MacAndrew, C., & Edgerton, R. (1969). *Drunken comportment: A social explanation.* New York: Aldine.

Madsen, W. (1979). Alcoholics Anonymous as a crisis cult. In M. Marshall (Ed.), *Beliefs, behaviors, & alcoholic beverages.* Ann Arbor: University of Michigan Press.

Marmo, M. (1983). Arbitrators view problem employees: Discipline or rehabilitation? *Journal of Contemporary Law, 9,* 41–79.

Marshall, M. (1979). *Weekend warriors: Alcohol in a Micronesian culture.* Palo Alto, CA: Mayfield.

Mothers Against Drunk Driving. (2008). *Some university presidents shirk responsibility to protect students from dangers of underage drinking* [MADD Media Center Press Releases]. Retrieved September 21, 2009, from http://www.madd.org/Media-Center/Media-Center/Press-Releases/PressView.aspx?press=150

Münch, R. (1994). *Sociological theory* (Vol. 1). Chicago: Nelson-Hall.

Oldenburg, R. (1991). *The great good place.* New York: Paragon.

Pittman, D. J. (1967). International overview: Social and cultural factors in drinking patterns, pathological and nonpathological. In D. J. Pittman (Ed.), *Alcoholism* (pp. 8–10). New York: Harper & Row.

Prus, R., & Irini, S. (1988). *Hookers, rounders, & desk clerks.* Salem, WI: Sheffield.

Ritzer, G. (2000). *Sociological theory* (5th ed.). New York: McGraw-Hill.

Scaff, L. (2000). Georg Simmel. In G. Ritzer (Ed.), *The Blackwell companion to major social theorists* (p. 253). Malden, MA: Blackwell.

Schmidt, L., & Weisner, C. (1993). Developments in alcoholism treatment. In M. Galanter (Ed.), *Recent developments in alcoholism* (Vol. 11). New York: Plenum.

Sellerberg, A.-M. (1994). *A blend of contradictions: Georg Simmel in theory and practice.* New Brunswick, NJ: Transaction.

Simmel, G. (1955). In K. H. Wolff & R. Bendix (Trans.), *Conflict & the web of group affiliations* (p. 88). New York: Free Press. (Original work published 1923)

Simmel, G. (1957). Fashion. *American Journal of Sociology, 62*(6), 541–558.

Simmel, G. (1964a). The isolated individual and the dyad. In K. H. Wolff (Ed. & Trans.), *The sociology of Georg Simmel* (pp. 123–124). New York: Free Press. (Original work published 1908)

Simmel, G. (1964b). The quantitative determination of group divisions and of certain groups. In K. H. Wolff (Ed. & Trans.), *The sociology of Georg Simmel* (pp. 111–114). New York: Free Press. (Original work published 1908)

Simmel, G. (1964c). *The sociology of Georg Simmel.* New York: Free Press. (Original work published 1908)

Simmel, G. (1964d). Superordination and subordination. In K. H. Wolff (Ed. & Trans.), *The sociology of Georg Simmel.* New York: Free Press. (Original work published 1908)

Simmel, G. (1971a). Sociability. In D. N. Levine (Ed. & Trans.), *On individuality and social forms* (pp. 132–133). Chicago: University of Chicago Press.

Simmel, G. (1971b). The stranger. In D. N. Levine (Ed. & Trans.), *On individuality and social forms*. Chicago: University of Chicago Press.

Simmel, G. (1971c). Subjective culture. In D. N. Levine (Ed. & Trans.), *On individuality and social forms*. Chicago: University of Chicago Press.

Simmel, G. (1990). Introduction to the translation. In G. Simmel, *The philosophy of money* (D. Frisby & T. Bottomore, Trans.). New York: Routledge. (Original work published 1900)

Staudenmeier, W. J., Jr. (1985, March). *Race and deviance: Blacks and alcohol in the age of temperance.* Paper presented at the meeting of the Midwest Sociological Society, St. Louis, MO.

Staudenmeier, W. J., Jr. (1987). Context and variation in employer policies on alcohol. *Journal of Drug Issues, 17,* 255–271.

Staudenmeier, W. J., Jr. (1994, October). *From moral entrepreneurs to economic entrepreneurs: Rationalization and disenchantment in the American social movement against alcoholism.* Paper presented at the 38th Scottish Alcohol Problems Research Symposium, Pitlochry, Scotland.

Trice, H. M. (1966). *Alcoholism in America.* New York: McGraw-Hill.

Trice, H. M., & Staudenmeier, W. J., Jr. (1989). A sociocultural history of Alcoholics Anonymous. In M. Galanter (Ed.), *Recent developments in alcoholism* (pp. 11–35). New York: Plenum.

Wagenaar, A. C., & Toomey, T. L. (2002). Effects of minimum drinking age laws: Review and analyses of the literature from 1960–2000. *Journal of Studies on Alcohol* (Suppl. No. 14), 206–225.

Wolff, K. H. (Ed. & Trans.). (1964). *The sociology of Georg Simmel.* New York: Free Press. (Original work published 1908)

DISCUSSION QUESTIONS

1. Think about the friendship dyads of which you have been a part. Apply Simmel's ideas about the dyad and triad from this chapter to one of your examples. What changes took place when a third person joined the group?

2. What are some of the current conflicts in American society over alcohol or other drugs or both? Do these conflicts, as Simmel suggests, temporarily bind the two parties together in intensive interaction? Does the conflict lead to greater centralization and unity within each party to the conflict? What other effects does the conflict seem to have on each of the groups? Defend your position.

3. Like clothes, academic majors and ideas come into and go out of fashion. What changes in fashion have occurred in the recent past on your campus? (Hint: Ask librarians and professors for their insights, and get the registrar's list of majors for various years.) Choose one example and apply Simmel's ideas on fashion to that case.

4. If Simmel were alive today, do you believe that he would be arguing against consumerism? Do the objects we crave and purchase reduce the chance for the development of what Simmel terms "subjective culture"? Explore these questions and give examples to illustrate your position.

5. In today's world, we are more likely to find ourselves among "strangers" and to be "strangers" ourselves. Look around you. What are the positive and negative consequences of this at your school or in your community? What actions might be taken within communities to transform "strangers" into "one of us"?

PART II

Contemporary Theories and Their Connections to the Classics

Introduction

Peter Kivisto

T he sociological imagination today is informed by numerous theoretical perspectives. A by no means inclusive list of some of the most influential theories in the discipline would include structural functionalism, systems theory, exchange theory, rational choice theory, poststructuralism, structuration theory, symbolic interactionism, ethnomethodology, dramaturgy, phenomenology, neo-Marxism, critical theory, feminist theory, globalization theory, and postmodernism.

Thus, unless I wanted to produce a multivolume collection, I was forced to make decisions about which theories would be included. All the previously noted theories have had a significant influence on contemporary sociology, and by making the decision to include particular theories while excluding others, I am not implicitly arguing that the ones selected for inclusion are somehow more important than the others. The main reason for selecting the particular theories represented in Part II is that, taken together, they afford the student reader the opportunity to get a sense of the range and variability of social theory.

If one were to divide all theories into two categories, it would be possible to do so by looking to see if the theories emphasize the role of humans (typically referred to as actors or agents) in creating their social conditions or the influence of social conditions (often called structures or forces) on individual attitudes and behaviors. The chapters included herein are equally divided between these two foci.

Chapter 5, coauthored by Paul Colomy and Laura Ross Greiner, is devoted to a neofunctionalist examination of institutional responses to adolescents and crime. Their theoretical perspective is a recent development that has arisen as an effort to both build on and revise older functionalist tradition in sociology. Functionalism was the dominant theoretical paradigm in sociology during the 1950s and 1960s, a period during which Harvard sociologist Talcott Parsons emerged as the most influential social theorist of his generation. However, by the 1970s, critics of functionalism had become increasingly vocal and dismissive. Many were prepared to claim that functionalism was dead, but a younger group of theorists associated with Yale sociologist Jeffrey Alexander concluded that although functionalism needed to be substantially revised, it would be a serious mistake to reject it. Instead, they argued on behalf of what has become known as "neofunctionalism." Colomy is one of the theorists responsible for the promotion of this perspective. After providing an overview of the key strengths and weaknesses of functionalism, the authors present a discussion of neofunctionalism's efforts to retain what was valuable about functionalism, while simultaneously showing how it has attempted to redress the problematic features of the tradition.

Colomy and Greiner employ a neofunctionalist perspective in their examination of the ways that American society has responded to adolescents who are chronic criminals or who have committed serious crimes. They seek to understand the circumstances in which the public and lawmakers have shifted from a perspective that treats youth as capable of rehabilitation to a viewpoint that increasingly wants to get tough by punishing them as adults. The particular case study that serves to highlight this topic focuses on the Youth Offender System that was passed into law in Colorado in 1993, after what was described—inaccurately, as it turns out—as an unprecedented "summer of violence." The chapter assesses the factors, from the cultural to the institutional, that put into motion and shaped the political response to these perceptions.

Christopher Prendergast, in Chapter 6, offers what he refers to as a structuralist explanation of why African Americans pay more for new cars than white people do. His theoretical perspective makes use of various interconnected theoretical strands, the most important of which include the exchange theory most closely associated with the work of the late Richard Emerson and the rational choice theory developed by the late James Coleman. In addition, he uses elements from a range of other theoretical perspectives, including those of French theorist Pierre Bourdieu, phenomenological theorist Alfred Schutz, and action theorist Carl Menger.

The reason for all this theory becomes evident in his presentation. Prendergast wants to show why we need an alternative to the most obvious explanation we are likely to offer for the answer to the above posited question: prejudice and discrimination. Given the racism of American society, this layperson's theoretical account would appear to be more than plausible. However, a closer examination of the process of car buying, from both the salesperson's and the customer's perspectives, reveals the shortcomings of this explanation and the need to look for an alternative. In the process of weaving together his structuralist explanation of the car price mystery, Prendergast makes a powerful case for the singular significance of this particular kind of theorizing for the sociological enterprise.

Chapter 7, by Steven P. Dandaneau, examines the critical theory of Jürgen Habermas. As will be evident immediately, the issues addressed in this article bear a close resemblance to those discussed in the chapter on Marx. This is not surprising because critical theory has been profoundly influenced by Marx's thought. Perhaps less obviously, critical theory has also been shaped by Weber's ideas. Critical theory was developed, beginning in the 1920s, by a number of German scholars who came to be identified as the Frankfurt School. Habermas is the most important inheritor of this tradition of social theory, and he is widely regarded as one of the three or four most important theorists in contemporary sociology.

Critical theorists have been particularly interested in the changing character of capitalist industrial society and in the struggle between democratic and authoritarian political systems. Critical theory often operates at a high level of abstraction that is difficult for students to both comprehend and connect to concrete events. Dandaneau, having studied the devastating impact of deindustrialization on his hometown of Flint, Michigan (the city featured in *Roger & Me*, the highly acclaimed first film by Michael Moore, who more recently directed *Bowling for Columbine* and *Fahrenheit 9/11*), has found that the insights from critical theory can be employed to make sense of the factors that have contributed to Flint's problems and to offer some sense of future possibilities. Thus, in this chapter, the focus is on social structural forces shaping the community.

Chapter 8, authored by Douglas Hartmann and Joyce M. Bell, is yet another instance of critical theory, in this case focusing on recent approaches to contemporary race relations. Race-based critical theories have emerged during the past half-century in the wake of the civil rights movement of the 1950s and 1960s, which constituted a watershed in black/white relations. Specifically, it signaled the demise of the Jim Crow era, which was defined in terms of social and cultural structures that served to perpetuate the political oppression, economic exploitation, and social exclusion of citizens of African descent. One can point to a number of significant advances that have since occurred, including the growth of the black middle class and declines in levels of traditional forms of prejudice and discrimination. By the latter part of the 20th century, in stark contrast to earlier times, a vast majority of white Americans expressed a belief that all groups in America were entitled to equal opportunities for success. For some, these advances suggested that we had entered a new, postracial era. However, by any measure of well-being, including income, wealth, life expectancy, housing quality, and so forth, blacks still lag considerably behind whites, and racism has clearly not disappeared. It's this reality that served as the stimulus to critically rethink the role of race in the post-civil rights era.

Hartmann and Bell provide a succinct and insightful overview of the key components of a race-based critical theory, introducing readers to some of the most important scholars associated with this approach. They then turn to a case study that serves to illustrate how such a critical theory interprets research findings.

Specifically, they make use of some of the findings from the American Mosaic Project (Hartmann has co-directed the study and Bell has served as a member of the research team), exploring the contradictory and ambivalent ways that many Americans address the reality of living in a society characterized increasingly by racial, ethnic, and religious diversity.

Chapter 9 is concerned with the role of actors in social construction, in this case, with the social construction of the body. Two eminent feminist scholars, Judith Lorber and Patricia Yancey Martin, have used various strands of contemporary feminist theory to explore such everyday life issues as gender and sport as well as problems associated with eating disorders.

Feminist theory (or more appropriately, perhaps, *theories*) appeared on the sociological scene in the past three decades, emerging out of the women's movement of the 1960s and closely associated with the establishment of programs of women's studies on college and university campuses. Given these origins, there are several unique features to feminist theory. First, it links efforts to better understand gender issues with political activism aimed at ending the various forms of patriarchal domination that have resulted in the subordination of women. Second, feminist theory is inherently interdisciplinary—reaching out not only to other social sciences but also to the arts and humanities. Third, because the classics tended to ignore or downplay the significance of gender relations, feminist theory is less indebted to the founders than are other theories (it should be noted in fairness to them, however, that both Simmel and Weber wrote rather perceptively on gender topics).

Lorber and Martin show how gender permeates social life. Gender definitions and distinctions tend to be taken for granted and are generally seen as universal and unchanging. Feminist theory is a powerful antidote to these views, having proven itself to be an effective tool in the process of making the invisible visible.

Chapters 10 and 11 are also actor, rather than structure, focused. In Chapter 10, David Schweingruber and Nancy Berns provide an overview of a distinctly American version of interpretive sociology known as symbolic interaction. The label of this school of thought was coined by Herbert Blumer, who taught at the University of Chicago and the University of California at Berkeley. This theory school is rooted in American pragmatist thought as developed by such philosophers as William James, Charles Peirce, John Dewey, and especially George Herbert Mead, as well as in the sociological approach advanced by Robert E. Park and others at the Chicago School of Sociology. According to Blumer, symbolic interaction theory begins with the assumption that people act in the social world on the basis of the meaning imputed to various situations and contexts. However, meaning is not simply an individual construct, but rather emerges out of interaction and via ongoing interpretive processes. The use of the word *symbol* in the label is significant insofar as it emphasizes the fact that humans rely on symbols as tools in the process of meaning creation.

Schweingruber and Berns illustrate the theoretical advantages of this perspective in their examination of a company that hires students as summer workers selling educational books door-to-door. Having been engaged in this business since shortly after the Civil War, the company appears to know well what it takes to inculcate in their temporary student workers attitudes about sales that are essential for success. Specifically, the authors describe the ways that managers work to communicate messages to students that are designed to assist them to come to define this line of work as meaningful, focusing on three key factors: (a) creating and maintaining a positive attitude, (b) understanding the significance of money, and (c) attempting to establish a "service-minded" approach to sales.

In Chapter 11, Peter Kivisto and Dan Pittman examine the dramaturgical sociology of Erving Goffman. There are clear similarities between this orientation and the approach in the preceding chapter. This is not surprising because Goffman was trained at the University of Chicago, which was a key center of symbolic interaction theory. Temperamentally, Goffman bears a decided resemblance to Simmel because both wrote with a unique ironic style. Somewhat surprisingly, however, given the fact that Durkheim is usually seen as a structuralist sociologist, Goffman has indicated his affinity with Durkheimian sociology. Essentially, Goffman is concerned with the ways people manage to act within the constraints imposed by preexisting social structures.

Thus, although interpretive sociology examines how people, individually and collectively, construct their social realities, the dramaturgical sociology advanced by Goffman examines how people fashion and act out various roles in what turns out to be a rather constricted set of options. Often, interpretive theorists tend to downplay the constraints of social structure by concentrating on the creative ability of people to shape and modify structures. In stark contrast, Goffman thinks that people operate within circumscribed social conditions: Their freedom of action appears much more limited.

For this reason, Kivisto and Pittman find his work particularly useful in exploring the highly scripted world of sales and service. Rather than emphasizing how actors freely create their roles, this chapter, in Goffmanesque fashion, explores how people manage and manipulate the roles they play in the interactional realm of consumer culture. Dramaturgical sociology highlights some of the dilemmas and tensions inherent in people's identification with or distance from the roles they play as well as some of the difficulties that arise as they attempt to effectively and convincingly embrace certain identities and perform various roles.

In Chapter 12, Kevin Fox Gotham provides an overview of postmodern theorizing. Actually, as he notes at the outset, his contribution seeks to explore the interstitial place where the modern and the postmodern meet, and thus where theories of modernity appropriately compete with theories of postmodernity. Postmodern theory comes in many variants, ranging from more radical articulations, as in the work of Jean Baudrillard, to more moderate versions, such as in the work of émigré scholar Zygmunt Bauman. Of particular significance in distinguishing the differences among postmodern theorists is the fact that some postmodernists posit the claim that the modern age has ended, giving way in its wake to the postmodern period, while on the other hand, other postmodernists contend that the modern and the postmodern can coexist, even if in an uneasy tension. Gotham opts for the latter position.

His chapter uses Mardi Gras in pre-Katrina New Orleans as a strategic research site for exploring the ways that a pre-Lenten, religiously inspired Carnival, characteristic of Catholic communities in many places throughout the world, was transformed in

New Orleans to both a commodity created for consumption in a capitalist marketplace and a spectacle. Gotham's particular take on postmodernism evidences a continuity with Marxist themes regarding the commodification of culture, particularly as these themes have been developed by critical theory—especially scholars associated with the Frankfurt School. In a sense, although the focus is on the postmodern, his version of postmodern theory can be seen as an effort to bring postmodernism and critical theory into fruitful dialogue. In the course of the chapter, readers are introduced to such postmodern concepts as simulacra, spectacle, implosion, and hyperreality.

Turning to Chapter 13, Anne F. Eisenberg invites readers to explore the work of Pierre Bourdieu in examining an organization committed to supporting the rights and interests of gays and lesbians. Bourdieu was arguably one of the three or four most important theorists in the world during the latter part of the past century (he died in 2002), his career culminating in his appointment to the Chair in Sociology at the Collège de France. His work builds on the classical tradition, being influenced in particular by Marx and Durkheim, but also by a wide range of theorists who appeared on the scene after these classical figures had departed. His theoretical contribution was also profoundly shaped by the empirical work in which he engaged throughout his life, work that was far reaching. He studied, for example, working-class Algerians in the postcolonial period and remained connected to events in that country throughout his life. At the same time, he conducted influential studies on social inequality, education, culture, art, and the mass media in contemporary France. All of this was grist for his theoretical mill.

Among the key concepts he developed are habitus and field, along with the related concepts of social positions and position-taking. Eisenberg summarizes the meaning and significance of these ideas and proceeds to illustrate their theoretical utility in exploring the history of an organization called Parents, Families and Friends of Lesbians and Gays (PFLAG). Her analysis traces the emergence of what was, at the beginning, perhaps no more than a support group but evolved into an organized agent for social change. Given that Bourdieu was, throughout his life, a public intellectual committed to progressive social change, it is particularly appropriate that his ideas are applied to this example, for his goal was to not simply advance sociology as a discipline but also to provide knowledge that agents of change can translate into practice.

In Chapter 14, William H. Swatos, Jr., examines another recent development in social theory: globalization. That people around the globe are more interconnected and interdependent than ever before is one of the hallmarks of our age. Globalization theory is an attempt to make sense of these developments. It attempts to provide a way of examining, for instance, the workings of the global economy, in which multinational corporations not only compete internationally but also appear to be severing the attachments they once had to the nations where they originally operated. Flint, Michigan, cannot be fully understood without also understanding what is happening in developing nations. Likewise, penetration into new markets is a characteristic feature of the global economy, as in the introduction of McDonald's and other fast-food restaurants into Russia and the rest of the former communist bloc.

Globalization, as Swatos indicates in his study of the impact of fundamentalist religious beliefs on world politics, is also having an impact on politics and culture. As a reaction to many aspects of modernity, religious fundamentalisms emanating from all of the major world religions have had an impact on politics, both nationally and transnationally. As Swatos reveals, this is nowhere more evident than in the contemporary Middle East, where the fundamentalist ideals of the three historical Occidental religions—Judaism, Christianity, and Islam—are engaged in a conflict of worldviews that has, in recent years, produced global political consequences.

Collectively, the 10 chapters in this section provide students with an appreciation of the diversity, adaptability, and value of a cross-section of major contemporary theoretical orientations. They reveal continuities with the topics and theoretical approaches of the classics. Building on them, but going beyond them, both in terms of what they study and in terms of the particular theoretical lenses that they have crafted, we see theorists today influenced by the same sociological imagination that inspired the founders of the discipline.

CHAPTER 5

Criminalizing Transgressing Youth

A Neofunctionalist Analysis of Institution Building

Paul Colomy and Laura Ross Greiner

Paul Colomy is Professor of Sociology at the University of Denver, where he teaches classic and contemporary theory. His research uses neofunctionalism and other theoretical traditions to examine the creation of new institutions and roles. He is particularly interested in understanding the origins and transformation of the juvenile justice system. He has edited The Dynamics of Social Systems *and co-edited* Differentiation Theory and Social Change.

Laura Ross Greiner is an independent writer and consultant working primarily for the Center for the Study and Prevention of Violence at the University of Colorado, Boulder. She helped establish the center in 1992, and her institution-building efforts have included assembling a national information house on youth violence. She received her MA from the University of Colorado and her PhD from the University of Denver. Her major research interests are youth violence, juvenile justice, and the sociology of mass media.

The past decade has witnessed a virtual sea change in the way American society responds to juveniles who commit chronic or serious crimes (Feld, 1999). For most of the 20th century, law-breaking youth were sent to juvenile courts and, if found delinquent, received relatively mild sanctions (compared to the punishments meted out to adults guilty of the same offense). Convinced that adolescents were malleable and could be redeemed, juvenile justice officials aspired to rehabilitate delinquent youth. Dubious about a youngster's ability to form criminal intent and explicitly rejecting the language of punishment and retribution, these officials were principally concerned with the child's best interests. These notions justified a separate system of justice in which adolescents were adjudicated (not tried) and were liable for no more than a 2-year term in a reform school where, in theory, they were treated (not punished). A cumbersome waiver hearing was reserved for the most extreme cases, which were sometimes transferred to adult criminal court. The very cumbersomeness of these hearings discouraged prosecutors and judges from requesting transfers and reaffirmed the presumption that juvenile court was the most appropriate forum for transgressing youth.

Today, that presumption has been largely discredited as soft-minded sentimentalism. Reacting to an apparently growing legion of really bad kids who commit shocking crimes and are reputedly contemptuous toward the juvenile justice system's ministrations, lawmakers across the country have approved, at breathtaking speed, a spate of far-reaching statutes. From 1992 to 1995, a total of 48 of 51 state legislatures (including the District of Columbia) enacted laws targeting serious juvenile offenders. In all but 10 states, these laws make it "easier to prosecute juveniles in criminal courts." In 25 states, new legislation gives judges additional sentencing options to incarcerate young people for longer periods of time. Openly espousing the language of punishment and retribution, 23 states now impose more severe penalties, including confinement in adult prisons, to sanction youth convicted in criminal courts (Torbet et al., 1996). Taken together, these innovations reflect a pattern of institutional and legal change that has been called "(re)criminalization," a process of relinquishing elements of the juvenile justice system (and certain categories of transgressing adolescents) to the adult criminal justice system (Singer, 1996).

This chapter analyzes how this process unfolded in a single state. On September 13, 1993, Colorado Governor Roy Romer signed a law establishing the Youthful Offender System. This legislation, along with several other measures, was introduced, debated, and amended during a 5-day special session of the Colorado General Assembly convened to address the problem of youth violence. Two elements of this measure are particularly noteworthy. First, the bill gives considerable discretion to district attorneys, who now decide whether to direct-file on young lawbreakers. (The direct-file provision effectively circumvents cumbersome judicial waiver hearings and makes it much easier to charge and try juveniles in adult court.) Second, the bill authorized construction of a new tier in the correctional apparatus. The 14- to 18-year-olds sent to the Youthful Offender System (YOS) are prosecuted as adults for crimes ranging from theft to manslaughter and, if convicted, are sentenced to the adult prison system. That sentence is suspended on the condition of completing a term ranging from 2 to 6 years in YOS. Those failing the program are returned to court for imposition of the original sentence and remanded to an adult correctional facility. With its no-nonsense military-like regimen, stringent discipline, and succeed-or-perish philosophy, YOS represents "the hammer" Colorado lawmakers said was necessary to combat serious juvenile crime. At the same time, legislators envisioned this new tier as a "second last chance" for youthful offenders, and the teens housed at YOS are provided with treatment and a variety of educational, vocational, cognitive-behavioral, life-skills, and mentoring programs. Believing that youth violence had become a critical problem requiring a forceful response, Colorado policymakers allocated substantial sums to this 480-bed facility: More than $37 million was spent to construct YOS; operating costs run another $10.2 million annually.

Although many other states have approved legislation similar to Colorado's YOS law, the passage of this bill was hardly inevitable. To the contrary, when initially proposed, the YOS statute was regarded as a dubious proposition. During its regular session, which concluded in mid-May 1993, the Colorado General Assembly rejected several bills that were moderate versions of the YOS measure approved 4 months later. Writing in early August, shortly after the special session on youth violence had been announced but a month before it opened, and distressed by the dismal prospect of a fruitless repeat performance, a reporter predicted that "lawmakers will have a sense of deja vu, already having considered—and killed—many of the issues expected to come before them again in the special session."[1] In the regular session, the legislature had rebuffed a provision that would have asked voters to consider a one-quarter-cent increase in the state's sales tax to generate additional revenue for prison construction. Another proposal recommended expanding "the seriously overcrowded Colorado Division of Youth Services [the agency responsible for the state's reform schools]," but while lawmakers approved this plan, they refused to fund it, thereby rendering the legislation an empty gesture.[2] Ironically, a cost-cutting statute approved in the regular session reduced sentences for some crimes to slow the growth of prisons. The governor, however, was not dissuaded by the seemingly long odds. Intuiting a fateful change, he sensed that similar, and even more costly and controversial, renditions of measures rejected in May were "more likely to pass" in September.[3] "There is a different atmosphere now than there was in the spring when the session was here," the governor assured the worried journalist, and in this altered environment, there was "a much more radical need for action."[4]

The governor was right. Between May and August 1993, a significant transformation had occurred, and there was mounting pressure on local and state officials to "do something" about street violence. From May 2, when a baby visiting the Denver Zoo was wounded by a stray bullet, to August 2, when an elementary school teacher was murdered in a suburban parking lot, print and electronic media gave extensive coverage to several "high-profile" violent crimes, a number of which were allegedly committed by gang-affiliated juveniles. These incidents became the centerpiece of an unfolding media event, eventually dubbed "the Summer of Violence" by the local press, which continued until mid-September when lawmakers concluded their deliberations. The unremitting coverage of this putative crime wave heightened fear of violence, prompting some residents to flee the supposedly deadly environs of Denver for the alluring (but ultimately elusive) safety of the suburbs, while others organized marches to "take back the streets" or badgered public officials to "crack down" on violent youth. This was the "different atmosphere" in which the governor divined "a much more radical need for action" and convened the special session.

Employing the neofunctionalist perspective, this chapter explains how new institutions, such as the Colorado YOS, are created. The founding of YOS is one instance of a general process known as "institution building," and neofunctionalists maintain that this process is profoundly shaped by both the encompassing social and cultural context and the efforts of institutional entrepreneurs—the individuals, groups, or organizations who assume leadership roles in episodes of institutional change. After outlining neofunctionalism's fundamental principles, the empirical part of this chapter uses content analysis and a qualitative assessment of the print media's coverage of the Summer of Violence to indicate how street crime became a visible social problem. We then discuss the crystallization of a new category of transgressing adolescents and the complementary claim that the existing juvenile justice system had failed to respond adequately to this novel "breed" of offender. Finally, we examine how a prominent institutional entrepreneur, Governor Roy Romer, mobilized support for a new institution (YOS) designed to control and treat serious juvenile lawbreakers.

Neofunctionalism

Neofunctionalism's central concepts are most effectively presented as a critical response to the functionalist tradition. The latter is a macrosociological perspective that examines the creation, maintenance, and alteration of enduring social practices, institutions, and entire societies. Émile Durkheim, a French sociologist who published several provocative books between 1890 and 1915, is often regarded as the classic founder of functionalism. This approach was articulated most forcefully, however, by a group of American sociologists, including Talcott Parsons, Robert K. Merton, Wilbert Moore, Bernard Barber, and Robin Williams, during the 25 years following World War II. Although functionalism dominated the sociological imagination from 1945 to 1970, it also spawned considerable controversy and critique. Acknowledging the merit of many (but not all) of these criticisms, a younger generation of scholars led by Jeffrey Alexander began (in the early 1980s) responding to the critics' legitimate objections by revising the postwar version of functionalism in significant ways (Alexander, 1985). Bringing together the valuable elements of orthodox functionalism with the insights of several other sociological traditions, these revisions have culminated in a substantially modified rendition of functionalism, a rendition its proponents call neofunctionalism. We discuss neofunctionalism in terms of four key notions: problem solving, structural differentiation, systems, and culture.

Problem Solving

Traditional functionalism likens societies (and all types of social units, stretching from dyads to world systems) to problem-solving entities. If a society is to persist, functionalists assert, it must address certain vital problems in a reasonably satisfactory way. (Several terms were coined to characterize these vital problems, including requirements, functions, needs, prerequisites, exigencies, and functional prerequisites.) An enduring society must, for example, socialize its youngest members, produce and distribute food and other essential goods and services, and devise mechanisms to control deviance and contain conflict. If a society does not satisfactorily address these (and other) prerequisites, it will experience considerable strain, and if its failure to address these problems continues, it will collapse.

A definitive catalog of the essential exigencies confronting all societies has never been compiled. Nevertheless, both proponents and critics of functionalism agree that Parsons offers the most incisive statement of functional requirements now available (Parsons & Smelser, 1956). Pitched at a high level of abstraction, Parsons's model identifies four universal problems confronting every social unit. *Adaptation,* the first function, refers to how a social system supports itself in relationship to an external environment. When societies are the unit of analysis, adaptation refers to the production and distribution of the basic necessities of life. *Goal attainment,* the second prerequisite, is concerned with the collective definition of goals and the mobilizing and coordinating processes associated with reaching these goals. *Integration* underscores the necessity of sustaining a minimal level of cohesion among members of the social unit. Finally, *latency* (or pattern maintenance) highlights the problem of maintaining basic value patterns. (An acronym, AGIL, is shorthand frequently used when discussing Parsons's analysis of adaptation, goal attainment, integration, and latency.) Parsons believed that social organizations of every size and type are built around these exigencies and claimed that the AGIL grid supplied an indispensable tool for comparative and historical studies of social life.

Extending the metaphor that likens societies to problem-solving entities, functionalists portray ongoing social practices and structures as provisional answers or solutions to fundamental prerequisites. Families and schools, for instance, are institutions that emerge to answer the problem of socializing and educating the young. (In Parsons's terminology, these institutions are organized around the problems of latency and integration.) Economic institutions such as the free market, however, address the problem of producing and distributing the basic necessities of life (the problem of adaptation). Political systems, whether democratic or totalitarian, attempt to articulate collective goals and mobilize citizens in support of shared objectives (the problem of goal attainment).

Neofunctionalists have recast the notion of problem solving. First, they suggest that the prerequisites discussed by Parsons identify only very broad, open-ended parameters, and these generalized exigencies alone cannot fully explain the particular practices and structures that emerge in a given society. Second, they supplement functionalism's characterization of institutions as problem-solving entities with the observation that problem solving is also a cognitive framework and a powerful rhetoric deeply rooted in modern societies. A pervasive, problem-solving schema, in other words, shapes the way many elites—reformers, citizens, and social scientists—think about and evaluate institutions. The rhetoric of problem solving is often used to justify existing practices, with supporters of the status quo insisting that established institutions serve vital functions. But the very same problem-solving rhetoric is also employed to assail current arrangements for their failure to fulfill essential tasks. Moreover, the perception that important needs are not being met effectively frequently fuels calls to reform existing institutions or to create new ones.

Third, neofunctionalists suggest that citizens and officials usually assess practices and institutions not by reference to abstract, universal functions (e.g., adaptation or latency) but in light of more specific concerns (e.g., an apparent rise in crime or a decline in students' test scores). These concrete problems are socially constructed, and episodes of institutional change cannot be considered apart from the processes by which such problems are identified and made publicly visible. Salient social problems that appear to exceed the problem-solving capacities of existing structures are a potent impetus to alter the established institutional order. Moreover, the socially defined character and scope of these unresolved problems vitally affect the types of alterations proposed and approved.

Structural Differentiation

Over the course of human history, societies have devised many different institutional arrangements to address the exigencies of social life. These variable institutional arrangements are not equally effective, however. In the long run, functionalists hypothesize, more specialized or differentiated institutions have responded more efficiently and effectively to functional perquisites than have multifunctional (or multipurpose) institutions. In an important sense, the proliferation of increasingly specialized structures represents a master trend of modern social change. Two hundred years ago, the family was a multifunctional institution, in that it fulfilled many different tasks, such as economic production, procreation, socialization, care for the infirm elderly, and social control. Today, many of these chores have been delegated to specialized institutions. Economic production, for instance, is no longer addressed by the family but by business enterprises legally and institutionally separated from family life, whereas crime control is increasingly delegated to differentiated social control agents such as police and courts. The family, too, has become a more specialized institution, one whose primary tasks include procreation, socialization of the very young, and emotional support for family members.

Functionalists attribute the growth of differentiated institutions to an imperative toward greater efficiency and effectiveness built into the very fabric of modern societies. The dissatisfaction that arises when functional requirements are not met effectively generates innumerable reform proposals (Smelser, 1959). Because more specialized institutions enable societies to operate more effectively and efficiently, reform programs advocating higher levels of differentiation tend to be, in the terms of neoevolutionary theory, "selected out" and "stabilized" (Parsons, 1966). Structural differentiation can be understood, then, as an unconsciously evolved device modern societies have "hit upon" to increase their overall effectiveness and efficiency.

Neofunctionalists agree that differentiation accurately describes something fundamental about the structure of modern societies. But they also argue that a satisfactory explanation of this master trend of social change must supplement allusions to increased efficiency and effectiveness with a consideration of how individuals and groups affect the course of institutional change. New institutional arrangements are due in part to the efforts of institutional entrepreneurs, the individuals, groups, and organizations that assume leadership roles in episodes of institutional change (Eisenstadt, 1964, 1995). These movers and shakers are not, moreover, altruistic agents of greater societal effectiveness or efficiency. To the contrary, their proposed reforms are impossible to separate from their own particular material and ideal interests. Not surprisingly, resource-rich elites and secondary elites, including powerful state actors and various professional groups, are disproportionately represented among successful entrepreneurial groups (Colomy, 1998). However, few elite groups possess the resources, power, and legitimation necessary to impose their institutional vision on the larger society unilaterally. Consequently, the success of many institution-building projects depends largely on entrepreneurial groups' ability to cultivate allies and defuse resistance. Coalitions, compromises, entreaties for public support, and recurring struggles with opponents are staples of institution building. As a result, the course of institutional change is shaped by political dynamics as much (or more) than it is by concerns for greater efficiency and effectiveness (Smelser, 1985).

Systems

Functionalism conceptualizes societies (and other social units) as systems comprising autonomous-but-interdependent institutions (or subsystems) (Parsons, 1971). This approach rejects reductionist theories, which claim that one subsystem (e.g., the economy or the state) dictates what transpires in other subsystems (e.g., law or religion). Each institution is guided, in large measure, by its own internal logic. Science, for example, is organized around distinctive premises and procedures, just as religion, politics, and the military are. These distinctive logics impart considerable (but not unlimited) autonomy to each institution. At the same time, these partially autonomous subsystems are interrelated in complex ways. Parsons's interchange model uses the terms *outputs* and *inputs* to describe the interdependent relations between different institutions (Parsons & Smelser, 1956). In essence, this model suggests that the operation of any single institution (e.g., schools) depends on the inputs it receives from other institutions (e.g., families, business, and government), while that institution, in turn, produces (part of) what the other subsystems require to perform effectively.

Neofunctionalists have extended the concept of systems in three ways. First, they caution that the notion of institutions regulated by a distinctive logic must not obscure the fact that different positions within the same institution frequently spawn disparate perceptions and interests (Smelser, 1974). For example, although the child's best interests and the preservation of public safety are the principal concerns of contemporary juvenile justice, this overarching institutional logic does not preclude chronic conflicts from arising between judges, probation officers, reform schools, residential care providers, parole officers, and other participants in this subsystem (Jacobs, 1990).

Second, noting that the interchange model is intended to describe the interworkings of a perfectly integrated social system—a conceptual ideal type that no actual society has ever approximated—neofunctionalists have supplemented Parsons's analysis of the mutually rewarding, interinstitutional exchanges with examinations of the tensions within and between institutions. When one subsystem fails to fulfill its particular exigencies, for example, other subsystems dependent on its outputs will be pressed to perform its functions, even though they often lack the necessary resources. Elementary school instructors, for instance, sometimes complain that they must devote inordinate time to attending to a few unruly pupils. Believing that these children's emotional, psychological, and medical needs are the responsibility of families and health care providers, these educators claim that when these unmet needs are displaced onto teachers (in the form of disruptive classroom conduct), it is nearly impossible to provide a quality education for all their students.

The lead-and-lag principle identifies another common source of institutional strain. Presuming a social system composed of several parts (or subsystems), the idea of leads and lags maintains that rapid alterations in any single subsystem can outstrip the responsive capacity of other (interdependent) subsystems. In the classic statement of this principle, William Ogburn (1922) wrote,

> Not all parts of our [society] are changing at the same speed or at the same time. Some are rapidly moving forward while others are lagging. These unequal rates of change in economic life, in government, in education, in science, and religion, make zones of danger and points of tension. (p. xiii)

Third, neofunctionalists recommend treating the notion of systems (and subsystems) as "environments of action" that shape the change-oriented activities of institutional entrepreneurs (Alexander, 1988; Colomy & Rhoades, 1994). Entrepreneurs' projects are not articulated in a sociological vacuum: Their indictment of the existing institutional order, their proposed alterations of that order, and their strategies for attracting allies and overcoming opponents are influenced by the environing systems in which they pursue their reforms. From the standpoint of entrepreneurs, these encompassing systems comprise a constellation of opportunities and constraints that render some reforms and some mobilizing strategies more feasible than others.

Culture

How do modern societies containing scores of specialized institutions and hundreds of heterogeneous subgroups manage to sustain themselves without dissolving into an anarchic "war of all against all"? Recognizing that coercion, artifice, and domination are indelible features of social life, functionalists nevertheless insist that these dynamics alone do not adequately account for the coherence of complex social orders. They attribute the modicum of social integration characteristic of many modern societies to two main mechanisms. First, an important product of increasing structural differentiation is the emergence of specialized, integrative institutions and processes—for example, inclusive citizenship rights, religious ceremonies, athletic contests, media events, and nationally celebrated holidays—that affirm some solidarity among people who otherwise might have little in common (Etzioni, 2000; Marshall, 1964). Second, as modern societies differentiate and as their populations (and the heterogeneity of these populations) expand, the values they espouse are generalized and universalized (Durkheim, 1893/1984). The prevailing value commitments of contemporary postindustrial societies, in other words, are abstract and are formulated in an inclusive way so that, in principle, they apply equally to every citizen. For example, some social scientists suggest that much of the continuity and change evident throughout American history is due to the fairly high level of agreement on the country's core values (values that are sometimes referred to as the American Creed), including individualism, freedom, equality, democracy, achievement, and work (Lipset, 1996). Incorporated into different institutions and internalized by individuals (during the course of their early socialization), these shared values enable the diverse components of a large, differentiated society to coexist and bond rather than disintegrate into chronic chaos (Parsons & Bales, 1955).

Neofunctionalists have rounded out the functionalist conception of culture in three ways. First, they supplement the analysis of consensus on core values with discussions of the cultural roots of conflict and change. They note, for example, that many cultural systems contain strikingly inconsistent elements. In American society, the inclusive values of freedom and equal opportunity for all are opposed by a potent exclusive tradition of sexism, homophobia, and racism, which historically has supported the privileged position of white, Anglo-Saxon, Protestant (WASP) males over women; gays and lesbians; and racial, ethnic, and religious minorities (Alexander, 1990; Glazer, 1975). Another source of contention and change is the wide gap between cherished cultural ideals (e.g., equality and freedom) and the actual realities of social life (e.g., marked inequalities and repression). When these cultural ideals are taken seriously, they can produce significant instability, fueling attacks on the way things are in the name of the way things should be (Huntington, 1981).

Neofunctionalists also contend that cultural systems are no less preoccupied with the negative than they are with the positive. Functionalist theories of culture focus on values, which are commonly defined as socially shared ideas about what is good, right, and desirable. But this equating of culture with positive, idealized imagery omits a critically important consideration: The bad, evil, and undesirable are key elements of every cultural system, and they are "symbolized every bit as elaborately as the good" (Alexander & Smith, 1993, p. 158). Inspired by Durkheim's classic analysis of religious systems, neofunctionalists suggest that the meanings and symbols most central to social life are frequently imbued with religious-like properties, frequently assuming a sacred or profane cast. Sacred symbols "provide images of purity and they charge those who are committed to them with protecting their referents from harm. Profane symbols embody this harm; they provide images of pollution, identifying actions, groups, and processes that must be defended against" (Alexander & Smith, 1993, p. 158). The sacred and profane are "highly charged" emotional symbols, and when they are used to classify particular acts as transgressions against the community's conception of the sacred and to portray the transgressors as embodiments of the profane, these highly charged symbols are likely to trigger a dramatic community response.

Third, neofunctionalists direct attention to the cultural dimensions of entrepreneurs' projects. When identifying crucial public problems or unmet social needs, criticizing current arrangements, and proposing alterations in the institutional order, entrepreneurs invoke, often in innovative ways, shared cultural traditions and symbol systems. In doing so, they treat culture as a tool kit, adroitly wielding its elements to construct persuasive rhetorical appeals (Swidler, 1986). However, it must be recognized that symbol systems have an internal logic of their own, one whose tacit assumptions and taken-for-granted status render culture partially opaque, even to those who use it competently (Williams, 1995). Consequently, explicating what can be called entrepreneurs' signifying or interpretive work (Snow & Benford, 1988) requires consideration of the meanings they consciously articulate, as well as an analysis that pushes below the surface, from intended meanings to the deeper, symbolic codes infusing their projects (Bellah, 1999).

Identifying a Problem: Making Street Violence Visible

The criminalization of transgressing youth is not the handiwork of a single individual, group, or organization. Rather, it evolves within the context of a complex division of labor, and several different institutions, entrepreneurial groups, and the general public contribute to this process. In Colorado, the news media—particularly the Denver news media (which are the largest and most influential news agencies in the state)—played an important part in this division of labor. Through continuous and prominent coverage of violent crime (particularly violent crime allegedly committed by juveniles) and the construction of an ongoing narrative that forged links between several isolated, "high-profile" incidents, journalists helped to make street crime much more salient than it had been only 3 or 4 months earlier. These news reports—which, in neofunctionalist terminology, can be construed as outputs of the media subsystem—established a new *significatory context* (or environment of action), one that supplied officials and reformers with compelling justifications for taking, in Governor Romer's words, "radical action" against serious young offenders.

There is little evidence that the press's voluminous reports reflected a sharp jump in the amount of street crime. The journalistic standard of newsworthiness, a standard central to the news media's unique institutional logic, provides a more persuasive explanation of the coverage. This criterion, which sets a premium on the novel and dramatic, occasionally fosters (factually) unwarranted inferences: A succession of atypical (and hence newsworthy) cases is depicted as an alarming crime wave, even when there is little or no change in the overall rate of offending. News organizations also have material interests: As privately (and often corporately) owned, profit-oriented ventures, the media are well aware that crime news is an appealing commodity. In addition, in medium-size markets like Denver (as compared to the much larger markets in New York, Chicago, and Los Angeles), competition among media outlets—evident in both journalists' ambition to break newsworthy stories and owners' interest in circulation, audience shares, and advertising dollars—fosters exhaustive coverage of the same events. This produces an amplification effect as print journalists, television anchors, and radio announcers inundate audiences with reports of the same crimes.

Our substantive discussion of the Denver media's accounts of the Summer of Violence is divided into two parts. First, we review the findings from a quantitative content analysis that documents the prominent and continuous newspaper coverage of youth and violent crime in the summer of 1993. Then, we discuss the general themes reporters devised to tell the story of that summer's violence.

Continuous and Prominent Coverage of Youth and Violent Crime

Newspapers are divided into sections and pages, and placing a story on a specific page in a specific section—like the decisions about a story's appropriate length and whether it should be accompanied by a photograph and, if so, how large a photograph—reflects a professional judgment about the story's newsworthiness. Moreover, because journalists place a premium on novelty, frequent reports about the same issue—particularly when they appear on the paper's front page and in its editorial section—also signal an assessment about that issue's significance. When the press plays, in effect, an initiating role in identifying a pressing public problem, it typically does so by devoting continuous and prominent coverage to a particular issue. This was clearly the case in Denver (and Colorado) during the summer of 1993, when both the print and electronic media gave extensive coverage to the problem of juvenile and violent crime.

Table 5.1 presents data generated from a content analysis of the *Denver Post*, the newspaper with the largest circulation in Denver (and Colorado). These data indicate that, depending on the particular indicator employed, juvenile and violent crime[5] received from 2 to over 10 times more coverage in the *Post* during the summer

Table 5.1 Number, Placement, and Length of Youth and Violent Crime Stories and Accompanying Photographs Appearing in the *Denver Post* by Summer

	Summer/Year		
	1992	*1993*	*1994*
Stories			
Total	73	196	61
Front page	2	44	6
Section A	2	73	10
Editorial page	3	48	5
Length of all stories[a]	1512.65	5606.87	1615.98
Photographs			
Total	29	106	32
Front page	0	32	3
Length of all photographs[b]	177.89	1153	495.89

a. Length of all stories is measured in column inches.
b. Length of all photographs is measured in column inches.

of 1993 than in either the previous or subsequent summer. For example, with 196 stories on youth and violent crime,[6] the 1993 summer clearly outpaced both the 1992 summer, during which 73 such articles were published, and the 1994 summer's publication of 61 stories. In addition, 44 front-page stories on juvenile and violent crime were published during the summer of 1993, whereas in the summers of 1992 and 1994, only 2 and 6 such stories, respectively, made the front page. Editorials about youth and violent crime were also much more common during the 1993 summer; similarly, the juvenile and violent crime articles printed in the 1993 summer were more likely to be accompanied by photographs, and these photographs were much more likely to appear on the front page.

As noted earlier, the extensive news coverage of youth and violent crime in the summer of 1993 was not due to a dramatic rise in the incidence of serious offenses. We consulted the official monthly reports of the Denver metro area's two largest police departments (Denver and Aurora), which are forwarded to the Federal Bureau of Investigation and summarized in its annually published *Crime in the United States: The Uniform Crime Report.* We used these monthly reports to calculate the amount of violent crime and the number of juvenile arrests for violent offenses in these two cities during the summer months of 1992, 1993, and 1994. The reports disclose a small and unspectacular upturn in violence during the summer of 1993. In the 1993 summer, Denver and Aurora police recorded two more homicides than they did in the summer of 1992 and three more than in the summer of 1994. The number of nonlethal violent offenses (i.e., forcible rape, robbery, and aggravated assault) in the summer of 1993 was about 3.5% higher than in the 1992 summer and roughly 5% to 10% higher than in the 1994 summer.[7] It appears highly improbable, however, that this modest increase in serious crime (including the slight increment in homicides) during the 1993 summer can fully account for the remarkable surge in media coverage that occurred then.

The available data on juvenile arrests (which both the Denver and Aurora police departments define as arrests of youth under 18 years old) belie the notion that the metro area experienced an explosion of youth crime in the 1993 summer. The monthly reports indicate that 5 juveniles were arrested by the two departments for homicide in the 1992 summer, 2 in the 1993 summer, and 1 in the 1994 summer. During the summer of 1992, Denver and Aurora police arrested 128 juveniles for other serious, nonlethal violent offenses; 159 juvenile arrests were made for these offenses in the 1993 summer, whereas in the summer of 1994, 186 juveniles were arrested for these crimes. This steady increase in juveniles arrested for serious, nonlethal crimes, coupled with the steady decline in juveniles apprehended for homicide over the three summers, stands in stark contrast to the undulating pattern of media coverage, with the relatively small number (and low priority) of news articles published in the summers of 1992 and 1994 interrupted by the dramatic spike of prominent juvenile crime stories in the 1993 summer.

Narrating the Summer of Violence[8]

Like the sheer volume and salience of media coverage, the actual content of reports written and broadcast during the 1993 summer heightened the visibility of juvenile violence. Journalists narrated an unfolding story, drawing meaningful, gestalt-like links between what could easily have been construed as unrelated or merely coincidental crimes and articulating overarching themes that offered a persuasive interpretation of the summer's violence. Four themes were central to the media's narration of the Summer of Violence: innocent victims, unprecedented violence, encroaching violence, and random violence.

Innocent Victims

The perceived innocence of select victims injured or killed by gun-toting assailants, many of them allegedly juveniles, was the anchoring theme in the media's coverage. Seven high-profile violent crimes, which received front-page coverage immediately after they occurred and, subsequently, were frequently mentioned and briefly recapitulated in reporters', columnists', and editorial writers' summary characterizations of the summer's violence, figured prominently in the elaboration of this theme. In four of these incidents, children ranging in age from 10 months to 6 years were victimized. In the other cases, four "exemplary adults" were killed or seriously injured.

The Denver press presented these crimes in graphic detail, conveying, to the extent that words, photographs, and videotape can, their destructive immediacy. Reporters described how a woman stood by helplessly as her husband was murdered and, moments later, after "falling to her knees," suffered a "savage beating" that caused her head to swell to twice its normal size.[9] They described how a bullet struck a 4-year-old in the cheek and traveled to the back of his throat,[10] and how a man shot in the side three times while driving home in the early morning hours bled to death as his car came to rest on a corner lawn.[11] Journalists offered their descriptions of these crimes and of the other high-profile incidents and victims as eye-grabbing and gut-wrenching examples of the general problem of street crime.

The victims' cultural-moral status made the violence appear even more ominous. Unequivocally, innocent victims of street crime are rare. Many victims act in a manner that contributes, unwittingly or not, to the sequence of events that results in their injury or death, and they are often not easily distinguished from those who attack or kill them (Christie, 1986; Luckenbill, 1977). Reporters are keenly attuned to moral character, and estimates about a victim's moral standing figure into their calculations about a crime's newsworthiness. In journalists' eyes, the children and adults attacked in the high-profile cases closely approximated the folk concept of the "ideal victim" (Christie, 1986, p. 25): These victims were innocent not merely in a technical, legal sense but in a morally and sociologically compelling way. The media were particularly sympathetic to the child victims, whom they regarded as morally pure and whose victimization qualified as eminently newsworthy. As one reporter[12] told us,

> The children. That was why there was so much coverage [of violent crime in the summer of 1993]. Little kids getting shot and killed. That put it [violence] on an entirely different level. Innocent blood. That's a tabloid statement, but it's true. . . . Children and animals are innocent. It brings outrage when this type of thing is done to innocents.

Given the reigning (Western) cultural conception of childhood (Zelizer, 1985), the young child victims' moral innocence could simply be assumed, by both the press and the public. The moral standing of the adult victims, however, could not be taken for granted, and journalists offered some interpretive work to affirm these men's and women's innocence. Quoting liberally from testimonials offered by these victims' families, friends, and colleagues, reporters constructed idealized mini-narratives attesting to these adults' exemplary character. For example, neighbors described an adult victim, Richard Prentice [pseudonyms are used for all victims], as "easygoing" and "as nice as can be."[13] He had volunteered as a Big Brother, and a friend recollected an occasion when the victim had taken "one of his charges to buy fishing equipment. The kid swiped some items. [Prentice] forced him to go back into the store and return the stolen goods and apologize. Then he bought the kid the stuff he stole."[14] The victim's boss described him as a man who, despite his imposing, 6-foot, 4-inch stature, was "a gentle guy who was very dependable and was the most likable cable marketer he ever had."[15] Prentice had graduated from a local college with a bachelor's degree in fine arts and often sold tickets to the Colorado Ballet, a company in which his wife was a well-known dancer. He recommended "works of Shelley and Keats that were [an] inspiration" for her performances.[16] "He'd always be standing in the wings," his wife said. "I would never go on stage without a hug and a kiss." Richard was, she added, "[m]y best friend. My confidant. My biggest supporter."[17]

The press portrayed the high-profile incidents as "typifying examples" (Best, 1990, pp. 28–29) of the summer's violence. In fact, the child and exemplary adult victims were, socially and demographically, strikingly different from the majority of those injured or killed by youth (or adult) violence in Denver (and Colorado) that summer. Statistically, the "average victim" was a "Hispanic male, 17.7 years old," who was also a gang member, "a high school dropout, and [himself] a perpetrator of youth violence."[18] The four child victims' ethnicity and race—three were Latino, the other African American—were similar to the average victim (73% of those victimized by juvenile violence were either Latino or African American), but the children differed markedly along nearly every other meaningful social attribute. The four exemplary adults, who ranged in age from 27 to 43 and who were all white, middle-class, and college-educated, were also starkly unrepresentative of those most likely to be victimized by street violence. The criterion of newsworthiness (which stipulates that typical crimes and victims merit minimal coverage) in conjunction with remnants of America's exclusive cultural tradition (which valorizes middle-class WASPs over people of color) prompted the media to give little attention to the statistically average victims while granting exhaustive coverage to the ideal victims. Consequently, despite their singular character, the high-profile incidents powerfully shaped the community's and officials' "perception of the problem" of youth violence (Best, 1990, pp. 28–29).

Unprecedented Violence

Although lacking corroborating statistical data from law enforcement agencies (or other sources), the local media claimed that juvenile (and adult) violence in Denver (and Colorado) was rising at an alarming rate during the 1993 summer. In the place of credible numeric evidence, journalists buttressed this claim by turning to presumably knowledgeable public officials and, uncritically quoting and para-phrasing their remarks, passed off their rough approximations and gut-level impressions as fact. In the wake of the first high-profile crime (which occurred in early May 1993), the Denver police chief, while conceding that he did not "have the statistics yet to prove it," nonetheless told reporters that "he believes violence is on the rise in Denver."[19] Drawing on interviews with several officers and gang-intervention workers, a front-page article titled "Police: Violence Escalating" indicated that the number of guns possessed by juveniles, the number of drive-by shootings, and the number of homicides were all on the rise.[20]

Reporters kept a running tabulation of the high-profile cases, a form of counting that, unlike a single summary statement of the crime rate, justified meticulous accounts of each new incident. Explicitly connecting each high-profile event to the others preceding it, this running tab also implied that the crimes cohered into a meaningful pattern and that the summer's violence represented something greater than the sum of its individual crimes. For instance, an article reporting the shooting of a 6-year-old began, "Yet another young child was fighting for his life last night."[21] Similarly, a story about the killing of an elementary school teacher opened with the line, "In what has become a deadly ritual in the metro area, yet another innocent victim was fatally shot."[22]

Using disquieting imagery and analogies, reporters dramatized the threat violence posed to the city and state. For example, medical personnel interviewed by the press frequently made analogies connecting the city's (and state's) street crime with international and civil wars. A Denver trauma surgeon compared "the recent sharp increase in [violent] incidents" to "a battle zone," adding that "this is like Korea or something."[23] Other reports insinuated that Denver was a city under siege. One appeared beneath the heading, "City a Hostage to Violence?"[24] A full-page (Sunday) editorial column about Denver's street violence was titled, "Under Siege: Living With Barbarians at the Gate."[25] Other journalists characterized the summer's violence with such emotionally charged images as "urban terrorism"[26]; "a seemingly endless, senseless plague of wanton violence"[27]; and, in a column titled "Where Are Our Leaders as Denver Dies?" a "city teetering on the edge of a murderous abyss."[28]

Characterizing the high-profile victims not only as individuals but also as symbols of collective life, the press alluded to another dimension of the summer's ostensibly unprecedented violence. Durkheim's (1912/1995) classic analysis of Aboriginal totems and other religious objects notes that they are "among the most preeminently sacred things" and, as a result, are bound up with "the collective fate of the entire clan" (pp. 118, 120). In the summer of 1993, the local media transfigured the child and exemplary adult victims, in their injuries and deaths, into symbolic emblems of Denver's (and Colorado's) communal life. For instance, after applauding the "overwhelming" public response to "the bounty fund" he had established to "persuade someone to turn in the punks who shot a 6-year-old boy," a columnist explained the child's totemic status:

> You [those who contributed to the fund] understood that the moment that bullet penetrated [the boy's] brain he became all of our sons, all our children, brown and yellow, pink and red, rich and poor.

He was our hope for a better tomorrow, our dreams and our aspirations for a better world. And you understood we couldn't sit by passively while the thugs stole that from us.[29]

With the media spotlight brightly focused on the high-profile cases, reporters suggested that a distinguishing feature of the Summer of Violence was a succession of assaults against cherished icons. These desecrations, the media intimated, constituted "a disaster, the greatest misfortune that can befall a group" (Durkheim, 1912/1995, p. 120). Amplifying the language of communal crisis, disorder, and dissolution—for example, "a city teetering on the edge of a murderous abyss"— journalists effectively conveyed the notion that transgressions against a community's quintessentially sacred objects represent symbolically "a retrogression to chaos" (Eliade, 1959, p. 48).

Encroaching Violence

During the summer of 1993, news agencies regularly remarked on the apparent movement of violence from the "streets" to purportedly idyllic social space. This media-conveyed sense of encroaching violence was frequently joined to the distinction many make between ostensibly "good" and "bad" parts of town, and the complementary expectation that serious, violent crime will be concentrated in a community's less reputable areas. Journalists hold a similar folk concept, tending to regard as commonplace the violence that occurs in what is regarded as the "socially disorganized, inner city" (or its analogues in smaller communities). More novel and newsworthy is street crime erupting in presumably "nice" residential neighborhoods or sacrosanct public space.

The notion of violence invading safe, inviolate space was elaborated in reports suggesting that violent crime had escaped its traditional confines and was trespassing on urban enclaves and into suburban areas that heretofore had been relatively unscathed by street violence. A state legislator, reflecting on the summer's shootings, succinctly summarized this sentiment: "I think we assumed for a long time that some neighborhoods are safe and some aren't. We can't assume that anymore."[30] This differentiation of (inner) city and suburban space infused newspaper (and television) coverage of several high-profile cases, while the more generalized motif of violence radiating from corrupt centers to pristine peripheries appeared in stories decrying the spread of street violence from Denver and its immediate environs (including its suburbs) to smaller cities and towns—for example, Colorado Springs, Durango, Grand Junction, and Pueblo—throughout the state.[31]

The theme of violence encroaching on sacrosanct social space was redeployed in other ways. Several articles deplored the spread of street violence to revered social institutions, including churches and schools, once regarded as sanctuaries sequestered from the tumult and dangers of the profane world. The Denver Zoo is not itself a sacred place, but its representational value as an emblem of civic pride and its powerful association with weekend family outings, often with young children in tow, renders it a potent symbol of public space. An editorial characterized the shooting of an infant, who was sitting in front of the zoo's celebrated polar bear exhibit, as a riveting reminder that no institution or public (or private) space is inviolate:

> The bullet that sent the youngster to Denver General Hospital . . . could serve as a metaphor for how violence robs this city's soul of its collective peace. . . . No citizen is safe anywhere as long as a predilection to violence remains prevalent. Drive-by shootings can happen anywhere an automobile can travel, and that includes any street in the core city or its suburbs. Gangs, drugs, and guns can infest any school, whether it is located in the inner city or in an upscale enclave. The failure of the city, the state, and the nation to cope with violence has come to haunt every corner of society—even the polar bear exhibit at the local zoo.[32]

Random Violence

Continually pointing to the seemingly unpredictable character of the seven high-profile incidents, reporters suggested that random violence threatened the entire community. Underscoring this theme, one article observed, "With tiny children shot, men murdered, [and] women beaten . . . the specter of random violence [is] taking center stage this summer."[33] Several distinct meanings were attached to the theme of random violence, but perhaps the most salient was its unpredictable character, the unnerving sense that "anyone could be the next victim."[34] A local talk-radio host we spoke with emphasized this element of random violence:

> It [the violence occurring during the summer of 1993] wasn't predictable. It could happen anywhere for no apparent reason, all of a sudden, out of the blue. People don't like that. If you've got a problem that people can identify and isolate, then they can adjust to it. You can't adjust to random violence.

The threat of random violence becomes psychologically salient only when the perception that "anyone could be the next victim" is interpreted as meaning "the next victim could be me or someone I care about." Personal identification with recent, actual victims of apparently random violence fostered this heightened sense of vulnerability. The print media suggested that many citizens identified strongly with one or more of the victims described in the high-profile cases. For example, shortly after the shooting at the zoo, a reporter interviewed a 14-year-old relaxing in City Park, which is immediately adjacent to the Denver Zoo. The boy said, "My mom's starting to worry about me. She's real hyper about this, real hesitant since the gunshots. She says that little kid [who was shot at the zoo] coulda been me."[35]

Several of the journalists we interviewed remarked that the high-profile incidents, with their detailed, dramatic descriptions, supplied readers with abundant opportunities for intuiting connections between themselves, or their immediate social circle, and the victims. Proximity, for example, whether calculated in terms of physical space or social networks, frequently elicits identification with a victim of crime. As one reporter said, "When it's somebody that your mother knows or it's two blocks from your home and he got shot in your neighborhood, suddenly it could be said, 'That could be me.'"

Common social and demographic attributes (e.g., age, class, ethnicity, race, gender, marital status) can spark a vivid recognition of the self-in-the-other. For example, the Coles (Bob Cole was murdered while Mary Cole survived a severe beating)—portrayed in news accounts as a dynamic, popular, loving, handsome young couple; recently married, with a newly acquired apartment of their own; and working hard to launch a successful business venture—embodied a social identity and trajectory that, several reporters speculated, mirrored the aspirations of many young adults in Denver (and Colorado) while eliciting the nodding approval of older residents.

It can be hypothesized, as many journalists did in their interviews with us, that the print media's idealized representations of victims, which emphasized their impeccable character and moral innocence, resonated with the way many people like to think about themselves and encouraged members of the public to see a critical similarity between themselves and the high-profile victims. The following conjecture, ventured by a reporter, describes the folk reasoning that may have connected readers to Ann Temple, a slain elementary school teacher:

> A teacher, who is from Eagle [a small mountain town, roughly 75 miles west of Denver], comes down to take a job in Denver. And it's her dream to teach in the school and everything. And she is staying with a girlfriend. She goes out to dinner and then drives to Safeway and gets something. And some gang members scope her and kill her in a parking lot as they try to rob her pocketbook. So here is another innocent victim, *like you and I*, killed in quote our safe neighborhoods of Denver. [Emphasis in original]

In brief, through their continuous and prominent coverage and their (melo)dramatic narrative of the Summer of Violence, the Denver media took the lead in identifying an apparently urgent problem. In effect, news reports democratized the risk of street violence, suggesting that anyone—regardless of class rank, moral standing, or demographic profile—could be violently assaulted. In addition, these reports intimated that the attacks on innocent children and "good" adults represented nothing less than transgressions against the community's conception of the sacred. However, acknowledging the media's leadership role in focusing public and policymaker attention on an issue does not imply that news agencies, by themselves, can simply mandate the existence of a serious social problem. Press accounts of problematic behaviors or harmful social arrangements are more accurately conceptualized as claims, which can be accepted, revised, or rejected by citizens, public officials, and other institutional elites. When media claims about allegedly troublesome conditions are broadly affirmed by significant segments of the public and by elites in other institutional sectors, a social problem is effectively ratified. This is exactly what occurred during the Summer of Violence.

In response to news reports about the Summer of Violence, local and state officials, as well as Colorado's congressional representatives, issued calls for forceful measures against street crime.[36] An array of opinion leaders, including luminaries in the business and professional communities, the archbishop of Denver, and Pope John Paul II (who traveled to the Mile High City to celebrate World Youth Day), confirmed that it was "time to take action."[37] At the grassroots level, frightened residents altered the routes they drove to and from work, suspended their daily jog, mowed their lawns in the early morning hours, refrained from sitting on the porch after dark, installed bars across the windows of their homes, put their young children to sleep in the bathtub to avoid stray bullets, imposed what their teenage children regarded as outrageously restrictive curfews, considered moving to safer locales, or took more precautions about locking car doors and looking over their shoulders while walking city streets.[38] Street violence became a prominent issue in a burgeoning public debate, with many concerned citizens sending letters to newspapers, calling local talk-radio programs, participating in town meetings, organizing protest marches to decry the violence, and contacting city and state officials, urging them to "do something."[39] The net and mutually reinforcing effect of these reactions, which themselves were circulated back into the media's unfolding narrative about the Summer of Violence, was to magnify the visibility of violent crime and reaffirm the perception that it constituted a vitally serious problem requiring immediate action.

Attributing Blame for the Problem: A New "Breed" of Transgressing Adolescent and the Juvenile Justice System

When pressing problems are identified and ratified, the problem-solving paradigm hardwired into modern societies supplies a powerful impetus to devise suitable remedies. These solutions take many forms, one of which is simply expanding the institutional sector whose purview of responsibility encompasses the problem that has been identified. When communities confront crime waves, for example, they often expand their social control agencies: They assign more police to troubled neighborhoods, pay officers to work overtime, or hire additional recruits. This kind of response, which can be called institutional expansion, was clearly evident during the Summer of Violence. The Denver mayor, for example, offered up to $1.1 million in overtime pay as incentive for police officers to work "around the clock."[40]

Institutional differentiation is a second type of response, and it involves devising specialized organizational arrangements and practices to address what is regarded as a significant and distinctive problem. Differentiation usually occurs when existing institutions (or the simple expansion of existing institutions) are deemed incapable of addressing the problem in a satisfactory way. The presumed incapacity of established institutions, in turn, becomes a warrant for proposing new arrangements that are typically heralded as much more efficient and effective than the structures they replace. In this vein, one of the most important legacies of the Summer of Violence was the crystallization of a new category of transgressing adolescent who, many believed, exceeded the problem-solving capacities of the existing juvenile justice system.

Denver journalists asserted that an "unholy trinity" of guns, gangs, and juvenile offenders was responsible for the Summer of Violence (Acland, 1995, p. 4). Reporters repeatedly insisted that the principal culprit was a gun-toting, gang-affiliated adolescent. The press did not arrive at this conclusion on its own. After focusing public and policymaker attention on a riveting issue (such as an apparent surge in street violence), the media typically turn to other respected institutions and groups (rather than to insurgents, radicals, and outsiders) for definitive characterizations of the sources of the problem (Gitlin, 1980). Relying heavily on interviews with select state legislators, juvenile court judges, public defenders, police, gang intervention workers, and district attorneys, the press sharply distinguished the juveniles blamed for the summer's violence from conventional delinquents. In fact, reporters rarely used the word "delinquent": In the more than 500 youth and crime stories published by the *Denver Post* and *Rocky Mountain News* from May through mid-September 1993, the terms "delinquent" and "delinquency" appear less than two dozen times. And when employed, these words were dubbed anachronisms: "delinquent" and "delinquency," reporters implied, conjured up forms of adolescent transgression characteristic of an earlier and more innocent time and place. Playing cultural entrepreneur, reporters coined dozens of clever catchwords to characterize an allegedly new breed of juvenile lawbreaker—for example, "criminal kids"; "kid gangsters"; "hard-core juvenile offenders"; "scary and dangerous youths"; "young thugs preying on their fellow citizens"; "the state's nastiest young felons"; "kids doing the criminal work of adults"; "greedy, self-serving, predatory street punks"; "an infestation of teenage evil"; and "tiny terrorists."

A rough sketch differentiating this hyper-threatening teen from the traditional delinquent complemented the slogans. This comparison held, first, that the "new breed of youthful offender" committed more serious crimes and engaged in more chronic law-breaking: Where delinquents filched cars and played mailbox baseball, youthful offenders "swagger out to kill motorists, passers-by, neighbors, each other. What isn't targeted for dead is fair game for robberies, rapes, carjackings, and drug dealing."[41]

A second contrast underscored the contemporary youthful offender's debased moral character. In the early decades of the 20th century, Denver had been the site of a remarkably compassionate characterization of the delinquent (Colomy & Kretzmann, 1995). Consistently affirming delinquents' basic humanity and fundamental, childlike innocence, Judge Ben B. Lindsey, the leading figure of the early Denver juvenile court, passionately proclaimed (in articles, books, and speeches) that the sins of young lawbreakers paled in significance when compared to the sins committed against them by negligent parents or a corrupt, hypocritical social order. In the summer of 1993, the Denver media, leaning on insights supplied by elected officials and professionals in the juvenile and criminal justice systems, repudiated this sympathetic conception of transgressing youth as sentimental, mushy-headed nostalgia. As an influential state representative observed, "We have a tendency to believe the Father Flanagan/Spencer Tracy Boys' Town thing, that there's no such thing as a bad boy. But that's a movie. Our reality today is that Spencer Tracy wasn't right."[42] Today, there are, added the governor's chief legal counsel, "really bad kids."[43]

Lacking essential moral attitudes and emotions, these bad kids struck journalists and public officials as not quite fully human. Denver's chief juvenile court judge told a reporter, "I see, in the youths who are appearing in court, a lack of valuation of life, a lack of respect for life . . . some scary, scary kids."[44] Others elaborated upon this observation, adding that contemporary young offenders are incapable of empathy or compassion. A former public defender said, "There is just a different attitude among the kids now. It's not just that they have no social conscience. It's almost like there is no morality. There is not any feeling toward other people."[45]

Elements of a powerful cultural code informed this burgeoning portrait of contemporary youthful offenders. Accounts of the high-profile cases assigned religious-like features to the juveniles suspected of injuring or killing ideal child and adult victims. Modern Western societies, according to Durkheim, are permeated by a "religion of humanity," which constitutes the "human person" as "sacred in the ritual sense of the word" and imbues the individual in general with "the transcendent majesty that churches of all time lend to their gods" (Durkheim, 1898/1973, p. 46). Like more orthodox forms of religiosity, however, the religion of humanity actually gravitates around two poles, the sacred and the anti-sacred, with the latter viewed as "evil and impure powers, bringers of disorder, causes of death and sickness, instigators of sacrilege" (Durkheim, 1912/1995, pp. 412–414). It is in this quasi-religious sense that Christie (1986) portrays ideal victims and ideal offenders as two sides of the same symbolic coin: "Ideal victims need—and create—ideal offenders. . . . The more ideal the victim is, the more ideal becomes the offender." Ideal victims personify innocence, and so ideal offenders embody evil; the ideal offender "is, morally speaking, black against the white victim" (p. 25). Ideal victims are symbolic icons of community life; ideal offenders are symbolic outsiders, strangers, foreigners, aliens, and intruders. "The more foreign the better," according to Christie, who adds that the ideal offender "is a dangerous man coming from far away." Ideal offenders, moreover, lack qualities essential for being regarded as fully human: The ideal offender "is a human being close to not being one" (Christie, 1986, pp. 26, 28). The religion of humanity implies, in other words, that those who desecrate innocent children and morally upstanding adults are something less than human beings, a sentiment aptly conveyed in the evocative phrases some Denver reporters used to describe violent youth: "ugly, creepy, putrid cockroaches"; "predators"; "wolves out looking for prey"; and "wild animals."

In addition to the religious-like contrast between ideal victims and ideal offenders, the exclusive tradition in American culture permeated the media's sociomoral profile of these dangerous teens. There is abundant evidence suggesting that "mainstream America"—particularly *white* mainstream America—associates (and has long associated) African American and Latino male adolescents and young adults with violence, danger, and disorder (Anderson, 1990; Sampson & Laub, 1993). There can be little doubt that this association, powerfully reinforced by continuous coverage of the high-profile attacks on children and exemplary (white) adults—assaults the media attributed explicitly and exclusively to young Latinos and African American males—figured significantly in the construction of a more ominous category of transgressing adolescent. This association, it is reasonable to surmise, also served as the potent cultural subtext for key themes in the media's account of the Summer of Violence, with the themes of unprecedented, encroaching, and random violence animated by the frightening specter of African American and Latino youth wreaking havoc on middle-class, Anglo lives and neighborhoods and in the public spaces Anglos share with other groups.

Although they incorporated the symbolic opposition between the ideal victim and the ideal offender and the exclusive tradition's stereotype linking minority males to street crime, media accounts did not depict juvenile offenders as unequivocal embodiments of evil. Rather, these accounts were infused with considerable ambivalence: Although assuredly a more forbidding figure than the joyriding, hubcap-stealing delinquent of yesteryear, the contemporary young offender was not (yet) a "hardened adult criminal." Journalists, like the officials and experts they interviewed, were unwilling to abandon completely the cultural precept that youthfulness mitigates, to an extent, the culpability of young offenders. Nor were they inclined to jettison entirely a belief in the presumed malleability of youth, a conviction that sustains hope that juvenile lawbreakers—even violent ones—can be redeemed. The youthfulness of the new type of transgressing adolescent did not prevent some columnists and reporters from likening violent juveniles to "bringers of disorder," but it also generated a nearly equal number of columns and reports that counterbalanced this demonology by describing the conditions—largely of familial, social, economic, and moral breakdown (Sasson, 1995)—that purportedly propel "our young people" to act "with so little regard for human life." As portrayed by the *Denver Post* and the *Rocky Mountain News* during the Summer of Violence, youthful offenders were not, as a group, completely credible icons of "dangerous men coming from far away."

If reporters and their sources expressed some ambivalence in their characterization of this new type of youthful offender, they displayed little equivocation in indicting the juvenile justice system for its inability to respond effectively to these hyper-threatening teens. Fashioning a commonsense version of the lead-and-lag principle, the press, along with several other entities (e.g., the governor, state legislators, social control agents, and gang intervention workers), observed that the system of juvenile justice had, in the words of a *Rocky Mountain News* editorial, originated back in "the palmier days when serious juvenile rebellion . . . meant filching a car and the term delinquent suggested only a temporary pause from civilized behavior."[46] At that time, it was widely acknowledged "that kids make mistakes" but ought not to be severely punished for their lack of judgment. Juvenile justice's firm-but-compassionate stance toward delinquents made perfect "sense so long as the offenses themselves were relatively minor."[47]

However, as the Summer of Violence seemed to demonstrate all too clearly, yesterday's delinquent had been eclipsed by a new brand of juvenile offender who commits heinous crimes and exhibits a viciousness unknown to adolescents of an earlier era. As a Denver assistant district attorney noted, "The type of kid we're talking about isn't your next-door neighbor. This is the kid who is robbing, raping, killing and shooting."[48] No less important was the fact that the juvenile justice system had proved incapable of responding effectively to this exceedingly dangerous youthful offender. Governor Romer's opening remarks to the special legislative session on youth violence zeroed in on this key point:

The fact is, the [traditional juvenile justice] system never contemplated and is totally unprepared to handle the problems we see today—kids shooting kids,

kids raping kids, kids terrorizing neighborhoods, kids running sophisticated criminal organizations that deal in drugs.[49]

Legislators, police, prosecutors, and many others elaborated upon the governor's claims. They noted, for example, that many teens confined in the Colorado Division of Youth Services (DYS) reform schools were much tougher than the facilities in which they were incarcerated and, consequently, were unfazed by the experience. In this vein, a state senator said,

> I went and talked to a bunch of kids . . . who have been in and out of DYS facilities. . . . They said if they are sent back to Montview [a reform school], it's like old home week and they go back and see their friends. There is no fear. . . . It doesn't bother them if they go in and out of this revolving door at DYS because they know they are not going to stay very long.[50]

A representative of the county sheriffs of Colorado made a similar claim: "Many of these kids, and we've seen some of the profiles on them, have been in and out of the Division of Youth Services five and six times. DYS for these kids is a joke."[51]

This endlessly reiterated version of the lead-and-lag principle—that young people had become more dangerous, deadly, and disdainful, while the juvenile justice system had utterly failed to keep pace with this new type of offender—led, inexorably, to a painfully obvious conclusion: "We can't keep doing things the same way because it's different than it was in the '50s. It's different than it was in the '70s. There's a new breed of kid out there that is not afraid of anything."[52]

Fixing the Problem: Creating and Mobilizing Support for the Youthful Offender System

The institutional logic of newsworthiness discourages news agencies from assuming political responsibility for the deleterious conditions their coverage highlights. Instead of assuming an obligation to ameliorate problems, the media's tack more commonly revolves around identifying "the responsible office or person" and assigning that party the chore of doing something about the problem, often using follow-up reports to hold the designated authority accountable for fulfilling that charge (Gusfield, 1981). Practicing a "trickle-up principle," journalists generally assign responsibility to individuals holding high-ranking positions in the pertinent public or private institution, especially when a serious problem allegedly occurs "during their watch" (Stallings, 1990, p. 90).

In a complex polity with multiple levels of governance, an abundance of civic groups, and numerous opportunities for activist citizens to voice their concerns and recommendations, a socially ratified problem commonly elicits a host of proposed remedies. The Summer of Violence proved no exception to this generalization. Providing seemingly incontrovertible evidence that the function of controlling juvenile crime was not being fulfilled effectively, the Summer of Violence generated dozens of "plans of action" aimed at fortifying social control institutions and stemming the apparent surge of youth violence (Blumer, 1971, p. 304).

The deeply felt urge to "do something" prompted Denver-area teens to form a group, Helping Young People Educate (HYPE), to assist adolescents and their families in coping with youth violence.[52] A charismatic community activist and former gang member, a city councilman, and several gang leaders attempted to negotiate a truce between rival gangs, an effort they called Operation Reconstruction.[53] Metro-area educators took steps—for example, closing off streets bordering a school during lunch periods to prevent drive-by shootings and encouraging school administrators to accompany students as they went to lunch off campus—to protect students from violent crime.[54] A 30-member committee, appointed by the Denver mayor and the Denver city council president, was asked to devise a plan to combat youth violence.[55] Aurora assigned 20 additional officers to its police gang unit,[56] whereas Adams County instituted a "zero tolerance policy" requiring that any juvenile committing a crime with a gun be jailed immediately,[57] and the city councils of Denver and Westminster approved ordinances "forbidding the possession of firearms by juveniles and imposing penalties upon adults who furnish minors with guns."[58] District attorneys representing Denver and seven nearby counties announced plans to "make violent crimes involving weapons our highest priority."[59] Congressman Bill Armstrong (from Colorado) argued that fighting juvenile and gang violence would require more money to hire additional police officers.[60] Congresswoman Pat Schroeder (also from Colorado) sought $4.4 million from Congress to fund a military-style program aimed at "reclaim[ing] America's youth."[61] Announcing that violent crime was the number one priority of the city police department, Denver Mayor Wellington Webb outlined a six-point plan, heavy on increased law enforcement, to combat gang and youth violence.

The summer's most ambitious (and successful) institutional entrepreneur, however, was Governor Roy Romer, whose 14-point strategy to curtail violent youth crime received the greatest attention from policymakers, news organizations, and the public. Promoting his plan as "an 'iron fist' against outlaw gangs and a 'helping hand' for Coloradans fighting to take back their neighborhoods," Romer urged the swift prosecution of gangs and of youth charged with violent offenses, targeted juveniles with guns, and recommended building a new youthful offender system.[62] He characterized YOS as a "middle tier" in the correctional apparatus, a tier carefully crafted to fit between the existing criminal and juvenile justice systems. Envisioned as a differentiated structure targeting a distinctive group of juvenile lawbreakers, YOS did not simply replicate existing adult prisons or juvenile reform schools. Rather, YOS is an instance of institution building, involving the creation of a new set of arrangements and practices aimed at controlling and treating a group of offenders who are neither hardened adult criminals nor malleable juvenile delinquents.

Devised as a response to an allegedly new type of transgressing adolescent, Romer's YOS mirrored the ambivalence permeating the youthful offender category itself. Just as juvenile offenders purportedly differ from traditional delinquents by posing a more ominous threat to public safety, so YOS differs from conventional (juvenile) reform schools in its more explicit commitment to punishment. Romer and other advocates of YOS asserted that juveniles committing serious, adult-like crimes forfeit any legitimate claim to be recognized and treated as juveniles by the community and courts. As one district attorney put it, "Let's differentiate juveniles [from adults] on the basis of their conduct, not on the basis of their age."[63] According to Romer, YOS originated, in part, "to impose the kind of punishment such [adult-like] crimes deserve."[64] Some of YOS's punitive elements were outlined earlier in this chapter—for example, the direct-file provision and the sentencing of (convicted) juveniles to adult prisons, a sentence suspended conditional on completing a 2- to 6-year term in YOS. The institution's explicitly punitive components are also manifested in the decision to place YOS under the administrative (and symbolic) purview of the (adult) Department of Corrections, not the (juvenile) Division of Youth Services. Programmatically, YOS includes a rigorous boot camp that tests inmates' physical and psychological limits. Chronically recalcitrant youth are sent to "readjustment centers," where they are locked up for 23 hours a day. Those who continually flout the institution's rules can be returned to court for imposition of the original sentence to adult prison.

Despite having committed a serious, violent offense and posing a genuine threat to public safety, the juvenile offender still possesses some of the cultural attributes ascribed to youth, attributes that entitle her or him to a "second last chance at rehabilitation." Thus, one proponent of YOS argued that youthful offenders

> are still children and so in that regard . . . we still have to hope that given as young as some of these kids are, that we can with some intensive programming and a very big stick over their heads, turn some of them around.[65]

Sounding a similar note, the bill's cosponsor, Senator Wham, said,

> We have to treat youngsters who are doing adult crimes with some punishment that is meaningful. At the same time, I think the [youthful offender] system says we're not giving up on you completely and maybe it's the second and last chance.[66]

The bill's other cosponsor, Representative Berry, maintained,

> We do recognize that young offenders are entitled, in many cases under constitutional provisions, and just in good common sense ought to have treatment and try to get them to change their attitude. . . . Hopefully, we can change the behavior. We can get their attention. We can in fact have it sink into their minds the seriousness of the conduct and of the attitude they have. Turn that around. And I think it is all of our hopes that when they come out they will not re-offend.[67]

To help ensure that YOS would not become merely a "prison for punks," the enabling legislation mandated that its staff must have at least a bachelor's degree—a requirement that effectively ruled out many correctional officers already employed by the (adult) Department of Corrections, officers who the YOS architects believed would be too preoccupied with custody and too little concerned with treatment.

Advocates of YOS also believed that requiring a college degree would be more likely to attract staff wholeheartedly committed to rehabilitating young people. Moreover, the three phases of the YOS program following the boot camp induction are, in theory, structured around an intensive form of compulsory resocialization. In Phase 1, inmates receive academic instruction, vocational training, and various forms of individual and group counseling. In Phase 2, they are moved to a community facility and prepared for reentry to community life. In the final phase, a parole officer provides YOS youth with intensive community supervision and support.

Romer championed YOS in large part because he sincerely believed that this new institution represented a potent antidote to serious juvenile crime. He was also convinced that by reacting forcefully to the Summer of Violence, he would restore credibility in government, demonstrating that public officials were attuned to the populace's concerns and were willing to take drastic action in response to a crisis. However, like other institutional entrepreneurs, Romer did not act solely as an altruistic agent of greater societal effectiveness or democratic governance. By presenting his 14-point plan, convening the special legislative session, and successfully securing passage of YOS and other initiatives, Governor Romer's public visibility and approval ratings soared. Throughout his tenure, Romer had been an enormously popular governor. However, some of his political capital had been depleted the previous year (1992), when he lobbied heavily on behalf of higher taxes for schools (a measure the public rejected decisively) and when he vehemently opposed an amendment to the state's constitution limiting government spending (a bill voters overwhelmingly approved).

Since 1994 was an election year, it is reasonable to suppose that Romer and his staff were fully aware that decisive action against street crime in the summer of 1993 would improve the governor's prospects for reelection. Moreover, the juvenile crime problem presented Romer, a Democrat, with an opportunity to seize an issue—law and order—that heretofore had been the preserve of conservative Republicans. By embracing a tough-on-crime stance, Romer enriched not only his own political fortunes but those of his party as well. Finally, in their interviews with us, several Romer staff members conceded that the governor relished the publicity and acclaim he received while leading the fight against youth crime. In the words of one respondent, "Roy Romer liked the spotlight, there's no question about that. . . . No man ever got more press than he did and no man ever wanted what he got more."

Proposing a new institution as a remedy to a socially ratified problem is one thing; mobilizing support for that proposal is another. Romer and his staff confronted several obstacles to winning approval for the YOS initiative. First, the Colorado governor is, in important respects, a constitutionally weak chief executive, with limited appointive powers, little authority over important state programs, and a lack of control over the state budget. Second, Romer had to ensure that the public's and policymakers' attention remained focused on youth violence. A third impediment involved defining youth violence as a credible, statewide issue and not just a problem confined to Denver. Fourth, both houses of the General Assembly were controlled by Republicans and, up until 1993, Colorado Republicans had "owned" the crime issue. Finally, YOS raised potentially divisive racial and ethnic issues, with some activist citizen groups predicting (correctly, as it turned out) that young Latinos and African Americans would be statistically overrepresented in the YOS population.

Romer's adroit use of the media and the bully pulpit of the governorship amply compensated for the constitutional infirmities of his office and enabled him to sustain citizens' and officials' focus on the issue of serious juvenile crime. In this regard, an expert on the state's politics notes that Colorado governors are well-positioned to serve as leaders of public opinion:

> The governor of Colorado is usually the best known public official in the state other than the president of the United States. The governor is frequently in the news and becomes a celebrity. He has only to notify the press that he intends to give a pint of blood to the Red Cross or pay his personal respects to a one-hundred-year-old grandmother and his performance will be broadcast across the state. This ability to reach the public with his message exceeds that of all other politicians in the state. . . . What the governor says is important if for no other reason than that it is heard far and wide. The legislature, on the other hand, speaks with a hundred voices, none of which begins to match the governor's command of public attention. This fact affects legislators, who understand very well that the governor is better equipped than they to reach the voters. (Lorch, 1983, p. 198)

During the summer of 1993, the governor spoke frequently about youth violence, and his remarks almost always made news. By late June 1993, he announced that serious juvenile crime was "the highest thing on my agenda now."[68] He met with family members of victims struck down by street crime and walked in protest marches denouncing the summer's violence. He convened "town meetings" with citizens across the state to discuss the problem of youth violence, soliciting participants' feedback and enlisting their support for his proposals. (His staff alerted news agencies to these meetings, which invariably received extensive coverage.) He spent a night in a jail cell, where he spoke to print and television reporters about the need for a tough, no-nonsense response to serious young offenders. An evening ride-along with the Aurora and Denver police netted a juvenile suspect packing two loaded firearms and front-page coverage in both Denver newspapers. His rhetorical hyperbole underscored both the seriousness of youth crime and the urgent need for a solution. He claimed, for example, that Colorado confronted a crisis unlike anything the state had seen and that absent dramatic, forceful action, "society's not going to hold together."[69]

While traveling across the state to speak to various groups about juvenile crime and other issues, Romer continually reiterated his belief that far from being confined to Denver, youth violence had erupted in every corner of Colorado and constituted a statewide problem. At a press conference, for example, the governor pulled out a recent newspaper article from the Pueblo Chieftain that he had been carrying. The article described a teen (living in the city of Pueblo) who was shot in the back while he slept, a murder police characterized as a retaliatory strike for the boy's reporting of another drive-by shooting to the authorities.[70] In his opening remarks to the special legislative session, Romer repeated this point: "This [youth violence] is not just a Denver problem. It's a problem throughout the state—in Colorado Springs, in Pueblo. We even had a drive-by shooting this summer in Lamar [a very small town in southeastern Colorado]."[71]

Romer used the pressure of public opinion, the goodwill he had cultivated earlier with legislators on both sides of the aisle, and traditional political horse-trading to garner cooperation from the Republican-controlled General Assembly. More than any other policymaker, Romer propelled youth violence to the top of the policy agenda while periodically entertaining the possibility of calling a special legislative session to address the issue. Legislators, particularly Republicans, were reticent about convening such a session and questioned whether anything significant could be accomplished in a 4- or 5-day session. In response, Romer continued to use his bully pulpit and the media to highlight the problem of juvenile crime while promising to consult Republican leaders before making a final decision about the special session. However, during the last week of July, when four high-profile incidents occurred in rapid succession (and were extensively covered by the media), and while several Republican lawmakers were in San Diego attending the National Conference of State Legislators, Romer announced that a special session would be held. Romer's failure to contact legislators before making this announcement angered Republicans, but the public clamor about juvenile violence and widespread calls to "do something" effectively precluded objections or organized resistance to the session. In the weeks leading up to the session, Romer aggressively pursued a bipartisan approach to win approval of his initiatives. He persuaded Dottie Wham, the powerful and highly respected Republican chairwoman of the Senate Judiciary Committee, and Chuck Berry, the Republican Speaker of the House, to cosponsor the YOS bill. With their help (given in exchange for future political rewards, including the prospect of augmenting their political capital by cosponsoring an important piece of legislation), in conjunction with the pressure he applied to members of his own political party, Romer successfully piloted the bill through the legislature.

Finally, some civil rights activists publicly predicted that minority youth would be disproportionately incarcerated in YOS. These predictions sounded a note of dissent within the Democratic coalition, a group Romer was counting on to deliver votes in support of YOS. Romer addressed this potentially divisive issue in three ways. First, he proclaimed that the problem of youth violence cut across racial, ethnic, and class lines and that violent young people existed in every community. In his opening address to the special session, Romer said, "This [youth violence] is not just a problem for any particular ethnic group. We are all in this together. Rural, urban, Black, Latino, Asian-American, and Anglo—our whole community is victimized by violence."[72]

Second, Romer met privately with leading representatives (political, social, and civic) of the African American and Latino communities. According to Romer's staff members, these leaders expressed concerns not only about the violence in their neighborhoods but also about police harassment. Romer assured these leaders that his legislative initiatives neither singled out minority youth nor gave police (or other social control agents) license to mistreat Latino or African American youth. He reiterated this point publicly in his opening remarks to the special session:

Let me say this right up front—this is a tough package we are about to discuss, and I hear and understand the concerns of parents and others in the communities of color that what we do here not be an excuse for the police to harass kids because of the color of their skin. We're not here to do that. We're trying to get the guns out of the hands of children so that they don't hurt one another, no matter what their color. I will work with you and with law enforcement agencies to ensure these laws are applied fairly. What we want to do is stop the violence, not harass innocent kids.[73]

Third, although Romer's role in this decision is not entirely clear, it is worth noting that the person appointed as the first director of YOS, Regis Groff, was a highly respected, liberal, African American state senator who, during the special session, delivered the single most powerful speech in support of the YOS measure. Groff's appointment provided YOS with a battle-tested leader, one whose strong ties to the legislature enhanced appreciably the new institution's prospects for future funding. This appointment also signaled that YOS would be keenly attuned to racial and ethnic disparities among its inmate population and that discrimination would not be tolerated.

Conclusion

This chapter has indicated how the recent trend toward criminalizing a subset of youth can be understood from a neofunctionalist perspective. This perspective maintains that new, differentiated institutions are often justified as a remedy for pressing problems and that successful episodes of institution building depend, in part, on the ability of entrepreneurs to mobilize support for new and purportedly more effective problem-solving structures. While successful entrepreneurs make institutional history, they do not, to paraphrase Marx, make it in circumstances of their own choosing. Accordingly, understanding entrepreneurs' institution-building efforts requires situating their change-oriented projects and mobilization strategies in a broader institutional and cultural context. Through a detailed examination of the Summer of Violence and the creation of the Colorado YOS, we have attempted to illustrate these general ideas.

Neofunctionalism's interest in the creation of new institutions can be profitably joined to traditional functionalism's concern with the consequences of long-standing structures and practices. It was, after all, a functionalist who first formulated "the law of unintended consequences" and pointed out that institutions, once established, operate in ways their originators never intended or anticipated (Merton, 1936, 1968). This chapter is not the place to present a comprehensive treatment of YOS's unintended consequences, but three issues pertinent to that type of analysis can be briefly considered. First, although YOS was touted as better equipped to address the problem of serious juvenile offenders, little systematic evidence has been generated to support this claim. A performance audit of YOS (published in August 1999) conducted by the Office of the Colorado State Auditor offered this observation:

More than five years have passed since the Youthful Offender System began accepting offenders. . . . Yet the Department [of Corrections] has not evaluated the effectiveness of the program or measured its outcomes. Consequently, the overall effectiveness of the program is unknown. This is particularly troubling because YOS was intended to be an innovative approach to turning youthful offenders around before it was too late—a second last chance. . . . However, the Department can provide no real evidence that YOS has been successful in achieving the goals for which it was created. (Report of the [Colorado] State Auditor, 1999)

The absence of a rigorous evaluation—despite the fact that the legislation creating YOS explicitly mandated such an evaluation—is not surprising. During the early stages of institution building, entrepreneurial groups and their allies herald newly proposed structures as much more effective and efficient problem solvers than the existing structures they are designed to replace. But once the new structures are in place, their management and staff resist systematic assessments of the institution's performance. With regard to YOS, the consequence of this "assessment avoidance" is that few people, and certainly not the general public, know whether the YOS program succeeds in resocializing its inmates and significantly reducing their rates of reoffending.

Second, the ambivalence built into YOS—the uneasy balance between punishment and treatment—seems to be inherently unstable and, in the long run, may be unsustainable. Like scores of previous correctional programs, YOS appears to be subordinating its commitment to treatment and rehabilitation while elevating its concern for control and custody.[74] This development may overlap with the pattern of assessment avoidance described in the previous paragraph: So long as YOS succeeds in controlling and incapacitating its inmates, little public or policymaker attention is likely to be given to whether the institution successfully treats young offenders.

Third, the continuing decline of violent juvenile crime in Colorado (and across the nation) raises an obvious question about the future of institutions like YOS that emerged in response to an apparent surge in the number of gang-affiliated, violent youth. Proponents of YOS presumed that high rates of violent juvenile offending would continue indefinitely and that the institution's 480 beds would be filled with dangerous young felons. What is likely to happen if there are not enough violent adolescents to occupy those beds? The sociology of prisons provides an answer: The beds will be filled, if not by hyper-violent gang members, then by some other type of transgressing adolescent, albeit not the "new breed of youthful offender" who was invoked to justify the construction of YOS in the first place.

Notes

1. *Denver Post,* August 8, 1993, p. 16A.
2. *Rocky Mountain News,* May 31, 1993, pp. 8A, 10A.
3. *Denver Post,* August 8, 1993, p. 16A.
4. *Denver Post,* August 8, 1993, p. 16A.
5. Youth and violent crime articles were identified through the *Denver Post Index* using several topical categories: crime, crime prevention, criminal law, criminal sentences, detention centers, gangs, juvenile delinquency, murder and murder attempts, victims of crime, violent crime, and violence. Every story in the category of juvenile delinquency was included in the sample. For the category gangs, every story was included with the exception of articles

describing adult mobster gangs. Stories for all other categories were included only if the index indicated that the article contained one or more of the following phrases: youth/juvenile violence, youth/juvenile offender, epidemic of violence, crime wave, town meetings/marches/protests/press conferences/church sermons on crime/violence, correctional facilities for youth, criminal/juvenile system and youth, gangs, gang prevention, random violence, reports on patterns/distributions/trends/rates of crime/violence, fear of crime/violence, and funds/resources/personnel allocated to crime/violence prevention programs.

6. We focus on youth and violent crime because this topic, more than any other, fueled local media coverage of the summer's violence.

7. The data for the 1994 summer are incomplete because the Aurora monthly report does not include aggravated assault figures for August of that year. Combining Denver's complete figures with the partial information supplied by Aurora, we inferred that nonlethal, violent offenses were roughly 5% to 10% lower in the 1994 summer compared to the 1993 summer.

8. Our qualitative assessment of the media's coverage of the Summer of Violence analyzed articles published in both the *Denver Post* and the *Rocky Mountain News*. The *Denver Post* has the largest circulation in the state, whereas the *Rocky Mountain News* boasts the second-largest circulation. Both papers are based in Denver.

9. *Denver Post* (1993, July 24), pp. A1, A2, A4; *Denver Post* (1993, July 28), p. A16; *Denver Post* (1993, July 24), pp. A1, A15; *Denver Post* (1993, July 31), p. A18.

10. *Denver Post* (1993, July 28), pp. A1, A4; *Denver Post* (1993, July 28), pp. A1, A11.

11. *Denver Post* (1993, July 29), pp. A1, A4; *Denver Post* (1993, July 29), pp. A1, A10.

12. We conducted interviews with 23 reporters, columnists, and editors involved in writing about youth crime for the *Denver Post* and the *Rocky Mountain News* during the 1993 summer. (We also conducted interviews with three local television reporters, a local talk-radio show host, and a reporter employed by *Westword*, an alternative Denver newspaper.) To protect confidentiality, we promised those who spoke with us that we would characterize all respondents generically as either journalists or reporters. The interviews were designed to elicit the meanings journalists were inviting their readers to accept, and reporters' comments and insights proved invaluable to our qualitative assessment of news themes.

13. *Denver Post* (1993, July 30), p. A16.

14. *Denver Post* (1993, July 31), p. A5.

15. *Denver Post* (1993, July 30), p. A15.

16. *Denver Post* (1993, July 31), p. A5.

17. *Denver Post* (1993, July 31), p. A5.

18. *Denver Post* (1993, December 19), pp. A4, A45. The author of this story based his account on a computer search of Denver police records, which revealed that juveniles "attacked" 210 people during June, July, and August of 1993. From the story's context, it appears that this journalist defined juvenile violence broadly to include victims of homicide, forcible rape, aggravated assault, and non-aggravated assault. (The latter category is often omitted from social-scientific discussions of serious youth violence.) Unfortunately, this reporter was killed in a traffic accident a year before we began our research, and consequently, we could not ask for clarification about the data and sources used for this article.

19. *Denver Post* (1993, May 5), p. A22.

20. *Denver Post* (1993, June 11), p. A1.

21. *Denver Post* (1993, June 10), p. A1.

22. *Denver Post* (1993, August 3), p. A1.

23. *Denver Post* (1993, June 11), p. A1.

24. *Denver Post* (1993, May 5), p. A1.

25. *Denver Post* (1993, August 8), p. A86.

26. *Denver Post* (1993, July 31), p. E1.

27. *Denver Post* (1993, August 12), p. A62.

28. *Denver Post* (1993, August 5), p. B9.

29. *Denver Post* (1993, July 13), p. B7.

30. *Denver Post* (1993, July 28), p. A13.

31. *Denver Post* (1993, June 15), p. A14; *Denver Post* (1993, June 23), pp. A1, A11; *Denver Post* (1993, July 1), pp. B1, B4.

32. *Denver Post* (1993, May 4), p. B6. Reprinted with permission.

33. *Denver Post* (1993, August 1), p. C4.

34. *Denver Post* (1993, August 8), p. D1.

35. *Denver Post* (1993, May 6), p. B1.

36. *Denver Post* (1993, June 11), pp. A1, A4, A6; *Denver Post* (1993, July 7), p. A5; *Denver Post* (1993, July 13), p. A6; *Denver Post* (1993, July 20), p. A12; *Denver Post* (1993, July 23), p. A1, A14; *Denver Post* (1993, June 17), p. A21; *Denver Post* (1993, June 23), p. A1; *Denver Post* (1993, July 2), p. A1; *Denver Post* (1993, July 3), p. B1; *Denver Post* (1993, July 30), p. A12; *Denver Post* (1993, July 31), p. A16; *Denver Post* (1993, August 20), p. B1.

37. *Denver Post* (1993, August 10), p. A12; *Denver Post* (1993, September 7), p. A33; *Denver Post* (1993, July 13), p. B3; *Denver Post* (1993, July 30), p. A1; *Denver Post* (1993, August 15), pp. A1, A4; *Denver Post* (1993, September 7), p. A12.

38. *Denver Post* (1993, June 11), p. A26; *Denver Post* (1993, July 29), p. A20; *Denver Post* (1993, July 29), p. A9; *Denver Post* (1993, August 1), C4; *Denver Post* (1993, August 4), pp. A1, A4, A6.

39. *Denver Post* (1993, July 17), pp. A1, A5; *Denver Post* (1993, July 22), p. A16; *Denver Post* (1993, July 25), pp. A1, A6, A26; *Denver Post* (1993, June 15), pp. A1, A4; *Denver Post* (1993, June 17), pp. A1, A27; *Denver Post* (1993, August 2), p. A1.

40. *Denver Post* (1993, July 7), p. A5.

41. *Denver Post* (1993, August 4), p. A32.

42. *Denver Post* (1993, July 12), p. A8.

43. *Denver Post* (1993, September 5), p. A93.

44. *Denver Post* (1993, September 1), pp. F1, F4.

45. *Denver Post* (1993, September 9), p. B7.

46. *Denver Post* (1993, August 4), p. A32.

47. *Denver Post* (1993, August 4), p. A32.

48. Colorado Special Session on Youth Violence. Remarks delivered to House Judiciary Committee (September 9, 1993).

49. Colorado Special Session on Youth Violence. Remarks delivered to Colorado House and Senate (September 7, 1993).

50. Colorado Special Session on Youth Violence. Remarks delivered to Senate Appropriations Committee (September 8, 1993).

51. Colorado Special Session on Youth Violence. Remarks delivered to House Judiciary Committee (September 9, 1993).

52. *Denver Post* (1993, June 23), p. B4.

53. *Denver Post* (1993, June 24), pp. A1, A4.

54. *Denver Post* (1993, September 5), pp. A20, A22.

55. *Denver Post* (1993, July 31), p. A16.

56. *Denver Post* (1993, July 20), p. A12.

57. *Denver Post* (1993, June 17), p. A21.

58. *Denver Post* (1993, July 13), p. A6.

59. *Denver Post* (1993, July 30), p. A12.

60. *Denver Post* (1993, July 3), p. B1.

61. *Denver Post* (1993, August 20), p. B1.

62. *Denver Post* (1993, July 23), pp. A1, A4; *Denver Post* (1993, July 23), p. A1.

63. *Denver Post* (1993, September 10), p. A11.

64. Colorado Special Session on Youth Violence. Remarks delivered to Joint Session (September 7, 1993).

65. Colorado Special Session on Youth Violence. Remarks delivered to Senate Judiciary Committee (September 7, 1993).

66. Colorado Special Session on Youth Violence. Remarks delivered to Senate Judiciary Committee (September 7, 1993).

67. Colorado Special Session on Youth Violence. Remarks delivered to House Appropriations Committee (September 10, 1993).

68. *Denver Post* (1993, June 23), p. A1.

69. *Denver Post* (1993, July 23), p. A1.

70. *Denver Post* (1993, July 1), pp. B1, B4.

71. Colorado Special Session on Youth Violence. Remarks delivered to Joint Session (September 7, 1993).

72. Colorado Special Session on Youth Violence. Remarks delivered to Joint Session (September 7, 1993).

73. Colorado Special Session on Youth Violence. Remarks delivered to Joint Session (September 7, 1993).

74. [Denver] *Westword* (1999, December 2–8), pp. 1, 24, 25, 27, 28, 30, 32.

References

Acland, C. R. (1995). *Youth, murder, spectacle: The cultural politics of "youth in crisis."* Boulder, CO: Westview.

Alexander, J. C. (Ed.). (1985). *Neofunctionalism*. Beverly Hills, CA: Sage.

Alexander, J. C. (1988). *Action and its environments: Toward a new synthesis*. New York: Columbia University Press.

Alexander, J. C. (1990). Core solidarity, ethnic out-groups, and social differentiation. In J. C. Alexander & P. Colomy (Eds.), *Differentiation theory and social change: Comparative and historical perspectives*. New York: Columbia University Press.

Alexander, J. C., & Smith, P. (1993). The discourse of American civil society: A new proposal for cultural studies. *Theory and Society, 22,* 151–207.

Anderson, E. (1990). *Streetwise: Race, class, and change in an urban community*. Chicago: University of Chicago Press.

Bellah, R. (1999, April 6). *Protestants, Catholics, and the common good*. Chester Alter Lecture delivered at Regis University, Denver, CO.

Best, J. (1990). *Threatened children: Rhetoric and concern about child-victims*. Chicago: University of Chicago Press.

Blumer, H. (1971). Social problems as collective behavior. *Social Problems, 18,* 298–306.

Christie, N. (1986). The ideal victim. In E. A. Fattah (Ed.), *From crime policy to victim policy: Reorienting the justice system* (pp. 17–30). New York: St. Martin's Press.

Colomy, P. (1998). Neofunctionalism and neoinstitutionalism: Human agency and interest in institutional change. *Sociological Forum, 13,* 265–300.

Colomy, P., & Kretzmann, M. (1995). Projects and institution building: Judge Ben B. Lindsey and the juvenile court movement. *Social Problems, 42,* 1191–1215.

Colomy, P., & Rhoades, G. (1994). Toward a micro corrective of structural differentiation theory. *Sociological Perspectives, 37,* 547–583.

Durkheim, É. (1973). In R. N. Bellah (Ed.), *Emile Durkheim: On morality and society*. Chicago: University of Chicago Press. (Original work published 1898)

Durkheim, É. (1984). *The division of labor in society.* New York: Free Press. (Original work published 1893)

Durkheim, É. (1995). *The elementary forms of religious life.* New York: Free Press. (Original work published 1912)

Eisenstadt, S. N. (1964). Social change, differentiation, and evolution. *American Sociological Review, 29,* 235–247.

Eisenstadt, S. N. (1995). *Power, trust, and meaning.* Chicago: University of Chicago Press.

Eliade, M. (1959). *The sacred and the profane: The nature of religion.* New York: Harcourt, Brace & World.

Etzioni, A. (2000). Toward a theory of public ritual. *Sociological Theory, 18,* 44–59.

Feld, B. C. (1999). *Bad kids: Race and the transformation of the juvenile court.* New York: Oxford University Press.

Gitlin, T. (1980). *The whole world is watching.* Berkeley: University of California Press.

Glazer, N. (1975). *Affirmative discrimination.* New York: Basic Books.

Gusfield, J. R. (1981). *The culture of public problems: Drinking-driving and the symbolic order.* Chicago: University of Chicago Press.

Huntington, S. (1981). *American politics: The promise of disharmony.* Cambridge, MA: Harvard University Press.

Jacobs, M. D. (1990). *Screwing the system and making it work: Juvenile justice in the no-fault society.* Chicago: University of Chicago Press.

Lipset, S. M. (1996). *American exceptionalism: A double-edged sword.* New York: Norton.

Lorch, R. S. (1983). *Colorado government.* Boulder: Colorado Associated University Press.

Luckenbill, D. (1977). Criminal homicide as a situation transaction. *Social Problems, 25,* 176–186.

Marshall, T. H. (1964). *Class, citizenship, and social development.* Chicago: University of Chicago Press.

Merton, R. K. (1936). The unanticipated consequences of social action. *American Sociological Review, 1,* 894–904.

Merton, R. K. (1968). *Social theory and social structure.* New York: Free Press.

Ogburn, W. F. (1922). *Social change: With respect to culture and original nature.* New York: B. W. Huebsch.

Parsons, T. (1966). *Societies: Evolutionary and comparative perspectives.* New York: Free Press.

Parsons, T. (1971). *The system of modern societies.* Englewood Cliffs, NJ: Prentice Hall.

Parsons, T., & Bales, R. F. (1955). *Family, socialization, and interaction process.* New York: Free Press.

Parsons, T., & Smelser, N. J. (1956). *Economy and society.* New York: Free Press.

Report of the [Colorado] State Auditor. (1999). *Performance audit of Department of Corrections: Youthful Offender System.* Denver: Legislative Services.

Sampson, R. J., & Laub, J. H. (1993). Structural variations in juvenile court processing: Inequality, the underclass, and social control. *Law and Society, 27,* 285–311.

Sasson, T. (1995). *Crime talk: How citizens construct a social problem.* New York: Aldine de Gruyter.

Singer, S. I. (1996). *Recriminalizing delinquency: Violent juvenile crime and juvenile justice reform.* Cambridge, UK: Cambridge University Press.

Smelser, N. (1959). *Social change in the Industrial Revolution.* Chicago: University of Chicago Press.

Smelser, N. (1974). Growth, structural change, and conflict in California higher education, 1950–1970. In N. Smelser & G. Almond (Eds.), *Public higher education in California* (pp. 9–141). Berkeley: University of California Press.

Smelser, N. (1985). Evaluating the model of structural differentiation. In J. C. Alexander (Ed.), *Neofunctionalism* (pp. 113–129). Beverly Hills, CA: Sage.

Snow, D. A., & Benford, R. D. (1988). Ideology, frame resonance, and participant mobilization. *International Social Movement Research, 1,* 197–217.

Stallings, R. A. (1990). Media discourse and the social construction of risk. *Social Problems, 37,* 80–95.

Swidler, A. (1986). Culture in action: Symbols and strategies. *American Sociological Review, 51,* 273–286.

Torbet, P., Gable, R., Hurst, H., IV, Montgomery, I., Szymanski, L., & Thomas, D. (1996). *State responses to serious and violent juvenile crime.* Washington, DC: Office of Juvenile Justice and Delinquency Prevention.

Williams, R. H. (1995). Constructing the public good: Social movements and cultural resources. *Social Problems, 42,* 124–144.

Zelizer, V. A. (1985). *Pricing the priceless child.* New York: Basic Books.

DISCUSSION QUESTIONS

1. This chapter argues that news organizations, like other institutions, are guided by a distinctive institutional logic. The media's institutional logic is structured around newsworthiness. How does the logic of newsworthiness affect the coverage of crime in your town or city? Do some crimes seem to receive substantially more coverage than other crimes? Why? How does the status of crime victims affect that coverage? How might the size of a city and the overall volume of crime influence news coverage? Finally, what distinctive logics inform the functioning of other institutions—for example, science, religion, family, and government?

2. The authors point to the fact that there has been "a virtual sea change in the way American society responds to juveniles who commit chronic or serious crimes." Discuss the logic of the rationale for treating young people differently from adults, and in fact creating a separate court and punishment system for juveniles. Why has this changed in recent years?

3. Many contemporary legislators and policymakers blamed a new breed of vicious teens for the surge in youth violence that occurred between the mid-1980s and mid-1990s. But the rates of youth violence have declined dramatically since 1995. What has happened to this supposedly new breed of offender? Did this new breed of offender ever really exist, or was it primarily a construction of the media and policymakers, a construction subsequently endorsed by the public?

4. Supporters of current "get tough" policies maintain that trying teens in adult (criminal) courts and sending those who are convicted to adult prisons (or to very punitive juvenile institutions) will deter both these offenders and other young people from committing crimes in the future. Do you agree with this argument? Why or why not? If you wanted to test this argument empirically, what type(s) of data would you gather?

5. This chapter makes a case for a neofunctionalist approach to the issue of juvenile offenders. Provide a summary of your understanding of neofunctionalism, including a discussion of how it is related to and how it differs from traditional functionalism. Offer a critical analysis of the way the authors advance their argument for the utility of a neofunctionalist perspective in interpreting Denver's Summer of Violence, the passage of the Youth Offender System, and the institutional form that legislation took.

CHAPTER 6

Why Do African Americans Pay More for New Cars?

A Structural Explanation

Christopher Prendergast

Christopher Prendergast received his BA from Brooklyn College (CUNY) in 1970 and then worked for the New York City Housing Authority for 2 years before pursuing an MA (1974) and a PhD (1979) from Southern Illinois University, Carbondale, where he concentrated on phenomenological sociology, Weber's methodology, Parsons, Lévi-Strauss, and the philosophy of science. For the past decade, he has centered his research on the concept of social structure in classical and contemporary social theory. He is Professor Emeritus of Sociology at Illinois Wesleyan University and a past president of the Midwest Sociological Society.

This chapter develops a structural explanation to account for a disquieting and, on closer inspection, puzzling social fact—that African Americans in the Chicago metropolitan area pay more for new cars of comparable size and quality than do whites—not a few dollars more, but hundreds of dollars more.

I define what a structural explanation is a bit later. For this chapter to succeed in its pedagogical purpose, however, readers should pause here and ask themselves, how is that possible? Most of you have some experience with the retail car business. What factors and circumstances could possibly account for this price disparity?

To spare you from heading off in the wrong direction altogether, I should inform you that the price differences were established by controlled experiment. Whites and blacks, matched for everything except race and gender, bargained for the same (or comparable) cars following the same bargaining script, and still the African Americans paid more—lots more.

While you are puzzling out the why and the how, I will discuss structural explanations in sociology and introduce a few of the concepts I use in this chapter.

Structural Explanation in Sociology

A *structural explanation* is a type of causal explanation that is specifically designed to account for patterns of human actions and choices. These patterns are usually formulated as statistical frequencies and correlations, but any observed regularity or sequence of human behavior and belief can be subject to a structural explanation. A structural explanation takes the observed pattern or outcome as the fact to be explained. It then accounts for the pattern by identifying the social process or processes that produce it. The process usually amounts to a sequence of social interactions that leads each party to make an interdependent choice from a shrinking, often familiar, and even institutionalized menu of options. The process or processes that ultimately account for the pattern operate within a system of social relationships, practices, and beliefs called, appropriately, a *social system.* The process is the way these relationships, practices, and beliefs operate dynamically to structure the choices and actions of individuals. The first step in a structural explanation is to describe the social system(s) whose processes generate the pattern, and the second is to forge a plausible link between the processes and the pattern.

That may sound simple enough, but in practice, both steps are fraught with challenges because social systems crisscross and overlay each other in complex ways. That complexity has to be disentangled by abstraction into a series of interrelated models of structure and process aligned in a causal sequence. In the following explanation, several systems of relationships, practices, and beliefs are aligned into two causal streams that merge in the automobile showroom. One stream flows into the buyer and the other into the seller. The buyer–seller relationship is the social system closest to the decision to pay X amount for a new car. However, it may not be the most important link in the causal sequence. In the following explanation, we will need to go back several levels in the social structure to get a sense of the overlapping social systems involved. On the seller's side, we need to consider the dealership as a social system—the network of dealerships in the metropolitan area; the relationship between dealers and manufacturers; and, ultimately, the dynamics of the international automobile industry as a whole. On the buyer's side, we need to differentiate buyers by social network, community, and class position. Buyer and seller greet one another as bearers and emblems of structural position.

A structural explanation leans heavily on objective structural conditions antecedent to the fact to be explained, but it cannot settle for correlations. It must describe the social processes that unfold in the social situations that structural conditions recurrently generate. The foremost process in our case is one of bargaining. Ultimately, a buyer agrees to pay X for a new car, and a seller agrees to accept that price. Out of those decisions arises the statistical price disparity that we wish to explain.

Bear in mind that the price disparity is an aggregate figure, an average cost difference per car. Because some African American buyers will get better deals than most whites, the explanation needs to identify the conditions and processes that produce that outcome as well as the opposite outcome. Some of these conditions and processes are bound up with individual performance, others with various kinds of empowerments (called social and cultural capital), and others with organizational characteristics and sales practices.

A model or, rather, a collection of models that tries to cover all the conditions and processes responsible for the price disparity would be too complex to present here, even if I had made a complete inventory of them. In fact, there are gaps even in crucial places. To forestall criticism, I admit that the explanation presented here reverts to guesswork in several places.

Because a structural explanation is a form of explanation, rather than a theory in its own right, it necessarily relies on a number of component theories to accomplish its task. The component theories employed here are represented by the following concepts: social capital, cultural capital, status characteristics, typification, power/dependency, and power-balancing operations.

The most important of these concepts, *power/dependency,* is taken from Richard Emerson's (1962) famous essay, "Power-Dependence Relations." Emerson's conception of power is entirely relational: One party's power in a relationship is equal to the other party's dependence on the rewards or resources derived from the relationship. It is significant that dependency is a two-sided concept. A's dependence on B increases proportionally to A's motivational investment in the goals or resources controlled by B, where *resources* refers to anything of value to A (e.g., a new car). Conversely, A's dependence on B decreases to the extent that A finds alternative suppliers of the resource controlled by B (i.e., another car dealer). When relationships are power imbalanced, the party with the greater power is tempted to seek a higher level of reward from the other, whereas the more dependent party is inclined to reduce dependency by seeking other exchange partners, forming a coalition with others in that dependent condition, or adjusting his or her desires and preferences. Emerson calls these strategic responses to dependency *power-balancing operations.* Being first cousin to the law of supply and demand, the concept of dependency provides a powerful conceptual bridge between structural conditions and bargaining processes.

For the concept of *cultural capital,* which refers to the quality and quantity of information that actors can deploy in social interaction, I draw on French sociologist Pierre Bourdieu (1984, 1985). For the concept of *social capital,* which refers to the pool of favors and obligations in one's social network (Prendergast, 2004a), I draw on James Coleman (1988, 1990). *Status characteristics* refers to the attributes commonly associated with statuses such as age, physical attractiveness, class, race, and gender. For my understanding of how status characteristics affect social interaction, I am indebted to Knottnerus (1994, 1997), Ridgeway (1991), Ridgeway and Berger (1988), and Wagner and Berger (1993).

The term *typification* is from Alfred Schutz (1962). It characterizes the degrees of knowledge that people have in different domains of experience. Some things we know in fine detail, others by name only. Both the salesperson and the customer can banter about the wonders of the "computer-controlled ignition system," but neither could explain how it works to an engineer. Having typifications of impressive depth and variety, and the linguistic competence to use them, is what cultural capital is all about. All status characteristics are known through typification.

Underlying the whole explanation is a theory of action derived from Carl Menger (1963) via Max Weber (1947) and developed further by March and Simon (1958), Kahneman, Slovic, and Tversky (1982), and White (1992). Social structure, understood as a phenomenon of levels (Prendergast, 2004b), can be fruitfully represented using the concepts and methods of social network analysis (Burt, 1982, 1992; Knoke & Guilarte, 1994; Willer, 1999). For the concept of structural explanation, I rely on Boudon (1987), Coleman (1987), and Little (1991). Finally, in emphasizing typifications and cultural capital, I try to avoid the pitfalls of structural determinism and reductionism identified by Rubinstein (1986, 2000).

Do these concepts belong together in the same explanation? They come from different theoretical traditions and schools of thought. Should not explanation stem from a single, *consistent* set of concepts, models, and generalizations? That was the belief and the ambition of the founders of sociology and of the great synthesizers who succeeded them. We can only admire these intellectual giants today. Specialized knowledge—the division of labor—makes it impossible for any individual or group of collaborators today to unify knowledge beyond the ramifying organization of the textbook or encyclopedia. To seek sociological explanation in this environment is to seek a scaffold upon which to assemble the concepts, models, generalizations, findings, and paradigmatic explanations that the explainer believes will account for the phenomenon of interest and withstand critical scrutiny.

My scaffold rests on four legs: structural conditions (geographic, demographic, and institutional); the levels of social structure (encapsulated social systems extending from the world system to interpersonal relationships); the social situations in which differentially empowered actors use typifications to make attributions and social comparisons; and the choices and actions that precipitate from these situations. Each leg of the scaffold makes indispensable contributions to the whole. I call the final product a structural explanation because structural conditions and the levels of social structure set up the recurrent social situations in which unfold the processes that, iteratively and over time, produce the social fact to be explained. Relying heavily on rational choice theory and social network analysis, Burt (1982) has called this approach to explanation the "structural theory of action." Because the social situation of choice is buffeted left and right and up and down by social psychological processes of typification, attribution, and social comparison, a more accurate name for the four-legged scaffold employed here might be "the structural-social psychological theory of social action." How's that for a catchy title? If you are wondering where culture fits on the scaffold, it is absorbed into the social psychology.

All that theory for one little explanation? You bet, and that is just the short list. Now let's get back on task. While I have been assembling the concepts that are essential for my explanation, have you been attempting to do something similar?

Some Background Information

So why do African Americans in the Chicago metropolitan area pay hundreds of dollars more for new cars? It must have something to do with race, but what?

Like most facts, this one comes to us preinterpreted. So our first task is to question the interpretation that envelops it. We then marshal some background knowledge and try to work up a sociological explanation of the sort that I am promoting in this chapter. Because much of the information that you need for an alternative explanation is widely known, you should be able to keep a step or two ahead of the argument. However, for those of you who are unfamiliar with the Chicago metropolitan area, let me share two essential bits of information.

First, the Chicago metropolitan area is highly segregated. According to the U.S. Bureau of the Census (1993, pp. 106–107), Chicago was 45% white and 39% black in 1990, whereas its suburbs were 87% white and 6.7% black. But that is just the tip of the iceberg. Most of the black population in Chicago is concentrated in two areas, south and west of downtown. The city is so segregated that 91% of the black population would have to move for everyone to live in an integrated neighborhood (Massey & Denton, 1993, p. 72). Segregation extends into the suburbs as well: The majority of black suburbanites live in segregated towns and neighborhoods just across the city line (Massey & Denton, 1993, pp. 67–74). Two of these suburbs, near the abandoned East Chicago steel mills, are among the 15 poorest suburbs in the entire country (McCarron, 1989, p. 7). The term *hypersegregation* was coined to describe the extreme isolation and concentration of African Americans in metropolitan areas such as Chicago (Massey & Denton, 1993, p. 74).

Segregation may concentrate African Americans geographically, but that does not mean the population is highly integrated. On the contrary, African American social networks tend to be shorter in length (i.e., they do not extend as far into the larger community or the nation); range less widely across the social spectrum; and have fewer links to brokers of jobs, opportunities, and information (Fernández-Kelly, 1995; Patterson, 1998). College graduates who reside in segregated neighborhoods inhabit social networks as contact poor and isolated as those of people who never attended college (Patterson, 1998, p. 153). If segregation undercuts the kind of social capital that grows out of interpersonal contacts across social boundaries, the poverty associated with segregation undercuts the kind of social capital that grows out of cohesive bonds with others. Even though their households include relatively more kin (Allen, 1979; Hays & Mindel, 1973), compared to non-Hispanic whites, African Americans give and receive less help from friends, coworkers, neighbors, and even parents and children, including less transportation assistance (Roschelle, 1997, p. 107). Mutual aid declines with socioeconomic status (Eggebeen & Hogan, 1990; Sarkisian & Gerstel, 2004, p. 829)—a social fact of great significance in Chicago, with its high concentration of poverty in majority black neighborhoods.

The second essential piece of information about Chicago is that the median income of African Americans living in the city was just $20,282 in 1995, compared to $39,520 for the median family in suburban Cook County, Illinois, and $60,686 for the median family in prosperous Du Page County (U.S. Department of Housing and Urban Development/U.S. Bureau of the Census, 1997, p. 23). As a result of both of these conditions, geographical concentration in areas served by public transportation and lower median income, fewer African Americans own cars. Slightly more than 60% of black households in Chicago owned an automobile in 1995. That is a major improvement over the late 1960s, when fewer than 30% owned an automobile (U.S. Department of Housing and Urban Development/U.S. Bureau of the Census, 1997, p. 17). But it is no match for the "collar counties" (a term applied to the five counties that surround the centrally located Cook County in the Chicago metropolitan area), where two- and three-car families are commonplace.

Interesting, you may say. But what do these facts have to do with African Americans paying more for new cars?

Car Price Mystery

Some years ago, economist and law professor Ian Ayres sent a number of "testers" to auto dealerships in the Chicago area. Testers are employees in an experiment designed to detect discrimination against minorities, usually in housing and hiring. In this case, the Ayres team was responding to reports that African Americans paid more for new cars than did whites.

As is customary in this type of study, pairs of testers were matched for age, physical attractiveness, speech, dress, and socioeconomic status (all presented themselves as young professionals). In this case, all of the pairs included a white male; the other member of the pair was a white female, a black male, or a black female. Each member of a tester pair went separately to 90 different dealerships in the metropolitan area. Although the testers did not actually purchase cars, they bargained for the best price they could get and left with an offer in hand. All followed the same negotiating script, which they rehearsed for 2 days to minimize differences in personality and bargaining style. The script called for them to quickly select a car in the predetermined price range, ask how much the seller wanted for it, counteroffer at the wholesale price, then split the difference on subsequent counteroffers. Counteroffering at the wholesale price was supposed to suggest that the tester had done a little homework. That may have worked for the white male testers, but after 180 deals in 90 showrooms, the African American testers wound up agreeing to markups two and three times higher than their white counterparts. The results of this study are shown in column 1 of Table 6.1.

Because only six testers were involved in the study, the reliability of the findings could be challenged. So Ayres replicated the study using 38 testers who struck 404 deals at 225 dealerships (column 2 of Table 6.1). This time, testers were allowed to look at nine types of vehicles, and the script allowed salespersons to talk them up to a bigger car (which is why the markups were higher in the second study). Table 6.1 shows the differences between the average invoice price (roughly the cost of the car to the dealer) and the final bid price by status of tester in the two studies.

Rather amazing and disturbing, isn't it? At the time the studies were undertaken, the income of the median black family in the city was nearly $20,000 less than that of the median family in suburban Cook County and $40,000 less than that of the

Table 6.1   Car Price Markups by Status of Buyer

	1991 Study	*1995 Study*
White male	+$362	+$564
White female	+$504	+$656
Black male	+$783	+$1,665
Black female	+$1,237	+$975

Source: Ayres (1991), Ayres and Siegelman (1995).

median family in Du Page County. Yet car dealers seemingly gave white families a break in price while taking black families to the cleaners. It looks like a prima facie case of discrimination. It certainly suggests that bias against African Americans must run pretty deep in the retail car business. Like exclusionary housing and hiring practices, price discrimination in car sales reinforces segregation and denies African Americans equal treatment and respect.

Yet there is something odd about this case, isn't there? Auto dealers are in the business of selling cars, not enforcing the color line. Salespeople rely on commissions for their livelihood. Both want to move product off the lot. Discriminatory pricing seems like a risky and self-penalizing way to express racial animosity. Even if one could avoid a lawsuit, what sense does it make to risk alienating a customer base as large as 40% of the population of Chicago?

Besides, just how does racial bias account for discriminatory pricing? Do dealers instruct salespeople to bargain in bad faith? Are they trying to enforce segregation by punishing those who cross the color line with higher prices? Do salespeople, acting on their own, just enjoy gouging their black customers? Is it company policy, maverick salespeople, or some deeply ingrained disposition on the part of whites to get the best of blacks when they have the chance?

Perhaps auto sales are like housing sales, where white homeowners may be united in their desire to exclude blacks and realtors who break the ban face retaliation. If the analogy holds, suburban auto dealers try to keep black customers off the lot to ease the discomfort of white buyers, whom they placate further by giving them better deals. If so, the tactic of discriminatory pricing seems as ineffective as it is risky. Black customers take as long as anyone else to strike a deal. As far as race-sensitive whites who come on the premises during the negotiations are concerned, the dealership *is* integrated, whether the deal is struck or not and regardless of the markup. Besides, realtors who discriminate do not just bargain harder with African American buyers. They steer them into black-majority neighborhoods. Car dealers cannot do that without losing the sale.

Chicago suburbs are among the most highly segregated in the country. However, the higher markups were not concentrated in the suburbs. They were just as high at dealerships located in and near majority black neighborhoods and at dealerships owned by blacks (Ayres, 1991, p. 847; Ayres & Siegelman, 1995, p. 315).

If protecting the color line is not the motive behind the higher prices, perhaps the explanation lies in the prejudice of individual salespeople. Everyone in this society has been exposed to racial stereotypes. Perhaps some white salespeople have passed these stereotypes back and forth within their social networks for so long that they cannot distinguish one African American from another anymore. All black customers are the same to them. They all fall for the same sales pitch. They are all equally gullible and uninformed and loose with their money. The testers' knowledge of what the dealer paid for the car, their professional middle-class status, and their businesslike manner of negotiating are all screened out. The biased salespeople just keep interacting with a stereotype. They hardly budge on the price, while the testers keep splitting the difference. Bias wins, and the black testers leave with higher final offers than white testers.

That is a plausible theory with much good social psychology behind it. Many studies of prejudice document an out-group homogeneity effect, an expectation effect, and an assimilation effect (Fiske, 1993; Hilton & von Hippel, 1996). Taken together, these effects mean that prejudiced people operate with stereotypes that resist disconfirmation. But these studies also suggest that these effects diminish through social interaction, that people use more accurate subtypes rather than global stereotypes in practical affairs, and that subtypes eventually displace stereotypes when these practical needs persist (Brewer, 1988). Outcome dependency (relying on a minority for an outcome such as making a sale) also undermines stereotypes (Riley & Fiske, 1991). So does competition (Matheson, Holmes, & Kristiansen, 1991). Finally, being accountable to third parties such as car manufacturers or the local civil rights commission also prompts people to attend to individual differences (Fiske, 1993, p. 174). All this suggests that car salespeople, biased or not, are occupationally predisposed to make finer, more accurate distinctions than the prejudice explanation requires.

However, there is an even stronger reason to doubt this line of explanation: African American testers buying cars from African American salespeople suffered the same markups. The same was true for female buyers and female sellers (Ayres, 1991, p. 847; Ayres & Siegelman, 1995, p. 316). You read that correctly. The race and gender of the salesperson, like the location of the dealership, had no statistically significant effect on the markups.

If higher markups do not kick in at the suburban boundary, and if black and female salespersons extract the same markups as white salesmen, the correlations between race, gender, and car price remain a mystery. Bias/discrimination is a plausible first hypothesis. But try as we might, we cannot figure out the causal process, the step-by-step progression from bias to higher car prices. Before we start formulating an alternative explanation, however, we might ask whether the Ayres team got its facts straight in the first place.

Despite all their precautions, could the testers inadvertently have provoked these results? After all, they were employed to test for discrimination. In a kind of self-fulfilling prophecy, could black and female testers have caved in early in the price negotiations, whereas white male testers held out longer? Perhaps this occurred in the first study, but it did not in the second. The testers in the second study thought they were studying negotiating tactics and did not know that they were being paired with testers of a different race and gender (Ayres & Siegelman, 1995, p. 307).

Alas, the Ayres studies just confirm what has been known since the early 1960s: Poor and minority residents living in segregated areas pay more for everything from furniture and appliances to rent, insurance, and loans (Caplovitz, 1967; see also Alwitt & Donley, 1996). Rather than pick apart the methodology, let us accept the price differentials as substantially correct and try to explain them differently.[1]

Bargaining Power, Capital, and Dependency

Let us begin by reviewing Table 6.1 again. Notice that among whites, the markup on new cars sold to women is also higher than it is for men—a full 40% higher in the first study. Why is that? When I ask my students this question, they usually point out that since they were kids, men and women have looked at cars differently. Notable exceptions aside, men are generally more interested in and knowledgeable about cars and car dealing than women of the same age. Women pay more, my students suggest, because they know less about car models and features, the frauds and bluffs of bargaining, and car culture generally, which has largely remained a male preserve. Studies have shown, however, that this handicap can be offset by coming from a two-car family or being coached by more knowledgeable family members or friends.

Could something like this affect African American car buyers? Here is where the fact that only 30% of black households in Chicago owned a car in the late 1960s, whereas 60% did 20 years later, comes in. Many African Americans going into the dealerships in the years before the Ayres study were first-time car buyers with all the informational deficits that implies. With fewer people in their social networks owning cars, the coaching factor was also minimized.

Do you know that you should research the invoice price of the car in which you are interested before going in for a test drive? I didn't when I bought my first car as a 23-year-old New Yorker. I paid the full sticker price plus a few options, without getting even the floor mats thrown in. According to the Consumer Federation of America (1990, p. 9), approximately one-third of white Americans are as naive about sticker prices as I was. Given their car-ownership rates, it is not surprising that three-fifths of African Americans are as well.

Being carless not only hurts African Americans in the information department, it also limits their ability to drive to the big suburban dealerships with the large inventories, low overhead, and high-volume sales to get a lower bid. Instead, they are stuck with a few dealerships close to home. These dealers soon come to know their customers and get used to pretending that the sticker price is an impartial measure of market value. That is what the testers confronted when they stepped into the showrooms: salespeople and managers accustomed to bargaining down from the sticker price, and not very steeply, either.

Let's call the practical knowledge of car buyers their cultural capital and the number of potential coaches and advisers in their networks their social capital. Let's call the condition of having fewer alternative sources of information, advice, and bids dependency. Capital and dependency are inversely related: Bargaining power increases with social and cultural capital and decreases with dependency. For reasons of residential segregation, median economic standing, network structure, and carlessness, many African American buyers enter the showrooms relatively low in bargaining power. That is just a hard fact, a statistical frequency. But it is a fact associated with race.

In the alternative explanation we are developing here, race is just a rude proxy for bargaining power. The causally relevant conditions on the buyer's side are all the things that affect bargaining power: information about invoice prices, comparable cars, and bargaining tactics; the capacity to visit different dealerships to compare bids and prices; and the quality of social and cultural capital in one's social network—for example, the availability of a "purchase pal" (Furse, Punj, & Stewart, 1984) more knowledgeable than oneself. If these conditions were equal among white and black buyers, price differences in a controlled study such as this would be due to individual differences in personality and negotiating style, situational contingencies, and conditions affecting the dealer's bargaining power and dependency.

Because these conditions are not equal, race *is* a proxy for bargaining power. That puts all African Americans at a disadvantage, even young Buppies (black urban professionals) like our testers. For all the dealers know, these young, well-dressed African Americans are just upwardly mobile, first-generation car buyers, not the savvy negotiators they claim to be. Perhaps that is why the black testers were two-and-a-half times more likely to be asked how they got to the dealership (Ayres, 1995, p. 139). When testers in the second study said that they did not own a car, the final bid was $127 higher. When they said that they had visited another dealership, it was $120 lower (Ayres, 1995, p. 139). Not owning a car means fewer opportunities for price comparison, less experience in price negotiation, and recent upward mobility (read: disposable income and status seeking).[2] In asking these questions, the sellers were seeking clues to dependency and trying to fine-tune their buyer categories.

Sound like we are onto something? Then let's take a quick look at a key social practice that we will return to soon: the sales commission. The higher the price, the higher the commission—that is well-known. But what is not is this: A full 50% of dealer profit comes from just 10% of buyers (Ayres, 1991, p. 854)—those who pay the full sticker price, or close to it, as I did years ago. Given this profit profile, salespeople are on the lookout for the young, the naive, the enchanted, the free spending, and the stuck—whatever their race, class, gender, or favorite breakfast cereal may be.

Rather than trying to protect the color line or being unable to distinguish one African American from another, in all likelihood, the dealerships were only too glad to see the testers—or rather, the demographic stratum that they represented—walk in the door. Young, upwardly mobile African Americans just establishing themselves in dynamic new careers—when asked, the testers described themselves as "systems analysts" in the banking business and as residents of Streeterville, a trendy, upper-middle-class neighborhood in the city—they had profit opportunity written all over them.

Statistically, the African American population in Chicago is relatively weak in bargaining power; race is associated with deficits in cultural and social capital and with greater dependency (i.e., less opportunity to get two or more dealerships into a bidding contest); and the testers represent a young, affluent stratum of the African American population that includes many inexperienced buyers, even if these particular customers seem to have done their homework. Tight-lipped, well-dressed white customers who split the difference between offers are readily typified as knowledgeable, self-reliant negotiators who could easily get a lower bid at another dealership. Socially and behaviorally similar black customers *should* be treated the same—in the abstract. But in the dealer's experience, this combination of buyer attributes is rather rare. To them, the testers' age, race, gender, and socioeconomic status signal "inexperienced buyer with money." Perhaps that is why, when they asked how much the dealer wanted for a car, 29% of the African American testers were told the full sticker price, as opposed to just 9% of white testers (Ayres, 1995, p. 141). In the end, the burden of proof was on them (on the burden of proof assumption, see Berger, Cohen, & Zelditch, 1966). The net result? Final bids that were $400 to $1,100 higher than white testers were offered for comparable new cars.

How does being African American or female fit into this explanation? To the extent that dealers associate these statuses with inadequate knowledge, less opportunity for price comparison, and lack of negotiating savvy, they matter a lot. If they also harbor typifications about the buyer's gullibility, spending habits, and cave-in point based on race and gender alone, they matter. But mostly, they count when the typical minority buyer *actually is* in a poor bargaining position. Residential segregation in areas of low economic opportunity, visible social mobility limited to members of two-income families and a small but growing upper middle class, relative carlessness, and weak advice networks—these are the structural conditions that make dark skin a rough-and-tumble proxy for low bargaining power. It is not an accurate measure or a sufficient one, and certainly not a fair one. However, it is a measure that hits the mark often enough to acquire presumptive validity.

The good news in this analysis, as opposed to the utter pessimism of the bias/discrimination account, is that a minority car buyer who is well informed, talks about offers tendered elsewhere, and is willing to walk out the door should prompt the salesperson to reflect on his or her own bargaining position: the other missed opportunities this week, the growing inventory problem, the lost commission, and the sales manager's chagrin. Projecting upper-middle-class standing and following a good bargaining script, as the testers did, is not enough. Given the structural handicaps of the African American population in the city as a whole, to get equal treatment one has to prove—through the social performance of bargaining—that one is no mere arriviste but someone with sufficient financial, social, and cultural capital to play the game well.

The alternative explanation we are developing here moves bias and discrimination to the periphery of the argument, but it does not deny their reality. Car dealers and salespeople may well hold overgeneralized, disparaging beliefs about African Americans. Such beliefs are easily grafted onto unequal outcomes and used to excuse the practices that generate them (Ridgeway & Berger, 1988). However, our alternative account can also explain why black and female salespeople seek the same markups; why women pay more; and why blacks with equal financial, social, and cultural capital bargain nearly as effectively as whites with similar resources. I say "nearly" because, statistically, a large portion of the African American community is in a poor bargaining position, and dealers hit the full-sticker jackpot too often to alter their bargaining approach. As a result, even savvy African American buyers are going to pay slightly more on average than comparable whites, whose racial status signals a better bargaining position before they utter a single word.

The Contexts of Dealer Dependency

My purpose in introducing the car price mystery is not just to tickle your sociological imagination but also to illustrate the principles of structural explanation in sociology. I did that so far by showing how background structural conditions, such as residential segregation, carlessness, and recent social mobility, increase buyer dependency; reduce the cultural and social capital of black social networks; and allow sellers to use external status characteristics, such as age, class, race, and gender, as indicators of bargaining power. Yet, aside from seller typifications, the axis of explanation mainly ran down the buyer's side of the relationship. For a proper structural explanation, we need to do at least two additional things: look at the dependencies on the seller's side of the relationship and contextualize the buyer-seller relationship by looking at the retail car business more globally. A good structural explanation always strives to chart all the lines of social causation that collapse on the immediate context of action—in this case, the bargaining situation.

Let us resume, then, where we left off—with the discovery that in the Chicago area, 50% of dealer profit comes from just 10% of buyers. As you recall, we used that statistic to explain why certain social statuses provoke so many full sticker-price offers. However, this statistic describes a condition of seller dependency as well. In the good old days of the 1950s, when the Big Three automakers had a swell little oligopoly going, dealers did not rely on 10% of sales for their livelihood. They expected, and got, markups in the 20% to 25% range, even more on hot new models (Yates, 1983, p. 220). There was some dickering over the price but not the wide disparities that we see today.

Flipped around, that statistic signifies a continental shift in dependency. Empowered by higher cultural and social capital and assisted by national organizations such as the Consumer Federation of America, which broadcasts coaching tips to its members, and credit unions, which provide wholesale car prices to their members for the asking, it has become increasingly more familiar for buyers to bargain dealers down to markups of just $300 to $500 per vehicle. During the mid-1990s, for example, members of the Chicago Automobile Association could order a new car through a dealer consortium for just 5% above the invoice price. One consequence of this new landscape of dealer dependency is the somewhat desperate attempt to exploit whatever buyer dependencies are left to dealers, such as the naïveté of first-time car buyers. We saw how that affects African Americans in Chicago, almost two-fifths of whom are still carless, but that is obviously a rearguard action. What happened to the retail car business since the glory days of 25% markups?

Competition happened, that's what. In 1950, the United States produced 80% of the world's automobiles; by 1980, the U.S. share fell to 30% (Yates, 1983, p. 15). In the spring of 1999, the world's top 40 car makers had enough industrial capacity to produce 23 million more cars a year than consumers could buy. With overcapacity like that, a price war would decimate the industry. To forestall that outcome, car makers are acquiring each other at an unprecedented rate. The mergers of Daimler-Chrysler, Ford-Volvo, and Nissan-Renault in 1998 and 1999 mark the beginning of a new merger wave that could end with just six or eight global firms dominating the industry ("The Car Industry," 1999, p. 24).

These trends first hit American shores in the 1970s, when European and Japanese imports began to crowd the domestic market. Smaller, cheaper, sleeker, more fuel-efficient, better engineered, and better assembled foreign imports forced the domestic car industry into a crisis of reengineering, marketing, and downsizing that lasted two decades, cost more than 400,000 jobs, and—in conjunction with similar developments in the steel industry—turned the ring of manufacturing cities around the Great Lakes into the Rust Belt.[3]

How did the crisis in manufacturing affect the retail car business? It left dealers holding the bag, for one thing. As Detroit mass produced one overpriced dud after another, dealers found themselves with unsold inventory, unhappy customers, and declining product loyalty. Each new model and engineering makeover also meant additional employee training, new service equipment, and more advertising—costs borne by the dealer and passed on to customers in annoying new fees and charges. Getting an edge on the competition often meant moving the dealership to a bigger and better location, keeping more inventory on hand, and borrowing at high interest rates to finance the upgrades. By the early 1990s, the cost of marketing a new car had risen to $1,500 per vehicle (Wysner, 1994, p. 95). With ever-rising prices, approximately 800 models to choose from, and a wide range of quality on the market, savvy consumers began to shop around and to seek the aid of guidebooks and consumer organizations.

Caught between manufacturers and consumers, both of whom wanted lower prices, dealers had little choice but to deal. As markups slipped, dealer profits slipped with them, from 9% in 1985 to 6.5% a decade later, a difference of approximately $300 per car (Darin, 1996). In 1985, new car sales accounted for 78.5% of dealer profit. Ten years later, they accounted for only 6.3% of dealer profit; used car sales and the parts and service business accounted for 47.8% and 45.9% of dealer profits, respectively (Naughton, 1996, p. 72). Many dealers did not make it. More than 1,000 closed their doors during the recession years of 1990 and 1991 alone ("Rabbit Is Poor," 1994, p. 68). Caught in the profit squeeze, many dealers either sold their franchise or used it to acquire trade-ins for their used car operations, where a quick turnaround could still garner a 25% markup, just like the old days.

The Social Structure of Dealer Dependency

Funny thing, context. Just flipping a statistic around or looking at a particular relationship from a more encompassing standpoint can dramatically alter your understanding of how things fit together. What have we learned from this contextualization of the buyer-seller relationship? Just this: The Ayres studies were undertaken at a particular point in time—in the midst of a recession that would close 1,000 dealerships, one of a series of recessions within a longer cycle of price deflation, industrial restructuring, dealership consolidation, and market segmentation. Dealership dependence was at a peak, but so was the need to exploit buyer dependence for every last buck. Despite the price differences shown in Table 6.1, in all likelihood, the markups for African Americans and women were lower at the time of the Ayres studies than at any time in American history.

Perhaps this thought occurred to you as well: Just as bargaining power varies among categories of consumer, so it must vary among categories of dealer. Insofar as the buyer-seller relationship (like any relationship) exhibits the property of power-dependence, various things can shift the balance of power one way or the other. We saw how buyers can overcome dependency: by finding a purchase pal more knowledgeable than themselves, by obtaining multiple bids, and by joining the Consumer Federation or a credit union. Dealers can lessen their dependence on consumers and manufacturers, too, by adopting the right power-balancing strategies. To the extent that they succeed, dealers can ride the trends, even prosper by them. To the extent that they fail, they suffocate under the combined weight of indebtedness, price competition, and consumer dissatisfaction.

The question for us is, to what extent do the markups in Table 6.1 reflect the array of dealer strategies for overcoming dependence? In the main, the answer should be clear: African Americans should do better with dealerships that are unable to devise successful power-balancing strategies. Now, I do not have the data to test this hypothesis, but I can at least lay out the logic behind it. Because my purpose is to illustrate the principles of structural explanation, that will be good enough, although hardly ideal.

What we might call "the social structure of dealer dependency" is a heuristic model of five types of dealership, differentiated by sales volume, organization of the sales staff, and degree of dependence. Each type of dealership adopted different power-balancing strategies for overcoming dependence, which vary in their effectiveness. I summarize the model in Table 6.2. In the last column, I estimate how buyer and seller dependencies intersect. That is, I *guess* what the markups by race and gender would be under the five conditions of dealer dependence, using the data in Ayres's (1995) second study as a guideline.

The first type of dealership is the traditional franchise, which comes in two varieties. The first is a low-volume, family-run operation with a small entrepreneurial sales staff whose income is derived from commissions (sometimes supplemented by a small salary). The traditional entrepreneurial salesperson is, in effect, an independent contractor hired by the dealer to resell merchandise for a cut of the profit (typically 25% of the markup). Highly vulnerable to price competition in recent years, the low-volume traditional franchise exploits buyer dependency where it finds it, but its own dependency is such that it must concede on price in the face of buyer resistance.

The second type of dealership is the traditional franchise as well, except it has a higher sales volume and its own niche of loyal, well-heeled customers. It survives on repeat business and customer service, making its customers feel special and elite—and disloyal and cheap for seeking bargains.

Table 6.2 Dealer Dependence by Type of Dealership

Sales Volume	Type of Dealership	Sales Force Organization	Power-Balancing Strategy	Dependence	Bargaining Strategy	Markups by Status of Buyer
Low	Traditional franchise	Entrepreneurial	None; withdrawal	High	Exploit dependence, cave-in	WM, $350 WF, $415 BF, $620 BM, $1,090
	Traditional franchise (niche)	Entrepreneurial	Status-giving	Low	"Fair price" for quality service	WM, $1,050 WF, $1,225 BF, $1,815 BM, $2,750
Medium	Dual-franchise (import)	Entrepreneurial or team	Network extension	Medium-high in weaker; low in stronger	Exploit, cave-in (weaker); "fair price" for quality car (stronger)	WM, $750 WF, $870 BF, $1,290 BM, $2,285 (average)
	High-volume (team)	Team concept	Coalition formation (internal)	Medium-high	Exploit dependence, hold the line, discount when necessary	WM, $500 WF, $585 BF, $860 BM, $1,490
High	Megadealer	Entrepreneurial in small shop; team in large shop	Coalition formation (external)	Medium (in 1990)	Strategy pegged to size of franchise; discount in high-volume shops	WM, $650 WF, $760 BF, $1,020 BM, $1,950

Note: Numerical values are hypothetical, reflecting the relative dependencies in column 5 (Dependence). WM indicates white male; WF, white female; BF, black female; BM, black male.

The third is the dual-franchise operation. Its response to the foreign competition is to hop on board. This strategy can produce headaches and higher costs; many dual-franchise operations had to build separate showrooms for their domestic and import lines to keep salespeople from talking up the high-markup imports at the expense of the domestic franchise (Yates, 1983, p. 227). But it allows the owner to shift resources to the stronger franchise as market conditions dictate.

The fourth type of dealership uses a "sales team" approach to increase the volume of transactions while keeping labor costs down. In this type of shop, the first salesperson you meet handles the car selection process and steers you into the office, where the "closer" and the sales manager work the angles to maximize dealer profit on each aspect of the transaction (car price, trade-in, financing, and down payment) (for an insider account, see Parrish, 1992). The commission is then split between the salesperson and the closer (and sometimes the sales manager). In effect, the team concept allows a coalition of insiders to corral commission income at the expense of entry-level personnel. Dealer dependency remains fairly high and markups fairly low, but the higher sales volume carries the company.

The final type of dealership seeks to control price competition by gaining a retail monopoly in the franchise. With 10 to 20 showrooms in its fleet, the megadealership can achieve economies of scale in personnel, inventory, and financing, not to mention greater leverage over manufacturers and consumers. In the future, the megadealer may go head-to-head with corporate retailers, selling all makes and models of cars on a fixed-price basis (for a discussion of this impending "revolution in retailing," see "Angst for the Angstroms," 1997, p. 56; Naughton, 1996). When this happens, the megadealer is likely to adopt similar sales and commission practices (Simison & Suris, 1997; Taylor, 1997). In the early 1990s, however, few high-volume dealers had anything approaching a retail monopoly. At that time, the nascent megadealership was indifferent to sales organization. It retained both entrepreneurial and sales team forms as it found them and relied on sales managers to limit and coordinate discounts.

So those were the kinds of dealership the testers approached with their common bargaining script during the recession of 1990 and 1991, matched for everything except race and gender. Some dealers were teetering on the edge of bankruptcy, others were cushioned by their import franchise or loyal customer base, and still others were learning to live with lower profit margins by reorganizing their sales staffs or acquiring the competition. Now, we can pull both sides of the explanation together. Where they meet is in the bargaining process. There, in the real-time, face-to-face situation of social interaction, buyer and seller dependencies confront each other, and seller typifications of buyers are put to the test.

From Both Sides Now: The Bargaining Process

The testers' bargaining script allows us to develop a simplified model of the bargaining process. In the model, the 60- to 75-minute interaction is divided into three phases. Phase 1, devoted to information exchange and car selection, concludes with the seller's initial offer. Phase 2 begins with the tester's counteroffer at the invoice price and concludes with the seller's second offer. Phase 3 includes all subsequent rounds of price negotiation, concluding with the seller's final offer.

Given the testers' split-the-difference method of price negotiation, the crucial moments in the bargaining process are all controlled by the seller: the initial offer, the second offer, and the final offer. That is just what we want, of course, but we do need a way to represent or model the seller's decision-making process. The seller is a composite of up to 225 salespeople, so our model has to be highly generalized and fitted to our explanatory purpose. It can be made slightly more concrete by taking into account the five types of dealership and their associated bargaining strategies. To the extent that there is a good fit between the salesperson and the organization, we then have five sellers, or rather, five models of seller decision processes. Finally, we need to put some thoughts inside the sellers' heads as they interact with the testers. The thoughts are mostly tactical in nature, but they also involve typifications of car buyers; external status characteristics such as race and gender (provisional proxies for bargaining power); and the expectations and reactions of others, especially peers and supervisors.

This is the final step of our long explanatory journey, where it all comes together. Let us walk through it phase by phase.

Phase 1

Recall that the testers quickly select a car. In the second study (the one we are following here), they also allow the sellers to talk them into the deluxe model or a larger car. During this phase, the salesperson gathers information about the tester's occupation, car knowledge, and ability to pay. The tester's speech, dress, and residential neighborhood also provide clues to socioeconomic status. What the salesperson, particularly the traditional entrepreneurial salesperson, is looking for is the "qualified buyer" (Parrish, 1992), a person with money who is ready to buy right away. A qualified buyer who has not shopped around much, is committed to a certain make and model of car, and knows or cares little about bargaining may be called a "prime profit opportunity." Young, first-time car buyers often fall into this category (Parrish, 1992). The testers do not ask for a test drive, nor do they want time to think it over. After selecting the car they want, they ask, "How much do you want for it?"

Qualified buyers, right? If the women sounded insecure or smitten, they would be prime profit opportunities, for sure. They do not, so their shopping alone could be a sign of self-confidence. Given the widely known problems of black unemployment and blocked social mobility, the black male's age and socioeconomic status suggest recent and perhaps dramatic social mobility. He could really want this car. As for the white guy, he seems a little taciturn and businesslike. Probably a "retail shopper" (Furse et al., 1984), a guy who shops around for a good price.

However, buyer typifications and typifications about age, race, class, and gender are not the only factors at work here. There is also the dealership's market position, its access to customers like the testers, its policy on discount pricing, and its sales targets for the week, not to mention the salesperson's stake in the matter, the sales commission. The greater the dealer dependence, the less it can afford to lose the sale. The niche and import dealers and some megadealer showrooms can afford to highball, but if the high-volume and low-volume shops try the same thing, they will have to back off quickly. Many African Americans coming into the dealerships are upwardly mobile, first-time car buyers. If anyone is to be highballed, it should be them.

Phase 2

A counteroffer at the wholesale price, a markup of zero! This is the crucial phase for the seller because buyer typifications have to be reassessed quickly. The salesperson's least favorite categories of buyer include "the negotiator" and "the retail shopper" (Furse et al., 1984). Both will walk away if they do not get a good bargain. The white guy now looks like a negotiator, and perhaps the white woman as well. The black woman moves up from profit opportunity to retail shopper, and the black male, too. How quickly the tables turn! How many low-markup sales did the sales manager approve this month? Not many to black males, that's for sure. Or to black females, for that matter. Then again, perhaps they have been coached. Or read that article in *Consumer Reports*—the white guy knows his way around, and the white woman is surely a feminist. How do these people stack up against our usual customers?

Phase 3

When the testers split the difference between their initial counteroffer and the seller's second offer, a minimum profit is assured at all dealerships. However, although that has become all too customary at the low-volume and high-volume (team) dealerships, it does not cut the mustard at the niche, import, and megadealer showrooms. By this time, the salesperson is committed to an array of buyer and status typifications, most of them reinforced by the prevailing occupational culture, particularly in shops in which exploiting buyer dependency is considered playing by the rules in a dog-eat-dog world. So the bargaining continues for another round or two until a deal is struck or the seller refuses to discount any further.

The last column of Table 6.2 shows how the balance of dependencies works out theoretically. The dollar figures are hypothetical. They are the markups I imagine the testers would receive at that type of dealership. In the middle of the table, you will find the terms *withdrawal, status-giving, network extension*, and *coalition formation*. These terms refer to the four power-balancing operations in Richard Emerson's (1962) theory of power dependency. The correspondence between the dealers' organizational adaptations and Emerson's four responses to dependency is striking.

Loose Ends

That completes the task I set for this chapter, but because we invested so much time in this explanation, perhaps we should use what we learned to tidy up a few loose ends.

Do you recall Ayres's finding that the race and gender of the salesperson had no effect on the markups? That is what led us to reject the bias/discrimination account. Does that finding make better sense now? I think it should, given what we learned about the types of dealership. The marginalization of the low-volume dealership and the spread of the sales team concept dramatically affected the occupation of car selling. Today, car salespeople have less autonomy than ever before and less room to vary their bargaining style. Their bargaining behavior is shaped by the kind of dealership they work for, particularly the way the sales force is organized. Three consequences of these occupational changes are relevant here.

One is lower income. Between 1974 and 1996, the inflation-adjusted income of car salespeople fell by 14% (Darin, 1996, p. 38). In commission-only shops today, the salesperson's salary averages just $24,000 to $28,000 a year, compared to the industrywide average of $35,000 (Henry, 1996, p. 54). Care to guess where the losses were concentrated? Right, in the smaller, traditional franchises and in entry-level positions in the high-volume dealerships. A second, related change is high employee turnover—50% in 1990 (Bohn, 1991, p. 1) and 61% during the economic recovery of 1993 to 1996 (Darin, 1996, p. 38).

A third trend follows directly from the previous two: the influx of female and African American salespeople. More than one-fifth of the salespeople in Ayres's second study were nonwhite (Ayres, 1995, p. 135). As the new faces on the lot, women and blacks would bear the brunt of the occupational restructuring and diminished income, a pattern often associated with occupational desegregation by race and gender (Reskin & Roos, 1990, p. 80).

Why do the race and gender of the salesperson have no effect on the markups? Female and African American salespeople hired by a megadealer follow the same script as other employees. Those joining the sales team suffer split commissions, so they need high markups just to scrape by. Those hired by traditional franchises either exploit buyer dependency or enjoy uncertain incomes of $24,000 to $28,000 a year or less. Those lucky enough to be hired by the low-dependency niche and import dealers find the testers' bargaining style—counteroffering at the invoice price—just as offensive as their white male colleagues do. In short, the occupational position of the salesperson, the position of the dealership in the marketplace, and the give and take of the bargaining process determine the deals that salespeople offer to their customers, not the seller's race and gender.

Like their white counterparts, female and African American salespeople have little control over structures, practices, and processes that predated their arrival—the franchise system, the sales commission, and the bargaining script—or the structural conditions affecting the industry in which they work—the distribution of social classes and populations across city and suburb, macroeconomic trends and conditions, or the social structure of dealer dependency. Nor do they control the social and cultural capital and dependency of their customers, black or white. Can we really expect these powerless newcomers to risk their own income and job security in a counter-institutional campaign to ensure that all customers pay the same price for the same car, regardless of their bargaining power or performance in the bargaining situation?

That would be a quixotic effort, given the institutions and practices of the industry. Yet the franchise system and all its associated practices may be swept away by the impending "revolution in retailing" (Naughton, 1996). That would be an ironic development because the initiators of this transformation are interested not in social justice but in the more efficient accumulation of capital. Nevertheless, the passage of a social system in which some people are compelled to exploit the lower social and cultural capital and higher dependency of others for a share of the markup will indicate a small step toward a society in which all people are afforded equal concern and respect.

Conclusion

I introduced the car price mystery to illustrate the principles of structural explanation in sociology. The explanation, such as it was, was highly informal. Normally, one would define concepts and diagram the cause-and-effect relations with greater precision. It was also highly generalized. The car buyers and salespeople we talked about were mere stick figures (for flesh and blood, see Lawson, 1996). Moreover, without original data on seller typifications of African American car buyers pegged to social class, the discussion of race as a proxy for bargaining power remains hypothetical. Finally, we do not know the characteristics of the Chicago dealerships (traditional franchise, sales team, etc.) that sell the largest number of cars to African Americans. As a result, we cannot connect the two strands of the explanation as tightly as we need to do. That step, too, was hypothetical. Despite these shortcomings, I think our explanation makes better sense of the data than the bias/discrimination account or Ayres's (1995) own "willingness to pay" explanation.[4]

Let me close with a few encouraging remarks to student readers and a hint to their professors. C. Wright Mills (1958) once came within a hairbreadth of identifying structural explanation with the sociological imagination. Perhaps he overstated the case, but structural explanation satisfies an intellectual imperative deeply rooted in the discipline. In contrast to psychology and economics, which are (subspecialties aside) individualistic, law seeking, and ahistorical, sociology has been historical, holistic, and process seeking since Auguste Comte first chatted about social statics and social dynamics in 1839. Nowhere more than in the United States is this true, where figures such as Cooley (1909, 1918) and Mead (1934) ditched the language of statics and dynamics in favor of social organization and social process and developed a sociological social psychology that made each a reciprocal phase of the other. Since then, every generation of social theorists and researchers has reworked the structure/process formula in different ways, trying to find the best mix of composite theories or the synthesis that will bring the search to an end. What I called above the "structural-social psychological theory of social action" is just another riff on this familiar melody.

If structural explanation is so central to the sociological imagination, perhaps undergraduates should be encouraged to try one on for size. As the car price mystery shows, the form is easy to adopt. All you need, for starters, is some conception of the levels of social structure; a knack for identifying social systems and mapping them onto the levels scheme; and a sense of how social relationships, beliefs, and practices fit together dynamically to generate the facts you seek to explain. (The simplest levels scheme is the bi-level one of macro and micro [Coleman, 1987]. Slightly more realism can be gained by the addition of a meso level [Maines, 1982].

A six-level scheme has an intuitive appeal all its own [Prendergast & Knottnerus, 1994]. Systems theorists are particularly adept at levels construction [Bertrand, 1972; Pattee, 1973; Simon, 1981].)

Of course, you need other things, as well as a load of factual information, some composite theories for understanding the key processes, and a lot of time for research. Oh, and a good problem to work on, too. To accumulate factual material and find something interesting to explain, students may wish to return to aspects of the same research problem in different courses—for example, why priest resignations in the Catholic Church spiked after Vatican II (Seidler, 1979). To assemble the composite theories, students may need to approach the theory course differently. Perhaps it is not just an exercise in intellectual history. Time is always scarce, but if two or three students work on the same explanation, using an effective division of labor . . .

There is one other thing students can do to make the task of structural explanation more manageable: develop simple models. Use Marx or Durkheim for the macrotheory and Mead, Emerson, or Dorothy Smith for the microtheory. Remember, you are trying to develop a chain of social causation. Pick the composite theories that get the job done. Which ones you select will depend in part on the social facts you want to explain. Cultural capital may not help you with priest resignations, although a theory of identity might. Just keep in mind Burt's (1992) dictum—"causation resides at the intersection of social relations" (p. 2)—if your theoretical musings wander far afield. Sociology allows enormous freedom in theory selection. Yet the choice of composite theories is never arbitrary. If you think otherwise, read Burt's dictum again.

The real payoff in structural explanation, even with the gaps and hypotheticals, is the way it pulls things together. When you finally assemble all the parts, you really *understand* something. You see how a social system *works*. And that is the point, isn't it?

Postscript (2004)

The explanation you just read was bounded in time, space, and scope by the car price data that law professor Ian Ayres collected in metropolitan Chicago in the early 1990s. Much has changed since then, far too much to review in a brief postscript. The changes would make worthy topics for collaborative student research, though. One team could examine the changes in African American communities, social networks, and social and cultural capital in order to estimate the degree of buyer dependency today. Another team could focus on the changes in the social structure of dealer dependency. With faculty help, both teams could develop better indicators of dependency than I employed. In this postscript, I limit myself to a simple empirical question: Do African Americans still pay more for new cars a decade after Ayres's studies, or has the racial disparity narrowed somewhat or even disappeared altogether?

The question continues to be researched, although no one has replicated the paired-testers methodology of Ayres's studies. That methodology has many virtues, but it failed to see that sending Buppie testers into the showrooms would trigger a target-specific set of seller typifications, even if the sellers were themselves African American. Other types of controlled comparison study using actual sales data were conducted in the late 1990s, however. I won't hold you in suspense. African Americans still pay hundreds of dollars more for cars of the same size and sticker price, even after controlling for a variety of differences among buyers that reduce the disparity somewhat.

In a well-designed study using a random sample of 700,000 car sales in 1999, Scott Morton, Zettelmeyer, and Silva-Risso (2003) found that African American car buyers paid $1,700 over invoice price relative to nonminority Americans, a markup bonus of 30%. Controlling for income, education, region, type of car, and a host of other things, they reduced the initial price difference to approximately $500 on the average car. They also found a residual "price premium" for women of $100 but did not report differences between African American males and females. The price disparity persists.[5]

Scott Morton et al. (2003) did not stop with that finding. They also obtained sales data from the top company in Internet referrals. This company has contracts with 5,000 of the country's 22,000 dealerships. In exchange for a fee paid by the dealer, it obtains basic information from the buyer and then solicits a bid for the make and model of car that the buyer is interested in from the nearest dealerships in its network. Race can be inferred from name and address, but apparently little of that occurred because *the price disparity virtually disappeared in online car shopping.*

Makes your head spin, doesn't it? If white Americans treat people of African ancestry differently just because they are black, name and address should be enough to trigger price discrimination. That does not happen because disparate treatment, to the extent that it exists, is situationally conditional. In online shopping, the buyer-seller relationship has been altered by the introduction of a third party. The largely impersonal relations between the referral company and its affiliated dealerships insulate minority buyers from predatory pricing. These dealerships establish Internet sales departments that, by contractual agreement, operate separately from the rest of the showroom. The Internet salesperson, who is not supposed to handle walk-in traffic, is paid by sales volume, not a percentage of the markup (Scott Morton et al., 2003). The sales process has been standardized and reduced to procedures. Most of the contact between the customer and the Internet salesperson occurs by phone over content dictated by the paperwork that the referral company helps the customer to fill out, up to and including the financing. Ideally, the online buyer just shows up at the dealership to sign the contract and pick up the car. After the sale, the referral company surveys buyers to gauge their satisfaction with the process. Dealerships that try to restructure the deal when they get the buyer on the premises may be dropped from the network, although referral company dependency often precludes that outcome. (Dealer compliance is the weak link in the system.) Finally, the dealers who affiliate with the network are precisely those high-volume dealerships known to underprice the competition slightly (Zettelmeyer, Scott Morton, & Silva-Risso, 2001).

In short, the relative anonymity and routinization of the sales process insulate minority buyers. Sellers are denied the opportunity to deploy their well-honed buyer typifications that, when confirmed, lead to the extraction of increasingly higher markup from the timid, the uninformed, and the credulous of all races and creeds. The key structural difference is the absence of bargaining. Online shopping is not color-blind, but it neutralizes buyer dependency arising from structural inequities in social and cultural capital. It does not offer the same vehicle to all customers at the same price, as the revolution in retailing promised to do, but it standardizes the bids that a single dealership makes to a third party (the referral company), which has the effect of equalizing prices among demographic groups.

Online shopping is no panacea. Few car sales are transacted online. Although more equalized, markups are higher than savvy bargainers can get on their own— that is, by dealing in person. Buying a car online saves consumers only approximately $450 on the average car (Scott Morton et al., 2003), but it benefits less savvy bargainers more (Zettelmeyer et al., 2001)—a real advantage for many buyers, particularly first-timers. Alas, like other resources, Internet access is unequally distributed by class, race, and region. Whereas 62% of Asian Americans and 43% of nonminority whites used the Internet for comparison shopping at the turn of the 21st century, only 39% of Hispanics and 27% of African Americans did so ("Minorities' Internet Usage," n.d.). The Internet may level the playing field for some, but the majority of African American buyers continue to have to fend off seller typifications in the showrooms.

They have a lot more fending off to do than we realized, too. It turns out that the price disparities we have been discussing—$564 to $1,665 in Ayres's 1995 study and $350 to $500 under different control conditions in the Scott Morton et al. 2001 and 2003 studies—*underestimate by half* the extent of the disparity because none of them factored in finance charges.

Car makers finance 45% to 50% of car sales through their own assurance operations (car financing operations). When you separate borrowers by race, and control for the usual sources of variation, the markups on African American borrowers are double those of whites—$970 per contract versus $462, a difference of $508, at one manufacturer's lending arm (Ayres, 2001). Part of the difference comes from poorer African Americans borrowing more money for longer periods of time. The rest comes from higher interest rates (after controlling for credit risk) and hidden charges. In the first controlled study that takes into account both sale price and finance charges, Ayres (2002) examined racial disparities in 1,000 "consummated sales" at a single dealership in Atlanta, Georgia. (Half of its customers were black and half were white.) He found that African American females paid markups that were $505 higher than white males on sale price and $589 higher in finance charges, all other things being equal. Excess profits on African American males were higher than on white males, too—$405 more on the car and $471 more on the financing.

African Americans continue to pay more for new cars. Economists have struggled for two decades to explain why. Hemmed in by the premises of rational choice and consumer sovereignty, the best they can offer is "willingness to pay." Perhaps sociologists, with our theoretical ears perked to issues of structure and process and a 70-year head start in social psychology, should give it a try.

Postscript (2010)

In the previous postscript, I reviewed the ongoing scholarship documenting the fact that African Americans pay more for new cars and the loans that finance them. In this postscript, I examine recent developments on the *seller's* side of the buyer-seller relationship, the side of the dealerships and manufacturers. If you saw the headlines coming out of Detroit in 2008 and 2009, you know the developments to which I am referring. Record quarterly losses in the billions of dollars. Nose-diving share prices. Disappearing cash reserves. Government bailouts of General Motors and Chrysler Motors. Bankruptcy. Restructuring under the stern guidance of a White House task force. Factory closings. Dealership terminations. Layoffs in the tens of thousands. Entire car brands extinguished or sold off.

The collapse of the U.S. automobile industry might have been the biggest story since 9/11, except it wasn't. It was overshadowed by an even bigger, more spectacular, and more terrifying story that coincided with it—the simultaneous (because they were interdependent) collapses of the housing bubble, the credit bubble, and the stock market bubble, which together almost brought the U.S. banking system to ruin. Nine trillion dollars of wealth evaporated into air as overleveraged financial titans scrambled to sell off toxic assets and recapitalize themselves by hoarding cash and tightening credit, thereby triggering a massive credit crunch that sucked the economy into recession and the two car makers into bankruptcy. My aim in this postscript will be to make both economic and sociological sense of these developments.

In some respects, the collapse of General Motors and Chrysler is an oft-told tale, a tale of overproduction, contraction, and "creative destruction" (Schumpeter, 1950). In other ways, it is a uniquely *postindustrial* story, the story of a crisis in "casino capitalism," a capitalism in which debts never get repaid, just refinanced, or better yet, repackaged and sold off as interest-bearing securities. I will narrate both stories, but I am more intrigued by the second. As I will recount, Chrysler and General Motors had a series of painful interactions with Wall Street firms shortly before the financial meltdown provoked the worst contraction in auto sales since the oil embargoes of the 1970s. I will close by exploring the consequences of these developments for the social structure of dealer dependency, the concept that played so prominent a role in the second half of this chapter. Between the credit crunch, the ensuing recession, and the restructurings of the two bankrupt car makers, nearly 2,500 dealerships went belly up, got acquired by an auto superstore, or had their franchise revoked by the manufacturer (Harris, 2009a; Sawyers, 2009). A disproportionate number of closings involved minority-owned dealerships (Sawyers, 2009). Given what you learned about the conditions affecting buyer *and* seller dependency, what effects might the new dealership landscape have on the postrecession prices that African Americans pay for new cars?

Overcapacity

The foremost structural condition underlying the dramatic events of 2008 and 2009 remains, as it has been since the 1960s, overcapacity. Automobile manufacturers in 2009 had the plant and equipment and skilled labor to produce 92 million cars (Linebaugh & Shirouzu, 2008), but fewer than 60 million were actually sold (Bissinger & Schulz, 2009). That is a "capacity utilization rate" of 65%. Car makers need to operate at 80% of capacity to survive, a level the industry is not expected to see again until 2014 (Linebaugh & Shirouzu, 2008). The vast majority of those 32 million extra cars were never built, of course. But the underutilized capacity puts manufacturers under constant pressure to increase productivity; niche-market their products more precisely; globalize their operations and workforces; and find creative ways to raise capital, harvest tax credits, and cut costs.

Overcapacity is not simply a matter of too many factories stamping out too many vehicles with too many workers. It is a condition relative to a competitive field and the various dimensions of that field. At bottom, the problem of overcapacity reduces to a company's comparative disadvantage relative to the competition on sunk costs of demonstrative importance at a given time.

Overcapacity may sound like an objective condition, but like anything factual, it needs to be "objectivated," that is, made into a known object through categorization and typification (Blumer, 1969, pp. 68–70; Schutz, 1967, pp. 78–83). As distinctions proliferate, a field of criticism and discourse comes into being about how comparative disadvantage on one or more dimensions of overcapacity can be remedied. Any sunk cost can be the target of stinging criticism simply by comparing it in the abstract with a competitor's superior performance on the same dimension. The clarity and persuasiveness of the comparative analysis, as perceived by the decision makers of the day, sets organizational reform into motion. Because no company maintains comparative advantage on every dimension of organizational success, and there are as many dimensions as there are sunk costs, organizational reform is often a matter of emulation rather than innovation (DiMaggio & Powell, 1983). The nearly 50-year-long struggle of the American auto industry with overcapacity provides numerous examples of ill-considered emulation—diversification, for example. Between 1984 and 1989, the Big Three spent $20 billion buying up electronics, aerospace, defense, and consumer finance companies, even a chain of savings and loans (Ingrassia, 2010, pp. 87–92). The idea was that these other businesses would generate profits to compensate for off years in the car business, and vice versa. Unfortunately, car guys don't know much about electronics or aerospace, and learning how to manage those businesses proved to be a distraction. Although diversification now looks like a strategic blunder, it reflected the conventional wisdom of the day (Fligstein, 1990).

Flash forward two decades to December 2008, when, by executive order, President George W. Bush bailed out GM and Chrysler and created the Automotive Task Force, which the Obama White House staffed and charged with the task of restoring two auto icons to profitability. Who served on the 15-member Automotive Task Force? Not politicians or government officials, but financial analysts, lawyers, bankers, and managers of private equity firms (Ingrassia, 2010, pp. 229–231). None had any experience in the auto business, but that is typical in private equity. What qualified them for the job? Their experience with evaluating companies' performance and potential, removing underperforming executives, and making hard decisions about the parts of companies to save and the parts to shut down. In effect, the government assembled its own private equity firm to dispose of the unprofitable parts of the companies it had rescued. There is a huge irony here. As I will show below, the actions of private equity firms, hedge funds, and investment banks played central roles in the collapse of the two companies. As they lay prostrate on the ground, to whom did the government turn to rebuild them? The same Wall Street firms that helped bring them down! As diversification was the conventional-wisdom solution to overcapacity in the 1980s, so private-equity restructuring under government authorization may well become the conventional-wisdom solution to overcapacity in the future. In such ways, a particularistic set of objectivations comes to be legitimated as the only rational way to manage the systemic crises of finance capitalism.

But that's the end of the story. Let's back up closer to the beginning.

The Long Learning Curve

As you probably know from general reading, the story of the decline of the U.S. auto industry begins with the recovery of Europe and Japan from the devastation of World War II, continues through the import threat of the 1960s and 1970s, and gains momentum through the design and safety failures of the 1980s and 1990s. Temporary salvation came in the form of the sports utility vehicle (SUV), the oversized engineering mediocrity that became the status emblem of the suburban household from the mid-1980s until the recent spike in gasoline prices. The first decade of the SUV era was a profitable one for the Big Three, and innovations in robotics, passenger comfort, and marketing kept investors content. Income and stock prices at Ford and GM hit record levels in 1999 and 2000, while Chrysler's strength in Jeeps and minivans prompted a "merger of equals" with the German luxury car maker Daimler-Benz in 1998 (Ingrassia, 2010, pp. 113-114). As Japanese transplants began building cheaper, better engineered, and virtually maintenance-free cars and SUVs in eight nonunion states in the South, however, that comparative advantage began to disappear. By 2002, the big three American firms were losing market share not only in small cars but in luxury cars and SUVs as well. Where Toyota was making $2000 per vehicle sale in 2003, GM was making $18 and Ford was losing $197 (Taylor, 2003).

It is easy to blame the decline of the American car business on mismanagement. The Big Three never did manage to produce attractive, fuel-efficient small cars. For 30 years, they fought national fuel-efficiency mandates as fiercely as they did safety and air pollution regulations, even as their cars became less reliable, less stylish, and more expensive. They retained a decentralized form of organization long after competitors like Toyota proved the superiority of centralized management. As late as 1992, General Motors still had seven manufacturing units each with its own engineering, marketing, and purchasing departments. Suppliers sold the same part to different units under different part numbers at different prices (Holstein, 2009, pp. 8–11). But as William J. Holstein shows in *Why GM Matters* (2009), in the decade before its bankruptcy, GM *had* overcome longstanding vulnerabilities.

What did it do? It centralized operations, took advantage of the North American Free Trade Agreement (NAFTA) by dispersing operations to Canada and Mexico, and trimmed tens of thousands of blue-collar and white-collar jobs in the Midwest. Adopting the lean production methods of Toyota, it built new plants in a T-shaped design, so that trucks could deliver parts to the appropriate places on the assembly line in a continuous flow. It adopted as well Toyota's team production methods and *kaizen,* the philosophy of continuous improvement in quality and efficiency. As a result of these changes, productivity, quality, and reliability improved measurably. But GM went further: It turned itself into a truly global corporation. Design and engineering for cars to be built in Mexico or Brazil were farmed out to specialized teams in Australia or Korea. A joint venture with a Chinese company gave birth to Shanghai GM, a state-of-the-art design, engineering, and manufacturing complex that made a redesigned Buick the best-selling car in China in 2004 and made China the car maker's second largest market after North America. Following the Walmart model, Shanghai GM now contracts with small provincial manufacturers in China to produce millions of car parts for shipment to subcontractors or to GM assembly lines around the world (Holstein, 2009, pp. 171–190).

Finally, it rolled back decades of contractual agreements with the United Auto Workers (UAW) in health care benefits, job security, and wage rates. GM had steadily reduced its workforce since 1979, when it employed 618,000 people ("General Motors Bankruptcy," 2010), so that by 2009, it had nearly five times as many retirees as active employees, all enrolled in what health care reformers in 2010 would label a "Cadillac" health insurance plan. In September 2007, GM moved $50 billion in health care liabilities off its accounting sheets and gifted them to a trust fund administered by the UAW. Employee and retiree health care coverage had been costing GM $7 billion a year, adding $1,500 to the price of a new car (Holstein, 2009). Although it agreed to endow the fund with cash and stock, once those contributions were made, GM would be off the hook for retiree health care. The UAW also allowed GM (and later Chrysler and Ford) to terminate Jobs Bank, a program dating from 1984 that paid laid-off workers 95% of their salary until a new job became available to them, an increasingly rare prospect in 2007. In the same contract, the UAW allowed GM to establish a two-tiered wage regime, with new employees starting at hourly rates 50% below the current pay scale, and agreed not to authorize a strike until 2015 (Holstein, 2009). The once-fierce UAW had become a company union for retired auto workers.

By 2008, General Motors could boast that its new plants could assemble a car in 32 hours (compared to 30 for Toyota), that these new cars matched Toyota's in quality and reliability, that its "legacy costs" had been contained, and that it was well-positioned to dominate the fastest growing car market in the world. It even had something in the pipeline to assuage its greenest critics: a fuel-efficient, greenhouse gas-reducing, plug-in electric car scheduled for mass production in 2010 (Holstein, 2009). During its 9 years under Daimler, Chrysler also invested in new plants, reduced its production hours per vehicle to near-Toyota levels, and improved the styling and reliability of its fleet ("Cerberus Takes Over," 2007).

So, what happened? How could a car company that had seemingly turned itself around suddenly start losing fantastic amounts of money, fall into bankruptcy, and wind up 60% owned by the taxpayers?

The Collapse

The theory of overproduction states that a saturated market sets into motion a spiral of falling prices, profits, and production as insufficient demand leaves more and more producers unable to recover the costs they incurred in bringing products to market (Roll, 1938, pp. 236–237). That describes what transpired in the U.S. auto industry around 2005–2006 rather well, up to a point. By 2003, the economy had rebounded from the recession of 2001–2002. Interest rates were low, stimulating (or, in retrospect, overstimulating) demand for cars and houses and giving investment banks, mortgage lenders, and hedge funds lots of cheap money to play with. In 2005, car makers sold a record number of vehicles worldwide, including 16.9 million in North America ("U.S. Auto Sales," 2006). But the North American numbers were down from a high of 17.4 million in 2000, and the Big Three continued to lose market share to imports and transplants (Snyder, 2010, p. 27). Spiking gasoline prices after Hurricane Katrina struck the Gulf Coast in August 2005 quelled the suburban family's affection for minivans and heavy SUVs, the only class of vehicles on which the Big Three were making money (Holstein, 2009, pp. x, 61). When the numbers slipped again in 2006, all three firms posted losses on the year (Bunkley, 2008).

Meanwhile, bad things were happening elsewhere in the economy. The housing bubble burst in 2006 as overextended home buyers couldn't make their balloon mortgage payments and banks declined to refinance their loans (the subprime mortgage crisis). A year later, in 2007, investment banks, having bundled subprime mortgage debts into securities and having hedged those securities against the risk of default by purchasing credit default swaps from other investment banks, suddenly found themselves awash in "toxic assets" (the banking crisis). Commercial banks and car finance companies started to protect their capital by hiking interest rates, tightening credit regulations, and denying credit applications (the credit crunch). Poorly capitalized auto dealerships seeking loans for next year's fleet of new cars couldn't get them (Harris, 2009b). Consumers started to cut back on spending. Car sales slowed, then slowed some more. Depending on how you measure profit and loss, in 2007, GM lost either $38.7 billion (counting charges against unused tax credits) or $23 billion (counting just plain-vanilla losses on operations) (Durbin, 2008). Ford lost $12.7 billion in 2006 and $2.7 billion in 2007 (Bunkley, 2008). (Chrysler no longer had to report losses because it was acquired by a private equity firm in May 2007; more on that soon.) With 2008 new cars already on the assembly line and a million unsold vehicles on dealers' lots, the Big Three auto makers' cash reserves flew out the door. On Wall Street, GM's shares fell 40% by year's end (Ingrassia, 2010, p. 203); Ford's fell 10.4% ("Ford Motor Company," 2010).

The sales and shares slumps continued into 2008, then turned horrific as the Federal Reserve Bank began bailing out brokerage houses, investment banks, and a pair of semi-private institutions (Fannie Mae and Freddie Mac) that bought mortgage debt from banks, thereby allowing the banks to borrow more and lend more than they otherwise could (Johnson & Kwak, 2010, pp. 144–146). When the Fed allowed one of the big banks to fail (Lehman Brothers), a full-fledged bank panic ensued. Credit froze up completely. GM lost $30 billion in 2008 ("Humbled GM," 2009), and Ford lost $14.6 billion (Vlasic, 2009). Things were so bad at Chrysler that its new owners offered to *give* the company to the government for free at the end of 2008 (Story, 2009). What Linebaugh and Shirouzu (2008) called "the worst downturn in global vehicle sales in the last 50 years" lasted 2 full years. Only Ford survived without taxpayer assistance. Overcapacity. Overproduction. Market saturation. Price deflation (via rebates and dealer incentives). Evaporating cash reserves. Bankruptcy.

Although the classic theory fits the facts well enough, it is doubtful that overproduction and market saturation themselves would have led to the bankruptcy of Chrysler and General Motors. Car makers have lived with overcapacity for nearly 50 years. They know how to respond to episodes of market saturation. They lay off workers, cut production, sell off assets, and spend down their cash reserves until demand picks up again. In a unique take on these tactics, in 2006, Ford *mortgaged the entire assets of the company* for $25 billion, which provided the cash cushion it needed to keep operations going during the downturn ("Humbled GM," 2009). Indeed, car makers use these periodic downturns to force their employees, suppliers, and dealers to accept new arrangements beneficial to themselves. The United Auto Workers union was the prime target of their arm-twisting this time around. Using such traditional methods, GM cut its losses from $10 billion in 2005 to $2 billion in 2006 despite lower revenues from declining sales (Durbin, 2008). The suddenness of the collapse, its resemblance to a crisis of confidence panic, and its timing relative to the collapse of the financial sector recall the onset of the preceding recession of 2001–2002. That recession was triggered by the implosion of highly leveraged companies (Enron and WorldCom) that had dazzled Wall Street with their ingenious debt-to-equity sleights of hand, involved a banking crisis, and provoked a recession through the tightening of credit on the real economy of goods and services (Partnoy, 2004). The classic overproduction account overlooks how easily industrial firms can become entangled in the high-stakes, high-risk practices of the financial sector.

In the space remaining, I will assemble evidence that one of the car companies' customary methods for surviving downturns—selling assets—entangled them in the strategies and practices of the investment banks, hedge funds, and private equity firms that increasingly dominate the financial sector of the economy. As I see it, the outcomes of these entanglements made it impossible for Chrysler and General Motors to recover from a serious, but familiar and manageable contraction in vehicle sales beginning in 2005. The account explores dependencies and dynamics at the interorganizational level of social structure (Prendergast & Knottnerus, 1994).

The Interorganizational Contexts of Bankruptcy

Let's start with the General Motors Acceptance Corporation (GMAC). This was the division of General Motors that lent money to car buyers and auto dealers to lease or purchase GM vehicles. Most buyers take out loans to purchase cars. Banks or credit unions could lend them the money, but most buyers let the car manufacturers profit a second time from their purchase. American car companies have been operating finance divisions since the 1920s. Although less profitable during periods of low interest rates, selling car loans is much like selling life insurance—one rarely loses money doing it. During the 1990s, an era of high interest rates, as price competition eroded profits in the manufacturing division, GMAC transferred $8 billion to the parent company. By 2000, GMAC, with more than $200 billion in assets, had become the seventh largest *home mortgage* lender in the country (England, 2004). Except for the recession years of 2001 and 2002, when low interest rates and the gimmick of zero-percent financing caused the unit to lose money, GMAC continued to prop up the industrial operations through 2005. Then, in 2006, GM started pouring cash into its financial arm by the hundreds of millions of dollars (Mildenberg, 2008). Care to guess why? Not zero-percent financing this time. Not the modest fall-off in sales that year. Right, the subprime mortgage mess.

Low interest rates make car financing less profitable, but they attract people to the housing market. So, like other mortgage lenders, GMAC began selling home mortgages to borrowers who either did not have the income to repay the loans or who were buying numbers of houses for quick resale in the rising market. Apparently, GMAC emulated the practices of the mortgage brokers and predatory lenders who gave subprime lending a bad name, for GM dealerships started to encounter car buyers who resented having to fill out a credit application. They got their home mortgage from GMAC on unverified "stated income" alone, so why not a mere car (Ingrassia, 2010, p. 163)? Like other finance companies, GMAC had been selling its auto debt and mortgage debt to Wall Street firms to securitize, thus allowing it to borrow more and lend more than it could have if those liabilities had remained on its books. When the housing bubble burst in 2006, the subprime mortgages it could no longer offload turned into toxic assets. In 2006, the home mortgage division lost $1.8 billion. It lost $4.3 billion more in 2007, but by then, GM had cut its losses in half by selling 51% of GMAC to a private equity firm called Cerberus Capital Management (Mildenberg, 2008).

We will return to GMAC shortly. I've already made the point that part of GM's difficulties in 2006 stemmed from its involvement in the relatively new practice of securitizing home mortgage debt, a problem independent of slipping auto sales. Now let's see if GM's relations with other actors in the world of high finance turned out any better. Let me introduce you to the private equity firm to which GM sold 51% of its finance operations, Cerberus Capital Management.

A private equity firm is an investment shop that specializes in buying and selling companies using borrowed money (Preston, 2008, pp. 28–33). For some of the companies in its portfolio, it raises capital for product development or expansion. For others, it arranges a merger or an acquisition by a new parent company. The rest tack this way or that until the private equity firm loses faith in them. The companies then get stripped of their assets and shut down. The assessment period is typically short—2 to 5 years (Preston, 2008, p. 29). When a private equity firm shows little or no interest in the long-term prospects of the companies it acquires, it is called a "corporate raider." Cerberus descends from the investment firm whose creative packaging of low-quality corporate debt (i.e., junk bonds) funded the most aggressive corporate raiders of the 1980s, Drexel Burnham Lambert (Moyer, 2009). Its stated philosophy, however, is "buy, build, and hold" ("Prepared Remarks of John W. Snow," 2007), and to that end, it has a staff of 150 former corporate executives who help run the portfolio companies until Cerberus decides which of the three disposal options will be most lucrative for the firm's partners.

When Cerberus buys a company, say, GMAC or Chrysler Motors (oh, yes, it did! Chrysler, too!), it assigns one of its executives to work alongside the CEO to make sure the company makes the kind of decisions that Cerberus considers beneficial to them both. At the time it acquired GMAC and Chrysler, none of its 150 executives had any experience in automobile manufacturing or car financing. The executive it assigned to GMAC, a partner in Cerberus, owned a private hedge fund (Wayne, 2009). A money guy, not a car guy. What transpired next can be explained in two ways, the money guy's ignorance of the car business and a pincer maneuver by Cerberus in a mergers-and-acquisitions offensive.

Whether giving up a controlling stake in GMAC was a smart move or a dumb one on GM's part was hotly debated in the business press (e.g., Crane, 2006). It was a disaster for GM dealers, three fourths of whom then obtained their inventory loans through GMAC (Mildenberg, 2008). Financing is part of the chain of interdependency that holds the auto industry together. When GM agreed to sell a majority stake in GMAC to Cerberus in November 2006, it severed the chain at a vital link. With car sales slumping, the last thing the old GMAC would have done is raise credit requirements. Cerberus did precisely that. When GM dealers applied for loans to finance their orders of 2008 vehicles, Cerberus demanded more guarantees of credit worthiness and higher interest rates. Banks were doing the same thing at the time, so dealers were caught between a rock and a hard place. Some couldn't afford the loans and turned themselves into used-car operations. Others relied on the sales of their other franchise, if they had one. Still others closed their doors (Harris, 2009a, 2009b, 2010). The credit embargo hurt GM badly. If sales were falling before the embargo, they were crashing now. With Cerberus's help, GM would lose $23 billion on operations alone in 2007 (Durbin, 2008).

Perhaps GM just shot itself in the foot by selling GMAC to a firm with no car-financing experience. But let's follow the other explanatory angle for a bit. Cerberus acquired an 80% stake in Chrysler Motors in 2007, when Daimler abruptly washed its hands of the company as the sales slump started to gather speed ("Cerberus Takes Over," 2007). The part of Chrysler it wanted was its financing unit, but it paid so little for the whole company it figured it could take a crack at turning it around (Story, 2009). Like GM, Chrysler *had* improved the productivity, quality, and marketability of its products in the previous decade ("Cerberus Takes Over," 2007). Timing is everything, however, and soon Chrysler was losing money as fast as GM was. Cerberus immediately stopped investing in Chrysler and started looking for merger partners, especially General Motors (Vlasic, 2008). This move fed speculation in the business press that Cerberus had deliberately placed a credit embargo on GM dealerships in order to force GM to sell Cerberus a larger share of GMAC (which it wanted to merge with Chrysler's financial arm) or to weaken GM to the point where it would agree to merge with Chrysler (Holstein, 2009, p. 242). Cerberus would either make a killing on the merger or have clear title to a giant auto financing operation, which it could sell to a Wall Street firm looking to expand its securitization business.

Whichever explanation of Cerberus's actions one accepts, GM's interactions with the private equity firm hurt the company badly. Not only did GM's revenues fall more steeply than they otherwise would have, the record-setting losses in 2007 sent distress signals to Wall Street. Coming on the heels of maverick investor Kirk Kerkorian's sell-off of 56 million shares of GM stock the year before ("Kerkorian Said to Bail Out of GM," 2006), big institutional investors and mutual funds began to pull their money out of the company. Kerkorian, owner of the biggest and grandest casinos in Las Vegas, operating through his private investment firm, had acquired nearly 10% of GM stock. When GM rejected his proposed merger with Renault-Nissan, he sold his entire stake within a month. Merger talk alone signals distress and the erosion of options. Merger talk coupled with record-setting losses, a gathering recession, and stock sell-offs signify impending collapse. Thus began the erosion of confidence that made it impossible for GM to raise sufficient capital to replenish its cash reserves and keep it operations going. The endgame was in sight.

This was not the endgame of an overproduction crisis, however, with desperate producers pricing themselves out of business, but the endgame of a financial crisis. For General Motors, the game ended, symbolically at least, with a coup de grâce executed by the very organizations that GMAC was striving to emulate in selling off its car loan and mortgage debt. Cut to the fall of 2008. Investment banks are imploding one after another, led by the fall of Lehmann Brothers, the largest bank failure in U.S. history. The Federal Reserve Bank and the U.S. Treasury Department are trying to contain the crisis by recapitalizing troubled banks, arranging mergers, and guaranteeing their assets against default (Johnson & Kwak, 2010, pp. 167–172). The stock market is tanking. As share prices fall, smart players can still make money selling "short." Short sellers borrow shares from investors who still value them; sell them at the current market price; hold them until the price falls further; then replace them with shares purchased at the new lower price, and pocket the difference (less fees paid to the brokerage house that lent the shares, the actual shareowners being neither informed nor rewarded for their part in the transaction) (Pozen, 2010, p. 104; see also Fabozzi & Mann, 2005). That is what the investment banks and hedge funds were doing to GM shares in the fall of 2008—borrowing shares from investors who were sticking with the company and selling them short (Holstein, 2009, p. 243).

Conclusions

Earlier in this chapter, I argued that, to explain the variance in the prices that African Americans pay for new cars relative to similarly qualified whites, one must examine the dependencies on the *seller's* side of the buyer-seller relationship as well as those on the buyer's side. I identified some of the conditions affecting dealer dependence, then explored the competitive relations between the manufacturers, which is where I first introduced the concept of overcapacity. Overcapacity is *the* condition underlying all the plant closings, layoffs, union give-backs, and charges of corporate mismanagement; the mergers, acquisitions, and joint ventures between firms; and the dispersal of automotive design, engineering, and production from Europe and America into emerging markets around the world. So, it is imminently reasonable to argue that overcapacity finally caught up with the dinosaurs of Detroit and would have put two of them out of business had not American and Canadian taxpayers invested $66 billion in their survival (and another $40 billion in the survival of their parts suppliers and GMAC) (Ingrassia, 2010, p. 275).

Overcapacity, however, differs from overproduction. The market for new cars in North America surely was saturated in 2005, but no car maker recklessly increased production and cut prices in a bid to grind the competition into the ground. Corporate capitalism abhors such behavior, and that is not what happened to Chrysler and GM. Rather, the financial sector of the economy—notoriously under-regulated and wildly inventive of new ways to convert debt into equity while circumventing capital requirements and hiding liabilities in off-account shell companies called "special-purpose vehicles" (Cassidy, 2009, pp. 214, 272)—spun itself into another financial crisis, the fourth in the past two decades, and pulled two American car companies under with it.

Chapter 11 bankruptcy is a legal process designed to protect the interests of creditors and bondholders while a distressed company restructures itself to compete again in the marketplace. In this case, the restructuring of GM and Chrysler was negotiated not with a bankruptcy court judge, but with the Automotive Task Force. Operating on private equity principles, the task force sought to hack the companies down to a size suitable to the competitive conditions it expected them to face after they emerged from bankruptcy protection. That meant a workforce of about 70,000 at GM, with management ranks pared by one third (Ingrassia, 2010, p. 278). The task force wanted GM to shut down or sell off six of its eight brands, but settled for four: Hummer, Saturn, Pontiac, and Saab. Chrysler agreed to cut its workforce by 6,500 and close eight factories (Ingrassia, 2010, p. 278). The task force also sought dealership terminations of one third at GM and one fourth at Chrysler. Finally, in classic private equity fashion, it arranged for the acquisition of Chrysler by the UAW and Fiat, which will manage the new entity (Ingrassia, 2010, p. 254). Acting decisively under the aegis of bankruptcy law, the task force achieved something completely unexpected: Make two thirds of a decaying oligarchy dance to Wall Street's tune.

Let me close by guesstimating the effects of the restructurings of Chrysler and General Motors on "the social structure of dealer dependency" and minority car buyers. At this point, it is unclear how many dealerships will lose their franchises because of restructuring, perhaps rather few. Most of the 3,000-plus terminations were rescinded after the National Auto Dealers Association prevailed upon Congress to pass legislation compelling GM and Chrysler to arbitrate each contested termination on a case-by-case basis (Faler, 2009). In the end, the credit crunch and the recession did the job that restructuring could not. The number of dealerships in the United States fell by 760 in 2008, with another 1,800 or so closing in 2009 (Harris, 2009a). Minority-owned dealerships shut their doors at a rate three times higher than the overall rate of dealership closings (Sawyers, 2009, p. 23). The number of franchises contracted to dealerships also fell by 9% in 2009, the largest decline in 40 years (Chappell, 2010, p. 21). Metropolitan areas suffered the worst of it (Harris, 2009a).

In terms of the categories of dealerships distinguished in Table 6.2, the chief victims of the recession (and also the chief targets for termination) were small, traditional dealerships that exploit buyer dependency to the hilt when they can but cave in on price when their lots fill with unsold product. Many neighborhood and minority-owned dealerships fall into this category. If minority-owned dealerships valiantly refused to exploit minority buyer dependency, the 15% decline in minority-run dealerships (Sawyers, 2009) would represent a significant setback for African American car buyers. Alas, the conditions of *dealer* dependency preclude such gestures of solidarity. The disappearance of hundreds of low-volume urban dealerships, however, means that African American car buyers will haggle with fewer dealers whose dependencies periodically outweigh their own. In that respect, the closure of so many minority-owned dealerships represents a small net increase in minority buyer dependency.

The high-volume, team-concept dealerships and the megadealerships of Table 6.2 are the types best prepared to scale up their operations in the way the Automotive Task Force envisioned and the manufacturers want. The key question for minority buyers is whether the institution of the sales commission will survive the scale-up. It seems that it will, for the National Auto Dealers Association succeeded in exempting car financing from oversight by the recently created Consumer Financial Protection Agency ("Financial Reform Conference," 2010). As a result, car buyers will still have to sit across the table from the closer with his (or her) myriad ploys for maximizing profit on the trade-in, the purchase price, and the financing. Minority buyer dependency will continue to be exploited in the showrooms for years to come.

How will all this affect the prices that African American car buyers pay for new cars? Just now, at the onset of a feeble economic recovery, dealer dependency is palpable (Harris, 2010). A minority car buyer with good credit embedded in a social network high in social and cultural capital will pay prices comparable to what white buyers with good credit will pay, but only if he or she comparison shops outside the neighborhood. Dealership consolidation, however, can tip the scales back the other way in short order. Once the recovery stabilizes and the high-volume dealerships put their weaker rivals out of business, minority car buyers will once again have to rely on *Consumer Reports,* purchase pals, and their own bargaining skills to negotiate a fair price for a new car or become adept at online car shopping.

Notes

1. For methodological and ideological criticisms of the study, see Goldberg (1996) and Epstein (1992), as well as Ayres's (1994) reply to Epstein.

2. First-time car buyers, by definition, fit into the seller's category of "inexperienced shoppers." (For seller typifications of car buyers, see Furse et al., 1984.) In his exposé of the

retail car business, Parrish (1992) answers the question, "Why are first-time car buyers so vulnerable?" as follows: "Firstly, the young car buyer will do almost anything to get into a car. Secondly, he/she is very inexperienced at negotiating. And these people usually have no credit record" (pp. 235–236).

3. The auto makers were not entirely responsible for their own troubles. Like housing, steel, and agriculture, the auto industry took a beating in the drive to control inflation. Among other destabilizing effects, inflation erodes the value of bonds and other long-term investments. With bank assets losing value, the Federal Reserve acted decisively in the late 1970s to raise interest rates and provoke a recession. At the height of the anti-inflation effort, from 1979 to 1982, auto industry unemployment reached 23%, and overall industrial output fell 12%. After 3 years of 18% to 20% interest rates, personal income from interest (86% of which goes to the wealthiest 10% of Americans) grew by $148 billion (67%), the largest banks registered record profits, and the effective tax rate on the banking industry was reduced to 3.8% (Greider, 1987, pp. 401, 413, 456). This abrupt redistribution of wealth fueled the great bull market in stocks that began at the end of 1982 and lasted for 18 years. Because cars are bought on credit, automakers, dealers, and customers alike paid heavily for the restoration of bank capital. As I will show in the second postscript below, the new financial organizations that Wall Street firms devised to capture the new wealth helped propel two American car makers into bankruptcy.

4. Ayres (1995, pp. 131–135) also rejects what he calls an "animus" explanation of his data. In the end, he favors a willingness-to-pay account, although he also sees some animus in the treatment of black males and some reluctance on the part of black females to bargain tough with sellers (p. 141). My emphasis on carlessness and restricted search opportunities overlaps what Ayres calls a "cost-based" account. He rejects this account because there were no statistically significant differences between the markups in black-majority neighborhoods (representing low search costs) and those in white-majority neighborhoods (representing high search costs) (p. 136). What Ayres considers low search costs I consider a condition of buyer dependency. Originally, I expected dealerships serving African American customers regularly (even if black owned) to charge higher markups. When they did not, I put proportionally more emphasis on the sources of dealer dependency. If dealerships serving African Americans are mainly older, smaller franchises with low sales volume, dealer dependency may actually outweigh buyer dependency, particularly during economic downturns. Indeed, as Ayres (p. 136) reports, dealers in black-majority neighborhoods did offer slightly lower prices to African American testers, although not low enough to be statistically significant at the .05 level. Why? Faced with customers of the tester's socioeconomic status and bargaining style, these low-volume dealers quickly abandoned full-sticker hopes and conceded more steeply in subsequent bargaining rounds, knowing that Buppie customers like the testers could and do shop outside the neighborhood.

5. The $500 price difference can be restated in percentage terms. So formulated, African Americans pay 1% more for the average new car. Some industry analysts are inclined to say "only 1% more" and to attribute the difference to African Americans' penchant for economizing on search costs. The price difference is statistically significant and reliable, and should be doubled to include the higher finance charges that African Americans pay. The price difference can be understood more critically as a power-based extraction of millions of dollars a year from a positionally disadvantaged population. To use a less neutral term from the economist's lexicon, the auto dealers' exploitation of buyer dependency amounts to "rent-seeking," an economic practice that has yet to find a persuasive apologist. In his most recent writings on price discrimination, Ayres (2001, 2002) discards his willingness-to-pay account (see note 4) in favor of rent-seeking behavior he calls supra-competitive pricing.

References

Allen, W. (1979). Class culture and family organization: The effects of class and race on family structure in urban America. *Journal of Comparative Family Studies, 10,* 301–313.

Alwitt, L. F., & Donley, T. D. (1996). *The lower-income consumer: Adjusting the balance of exchange.* Thousand Oaks, CA: Sage.

Angst for the angstroms. (1997, July 12). *The Economist,* pp. 56–57.

Ayres, I. (1991, February). Fair driving: Gender and race discrimination in retail car negotiations. *Harvard Law Review, 104*(4), 817–872.

Ayres, I. (1994). Alternative grounds: Epstein's discrimination analysis in other market settings. *San Diego Law Review, 31,* 67–87.

Ayres, I. (1995). Further evidence of discrimination in new car negotiations and estimates of its cause. *Michigan Law Review, 94,* 109–147.

Ayres, I. (2001). *Expert testimony of Ian Ayres.* Boston: National Consumer Law Center. Retrieved from http://www.nclc.org

Ayres, I. (2002). *Pervasive prejudice? Unconventional evidence of race and gender discrimination.* Chicago: University of Chicago Press.

Ayres, I., & Siegelman, P. (1995). Race and gender discrimination in bargaining for a new car. *American Economic Review, 85*(3), 304–321.

Berger, J., Cohen, B. P., & Zelditch, M., Jr. (1966). Status characteristics and expectation states. In J. Berger, M. Zelditch, Jr., & B. Anderson (Eds.), *Sociological theories in progress* (pp. 29–46). Boston: Houghton Mifflin.

Bertrand, A. L. (1972). *Social organization: A general systems and role theory perspective.* Philadelphia: Davis.

Bissinger, M., & Schulz, R. (2009, October 5). The global automobile industry's long road to recovery. Retrieved from http://www.businessweek.com/investor/content/oct2009/pi2009105_817245_page2.htm

Blumer, H. (1969). *Symbolic interactionism: Perspective and method.* Englewood Cliffs, NJ: Prentice Hall.

Bohn, J. (1991, September 16). Half the sales staff is quitting. *Automotive News,* pp. 1, 49.

Boudon, R. (1987). The individualistic tradition in sociology. In J. C. Alexander, B. Giesen, R. Münch, & N. J. Smelser (Eds.), *The micro-macro link* (pp. 45–70). Berkeley: University of California Press.

Bourdieu, P. (1984). *Distinction: A social critique of the judgement of taste* (R. Nice, Trans.). Cambridge, MA: Harvard University Press.

Bourdieu, P. (1985). The forms of capital. In J. G. Richardson (Ed.), *Handbook of theory and research for the sociology of education* (pp. 241–258). Westport, CT: Greenwood.

Brewer, M. B. (1988). A dual process model of impression formation. In T. K. Srull & R. S. Wyer (Eds.), *Advances in social cognition* (Vol. 1, pp. 1–36). Hillsdale, NJ: Lawrence Erlbaum.

Bunkley, N. (2008, January 25). Ford narrows loss for 2007. Retrieved from http://www.nytimes.com/2008/01/25/business/25ford-web.html

Burt, R. S. (1982). *Toward a structural theory of action.* New York: Academic Press.

Burt, R. S. (1992). *Structural holes: The social structure of competition.* Cambridge, MA: Harvard University Press.

Caplovitz, D. (1967). *The poor pay more: Consumer practices of low-income families.* New York: Free Press.

The car industry: Barbarians at Bavarians' gates. (1999, February 13). *The Economist,* pp. 23–25.

Cassidy, J. (2009). *How markets fail: The logic of economic calamities.* New York: Farrar, Straus & Giroux.

Cerberus takes over majority interest in Chrysler Group and related financial services business for $7.4 billion from DaimlerChrysler [Press release]. (2007, May 14). Retrieved from http://www.cerberuscapital.com/news_press_release_07132007.html

Chappell, L. (2010, April 12). Imports cut stores too. *Automotive News,* pp. 1, 21.

Coleman, J. S. (1987). Microfoundations and macrosocial behavior. In J. C. Alexander, B. Giesen, R. Münch, & N. J. Smelser (Eds.), *The micro-macro link* (pp. 153–173). Berkeley: University of California Press.

Coleman, J. S. (1988). Social capital in creation of human capital. *American Journal of Sociology, 94,* S95–S120.

Coleman, J. S. (1990). *The foundations of social theory.* Cambridge, MA: Harvard University Press.

Consumer Federation of America. (1990). *U.S. consumer knowledge: The results of a nationwide test.* Washington, DC: Author.

Cooley, C. H. (1909). *Social organization: A study of the larger mind.* New York: Scribner's.

Cooley, C. H. (1918). *Social process.* New York: Scribner's.

Crane, M. (2006, April 4). GMAC sale to Cerberus criticized. Retrieved from http://www.forbes.com/2006/04/04/general-motors-gmac-0404markets15.html

Darin, A. T. (1996, November 11). Hiring, keeping sales people is nearly impossible. *Automotive News,* p. 38.

DiMaggio, P. J., & Powell, W. W. (1983). The iron cage revisited: Institutional isomorphism and collective rationality. *American Sociological Review, 48,* 147–160.

Durbin, D. (2008, February 13). $38.7 billion loss for General Motors is industry record. Retrieved from http://articles.sfgate.com/2008-02-13/business/17142258_1_gm-s-annual-loss-gm-s-offer-gm-s-allison-transmission

Eggebeen, D. J., & Hogan, D. P. (1990). *Giving between the generations in American families.* University Park: Pennsylvania State University Press.

Emerson, R. M. (1962). Power-dependence relations. *American Sociological Review, 27,* 31–41.

England, R. S. (2004, May 1). How GMAC built a lending powerhouse. Retrieved from http://www.allbusiness.com/finance/3595744-1.html

Epstein, R. A. (1992). *Forbidden grounds: The case against employment discrimination laws.* Cambridge, MA: Harvard University Press.

Fabozzi, F. J., & Mann, S. V. (2005). *Securities finance: Securities lending and repurchase agreements.* Hoboken, NJ: Wiley.

Faler, B. (2009, December 9). Legislation offers arbitration to former auto dealers. Retrieved from http://www.bloomberg.com/apps/news?pid=newsarchive&sid=aOZFeFXgC3BQ

Fernández-Kelly, M. P. (1995). Social and cultural capital in the urban ghetto: Implications for the economic sociology of immigration. In A. Portes (Ed.), *The economic sociology of immigration: Essays on networks, ethnicity, and entrepreneurship* (pp. 213–247). New York: Russell Sage.

Financial reform conference: Auto dealers beat Obama, win exemption from consumer protection agency. (2010, June 22). Retrieved from http://huffingtonpost.com/2010/06/22/auto-dealers-beat-Obama_n_621692.html

Fiske, S. T. (1993). Social cognition and social deception. *Annual Review of Psychology, 44,* 155–194.

Fligstein, N. (1990). *The transformation of corporate control.* Cambridge, MA: Harvard University Press.

Ford Motor Company. (2010, May 26). Retrieved from http://quicktake.morningstar.com/stocknet/stockReturns.aspx?symbol=F

Furse, D. H., Punj, G. N., & Stewart, D. W. (1984). A typology of individual search strategies among purchasers of new automobiles. *Journal of Consumer Research, 10,* 417–431.

General Motors' bankruptcy by the numbers. (2010, May 27). Retrieved from http://www.crikey.com.av/2009/06/02/general motors-bankruptcy-by-the-numbers

Goldberg, P. K. (1996). Dealer price discrimination in new car purchases: Evidence from the consumer expenditure survey. *Journal of Political Economy, 104,* 622–654.

Greider, W. (1987). *Secrets of the temple: How the Federal Reserve runs the country.* New York: Simon & Schuster.

Harris, D. (2009a, September 7). Confidence of dealers is at 29-yr. low. *Automotive News,* p. 23.

Harris, D. (2009b, September 14). Deep freeze for dealership deals. *Automotive News,* pp. 1, 30.

Harris, D. (2010, February 15). New retail model: Slash your way to net profits. *Automotive News,* pp. 1, 49.

Hays, W. C., & Mindel, C. H. (1973). Extended kinship relations in black and white families. *Journal of Marriage and the Family, 35,* 51–57.

Henry, J. (1996, May 27). Kicking the commission habit: Land Rover backs salary plan. *Automotive News,* pp. 3, 54.

Hilton, J. L., & von Hippel, W. (1996). Stereotypes. *Annual Review of Psychology, 47,* 237–271.

Holstein, W. J. (2009). *Why GM matters: Inside the race to transform an American icon.* New York: Walker.

Humbled GM files for bankruptcy protection. (2009, June 1). Retrieved from http://www.msnbc.msn.com/id/31030038/ns/business-autos.html

Ingrassia, P. (2010). *Crash course: The American automobile industry's road from glory to disaster.* New York: Random House.

Johnson, S., & Kwak, J. (2010). *13 bankers: The Wall Street takeover and the next financial meltdown.* New York: Pantheon.

Kahneman, D., Slovic, P., & Tversky, A. (1982). *Judgment under uncertainty: Heuristics and biases.* New York: Cambridge University Press.

Kerkorian said to bail out of GM. (2006, December 1). Retrieved from http://money.cnn.com/2006/12/01/news/companies/kerkorian_gm/index.htm

Knoke, D., & Guilarte, M. (1994). Networks in organizational structures and strategies. In J. D. Knottnerus & C. Prendergast (Eds.), *Current perspectives in social theory: Supplement 1. Recent developments in the theory of social structure* (pp. 77–115). Greenwich, CT: JAI.

Knottnerus, J. D. (1994). Expectation states theory and the analysis of group processes and structures. In J. D. Knottnerus & C. Prendergast (Eds.), *Current perspectives in social theory: Supplement 1. Recent developments in the theory of social structure* (pp. 49–74). Greenwich, CT: JAI.

Knottnerus, J. D. (1997). Social structural analysis and status generalization: The contributions and potential of expectation states theory. In J. Szmatka, J. Skvoretz, & J. Berger (Eds.), *Status, network, and structure: Theory development in group processes* (pp. 119–136). Stanford, CA: Stanford University Press.

Lawson, H. M. (1996). Car saleswomen: Expanding the scope of salesmanship. *Current Research on Occupations and Professions, 9,* 53–71.

Linebaugh, K., & Shirouzu, N. (2008, December 13). Global auto contraction ahead. Retrieved from http://online.wsj.com/article/SB122909314171801757.html?KEYWORDS=Global+auto+contraction+ahead

Little, D. (1991). *Varieties of social explanation: An introduction to the philosophy of social science.* Boulder, CO: Westview.

Maines, D. R. (1982). In search of mesostructure: Studies in the negotiated order. *Urban Life, 11,* 267–279.

March, J. G., & Simon, H. A. (1958). *Organizations.* New York: John Wiley.

Massey, D. S., & Denton, N. A. (1993). *American apartheid: Segregation and the making of the underclass.* Cambridge, MA: Harvard University Press.

Matheson, K., Holmes, J. G., & Kristiansen, C. M. (1991). Observational goals and the integration of trait perceptions and behavior: Behavioral prediction vs. impression formation. *Journal of Experimental Social Psychology, 27,* 138–160.

McCarron, J. (1989, June 5). Chicago has both poorest, richest suburbs. *Chicago Tribune,* pp. 1, 7.

Mead, G. H. (1934). *Mind, self, and society: From the standpoint of a social behaviorist.* Chicago: University of Chicago Press.

Menger, C. (1963). *Problems of economics and sociology* (F. J. Nock, Trans.). Urbana: University of Illinois Press.

Mildenberg, D. (2008, February 5). GMAC posts $729 million loss as home loans sour. Retrieved from http://www.bloomberg.com/apps/news?pid=2060187+sid=ap3VsENQaoyE&refer=home

Mills, C. W. (1958). *The sociological imagination.* New York: Oxford University Press.

Minorities' Internet usage. (n.d.). *Automotive Retailing Today.* Available at http://www.autoretailing.org/research

Moyer, L. (2009, May 1). How Chrysler put the bite on Cerberus. Retrieved from http://www.forbes.com/2009/05/01/bankruptcy-cerberus-chrysler-business-autos-cerberus.html

Naughton, K. (1996, February 19). Revolution in the show room. *Business Week,* pp. 70–76.

Parrish, D. (1992). *The car buyer's art: How to beat the salesman at his own game.* Bellflower, CA: Book Express.

Partnoy, F. (2004). *Infectious greed: How deceit and risk corrupted the financial markets.* New York: Times Books.

Pattee, H. H. (Ed.). (1973). *Hierarchy theory: The challenge of complex systems.* New York: Braziller.

Patterson, O. (1998). *Rituals of blood: Consequences of slavery in two centuries.* Washington, DC: Civitas/Counterpoint.

Pozen, R. (2010). *Too big to save? How to fix the U.S. financial system.* Hoboken, NJ: Wiley.

Prepared remarks of John W. Snow before the National Press Club [Press release]. (2007, July 18). Retrieved from http://www.cerberuscapital.com/news_press_release_07202007.html

Prendergast, C. (2004a). Levels of social structure. In G. Ritzer (Ed.), *Encyclopedia of social theory* (Vol. 1, pp. 441–443). Thousand Oaks, CA: Sage.

Prendergast, C. (2004b). Social capital. In G. Ritzer (Ed.), *Encyclopedia of social theory* (Vol. 2, pp. 715–717). Thousand Oaks, CA: Sage.

Prendergast, C., & Knottnerus, J. D. (1994). Recent developments in the theory of social structure: Introduction and overview. In J. D. Knottnerus & C. Prendergast (Eds.), *Current perspectives in social theory: Supplement 1. Recent development in the theory of social structure* (pp. 1–26). Greenwich, CT: JAI.

Preston, R. (2008). *Who runs Britain? How Britain's new elite are changing our lives.* London: Hodder & Stoughton.

Puzzanghera, J. (2010, May 25). Financial overhaul on deck. *Chicago Tribune,* p. 4.

Rabbit is poor. (1994, February 26). *The Economist,* p. 68.

Reskin, B., & Roos, P. (1990). *Job queues, gender queues: Explaining women's inroads into male occupations.* Philadelphia: Temple University Press.

Ridgeway, C. L. (1991). The social construction of status value: Gender and other nominal characteristics. *Social Forces, 70,* 367–386.

Ridgeway, C. L., & Berger, J. (1988). The legitimation of power and prestige orders in task groups. In M. Webster, Jr., & M. Foschi (Eds.), *Status generalization: New theory and research* (pp. 207–231). Stanford, CA: Stanford University Press.

Riley, T., & Fiske, S. T. (1991). Interdependence and the social context of impression formation. *European Bulletin of Cognitive Psychology, 11,* 173–192.

Roll, E. (1938). *A history of economic thought.* London: Faber and Faber.

Roschelle, A. R. (1997). *No more kin: Exploring race, class, and gender in family networks.* Thousand Oaks, CA: Sage.

Rubinstein, D. (1986). The concept of structure in sociology. In M. L. Wardell & S. P. Turner (Eds.), *Sociological theory in transition* (pp. 80–94). Boston: Allen & Unwin.

Rubinstein, D. (2000). *Culture, structure, and agency: Toward a truly multidimensional sociology.* Thousand Oaks, CA: Sage.

Sarkisian, N., & Gerstel, N. (2004). Kin support among blacks and whites: Race and family organization. *American Sociological Review, 69,* 812–837.

Sawyers, A. (2009, November 16). Struggle to stay afloat. *Automotive News,* pp. 1, 23.

Schumpeter, J. A. (1950). *Capitalism, socialism and democracy* (3rd ed.). New York: Harper Torchbooks.

Schutz, A. (1962). *Collected papers I: The problem of social reality* (M. Natanson, Ed.). The Hague, Netherlands: Nijhoff.

Schutz, A. (1967). *The phenomenology of the social world* (G. Walsh & F. Lehnert, Trans.). Evanston, IL: Northwestern University Press.

Scott Morton, F., Zettelmeyer, F., & Silva-Risso, J. (2003). Consumer information and discrimination: Does the Internet affect the pricing of new cars to women and minorities? *Quantitative Marketing and Economics, 1,* 65–92.

Seidler, J. S. (1979). Priest resignations in a lazy monopoly. *American Sociological Review, 44,* 763–783.

Simison, R. L., & Suris, O. (1997, January 31). U.S. car buying practices are getting a big overhaul: Dealer consolidations, big chains indicate good news for customers. *Wall Street Journal* (Eastern ed.), p. B4.

Simon, H. A. (1981). The architecture of complexity. In H. A. Simon (Ed.), *The sciences of the artificial* (2nd ed., pp. 193–229). Cambridge: MIT Press.

Snyder, J. (2010, January 11). Detroit's dismal decade. *Automotive News,* pp. 1, 27.

Story, L. (2009, August 8). For private equity, a very public disaster. Retrieved from http://www.nytimes.com/2009/08/09/business/09cerb.html?_r=1

Taylor, A. (1997, June 9). Car wars: Wayne Huizenga vs. everybody. *Fortune, 135,* 92–94.

Taylor, A. (2003, December 8). The Americanization of Toyota. *Fortune, 141,* 165–170.

U.S. auto sales reach 16.9 million in 2005. (2006, January 5). Retrieved from http://www.autoweek.com/article/20060105/FREE/60105002

U.S. Bureau of the Census. (1993). *1990 census of the population, social and economic characteristics, urbanized areas.* Washington, DC: U.S. Government Printing Office.

U.S. Department of Housing and Urban Development/Bureau of the Census. (1997). *American housing survey for the Chicago metropolitan area in 1995.* Washington, DC: U.S. Government Printing Office.

Vlasic, B. (2008, October 14). Cerberus's role crucial as GM-Chrysler merger talks continue. Retrieved from http://www.nytimes.com/2008/10/14/business/worldbusiness/14iht-14auto.16922509.html

Vlasic, B. (2009, January 29). Ford reports a record $14.6 billion loss for 2008. Retrieved from http://www.nytimes.com/2009/01/30/business/30ford.html

Wagner, D. G., & Berger, J. (1993). Status characteristics theory: The growth of a program. In J. Berger & M. Zelditch, Jr. (Eds.), *Theoretical research programs* (pp. 23–63). Stanford, CA: Stanford University Press.

Wayne, L. (2009, January 10). GMAC chairman with ties to Madoff steps down. Retrieved from http://nytimes.com/2009/01/10/business/10gmac.html

Weber, M. (1947). *The theory of economic and social organization* (A. M. Henderson & T. Parsons, Trans.). New York: Free Press.

White, H. C. (1992). *Identity and control: A structural theory of social action.* Princeton, NJ: Princeton University Press.

Willer, D. (Ed.). (1999). *Network exchange theory.* Westport, CT: Praeger.

Wysner, J. W. (1994). *Every purse and purpose: General Motors and the automobile business.* Davisburg, MI: Wilderness Adventure Books.

Yates, B. (1983). *The decline and fall of the American automobile industry.* New York: Empire Books.

Zettelmeyer, F., Scott Morton, F., & Silva-Risso, J. (2001). *Cowboys or cowards: Why are Internet car prices lower?* (Working Paper No. 8667). Cambridge, MA: National Bureau of Economic Research. Available at http://faculty.haas.berkeley.edu/forian/

DISCUSSION QUESTIONS

1. What is structural explanation in sociology? Define and expound on the idea of structural explanation. In what respect does structural explanation fulfill the promise of "the sociological imagination," as C. Wright Mills conceived it?

2. The author's approach to structural explanation does not stem from a single theoretical standpoint or tradition. Instead, he develops a four-legged "scaffold" he calls the "structural-social psychological theory of social action." Discuss the four legs of the scaffold individually and show how they fit together in constructing structural explanations of social facts.

3. The author uses a number of concepts from a variety of theorists and theoretical research programs to explain why African Americans pay more for new cars than do European Americans. Chief among these concepts are social capital, cultural capital, status characteristics, typifications, power dependence, and power-balancing operations. Define these terms in your own words. Then, suggest how some or all of them can be used to explain a curious social fact that interests you.

4. The author insists that a proper structural explanation of the car price mystery requires the sociologist to track the chains of social causation that operate on both sides of the buyer–seller relationship, right down to the face-to-face bargaining situation. Setting aside issues of seller dependency, trace the chain of social causation operating on the buyer's side of the relationship, focusing on the case of African Americans in Chicago.

5. In the section called "Loose Ends," the author tries to explain why the race and gender of the salesperson had no effect on the markups extracted from African American car buyers. That is a counterintuitive finding. Surely, African American salespersons are not biased against African Americans. So why do their African American customers pay the same $450–$500 price premium per sale?

CHAPTER 7

Critical Theory, Legitimation Crisis, and the Deindustrialization of Flint, Michigan

Steven P. Dandaneau

Steven P. Dandaneau is Associate Professor of Sociology and Director of the Chancellor's Honors and Haslam Scholars Programs at the University of Tennessee, Knoxville. He has taught social theory at the undergraduate level since receiving his doctorate in sociology from Brandeis University in 1992. His contribution to this volume is based on his book A Town Abandoned: Flint, Michigan, Confronts Deindustrialization *(1996), whereas his continuing interest in applied critical theory is exemplified in the book* A Wrong Life: Studies in Lifeworld-Grounded Critical Theory *(1998), of which he is coauthor with Maude C. Falcone, and in his Pine Forge Press book* Taking It Big: Developing a Sociological Consciousness in Postmodern Times *(2001).*

In this chapter, I will apply the famous legitimation crisis theory of Jürgen Habermas (1929–), the world's leading contemporary exponent of critical theory, to the phenomenon of deindustrialization in Flint, Michigan.[1] Growing from, but also fundamentally revising, Marx's original theory of capitalist economic crisis, Habermas and other 20th-century critical theorists attempted to understand and explain the changing nature of capitalist society since Marx's time.[2] In agreement with Marx, critical theorists view capitalism as an irrational, contradictory, and oppressive, albeit dynamic and productive, economic system. It is therefore understood as a leading cause of contemporary social problems, crisis, and domination, as well as a source of rapid social change and technological advancement. However, critical theorists have found it necessary to go beyond Marx's primary analytical focus on the internal dynamics of the capitalist economic system per se to include analyses of the political and cultural processes increasingly essential to the sustained and legitimate reproduction of 20th-century capitalist society.[3] Attention to the case of a medium-size midwestern American city's staggering loss of auto industry jobs more than four decades ago—and in 2009, the bankruptcy and government bailout of Flint's home-grown General Motors Corporation—allows us to better understand not only the complexities of contemporary capitalism but also the need for criticism and fundamental social change in our society. Indeed, Habermas's (1981/1987) theory of legitimation crisis ultimately helps us see a variety of ways in which the continuation of capitalism as we know it causes unnecessary and unjustifiable social disruption and human suffering, damaging what Habermas dubs, in a poetic turn of phrase, the "grammar of forms of life" (p. 392).[4]

The student should know that Habermas's theoretical works are notoriously difficult, even for professional social theorists. Writing about Habermas has already caused me to use a host of difficult concepts, such as capitalism, legitimation, deindustrialization, and the notion of critical theory itself. Also, what might Habermas mean by the phrase "grammar of forms of life"? I would not blame the reader for thinking, "If this is the first paragraph, what lies in store?" Never fear, however; this chapter, like *Illuminating Social Life* as a whole, is premised on the idea that a good way to begin to understand abstract social theories is to witness their power in action with respect to a concrete case in point.

What Is Critical Theory (Doing in Flint)?

At first blush, the experience of the people of Flint, Michigan, is quite revealing and easy to appreciate.[5] This city of 124,943 (according to the U.S. Census, 2000) is approximately 50 miles northwest of Detroit, Michigan, and is the historic hometown of both the General Motors (GM) Corporation (founded in 1908), historically America's largest and perhaps most recognized industrial firm, and the United Auto Workers (founded in 1937), America's largest industrial union. Flint is also the focus of Michael Moore's first major film, *Roger & Me* (1989), which depicts a decade's worth of the devastation and mayhem caused by massive unemployment in Flint.[6] Indeed, throughout its history, Flint's local experience has been an exaggeration of the main crisis tendencies of American capitalism such that close attention to its particulars brings into sharp relief the structure and dynamics of this complex societal subsystem. One Flint resident noted,

> Flint would be to life what a cowboy movie is to life or [what] a football game is to life: It is uniquely and usefully simplified. So, we're anything but a microcosm. We are the essence of the issues with all the extraneous stuff stripped away.[7]

As Habermas's theory of legitimation crisis predicts, however, Flint also has a rich experience of displacing and transforming the effects of economic crisis into spheres of social life once largely free of direct integration into the capitalist system, such as family life and the educational system. Habermas's perspective not only draws our attention to this displacement tendency but also thereby allows us to view Flint as a community with a history and a story to tell rather than, through the imagery of economic science, as one abstract location of factories and jobs among others.

Before going beyond these prefatory remarks, it is also essential to reveal that Flint is my hometown. In reviewing what Habermas and others have to say about the "Flints" of the world, I am trying to make better sense of my own life's experiences as much as I am simply trying to understand and teach yet another social theory. Importantly, this reflexive approach[8] to theorizing is consistent with the spirit and purpose of critical theory because this term broadly applies to theories that set as their ultimate goal the emancipation of people from both historically specific situations that prevent them from realizing their human freedom and the kind of thinking that muddies their ability to fully understand the sources of their "unfreedom."[9] If we call the former domination and the latter ideology, then we can say that critical theories are distinct from other types of contemporary social theory inasmuch as critical theories explicitly and purposely work from within conditions of domination and ideology to oppose domination and ideology.[10] In this sense, critical theories are partisan.[11] I write about critical theory and Flint primarily because my experience tells me that domination and ideology (bound together in a process of deindustrialization) are an important part of Flint's experience. Luckily, there is a rich theoretical tradition from which I can draw inspiration and orientation in my opposition to this state of affairs.

The two most important originators of critical theory are Karl Marx (1818–1883) and Sigmund Freud (1856–1939). Even though Marx thought of himself as a philosopher-turned-scientist, he could be understood to have created a new type of theory that was irreducible to either science or philosophy. Rather, as in the title of Habermas's famous treatise on the subject, Marx seemed to move "between philosophy and science" to "critique."[12] With the critical impulses of the Enlightenment tradition of Kant and Hegel, the French Revolution and its aftermath, and an emerging economic science serving as major influences, Marx developed a unique version of critique that meant self-conscious theoretical activity aiming to educate humanity about its actual and potential participation in history making.[13] How could humanity make its future? What prevented humanity from realizing, in Marx's (1972) youthful expression, "the meaning of its own struggle and its own desires"? Whereas mainstream labor economics and "scientific management" theory view workers as mere labor commodities to be bought and sold like any market commodity and then fit like cogs into the machinery of industrial production, Marx's economics became, as in the subtitle of his greatest work, *Capital* (1867), a "critique of political economy."[14] In other words, Marx formulated his economics in opposition to the economic orthodoxy of early British and French political economy, which he regarded as benefiting the capitalist class by envisioning a social order in accordance with its interests. If this mainstream economic theory could be criticized and, thereby, in the minds of the majority working class, delegitimized, then such critique would affect the course of history by encouraging revolutionary social change. Paraphrasing his famous "Eleventh Thesis on Feuerbach" (1843), Marx discerned that philosophers had only interpreted the world, whereas in modern, scientific times, the point was to change it.[15]

Sigmund Freud thought of himself as a medical doctor treating psychological illness, but his new psychoanalytic method had similar revolutionary implications inasmuch as it aimed to dispel self-deception through a form of dialogical analysis.[16] His innovative "talking cure" treated humans as communicatively competent participants in their own illness and cure and is to be contrasted with other approaches, such as the use of drugs, lobotomies, shock therapies, and all manner of behaviorist conditioning, that treat humans as thing-like phenomena to be manipulated. Freud's emancipatory theory and method sought to lessen the grip of irrational and unnecessary forms of repression that limited individual human self-development, much like Marx's critique of prevailing economic theory was meant to open space for theory and practice that was true to the experience of the working class and to the potentials of history making in his time. Also, much as Marx viewed the early industrial working class as a potentially self-directed (class-conscious) political force necessary to any sustainable and liberatory social revolution, Freud saw people as necessary participants in their own cure. Inspired by Marx and Freud, critical theorists oppose "bourgeois" economic and management theory and behaviorist psychology inasmuch as these theories lack reflexivity and thus fail to understand their own participation in a society ultimately based on the domination of humans by other humans.

Even though they are credited with forging a new type of emancipatory social theory, neither Marx nor Freud fully appreciated what he had achieved. Such a consistent self-understanding had to wait for Max Horkheimer's (1895–1973) seminal 1937 essay, "Traditional and Critical Theory" (Horkheimer, 1972).[17] Horkheimer was a German philosopher and social theorist, and, beginning in 1931, director of the Institute for Social Research affiliated with the University of Frankfurt. Horkheimer coined the term *critical theory* to call attention to his goal to offer a self-conscious and generalized approach to social theory that would transcend its particular origins in Marx, Freud, and others. In part, too, Horkheimer found in the new terminology a politically useful euphemism for studies inspired by one so radical and controversial as Marx. Working from within the devastation that was Germany after the Great War (World War I) and anticipating the rise of such movements as Hitler's National Socialism, Horkheimer set out to update and synthesize the best that modern social theory could offer to put this critical social theory to work for his contemporaries, who, in his view, were in need of liberation from capitalist domination and the irrationalist ideology of an emergent German fascism.

The notion, then, of a "critical theory of society" is intimately associated with Horkheimer and his luminous "Frankfurt School" colleagues from this period.[18] Horkheimer's most prominent colleagues included Theodor W. Adorno (1903–1969), Herbert Marcuse (1898–1979), and Walter Benjamin (1892–1940). Each of these social theorists made scores of significant contributions to 20th-century philosophy and social theory. Each, like Jean-Paul Sartre, Albert Camus, and Michel Foucault, would be considered among the leading intellectual figures of the 20th century. Even though this chapter treats only one important specific theory from today's preeminent living critical theorist, Jürgen Habermas, I encourage students to investigate the lives and work of Habermas's vitally important teachers and predecessors.[19]

Habermas and Legitimation Crisis

We may now consider the essentials of Habermas's theory of legitimation crisis and its applicability to the case of Flint. Although there are many discussions and explications of Habermas's theory, this study's empirical orientation seeks to direct attention to the concrete experience of Flint's citizens to illustrate the ongoing significance of Habermas's perspective. This discussion is, therefore, an attempt to demonstrate not only the continuing importance of Marx's original critique of capitalist society but also the need to extend and revise the Marxian analysis, as Habermas has done, to meet the challenges of today's "late capitalist" society.

Flint is today a notorious case of a depressed, midwestern, Rust Belt community. So devastated is Flint that, in 2009, the *New York Times* featured a prominent local official advocating "shutting down quadrants of the city" in an effort to return it, in the words of the article, to "the forest primeval" from whence it emerged.[20] But Flint was not always a city in steep decline. Indeed, it is possible to identify three distinct periods in Flint's 20th-century social and economic history, each of which corresponds to significant changes in the American capitalist-industrial system, and each of which is discussed by Habermas in his 1973 book *Legitimation Crisis.* By way of further introduction to Habermas via Flint and its telling contemporary experience, I briefly describe the periods of liberal, advanced, and late capitalism through their manifestation in 20th-century Flint.

Capitalism in Flint

The period of liberal or laissez-faire industrial capitalism occurred in Flint between the development of the horse-drawn carriage, and later, the automobile industry, and the Great Sit-Down Strike of 1936–1937. Carriage production mushroomed in late 19th-century Flint. By 1904, Flint was the world's leading center of horse-drawn carriage production, producing more than 150,000 carriages per year. In 1908, Henry Ford rolled out the first of his Model Ts in Detroit, while in Flint, Billy Durant founded the GM Corporation. As a result of the rapid expansion of its local automobile industry, Flint quickly became an amazing boomtown, so much so that the city's population more than tripled between 1900 and 1930. As historian Ronald Edsforth documents, the automobile was the "primary driving force" behind America's 20th-century "second industrial revolution."[21] Flint was in the thick of these momentous developments, with the likes of Fisher Body, Chevrolet, Buick, AC Sparkplug, Cadillac, and DuPont fortifying the city's economic expansion.

This was still a time in American society when entrepreneurs like Durant had a relatively free hand in deciding where, when, and how to run their private businesses—hence the notion of *laissez-faire,* which refers to the doctrine of government noninterference in the workings of the economic system.[22] Although it is true that the American economy by this time was characterized by very notable economic concentration (including the infamous "trusts" in steel, railroads, oil, and banking and the social struggles by immigrant workers, farmers, and other groups against these monopolies) in newly forming industries, such as Flint's fledgling automotive industry, independent inventor-entrepreneurs still played a vital role. Indeed, their ingenuity and inventiveness, their willingness to take risks, and their ultimate success at creating vast wealth are regularly celebrated by proponents of capitalism as proof of the system's robust social virtues.

In this period, capitalists such as Durant not only ruled over their own private property but also sought and obtained considerable power beyond their workplaces. This was certainly true in Flint. For example, in 1910, when a socialist, John H. Menton, was popularly elected as Flint's mayor, local business leaders rallied to defeat this challenge by electing in the following year one of their own, multimillionaire and GM board member Charles Stewart Mott. From 1911 to 1973, when Mott died as one of America's richest men, no other person exerted more influence in or over Flint. Mott's personal significance is suggestive of GM's structural dominance in Flint as the city's primary employer, just as GM's role in Flint is suggestive of big business's dominant place in American society as a whole. The era of liberal capitalism was a time of relatively little government interference with the workings of the private market economy, and a time when the social power of America's dominant capitalist class was effectively unquestioned.

The second period of 20th-century capitalist development began with the onset of capitalism's worst hour: the Great Depression. After the infamous stock market crash of 1929, the laissez-faire capitalist economy collapsed, causing widespread hardship in Flint and throughout America and the world. The private ownership of wealth and its use in the private pursuit of profit (capitalism) did not generate, as Adam Smith's theory of the "invisible hand" predicted, a new round of entrepreneurship, employment, and economic growth. Thus, the Great Depression was not only a pressing practical problem but also an ideological problem that threatened the economic theory that legitimized capitalism as a whole. The workings of the market "mechanism" had been touted by economists since Smith as a nature-like system (*ordre naturel*) that, if left to correct its own imbalances, should have moved to a state of full-employment equilibrium. Much to the chagrin of economists, however, the market was unable to pull itself up by its own bootstraps, and, in Flint as elsewhere in America, the very real threat of social upheaval meant that something had to be done.

It is no surprise that Franklin Delano Roosevelt's activist New Deal program was enthusiastically welcomed by Flint's working class. Elected twice to the presidency in the 1930s with the strong backing of Flint's industrial workers and other minorities, Roosevelt dramatically reversed the Hoover administration's traditional do-nothing policy toward the Great Depression in favor of an unprecedented surge in government involvement in economic affairs. In establishing his so-called alphabet soup of government job creation and economic stimulus programs, and in supporting the rights of workers to unionize and claim power in the workplace as well as in the wider political arena (e.g., by supporting the National Labor Relations Act and castigating the nation's wealthy elite as an illegitimate "plutocracy"), Roosevelt forcefully challenged the exclusive power of the capitalist class to manage America's economic growth. In this era, there arose a new type of capitalist system significantly different from the liberal capitalism that collapsed into economic depression. Habermas calls this second phase of 20th-century capitalism "advanced capitalism." It is also known as organized capitalism, monopoly capitalism, and, more popularly, "welfare state" capitalism.

Although the welfare state developed sooner and grew much larger in Europe, it could be said that America's period of advanced capitalism was born in Flint precisely when, during the Great Sit-Down Strike of 1936 and 1937, Michigan's New Deal governor placed National Guard troops *between* striking workers at Flint's GM facilities and the GM-controlled local police force, which was attacking the "sit-down" strikers in an effort to rout them from their held positions in the factories. The workers had struck the corporation primarily as a result of the physically intolerable working conditions but also because of the arbitrary and unjust use of managerial authority and the widespread insecurity and suffering that 6 years of economic depression had wrought—not, of course, on Mr. Mott and associates, but on the workers and their families, who owned little but their ability to labor. In a sense, then, the workers sat down in the factories to stand up for their rights as human beings and not mere factors of production. In total, 11 strikers were wounded by police gunfire during the 44 days of the strike action as thousands of fellow workers and strike sympathizers poured into Flint and filled the streets in a jarring conflict that garnered the attention of the nation and the world. As depicted in the Academy Award–nominated film *With Babies and Banners,* even members of the United Auto Workers' (UAW) Women's Emergency Brigade took the unusual and courageous step of placing themselves between the strikers and police, suggesting the depth of commitment and solidarity emerging from within Flint's working-class community (Bohlen, Goldfarb, & Gray, 1978).[23]

With the blessing of President Roosevelt and his secretary of labor, Frances Perkins, Michigan Governor Frank Murphy moved to protect the strikers and encouraged the negotiation of a settlement in which GM would for the first time recognize the UAW and thereby its workers' right to unionize. This development was part of a larger movement in American society to mitigate and in doing so salvage, if not laissez-faire capitalism, then at least capitalism in some form. While many capitalists at the time, such as Charles Stewart Mott, disliked Roosevelt's New Deal (and they *did* very much dislike it[24]), its ultimate effect was to bring a greater balance of power between capital and labor and thus save American society from more extreme forms of political revolution, such as those that occurred at the time in Germany and earlier in Russia.

U.S.-advanced capitalism emerged from World War II virtually unscathed and, indeed, strengthened by worldwide military conflict. In the sardonic phrase of the sociologist C. Wright Mills (1979), this was a time of an "American celebration." Postwar America was a society that easily delivered the proverbial goods, creating material abundance for a growing and stabilizing middle class. The overt political upheavals associated with the "labor wars" of the 1930s were replaced by a postwar mass democracy that created political stability and ideological conformity. Aided by Cold War tensions abroad and McCarthyism at home, this "culture of abundance" encouraged, in Edsforth's phrase, the emergence of a "cultural consensus."

As a shining example of the celebration of postwar American prosperity, Flint enjoyed its *Leave It to Beaver* heyday. As Edsforth documents, one magazine in 1956 went as far as to dub Flint "The Happiest Town in Michigan."[25] In this new era of (as it turned out, temporary) consensus, the American automobile industry dominated the world's market for cars and trucks, providing an abundance of jobs and economic growth. The UAW, for its part, negotiated steadily increasing wages, benefits, and improved working conditions. This steady rise in income created the conditions for a parallel rise in consumption. It was not uncommon for Flint's working people to own a home, two or more cars, a boat, and perhaps a cabin "up north" where families might regularly vacation, and for parents to ponder the likelihood of sending their children to the local college or one of the expanding state universities. Not only were individuals realizing what, at the time, constituted the "American Dream," but also whole communities were sprouting, as was Flint, all manner of museums, theaters, sports facilities, superhighways, libraries, and music halls. From 1945 to the late 1960s, the Big Business/Big Labor/Big Government advanced capitalist economy was good for GM and was absolutely great for Flint.

From the early 1970s onward, however, the stability of the advanced capitalist system began to erode, so much so that we may distinguish this period as the third phase of 20th-century capitalism. With the 1973 publication of *Legitimation Crisis* and its English translation 2 years later, Habermas helped to initiate discussion of late capitalism in terms of the "crisis tendencies of advanced capitalism." Because it is the burden of the remaining discussion to fully explain Habermas's theory of these "crisis tendencies," including, in particular, the potential in our time for "legitimation crisis," I conclude this background discussion of the changing shape of American capitalism by simply describing the emergence of late capitalism in Flint.

Once an expanding metropolis and a veritable boomtown, Flint is today closer to a ghost town.[26] As sociologist Paul J. Draus notes, cities like Flint have been hit by "slow-motion disasters."[27] According to one study, "General Motors [at its peak local employment in 1978] *directly* contributed 42.4 percent of the county's jobs and indirectly significant other auto-related jobs."[28] Auto industry jobs have been crucial to the vitality of the area's economy for 100 years in large part because the typical pay and benefit level for these jobs significantly exceeded the national average. In fact, auto industry jobs remain better paying than almost every other type of industrial job. For example, in 1987, automotive manufacturing occupations had annual average earnings of $39,500, which was in that year $13,800 more than the average manufacturing wage (Grimes, 1990, p. 2). By 2009, GM's workforce in Flint was still able to earn an estimated $28 per hour and annual incomes of $60,000, plus benefits packages that included extensive medical insurance coverage and retirement pensions. In comparison to minimum-wage, service-sector employment, auto industry jobs have always been, and those that remain are, a gold mine. Since 1978, however, GM has cut its Flint workforce by the staggering figure of

75,000 (from 80,000 in 1978 to roughly 5,000 in 2009).[29] This massive reduction of once-secure, high-wage jobs has resulted in ripple effects through the community, which register in Flint as a panoply of apparently disparate social problems (Bluestone & Harrison, 1982).[30]

In *The Deindustrialization of America: Plant Closings, Community Abandonment, and the Dismantling of Basic Industry* (1982), economists Barry Bluestone and Bennett Harrison describe this general process as deindustrialization. They define deindustrialization as "the widespread, systemic disinvestment in the nation's basic productive capacity" (p. 6), which, they argue,

> can be traced to the way capital—in the forms of financial resources and of real plant and equipment—has been diverted from productive investment in our basic national industries into unproductive speculations, mergers and acquisitions, and foreign investment. (ibid.)

For Bluestone and Harrison (1982), deindustrialization has led to "shuttered factories, displaced workers, and a newly emerging group of ghost towns" (p. 6). Sadly, Flint's experience is an exaggeration of these tendencies.

Although scratching only the surface of the human dimensions of widespread and sustained unemployment, a rehearsal of social statistics is one way to spark the imagination. According to a 1991 memorandum authored by staff at the Flint branch of Michigan's Department of Social Services, titled "State of Flint," Flint lost a quarter of its population in the 20-year period from 1970 to 1990. Since 1990, Flint's population has declined even further, from 141,367 to an estimated 110,000 in 2009.[31] In 1990, Flint had more vacant businesses and boarded-up homes than at any time in its history, as well as the tenth highest infant mortality rate in the nation. In this same year, Flint recorded an unemployment rate for black youth of nearly 60%. According to this source, public assistance caseloads in the Flint area increased by 79.6% during the period between 1973 and 1989, with the result that slightly more than 40% of Flint's total population was receiving some form of public assistance.[32]

Crime, not surprisingly, is also a problem. For example, in 1989, Genesee County, where Flint is situated, ranked third highest of the 333 largest U.S. metropolitan areas in the number of violent and property crimes committed.[33] In the 1980s, while Genesee County's overall youth unemployment rate grew to 25%, its homicide rate for youth rose 400%.[34] By 1990, Flint had the highest serious crime rates of any Michigan city, including Detroit. In 2006, St. Louis, Detroit, and Flint were ranked the first, second and third "most dangerous cities" in the United States, while in 2008, burglaries and robberies increased even as violent crime declined along with population.[35]

Additional indicators of Flint's depressed condition during the period of its most rapid job loss include statistics that document the following: Suicide rates for Genesee County's 15- to 19-year-olds increased 300% from 1982 to 1987; adolescent substance abuse increased by nearly 20% between 1988 and 1990; the number of domestic violence clients increased tenfold in the period from 1984 to 1991; Genesee County's divorce rate was in this period 66% higher than the national average; reported cases of child abuse and neglect increased by more than 20% during the 1980s; and, finally, by the early 1990s, 58% of Flint's children were raised in single-parent households, which, research documents, are household types that suffer disproportionately from persistent poverty.[36] In 1987, *Money* magazine ranked Flint the least desirable American city in which to live.[37] By 1995, Flint's most depressed neighborhoods, populated disproportionately by Flint's African American citizens, had unemployment rates above 25% and concentrated rates of poverty ranging above 40%. Indeed, as Jonathan Mahler stressed in his 2009 *New York Times Magazine* story of the subject, the collapse of the U.S. auto industry threatened "the fall of the black middle class."[38] By 2000, Flint's overall rate of poverty among individuals held steady at 26.4%, but by 2007, after additional layoffs, plant closings, and population loss, Flint's poverty rate had climbed to a truly stunning 33.2%.[39] Perhaps even more telling than 1 in 3 Flint residents living in poverty is the fact that nearly 1 in 2 of Flint's citizens survived in 2000 on just 200% of the official poverty income level, while nearly 1 in 8 earned less than 50% of the already grossly inadequate annual poverty income threshold.[40]

Because Flint is singularly dependent on GM employment—an extreme case of the proverbial one-horse town—Flint's high rates of sustained, structural unemployment, as well as the social problems predictably related to this condition, are easily attributable to GM's local downsizing.[41] GM is not, however, legally or politically held responsible for Flint's economic ruination. GM was not, for example, charged with premeditated murder when Flint's crime and suicide rates shot up as an indirect, but predictable, result of massive local unemployment. Nor did the federal, state, or local governments ask GM to pay increased taxes to cover the soaring expenditures for social services caused by GM's widespread layoffs. On the contrary, governments at all levels are much more likely to grant tax breaks and provide other incentives in an effort to entice corporations to retain the reduced number of jobs remaining after a round of downsizing.

This was certainly the case in Flint, where GM received $400 million in local tax breaks during the 1980s, even as the company slashed its Flint-based employment.[42] The Flint City Council continued to approve GM tax abatement requests, including eight abatement requests for a building constructed on top of the demolished GM factory recognized as the historic site of Flint's Great Sit-Down Strike. In the early 1990s, GM announced a new round of layoffs and local plant closings in Flint, and the local business class grew desperate.[43] By 1996, Flint-area business and political leaders predicted that local GM employment could drop to "between 26,000 and 15,000 by the end of the decade," causing the head of the Flint-Genesee Economic Growth Alliance to speculate that Flint should consider following the lead of Amarillo, Texas, which taxes its citizens to pay prospective businesses a "bounty on jobs," as much as $10,000 up front for every $12-per-hour job they promise to create.[44] As it turned out, these predictions were too rosy. By the decade's end, GM had gone in and, thanks primarily to U.S. taxpayers, out of bankruptcy, while Flint's GM workforce had shrunk to 5,000, not 15,000. It seemed as though the dominance of capitalism in Flint had in some sense come full circle: Instead of GM paying Flint's workers for their labor power and creating prosperity in the community, Flint's workers were being asked to consider paying GM for the privilege of holding a job, and, once the corporation finally became insolvent, they were asked to pony up $60 billion to save the company—the symbol of capitalist might—from liquidation.[45]

A poignant moment in *Roger & Me* may serve to capture the deep social conflict engendered by capitalism. After years of trying, Michael Moore finally corners then–GM Chairman Roger Smith and asks him to come to Flint to witness the devastation caused by Smith's disinvestment decisions. Suggesting GM's legal and political unaccountability to the people of Flint, as well as, perhaps, the arrogance and sheer might of transnational capital in the increasingly freewheeling era of late capitalism, Smith tersely says to Moore, "I cannot come to Flint, I'm sorry," before he abruptly turns his back. In its bankruptcy, however, GM did come to Flint, and to all the citizens of the United States and even those of Canada, hat in hand and, one imagines, grinning like the Cheshire Cat.

Habermas's Theory of Legitimation Crisis: Systems Crisis

Although Flint has experienced, as has been shown, something approaching Depression-like conditions during the past three decades, there has been no repeat of the kind of grassroots militancy and social upheaval that characterized Flint in the Great Depression. In Flint, there is no manifest development of a "proletarian" revolutionary consciousness; nothing like the class struggle predicted in the imagery of Marx's original theory of capitalist crisis; and no repeat of the Great Sit-Down Strike of 1936 and 1937.

Drawing from *Legitimation Crisis* as well as Habermas's two-volume magnum opus, *The Theory of Communicative Action* (1981/1987), and other writings, we can make sense of this apparent departure from Marxian expectations by first taking into account the important changes in the capitalist system since Marx's time.[46] In contrast to Marx's original critique of liberal capitalism, Habermas directs our attention to advanced capitalism's integration of economic and political systems and, thus, to the displacement or shifting of the potential for economic crisis into a potential for political or government crisis, or what Habermas calls the tendency toward "rationality crisis." Unlike the situation in Marx's own time, governments since the Great Depression and the rise of the welfare state have taken explicit responsibility for smoothing out economic cycles and ameliorating income disparities. Agreeing with Marx, Habermas sees these types of crises—the vagaries of the capitalist market—as endemic to the class-based structure of liberal capitalist society.[47] But what of advanced capitalism? Thanks to the famous suggestion by economist John Maynard Keynes that government involvement in the capitalist economy could be a good and, from time to time, necessary thing, advanced capitalist governments had an economic theory that legitimized their attempts to manage economic growth (using fiscal and monetary policy, international trade policy, regulation of stock and bond markets, the expertise of the president's Council of Economic Advisors, etc.). This was especially the case in postwar Europe and in Japan, but it was also true to an important extent in the United States. Indeed, as we have seen, the postwar boom that made Flint "The Happiest Town in Michigan" also made it seem as though mass production and mass consumption, along with the government's Keynesian economics, had forever and peacefully solved the same contradictions of capitalism that, in *Capital*, Marx had suggested were resolvable only through wrenching class revolution.[48]

As a consequence of government intervention, Habermas observes that attempts to manage economic growth politicize that which had previously been seen as the nature-like, impersonal workings of the free market system. The results of Adam Smith's "invisible hand" became the all-too-visible outcomes of public policy decisions and labor-management collective bargaining. Constitutionally charged with promoting the general welfare, the post–New Deal federal government was called on to mitigate the short-term effects of unemployment and various other social problems and to create what today is often called the "social safety net." This implicit guarantee by the government to promote full employment and to protect individuals from the worst vicissitudes of the market is paid for by tax dollars and administered by government bureaucracies. Today, the expansion or contraction of this safety net is a matter of continual political debate, as is suggested by the title of Laura Meckler's 2009 article in the *Wall Street Journal*, "Public Wary of Deficit, Economic Intervention," which documented that nearly 7 in 10 Americans "had concerns about federal intervention into the economy, including Mr. Obama's decision to take an ownership stake in General Motors Corp., limits on executive compensation and the prospect of more government involvement in health care."[49]

In this regard, Habermas (1981/1987) writes, "between capitalism and democracy there is an *indissoluble* tension; in them two opposed principles of societal integration compete for primacy" (emphasis original). As economic crises grow and multiply (as in Flint since the advent of GM's downsizing and eventual bankruptcy), the democratic governments of late capitalist society are expected to provide more and more relief and protection from the harm engendered by economic crisis. Recall that it is not unusual for 40% of Flint's citizens to receive some form of public assistance. Governments, however, can provide and administer more services (e.g., increased unemployment benefits, medical care, educational benefits, and welfare services) only by increasing tax revenues or by borrowing to match the expenses caused by a rise in the number of "clients" of various government bureaucracies (such as the patients in veterans' hospitals, senior citizens requiring government health care assistance, prisoners in America's jails, the recipients of food stamps, and even the once-mightiest industrial corporation in the world). Economic problems are, in this way, translated into political problems to be solved through the administration of welfare-state bureaucracies.

It is also a problem because not only do average citizens generally dislike increased taxation, which diminishes the money they have to spend on themselves, but also increased taxation on business diminishes profits and, in so doing, discourages capitalist investment. Because capitalists invest, after all, to reap maximum private profits, capitalists might reasonably ask themselves, "Why invest (and create jobs and new products and services) if the government is just going to take a large share of my profits to pay for other people's problems" (e.g., the problems experienced by the people of Flint)? or "Why invest in GM stock, and thereby increase GM's ability to expand and improve its business, if the corporation's profits are just going to be redirected through government taxation and spending policies back to the people of Flint instead of into my personal bank account as stock dividends?" Even more plausibly, what is to prevent an investor from looking to make money in other countries, particularly those with more favorable "business climates" (i.e., countries with lower taxes, less government regulation to protect workers' rights and the environment, and a less powerful workforce, which is therefore less able to bargain or demand wage and benefit increases and less able to elect political leaders who will tax business and the wealthy to provide social services)? In any case, it stands to reason that the U.S. economy would suffer a loss of investment, which could lead to a vicious cycle of decline: Less domestic investment or investment "offshore" means more domestic unemployment; more unemployment means more social problems; increasing social problems mean more pressure on government to increase social services to ameliorate the problems; but increased taxes could mean less investment, and so on.

There is also the possibility that this contradiction could cause political unrest, such as "tax revolts," in which voters reject local school millage increases, human service levies, property taxes, and candidates at all levels of government who would dare advocate increased taxation. In America, it is just this contradiction that produced the much-debated problem of the national debt. Although Reagan- and Bush II-era tax cuts were in themselves politically popular, they were not balanced by reductions in government spending, which, because so many depend on forms of government spending, tend to be politically unpopular. The resulting indebtedness of the government, which requires that an increasing proportion of the yearly budget go to paying interest on the debt, hinders the political system's ability to address social problems. Many are concerned that a "reformed" U.S. health care system will result in the same problem. For Habermas, this "crisis of the welfare state" is caused by the displacement of the contradictions in the capitalist system into the realm of politics, where they emerge in a different form. In Habermas's view, the contradictions of liberal capitalism (identified more or less correctly by Marx as rooted in the class structure of capitalist society[50]) are, in advanced capitalism, transformed into the persistent contradictions of the welfare state.

So, why is it that GM is able to reduce its Flint-based employment by 75,000 jobs without sparking "class struggle"? Deindustrialization is a relatively smooth process, in part because the government is expected to ameliorate hardship, absorb the social costs, and diffuse the frustration and anger caused by GM's private business decision and market failures. It is expected, furthermore, that politicians will not explicitly discuss the class basis of capitalism or bring into question the legitimacy of the capitalist system as a whole. Instead, mainstream political leaders are expected to present this conflict in a technical or administrative light, for example, as a debate over "balancing the budget" or saving specific companies that are "too big to fail." This type of discourse calls attention only to the conflict between tax increases and the pressures on government spending as well as the strategic position of specific firms in specific industries, not conflict between social classes as such or concern for the viability, much less the desirability, of the system—the worldwide system—as a whole. Thus, this kind of discourse tends to leave citizens demanding contradictions (e.g., more government-provided benefits and less taxation, more economic growth and less ecological destruction, more economic security and less government intervention in economic affairs, etc.). This explains, in part, why political leaders as divergent as Ronald Reagan and Jesse Jackson could, in the 1980s, simultaneously be very popular in Flint: Each spoke to a different dimension of Flint's experienced crisis, much as today's Sarah Palin and Barack Obama do.

Although the preceding discussion broadly captures what Habermas calls the rationality crisis of governments at the national and state levels, it is also instructive to examine for a moment the details of Flint's local response to its GM-based deindustrialization. Even though Flint had for decades been overwhelmingly dependent on GM employment, Flint's government and community leaders showed surprising inventiveness and industry of their own in devising a plan to replace the permanently lost GM jobs. Acting in accordance with their implicit responsibility to promote the general welfare, and with more than $200 million in investment capital (including $80 million in backing from the Flint-headquartered Charles Stewart Mott Foundation, one of the country's largest charitable foundations), Flint's leaders set about to reinvent the city's image and economy.

Beginning in the late 1970s, and gaining steam with Reagan-era optimism and deficit spending, Flint's leaders hoped to take Flint from what it was, a decaying, Rust Belt, industrial city heavily dependent on its remaining and still substantial GM base, to, as one commentator put it, the "tourist and convention mecca of the Midwest" (Zwerdling, 1982, p. 35). The centerpiece of this would-be phoenix-like rebirth was "AutoWorld," an indoor theme park designed to attract more than 1 million visitors per year to Flint. Tax dollars also funded the construction of a new hotel in downtown Flint. With several additional developments, including a James Rouse–designed "festival marketplace," Flint readied itself to emerge as a 1980s family vacation destination.

Of course, as *Roger & Me* depicts with such great effect, this government-inspired and government-administered convention and tourism plan was a tremendous flop. The only conventions Flint could attract were on the order of statewide meetings of Scrabble players, and AutoWorld, the $80-million theme park, closed within 6 months of its opening due to lack of visitors. Apparently, the attraction of riding the world's largest indoor Ferris wheel and the sheen of Flint's new slogan "Flint: Our Spark Will Surprise You!" could not offset people's commonsense understanding of the bitter-hard realities of a Rust Belt auto town. Flint's downtown hotel eventually went bankrupt (although it has since reopened under new, religiously oriented management), and its so-called festival marketplace was transferred to the University of Michigan at Flint for a token sum. As Michael Moore pointed out in his *Roger & Me* narration,

> Expecting a million people to come to Flint was a little like expecting a million people to go to New Jersey to "ChemicalWorld," or to Valdez, Alaska, to "ExxonWorld." Some people just don't like to celebrate human tragedy while on vacation.[51]

Flint's community leaders' failed attempt at economic development exemplifies Habermas's notion of rationality crisis. With a grant from the C.S. Mott Foundation, tax dollars, and additional borrowing, the city tried to replace what it lost when GM removed so many jobs from the community. Instead of a viable alternative to capitalist development, however, Flint succeeded only in bringing the political nature of economic development into the open and placing in question the competence of government planners. Some years later, in a moment of frustration, Mark S. Davis, the head of Flint's new post–AutoWorld private business–led economic development coalition, exclaimed, "I mean, for God's sake, this is the town that built AutoWorld!"[52] Even for Davis, no radical social theorist of the Frankfurt School variety, AutoWorld was symbolic of the inability of technically oriented government administrators to fundamentally solve the contradictions of capitalism. It is no wonder, then, that AutoWorld was eventually demolished, for it stood as a constant reminder that the old solutions to America's social problems have been eclipsed by the new realities of late capitalism. It remains to be seen whether the politically orchestrated bailout of GM in 2009 will result in similarly disheartening consequences, although on a much grander scale.

Habermas's Theory of Legitimation Crisis: The Lifeworld

To this point, I have not addressed the especially unique aspect of Habermas's theory. Habermas in particular argues that a further displacement of the potential for crisis can and does occur, this time not as an exchange from the integrated economic and political systems (as previously described) but rather as an exchange from these machine-like societal subsystems to our community and personal lives, or to what Habermas calls the *sociocultural system* or *lifeworld*. For Habermas, the truly unsettling crises of late capitalism are likely to occur along the "seams" between our contradiction-ridden social systems and the traditional, taken-for-granted cultural patterns (norms, values, and beliefs) that anchor our sense of reality and our personal identity, and that guide and regulate our motivation as social actors.[53] In this way, Habermas moves the analysis of late capitalism in a distinctly sociological direction.[54] Drawing on the classic sociological theories of Durkheim, Mead, Parsons, and others, Habermas refocuses critical theory toward the tenuous and vulnerable processes of the symbolically mediated dialectic between self and society and the shared moral fabric that undergirds the abstract functioning of formal social systems. In *Legitimation Crisis*, Habermas names both the legitimation and motivation crisis tendencies associated with this part of his argument as types of identity crisis. This part of Habermas's theory has more in common with Durkheim's theory of anomie than it does, for example, with Marx's economistic concern for the so-called *laws of capital accumulation* and the *falling rate of profit*. What is at stake in Habermas's attention to the lifeworld is the nonrational underbelly of functionally differentiated social systems, which provides societies with their coherence and collective identity.[55]

Before applying this aspect of Habermas's theory to the case of Flint, it is necessary to point out that Habermas's theoretical approach is unique (and made even more complex!) because Habermas also identifies a type of top-down response to the crisis tendencies undermining late capitalism from below.[56] In effect, Habermas asks the following: If the New Deal welfare state (Big Government), increased unionization (Big Labor), and America's postwar global hegemony, among other factors, temporarily resolved the crisis of America's laissez-faire capitalism by creating a new type of advanced capitalism, then what might contemporaries do in response to the crises of advanced capitalism that continue despite government attempts to ameliorate them? Habermas's answer to this question allows us to make sense of the latest elite-driven responses to Flint's woes. As I have already intimated, Flint did not sit idly by after the AutoWorld debacle and watch while its fortunes declined. Instead, there arose a new set of strategies designed to extend the tentacles of economic and political elites deep into the social and cultural fabric so as to vitiate the destabilizing effects of the crises of advanced capitalism.

Habermas uses the phrase "colonization of the lifeworld" to describe the tendency of corporations and government entities to work together in a desperate attempt to stabilize and reproduce late capitalism by attempting to manage and control more and more of everyday life.[57] The question then becomes, how much of everyday life can be successfully integrated into the operation of these social systems before new social and cultural pathologies are engendered as a result? Can people come to think of themselves, their families, and their community as mere cogs in turbulent bureaucratic corporations and mass political and economic systems and, at the same time, continue in good faith to wholeheartedly participate in such a society? Can people function, asks Habermas (1981/1987), when their "everyday consciousness is robbed of its power to synthesize; [when] it becomes fragmented"?

Habermas does not think so. He sees a fundamental contradiction between the abstract calculus of instrumental rationality, which guides both the profit-maximizing firm and bureaucratic government, and the textured communicative rationality of everyday life, which guides us in our "action oriented to reaching understanding" and, in this way, secures and reproduces the integration of social life.[58] In other words, for Habermas, it is not possible to replace traditional values and beliefs with an artificial culture constructed only to further some corporation's profit maximization strategy or some government's legitimacy. People cannot live as members of the "MTV" or "Pepsi Generation," at least not without serious and dysfunctional consequences. What Habermas calls the *internal colonization* of the lifeworld is, therefore, a contradictory process because it threatens to create forms of social *dis*integration, such as individual psychopathologies and collective anomie, even though its purpose is to stabilize and reproduce a coherent and integrated social order.[59]

This is where Habermas's (1982) theories of legitimation and motivation crisis become germane. We may think of these as crisis tendencies "from below" inasmuch as both refer to people's withdrawal of their connection to the society's institutionalized social systems. In particular, Habermas understands the potential for people to lose confidence in a mass political system that is democratic in name but that in myriad ways discourages genuine participation and denies average citizens a meaningful political voice. Everyone knows, for example, that a "televised town meeting" is not a real town meeting but is instead a format designed to stage the appearance of participatory democracy for a mass viewing audience. Moreover, because the political system regularly fails to solve the fundamental problems caused by a contradictory capitalist system (in part because the true nature of the problems cannot be openly identified and debated), citizens become disaffected, apathetic, and resigned, even if they are not consciously aware of the source of their disaffection and its relation to the prohibition against class-based political debate. Also, because the political and economic systems have become so tightly integrated, when both fail, and when the "colonization" tendencies identified by Habermas are, as a result, intensified, then torn and frayed is the very fabric of traditional values and beliefs that once motivated people to give over their lives to participation in the risky and difficult workings of the marketplace. For Habermas, this set of motivational resources includes a variety of specific dimensions, such as "civil" and "familial-vocational privatism," or the tendencies toward political nonparticipation in favor of attention to leisure, consumption, and status competition through careerism.[60]

For Habermas, there are no easy functional replacements for these traditional guiding values and norms, and it remains an open question whether the social systems can reproduce themselves without recourse to a pre-reflective, always implicit, and shared culture. Habermas calls the withdrawal of mass political loyalty *legitimation crisis* and the withdrawal of motivation, especially the motivation toward achievement and participation in the occupational system, *motivation crisis*.[61] A combined realization of these closely related crisis tendencies would portend a radical transformation of society.

The development in 1989 of the Genesee Economic Area Revitalization, Incorporated (GEAR), a new umbrella public-private economic development partnership for the Flint area, illustrates Flint's colonizing response to the possibility of legitimation and motivation crises. Facing more GM downsizing (economic crisis) and stung by the AutoWorld debacle (rationality crisis), Flint's reeling elites implicitly sought (or so I argue) to ward off legitimation and motivation crises by adopting the attitude that any future economic development would have to be strategically, that is, self-consciously and systematically, tied to a human resource strategy and an education strategy.[62] In other words, GEAR's economic development mission involved what its executive director, Mark S. Davis, colorfully described as "defining" and "improving the product." Davis explained,

> The economic reality of GM shutting down jobs during the last couple of decades has created a political environment that has many effects on the social economy, the social fabric.
>
> But everybody in the past has been focused on the god-damned public sector. . . . For a long time, the way things got decided in our community was people waited for GM, the UAW, and the Mott Foundation to tell them what to do.

> What's happening now, though, is there are massive structural changes in the economy taking place. So, as a community, we're recognizing, in a way, the ascendancy of the private sector in economic development in a way that has never been understood before.
>
> My message here is economic development cannot succeed unless we improve the product. A community is a product. The product is the summation of what we are. What we have to offer to a business, to an employer, to an investor, is the summation of what we are. That is our product.[63]

Davis's notion that "a community is a product," or that a community's market or economic value to business is the "summation" of what a community is, jibes with Habermas's claim that the lifeworld (Davis's "social economy, the social fabric") is increasingly the focus of capitalism's efforts to stabilize itself.

If we follow the logic of this position, then everything that reproduces and characterizes human society becomes a potential object of manipulation. GEAR's colonizing framework even defines Flint's evident social problems primarily in terms of their negative effect on the ability of "the product" to retain or attract outside business. For example, GEAR's 1991 strategic economic development plan states the following with regard to Flint's poverty: "Persistent poverty breeds understandable social resentment and conflict, dividing communities and prohibiting effective common action, *conditions that discourage enterprise and outside investment* [italics added]."[64] The following is also from this same document:

> Finally, but perhaps most importantly, there is the central issue of the human resource challenges in the Flint/Genesee County community that must be met if our economic future is to be bright.
>
> Unless our people are provided with the material and spiritual resources needed to build a healthy, safe, and prosperous community—one in which people are permitted to dream and make choices about their futures—the prospect for more jobs is nothing but a hollow promise.
>
> Poverty, inadequate health care, poor nutrition, racial discrimination, dysfunctional families, substandard housing, unsafe neighborhoods, drug and alcohol dependence and human despair: All are powerful enemies of economic development.
>
> Therefore, we are of a strong and unanimous voice in recommending to the GEAR Board that the achievement of our vision for Flint/Genesee County's future requires that a human resources strategy be integrated with the economic development strategy we propose today.[65]

GEAR's Mark Davis puts this logic more simply and directly, and perhaps more honestly:

> We better have a better educated workforce, we better have babies that come to school healthy, because no amount of slick marketing on my part is going

to succeed in attracting a company from the outside unless we have a product that's competitive.[66]

In other words, GEAR recognized that its "product" is initially produced by individuals, families, and neighborhoods. As an economic planning organization, however, GEAR had little or no direct control over these spheres of life. GEAR may have had influence in the economic and political systems, but its influence in Flint's social-cultural system was scant. Hence, GEAR proposed that a "human resources strategy be integrated with [its] economic development strategy," presumably to better integrate human and economic development. In this way, GEAR treats people's lives as variables in a strategic plan. GEAR's social engineers are not so much worried about poverty or young children's health in and of themselves—as though people were of intrinsic value, their suffering itself a matter of concern, and as though the people of Flint were subjects with whom one would speak and argue in the hope of reaching mutual understanding and perhaps even agreement and consensus. Rather, GEAR weighs people and their life experience in an instrumental, cost-benefit calculus, adequate, at best, to the workings of social systems. A member of GEAR stated, "It doesn't make sense to try to drag in all this baggage, all these disenfranchised people."[67]

What if, however, in a different situation, it did "make sense" to drag in the "baggage" of disenfranchised people? What if it made good economic sense to employ workers in Mexico or China for $50 per week? Having eschewed an understanding of Flint as a community in favor of treating it as a product, GEAR took the strategic position that it could not in a cost-effective fashion sell Flint to prospective businesses unless Flint's people were competitively engineered at all stages of their socialization. It was decided, in other words, that Flint would "improve its product" and not ready it for a fire sale. Flint would set its sights high in hopes of attracting a handsome price. This would require strategic attention to the educational experience of Flint's citizens.

One might suppose that your study of the book in your hands is meant in some way to contribute to something as lofty as your full development as an intellectually empowered human being. Not surprisingly, perhaps, GEAR adopted a different way of looking at education. Because an important part of GEAR's early 1990s economic development strategy was to make Flint a "world center for applying information technology to manufacturing," GEAR recognized that this required Flint to also become home to a "world-class workforce."[68] The GEAR plan states the following:

> Every local economy must have a competitive advantage if it wishes to prosper in a global economy. In addition to the unique concentration of technically skilled workers that Flint/Genesee County proposes to create, the area has decided to develop a competitive advantage as a place where people know more about using information technologies and new organizational techniques in factory settings *than anywhere else in the world* [italics added].[69]

Because Flint's public educational system has the typical problems of school systems in most depressed urban areas, and because there are no major universities in

Flint, one might reasonably ask how GEAR planned to "create" this base of "technically skilled workers." The answer is given in the strategic plan as follows:

> The challenge of improving our work skills is great, because it will require that *every adult and youth* [italics added]—men and women already in the work force as well as young people still in school—acquire the learning skills, social skills and job skills to earn a middle-class living and retain and attract good jobs to Flint/Genesee County. To meet this goal, *each person must better their individual skills, and have a positive attitude about work, family and education* [italics added].[70]

From GEAR's perspective, then, the educational system in Flint should not so much be concerned with the students' enlightenment and personal growth, but should instead focus its institutional power on developing job skills and even "positive attitudes" sufficient to "retain and attract good jobs" to the area. In this way, the value of "liberal education" (a conversation about ideas?) is erased in favor of the integration of educational institutions as a means to the larger economic end of an improved product. Indeed, the surprising emphasis given to "a positive attitude about work, family and education" is indicative of GEAR's attention to Flint's sociocultural system. In this regard, GEAR's plan for the reform of Flint's educational system is exactly akin to its human resources strategy—it's all about improving the product.

From Habermas's perspective, it is, however, doubtful whether GEAR's colonization strategy could ever be successful. Although this type of top-down manipulation of everyday life may not engender a response such as the class struggle that spilled into the streets of Depression-era Flint, neither is it likely that such a cynical program as GEAR's—which, for example, conceives of a baby's health in terms of its cost benefit to prospective profit-maximizing business—will come to smoothly recast Flint's lifeworld in the form of a production process. As Habermas observes, culture is "peculiarly resistant" to such bureaucratic control.[71] It is simply too easy for people to see through such schemes to the cynicism concerning human life that lies at the heart of capitalism and any administrative attempts to contain the crises generated therein. Inasmuch as people, in solidarity with one another as human beings of intrinsic worth, do in fact resist the intrusion of such instrumental or "strategic" rationality into their lives, they withdraw their legitimation and their motivation from the integrated political and economic system that lives on little else.[72] In Habermas's view, and taking a more proactive stance, the protection and free development of the distinct form of human solidarity characteristic of the lifeworld necessitates the struggle against the colonizing tendencies of late capitalist society.[73]

Conclusion

Not surprisingly, as Flint's employment mainstays, the bankrupt General Motors and Delphi Corporations, struggled to maintain not so much profitability as their very existence by closing North American factories, shedding high-wage workers, and reneging on union contracts, Flint further declined as a city and community. Flint's last remaining factories are at risk of permanent closure, while most of its closed factories have been razed, the sites that once employed thousands now bare concrete floors as far as the eye can see. In 2009, Flint remains synonymous with economic wasteland, a veritable poster child of deindustrialization. And as though he had learned nothing except the exactly wrong lesson from the experience, Dan Kildee, Genesee County's treasurer and the local leader who the *New York Times* describes as the "chief spokesperson for the movement to shrink Flint," stated that "decline in Flint is like gravity, a fact of life."[74]

But this chapter is not about economic ruination per se. Habermas's theory leads us to consider how and why people respond—or, more to the point and per the example of Mr. Kildee—do not respond to the causes and effects of managed social processes like deindustrialization. While 21st-century scholars and activists continue to document the plight of Flint and similar cities, 21st-century citizens appear resigned to a postindustrial, although wholly capitalist, way of life.

There are exceptions. There is the person of Lawrence Marks, the 38-year-old African American Flint resident interviewed by Steve Mellon in his elegy *After the Smoke Clears: Struggling to Get by in Rustbelt America* (2002). "When he was young," writes Mellon, "Marks thought athletics would get him out of Flint" (p. 129). When that didn't work out, Marks enlisted in the Army, and when that didn't work out either, he held a string of odd jobs, including working as a security guard at AutoWorld. When Mellon encountered Marks, he had just recently been named senior co-pastor of Flint's All Equal Center, an organization officially dedicated to "combat and dispel all rumors, hearsay and innuendoes for the sole purpose of making this world a better place to live" (p. 130). Marks explained the Center's work thusly:

> If you're being discharged from your job, or have a workman's comp claim, we can look at the situation, gather information, put it all together. And if you need anything, we'll refer you to the proper agency. (p. 130)

Before taking leave of Flint, Mellon encountered Marks again at a downtown restaurant. Marks was carrying college textbooks and told Mellon that he was studying to earn an associate's degree. "'The field I'm interested in is criminal justice,' Marks said while standing in line. 'Then I'll go into sociology'" (Mellon, 2002, p. 130).

What if, indeed, Habermas's sociological theory informed the consciousness of everyday Flint citizens like Lawrence Marks? It seems appropriate to pose such questions in conclusion to this application of Jürgen Habermas's critical theory of legitimation crisis. Will withdrawal of motivation and legitimation create conditions for fundamental social change? Will the colonization of the lifeworld disrupt the symbolic reproduction through which social integration is maintained? Is the All Equal Center a harbinger of things to come, not only in Flint but in the United States and the capitalist world as a whole? If Habermas's theory is correct, it is as difficult to answer these questions as it is to ascertain the point at which an individual's or community's self-understanding as an administered and commodified product becomes unbearable, or to know why or even how these new conditions lead to self-debilitating or self-transformative responses or even to a radical political revolution—or to something in between, novel, or unprecedented.

What is clear, however, and what is appropriate to reveal, is that as a participant in the life of my hometown—which is to me, therefore, no mere product—I have a special interest in not further exposing Flint's lifeworld to any more top-down scrutiny than it has already received. In other words, as a reflexive critical theorist, I pursue sociology in a way that is mindful of how sociological knowledge can itself contribute to the "colonization of the lifeworld."

Therefore, I choose to underscore but a single point. This discussion suggests that Flint's leaders have long been at least tacitly aware of the crisis tendencies identified by Habermas as flaring up along the seams between system and lifeworld. Just as Habermas's analysis would lead us to predict "the repoliticization of the public sphere"[75] as the most probable crisis tendency to emerge out of a full-blown collapse of late capitalism, Mark Davis's following answer to my query concerning the origin of the GEAR board of directors' authority to manipulate Flint's "social fabric" suggests a parallel concern:

> To be honest, I've never looked, it wasn't important, and it's not important. It's only important to academics. In the real world, what is important is what are they doing, OK? And if we're going to get into legitimacy, and all these other sorts of stuff, I'm going to [pause]. I don't play that game because it's bullshit! (Dandaneau, 1996, p. 199)

At this point, Davis threatened to short-circuit our pursuit of "mutual understanding" by ending my interview. Although Davis's wariness about questions of legitimacy does not, of course, verify the validity of Habermas's legitimation crisis theory, his concern suggests at least the salience of Habermas's line of questioning. As Habermas (1982) at one point dryly notes, in the absence of a rational, democratic response to the crisis tendencies of late capitalism, we should realize that "the scope of tolerance for merely instrumental attitudes, indifference or cynicism, is expanded" (p. 281).[76]

Notes

1. This chapter is based on my work *A town abandoned: Flint, Michigan, confronts deindustrialization.* (1996). Albany: State University of New York Press. The main sources of Habermas's legitimation crisis theory are the following: Habermas, J. (1975). *Legitimation crisis* (T. McCarthy, Trans.). Boston: Beacon Press. (Original work published 1973); Habermas, J. (1979). Legitimation problems in the modern state. In T. McCarthy (Trans.), *Communication and the evolution of society* (pp. 178–205). Boston: Beacon Press. (Original work published 1976); Habermas, J. (1982). A reply to my critics. In J. B. Thompson & D. Held (Eds.), *Habermas: Critical debates* (pp. 219–283). Cambridge: MIT Press; Habermas, J. (1984). *The theory of*

communicative action: Volume I: Reason and the rationalization of society (T. McCarthy, Trans.). Boston: Beacon Press. (Original work published 1981); Habermas, J. (1987). *The theory of communicative action: Volume II: Lifeworld and system: A critique of functionalist reason* (T. McCarthy, Trans.). Boston: Beacon Press. (Original work published 1981)

2. In addition to the original works of Karl Marx, the beginning student might profitably consult the following: Tucker, R. C. (Ed.). (1972). *The Marx-Engels reader.* New York: Norton. A selection of prominent 20th-century analyses of Marxian crisis theory would include the following: Sweezy, P. M. (1942). *The theory of capitalist development.* New York: Monthly Review Press; Sweezy, P. M., & Baran, P. A. (1966). *Monopoly capital.* New York: Monthly Review Press; O'Conner, J. (1973). *The fiscal crisis of the state.* New York: St. Martin's Press; Offe, C. (1984). *Contradictions of the welfare state* (J. Keane, Ed.). Cambridge: MIT Press; Harvey, D. (1989). *The condition of postmodernity.* Cambridge, UK: Basil Blackwell.

3. For an excellent introduction to the distinctive Frankfurt School perspective on 20th-century capitalism, see the following: Held, D. (1980). *Introduction to critical theory: Horkheimer to Habermas* (pp. 40–76). Berkeley: University of California Press.

4. Habermas (1987), *The theory of communicative action* (Vol. 2), p. 392.

5. In addition to *A town abandoned* (Dandaneau, 1996), key sources for the analysis of Flint's social and economic history include the following: Edsforth, E. (1987). *Class conflict and cultural consensus: The making of a mass consumer society in Flint, Michigan.* New Brunswick, NJ: Rutgers University Press; Lord, G. F., & Price, A. C. (1992, May). Growth ideology in a period of decline: Deindustrialization and restructuring, Flint style. *Social Problems, 39*(2), 155–169. The following are also informative because both books are grounded in Flint's experience: Hamper, B. (1991). *Rivethead: Tales from the assembly line.* New York: Warner; Kearns, J. (1990). *Life after the line.* Detroit, MI: Wayne State University Press.

6. Moore, M. (Producer & Director). (1989). *Roger & me* [Film]. Dog Eat Dog Productions, released by Warner Brothers. For an extensive analysis of this film, see Dandaneau (1996), *A town abandoned,* pp. 107–157. For related sociological statements by Moore, see the following: Moore, M. (1989). GM and Flint, Michigan. In D. S. Eitzen & M. B. Zinn (Eds.), *The reshaping of America: Social consequences of the changing economy* (pp. 329–333). Englewood Cliffs, NJ: Prentice Hall; Moore, M. (1996). *Downsize this! Random threats from an unarmed American.* New York: Crown.

7. From a 1991 interview with D. C. Dort, in Dandaneau (1996), *A town abandoned* (p. xix).

8. "Important to Habermas's work is the claim that critical theory is reflexive" (Held, D. [1978, February]. Extended review. *Sociological Review, 26,* 190). In other words, critical theory must account for itself; it must understand its own position in the world and the history that it criticizes.

9. On the general notion of critical theory, see Geuss, R. (1981). *The idea of a critical theory: Habermas and the Frankfurt School.* Cambridge, UK: Cambridge University Press. Geuss writes, "A critical theory . . . is a reflective theory which gives agents a kind of knowledge inherently productive of enlightenment and emancipation" (p. 2). Similar works include the following: Kortian, G. (1980). *Metacritique: The philosophical argument of Jürgen Habermas.* Cambridge, UK: Cambridge University Press; Wellmer, A. (1971). *Critical theory of society* (J. Cumming, Trans.). New York: Continuum. (Original work published 1969); Bernstein, R. J. (1976). *The restructuring of social and political theory.* Philadelphia: University of Pennsylvania Press.

10. The notion of "ideology" is notoriously vague. See Geuss (1981), *The idea of a critical theory;* also see Thompson, J. B. (1990). *Ideology and modern culture.* Stanford, CA: Stanford University Press. I have chosen to stress the "immanent" nature of most critical theoretical

activities, famously stated by Adorno, for example, as the need to "break out of the objective context of delusion *from within*" [italics added] (p. 406); Adorno, T. W. (1973). *Negative dialectics* (E. B. Ashton, Trans.). New York: Continuum. (Original work published 1966)

11. In this regard, note Nancy Fraser's concise discussion of the meaning of critical theory. She writes, "To my mind, no one has yet improved on Marx's 1843 definition of Critical Theory as 'the self-clarification of the struggles and wishes of the age.' What is so appealing about this definition is its straightforwardly political character. It makes no claim to any special epistemological status but, rather, supposes that with respect to justification, there is no philosophically interesting difference between a critical theory of society and an uncritical one. But there is, according to this definition, an important political difference. A critical social theory frames its research programme and its conceptual framework with an eye to the aims and activities of those oppositional social movements with which it has a partisan though not uncritical identification. The questions it asks and the models it designs are informed by that identification and interest. Thus, for example, if struggles contesting the subordination of women figured among the most significant of a given age, then a critical social theory for that time would aim, among other things, to shed light on the character and bases of such subordination. It would employ categories and explanatory models that revealed rather than occluded relations of male dominance and female subordination. And it would demystify as ideological rival approaches that obfuscated or rationalized those relations. In this situation, then, one of the standards for assessing a critical theory, once it had been subjected to all the usual tests of empirical adequacy, would be: how well does it theorize the situation and prospects of the feminist movement? To what extent does it serve the self-clarification of the struggles and wishes of contemporary women?" (p. 31); Fraser, N. (1987). What's critical about critical theory? The case of Habermas and gender. In S. Benhabib & D. Cornel (Eds.), *Feminism as critique* (pp. 31–56). Minneapolis: University of Minnesota Press.

12. See Habermas, J. (1973).

13. This interpretation of the influences on Marx follows the classic triad introduced by V. I. Lenin, who wrote that "the Marxist doctrine . . . is the legitimate successor to the best that man produced in the 19th century, as represented by German philosophy, English political economy [i.e., economics] and French socialism" (p. 20); Lenin, V. I. (1977). The three sources and three component parts of Marxism. In *Lenin: Selected works* (pp. 20–24). Moscow: Progress Publishers.

14. Consider the description of labor found in one recent labor economics textbook: "There is a rumor that one recent Secretary of Labor attempted to abolish the term 'labor market' from departmental publications. He believed it demeaned workers to regard labor as being bought and sold like so much grain, oil, or steel. *True, labor is somewhat unique* [!] [italics added]. Labor services can only be rented; workers themselves cannot be bought and sold" (p. 2); Ehrenberg, R. G., & Smith, R. S. (1991). *Modern labor economics* (4th ed.). New York: HarperCollins. Marxian theorists believe that humans and their ability to work are more than "somewhat unique." For the classic Marxian critique of Frederick Winslow Taylor's "scientific management" and an exemplary use of Marx's alienation theory, see Braverman, H. (1974). *Labor and monopoly capital: The degradation of work in the twentieth century*. New York: Monthly Review Press. For a comprehensive analysis of the "Taylor Paradigm," see Bushnell, P. T. (1994). *The transformation of the American manufacturing paradigm*. New York: Garland.

15. See Marx (1972), in *The Marx-Engels Reader*, pp. 107–109. Thesis XI reads as follows: "The philosophers have only *interpreted* the world, in various ways; the point, however, is to *change* it" (italics original). For a noted discussion of Marx's modern historicity (or the reflexive

use of historical self-understanding in the project of historical change itself), see Berman, M. (1982). *All that is solid melts into air.* New York: Simon & Schuster.

16. The parallels between Marx and Freud as originators of critical theory are discussed in Geuss (1981), *The idea of a critical theory,* and Held (1980), *Introduction to critical theory.* A sampling of the various competing discussions of Freud among Frankfurt School critical theorists includes the following: Marcuse, H. (1955). *Eros and civilization: A philosophical inquiry into Freud.* Boston: Beacon Press; Fromm, E. (1962). *Beyond the chains of illusion: My encounter with Marx and Freud.* New York: Simon & Schuster; and Habermas's sympathetic treatment of Freud in Habermas, J. (1971). *Knowledge and human interests* (J. Shapiro, Trans.). Boston: Beacon Press. (Original work published 1968) (see especially Chapters 10–12).

17. Additional collections of Horkheimer's work from this period include the following: Horkheimer, M. (1978). *Dawn and decline: Notes 1926–1931, 1950–1969* (M. Shaw, Trans.). New York: Seabury Press. (Original work published 1974); Horkheimer, M. (1993). *Between philosophy and social science: Selected early writings* (G. F. Hunter, M. S. Kramer, & J. Torpey, Trans.). Cambridge: MIT Press. Also see Horkheimer's magnum opus, with Theodor W. Adorno (1972). *Dialectic of enlightenment* (J. Cumming, Trans.). New York: Herder & Herder. (Original work published 1944)

18. In addition to previously cited sources, see the following: Jay, M. (1973). *The dialectical imagination: A history of the Frankfurt School and the Institute of Social Research, 1923–1950.* Boston: Little, Brown; Wiggershaus, R. (1994). *The Frankfurt School: Its history, theories, and political significance* (M. Robertson, Trans.). Cambridge: MIT Press. (Original work published 1986)

19. Still the single best collective introduction to the work of Adorno, Horkheimer, Marcuse, and Benjamin is the following: Held (1980), *Introduction to critical theory.* For Habermas's own reflections on his predecessors, see Habermas, J. (1987). *The philosophical discourses on modernity* (F. Lawrence, Trans.). Cambridge: MIT Press. (Original work published 1985); Habermas, J. (1985). *Philosophical-political profiles* (F. G. Lawrence, Trans.). Cambridge, MA: MIT Press. (Original work published 1981); Habermas, J. (1985). Psychic thermidor and the rebirth of rebellious subjectivity. In R. J. Bernstein (Ed.), *Habermas and modernity* (pp. 67–77). Cambridge: MIT Press.

20. Streitfeld, D. (2009, April 22). An effort to save Flint, Mich., by shrinking it. *New York Times,* p. A12.

21. For population and other data, see Edsforth (1987), *Class conflict and cultural consensus,* p. 13.

22. See Gordon, H. S. (1986). Laissez-faire. In D. L. Sills (Ed.), *International encyclopedia of the social sciences* (Vol. 8, pp. 546–549). New York: Macmillan/Free Press.

23. On Flint's Great Sit-Down Strike, see Kraus, H. (1985). *The many and the few* (2nd ed., with an introduction by N. O. Leighton, W. J. Meyer, & N. Pendrell). Urbana: University of Illinois Press. (Original work published 1947); Fine, S. (1969). *Sit-down: The General Motors strike of 1936–1937.* Ann Arbor: University of Michigan Press; Reuther, V. (1976). *The brothers Reuther and the story of the UAW.* Boston: Houghton Mifflin; Edsforth (1987), *Class conflict and cultural consensus.*

24. In a 1970 interview with Studs Terkel, Mott derided Franklin Delano Roosevelt as "the great destroyer." Concerning the Great Sit-Down Strike, Mott stated, "[Frank Murphy] was the governor during the sit-down strikes, and he didn't do his job. He didn't enforce the law. He kept his hands off. He didn't protect our property. They should have said [to the strikers], 'Stop that thing. Move on, or we'll shoot.' And if they didn't, they should have been shot" (p. 135); Terkel, S. (1970). *Hard times: An oral history of the Great Depression.* New York: Pantheon.

25. See Edsforth (1987), *Class conflict and cultural consensus*, p. 218: Edsforth writes, "In articles like *U.S. News & World Report's* 'Labor Peace: It's Wonderful' (July 1950), *Look's* 'All American City' (February 1954), and *Coronet's* 'Happiest Town in Michigan' (June 1956), the national news media used Flint as an example of how the country had transcended the bitter, divisive class conflicts of the 1930s and early 1940s to enter a new era of consumer-oriented normalcy. Such publicity further legitimized the 'civilized relationship' between GM and the UAW, and it furthered the alienation of Flint's auto workers from their own union."

26. Flint is described as a ghost town in Zwerdling, D. (1982, July). And then there's the Disneyland solution. *The Progressive*, pp. 34–35. Zwerdling writes, "To see what 25 percent unemployment does to a community, take a stroll down Saginaw Street to the middle of town. It used to be a lovely place, lined with old brick buildings, with the kind of turn-of-the-century masonry you don't see much of any more. Saginaw, the main street, is paved with bricks, and the sidewalks are shaded by awnings. But there is almost nobody and nothing here. Virtually every second store is boarded up with plywood. Some businesses have fled to suburban malls, the rest of them have simply folded. Flint is a 1982 ghost town" (p. 34).

27. Draus, P. J. (2009). Substance abuse and slow-motion disasters: The case of Detroit. *Sociological Quarterly, 50*(2), 360–382.

28. Data for the following section are drawn mainly from research documents produced by and for Flint-area organizations. For the most part, these are not sources readily available for public access and review. In this case, I label the source "document" and describe its organizational sponsor. The first case in point is *The Genesis Project* report (document) (p. 4), prepared for the Genesee Area Economic Revitalization, Inc., by PriceWaterhouse, Inc.

29. See Ananich, J. D., Leighton, N. O., & Weber, C. T. (1989, May). *Economic impact of GM plant closings in Flint, Michigan* (document), sponsored by PURA at the University of Michigan at Flint; Grimes (1990), *Diversification trends*. Indeed, near-term projections for Flint-area GM employment are as low as 22,000. See Buss, D. D. (1999, June). GM's company town. *Automotive News*, pp. 26–28; (1999, July). City's boom replaced by hollow thud. *Automotive News*, pp. 34–35. Also, see Agrassia, P. I. (1998, June 30). A long road to good labor relations at GM. *Wall Street Journal*, p. A18. For a discussion of the "ripple effects" of plant closings, see Perrucci, C. C., Perrucci, R., Targ, D. B., & Targ, H. R. (1988). *Plant closings: International contexts and social costs*. Hawthorne, NY: Aldine. Also, Vilasic, B., & Bunkley, N. (2009, May 21). The last holdouts cast their lot with G.M. *New York Times*, p. B1.

30. On deindustrialization and critical theory, see Agger, B. (1985). The dialectic of deindustrialization: An essay on advanced capitalism. In J. Forester (Ed.), *Critical theory of public life* (pp. 3–21). Cambridge: MIT Press; Cowie, J., & Heathcott, J. (Eds.). (2003). *Beyond the ruins: The meaning of deindustrialization*. Ithaca, NY: ILR Press; High, S. (2003). *Industrial sunset: The making of North America's rust belt, 1969–1984*. Toronto: University of Toronto Press.

31. Streitfeld (2009), An effort to save Flint, Mich., by shrinking it, p. A12.

32. From a document titled "State of Flint," a 1991 memorandum from the State of Michigan Department of Social Services, Flint branch.

33. *The Genesis Project* report, p. 8.

34. From *The quality of life for children and their families in Genesee County* (document) (1991, June), sponsored by Priority '90s; see especially pp. 29–34.

35. Flint leads state in 1990 per-capita crime rate—FBI. (1991, August 11). *The Flint Journal*, pp. A1, A10; FBI figures still place Flint among most violent cities. (1992, April 26). *The Flint Journal*, pp. A1, A14. Morgan Quitno Awards: 13th Annual Safest (and Most Dangerous) Cities Award (n.d.). Retrieved October 30, 2006, from www.morganquitno .com/cit07pop.htm. Also, see Murphy, S. (2008, March 1). In Flint, Michigan, burglaries and

robberies on the rise as violent crimes decline. *The Flint Journal.* Retrieved December 28, 2009, from http://www.mlive.com/news/index.ssf/2008/03/in_flint_michigan_burglaries _a.html

36. *The quality of life for children and their families in Genesee County* (pp. 12–13, 20, 28– 30, and "Summary: Changing social and economic conditions"). Also see Poverty spreads in Michigan. (1991, September 27). *The Flint Journal,* p. A3. A classic scholarly statement on the causes and effects of concentrated poverty is provided in the following: Wilson, W. J. (1987). *The truly disadvantaged.* Chicago: University of Chicago Press. This analysis has been carried forward in Wilson, W. J. (1996). *When work disappears: The world of the new urban poor.* New York: Knopf.

37. For an interesting reflection on this event, see Moore, M. (1996, July). Flint & me: Michael Moore returns to our first last-place city. *Money,* pp. 86–87.

38. Mahler, J. (2009, June 28). G.M., Detroit and the fall of the black middle class. *New York Times Magazine,* p. MM30.

39. For 2007 data, see Flint city, Michigan Fact Sheet, U.S. Census Bureau. Viewed June 28, 2009, at http://factfinder.census.gov

40. See *Synopsis of Flint area Enterprise Community Program* (document) (1995, March 6), provided by the City of Flint Department of Community & Economic Development; Dandaneau, S. P. (2006, August). *Mills, Michigan, and me.* Unpublished manuscript.

41. Flint's dependency on GM employment is suggested by the fact that GM's local Flint payroll in 1988 exceeded $2 billion. See *Facts on Flint* (document) (1990, September 28), Office of the Mayor, City of Flint, Michigan.

42. See Lord and Price (1992).

43. See A city where hope runs on empty. (1992, February 26). *New York Times,* p. A8; Flint, Willow Run take hit. (1994, February 11). *The Flint Journal,* pp. A1–A2; Hurting: The GM fallout; Thousands still reel from impact of closings. (1992, February 25). *The Flint Journal,* pp. A1, A10; GM slashes—Michigan bleeds. (1992, February 25). *Lansing State Journal,* p. A1; Dupont leaving Flint, affecting 250 workers. (1992, January 14). *The Flint Journal,* pp. A1–A2.

44. See Flint preparing "bold" package to keep GM jobs. (1996, June 21). *The Flint Journal,* pp. A1, A9. This estimate has, unfortunately, proven to be accurate since Flint-area GM employment is expected to dip below 26,000 in the next few years.

45. King, N., & Terlep, S. (2009, June 2). GM collapses into government's arms. *Wall Street Journal,* p. A1.

46. In addition to major sources cited elsewhere, I have also consulted the following: Miller, J. (1975, Fall). A review of Jürgen Habermas, "legitimation crisis." *Telos, 25,* 210–220; Shapiro, J. J. (1976, Spring). Reply to Miller's review of Habermas's "legitimation crisis." *Telos, 27,* 170–176; Held, D., & Simon, L. (1976, Winter). Toward understanding Habermas. *New German Critique, 7,* 136–145; Schroyer, T. (1975, Spring). The re-politicization of the relations of production: An interpretation of Jürgen Habermas's analytic theory of late capitalist development. *New German Critique, 5,* 107–128; Laska, P. (1974, Fall). A note on Habermas and the labor theory of value. *New German Critique, 3,* 154–162; Keane, J. (1975, Winter). On belaboring the theory of economic crisis: A reply to Laska. *New German Critique, 4,* 125–130; Camilleri, J. (1981, Summer). The advanced capitalist state and the contemporary world crisis. *Science and Society, 45*(2), 130–158; Roderick, R. (1986). *Habermas and the foundations of critical theory.* New York: St. Martin's Press; Alway, J. (1995). *Critical theory and political possibilities.* Westport, CT: Greenwood; Aune, J. A. (1994). *Rhetoric and Marxism.* Boulder, CO: Westview; White, S. K. (Ed.). (1995). *The Cambridge companion to Habermas.* Cambridge, UK: Cambridge University Press.

47. On this point, as well as for the explication of Habermas's "legitimation crisis" in its entirety, see McCarthy, T. (1978). *The critical theory of Jürgen Habermas.* Cambridge: MIT Press (see especially Chapter 5). McCarthy writes, "Whatever its merits as an analysis of liberal capitalism—and Habermas holds them to be considerable—Marx's critique of political economy can no longer be applied to organized capitalism. There are a number of reasons for this, the primary among them being the changed relationship between the state and the economy; the latter no longer has the degree of autonomy that justified the exclusivity of Marx's focus" (p. 363).

48. Marx did, however, hold for the possibility of a peaceful movement to socialism. See The possibility of nonviolent revolution (1872) in *The Marx-Engels reader* (1972), pp. 522–524: Marx states, "Institutions, mores, and traditions of various countries must be taken into consideration, and we do not deny that there are countries such as America [and] England . . . where the workers can attain their goal by peaceful means" (p. 523).

49. Meckler, L. (2009, June 18). Public wary of deficit, economic intervention. *Wall Street Journal,* p. A1.

50. For example, in *Legitimation crisis,* Habermas (1973/1975) writes, "In the final analysis, [the] class structure is the source of the legitimation deficit" (p. 73).

51. Transcription by the author.

52. See Dandaneau (1996), *A town abandoned,* p. 228.

53. See Habermas (1981/1987), *The theory of communicative action: Volume II,* in which Habermas writes, "The new conflicts arise along the seams between system and lifeworld" (p. 395).

54. See Habermas (1981/1987), *The theory of communicative action: Volume II,* pp. 332–403.

55. See Habermas (1973/1975), *Legitimation crisis,* p. 45.

56. Habermas also discusses the "new social movements" that might arise in response to the predicted tendency toward a colonization of the lifeworld. In *A Town Abandoned,* Dandaneau (1996) treats *Roger & Me,* the UAW-New Directions Movement (a dissident faction seeking to return the union to its radical roots in the Great Sit-Down Strike), and Flint's Center for New Work (1984–1988; organized by two university philosophy professors to teach Flint's unemployed and underemployed how to make the best use of nonworking time in the pursuit of "new," more meaningful forms of work) as examples of bottom-up local responses to Flint's economic and rationality crises.

57. See, for example, Habermas (1981/1987), *The theory of communicative action: Volume II,* p. 355.

58. See Habermas's important discussion of "universal pragmatics" in *Communication and the evolution of society* (1976/1979, pp. 1–68), which is further elaborated and updated in Habermas (1981/1984), *The theory of communicative action: Volume I* and Habermas (1981/1987), *The theory of communicative action: Volume II.*

59. A succinct statement of this position is found in "Reply to my critics" in *Habermas: Critical debates* (1982), in which Habermas discusses the primary importance of "the loss of meaning, anomie, and personality disorders" that result from the "colonisation of the lifeworld" (pp. 280–281).

60. See Habermas (1973/1975), *Legitimation crisis,* pp. 75–92.

61. Note Habermas's 1982 (*Habermas: Critical debates*) clarification of his original argument in *Legitimation crisis*: "It is necessary to make a clear distinction that still escaped me in *Legitimation crisis*: A distinction between the deficits that inflexible structures of the lifeworld can give rise to in maintaining the economic and political systems on the one hand, and manifestations of deficiencies in the reproduction of the life-world itself on the other.

Empirically the two are connected in a feedback process; but it makes sense to separate analytically the *withdrawal of motivation* affecting the occupational system and the *withdrawal of legitimation* affecting the system of domination, on the one side, from the *colonization of the life-world* that is manifested primarily in phenomena of loss of meaning, anomie, and personality disorders, on the other side. In 1973 I used the misleading catchphrase 'motivation crisis' for deformations of the life-world which make themselves felt in modern societies as the destruction of traditional forms of life, as attacks on the communicative infrastructure of life-worlds, as the rigidity of a one-sidedly rationalised everyday practice, and which come to expression in the consequences of impoverished cultural traditions and disturbed socialisation processes. Now I would rather conceive of motivation crisis as a parallel case to legitimation crisis; and I would want to distinguish from both of these the pathological manifestations of a colonialised life-world" (pp. 280–281).

62. This discussion is drawn from Dandaneau (1996), *A town abandoned*, especially Chapter 7.

63. See Dandaneau (1996), *A town abandoned*, pp. 208–209, 212.

64. See Dandaneau (1996), *A town abandoned*, pp. 208–209, 212.

65. See Dandaneau (1996), *A town abandoned*, p. 212.

66. See Dandaneau (1996), *A town abandoned*, p. 212.

67. See Dandaneau (1996), *A town abandoned*, p. 213.

68. See Dandaneau (1996), *A town abandoned*, p. 206.

69. See Dandaneau (1996), *A town abandoned*, p. 207.

70. See Dandaneau (1996), *A town abandoned*, p. 211.

71. See McCarthy (1978), *The critical theory of Jürgen Habermas,* for a discussion of this point. McCarthy quotes Habermas: "There is no administrative production of meaning. The commercial production and administrative planning of symbols exhausts the normative force of counterfactual validity claims. The procurement of legitimation is self-defeating as soon as the mode of procurement is seen through" (p. 370). See especially Habermas (1976/1979), *Communication and the evolution of society,* pp. 178–204.

72. See Habermas (1982), *Habermas: Critical debates,* in which, in a concise statement, Habermas identifies the unacknowledged intrusion of strategic interaction into the realm of communicative interaction as the source for what he famously dubs "systematically distorted communication" (p. 264).

73. Habermas writes in support of "counterinstitutions" that are "intended to dedifferentiate some parts of the formally organized domains of action, remove them from the clutches of the steering media, and return these 'liberated areas' to the action-coordinating mechanism of reaching understanding" (Habermas [1981/1987], *The theory of communicative action: Volume II,* p. 396). He identifies a "new politics" in which "the issue is not primarily one of compensations that the welfare state can provide, but of defending and restoring endangered ways of life" (p. 392); "In terms of social statistics, the 'old politics' is more strongly supported by employers, workers, and middle-class tradesmen, whereas the new politics finds stronger support in the new middle classes, among the younger generation, and in groups with more formal education" (p. 392); "The following catchphrases serve at the moment to identify the various currents in the Federal Republic of Germany [the former West Germany]; the antinuclear and environmental movements; the peace movement (including the theme of north-south conflict); single-issue and local movements; the alternative movement (which encompasses the urban 'scene,' with its squatters and alternative projects, as well as the rural communes); the minorities (the elderly, gays, handicapped, and so forth); the psychoscene, with support groups and youth sects; religious fundamentalism; the tax-protest movement, school protest by parents' associations, resistance to 'modernist'

reforms; and, finally, the women's movement. Of international significance are the autonomy movements struggling for regional, linguistic, cultural, and also religious independence" (p. 393). Also see Habermas, J. (1990). *Moral consciousness and communicative action* (C. Lenhardt & S. Weber Nicholsen, Trans.). Cambridge: MIT Press. (Original work published 1983)

74. Streitfeld (2009), An effort to save Flint, Mich., by shrinking it, p. A12.

75. This is Thomas McCarthy's formulation of "legitimation crisis." See McCarthy (1978), *The critical theory of Jürgen Habermas*, p. 385.

76. On June 20, 1996, Flint's mayor joined spokespeople for GM, the C. S. Mott Foundation, and the UAW to announce the formation of the "Billy Durant Automotive Commission," whose cynical raison d'être is well captured by one of its most intelligent members' terse summary of Flint's current situation: "The facts are simple. Most of our plants are obsolete. They are 40 years old with 30-year-old equipment, processes and systems. We are not competing effectively. The challenge is to persuade our major customer [who buys the product!], the GM corporation, that this community and its workers will partner up with the company to become absolutely best in class in everything we do. *We have no other option*." Or so argues William Donohue, president of the Genesee Area Focus Council, as quoted in Billy Durant Automotive Commission formed to deal with GM losses in Genesee County (1996, June 27). *Headlight* (newsletter of the UAW Local 599), p. 1.

References

Bluestone, B., & Harrison, B. (1982). *The deindustrialization of America: Plant closings, community abandonment, and the dismantling of basic industry.* New York: Basic Books.

Bohlen, A., Goldfarb, L. (Producers), & Gray, L. (Director). (1978). *With babies and banners: The story of the women's emergency brigade* [Motion picture]. United States: Women's Labor History Film Project.

Dandaneau, S. P. (1996). *A town abandoned: Flint, Michigan, confronts deindustrialization.* Albany: State University of New York Press.

Grimes, D. (1990). *Diversification trends in Genesee County* [Document]. Sponsored by the Project for Urban and Regional Affairs (PURA), University of Michigan at Flint.

Habermas, J. (1973). *Theory and practice.* Boston: Beacon.

Habermas, J. (1982). *Habermas: Critical debates.* Cambridge: MIT Press.

Habermas, J. (1987). *The theory of communicative action: Volume II* (T. McCarthy, Trans.). Boston: Beacon Press. (Original work published 1981)

Held, D. (1980). *Introduction to critical theory: Horkheimer to Habermas.* Berkeley: University of California Press.

Horkheimer, M. (1972). *Critical theory: Selected essays* (M. J. O'Connell et al., Trans.). New York: Herder & Herder.

Marx, K. (1972). For a ruthless criticism of everything existing [a.k.a. Letter to Arnold Ruge, 1843]. In R. C. Tucker (Ed.), *The Marx-Engels reader* (2nd ed., pp. 12–15). New York: Norton.

Mellon, S. (2002). *After the smoke clears: Struggling to get by in rust belt America.* Pittsburgh: University of Pittsburgh Press.

Mills, C. W. (1979). On knowledge and power. In I. L. Horowitz (Ed.), *Power, politics, & people* (pp. 599–613). Oxford, UK: Oxford University Press. (Original work published 1963)

Zwerdling, D. (1982, July). And then there's the Disneyland solution. *The Progressive*, pp. 34–35.

DISCUSSION QUESTIONS

1. What makes critical theory a distinctive type of social theory?

2. In what ways does Jürgen Habermas's theory of the legitimation crisis exemplify the essential features of critical theory?

3. Think about your own community. How similar to or how different from Flint is it? Can you apply the four crisis tendencies of late capitalism discussed in the chapter to phenomena present in your community?

4. Habermas originally published his book on the legitimation crisis more than three decades ago. Obviously, much has changed in the world since that time. Do you think that there are features of Habermas's theory that need to be reformulated in light of those changes? Defend your position.

5. Marx and Engels speculated famously that, in capitalist society, "all that is solid melts into air." Is it fair to use the eclipse of Flint, Michigan, as an industrial city to draw critical conclusions about capitalism as a whole?

CHAPTER 8

Race-Based Critical Theory and the "Happy Talk" of Diversity in America

Douglas Hartmann and Joyce M. Bell

Douglas Hartmann is Professor and Associate Chair of Sociology at the University of Minnesota. He is author of Race, Culture, and the Revolt of the Black Athlete: The 1968 Olympic Protests and Their Aftermath *(University of Chicago, 2003), coauthor of* Ethnicity and Race: Making Identities in a Changing World *(Pine Forge, 2007), and co-editor of* Contexts, *the ASA publication that brings sociology to public audiences. His current research addresses sports-based crime prevention, American pluralism, and social science in the public sphere.*

Joyce M. Bell is an Assistant Professor of Sociology at the University of Pittsburgh. Her research interests include social change, social movements, and American race relations focusing on the civil rights era and its impact on social organizations. Her current work examines the relationship between the civil rights movement, social welfare, and community-based social work organizations, 1966–1976.

Introduction: Critical Theory and Conventional Social Science

Much sociological research, writing, and theory tries to describe and explain the social world as accurately, completely, and objectively as possible—identifying key social groups and institutions, documenting norms and cultural beliefs, measuring social forces, mapping relationships and the distribution of resources as well as patterns of continuity and change, and so on. In this vision, the social scientist and social theorist is usually conceived of (or conceives her- or himself) as a detached, objective observer whose goal is to provide a neutral, unbiased picture of how things really are. The information and insight produced by such an approach may (and often does) have broader social value and practical application; nevertheless, it is not the job of the social analyst to ensure that this is the case.

Critical theory has a much different, almost diametrically opposed, orientation and objective.[1] In contrast to conventional social thinking, critical social analysis takes as its starting point the understanding that social scientists are always part of the world(s) they are trying to depict and analyze. Rather than trying to set aside or overcome their particular position and corresponding viewpoints, critical theorists believe it is best to acknowledge their orientation and incorporate it into their analytical vision of the social world. The recognition of one's own positionality is not seen as a weakness but a strength; indeed, it is believed that self-conscious, systematic attention to one's own standpoint provides a clear perspective from which one can better describe, analyze, and apprehend the social world taken as a whole.

A critical theoretical perspective is not just any old point of view, however. At least two characteristics set a critical theoretical perspective apart from the opinions and viewpoints of everyday, ordinary people. One is that it is—or at least tries to be—wholistic or systemic; that is, it strives to be aware of itself and its relationship to others as well as attentive to a vision of society as a whole. Such a vision is, in other words, formulated in the context of the broader social world that it is trying to comprehend and of which it is part and parcel. A critical theoretical orientation is also (and this is the second defining characteristic) explicitly normative, evaluative, or moralistic. In sociology, the ethical orientation most often associated with critical theory focuses on inequality, oppression, and exploitation. But the key point is that a critical theory is guided by a set of principles, a moral vision of what is good, right, and appropriate in society as well as where the problems are and how things might be made better, more equitable, just, or sustainable. Its analysis is, in short, predicated on a comparative moral sense of how things might be different.

As an alternative vision of society, critical social theory regularly breaks with the conscious understanding and awareness of members of society themselves, especially those in positions of power and privilege. This ability to be critical of how things are and how different people in society understand and interpret their own role in the world is one of the defining characteristics and real strengths of social scientific research informed by critical theory. Critical theory also often delves into the silences, commonsense assumptions, or unseen forces and processes that organize, structure, and reproduce the status quo as we know it. It urges analysts to see things that are otherwise taken for granted; see through ideas and arrangements that otherwise seem rational or defensible; and call out claims that perpetuate—often unintentionally—problems, inequalities, and injustices. It isn't afraid, to use Eviatar Zerubavel's (2006) provocative metaphor, to call out the elephants in the room.

Extending from this, critical theoretical work also tends to be oriented toward activism and social change. With the well-known aphorism that social analysis is not only to understand the world but to change it, the more political, activist side of critical theory's orientation to change is probably what gets the most attention (and both of us have been involved with organizations, initiatives, and movements whose goals are to make the world a better place). But whether or not one is directly involved in making social change, the attention to change as an object of analysis serves a key analytical function. (And both of us have done plenty of this as well—Hartmann wrote a book on African American athletes who contributed to the struggle for racial justice and equality in the 1960s; Bell is writing a book on African American social workers who sought changes in their own professions in the 1970s). Studying movements like these helps us figure out not just how the social world is organized but *why* it is that way—the historical forces and social mechanisms that continue to make and shape the world as it is. Even to theorists who do not see themselves as activists per se, the analytical attention to movements and change provides a fuller, more concrete understandings of the mechanisms, processes, and forces that have made and continue to maintain the social status quo.

In its earliest social scientific manifestations, critical theory was largely focused on the inequalities generated by market-based, capitalist economies. It was, in short, all about class—economic-based exploitation, oppression, and stratification. Indeed, throughout the second half of the 20th century, the phrase "critical theory" was essentially synonymous with Marxism itself, the very term having been invented by German socialist critics such as Max Horkheimer and Theodor Adorno, who had fled Nazi Germany for the United States, where Marxist thought was about as popular as fascism. Despite the fact that early critical theory was inattentive to race, the basic tenets of critical theory began to be expanded and reworked to apply to other forms of social inequality and oppression in response to the social unrest and tumult of the 1960s in the United States and all over the world. Feminist theory, queer theory, postcolonial theory, subaltern studies, and intersectional (race-class-gender) analyses are all examples of more contemporary manifestations of critical theory.

In this chapter, we address one of the major strands of this thought, what we will call *race-based critical theory*. A race-based critical theory can be defined as critical theory that puts race—not just racial injustices and inequalities but racial ideologies and identities as well as racialized ways of thinking about and rationalizing existing social arrangements more generally—at the forefront of its analytic lens onto the social world. It starts from the presupposition that the modern world is organized by and structured through race, both as a principle for the (unequal) distribution of resources and power as well as a mode for thinking about culture and social life in general. It further insists that the racial organization of society and culture is neither just nor inevitable, and that the task of the social analyst is to identify, explicate, and deconstruct the often unseen or misunderstood social processes and cultural beliefs that maintain existing racial formations and inequalities. Its ultimate goals are to better understand the beliefs and processes that reproduce these inequalities and injustices and that would necessarily, then, be the target of challenge.

In what follows, we will further discuss the basic characteristics of this brand of critical theory, along with some of the scholars and scholarly bodies of work that have contributed to it. We pay special attention to the underlying cultural beliefs and ways of thinking and talking about race that account for the persistence and perpetuation of racial differences and inequalities in an era that often promotes itself as and appears to be thoroughly antiracism. To illustrate and further develop these insights, we will draw upon a recent study we conducted of the seemingly positive and upbeat ways Americans have of talking about diversity in social life. Informed by race-based critical theory and interviews with 150 Americans in four different metropolitan areas, we argue that the discourse of diversity—what we call "happy talk"—obscures the difficulties and deep inequalities associated with race in contemporary American society. It serves these functions, we further suggest, because of the color-blind ideals and white normativity underlying these ostensibly positive ways of thinking and talking. These findings and analyses not only help us understand the racial structure and function of the diversity discourse, they constitute key components of contemporary race-based critical theory.

Race-Based Critical Theory: Some Basics

Working from the basic definition offered above, we can break down race-based critical theory into four key components or propositions: (a) Race is a defining and foundational feature of modern society; (b) current racial arrangements and relationships are inequitable and unjust; (c) racial differences and inequalities are constructed in social relationships and not reducible to other forms of stratification; and (d) contemporary racial formations are maintained and reproduced through cultural mechanisms and social processes that are subtle and systemic, and often difficult for ordinary, even well-meaning people to appreciate and comprehend.

We will begin with the proposition that race is a fundamental and defining feature of modern social life. The idea here is that race and racism are deeply ingrained in modern world history and contemporary social life, in terms of both how they organize social relationships and the distribution of resources as well as how they structure culture and consciousness and how modern people think about themselves and the world around them. This latter emphasis on race's deep impacts on culture is one of the features that marks race-based critical theory as unique and uniquely challenging among scholarly conceptions of race. For example, the critical race theorists who came out of legal studies programs and law schools in the late 1980s and early 1990s (and helped launch race-based critical theory) argued that racial ideologies were indeed constitutive of American conceptions of the law and social justice. More specifically, they worked to demonstrate that ostensibly meritocratic, universalistic individualist ideals of fairness and ownership were based upon the worldviews and privileges of white male property owners (Crenshaw et al., 1996; Delgado & Stefancic, 2001). Philosophers such as David Theo Goldberg (1993) took the idea even further, arguing that racial ideologies and distinctions actually played a crucial role in the emergence of modernity itself, creating the social justifications for Enlightenment and its social and political conceptions of progress, freedom, rationality, and science.

To a certain extent, this claim that race and racism structure so much of modern life so thoroughly is an ethical proposition, a critical, orientating presupposition on modern history and contemporary social life. But it is also more than that. In fact, it is an empirical claim as much as an ethical assertion, a claim based upon both the facts of history (colonialism and apartheid in the international context; slavery, Jim Crow laws, and segregation on the American side) as well as the realities of contemporary social life, realities that systematically privilege whites over non-whites, Westerners over non-Westerners. On this latter front in particular, critical theory meets up with and draws upon conventional social science, which has clearly and convincingly documented racial inequalities and disparities across a whole range of social domains. In the United States, for instance, researchers have shown that African American men are eight times more likely than their white peers to be imprisoned (Latino men are incarcerated at four times the white male rate). Blacks and Latinos suffer poverty rates nearly three times that of the white majority, with nearly one in three of the children from these groups living in poverty. Individuals from these communities suffer from lower wages and higher rates of unemployment and underemployment, and they have significantly less wealth in their family networks to support their lives and sustain them in difficult times. People of color are far more likely to live in segregated neighborhoods and attend segregated schools. Minority kids also lag well behind their majority peers in terms of academic achievement—whether measured in terms of test scores, grades, performance on standardized tests, dropout rates, graduation rates, or likelihood of college attendance and completion.[2]

The second characteristic of race-based critical theory—that the current racial arrangements are inequitable and unjust—might seem like an obvious and easy point, one that should merit little or no controversy. But this relative absence of contention and debate in the contemporary culture is, in many respects, precisely the problem for the critical theorist. In the aftermath of the successes of the American civil rights movement and the end of colonialism in the 1960s, and the collapse of apartheid more recently, we live in a world that almost universally disavows racism, racial prejudice, and discrimination, and at times almost any form of racial differentiation or distinction. And yet racial inequities and injustices persist and are pervasive in the United States and all over the world. How can this be? The challenge and objective of race-based critical theory is to try to answer this question—to grasp how and why racial inequalities and injustices can be so pervasive in the face of social transformations that eliminated and discredited the most egregious legal systems and institutional structures that had maintained rigid racial hierarchies throughout the world. This paradoxical social context constitutes the crux of the critical theoretical challenge and the heart of the enterprise—and helps explain why race-based critical theory has really exploded as an intellectual force in recent decades.

The starting point for answering the paradox of a world that disavows race and racism, on one hand, and is yet marked so decisively by racial differences and inequalities on the other, brings us to the third core aspect of race-based critical theory—namely, the recognition that racial identities and inequalities are not natural or inevitable but constructed in social relationships and by social forces that are independent of other forms of social stratification. The idea that race is a social construction is not unique to race-based critical theory; indeed, most racial scholars today are unanimous in the belief that racial categories, identities, and differences are not natural or inevitable but are instead the product of historical forces and social processes (Cornell & Hartmann, 2007). However, several characteristics distinguish the critical theorists' thinking on this topic. One is the basic attention to causation and causal mechanisms.

For all its talk of social construction, and as effective as mainstream social science has been in documenting racial injustices and inequalities, it has not been particularly successful in explaining the sources of these patterns. One of the reasons for this failure involves a relative tendency, often defended under the guise of scientific objectivity, to focus on individual actions and beliefs as the proper unit of sociological data and analysis—to look for overt racial bias and intent, on one hand, and concerted individual action on the other.[3] In the case of race relations, however, such models often overlook the more complicated, insidious, and structural forces behind the production and perpetuation of racial differences and inequalities. For instance, Omi and Winant's (1994) influential racial formation theory highlighted how movements and programs intended to alleviate racial inequalities in American society were often co-opted by more conservative interests and actors in ways that muted their effects or even manipulated them into having effects entirely the opposite of their original intent.

And then there is the challenge of understanding how race is constructed in social relationships. With its emphasis on race relations, sociology has long been a leader in thinking about race as relationships between different groups of people—where questions of inequality always necessarily imply privilege as well as disadvantage, domination as well as subordination. Nevertheless, mainstream sociology too often thinks about race or racial inequality as the problem of a minority or disadvantaged community, rather than the result of a particular set of historical relationships and arrangements that benefits some even as it disadvantages others (Emirbayer, 1997). With its emphasis on critique and attention to oppression, domination, and injustice, race-based critical theory always puts these unequal relationships front and center in thinking about what accounts for racial differences and inequalities (see also Desmond & Emirbayer, 2010).

Another, subtler reason for the inability of conventional social science to fully grasp and explain the social construction of race in contemporary social life has to do with the tendency to see race as "epiphenomenal," the by-product of other social forces or inequalities such as class or nationalism. Many scholars from a variety of theoretical traditions (critical and otherwise) have attempted to explain the power and persistence of race and racial inequalities in terms of their connection with other forms of injustice and exploitation—seeing race and racism as a function of class-based inequities, for example, or the product of power differentials between nations where the racial order of societies has been unfortunately mapped onto the history of national expansion all over the world. Such perspectives are important. Race and racism are, indeed, related to and often interrelated with other forms of inequality and oppression (class, nationalism, gender), but they cannot be reduced to these forms and forces. Racialized patterns need to be analyzed, explained, and understood in ways that do not reduce racial inequalities to the by-product of other social forces as well as ways that grapple with the often unseen and invisible forces that reproduce them. Thus, the point is to figure out the unique mechanisms and processes that collude and cohere to create racial differences and inequalities as unique and irreducible social phenomena.

This brings us to the fourth and arguably most important point about contemporary race-based critical theory in the contemporary world—that racial formations are reproduced in ways and through processes that are subtle and systemic, yet difficult for ordinary, even well-meaning people to see. This point harkens back to the insistence that a critical orientation is especially important in the post-civil rights, post-colonial, post-apartheid context. In the so-called absence of legal de jure inequality, it is essential to understand the social mechanisms and forces that account for the continued perpetuation of racial injustices and inequalities. In the context of national and global cultures that appear to no longer be tolerant of unequal racial arrangements, it is critical to focus on mechanisms of production and reproduction, especially those that escape the attention and understanding of the agents themselves who act them out. Indeed, this is precisely why we got interested in the strange way in which so many Americans seemed to be talking about difference and diversity in American culture in such seemingly positive and optimistic ways. We became suspicious of such empty positive language about difference in a society that we see as at least partially founded and structured on racial inequality.

A key point in all of these elements is that racial hierarchies are not just reproduced in the contemporary world by old-fashioned prejudice and discrimination (where prejudice can be defined as beliefs about racial difference and inferiority, and discrimination involves activities and behaviors that produce and reproduce racial inequalities). Rather, racial inequalities are maintained and reproduced within institutional structures and cultural ways of thinking that allow race and racism to be reproduced whether or not individuals see it (see Table 8.1).

Mechanisms of Racial Reproduction

Probably the most typical, mainstream explanation for persistent racial inequalities and injustice has to do with overt prejudice and explicit discrimination—the persistence of overt racial biases against people of certain races and behaviors that translate into differential treatments and behaviors and thus eventually disparate outcomes. To be sure, prejudice and discrimination still exist. However, they cannot fully explain the persistence of contemporary racial formations. The problem with these traditional explanations for accounting for race in the contemporary world is twofold. On one hand, it appears that many of the most blatant forms of prejudice and discrimination have declined precipitously and are no longer legally or socially acceptable. On the other hand, to the extent that older, more traditional forms of prejudice and discrimination live on—which they do—it is difficult to collect data and information to verify and analyze them. For example, it has been noted that it is difficult to measure prejudice on attitudinal surveys (Schuman, Steeh, Bobo, & Krysan, 1997). People know how to respond to such

Table 8.1   Key Contributors to Race-Based Critical Theory

Body of Work	Core Insights	Key Theorists
Critical race theory	• Race is central to U.S. law and policy • Racial inequalities are reproduced in and through strict adherence to individualist, universalistic standards of fairness • Interest is in studying and transforming race/racism and standards of justice	Derrick Bell, Kimberle Crenshaw, Richard Delgado, David Theo Goldberg, Neil Gotanda, Cheryl Harris, Ian Haney Lopez, Patricia Williams
Racial formation theory	• Race is socially constructed and continually reproduced • The content and importance of racial categories are determined by social, economic, and political forces • Social programs are often co-opted and rearticulated by forces of status quo	Michael Omi and Howard Winant (1994)
Color-blind racism framework	• Adherence to color-blind ideals gets in the way of clear thinking and social policy addressing contemporary racial inequalities • Racism in the post-civil rights era is increasingly covert and expressed through an ideology that purports to be race neutral	Eduardo Bonilla-Silva (2001, 2003), Leslie Carr (1997), Charles Gallagher (2003)
Critical whiteness studies	• Whiteness is normalized in U.S. culture in a way that masks the real sources of inequality and maintains white privilege • White people are the beneficiaries of racial privilege	Joe Feagin (2006), Ruth Frankenberg (1993), Henry Giroux (1997), George Lipsitz (1998), Peggy McIntosh (1989), Toni Morrison (1992), David Roediger (1991, 2002)

questions now, in ways that are socially acceptable. Folks won't admit to or acknowledge their biases in polite public company, much less the company of liberal researchers. In other words, precisely because the most direct and traditional forms of racism have been socially discredited, they have gone underground. This is where some basic, critical thinking comes in to much standard research on racial inequalities.

One response to this on the part of researchers has been to ask questions about race designed to reveal and expose more deeply rooted racial prejudices, biases, and stereotypes. For example, social thermometer scales, where respondents are asked about how warm or cold they feel toward different groups of people, or questions about racial intermarriage for one's kids, measure how different or far away from various groups an individual feels and can serve as a proxy for underlying bias. A related methodological response is to pit the ideals of majority white respondents against their support for social policies or programs. In this line of research, analysts ask not only about beliefs about racial others but also about respondents' willingness to support social programs based on their own stated principles or ideals. For example, in the 1980s, researchers such as Larry Bobo (1988) asked respondents questions that gauged their support for affirmative action as a proxy for underlying racial stereotypes or attitudes. More recently, Bobo and his colleagues (Bobo, Kluegel, & Smith, 1997) interpreted blasé attitudes toward public policy as a kind of laissez-faire racism, stemming from an unwillingness to support social programs that would make good on their expressed ideals as well as subtle, unspoken, anti-black biases and sentiments. In many ways, such methods are predicated upon critical theories about race—an analysis that assumes that persons with no bias or prejudice would not exhibit racialized patterns. Thus, when such attitudinal patterns do emerge, we are presented with empirical data that give us evidence of deep-seated, group-based stereotypes or biases.

Another body of work that contributes to our understanding of racial mechanisms of reproduction is research on what is called institutional racism or institutional discrimination. The explanation for persistent racial inequalities in this tradition has less to do with underlying biases and beliefs and more to do with historical and existing social arrangements—in other words, how racial disparities are embedded in historical artifacts and current institutional arrangements. For example, as the work of William Julius Wilson (1987) and others have described, many racial minorities in the United States live in fairly depressed, segregated urban areas where they and their children lack access to public goods such as good schools, well-paying jobs, and quality health care. The absence of these resources stems, of course, from a variety of historical forces and factors associated with America's own history of slavery and segregation. But today, these conditions have taken on lives of their own and persist not so much because of overt prejudice and discrimination but because of the combined institutional effects of segregation, poverty, underfunded public policy, and the like. Racial inequality, in this case, is perpetuated in historical arrangements and institutions that continue to produce racial inequality even in the absence of overt prejudice or intentionally discriminatory treatment. Again, the point here is to see the attention to mechanisms and the often unrealized or underappreciated critical foundations of these approaches in the sense that these explanations and analyses break with the usual rationalistic, individualistic descriptions and accounts of social arrangements in modern society.

Whereas this research seeks to expose the underlying biases and institutional practices that perpetuate racial inequalities, more recent critical race theories add to these by digging deeper into cultural ideologies that maintain and reproduce racism and racial injustice. A key insight of these more culturally orientated critiques is that of a racialized society where racism and racial stratification are so entrenched that they seem natural, normal, and commonsensical. In this context, critical race theorists have focused on the "ideas, ideals, ideologies, and discourses that are not fully understood or consciously recognized by their advocates and adherents and that, in their unthinking embrace, serve to mystify, misconstrue, and ultimately legitimate the realities of race in the U.S." (Hartmann, 2007, p. 56). Although critical theorists in the sociology of race have written about a multitude of ways in which racial inequality is embedded in social structure and culture, we want to discuss two specific mechanisms here: color blindness and white normativity.

Color Blindness. The color-blind critique starts from the proposition that some of America's highest ideals and principles about individualism, meritocracy, and race neutrality are actually at the core of the American inability to recognize the persistence of racial inequality and injustice in the United States. The color-blind ideology, to put it somewhat differently, rests on the assumption that race should not be important in contemporary society and that today, it is most important to move beyond color and deal with people as individuals, not groups. However in the context of a racialized social structure characterized by white supremacy, the color-blind ideology works to mask racial inequality (Bonilla-Silva, 2003). The color-blind ideology makes it difficult, if not impossible, for social actors to recognize persistent racial inequalities and injustices as anything other than the result of poor decisions and actions on the part of disadvantaged people themselves. The color-blind ideology has no room for a larger structural analysis. Ideals get in the way of reality. As such, any attempts at explaining inequality within this framework end up blaming the victim. In this way, not only does it blind people to existing racial inequalities and injustices, it also legitimates and justifies the racial status quo and existing inequalities by explaining them in terms of deficiencies (Bonilla-Silva, 2001; Carr, 1997; Crenshaw, 1997). Here it is important to stress that the ideal (or dream) of a color-blind society that has moved past race and transcended racial inequalities and injustices may be a noble one; however, it is quite far from an accurate depiction of contemporary social life, and as such a deeply problematic conceptual frame for trying to make sense of the realities that are in place.

White Normativity. In recent years, there has been an explosion of the study of white culture and identity (Doane & Bonilla Silva, 2003; Fine, Weis, Powell, & Wong, 1997; Frankenberg, 1997; Hill, 1997; Kincheloe, Steinberg, Rodriguez, & Chennault, 1998). One of the key points is the relational point that understanding race and racial inequity is a matter of understanding not just inequalities and disadvantages, but also privilege and advantage. The study of white culture and identity locates the focus of racial analysis on the group empowered and advantaged by existing racial hierarchies and relationships. Critical whiteness studies focus their thought and analysis on majority white culture and consciousness, arguing that it is especially the attitudes, beliefs, and activities of the dominant group—about racial minorities but also about itself—that allows for the continued perpetuation of contemporary racial formations. Whiteness, in the critical conception, is not just a matter of political authority or material power but also a cultural vantage point so deeply privileged and culturally ingrained that it is able to disavow its own social privilege and cultural specificity (Goldberg, 2002). The idea behind the concept of white normativity is that there exists an assumption that the way of thinking, acting, and being in the world of the dominant group is not only acceptable but normal—the cultural mode to which everyone else must accommodate and aspire. Moreover, this centering of whiteness affirms the dominant social and cultural position of whites, of whiteness.

One version of this line of thinking is contained in Joe Feagin's (2006) concept of the white racial frame. Feagin defines the white racial frame as "an organized set of racialized ideas, emotions and inclinations, as well as recurring or habitual discriminatory actions, that are consciously or unconsciously expressed in and constitutive of the routine operations and racist institutions of US society" (p. 23). The white racial frame serves as a master frame for understanding race in the United States—a frame that "centers whiteness and a white perspective, thereby normalizing and justifying both white superiority and black inferiority" (Moore & Bell, in press). "Whiteness," in the critical frame, is therefore not so much about white culture and identity, but about how white culture and identity function to promote and preserve white privilege and the racial status quo. It is a whole set of ideologies, discourses, and identities that serves to produce and perpetuate existing racial hierarchies and white domination more specifically.

A Critical Analysis of American Diversity Discourse

To illustrate and further develop these ideas about the cultural mechanisms that contribute to the reproduction of racial injustices and inequalities in the context of contemporary American society, we will draw upon a recent study of American discourse on diversity that we conducted in four major metropolitan areas across the United States (Bell & Hartmann, 2007). The data for this study were drawn from 166 in-depth interviews conducted in Atlanta, Boston, Los Angeles, and the Twin Cities of Minnesota as a part of the American Mosaic Project, a multiyear, multimethod study of race, religion, and multiculturalism in the contemporary United States (see Edgell, Gerteis, & Hartmann, 2006). The interviews were designed to follow up, probe, and provide context for key issues that emerged from the telephone survey and fieldwork. Interviews lasted between 1½ and 3 hours, and one section of the interview focused specifically on understandings of diversity. Interviewees were recruited from three specific institutional locations in each city: neighborhood organizations, interfaith religious initiatives, and ethnic cultural festivals. Both rank-and-file members and persons in positions of leadership were interviewed. About a third of our sample was drawn from each setting. Two-thirds of our respondents were white; the sample was gender balanced, and respondents ranged from 20 to 75 years old.

It is important to emphasize that the interview population was not a random sample of Americans (as was the case with the telephone survey) but rather a purposive one, targeted to respondents who were actively and self-consciously grappling with issues of difference in their lives and who were thus both well-informed and articulate about diversity. We talked with them at length about their understandings of the term *diversity*. We asked about this term, on one hand, because few words in the current American lexicon related to race are as ubiquitous and ostensibly uplifting as diversity. At the same time, we became convinced that actual meanings and functions of the term are difficult to pinpoint and potentially quite a bit more problematic than that. The use of in-depth interviews, open-ended questions, and strategic probing allowed us to explore *why* people held certain beliefs about diversity; *how* certain experiences affected them; and what implications all of this had for understandings of race, racism, and inequality in contemporary American culture and society.

Some of our initial findings and results were fairly basic and straightforward. We discovered that Americans were very positive, proud, upbeat, and optimistic about diversity; however, we also found that they sometimes found it difficult to define what diversity really was, offering general platitudes or a laundry list of differences it was purported to include. Our respondents found it especially difficult to explain *why* they believed that diversity was positive and important. This inability became especially interesting to reflect upon as we realized that many of our respondents grew quite animated in talking about the problems of diversity and difference in American culture. Indeed, they were far more willing and able to talk about problems than they were about benefits.

Analyzing their responses more carefully, we saw that there were several reasons for this. For one thing, there is a tension in American culture between understanding difference as an individual status or as a group-level phenomenon. In other words, our respondents mostly wanted to assert each person's right to individuality as expressed in any multitude of identities, but had difficulty affirming group-level differences of experience or identity based on things like race.[4] More than this, as we pushed our respondents to give examples and stories that illustrated their own conceptions of diversity and the problems of difference that they had encountered, we found that the vast majority of these stories and anecdotes were about race. Race, in other words, completely dominated and even overdetermined American conceptions of and attitudes about difference and diversity. Indeed, in the vast majority of cases, we would suggest that diversity was actually used as a synonym for talking about race.

In and of itself, there is nothing necessarily or inherently wrong with substituting the language of diversity for the rhetoric of race. The more we critically analyzed how this language functioned, however, the more we came to realize that it overshadowed the very real problem of racial inequality. In other words, even though the diversity discourse was largely informed by understandings of race, it did not allow respondents to deal directly and explicitly with race itself. This was especially clear when it came to the inequalities and injustices we know to be associated with racial difference in the United States.

When we tried, explicitly and directly, to get our interviewees talking about inequality or injustice in the context of these discussions about diversity, our conversations often quickly ground to a halt. Folks just got so confused or agitated or angry that we had to shift the topic of conversation altogether or risk ending the interview. This was particularly striking for us because many of our respondents were actually quite political and articulate on issues of inequality in other settings and on other topics. Yet somehow, we came to realize, the language of diversity made it difficult, if not impossible, for them to talk about inequality and race at the same time.

These Americans mostly preferred this more abstract, and ostensibly more optimistic, uplifting language when discussing the issue of race. All of this, in our view, made it more difficult to recognize and grapple with problems of race. In short, the diversity discourse seems to mystify and obfuscate rather than illuminate issues of racial inequality. When asked what he thinks the general public thinks diversity is, one of our more enlightened respondents said,

> Well you know, it's a word that's in vogue, it's overused. Most of them don't know what they're talking about. But other than the fact that, you know, it conjures up ideas of the workplace or the community, that, where, you know, women have a place and men have a place and ethnic minorities have a place and somehow that the melting pot is working and everything's and everybody's happy ever after. And that's what the—that's happy talk, yeah.

His analysis of the function of the diversity discourse is that it almost serves as a euphemism for race. This idea is certainly echoed throughout the interviews we analyzed.

Our critical analysis of this happy talk led us to conclude that in talking a certain way about diversity, Americans are actually missing or misunderstanding racial inequalities and, moreover, allowing themselves to accept and even celebrate existing racial arrangements. Of course, the real analytical challenge, then, became to explain how and why Americans can adopt and perpetuate such ways of thinking and talking. This is where the race-based critical concepts of color blindness and white normativity became so useful, taking us deeper into understanding these discourses and ideologies.

In terms of the concept of color blindness, we found that the diversity discourse reflects the color-blind ideology in that it sees race only to the extent that race is an element of individual identities that should be tolerated, perhaps even celebrated, but not as the basis for complaints about inequality or group-based interests. For example, one of our respondents, Alice, a white Midwesterner in her 50s, felt that diversity was positive because it "reflects the values and traditions, and ethnicity, and religious backgrounds, skin color of everybody and it welcomes them, makes them feel that they're part of the group, that they're welcome." When discussing the positives of diversity, she talked about people as individuals, but when Alice talked about the drawbacks of diversity, her language switched to group-level differences:

> You have to constantly be thinking about if you're, I see it mostly, I think, when you're doing, like if you want to do the best summer reading for 2004, your instinct is to list all the top authors, and they're, surprise, all white. And oh my goodness, we didn't pick up any minorities, or any nonwhite people, we have to go back and do this and make sure we include them. And I think it's unfortunate that they are just right there to begin with, that we have to target out, we have to categorize our brains that way.

Ideally, for Alice, a commitment to diversity would make people feel welcome despite their various differences, but group-level differences—those that cause us to "categorize our brains"—can create problems.

Second, we turned to the question of white normativity. In our conception, once again, white normativity refers to the "reality of the racial structure of the United States in which whites occupy an unquestioned and unexamined place of esteem, power and privilege" (Bell & Hartmann, 2007, p. 907). Our analysis suggests that the diversity discourse rests on a white normative perspective and as such masks white privilege and racial inequality. We identify two elements of the diversity discourse that point to white normativity: the existence of assimilationist expectations, and that whiteness is centered within the discourse.

In terms of the first element, many of our respondents conditioned their positive assessment of diversity with appeals to cultural assimilation. For example, Melissa, a white southerner, talked about needing to "respect one another's differences and backgrounds . . . and be tolerant of one another." But she continued to say,

> But by the same token, you know, there has to be a defining thread somewhere whether it be, you know, political, whether it be a language that unifies us, you know. Because, you know, without . . . just a few strongholds of the nation, it's like that diversity is not gonna . . . work, you know.

Her sentiment was echoed by several other respondents, many of whom also referred to language as a necessary common thread. In this way, we find that behind an initial acceptance of diversity, there remains a call to conformity to the dominant culture in the United States.

Connected with and underlying this assimilationist sentiment is the assumption that the diversity discourse also has an implicit white center. During our analysis, we noted that when talking about diversity, people often used the language of "welcoming people from different backgrounds" or "respecting people who are different" and were forced to ask "different from what?" What gets left unspoken is who is doing the welcoming, who is doing the respecting. This language gives agency—the ability to welcome or respect or tolerate—to an undefined, but implied, "we." We make the case that this presumably neutral "we" is anything but neutral. In fact, one of our respondents, Jill, names this generally unnamed center by saying this:

> I don't know. I mean, it's almost like out of this sense, it's going to sound terrible coming out . . . almost like a sense of because I am in this privileged state of having a white skin, ah, but in a regard I have privilege, a perceived privilege as therefore obligating me to make sure that other, to extend to others regardless of their skin color, the same benefits and privileges that I have. But it puts, I mean, it's almost like I'm in the host or hostess position. And that's terrible, it's terrible to think of people who are black and brown as you know, having to be guests. Because basically nobody should be, um, I mean I wish it were, I wish that the reality were that it really didn't matter.

In seeing whites as "the hosts" and people of color as "the guests," Jill exposes that the diversity discourse is not race neutral. When we understand this discourse, not in an abstract sense, but in its actual context—referring to the racial reality of society structured by white supremacy—it becomes much clearer that this way of doing race affirms the centrality of whiteness and its ability to obscure racial inequality. As Estrada and McLaren (1993) explain, "Those who occupy privileged positions in our society forge a universalized, sanitized and naturalized 'we' that prevents the 'they' from speaking for themselves" (p. 29). We argue that ideas about "different" cultures, languages, and values simply cannot be separated from a cultural context in which whites occupy a place of higher power, prestige, and social esteem.

Conclusion: Critical Theory and Racial Change

In the sociological tradition, critical theory has served as a counterpoint to traditional social theory, one that seeks to not only describe the world as it is, but to capture the world in a way that provides a critical lens on how things are and how they might be different. In his classic treatise on critical theory, Max Horkheimer (1937/1982) describes this two-fold aim of critical theory with the following:

> The aim of [critical theory] is not simply to eliminate one or other abuse, for it regards such abuses as necessarily connected with the way in which the social structure is organized. Although it itself emerges from the social structure, its purpose is not, either in its conscious intention or in its objective significance, the better functioning of any element in the structure. On the contrary, it is suspicious of the very categories of better, useful, appropriate, productive, and valuable, as these are understood in the present order, and refuses to take them as nonscientific presuppositions about which one can do nothing. (p. 207)

In other words, critical theory presupposes that oppression is central to the social structure and, as a result, offers a critique of social structure in such a way to expose the inherent inequality in society. Furthermore, critical theories, in their challenges to oppression and social inequality, either explicitly or implicitly point to the need for change. In these ways, critical theory aims to illuminate the underlying ideas, cultural formations, and structural realities that create, maintain, and reproduce unequal power relations in society.

The fact that our research on diversity is informed by critical theory helps us to reveal that race informs much of our American thinking about diversity, yet it is also clearly limited in understanding and often simply misunderstood. Taking a critical perspective allowed us to analyze the language of diversity in a way that took into consideration the larger racialized structure and culture of the United States. In other words, it was important to use the larger frames of race-based critical theory to analyze the words that were being spoken. From a more mainstream, less critical point of view, we could have written a very different paper—one that said that people mostly like diversity and that diversity is really about accepting everyone. But as critical theorists, it was essential that we deconstructed taken-for-granted notions and underpinning cultural ideologies that serve to perpetuate and maintain existing power relations and inequalities.

Whereas the journal version of this research focused mostly on exploring the discourse itself and its problematic relationship to race and equality, we end this chapter with a call to reform the way we think about and practice diversity. To the extent that diversity is a central racial project in the 21st century, and we think that it is (see Hartmann & Gerteis, 2005), we were interested in giving some guidance to how we could change it.

One point, which we have not been able to develop in depth here, is the need to understand the independent, irreducible force of race in the modern world but also begin to see and understand how race also maps onto and interacts with other forms of stratification and inequality. The pitch here is for the more intersectional type of critical theory advocated by Patricia Hill Collins (2000), Margaret Andersen (2001), and others in recent years. But at the root of both these critiques and race-based critical theory is that all of our thinking about difference and diversity needs to be situated in a structural context, one that emphasizes the social inequalities and disparities associated with many forms of differentiation in the modern world. This is a second key point. We must pay attention to how these inequities are constructed and who they benefit. We must, in short, understand how diversity and equality are and must be interrelated.

And here is where some of our respondents did give some guidance. As Maryanne, a 75-year-old white Bostonian, said, "Well, I think diversity is kind of an unusual term in that equality is a better way of looking at it. No matter how different you are, you have the same rights as anybody else has. . . . I think equality is almost better than diversity." Maryanne and the other critics in our respondent pool help us to understand the limitations of the current diversity discourse and the extent to which it needs to be transformed. In this way, we conclude that we must both celebrate difference and recognize, for the purpose of dismantling inequalities, the unequal realities of race in the United States.

Notes

1. This brief, schematic overview is inspired by and draws upon many different sources, chief among them Craig Calhoun's (1995) thorough treatment of classical and contemporary critical theory.

2. Although a full accounting of the facts of racial inequality and injustice are well beyond the scope of this chapter, some selected sources include Western (2006) and Pager (2003) on arrest and imprisonment, Oliver and Shapiro (1997) or Conley (1999) on wealth, Massey and Denton (1993) on segregation and poverty, and Neckerman (2007) or Oaks (2005) on education.

3. For studies of conventional social scientific work on race, see Niemonen (1997) and Hartmann, Croll, and Guenther (2003). For more developed methodological criticisms, see Zuberi and Bonilla-Silva (2008) and Zuberi (2001).

4. In *On Toleration*, in fact, Michael Walzer (1997) argues that the central problem of contemporary American culture is not between diversity versus unity, but the diversity of groups versus the freedom of individuals.

References

Andersen, M. L. (2001). Restructuring for whom? Race, class, gender, and the ideology of invisibility. *Sociological Forum, 16*(2), 181–201.

Bell, J., & Hartmann, D. (2007). Diversity in everyday discourse: The cultural ambiguities and consequences of "happy talk." *American Sociological Review, 72,* 895–914.

Bobo, L. (1988). Group conflict, prejudice, and the paradox of contemporary racial attitudes. In P. A. Katz & D. A. Taylor (Eds.), *Eliminating racism: Profiles in controversy* (pp. 85–114). New York: Plenum.

Bobo, L., Kluegel, J., & Smith, R. (1997). Laissez-faire racism: The crystallization of a kinder, gentler, antiblack ideology. In S. Tuch & J. Martin (Eds.), *Racial attitudes in the 1990s: Continuity and change* (pp. 15–44). Westport, CT: Praeger.

Bonilla-Silva, E. (2001). *White supremacy and racism in the post-civil rights era.* Boulder, CO: Lynne Reinner.

Bonilla-Silva, E. (2003). *Racism without racists: Color-blind racism and the persistence of racial inequality in the United States.* Lanham, MD: Rowman & Littlefield.

Calhoun, C. (1995). *Critical social theory: Culture, history, and the challenge of difference.* Oxford, UK: Blackwell.

Carr, L. G. (1997). *Colorblind racism.* Thousand Oaks, CA: Sage.

Conley, D. (1999). *Being black, living in the red.* Berkeley: University of California Press.

Cornell, S., & Hartmann, D. (2007). *Ethnicity and race: Making identities in a changing world* (2nd ed.). Thousand Oaks, CA: Pine Forge.

Crenshaw, K. W. (1997). Colorblind dreams and racial nightmares: Reconfiguring racism in the post-civil rights era. In T. Morrison & C. B. Lacour (Eds.), *Birth of a nation 'hood* (pp. 97–168). New York: Pantheon.

Crenshaw, K., Gotanda, N., Peller, G., & Thomas, K. (Eds.). (1996). *Critical race theory: The key writings that formed the movement.* New York: New Press.

Delgado, R., & Stefancic, J. (2001). *Critical race theory: An introduction.* New York: New York University Press.

Desmond, M., & Emirbayer, M. (2010). *Racial domination, racial progress: The sociology of race in America.* New York: McGraw Hill.

Doane, A. W., & Bonilla-Silva, E. (2003). *White out: The continuing significance of racism.* New York: Routledge.

Edgell, P., Gerteis, J., & Hartmann, D. (2006). Atheists as "other": Moral boundaries and cultural membership in American society. *American Sociological Review, 71,* 211–234.

Emirbayer, M. (1997). Manifesto for relational sociology. *American Journal of Sociology, 103,* 281–317.

Estrada, K., & McLaren, P. (1993). A dialogue on multiculturalism and democratic culture. *Educational Researcher, 22*(3), 27–33.

Feagin, J. (2006). *Systemic racism: A theory of oppression.* New York: Taylor & Francis.

Fine, M., Weis, L., Powell, L. C., & Wong, L. M. (Eds.). (1997). *Off white: Readings on race, power, and society.* New York: Routledge.

Frankenberg, R. (1993). *White women, race matters: The social construction of whiteness.* Minneapolis: University of Minnesota Press.

Frankenberg, R. (Ed.). (1997). *Displacing whiteness.* Durham, NC: Duke University Press.

Gallagher, C. A. (2003). Color-blind privilege: The social and political functions of erasing the color line in post race America. *Race, Gender, and Class, 10*(4), 22–37.

Giroux, H. A. (1997). Racial politics and the pedagogy of whiteness. In M. Hill (Ed.), *Whiteness: A critical reader* (pp. 294–315). New York: New York University Press.

Goldberg, D. T. (1993). *Racist culture: Philosophy and the politics of meaning.* Cambridge, MA: Blackwell.

Goldberg, D. T. (2002). *The racial state.* Oxford: Blackwell.

Hartmann, D. (2007). Rush Limbaugh, Donovan McNabb, and "a little social concern": Reflections on the problems of whiteness in contemporary American sport. *Journal of Sport and Social Issues, 31*(1), 45–60.

Hartmann, D., & Gerteis, J. (2005). Dealing with diversity: Mapping multiculturalism in sociological terms. *Sociological Theory, 23,* 218–240.

Hartmann, D., Croll, P. R., & Guenther, K. (2003). The race relations "problematic" in American sociology: Revisiting Niemonen's case study and critique. *American Sociologist, 34,* 20–55.

Hill, M. (Ed.). (1997). *Whiteness: A critical reader.* New York: New York University Press.

Hill Collins, P. (2000). *Black feminist thought: Knowledge, consciousness, and the politics of empowerment.* New York: Routledge.

Horkheimer, M. (1982). Traditional and critical theory. In *Critical theory: Selected essays* (pp. 188–243). New York: Continuum. (Original work published 1937)

Kincheloe, J. L., Steinberg, S. R., Rodriguez, N. M., & Chennault, R. E. (Eds.). (1998). *White reign: Deploying whiteness in America.* New York: St. Martin's.

Lipsitz, G. (1998). *The possessive investment in whiteness: How white people profit from identity politics.* Philadelphia: Temple University Press.

Massey, D., & Denton, N. (1993). *American apartheid.* Cambridge, MA: Harvard University Press.

McIntosh, P. (1989, July-August). White privilege: Unpacking the invisible knapsack. *Peace and Freedom,* pp. 10–12.

Moore, W., & Bell, J. M. (in press). Maneuvers of whiteness: "Diversity" as a mechanism of retrenchment in the affirmative action discourse. *Critical Sociology.*

Morrison, T. (1992). *Playing in the dark: Whiteness and the literary imagination.* Cambridge, MA: Harvard University Press.

Neckerman, K. (2007). *Schools betrayed: Roots of failure in inner city education.* Chicago: University of Chicago Press.

Niemonen, J. (1997). The race relations problematic in American sociology: A case study and critique. *American Sociologist, 28*(1), 15–54.

Oaks, J. (2005). *Keeping track: How schools structure inequality* (2nd ed.). New Haven, CT: Yale University Press.

Oliver, M., & Shapiro, T. (1997). *Black wealth/white wealth.* New York: Routledge.

Omi, M., & Winant, H. (1994). *Racial formation in the United States: From the 1960s to the 1990s.* New York: Routledge.

Pager, D. (2003). The mark of a criminal record. *American Journal of Sociology, 108,* 937–975.

Roediger, D. (1991). *The wages of whiteness: Race and the making of the American working class.* London: Verso.

Roediger, D. (2002). *Colored white: Transcending the racial past.* Berkeley: University of California Press.

Schuman, H., Steeh, C., Bobo, L., & Krysan, M. (1997). *Racial attitudes in America: Trends and interpretations.* Cambridge, MA: Harvard University Press.

Walzer, M. (1997). *On toleration.* New Haven, CT: Yale University Press.

Western, B. (2006). *Punishment and inequality in America.* New York: Russell Sage.

Wilson, W. J. (1987). *The truly disadvantaged.* Chicago: University of Chicago Press.

Zerubavel, E. (2006). *The elephant in the room: Silence and denial in everyday life.* New York: Oxford University Press.

Zuberi, T. (2001). *Thicker than blood: How racial statistics lie.* Minneapolis: University of Minnesota Press.

Zuberi, T., & Bonilla Silva, E. (Eds.). (2008). *White logic, white methods.* New York: Rowman & Littlefield.

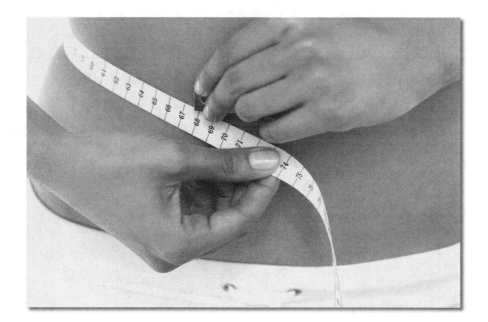

CHAPTER 9

The Socially Constructed Body

Insights From Feminist Theory

Judith Lorber and Patricia Yancey Martin

Judith Lorber *is Professor Emerita of Sociology and Women's Studies at Brooklyn College and the Graduate School, City University of New York. She is the author of* Breaking the Bowls: Degendering and Feminist Change *(2005);* Gender Inequality: Feminist Theories and Politics *(4th edition, 2009);* Paradoxes of Gender *(1994); and* Women Physicians: Careers, Status and Power *(1984). With Lisa Jean Moore, she is the coauthor of* Gendered Bodies: Feminist Perspectives *(2nd edition, 2011) and* Gender and the Social Construction of Illness *(2nd edition, 2002). She is coeditor of* Handbook of Gender and Women's Studies *(2006, with Kathy Davis and Mary Evans);* Revisioning Gender *(1999, with Myra Marx Ferree and Beth B. Hess); and* The Social Construction of Gender *(1991, with Susan A. Farrell). She is the Founding Editor of* Gender & Society, *the official publication of Sociologists for Women in Society. She received the American Sociological Association's Jessie Bernard Award in 1996.*

Patricia Yancey Martin *is Emerita Daisy Parker Flory Professor of Sociology at Florida State University. Her interests are gender and organizations, qualitative methods, and the second wave women's movement. She has written* Rape Work:

Source: Some of the material in this chapter was adapted from Lorber, J. (1994). *Paradoxes of gender.* New Haven, CT: Yale University Press; Lorber, J. (2001). *Gender inequality: Feminist theories and politics.* Los Angeles: Roxbury; Lorber, J., & Moore, L. J. (2002). *Gender and the social construction of illness.* Walnut Creek, CA: AltaMira; Lorber, J., & Moore, L. J. (2011). *Gendered bodies: Feminist perspectives* (2nd ed.). New York: Oxford University Press.

Victims, Gender, and Emotions in Organizations and Communities *(2005), exploring how police, medical personnel, prosecutors, and rape crisis centers are influenced by their organizations to treat victims unresponsively. She co-edited* Feminist Organizations: Harvest of the New Women's Movement *(1995, with Myra Marx Ferree). Her recent work focuses on rape crisis centers, aesthetics of bodies in residential organizations, "practicing" of gender at work, the fear standard in crimes of stalking, adolescent girls' "body project" issues relative to race and ethnicity, and "emotion work" by professionals who deal with rape victims. She received the American Sociological Association's Jessie Bernard Award in 2007, a CIES Fulbright Fellowship to Sweden in 2007, and the Distinguished Feminist Activism Award from Sociologists for Women in Society (SWS) in 2006.*

> *Body-reflexive practices . . . are not internal to the individual. They involve social relations and symbolism; they may well involve large-scale institutions. Particular versions of masculinity [and femininity] are constituted in their circuits as meaningful bodies and embodied meanings. Through body-reflexive practices, more than individual lives are formed: A social world is formed.*
>
> Connell (1995, p. 64)

I n an undergraduate course on the sociology of gender, one of us invited some young bodybuilders to speak to the class. Two speakers were a married couple who did "customized" coaching of people who wanted to "improve" their bodies in various ways. The husband coached young fat or skinny boys whose parents wanted them to be thinner or heavier, and the wife coached women who wanted to be "more defined," meaning they wanted muscles that were visible when their bodies were at rest. The third bodybuilder was a tall, muscular 20-year-old man.

All three speakers had been given questions in advance to think about for addressing the class. The 20-year-old had written his comments, and when his turn came to speak, he held the paper in front of him with both hands, looked down at it instead of at the students and in a voice choked with emotion, said:

> When I was 12 years old, my dad walked out on my mother and brother and me. I knew from that day I was now the "man of the house." So I had to do something. I started working out. I tried to get big so I could fill his shoes. I've never stopped working out. I have a kid today and I know I have to be there for her, be strong, be a man.

The class of 230 students sat in silence, touched by this unexpected confession. The speaker had, as a boy, decided that having muscles and being "big" made him into the man of the house he was required to be because of his father's departure. To be a man, he felt he had to "get big."

The equation of big size, strong muscles, and "true masculinity" is a pervasive *theme* theme in U.S. culture. It is so ingrained that many celebrity athletes secretly use body-building steroids, and up to 1 million adolescent athletes do too to attain muscular bulk. Young people using steroids can suffer premature stunting of bone growth and height loss, and there have been reports of depression leading to suicide. The long-term effects can be infertility, liver damage, high blood pressure, and other physiological problems, including impotence in men. But the desire to look "masculine" and be able to perform well as an athlete often outweighs regard for physical health (Klein, 1993).[1]

The young man's story illustrates a theme of this chapter: Members of a society construct their bodies in ways that comply with accepted views of gender—that is, norms of masculinity and femininity. They try to shape and use their bodies to conform to their culture's or racial ethnic group's expectations of how a woman's body, a man's body, a girl's body, or a boy's body should look. This point does not deny the distinctiveness of material bodies, with varying physical shapes, sizes, strengths, and weaknesses. It does emphasize, however, that members of a society, not genes or biology, determine the "proper" shape and usage of women's, men's, boys', and girls' bodies.

Genes only partially determine physiological development, while environmental factors such as nutrition, health regimens, prevention and treatment of illnesses, exercise, air, water, and general living conditions are the other part. Beyond physiology are cultural and social factors that are the focus of this chapter—the attitudes and values attached to gendered body practices. Such practices produce bodies that one's social group considers properly "masculine" or "feminine" and for which one is regularly rewarded or criticized.

The search for better-looking bodies fuels the popularity of cosmetic surgery, growth hormones, anabolic steroids, bodybuilding, and fitness regimens for men and women. For example, men are the targeted market of plastic surgeons for gynecomastia, or enlarged breasts. One ad said that "as many as one of three males are affected by this embarrassing problem" and that breast reduction surgery can remove the "undesirable contour . . . restoring the normal male breast shape." For women, the "normal female breast shape" is large, but not too large, firm and lifted, so they get targeted with ads for "breast augmentation" and "breast reduction/lift" as well as reshaping faces, noses, lips, tummies, and buttocks. The ads for body and facial surgery encourage men and women to judge their appearance against images that are culturally admired but that many, if not most, people find difficult to meet (Pitts-Taylor, 2007).[2]

According to the American Society of Plastic Surgeons, 12.5 million cosmetic procedures were performed in the United States in 2009, down 1% from the previous year but up 69% from 2000. Most 2009 procedures were minimally invasive (e.g., botulinum injections, chemical peels, or laser hair removal), but 1.5 million were surgical. In 2009, the top five surgical procedures were breast augmentation, nose reshaping, eyelid surgery, liposuction, and tummy tucks. Of the total procedures, women had 91%, men 9%. Only women had breast augmentation surgery, but women predominated in other categories, too—74% for nose reshaping,

85% for eyelid surgery, 89% for liposuction, and 98% for tummy tucks. Face lifts were the top cosmetic surgery between 2000 and 2004; in 2005, tummy tucks became number one as "more people turned toward body contouring and minimally invasive treatments for facial rejuvenation."[3]

Given their tendency to cause health problems, it seems unfortunate that fully one half of all breast augmentation surgeries in 2009 (there were 289,328 nationwide) involved silicone implants. The top surgical procedures for men in 2009 were nose reshaping (66,334, or 36% of the total), hair implants (12,973, or 63% of the total), and chin implants (6,272, or 48% of the total). Whites had almost two thirds of the procedures, followed by Asian Americans (17%), Hispanics (12%), and African Americans (5%). Somewhat amazingly, a 2010 survey of more than 2,000 U.S. residents who were asked about their interest in undergoing cosmetic surgery or related treatments showed a high level of enthusiasm.[4]

According to the American Society of Plastic Surgeons, cosmetic breast surgery rates fell about 6% between 2008 and 2009. Feminists may hope that this decrease signals changing attitudes toward surgically altering women's bodies in general and breasts in particular, but it more likely reflects our current economic crisis. In fact, when we look at trends over the past decade, breast augmentation (i.e., inserting breast implants) and breast lift (i.e., surgically altering the shape of the breasts) rates have increased 36% and 65%, respectively, since 2000. Thus, even though recent statistics show declines in cosmetic breast surgery, it is too early to know if the trend is due to changing attitudes about body modification or a reflection of a decrease in women's disposable income.

Given its high cost, cosmetic surgery appears to be a method used mostly by affluent white women in their quest for the "perfect" shape, size, or look. But the popularity of expensive exercise clubs and home exercise equipment indicates that men and women of all racial and ethnic groups are preoccupied with the search for the "perfect body" (Boyd, Reynolds, Tillman, & Martin, 2010). This preoccupation is not just about good looks but also success.

How Bodies Matter: Appearance and Success

We may say that intelligence and competence count for much more than physical appearance, but only a few presidents of the United States have been shorter than 6 feet tall, and research on corporations has shown that approximately 10% of a man's earnings can be accounted for by his height (Collins & Zebrowitz, 1995; Hall, 2006; Hensley & Cooper, 1987).

When one of the authors was doing interviews in the headquarters of a large, multinational corporation, she noticed that the men she interviewed were tall. As one interview with a man who was 6½ feet tall was about to begin, she asked, as a joke, "Are all the men at [the company] tall?" He smiled and said, "Well, a lot of us are," and he proceeded to explain that he has a bias toward tall people—men and women. He stated, "The last two women I've hired have been over 6 feet tall." He described his department's "winning" volleyball team and its "need [for] tall people to win." His comments may indeed reflect a preference for tall volleyball players by his department, but they may also reflect society's general preference for tall men. He may see tall men as superior, given society's valorization of height in men. Then his concern to avoid gender bias leads him to favor tall women as well.

When it comes to filling positions of authority, the male sports hero, astronaut, and combat soldier—symbols of the "right stuff"—are often the first choices. Their physical strength, coolness under fire, motivation to succeed, and combination of self-promotion and team support are thought to make them the exemplars of leadership. Their exemplary characteristics are displayed, we believe, on their faces and bodies.

A very large oil portrait, 50 feet wide by 30 feet high, of World War I British military officers in the National Portrait Gallery in London shows approximately 50 men in their military uniform finery. With the exception of two somewhat shorter, rotund men, all are tall and thin in physique. Furthermore, all have square jaws, strong chins, similar hair styles (short cropped and no beards), and conventional "good" looks. The idea may seem fantastical that military officers are chosen on the basis of height, weight, race, and jaw shape, given ideological claims in Western societies that ability, knowledge, and a track record of competence form the basis for such decisions. Recent research, however, shows that the shape of a man's jaw—for example, whether he has a receding or perpendicular chin—is a determinative factor in being chosen for high-ranking military office (Mueller & Mazur, 1996). "Weak-faced" men are rarely advanced to the highest ranks.

West Point's curriculum is devised to produce military leaders, and physical competence is used as a significant measure of leadership ability. When women were first accepted as cadets, it became clear that the tests of physical competence, such as the ability to scale an 8-foot wall rapidly, had been constructed for male physiques—pulling oneself up and over and using upper-body strength. Rather than devise tests of physical competence for women, West Point provided boosters that mostly women used but that lost them test points (in the case of the wall, West Point added a platform). Finally, the women figured out how to use their bodies successfully. Janice Yoder (1989) describes this situation as follows:

> I was observing this obstacle one day, when a woman approached the wall in the old prescribed way, got her fingertips grip, and did an unusual thing: She walked her dangling legs up the wall until she was in a position where both her hands and feet were atop the wall. She then simply pulled up her sagging bottom and went over. She solved the problem by capitalizing on one of women's physical assets: lower-body strength. (p. 530)

Thus, if West Point is going to measure leadership capability by physical strength, women's thighs and pelvises will do just as well as men's arms and shoulders.

The Social Construction of Gendered Bodies

Social construction feminism singles out gender as one of the most significant factors in the transformation of physical bodies to fit cultural ideals of feminine beauty and masculine strength. This feminist view argues that bodies are socially constructed in material and cultural worlds, which means they are physical and symbolic at one and the same time. To say that bodies are socially constructed is not to deny their material reality or universality. Bodies are born, and bodies die. Female breasts are usually able to produce milk for nursing infants, whereas male breasts usually cannot. Female mammals gestate and give birth; male mammals do not. Male bodies usually have less fat and more muscle than female bodies. But when we ask which women's and men's bodies are beautiful, or what the physical capacities are of human men and women in physical labor and sports, we are asking questions about social practices and judgments that vary by culture and ethnicity, time and place, and that differ for the rich and the poor.

Social practices exaggerate and minimize differences and similarities among people, creating, through physical labor, exercise, sports, and surgery, the various masculine and feminine bodies that social groups admire. Cultural views about the body are more than aesthetic; they are moral judgments, too. When a person's body contradicts social conventions regarding weight, height, and shape, that person may be viewed as lacking in self-control and self-respect. Conversely, people whose bodies comply with valued conventions are admired, praised, and held up to others as ideals to be emulated. In short, by judging, rewarding, and punishing people of different body sizes, shapes, weights, and musculature, members of a social group persuade and coerce each other to construct socially acceptable (and similar-looking) bodies.

Gender is one of the most significant factors in the transformation, via social construction dynamics, of physical bodies into social bodies (Fausto-Sterling, 2000). In Western culture, dieting, breast enhancement, and facelifts are ways that women have changed their appearance to fit ideals of feminine beauty, whereas men lift weights, get hair transplants, and undergo cosmetic surgery to mold their bodies and faces to a masculine ideal. These practices may lead to illnesses, such as eating disorders, infections, and systemic damage from leaking silicone implants, but by themselves they are not considered abnormal because they are responses to culturally idealized views of how women's and men's bodies should look (Blum, 2003; Bordo, 2005; Davis, 1995; Gilman, 1999; Gullette, 1993; Hesse-Biber, 1996; Pope, Phillips, & Olivardia, 2000).

Because bodies are socially constructed in deeply gendered societies, they will, of necessity, be gendered because a gender-neutral or androgynous or "unisex" body is anathema in a world in which people must know quickly and precisely where to place others they encounter for the first time or in brief, face-to-face interactions. How you look to the other person (masculine or feminine) is tied to who you are (woman or man). Your social identity is a gendered identity, and your identity papers and bureaucratic records document your gender over and over again. Who you are is therefore gendered. We will never know how much of this gendering is biology and how much is social construction unless we have a degendered society that does not produce or exaggerate differences through markedly different treatment and expectations of boys and girls.

Thus, although you may think the natural physiology and anatomy of female and male bodies dictates the ways women's and men's bodies look and are used, social constructionist feminist theory argues that the "ideal types" of bodies that we are encouraged to emulate are the product of society's gender ideology, practices, and stratification system. Western societies expect men to be aggressive initiators of action and protectors of women and children; therefore, men's bodies should be muscular and strong. Women are expected to be nurturant and emotionally giving, willing to subordinate their desires to please men and their interests to take care of children. Therefore, women's bodies should be yielding and sexually appealing to men when they are young, and plumply maternal when they are older.

Of course, many perfectly acceptable variations of women's and men's bodies exist, including well-muscled female athletes and graceful male ballet dancers. The underlying norms seep through, however. Male ballet dancers, such as Nijinsky, Nureyev, and Baryshnikov, awed audiences with their phenomenal leaps and turns, the specialty of male dancers. Accomplished women athletes pose provocatively for magazine covers in sexy clothes.

Gendered Bodies and Social Power

Feminist research has increased awareness of the social construction of *gendered bodies* by making visible cultural and social dynamics that generally are invisible to members of a society. Using these data, feminists have called into question many accepted "truths" about gender and bodies and have challenged the evidence on which dubious claims about men's physical superiority are based. In addition, feminists' political activism seeks to improve the status and treatment of women and girls by valuing women's bodies as much as men's bodies (Butler, 1993; Lorber & Moore, 2011; Price & Shildrick, 1999; Weitz, 2009).

Claims about gender, which include bodies, fit into the social arrangements and cultural beliefs that constitute gender as a social institution (Lorber, 1994; Martin, 2004). As a social institution, gender produces two categories of people, "men" and "women," with different characteristics, skills, personalities, and body types. These gendered attributes, which we call "manliness" or "masculinity" and "womanliness" or "femininity," are designed to fit people into adult social roles, such as "mother," "father," "nurse," or "construction worker."

The institution of gender has many facets, from the societal patterns that put men into most of the positions of power in government and corporations to intimate relationships in which men have more power over women than women have over men. There are racial, ethnic, and class differences among women and among men, but gender similarities still exist. These similarities are socially produced, but their pervasiveness makes it seem as if they are biologically linked. Thus, women's learned emotional sensitiveness will be considered as evidence that they are naturally maternal, and men's learned coolness and objectivity will be considered as evidence that they are naturally logical and scientific. Yet recent events have shown that men do cry, and women can be heroes, warriors, or terrorists (Lorber, 2002).

Another common pattern is that men's characteristics are, for the most part, considered superior to women's, thus justifying men's social dominance. Cockburn (1985) notes that men's supposed greater strength rationalizes the gendered division of labor, even when it is machinery that does the actual physical labor:

> Two qualities are combined in men's work: physical competence and technical competence. The men bind these two together and appropriate both qualities for masculinity. Each affords a little power. Not much, just a modicum of power that is enough to enable men to leverage more pay, less supervision, and more freedom out of management. (p. 100)

Cockburn (1983; also Martin, 2001) further notes that men's greater strength is socially constructed, and it builds into gender stratification at work and in society in general:

> Females are born a little smaller than males. This difference is exaggerated by upbringing, so that women grow into adults who are less physically strong and competent than they could be. They are then excluded from a range of manual occupations and, by extension, from the control of technology. The effect spills over into everyday life: Ultimately women have become dependent on men to change the wheel of a car, reglaze a broken window, or replace a smashed roof slate. Worse, women are physically harassed and violated by men: Women are first rendered relatively weak; the weakness is transformed to vulnerability; and vulnerability opens the way to intimidation and exploitation. It is difficult to exaggerate the scale and longevity of the oppression that has resulted. (p. 204)

Feminists argue that a system of domination requires difference. Thus, claims that women and men are different become fodder for the development and perpetuation of a gender hierarchy or a dominance system favoring men over women.

On Telling Men From Women

Imagery, ideology, and practice are the social processes by which supposedly natural bodies are socially constructed. One of the most crucial aspects of the social construction of gendered bodies is that women and men should be easy to tell apart. You may say that anyone can tell a female from a male. Physical differences between male and female bodies certainly exist—a roomful of naked people or a walk on the beach would tell us at least that. However, when dressed in unisex clothing, their differences are not as obvious as one may assume.

When four female students were admitted to the formerly all-male military academy, The Citadel, they were warned that they would have to have "nob" haircuts (shaved heads). Soon thereafter, however, they were told that they would have only very short haircuts in a "feminine" style. Unhappy with this distinction, three of the four women cadets shaved each other's heads and were disciplined for it (Allen, 1996). Although the commander insisted it was so that the women would not be humiliated, a picture of a woman Citadel cadet with her regulation hat showed how difficult it would be to tell the boys from the girls unless they had a visible gender marker such as longer hair. Christine Williams (1989) found that the U.S. Marines required women to wear skirts and make-up for similar reasons—to differentiate them from men.

In most situations involving bodies, women and men are physically marked and physically separated, and overlaps between female and male bodies are ignored. Separating women from men is not such a simple matter. In the past, chromosomal testing was thought to be an infallible sex detector. But an anomaly common enough to be found in several feminine-looking women competing at every major international sports event is the existence of XY chromosomes that have not produced male anatomy or physiology because of other genetic input. Even with evidence of overlapping physiology and physical capabilities, sports authorities continue to uphold the principle of separate competitions for women and men. Part of the reason is that men's sports have higher prestige, more extensive media coverage, and greater economic rewards.

The furor in 2009, when Caster Semenya, an 18-year-old South African woman, won the 800-meter race at the World Championships in Athletics in Berlin, and her womanhood was challenged by one of her competitors, is an example of the difficulties and persistence in trying to find a perfect gender verification test (Clarey & Kolata, 2009). Semenya won with a time of 1 minute 55.45 seconds, the best in the world in 2009, beating the defending champion by 2.45 seconds. Her time was not the all-time fastest, yet no other champions had to prove they were women. Semenya was described in one news report as having "an unusually developed muscular frame and a deep voice" (Kessel, 2009), hardly accurate criteria for gender verification. After extensive testing, Semenya was allowed to keep her medal, but the results of the tests were not made public (Longman, 2009). She won again a year later, amid persistent complaints about her gender (Clarey, 2010).

Trying to develop "simple rules for complex gender realities" presents a challenge to gender segregation, wrote Alice Dreger (2009), professor of clinical medical humanities and bioethics at Northwestern University. Genes don't tell you how a body functions physically. Measuring testosterone levels might give an indication of muscle mass, but testosterone levels aren't criteria for gender division. Men with low testosterone levels don't compete with women who have similar levels; rather, men are allowed to boost their levels. Dreger says the variation in biological sex challenges the belief that sex is clearly binary, with clearly distinguishable markers of female and male.

Sports is a prime cultural arena for the social construction of men's and women's bodies. In sports, men's bodies have an extremely high value, paying off in prestige and income. Women's sports do not pay off as well, even though the bodies of women athletes have physical capabilities most ordinary men and women could not emulate (McDonagh & Pappano, 2008). Another area in which gender norms affect bodies is health and illness. Here, men are more disadvantaged. Young men put themselves at risk for accidents, homicides, and drug and alcohol abuse, which reduce their life span. Young women with eating disorders also put themselves at risk, but the death rates are not as high. Regarding risk of HIV/AIDS, young women are becoming even more vulnerable than young men. Both women and men are disadvantaged by physical disability, but gender norms affect them in somewhat different ways. In the following sections, we detail the gendered aspects of sports, risk behavior, weight and eating problems, and able-bodiedness.

Gender and Sports

Sports competitions are almost always gendered, and different kinds of sports construct different kinds of women's and men's bodies. In the process, they also construct masculinity and femininity and men's superior status (Hargreaves, 1994; Heywood & Dworkin, 2003; McDonagh & Pappano, 2008; Messner, 2002; Messner & Sabo, 1994). Exactly how women and men are segregated in sports is easy to list: Many sports are gender-typed—few women in the United States play football, and few men are synchronized swimmers. Where women and men play the same popular sports, such as tennis, golf, and gymnastics, the rules and events are different. The women front-runners in marathons, who have beaten the times of a couple of hundred men, are compared only to the men front-runners, who run faster, although women are quickly catching up to them (McDonagh & Pappano, 2008, pp. 71–74). Talent for sports seems to show itself early, but it is carefully encouraged in the United States—and it is carefully gendered.

Many gendered body characteristics we think of as inborn are the result of social practices. The phenomena of boys' boisterousness and girls' physical awkwardness in Western societies are examples. When little boys run around noisily, we say, "Boys will be boys," meaning that their physical assertiveness has to be in the Y chromosome because it is manifest so early and so commonly in boys. Boys the world over, however, are not boldly physical—just those who are encouraged to use their bodies freely, cover space, take risks, and play outdoors at all kinds of games and sports. Conversely, what do we mean when we say, "She throws like a girl"? We usually mean that she throws like a female child, a carrier of XX chromosomes. After all, she is only 4 or 5 years old, so how could she have learned to be so awkward? In fact, as Young (1990) notes, she throws like a person who has already been taught to restrict her movements, to protect her body, and to use her body in ways that are approved of as feminine:

> Not only is there a typical style of throwing like a girl, but there is a more or less typical style of running like a girl, climbing like a girl, swinging like a girl, hitting like a girl. They have in common first that the whole body is not put into fluid and directed motion, but rather . . . the motion is concentrated in one body part; and . . . tends not to reach, extend, lean, stretch, and follow through in the direction of her intention. (p. 146)

The girl who experiences her body in such a limited way at an early age is a product of her culture and time. As she learns to restrict her moves, she simultaneously closes opportunities to develop the fluid, whole-bodied, unconstrained moves that are associated with outstanding achievement in sports. As social practices change, and girls are encouraged to use their bodies the way boys do, they become formidable sports competitors.

What has particularly changed women's bodies are the norms and expectations of their capabilities. For example, before Fanny Blankers-Koen, two-time mother, won four gold medals in sprinting in the 1948 Olympics, it was thought that childbirth ruined the female athlete's body. In 1952, June Irwin won a bronze medal in diving while she was 3.5 months pregnant (Wallechinsky, 1996). The rules governing women's competitions, however, have not always recognized their strength. In the Grand Slam tennis contests, men must win three of five games, whereas women must win two of three. In response to Martina Navratilova's call for the same rules for women as men (and the same prize money), journalist and tennis reporter Bud Collins stated in a letter to the *New York Times* that approximately 100 years ago, women played three-out-of-five-set matches (and in much more clothing). Their ability to match men's endurance "alarmed" the U.S. Tennis Association officials (all of whom were men), and they downgraded women's abilities by reducing the number of games they had to play to win a match (Collins, 1996).

An important part of the changed view of women athletes is that they are no longer seen as masculinized oddballs (Cahn, 1994). Muscles on women are now viewed as sexy. Holly Brubach (1996), in "The Athletic Esthetic," the "style" piece in a special issue of the *New York Times*, stated the following:

> Muscles bestow on a woman a grace in motion that is absent from fashion photographs and other images in which the impact resides in a carefully orchestrated, static pose. Muscles also impart a sense of self-possession, a quality that is unfailingly attractive. (p. 51)

Television broadcasts of the Olympics, news and magazine photos, product endorsements, and other popular media depictions make new images of women's bodies routine and everyday. No one would think of organizing an all-male Olympics anymore. Not only would it be unthinkable, but also it would be unprofitable. Olympic women athletes are good business; they attract audiences, men as well as women, and they sell products. But the prestige and financial rewards of sports for women are far less than for men, even though women—like men—sustain many injuries, play through pain, and undergo orthopedic surgery and other such procedures (Sokolove, 2008). For women, pain and injuries are the price of high-level competition. For men, they are marks of manhood. If male sports stars fail to ignore injuries and pain and refuse to use their bodies aggressively on the field, their masculinity is impugned by coaches and fellow players (Messner, 1992).

Sports is a path to upward mobility for poor and working-class boys, even though few become professional athletes. Those who break into professional teams have only a few years to make it, and they cannot afford to be sidelined by injuries. Alcoholism, drug abuse, obesity, and heart disease also take their toll. The life expectancy of professional football players in the United States is approximately 15 years less than that of other men (Messner, 1992), and repeated head traumas result in early dementia (Schwarz, 2009). Their payoff, and that of all successful athletes in men's sports, is very high income and fame, but they come at a physical and mental cost (Prior, 2006). Successful women athletes do not get the same amount of income, media coverage, or prestige.

Messner, Duncan, and Jensen (1993) found that in 1989 in the United States, men's sports received 92% of the television coverage and women's sports 5%, with the remaining 3% mixed or gender-neutral. In 1990, in four of the top-selling newspapers in the United States, stories on men's sports outnumbered those on women's sports 23 to 1. There is an implicit hierarchy in naming, with female athletes most likely to be called by first names, followed by African American male athletes, with only white male athletes routinely referred to by their last names.[5] Similarly, women's collegiate sports teams are named or marked in ways that symbolically feminize and trivialize them—for example, the men's team is called Tigers, whereas the women's team is called Kittens or Lady Tigers, with all the gendered meanings of the term *lady* (Eitzen & Zinn, 1989).

The ideological subtext in Western culture is that physical strength, as demonstrated in sports, the military, and bodybuilding, is men's prerogative and justifies men's physical and sexual domination of women (Hargreaves, 1986; Izraeli, 1997; Messner, 2002; Theberge, 1987). Women's physical capabilities challenge these assumptions. As MacKinnon (1987) says,

> It's threatening to one's takeability, one's rapeability, one's femininity, to be strong and physically self-possessed. To be able to resist rape, not to communicate rapeability with one's body, to hold one's body for uses and meanings other than that can transform what being a woman means. (p. 122)

Resistance to that transformation was evident in the policies of American women physical education professionals throughout most of the 20th century. They minimized exertion, maximized a feminine appearance and manner, and left organized sports competition to men for a long time (Mangan & Park, 1987).

Today, when girls and women are professional and amateur players in all kinds of sports, women and men are not allowed to compete against each other, so actual comparisons of men's and women's and boys' and girls' physical prowess are rarely made (McDonagh & Pappano, 2008). One student in one of our introductory sociology classes noted that he and the other boys were glad that they did not have to play against the best athlete in their elementary school—a girl. Sex segregation of sports by school officials kept her from playing with the boys and probably from showing them up. Another young man, who had played Little League baseball with girls, believed that most girls were "no good"—even though three or four girls were very good. The girls who played well were ignored by the boys. He said,

> About this time I participated in Little League baseball. This was a boy-dominated organization where a team was "unlucky" to have a girl teammate. Approximately 1 out of every 12 kids in Little League at that time [was a girl]. I remember them quite well. Most were really not that good at baseball. They would usually play at the end of the game and bat last in the lineup. Then there

were the three or four girls who stuck out in the league. They competed with the best of us. They could outhit just about any boy and played aggressively. Although they were good, they were also outcasts. Everyone considered them "tomboys" because they would dive for a fly ball or slide headfirst into home plate. Their teammates loved them on the field but once the game was over, so was the friendship. Girls just didn't fit into the norms of Little League. I have always wondered what it was like for those girls to play a boy-dominated sport.

The girls' willingness and ability to "play like boys" were valued and celebrated on the field, but the same boys who praised them on the field viewed these girls as "freaks" off the field.

If gender ideology about girls' and boys' bodies says girls are not athletically skilled, at least in sports defined as appropriate for boys, girls who do well in these sports are viewed as deviant. If teachers and principals forbid gender-mixed teams in schools, and if boys will not recognize girls' abilities when they play on teams outside of school, there is little opportunity to challenge the stereotypes of girls' versus boys' physical prowess (Fine, 1987; Grasmuck, 2005; Messner, 2002).

The belief that only men are "true athletes" plays out in media representation of women's and men's sports and in unequal distribution of financial rewards and prizes. Media images of modern male athletes glorify their strength and power, even their violence. Media images of modern female athletes tend to focus on their feminine beauty and grace (so they are not really athletes) or on their thin, small, wiry androgynous bodies (so they are not really women). As Lorber notes, "believing is seeing" (Lorber, 1993). If members of society are told repeatedly that women's bodily limitations prevent them from doing sports as well as men, they come to believe it and the belief is reinforced by the media. One result is that even women's championship teams often falter and fail (Longman, 2003; Vecsey, 2003).

Risk Behavior

The masculine code of physical strength valorized in men's sports is part of the body imagery of men generally. Men in the working class prove their masculinity by being tough, making fun of danger or hardship on the job, and lording it over women and weaker men. For the middle-class man, power over resources and people is a primary route to proving oneself a man (Martin, 2001). To get that power, a man may have to push himself so hard on the job that he ends up with a heart attack. Even more vulnerable than the "Type A" executive is the working-class African American, the "John Henry" who pits himself against impossible obstacles to try to make a decent living (Riska, 2004).[6]

Because of multiple risk factors, young African American men living in disadvantaged environments are the most likely group to die before reaching adulthood. In 2006, the leading cause of death for U.S. residents in the 5- to 44-year-old age range was accidents, largely due to motor vehicles (accidents of all kinds was fifth among the 10 most prevalent causes of death). However, the leading cause of death for young African American men ages 15 to 34 was homicide, and homicide was second in prevalence for African American boys aged 10 to 14 (Heron, 2010). Because of a high level of deaths due to homicides, accidents, and suicides, young African American men have been called an endangered species (Gibbs, 1988; Staples, 1995).

Young men's "taste for risk" has been attributed to sociobiological factors, but more plausible explanations are the seductiveness of danger; displays of masculinity; and, for African American men, despair about restricted opportunities and the future. If a man cannot honorably walk away from a fight, he may end up as a homicide statistic. One research study analyzed 80 cases in which a man killed a total stranger (another man) after what the assailant perceived as an insult or challenge to him made in front of his peers (Polk, 1994). Apparently, the attacker—often either working class or unemployed—attacked the insulter in order to "protect his honor."

Unsafe sex practices and shared needles in illegal drug use place both women and men at risk for AIDS. In the United States, the estimated number of people with HIV/AIDS as of 2007 was 1.1 million, 25% of whom were women (Centers for Disease Control and Prevention, 2010a, 2010b). Heterosexual contact accounted for 31% of the new cases in that year; 53% were the result of men having sex with men; 12% due to injection drug use; 4% from multiple forms of transmission. Officials had formerly said the United States has 40,000 new HIV cases per year, but recent data show considerably more—56,300 in 2006, almost half of whom were African American.

African Americans are only 12% of the U.S. population, yet according to the Centers for Disease Control and Prevention, 41% of U.S. men and 64% of U.S. women who have AIDS are African American (Centers for Disease Control and Prevention, n.d.). Many African American women with AIDS live in the rural southern United States, where joblessness, substance abuse, teenage pregnancy, sexually transmitted diseases, inadequate schools, minimal access to health care, and entrenched poverty add up to their high-risk status. Furthermore, both men and women who live in such conditions have less access to health care and are more apt to die sooner from AIDS than more privileged people.

Two recent trends are particularly alarming: the increase in the number of cases of HIV due to heterosexual contact and the growing numbers of young women and men with reported cases of full-blown AIDS. There is increasingly little difference in the number of reported HIV cases by sex. There is a possible second wave of infection among young homosexual men who, believing that AIDS is now treatable, are less vigilant about safe sex practices. A similar denial of vulnerability may be occurring among young heterosexual men and women as well. Transmission of HIV/AIDS is embedded in relationships, and whether heterosexual or homosexual, the closer the relationship, the less likely partners are to practice safe sex (Browne & Minichiello, 1996; Lear, 1995). More than 16,000 Americans die of AIDS each year, the majority of whom are men who have (or have had) sex with men. Although only 1% of the population is estimated to have HIV/AIDS, more than 546,000 Americans have died already, and the United States has the highest annual rate of new cases of any developed nation (Centers for Disease Control and Prevention, 2010b).

Health-threatening behaviors, such as smoking, drinking, illegal drug use, and unsafe sex, are influenced by social norms expressed in peer group pressures on young men and women of all racial and ethnic groups. According to a report of the National Institute on Alcohol Abuse and Alcoholism's Task Force on College Drinking, college students and other 18- to 24-year-olds are indulging in binge drinking and driving while intoxicated at a higher rate since 1998. The number of alcohol-related deaths has also increased. In 2001, there were an estimated 1,700 alcohol-related unintentional injury deaths among students 18–24, an increase of 6% among college students since 1998. Other adverse effects are assaults (more than 696,000 students per year) and alcohol-related sexual assault or date rape (more than 97,000 students per year) ("What Colleges Need to Know Now," 2007).

Young women tend to adopt a somewhat healthier lifestyle than young men on such measures as using seat belts, getting adequate amounts of sleep and exercise, eating a healthy diet, taking care of their teeth, and managing stress. Young middle-class women, however, are vulnerable to eating disorders, such as anorexia nervosa and bulimia, especially in the college years, and they are doing more binge drinking than previously. Although eating disorders are usually direct reflections of gender norms (Lovejoy, 2001; Markey, 2004; Miller & Pumariega, 2001), young women's greater indulgence in binge drinking appears to reflect an effort to "keep up with the boys," perhaps to the detriment of their health, both physical and emotional.

Weight and Eating Disorders

If a young woman's boyfriend sees a photo of her in a majorette uniform, in which she had thought she looked both pretty and important, and says, "You look like a whale," she may stop eating to control her weight and thus, in time, develop a medically recognized eating disorder, as well as depression and low self-esteem.

Many students are surprised at how body norms change. The average weight of Miss America contestants has declined by more than 20 pounds since the 1970s. The average adult in the United States, however, weighs 10 pounds more than he or she weighed a decade ago. Therefore, if women are fatter, but Miss Americas are thinner, there is going to be much dissatisfaction with bodies. When Rubens painted naked women in the 17th century, fleshy women with large stomachs, butts, and breasts had ideal bodies. Many current cultures want the most marriageable women to be full-breasted and full-hipped; their weight shows that they are fertile and healthy and that their families are prosperous. In other times, thinness in women showed religiosity. Sometimes, it is men who starve themselves for beauty; other times, it is women (Miller & Pumariega, 2001; Thompson, 1994). Obesity is a major health problem in the United States, but the stigma of "fatness" is equally problematic (Kirkland, 2008; Rothblum & Solovay, 2009).

Anorexia (self-starvation) and bulimia (binge eating and induced vomiting) are extreme ways to lose weight to meet Western cultural standards of beauty and to maintain control over one's body. Eating disorders are extremely difficult to reverse and can lead to hospitalizations and even death. Otherwise well-protected against health risks, young, white, middle-class college women who are dissatisfied with their body image are vulnerable to eating disorders (Ben-Tovim, Walker, Gilchrist, et al., 2001; Bordo, 2005; Brumberg, 1988; Cooley & Toray, 2001; Gremillion, 2002; Hesse-Biber, 1996). A study of teenagers found that more than 50% of girls in a national sample were trying to alter their weight by dieting, exercising, or using more extreme measures (pills, vomiting, etc.)—a pattern that was most pronounced among girls who made good grades, were more involved in school activities, and had more friends (Boyd et al., 2010). These findings suggest that pressure to have a "conforming" body begins early in life, at least for girls.

The significance of society's views of compulsory heterosexuality and femininity is highlighted by research comparing heterosexual women, who are subject to pressure from the media and the significant men in their lives to stay thin to be sexually attractive, and lesbians, whose views of beauty are not influenced by men's opinions. Lesbians are heavier than comparable heterosexual women, more satisfied with their bodies, and less likely to have eating disorders (Herzog, Newman, Yeh, & Warshaw, 1992). Men's idealized body image may also encourage anorexia and bulimia, especially those who have sexual conflicts or identify as homosexual (Herzog, Bradburn, & Newman, 1990; Herzog, Norman, Gordon, & Pepose, 1984; Kearney-Cooke & Steichen-Asch, 1990).

Women and men college athletes are prone to anorexia and bulimia when they must diet to stay in a weight class (Black, 1991). A study of 695 athletes in 15 college sports found that 1.6% of the men and 4.2% of the women met the American Psychiatric Association's criteria for anorexia, and 14.2% of men and 39.2% of women met the criteria for bulimia (Burckes-Miller & Black, 1991). The reasons for strict weight control are not standards of beauty but the pressures of competition, to meet weight category requirements, to increase speed and height, and to be able to be lifted and carried easily in performances. Eating disorders here are an occupational risk taken not only by young athletes but also by dancers, models, jockeys, and fitness instructors, as well as professional gymnasts, figure skaters, runners, swimmers, and wrestlers.

The norms about weight and thinness as markers of beauty and strength are part of a larger issue in the social construction of gendered bodies: What is a "good body"? What is an "able body"?

What Is an Able Body?

Able-bodiedness is a relative concept, dependent on the physical environment and social supports. When the physical environment is adapted to a range of needs, and technological devices that enhance hearing, speech, sight, and dexterity are available on a widespread basis, people with all kinds of bodies and physical capabilities can work, travel, and socialize. John Hockenberry (1995), a paraplegic due to an automobile accident, has gone around the world as a reporter in his wheelchair, openly flaunting his physical state and constructing an image of masculine strength. "Murderball" is a documentary of paraplegic athletes playing wheelchair rugby, in which the players "perform remarkable feats of wheeling and spinning, executing artful feints and lobbing courtwide passes to one another" (McGrath, 2005, p. B7).

Women, too, can enhance their self-image by overcoming adversity. Nancy Mairs (1986), who has multiple sclerosis, says she prefers to consider herself a cripple rather than disabled or handicapped:

> People—crippled or not—wince at the word "cripple," as they do not at "handicapped" or "disabled." Perhaps I want them to wince. I want them to see me as a tough customer, one to whom the fates/gods/viruses have not been kind, but who can face the brutal truth of her existence squarely. As a cripple, I swagger. (p. 9)

Unlike Hockenberry, who wants to present a strong, masculine image, Mairs's presentation of self is "tough"—a stance for women or men who want to confront the world on their own terms. One who did was Diana Golden Brosnihan, who died of cancer at 38. A skier from the age of 5, she developed bone cancer when she was 12 and resumed skiing 6 months after her right leg was amputated above the knee. Skiing on one leg with regular ski poles, she competed against two-legged skiers and won a gold medal in the giant slalom in the 1988 Winter Olympics, as well as 10 world and 19 U.S. championships from 1986 to 1990, skiing against others with disabilities. In recognition of her fight for equal status, her citation when she was inducted into the Women's Sports Foundation International Hall of Fame in 1997 read, "She persuaded the ski world to treat all athletes the same, regardless of ability or, in her case, disability" (Litsky, 2001, p. D7).

The conventional norms of femininity lock women with disabilities into a paradoxical situation: As women, it is all right for them to be helpless and dependent, but because they are disabled, they are unlikely to have a man to take care of them. Feminists have argued that norms of independence and economic self-support provide a better model for all women, and that giving women with disabilities the means to accomplish these goals would go a long way toward enhancing their self-esteem and quality of life (Asch & Fine, 1988).

For men with disabilities, change must come in challenges to conventional masculinity. Examining the problem of masculinity and physical disability in the lives of 10 men, one study discovered three strategies: reliance on conventional norms and expectations of manhood, reformulation of these norms, and creation of new norms (Gerschick & Miller, 1994). The men who relied on the predominant ideals of masculinity believed they had to demonstrate physical strength, athleticism, sexual prowess, and independence. Their self-image was tied to heroics and risk taking, but they often felt inadequate and incomplete because they could not do what they wanted or go where they wanted. The men who reformulated these norms defined their ways of coping with their physical limitations as demonstrations of strength and independence. For example, two quadriplegics who needed round-the-clock personal care assistants did not believe they were dependent on others but, rather, had hired helpers whom they directed and controlled. The men who rejected the standard version of masculinity put more emphasis on relationships than on individual accomplishments.

To erase the status dilemmas of women and men with physical disabilities, conventional norms about bodies, functions, and beauty need to be reexamined.

A woman without arms or legs claimed the statue of Venus de Milo as her model of beauty (Frank, 2000; Wendell, 1996). At the opening ceremony of the 1996 Olympics in Atlanta, the torch was lit by Muhammad Ali, the famous heavyweight champion and 1960 gold medalist. Weakened by Parkinson's disease, his left arm shook, his face was immobilized, and he could hardly walk. Why was he chosen to represent the spirit of athleticism when he seemed its very contradiction? As a man who was overcoming the limits of his body, he was celebrated once more as a hero (Vecsey, 1996).

Able-bodiedness is an impermanent state because illness, traumas, pregnancy, and old age render all of us disabled at one time or another. At the 1996 Academy Awards ceremony in Hollywood, the appearance on stage of two men, one young and one old, dramatized the body's fragility. Kirk Douglas, receiving a lifetime career award, was clearly counteracting the effects of a stroke in his walk and thank-you speech. Later, the curtain went up on Christopher Reeve, paralyzed from the effects of a fall from a horse. He was completely propped up and spoke with the aid of a breathing tube. When the mostly young audience members, gorgeous in body and face, rose to applaud these men, each must have had a sinking feeling in the pits of their stomachs and a whisper on their lips asking whatever higher being they believed in to spare them these fates, at least for a long while.

Degendering Social Bodies

Feminists do not deny that bodily differences between women and men exist; rather, they claim that many, if not most, of the uses of these differences are ideological. They oppose the use of bodily differences to benefit men and exclude or oppress women.

Changing the social construction of gendered bodies is difficult because identities are tied up with how bodies look and act or perform. Self-identity as a woman or man and self-esteem are translated into bodily markers. Sometimes, self-pride is exaggerated—we talk of strutting, swaggering, preening, and flaunting it. The playing field is not level for women and men, however: "For men, as for women, the world formed by the body-reflexive practices of gender is a domain of politics—the struggle of interests in a context of inequality. Gender politics is an embodied-social politics" (Connell, 1995, p. 66).

Men have the advantage because all men's bodies are stereotyped as bigger, stronger, and physically more capable than any woman's body. Realistically, we know that a well-trained woman, a tall and muscular woman, a woman who has learned the arts of self-defense, a woman soldier, or a woman astronaut is a match for most men. If women and men of the same size and training are matched, men may not necessarily be physically superior because women have greater endurance, balance, and flexibility. The type of competition makes a difference; most sports are made for men—that is, they are organized around men's bodily capacities.

Although feminists have different views regarding how much and in what ways men's and women's bodies differ, all object to claims that bodily differences between the sexes confirm men's superiority. Feminists who believe that women's and men's bodies are different tend to view women as superior in some ways and men as superior in others. They challenge assertions that differences between women and men require them to occupy different social positions or have different opportunities in society. They view claims about bodily differences between women and men as social rather than biological in character, meaning that, like the clothing that individuals put on to cover their bodies, cultural beliefs about bodies are put on or imposed by society onto the bodies of women and men, through gendered beliefs and practices, as part of the society's gender order (Davis, 1997).

A second theme of feminist analysis of the body is dominance with regard to questions of power, gender hierarchy, privilege, and oppression. Who says men's or women's bodies are one way or another? How many women MTV producers and Hollywood film directors decide how bodies are depicted in videos and movies? Who benefits when the media depict women's bodies as sexy and fragile, but strong enough to lift children, clean houses, and carry home the groceries (and work to pay for them, too)? Feminists assert that most of the naming, depicting, and promoting of the images of women are done by powerful, privileged men. Although only some men—white, economically privileged, powerful, middle-aged, and ostensibly heterosexual—create cultural images of women, all men benefit if the images influence most women to seek men's approval; cling to one man to receive protection from the rest; doubt their physical abilities because of their "feminine limitations"; or quit trying to get high-paying jobs in construction, mining, and truck driving.

A third aspect of feminist analysis of the body concerns subversion and relates to feminism's political agenda. Subversion refers to resistance to and undermining of cultural ideals and practices. Women may be depicted as less talented sports figures than men, but nevertheless, outstanding women athletes are "girls" who "play like boys," developing their bodies and skills to the maximum. Some women refuse to shave their legs or wear makeup, much less submit to liposuction or breast implant surgery. Some men refuse to worry about balding, height, and body shape, and many support women who compete in athletic events and apply for combat roles in the military. People who dress as "punks" resist mainstream society's views about tattooing and body piercing (Thomson, 1996). Resisting cultural pressures to adorn, shape, and judge bodies according to conventional standards, especially in relation to gender, is a subversive act.

Conclusion

What is beautiful, admired, rejected, or unattractive about women's and men's bodies? What is normal? What are the body's capacities?

Feminists raise these questions in an attempt to unveil the social processes that produce and maintain the invisible gender-related assumptions and beliefs that undergird so many claims about women's and men's bodies. The most important process is the maintenance of power differences. When we ask, "Who says? Who decides? Who benefits? Who is harmed?" we are asking who has the power.

Currently, men's greater power in society allows them to represent women's bodies in ways that are often untrue and harmful to girls and women. In questioning power in gender relations, feminists also ask questions about racial and ethnic hierarchies, social class, sexual orientation, age, and able-bodiedness, in addition to gender. When the "woman question" exposes women's exclusion or representation as inferior, awareness of the situation raises questions about who else is excluded. By questioning accepted norms and challenging the prerogatives of the powerful to set standards, feminists make room for differences in bodies and in behavior but do not allow these differences to result in hierarchies of power or prestige.

Notes

1. For a detailed account of drug use in sports and predictions of genetic manipulation of bodies to produce superathletes, see Sokolove (2004). For accounts of steroid and other banned substance use, see recent revelations by men and women athletes in many sports.

2. The ad for men appeared in *New York Times Magazine* (1997, January 5), p. 56. For comments on breast surgery for women, see Goodman (2003) and Kolata (2003).

3. American Society for Aesthetic Plastic Surgery: http://www.plasticsurgery.org/Documents/Media/statistics/2009-cosmetic-reconstructive-plastic-surgery-minimally-invasive-statistics.pdf

4. RealSelf.com at http://www.plasticsurgery.org/Media/Press/8/23/2010.

5. For an update, see Duncan, M. C., & Messner, M. (2005). *Gender in televised sports: News and highlights shows, 1989–2004.* Retrieved from http://www.la84foundation.org/9arr/ResearchReports/tv2004.pdf

6. John Henry is an African American folk hero, an early 20th-century laborer who raced against the newly invented mechanical steam shovel, won, and died.

References

Allen, M. (1996, November 9). Women at The Citadel get shorter hair, and in trouble. *New York Times,* Section 1, p. 9.

Asch, A., & Fine, M. (1988). Introduction: Beyond pedestals. In M. Fine & A. Asch (Eds.), *Women with disabilities: Essays in psychology, culture, and politics* (pp. 1–37). Philadelphia: Temple University Press.

Ben-Tovim, D. I., Walker, K., Gilchrist, P., et al. (2001, April 21). Outcome in patients with eating disorders: A 5-year study. *Lancet, 357,* 1254–1257.

Black, D. R. (Ed.). (1991). *Eating disorders among athletes.* Reston, VA: American Alliance for Health, Physical Education, Recreation and Dance.

Blum, V. (2003). *Flesh wounds: The culture of cosmetic surgery.* Berkeley: University of California Press.

Bordo, S. R. (2005). *Unbearable weight: Feminism, Western culture, and the body.* Berkeley: University of California Press.

Boyd, E., Reynolds, J., Tillman, K., & Martin, P. Y. (2010). *Adolescent girls' race/ethnic status, identities, and drive for thinness.* Unpublished manuscript, Department of Sociology, Florida State University, Tallahassee.

Browne, J., & Minichiello, V. (1996). Condoms: Dilemmas of caring and autonomy in heterosexual safe sex practices. *Venereology: Interdisciplinary International Journal of Sexual Health, 9,* 24–33.

Brubach, H. (1996, June 23). The athletic esthetic. *New York Times Magazine,* p. 51.

Brumberg, J. J. (1988). *Fasting girls: The emergence of anorexia nervosa as a modern disease.* Cambridge, MA: Harvard University Press.

Burckes-Miller, M. E., & Black, D. R. (1991). College athletes and eating disorders: A theoretical context. In D. R. Black (Ed.), *Eating disorders among athletes* (pp. 11–26). Reston, VA: American Alliance for Health, Physical Education, Recreation and Dance.

Butler, J. (1993). *Bodies that matter: On the discursive limits of "sex."* New York: Routledge.

Cahn, S. K. (1994). *Coming on strong: Gender and sexuality in twentieth-century women's sport.* New York: Free Press.

Centers for Disease Control and Prevention. (2010a). HIV and AIDS in the United States. *Fact Sheet.* Retrieved August 25, 2010, from http://www.cdc.gov/hiv/resources/factsheets/print/us.htm/

Centers for Disease Control and Prevention. (2010b). Projecting possible future courses of the HIV epidemic in the United States. Retrieved August 25, 2010, from http://www.cdc.gov/hiv/resources/factsheets/us-epi-future-courses.htm

Centers for Disease Control and Prevention. (n.d.). HIV/AIDS and African Americans. Retrieved August 25, 2010, from http://www.cdc.gov/hiv/topics/aa/index.htm

Clarey, C. (2010, August 23). Semenya returns, and so do questions. *New York Times,* pp. D1, D6.

Clarey, C., & Kolata, G. (2009, August 21). Gold is awarded, but dispute over runner's sex intensifies. *New York Times,* pp. B9, B11.

Cockburn, C. (1983). *Brothers: Male dominance and technological change.* London: Pluto.

Cockburn, C. (1985). *Machinery of dominance: Women, men, and technical know-how.* London: Pluto.

Collins, B. (1996, September 2). Navratilova against history: Love–15 [Letter to the Editor]. *New York Times,* Section 1, p. 27.

Collins, M. A., & Zebrowitz, L. A. (1995). The contributions of appearance to occupational outcomes in civilian and military settings. *Journal of Applied Social Psychology, 25,* 129–163.

Connell, R. (1995). *Masculinities.* Berkeley: University of California Press.

Cooley, E., & Toray, T. (2001). Body image and personality predictors of eating disorder symptoms during the college years. *International Journal of Eating Disorders, 30,* 28–36.

Davis, K. (1995). *Reshaping the female body: The dilemma of cosmetic surgery.* New York: Routledge.

Davis, K. (1997). Embodying theory: Beyond modernist and postmodernist readings of the body. In K. Davis (Ed.), *Embodied practices.* London: Sage.

Dreger, A. (2009, August 22). Where's the rulebook for sex verification? *New York Times,* pp. D1, D3.

Eitzen, S. D., & Zinn, M. B. (1989). The de-athleticization of women: The naming and gender marking of collegiate sport teams. *Sociology of Sport Journal, 6,* 362–370.

Fausto-Sterling, A. (2000). *Sexing the body: Gender politics and the construction of sexuality.* New York: Basic Books.

Fine, G. A. (1987). *With the boys: Little League baseball and preadolescent culture.* Chicago: University of Chicago Press.

Frank, G. (2000). *Venus on wheels: Two decades of dialogue on disability, biography, and being female in America.* Berkeley: University of California Press.

Gerschick, T. J., & Miller, A. S. (1994). Gender identities at the crossroads of masculinity and physical disability. *Masculinities, 2,* 34–55.

Gibbs, J. T. (Ed.). (1988). *Young, black, and male in America: An endangered species.* Dover, MA: Auburn House.

Gilman, S. (1999). *Making the body beautiful: A cultural history of aesthetic surgery.* Princeton, NJ: Princeton University Press.

Goodman, E. (2003, November 2). Beauty and the breast. *Boston Globe,* p. G11.

Grasmuck, S. (2005). *Protecting home: Class, race, and masculinity in boys' baseball.* New Brunswick, NJ: Rutgers University Press.

Gremillion, H. (2002). In fitness and in health: Crafting bodies in the treatment of anorexia nervosa. *Signs, 27,* 381–414.

Gullette, M. M. (1993). All together now: The new sexual politics of midlife bodies. *Michigan Quarterly Review, 32,* 669–695.

Hall, S. S. (2006). *Size matters: How height affects the health, happiness, and success of boys— and the men they become.* Orlando, FL: Houghton Mifflin.

Hargreaves, J. A. (1986). Where's the virtue? Where's the grace? A discussion of the social production of gender relations in and through sport. *Theory, Culture, and Society, 3,* 109–121.

Hargreaves, J. A. (1994). *Sporting females: Critical issues in the history and sociology of women's sports.* New York: Routledge.

Hensley, W. E., & Cooper, R. (1987). Height and occupational success: A review and a critique. *Psychological Reports, 60,* 843–849.

Heron, M. (2010, March 31). Deaths: Leading causes for 2006. *National Vital Statistics Reports, 58*(14). Retrieved from http://www.cdc.gov/nchs/data/nvsr/nvsr58/nvsr58_14.pdf

Herzog, D. B., Bradburn, I., & Newman, K. (1990). Sexuality in males with eating disorders. In A. E. Andersen (Ed.), *Males with eating disorders* (pp. 40–53). New York: Brunner/ Mazel.

Herzog, D. B., Newman, K. L., Yeh, C. J., & Warshaw, M. (1992). Body image satisfaction in homosexual and heterosexual women. *International Journal of Eating Disorders, 11,* 391–396.

Herzog, D. B., Norman, D. K., Gordon, C., & Pepose, M. (1984). Sexual conflict and eating disorders in 27 males. *American Journal of Psychiatry, 141,* 989–990.

Hesse-Biber, S. (1996). *Am I thin enough yet? The cult of thinness and the commercialization of identity.* New York: Oxford University Press.

Heywood, L., & Dworkin, S. (2003). *Built to win: The female athlete as cultural icon.* Minneapolis: University of Minnesota Press.

Hockenberry, J. (1995). *Moving violations: War zones, wheelchairs, and declarations of independence.* New York: Hyperion.

Izraeli, D. (1997). Gendering military service in the Israeli Defense Forces. *Israel Social Science Research, 12,* 129–166.

Kearney-Cooke, A., & Steichen-Asch, P. (1990). Men, body image, and eating disorders. In A. E. Andersen (Ed.), *Males with eating disorders* (pp. 54–74). New York: Brunner/ Mazel.

Kessel, A. (2009, August 19). Gold medal athlete Caster Semenya told to prove she is a woman. *Guardian.* Retrieved from http://www.guardian.co.uk/sport/2009/aug/19/castersemenya-gender-verification-test

Kirkland, A. (2008). *Fat rights: Dilemmas of difference and personhood.* New York: New York University Press.

Klein, A. M. (1993). *Little big men: Bodybuilding subculture and gender construction*. Albany: State University of New York Press.

Kolata, G. (2003, October 19). A sexual subtext to the debate over breast implants. *New York Times*, p. 4.

Lear, D. (1995). Sexual communication in the age of AIDS: The construction of risk and trust among young adults. *Social Science and Medicine, 41*, 1311–1323.

Litsky, F. (2001, August 28). Diana Golden Brosnihan, skier, dies at 38. *New York Times*, p. D7.

Longman, J. (2003, September 16). Women's soccer league folds on World Cup eve. *New York Times*, pp. A1, D6.

Longman, J. (2009, November 20). South African runner's sex-verification result won't be public. *New York Times*, pp. B10, B15.

Lorber, J. (1993). Believing is seeing: Biology as ideology. *Gender & Society, 7*, 568–581.

Lorber, J. (1994). *Paradoxes of gender*. New Haven, CT: Yale University Press.

Lorber, J. (2002). Heroes, warriors, and burqas: A feminist sociologist's reflections on September 11. *Sociological Forum, 17*, 377–396.

Lorber, J., & Moore, L. J. (2011). *Gendered bodies: Feminist perspectives* (2nd ed.). New York: Oxford University Press.

Lovejoy, M. (2001). Disturbances in the social body: Differences in body image and eating problems among African American and White women. *Gender & Society, 15*, 239–261.

MacKinnon, C. A. (1987). *Feminism unmodified*. Cambridge, MA: Harvard University Press.

Mairs, N. (1986). *Plaintext*. Tucson: University of Arizona Press.

Mangan, J. A., & Park, R. J. (1987). *From fair sex to feminism: Sport and the socialization of women in the industrial and post-industrial eras*. London: Cass.

Markey, C. (2004). Culture and the development of eating disorders: A tripartite model. *Eating Disorders: Journal of Treatment and Prevention, 12*, 139–156.

Martin, P. Y. (2001). "Mobilizing masculinities": Women's experiences of men at work. *Organization, 8*, 587-618.

Martin, P. Y. (2004). Gender as social institution. *Social Forces, 82*, 1249–1273.

McDonagh, E., & Pappano, L. (2008). *Playing with the boys: Why separate is not equal in sports*. New York: Oxford University Press.

McGrath, C. (2005, March 26). Hell on wheels. *New York Times*, pp. B7, B13.

Messner, M. A. (1992). *Power at play: Sports and the problem of masculinity*. Boston: Beacon.

Messner, M. A. (2002). *Taking the field: Women, men, and sports*. Minneapolis: University of Minnesota Press.

Messner, M. A., Duncan, M. C., & Jensen, K. (1993). Separating the men from the girls: The gendered language of televised sports. *Gender & Society, 7*, 121–137.

Messner, M. A., & Sabo, D. F. (1994). *Sex, violence, and power in sports: Rethinking masculinity*. Freedom, CA: Crossing Press.

Miller, M. N., & Pumariega, A. J. (2001). Culture and eating disorders: A historical and cross-cultural review. *Psychiatry, 64*, 93–110.

Mueller, U., & Mazur, A. (1996). Facial dominance of West Point cadets as a predictor of later military rank. *Social Forces, 74*, 823–850.

Pitts-Taylor, V. (2007). *Surgery junkies: Wellness and pathology in cosmetic culture*. New Brunswick, NJ: Rutgers University Press.

Polk, K. (1994). Masculinity, honor, and confrontational homicide. In T. Newburn & E. Stanko (Eds.), *Just boys doing business: Men, masculinities, and crime*. New York: Routledge.

Pope, H. G., Jr., Phillips, K. A., & Olivardia, R. (2000). *The Adonis complex: The secret crisis of male body obsession*. New York: Free Press.

Price, J., & Shildrick, M. (Eds.). (1999). *Feminist theory and the body.* New York: Routledge.

Prior, A. E. (2006). *The slave side of Sunday.* Charleston, SC: BookSurge.

Riska, E. (2004). *Masculinity and men's health: Coronary heart disease in medical and public discourse.* Lanham, MD: Rowman & Littlefield.

Rothblum, E., & Solovay, S. (Eds.). (2009). *The fat studies reader.* New York: New York University Press.

Schwarz, A. (2009, December 21). N.F.L. acknowledges long-term concussion effects. *New York Times,* pp. D1, D6.

Sokolove, M. (2004, January 18). The lab animal: In pursuit of doped excellence. *New York Times Magazine,* pp. 28–33, 54, 58.

Sokolove, M. (2008). *Warrior girls: Protecting our daughters against the injury epidemic in women's sports.* New York: Simon and Schuster.

Staples, R. (1995). Health among Afro-American males. In D. Sabo & D. F. Gordon (Eds.), *Men's health and illness: Gender, power and the body* (pp. 121–138). Thousand Oaks, CA: Sage.

Theberge, N. (1987). Sport and women's empowerment. *Women's Studies International Forum, 10,* 387–393.

Thompson, B. W. (1994). *A hunger so wide and so deep: American women speak out on eating problems.* Minneapolis: University of Minnesota Press.

Thomson, R. G. (Ed.). (1996). *Freakery: Cultural spectacles of the extraordinary body.* New York: New York University Press.

Vecsey, G. (1996, July 21). Choosing Ali elevated these games. *New York Times,* Sports section, p. 1.

Vecsey, G. (2003, November 16). Great sport had bad bottom line. *New York Times,* pp. D1, D6.

Wallechinsky, D. (1996, June 23). Vaults, leaps, and dashes. *New York Times Magazine,* pp. 46–47.

Weitz, R. (Ed.). (2009). *The politics of women's bodies: Sexuality, appearance, and behavior* (3rd ed.). New York: Oxford University Press.

Wendell, S. (1996). *The rejected body: Feminist philosophical reflections on disability.* New York: Routledge.

What colleges need to know now: An update on college drinking research. (2007). Retrieved from http://www.collegedrinkingprevention.gov/1College_Bulletin-508_361C4E.pdf

Williams, C. (1989). *Gender differences at work: Women and men in nontraditional occupations.* Berkeley: University of California Press.

Yoder, J. D. (1989). Women at West Point: Lessons for token women in male-dominated occupations. In J. Freeman (Ed.), *Women: A feminist perspective* (4th ed., pp. 523–537). Mountain View, CA: Mayfield.

Young, I. M. (1990). *Throwing like a girl and other essays in feminist philosophy and social theory.* Bloomington: Indiana University Press.

DISCUSSION QUESTIONS

1. What does your culture or racial or ethnic group think is the ideal body for a man and a woman? Address such features as the ideal weight, height, musculature, and so on. What attributes about the person are those ideal body norms supposed to show others?

2. Imagine that tomorrow you wake up in a body that is the opposite of yours in gender and of a different skin color. What would be the same about your daily life? What would be different?

3. How do men in feminized sports, such as figure skating, physically demonstrate masculinity? How do women in male-identified sports, such as basketball, physically demonstrate femininity?

4. List all the businesses and professions you can think of that profit from the social construction of idealized bodies in the United States.

5. In a typical day, how much time do you spend grooming your body, including washing, dressing, putting on makeup, combing your hair, exercising, and other body practices? How much time and money do you spend in a month on professional hair and body care, exercise, weight control, and similar body-related activities?

CHAPTER 10

Organizing Door-to-Door Sales

A Symbolic Interactionist Analysis

David Schweingruber and Nancy Berns

David Schweingruber is Associate Professor of Sociology at Iowa State University. He received his BA from Bluffton College and his PhD from the University of Illinois at Urbana-Champaign. His research, in the symbolic interactionist tradition, is concerned with the cultural and cognitive premises that guide social behavior in a variety of settings, including formal organizations, political demonstrations, and romantic events.

Nancy Berns is Associate Professor of Sociology at Drake University. She received her BA from Doane College and her PhD from the University of Illinois at Urbana-Champaign. Her teaching and research interests are in the areas of violence, media, social justice, grief, death, and social constructionism. She is the author of Framing the Victim: Domestic Violence, Media and Social Problems *(Aldine de Gruyter, 2004).*

Imagine you're looking for a summer job after your first year of college. A friend tells you about a sales job he had the year before and claims he earned a lot of money. He suggests you come to an interview with his sales manager, who will be visiting campus. Your friend doesn't want to give you many details, but when you press him, he tells you about life in the "book field." You are astonished at his description of the job because it doesn't sound anything like how you want to spend your summer.

Your job will be to sell educational books door-to-door on a commission. You will be sent somewhere in the United States far from home. You will be expected to work at least 13½ hours a day six days a week, including holidays, regardless of the weather. You need to knock on your first door by 7:59 a.m. and not finish your last sales call before 9:30 p.m. You should run in between houses so you don't waste time—even though you'll be carrying a heavy sample case. Most people won't let you into their houses and some will be rude to you. Most days you'll sell something, but sometimes you'll have a "zero day"—13½ hours of work with no sales and no pay. The job is so unpleasant that around a third of the salespeople quit each summer. Are you interested in this job? Is there any way your friend and his manager could convince you to sign up?

We are familiar with this door-to-door sales company—we refer to it as the Enterprise Company—because we conducted a sociological study of it using the perspective of symbolic interactionism to guide us (Schweingruber, 2006a, 2006b; Schweingruber & Berns, 2003, 2005). Symbolic interactionists believe that the key to comprehending a social world is to understand it from the perspective of the people actively engaged in it. Each year, Enterprise Company managers recruit thousands of college students to sell books. Most have the same reaction you might have—this job doesn't make any sense. Even some who take the job can't seem to make it work for them. But for many of these young salespersons, the social world of the Enterprise Company begins to make sense. This complicated social arrangement functions well enough that the company continues to successfully recruit students, sell books, and make a profit. The focus of our study was how this happens. How can company managers and salespersons construct a social world where a grueling door-to-door sales job not only is bearable, but can, as many of them claim, lead to the creation of a better self? By explaining how the social world of door-to-door sales works, we hope to illustrate how symbolic interactionist sociologists study social life.

But before focusing on this one company, let's consider some more basic questions of interest to interactionist sociology: How is any social arrangement possible? How can people fit their actions together to accomplish anything they could not do alone? How are people able to put together complicated institutions, like governments, corporations, universities, social movements—and door-to-door sales companies? How is human society possible?

Sociology is the social science of modernity. It arose as people struggled to understand the rise of capitalism, industrialization, and urbanization. Humans are inherently social, but these facets of the modern world we take for granted were not inevitable. Human beings have been around for a couple hundred thousand years, and for the first 190,000 or so of them, people lived in tiny bands. The social institutions that dominate our lives today are exceptional, having been invented during a relatively short time in the history of humanity (Couch, 1984). Although sociologists regularly examine the problems of living together, less attention is focused on how living together is even possible. The sociological perspective of symbolic interactionism offers an exception to this pattern. Symbolic interactionism, often called just interactionism or SI, directs our attention to certain human attributes that make social life both possible and difficult. Interactionists believe that people are purposive and that they are capable of creative problem solving in pursuit of their purposes. Creativity is required to invent new and better ways of doing things together. It is required to build innovative social institutions. But it also makes people potentially unpredictable and untrustworthy (Stewart, 1998). Because people are purposive and creative, they can decide to do something different from what is expected of them. They can decide to pursue their own goals rather than the ends of the group.

Interactionists take seriously the proposition that human beings are creative problem solvers. We are not stuck with the world as it presents itself to us. We can evaluate our situations, mull over what to do about them, and formulate plans for changing them. We are not stuck with the way we are, either. We can shift identities as we move from one situation to another and, more dramatically, reinvent ourselves. In other words, people have selves. Symbolic interactionism is the sociological perspective that takes selves seriously, and this focus has led to a useful and—we think—fascinating way of looking at and thinking about social life.

Before diving into our study of door-to-door sales, we will lay out some of the principles of symbolic interactionist sociology and some implications of these principles.

Basic Principles

Symbolic interactionism has its roots in the work of the pragmatist philosopher George Herbert Mead, who taught a famous graduate social psychology course at the University of Chicago. After his death, his students turned their course notes into the book *Mind, Self and Society,* which is the source of some key interactionist ideas, like "taking the attitude of the other" (Mead, 1934). Mead's student Herbert Blumer coined the term *symbolic interactionism* in 1937 (Blumer, 1969b). Blumer was primarily a theorist, not a researcher, but another University of Chicago sociologist, Everett C. Hughes, was one of the leading advocates of ethnographic field work (Hughes, 1958, 1971). This combination of Mead's social psychology (as interpreted by Blumer) and extensive field work directed by Hughes produced some of the earliest interactionist studies, including research by Howard Becker, which we will discuss. Blumer laid out three premises of symbolic interactionism, which remain a useful starting place for explaining the perspective (Blumer, 1969a). But first we should discuss interactionists' understanding of people's relationship to the world that underlies those premises.

Symbolic interactionism is a social constructionist sociological perspective. This means that symbolic interactionists are interested in how people create social worlds by making meanings. We live in two worlds. The first is the world of physical things, and the second is the world of meanings (Loseke, 2003). Our physical environment exerts influences on our actions that we cannot imagine away. We cannot, for instance, walk through a closed door. However, there is no inherent meaning to the closed door or any other objects in our physical environment. The closed door would likely mean very different things for a locked-out homeowner, a locksmith, a burglar, a designer, a carpenter, and a door-to-door salesperson. (The door-to-door salespersons we studied liked to say that "the solution to every problem lies behind the next door.")

Interactionists claim that there is nothing in the physical world that has inherent meaning, an assumption shared by other brands of social constructionism. Meaning comes from people. We construct the worlds in which we live by giving them meaning. What is true for the door is true for everything else in our environment. Scott Harris, an interactionist sociologist, calls this the "zero premise": "The meaning of things is not inherent" (Harris, 2006, 2010).

Blumer's First Premise

Blumer's three premises build on the social constructionist insight about the inherently meaningless world. His first premise is that *human beings act toward things on the basis of the meanings that the things have for them.* There is a lot going on in this premise, so let's pick it apart.

- *Human beings act*: Human beings are active, purposive creatures. Our behavior is not merely the outcome of social forces playing on us, nor do we just respond to these forces.
- Human beings act *toward things*: Things include physical objects, but also other human beings and categories of human beings, institutions, ideas, activities, and situations.
- Human beings act toward things *on the basis of the meanings that the things have*: People's actions toward things are not dictated by anything inherent in those things, such as their physical properties. People's actions are guided by the meaning we give those things.
- Human beings act toward things on the basis of the meanings that the things have *for them*: These last two words, "for them," are easy to overlook, but they are central to SI's distinctive approach to understanding society. If we want to understand people's actions, we need to understand the meaning of things "for them." It is common, for social scientists as well as for everyone else, to make assumptions about the meaning of something for other people. Symbolic interactionists believe that in order to understand other people, we need to develop what Max Weber called *verstehen*, or "understanding." Because of this, interactionists prefer research methods such as participant observation and in-depth, open-ended interviews that allow subjects to describe the meanings of things "for them."

Blumer's Second Premise

Blumer's second premise is that *the meaning of such things is derived from, or arises out of, the social interaction that one has with other people.*[1] Because meanings are not inherent, we need to get them from someplace. People are capable of generating new meanings (as we shall see in the third premise), but for the most part, we start with meanings that we get from other people. Babies are born into social worlds—worlds of meaning—and the journey from helpless infant to competent member of a society involves learning the meanings of that society, its knowledge. This knowledge includes the language (or languages) of the society, the categories (built into the language) for making sense of the world, standard recipes of action for getting things done, and the society's values—what is right/wrong, beautiful/ugly, and so on. This is called primary socialization. Learning meanings does not end with primary socialization, though. As people enter new institutions and new situations—like a door-to-door sales job—they continue to learn meanings from the people they encounter there. Symbolic interactionism's name comes from this focus on meanings being derived from social interaction, with "symbolic" referring to the importance of language in their creation and transmission.

Blumer's Third Premise

Blumer's third premise is the one that makes explicit the creative potential of human beings. *These meanings are handled in, and modified through, an interpretive process used by the person in dealing with the things he or she encounters.* This is another complicated premise worth breaking into parts.

- *These meanings are handled and modified*: People do not merely take the meanings that society offers us and act on them. People are capable of changing the meaning of things and do so all the time.
- These meanings are handled in, and modified through, *an interpretive process*: Interactionists emphasize the importance in people's ability to actively think about things: to consider, ponder, question, imagine, and so on. This remarkable human ability is central to interactionism's understanding of social behavior.
- These meanings are handled in, and modified through, an interpretive process *used by the person in dealing with the things he or she encounters*: Humans are problem-solving creatures, and people use their remarkable ability to interpret and change meanings to deal with the problems, big and small, that they encounter every day. It is when people encounter obstacles to their goals that their creative problem-solving abilities are most evident.

Three Implications of the Symbolic Interactionist Perspective

If Blumer's premises are a good description of the relationship between people and the world, they raise some implications that social scientists have to deal with as we study social life. Three of these implications are the nature of the self, the nature of social life, and the nature of society.

Selves Are Self-Conscious, Processual, and Situated

Blumer's first premise is that *human beings act toward things on the basis of the meanings that the things have for them.* One of the most important of these "things" is one's own self. In fact, interactionists claim that to have a self means to have self-consciousness, to be able to give meaning to yourself. You can like yourself, be upset with yourself, or want to improve yourself. You can evaluate yourself in the categories of the social worlds you inhabit. You can think of yourself as a good son or daughter, a poor student, an up-and-coming employee, an attractive or unattractive specimen, and so on. If you are a door-to-door salesperson, you can learn to evaluate yourself using the categories provided to you in your training, like being a "finisher" rather than a "quitter" and developing a "positive mental attitude." In other words, you can become an object to yourself.

You can also interact with yourself. One key way humans think is through internal conversation—an interaction with one's self. You are capable of questioning yourself about your situation and your plans. You can also ask yourself questions like, "If I did this, what would people do?" and "If I did this, what would Mom [or Dad, my boyfriend or girlfriend, the police officer, the sales prospect, and so on] do?"

This is a key way that we are shaped by society. We have internal conversations in which we anticipate how other people will react to us. First, we learn how specific people will react to us, especially our parents and siblings. These people are known as *significant others*. However, being able to anticipate the actions of just a handful of people becomes limited as we venture into different institutions and groups of people. Thus, people learn to have conversations with *generalized others*, the voices of the larger society or some part of it. In other words, we carry around in our heads the voices of society and can converse with them.

As neurologists continue to learn more and more about the complexity of the brain, it is becoming clear how complicated our mental processes are and how much goes on under our conscious awareness. People experience having desires, urges, impulses, ideas, and fantasies, and we often don't know where they come from. There are brands of behavioral science that try to explain human behavior based on these subconscious forces. For instance, evolutionary psychologists explain differences in male and female sexual behavior based on genetic differences between men and women that became encoded in our genes during the evolution of humans.

The shortcoming of this type of explanation is that humans' evolutionary legacy also includes the remarkable ability to examine all of our desires, inclinations, and plans—whatever their sources—and to evaluate them based on the values and goals of the social worlds we inhabit. This is not to say that people always carry out this type of evaluation. That's why we worry about the effects of drugs and alcohol on people's ability to evaluate their impulses, and why we say that some people have "poor impulse control" and label others "sociopaths." Having internal conversations with internalized others is not the only way that humans can think—and some people seem to have trouble doing it well—but this type of thinking plays an important role in making society possible.

Although Mead did not have the knowledge of the brain we do today, he did recognize that part of the self is unpredictable. He referred to this as the "I." The impulses and ideas of the "I" engage in conversation with the socialized "me" (related to the idea of significant and generalized others). Mead saw this type of internal conversation as central to the self. Thus, the self can be thought of as a process.

The internal conversation between the "I" and "me" is related to another key idea from Mead, "taking the attitude of the other," which is an interactionist term for being able to see the world from the perspective of someone else and to make a more-or-less reliable prediction of his or her behavior. Mead was fond of using baseball as an example of taking the attitude of the other. Suppose you are playing shortstop. A runner is on first and the ball is hit to you. If you have a knowledge of baseball, you can throw the ball to second base even if no one is covering the base because you know that by the time the ball gets to the base, the second baseman will be there. Baseball makes sense to someone who grew up watching the game, but for someone who has not, trying to make sense of what is going on can be mystifying. (Or think of an American baseball fan watching a game of cricket.) Being able to enjoy watching the game also requires taking the attitude of the players. If you do not understand what their goals are and how they fit together, you will not understand what is going on in the field. The same is true for interactionist research. Symbolic interactionists believe that to understand social life, they need to learn to see the world from the perspective of the people involved in the action.

Another related implication of the symbolic interactionist understanding of the self is that the self has multiple identities. (Some interactionists refer to people having multiple selves. Others refer to a self consisting of multiple identities.) When you are involved in the social world of your family (you are with your family or planning something related to them), your internal conversation probably involves the voices of specific members of your family as well as the generalized other of this social world. The way you talk around your family and the way you conduct yourself are going to be different, at least to some extent, from the way you talk and conduct yourself around your friends or at your job.

Not only do we have multiple identities, but these identities are "situated"—made real only in particular situations. The interactionist conception of the self is not of a stable entity, but a fluid one that is made real as specific identities play out in actual interactions in the social worlds we inhabit. Selves are situated in particular interactions, and they are also situated within elements of social structure. For instance, your identity as a student becomes salient in particular situations, such as the classroom or a conversation with your professor. That identity is also situated within a particular university and within a shared cultural understanding of the role of a college student.

Social Life Is Processual and Indeterminate

A second implication of Blumer's premises is that social life is indeterminate—it is not predetermined and is, to some extent, unpredictable. Things do not always turn out the way we expect or the way we plan. People, being creative and having their own purposes, may not do what we expect them to do. Even when people are trying to cooperate, communication may break down or people may forget or misunderstand what they are supposed to do. Interactionism highlights the troubles people have working together. Because social life is indeterminate and involves people negotiating the problems that arise during interaction, interactionists are interested not just in *what* people accomplish (or don't accomplish), but also in *how* they accomplish it. In other words, interactionism views social life as a process.

This perspective on social life is illustrated by a classic interactionist study, "Becoming a Marihuana User," which was conducted in the 1950s by Howard

Becker (1953). Becker, guided by Blumer's three premises, attempted to uncover the meanings that make using marijuana for pleasure possible, how people learn these meanings from peers, and how they interpret or make sense of them. He found that although the drug may have a physical effect, people will not continue using it for pleasure unless they connect the effect to the drug. In other words, people could be "high" and not know it. Once they figured out they were high, they had to interpret the high as a pleasurable experience. Both of these meanings are developed during interactions with other users and require interpretation. These more experienced users point out the effects of the drug and highlight the pleasurable aspects of it.

This interactionist approach is quite different from a conventional approach to drug abuse that takes the perspective of an outsider—rather than the meaning of marijuana for the actual users—and assumes that drug use is bad. Such an approach asks what independent variables lead to the dependent variable of drug use. For instance, what life experiences or individual attributes lead to using marijuana? The interactionist approach takes seriously that purposive actors are trying to get some things done and may or may not be successful. Becker showed that someone may attempt to become a marijuana user and fail to do so. Likewise, someone may attempt to become a door-to-door salesperson and fail. This is, in fact, one of the most important dynamics among Enterprise salespersons. Company managers provide the salespersons with many strategies for giving meaning to the "things" they will deal with in the book field—uninterested sales prospects, bad weather, feelings of hopelessness—and many salespersons make an effort to apply these meanings. But many of them fail.

Interactionists often use the word "work" to describe the processual and indeterminate nature of social life (Harris, 2010). Someone may attempt to do the interpretive work of, for instance, trying to smoke marijuana for pleasure, and fail. We will illustrate this idea with two types of work performed by the Enterprise salespersons: *emotion work*, a term coined by the sociologist Arlie Hochschild to describe people's attempt to make their emotions match cultural "feeling rules"; and *money work*, our term for people's use of money meanings to get things done, like selling books door-to-door. The work that interactionists describe usually involves people's interpretive work as they attach meanings to things they encounter in their environments.

Society Consists of Joint Action Made Possible by Social Arrangements

A third implication of Blumer's premises is that society can best be understood as people doing things together (Becker, 1986). Social institutions and social structures are not viewed primarily as forces that impinge on individual lives—although they can do this—but as the manifestation of people fitting their individual lines of action together. As we stated at the start of the chapter, this is not inevitable. People can act together only because they have developed social arrangements for doing so. Social arrangements consist of packages of shared meanings that allow people to be able to take the perspective of other people and predict their behavior.

A stoplight is a simple example of a social arrangement. Without stoplights and other traffic-related social arrangements, people would drive their cars into each other. The stoplight involves a simple mechanism and a simple set of meanings—of red, yellow, and green—and allows a driver to predict what other drivers will do. Even such a simple arrangement does not always work, and people may develop additional meanings not planned by the original designers. For instance, "It's okay to run a red light if nobody else is around" and "Speed up during a yellow light to get through in time." Social arrangements include the taken-for-granted rules that allow us to mostly avoid walking into other people on the sidewalk, talking at the same time during a conversation, or threatening people's safety or sense of decorum. The bureaucratic institutions that dominate modern life are complicated social arrangements involving both formal rules and informal understandings that allow people to fit their actions together in a complicated division of labor.

Some of the most complicated social arrangements are "social worlds." Think of the profession you hope to have in the future. You likely will work in a bureaucratic institution, such as a business, school, or government agency, and it will probably be one of many similar institutions that share many ways of doing things. These will be linked to other institutions that engage in some cooperation, such as a manufacturing firm, its suppliers, and its customers, or a county court with the police department, county jail, county prosecutors, and defense attorneys (Ulmer, 1997). You may be a member of a professional association and attend conferences with people outside your own institution. The shared understandings that will shape your social world will include not just formal rules, but also professional lore, jokes, rules of thumb, and various "lenses" for seeing the world differently from outsiders.

The idea of social worlds is exemplified by Howard Becker's (1982) study of "art worlds." Artists create art by making use of existing art conventions and personnel who follow them. Composers can write notes using a standard notation system that standardized groups of performers (e.g., a symphony orchestra, barbershop quartet, or rock band) can play using existing instruments designed to play standard notes (e.g., the Western chromatic musical scale). Becker tells the story of the composer Harry Partch, who wrote unconventional music that used 42 tones between octaves rather than the standard 12. This was possible, but it required Partch to invent and build new instruments, invent a new musical notation system, and locate and train musicians willing to learn to play entirely differently from the way they had been trained. As a consequence, it took 8 months of work to prepare for a 2-hour concert rather than the 8 hours of rehearsal it would take using standard music. Social worlds do not make people do anything, but they make some things easier to do and other things more difficult.

Social worlds consist of both a set of complicated meanings and also the actions of the people who are guided by those meanings. A typical symbolic interactionist study involves getting into some social world, such as a door-to-door sales company; figuring out what the relevant meanings are; and seeing how they work in practice, not just in theory. Interactionists study the messy reality of social life.

Studying Door-to-Door Sales

We are going to illustrate some principles of symbolic interactionism with our study of a company that hires college students to sell educational books door-to-door during their summer vacations. We call the company The Enterprise Company, and it is the oldest extant door-to-door sales company in the United States. Its student sales program began following the Civil War to help young Southern men earn money for college by selling Bibles and other religious books during the summer. Although the company still offers some religious books, its main product line now consists of educational books designed to help elementary and high school students with their schoolwork.

Potential salespersons are recruited on their college campuses, often by students who sold the previous summer. Following the end of the school year, these students travel to company headquarters for a weeklong sales school. They are then sent with a team, which usually includes other students from their school, to an assigned sales area somewhere in the United States. They work 6 days a week; on Sundays, they meet with their team for additional training and management and engage in some group recreational activity. As we mentioned above, the company asks its student dealers to follow a grueling work schedule (13½ hours a day, 6 days a week). They encounter continual rejection and struggle with many negative emotions caused by the job.

Symbolic interactionists argue that all social organization requires shared meanings for people to fit their actions together. However, a door-to-door sales company has the added complication that its members are working alone, without their fellow workers to help them maintain their prescribed reality. Because of this constraint, however, when managers and salespersons were together, they talked about the meanings of door-to-door sales constantly, making it easier for us to learn about them.

Like other symbolic interactionist studies, ours was shaped by Blumer's three premises. First, because people act toward things based on the meaning of those things for them, we needed to learn the meanings that things have for people in the company. To do this, we conducted interviews with managers and salespersons before, during, and after the summer; read company manuals (which presented the official set of meanings); and listened to audiotapes the company distributed to its sales force. Second, meanings derive from interactions with other people. To learn about how meanings developed and transmitted, we conducted participant observation of many interactions, including recruiting sessions, training sessions, and team meetings. Third, because people handle and modify meanings through an interpretive process as they deal with the things they encounter, it was important to observe salespersons using and modifying the meanings they had been taught as they went door-to-door.

Our discussion of our findings will begin by discussing three key meanings that people in the social world of Enterprise construct and connect to their work: (a) the importance of keeping a positive mental attitude, (b) the meaning of money, and (c) the meaning of having a service-minded attitude. We then discuss the role that taking the attitude of others plays in door-to-door sales work and how salespersons attempt to create new selves.

Positive Mental Attitude

One of the most important skills that student dealers were supposed to develop was the ability to maintain a positive mental attitude. Life in the book field is full of obstacles and troubles that would lead anyone to think about not knocking on the next door. But people with a positive mental attitude—people who have adopted the identity of a positive person—will, according to Enterprise managers, be able to transform negative experiences into positive ones.

Some background in the symbolic interactionist approach to emotions will help to make sense of how positive mental attitude works. Emotions are one of the "things" that people act toward based on their meaning. People experience emotions, but they are also able to interpret those emotions. Like everything else, the meaning of emotions is both social—learned from other people—and situated—dependent on the situation. Arlie Hochschild (1983) coined the term "feeling rules" to describe this approach to emotions. Social arrangements include rules about what emotions people should experience in specific situations. People whose feelings do not match the rules are expected to change them. Sometimes, people may fake their emotions. We expect children to act grateful about receiving gifts even if they do not really feel grateful. But we also think people really ought to feel grateful because we believe that "it's the thought that counts." So someone who does not feel grateful about an unwanted gift may feel guilty about being ungrateful. People act all the time to make their feelings match feeling rules. They get psyched up for the big game, suppress their anger when showing it would be inappropriate, and try to feel love for a family member they dislike. The process of attempting to make your feelings match feeling rules is called "emotion work."

Enterprise's primary feeling rule is that student dealers are supposed to have positive feelings in the book field. Negative feelings are supposed to be transformed into positive ones. These rules find expression in the idea of the positive mental attitude, or PMA. Enterprise did not come up with this concept. *Success Through a Positive Mental Attitude* is the title of a classic motivation book by Napoleon Hill and W. Clement Stone (1960). Their basic claim is that positive thinking will always lead to positive outcomes. They are not alone in making this claim. Their work is part of an American positive thinking tradition found in many motivational and self-help books. However, this tradition has come in for heavy criticism, with skeptics calling it naïve wish fulfillment and victim blaming. As sociologists, we are inclined to accept this critique. Social institutions pose obstacles for people that often cannot be overcome by wishing them away.

However, a symbolic interactionist approach requires us to look deeper. We need to understand the meaning of PMA for people who use it to deal with problems they encounter. We need to understand how PMA works in practice. What we discovered during our research is that PMA provides student dealers with a toolkit of techniques for dealing with problems they encounter in the book field. These range from routine problems, such as people closing doors in your face or unpleasant weather, to more exceptional problems, such as being dumped by a boyfriend or girlfriend back home or experiencing a death in the family. These problems create temptations for dealers to get "off schedule," which might mean taking a lengthy break, spending too long inside an air-conditioned home, or ending the day early. It may also create temptations to quit the job. Dealers use PMA techniques to reframe these situations as positive ones. In doing so, they follow the basic Enterprise feeling rule that negative thoughts are not allowed.

Dealers practice this type of positive thinking during sales school exercises in which they are expected to reframe negative situations they may encounter in the book field as positive ones. Managers describe to trainees particular scenarios they may face— rain, dog bites, slamming doors—and discuss not just how they should react to them, but how they can see them in a positive light. A broken car, for instance, means you will get some exercise. Rain means sympathetic people will let you into their homes. A natural disaster that destroys your sales territory means that people will need new books. Whenever something bad happens in the book field, dealers are supposed to come up with three of these positive reframings. Teaching how to achieve the right emotions—those that correspond to Enterprise feeling rules—is so important to Enterprise managers that they refer to much of the training they do as "emotional training."

Once dealers get into the book field, they use a variety of practices to keep thinking positive thoughts. They are supposed to read positive material, such as self-help books the company provides them; they are supposed to talk only about positive things with their fellow salespersons, and they participate in group activities designed to foster positive thinking.

One of the most popular motivational practices is repeating positive phrases aloud, a form of internal conversation. Enterprise managers recommend that dealers continually repeat positive phrases, or affirmations, between doors because "it's impossible to think a negative thought when saying a positive phrase." Dealers report two different benefits the phrases have on their thinking. First, the positive phrases help them focus on whatever they are saying. According to one dealer,

> It was so weird at first, like "This is going to be the greatest day," "I love people, I love my job." At first I'd say it and I'm like "Oh, my God, what am I doing," but the more you say it, the more you actually start believing it. So that helped me out tons. Also, the weeks that were just terrible were when I wasn't positive, when I never even said them. (white female, first-year dealer)

Second, saying prescribed positive phrases keeps nonprescribed thoughts from creeping into their minds or drive out negative thoughts that have already begun to form. According to another student dealer,

> Positive phrases have made a really big effect on me. I just say them constantly. Like whenever I'd get a negative thought in my head out in the book field, I'd just force myself to say [a positive phrase]. Say it over and over, I scream it or whatever. That really helps quite a bit. (white male, first-year dealer)

Many of these phrases are reminders that the dealer is having or will have great success in the book field. These include phrases such as "Everyone's getting them," "Who's next," and "Get your checkbook ready—here I come." Others express the salesperson's love of the job, for example, "It's a great day to be a bookie" and "I love people and I love my job." Another category of phrases prepares dealers to recover from rejection, for example, "Meet a neg, shake a leg" and "I don't care if I sell one unit today—I'm just going to have a blast." A phrase can also redefine a potentially negative facet of the job, like the heat, in a positive way, for example, "I love the sun, for it warms my soul."

Money

Money is an interesting example of socially constructed meaning. A dollar bill's value is not inherent in the bill itself but in the meaning people assign to it. Because this meaning is shared by so many people, as well as institutionalized by governments, banks, and businesses, we can use it to buy goods and services. However, like other meanings, the meaning of money is derived from social interaction, varies from one context to another, and is used and modified by people as they encounter problems. We found that Enterprise managers and salespersons engage in what we call "money work": They used money meanings to get things done in the book field.

Enterprise managers attempt to construct different, and often contradictory, meanings of money for different situations student dealers may encounter. When managers are recruiting and training college students, one of the biggest obstacles they face is that potential recruits do not believe they can make money selling books door-to-door. During this period, the potential of making money must be emphasized. During recruiting sessions, Enterprise managers showed recruits photos of students who have made large sums of money the previous year, they display statistics showing the average amount made by students the previous summer (an average of $5,600 for first-year dealers when we studied the company), and they receive instructions about "how the money works." Because dealers are paid a 40% commission on their sales, a dealer can exceed average earnings by selling just two lead products (multivolume book sets) a day. An audience participation device relied on the prospects' inflated idea of how many books they could sell and explained the commission system. After watching a sample sales demonstration, managers asked the students how many sales they could make if they gave 30 demonstrations. Their answers typically ranged from 10 to 15. The interviewer then informed them that they had to sell only two sets a day to earn $6,500 for the summer. They would sell two a day because of the "law of averages." According to this law, 2 out of 30 prospects will buy the books regardless of the dealer's selling ability. One manager used this device when she explained to her prospects:

> I can't teach you to sell 20, 15, 10, or even 5. I can teach you to show to 30 families. If you do this, the law of averages says you will sell to two. If you sell to two, you will save $6,500. Would your coach put you in the game if you shot 2 of 30 in basketball? Would you be happy if you scored 2 of 30 on a quiz? This is bad sales ability, but there is a good commission. . . . You don't have to sell a lot to do well. . . . Could you sell two a day? They sell themselves. [A company official] said you could tie the books to a dog's butt and send it around the neighborhood and it would sell two a day.

Enterprise managers tend to be skillful storytellers, but they are mostly unsuccessful in this meaning construction. Most potential recruits do not sign up. However, those that do begin to receive some additional, potentially contradictory money meanings. This is because Enterprise managers don't believe that money is a good motivator when dealers are in the book field. One reason for this is that dealers may work hours without making any sales. In fact, it is not uncommon for first-year dealers to have a "zero day"—one with no sales. If money is the focus for dealers who aren't making any money, it will be impossible to maintain a positive mental attitude. Thus, managers urge dealers to develop "emotional purposes" for selling books. Often described as a "reason to keep you going when the money no longer does," an emotional purpose, by definition, excludes money. Some of these may involve focusing on something money can buy rather than the money itself. According to one dealer,

> You have to say, "I'm out here selling books so I can pay off my credit card debts" or "I'm out here selling books so I can pay for tuition." Or something like that that's more emotional. Because if you just do it for money, it's nothing. You can't think moneywise. You have to think about what the outcome is. (Asian female, first-year dealer)

The other reason Enterprise managers attempt to construct selling as a non-monetary activity is that focusing on money interferes with effective interaction with prospects. Enterprise advocates using a "soft sell" approach to selling because "people love to buy things, but they hate to be sold," and because "when they're free to say no, their mind opens up, and they can say yes." The process of convincing prospects that the salesperson does not care whether they buy is called "creating a buying atmosphere." Just before the demonstration begins, dealers use these key lines in the sales talk to create a buying atmosphere:

> Let me just give you a real quick look at how it works and you can tell me what you think, okay? If you like it, fine, I take orders today and deliver them at the end of the summer. If not, that's okay too. Whatever you decide is fine with me but since I am trying to show this to thirty moms every day, you could just let me know yes or no when I am finished. Fair enough? Actually, most moms I talk with don't mind getting something helpful if the kids will really use it. So kids, take a close look and let me and your mom know when we get through if it is something you think you would use. Will you do that? Great! (Enterprise sales manual)

Dealers find that convincing a customer that they do not care about the sale is much easier if they can convince themselves first. According to one dealer, "All I would think about was money. So I would go to a door and dollar bills were in my eyes. And people can see that. . . . Money did not help me out at all" (white female, first-year dealer).

Here it is useful to mention the work of Erving Goffman (see Chapter 11). Although Goffman didn't consider himself a symbolic interactionist, his dramaturgical perspective and idea of "impression management" have been extremely influential among interactionists. Goffman (1959) argued that performers attempt to make sure

Goffman

> that as many as possible of the minor events in the performance, however instrumentally inconsequential these events may be, will occur in such a way as to convey either no impression or an impression that is compatible and consistent with the over-all definition of the situation that is being fostered. (p. 51)

This is especially a concern when "the audience is known to be secretly skeptical of the reality that is being impressed upon them" because they tend to "pounce on trifling flaws as a sign that the whole show is false." When dealers reveal "dollar signs" in their eyes or through facial expressions, style of speech, or choice of words, they are examples of what Goffman called "unmeant gestures" that can ruin a performance. Thinking about money can lead to several mistakes in the demonstration, including going too fast, putting too much pressure on the prospect, and creating frustration that can carry over to the next approach.

This section describes just two important money meanings—and types of money work—for Enterprise salespersons. During recruiting, Enterprise managers attempt to construct money as a motive for selling books door-to-door. During most of the summer, though, dealers are not supposed to think about money. There are additional complications—for instance, during designated times during the summer dealers can discuss and even celebrate money—but hopefully this account has given a taste of how the meaning of money can be constructed. The two major money meanings described here may appear to be contradictory, but money meanings, like all meanings, are situated in particular contexts. A symbolic interactionist approach forces us to examine the situations and see how people make use of money meanings as they deal with the things they encounter there.

Service-Minded Attitude

So what should students think about in the book field if they can't think about money? One important "emotional purpose" that Enterprise managers advise dealers to think about is "service-mindedness." Dealers who focus on service-mindedness attempt to keep in mind the valuable service that they are performing for their sales prospects. The claim that door-to-door salespersons provide valuable services seems even less believable than the idea that you can make money doing it. Door-to-door salespersons are burdened with a reputation of being dishonest and using high-pressure tactics. Many Enterprise student dealers struggle with their own perception that they fit this stereotype. How is Enterprise able to construct "service provider" as one of the meanings of door-to-door sales?

Dealers told us about three different "services" they could perform going door-to-door. First, selling educational books helps kids in school. Although managers tell student dealers not to oversell their products by making sensational claims, many dealers encounter families they believe will undergo a dramatic transformation because of the Enterprise books. For instance, one dealer described demonstrating books to a boy who was going to repeat the sixth grade:

> And Ray was so excited. He saw these books and he saw that they could really make a difference. They could help him get back to where he needed to be. He just got so excited that I was there and that these books were available. They weren't a real well-to-do family and I'm sure that $300 for a set of five books for them might have been a little bit of a stretch. . . . Whenever I had problems wanting to sell, I'd think back and I'd say there's a kid like Ray somewhere in this territory whose train has been derailed and he wants to get back on and really doesn't know how and these books can help him do that. Nobody has the right to ruin another person's dreams and I felt like I would help fulfill those dreams. (white male, first-year dealer)

Dealers also thought they could perform services for prospects who did not even buy the books. They believed that many of the parents they visited were uninterested in their children's education, and in fact, their sales visit may be the only conversation a family has about education all year. They supported this view with the fact that most parents don't buy Enterprise books. However, even these families may gain a new appreciation for education because of the salesperson's visit.

Finally, dealers claim that they can exert a profound influence on prospects through their positive approach. Whether or not prospects buy the books, they can see that the dealers are special. This idea is expressed in a popular affirmation that is printed on a large red card included in dealers' sales kits: "This is the best day I've ever had! I can, I will, and I'm going to help 30 people today live a richer, fuller, more meaningful life because I stopped by and showed them my books."

Taking the Attitude of Distant Others

Service-mindedness is an example of an emotional purpose that involves another person, in this case, the potential customer who will be served by the salesperson. Dealers may also attempt to focus on other people to motivate them to sell books, including teammates, who they don't want to let down, and future employers, who will be impressed by their sales record. It is important to remember that Enterprise salespersons usually sell all alone. The sales prospects with whom they interact aren't usually encouraging them; they are shutting doors in their faces. Enterprise salespersons rely on internal conversations with people who aren't present to construct reasons for selling books. This section will mention two methods for dealing with people back home: dedications and skeptics.

One way that these distant loved ones, especially those supportive of the salesperson, are made real is by symbolically dedicating all or part of the summer to them. The most organized system of dedications is the "Mom's Week" or "Dad's Week" that many sales manager organizations sponsor. During these weeks, dealers sell "for Dad" or "for Mom," instead of for themselves. Dealers attempt to think about all of the sacrifices that Mom and Dad have made for them, as this dealer reported:

I dedicated a week to my dad. I would tell myself, "Dad worked so hard for me all these years. He went to work so many days that he didn't want to work just because he knew he had to provide for me. That's love and I need to show him how good of a job he did." (white female, second-year dealer)

To help keep Mom or Dad in mind, dealers may post a picture of them in their car or even call them in the morning to tell them they will be selling for them that day. Some pretend the recipient of the dedication is present and have imaginary conversations with him or her.

Like all emotional purposes, dedications do not work for some dealers. One problem with dedications is that they may make dealers homesick. Another is that Mom or Dad may believe that selling books for Enterprise is a foolish way to spend the summer. Family or friends with this opinion—skeptics—may be the focus of another emotional purpose.

Selling for skeptics is the flip side of a dedication. Both involve selling for friends or family back home. But, whereas dedications are aimed at supportive friends or family, the use of skeptics as an emotional purpose is directed at those who doubt the ability of the student dealer to earn money selling books door-to-door. For some salespersons, skeptics can be a powerful motivation, as they were with this dealer:

My biggest thing was my dad told me that this was the stupidest decision I was ever going to make in my life. I'm going to go out there and waste a few weeks of my summer, come back, and he's going to tell me, "I told you so." So even when the slightest thought of why am I here came to my mind, I was like "To prove my dad wrong. I can do this. It may be hard, but I bet you my dad couldn't do this." Which is just stupid, but that was the big thing. That was my big thing all summer. (white female, first-year dealer)

Dealers use similar methods to keep skeptics in their minds that they use for dedications, including posting a picture of the skeptic in a car or bedroom. Dealers also attempt to visualize skeptics' reactions to their return home. If a dealer quit the job, her skeptics would say, "I told you so." If a dealer finishes the summer, though, she will be able to show her parents her "big check" (Enterprise jargon for a profit of over $5,000). She will be able to ask her friends what they did during the summer and then tell them how great her summer was and, incidentally, how much money she made. Dealers are supposed to visualize these differing scenarios when they are considering quitting.

Although these two types of distant others, the skeptic and the recipient of a dedication, are used differently in the book field, they both rely on taking the attitude of another person, a key interactionist concept that allows us to make sense of the social world of door-to-door sales.

Constructing a New Self

Recall that the self is one of the "things" that we act toward based on the meaning of it for us. One of the most interesting recent developments in symbolic interactionism is the concept of the "narrative self," the idea that some of the most important meanings we attach to the self are stories (Gubrium & Holstein, 2000; Holstein & Gubrium, 1999). We all tell stories about who we are. As we engage in internal conversation, we can run these stories by the generalized others from our different social worlds. As we engage in actual interactions, people may accept or reject the stories we tell about ourselves. One of the ways that institutions shape us is by selecting which stories people are allowed to tell and which are discouraged.

One of the claims Enterprise managers make to student dealers is that selling books door-to-door will "build character," that it will help them build a better self. According to the company sales manual:

> What kind of person do you want to be a year from now? Or two years from now? Or five years from now? Or 10? Or 20? Right now you are in the process of becoming the person you will be in a year, or two, or five, or 10 or 20 years from now. The habits you have now will determine the kind of person you will become unless you change those habits now.

Enterprise facilitates this self creation by promoting some stories about selves and discouraging others. During the training process, managers meet with student dealers and find out about their personality and goals. Together, they come up with a personal set of "emotional purposes." These emotional purposes form a bridge between the existing self and a new and improved self that is supposed to be created during the summer.

Positive stories focus on approved emotional purposes, such as having a positive mental attitude, being service-minded, and improving relationships with other people. Student dealers are exposed to positive stories in the form of motivational speeches. During sales school, former dealers describe how sticking with the job resulted in personal growth, self-confidence, money, success in future jobs, and healing of family conflict. These stories are intended to provide model narratives that student dealers can draw upon to make sense of their experiences in the book field.

During training, student dealers also learn about stories they need to reject if they are to be successful and develop a better self. Inappropriate stories are often personified as Mr. Mediocrity (or Mr. M), who appears in company materials as a little green man and is said to sit on students' shoulders saying things like, "This isn't working out, is it?" These are the sort of stories students aren't supposed to be telling themselves. They are supposed to (figuratively) knock Mr. M off their shoulders and stomp on him.

Negative stories are also forbidden in the book field. Student dealers are supposed to share only positive stories with each other. For instance, at the end of the day, roommates are not supposed to tell any "negative stories." They are not to indicate how well they sold that day because their failures are negative and their successes can be negative for someone who is not doing as well. The need to tell nonapproved stories—gripes, complaints, accusations—is met during Sundays when student dealers have one-on-one "personal conferences" with student managers. During these conversations, managers listen to dealers' stories and then attempt to reframe negative narratives as positive ones, such as by explaining how surviving their ordeals will make them stronger in the future.

Recall that for interactionists, the self can be thought of as a process, an internal conversation. By offering people new stories to tell, institutions help foster the creation of new selves. The self offered by Enterprise is designed to better sell books, but is also sold as a way to be more positive and successful in other social worlds.

Conclusion

We hope that the findings of our study give you a glimpse of some of the benefits of an interactionist approach to studying social life. Every social world contains a large number of interconnected meanings—categories, symbols, rules, shared assumptions, and so on—and the key to understanding the social world is understanding these meanings and how they are used by people in the course of getting things done. This is the approach of symbolic interactionist research.

We have illustrated this research with the social world of door-to-door sales. The organizers of this social world—Enterprise Company managers—have created a set of meanings designed to promote selling books door-to-door successfully. However, their task, like the task of all organizers, is made difficult by the fact that they are organizing humans, who are self-directed and creative. Organizers can't plant goals into people's heads; they need to communicate those goals with symbols and create social worlds where those goals are worth pursuing.

As college students attempt to sell books door-to-door, some of them are able to use meanings adopted from Enterprise to make sense of what they are doing and continue to the next door. Some of the students try to find a positive meaning in the job, but are unable to do so. They cannot frame the difficulties of the job in a positive light as they have been taught. Some students don't buy into the meanings offered by Enterprise at all. About a third of salespersons quit before the end of the summer, and most of those who did finish the summer fell well short of the ideal salesperson described in sales school.

Social life is messy and difficult because people are purposive and creative. But these same qualities make social organization and society possible. The social world of Enterprise is a strange world, with its frantic work schedule and unusual practices for promoting positive behavior. But all social worlds are strange to those unfamiliar with their meanings. Symbolic interactionist research aims to make sense of social worlds by taking seriously these meanings and how they are used by their inhabitants.

The goal of symbolic interactionist research isn't just to understand specific social worlds. Like other sociological perspectives, interactionist research builds on previous research. Interactionist sociologists attempt to discover processes that may be found in other social settings. For instance, in our research, we draw upon ideas like "feeling rules" (from Arlie Hochschild) and "impression management" (from Erving Goffman) that other sociologists have developed. In turn, we hope that some of our findings and concepts, like "money work," will be useful to sociologists studying other social worlds.

Note

1. We've substituted "other people" for Blumer's "one's fellows."

References

Becker, H. S. (1953). Becoming a marihuana user. *American Journal of Sociology, 59,* 235–242.

Becker, H. S. (1982). *Art worlds.* Berkeley: University of California Press.

Becker, H. S. (1986). *Doing things together.* Evanston, IL: Northwestern University Press.

Blumer, H. (1969a). The methodological position of symbolic interactionism. In *Symbolic interactionism: Perspective and method.* Berkeley: University of California Press.

Blumer, H. (1969b). *Symbolic interactionism: Perspective and method.* Berkeley: University of California Press.

Couch, C. J. (1984). *Constructing civilizations* (Vol. 5). Greenwich, CT: JAI.

Goffman, E. (1959). *The presentation of self in everyday life.* New York: Doubleday-Anchor.

Gubrium, J. F., & Holstein, J. A. (Eds.). (2000). *Institutional selves: Troubled identities in a postmodern world.* New York: Oxford University Press.

Harris, S. (2006). *The meanings of marital inequality.* Albany: State University of New York Press.

Harris, S. (2010). *What is constructionism? Navigating its use in sociology.* Boulder, CO: Lynne Rienner.

Hill, N., & Stone, W. C. (1960). *Success through a positive mental attitude.* New York: Pocket Books.

Hochschild, A. (1983). *The managed heart.* Berkeley: University of California Press.

Holstein, J. A., & Gubrium, J. F. (1999). *The self we live by: Narrative identity in a postmodern world.* New York: Oxford University Press.

Hughes, E. C. (1958). *Men and their work.* Glencoe, IL: Free Press.

Hughes, E. C. (1971). *The sociological eye.* New Brunswick, NJ: Transaction Books.

Loseke, D. R. (2003). *Thinking about social problems.* New York: Aldine de Gruyter.

Mead, G. H. (1934). *Mind, self, and society.* Chicago: University of Chicago Press.

Schweingruber, D. (2006a). Success through a positive mental attitude? The role of positive thinking in door-to-door sales. *Sociological Quarterly, 47*(1), 41-68.

Schweingruber. D. (2006b). The why, what and how of selling door-to-door: Levels of purpose and perception in a sales company." In K. McClelland & T. J. Fararo (Eds.) *Perception, meaning, and action: Control systems theories in sociology.* New York: Palgrave Macmillan.

Schweingruber, D., & Berns, N. (2003). Doing money work in a door-to-door sales organization. *Symbolic Interaction, 26*(3), 447–471.

Schweingruber, D., & Berns, N. (2005). Shaping the selves of young salespeople through emotion management. *Journal of Contemporary Ethnography, 34*(6), 679–706.

Stewart, R. L. (1998). *Living and acting together: An essay in social psychology.* Dix Hills, NY: General Hall.

Ulmer, J. T. (1997). *Social worlds of sentencing: Court communities under sentencing guidelines.* Albany: State University of New York Press.

DISCUSSION QUESTIONS

1. Provide a brief summary of your understanding of symbolic interactionism, analyzing in turn the three premises of this theoretical position as articulated by Herbert Blumer, who attempted to translate the philosophical thought of George Herbert Mead into a useful approach for social

analysis. As is made clear in the discussion of his thinking, treating action as meaningful is the central tenet of this approach. What do you think of this claim? Is all action meaningful? Does an actor have to be consciously aware of his or her actions for them to be meaningful?

2. Looking specifically at Blumer's second and third premises, it is claimed that meaning doesn't arise out of the mind of the solitary individual, but rather is the product of social interaction, and as such is a collective rather than individual accomplishment. However, the individual has the ability to interpret and thus to modify meaning. We are all born into social worlds that provide us with a world of meaning, although we can react to it in varied ways. Think about your own religious beliefs. Analyze those beliefs in terms of your own socialization, paying attention to the sorts of social interaction that shaped them and to the way you ultimately responded, whether it be by embracing, rejecting, or modifying them.

3. George Herbert Mead famously contrasts the "I" and the "me." Explain in your own words what he meant by making this distinction. Is it similar to Freud's discussion of the conscious and unconscious self, or are they fundamentally different conceptualizations of the human mind? Explain your position.

4. Symbolic interactionists contend that social life is indeterminate, with an emphasis placed on treating society not as a fixed entity, but as an open, fluid, ongoing accomplishment. As such, this theoretical position places a premium on the significance of human agency. Critics sometimes contend that in focusing on agency, social structures are either ignored or underappreciated, and as such the theory is not able to account for constraints on agency or the more enduring, unchanging aspects of social life. Where do you stand on this debate and why?

5. The second half of the chapter is devoted to an in-depth discussion of the world of door-to-door sales, employing the elements of a symbolic interactionist analysis to understand the process by which college students become salespersons. Take an example from your own life and perform a similar analysis, making explicit use of the three premises discussed earlier in the chapter. Focus on how you achieved a new role as part of that repertoire of multiple identities that constitute the self. This might be a summer job work role comparable to door-to-door sales, or it might involve becoming a member of a sports team, a Greek organization, or some other college organization.

CHAPTER 11

Goffman's Dramaturgical Sociology

Personal Sales and Service in a Commodified World

Peter Kivisto and Dan Pittman

Peter Kivisto is the Richard Swanson Professor of Social Thought and Chair of Sociology at Augustana College, in Rock Island, Illinois, where he has taught continuously since obtaining his PhD in sociology from the New School for Social Research in New York City. It was in the unique environment of the New School that he came to appreciate the importance of social theory for making sense of the social issues that are important to him. His major interests revolve around exploring the implications of racial and ethnic groups living in a society that is both capitalist and democratic. His dissertation research, for example, involved a historical excursion into the world created by Finnish American political radicals, which appeared as his first book, Immigrant Socialists in the United States *(1984). He coauthored, with Ronald Glassman and William H. Swatos, Jr.,* For Democracy *(1993) and published* Multiculturalism in a Global Society *(2002). He has recently published a third edition of his brief theory text for Pine Forge titled* Key Ideas in Sociology *(2011). He and his coauthor Thomas Faist recently published* Beyond a Border: The Causes and Consequences of Contemporary Immigration *(2010). In 2009, he began a 4-year position as Finland Distinguished Professor at the University of Turku, Finland.*

Dan Pittman grew up in an academic environment in Iowa City. He is a Phi Beta Kappa graduate of Augustana College, where he majored in sociology and philosophy. He received his JD from New York University School of Law, where he served as a staff editor for the Annual Survey of American Law. *He is a member of the New York bar and the U.S. Tax*

Court, and is employed as an Associate by the New York City law firm of Carter, Ledyard, and Milburn. He completed an LLM degree in taxation at NYU in 2006. He has produced a number of publications on tax law and recently presented a lecture at the Maritime Law Association of the United States. As an avocation, he remains engaged in a project concerned with the cultural roots of the blues, in which he examines the movement of the blues out of its rural origins in the Mississippi Delta to northern cities.

The original inspiration for dramaturgical sociology, the subject of this chapter, derives from the greatest playwright in the English language: William Shakespeare. It was Shakespeare who adorned London's famous Globe Theater with the Latin motto *Totus Mundus Agit Histrionem* (All the World Is a Theater) and who wrote the following lines for Jacques in *As You Like It:* "All the world's a stage, and all the men and women merely players."

For Erving Goffman (1922–1982), arguably the most original American theorist of the second half of the 20th century, the metaphor of life as theater is rich in meaning. He sees all human interaction as, in some ways, very much like a grand play. He is not, however, as concerned with sweeping generalizations about the human condition as he is with the particulars of daily life—the micro-level interactions between individuals that, when taken together, constitute the human experience. At this micro level, he argues, the world is much more like a stage than we commonly realize.

For Goffman, the subject matter of dramaturgical sociology is the creation, maintenance, and destruction of common understandings of reality by people working individually and collectively to present a shared and unified image of that reality. The brilliant insight that makes Goffman's book *The Presentation of Self in Everyday Life* (1959) so significant is that this process, which he believes lies concealed deep within every interaction, is familiar to all of us in the form of the theater. In a play, actors try to convey to an audience a particular impression of the world around them. Through the use of scripted dialogue, gestures, props, costumes, and so on, actors create a new reality for the audience to consider.

It is Goffman's claim that if we understand how a contemporary American actor can convey an impression of an angst-ridden Danish prince during a presentation of *Hamlet,* we can also understand how an insurance agent tries to act like a professional operating with a combination of expert knowledge and goodwill. If we can understand how a small stage can be used to represent all of Rome and Egypt in *Antony and Cleopatra,* we can also understand how the Disney Store creates a sense of adventure and wonder in any local mall. Also, if we can understand the process by which two paid actors convince us that they are madly in love in *Romeo and Juliet,* we can understand how flight attendants manage and use their emotions for commercial gain. In this chapter, we will attempt to explain aspects of Goffman's metaphor by taking insurance agents, employees of the Walt Disney corporation, flight attendants, and car salespeople as examples of how people create alternate realities. Beyond the metaphor of social life as dramatic ritual, Goffman sensed the potential for alienation brought about because of the problems of authentically embracing a role rather than feeling a certain ambivalence or distance from it. This alienation is also critical to Goffman's analysis.

Before directly reviewing Goffman's dramaturgical analysis of social interaction, we must briefly consider his rather unique conception of selfhood because it is crucial to his method of analysis. Goffman does not believe in a "self" in the traditional sense; he does not think that we can discuss people's selves abstracted from their social situations. He writes,

> This self itself does not derive from its possessor, but from the whole scene of his action . . . this self is a product of a scene that comes off, and not a cause of it. The self, then, as a performed character, is not an organic thing that has specific location . . . [the individual and his body] merely provide the peg on which something of collaborative manufacture will be hung for a time. And the means for producing and maintaining selves do not reside inside the peg. (Goffman, 1959, pp. 252–253)[1]

Goffman is arguing here that the self is not an entity that is in some sense antecedent to its enactment, but rather that it arises in the very process of performance. What is crucial is a recognition that, for Goffman, talking about the individual as some sort of autonomous agent is incorrect; rather, the individual should be thought of always in relationship to a social whole. Thus, the fundamental unit of social analysis, for Goffman (1959), is not the individual but rather what he refers to as the "team." He writes, "A teammate is someone whose dramaturgical cooperation one is dependent upon in fostering a given definition of the situation" (p. 83). Teams, then, are responsible for the creation of perceptions of reality in social settings. The crux of his dramaturgical social theory is that the analysis of how teams cooperate to foster particular impressions of reality reveals a complex system of interactions that, in many ways, is like the presentation of a play.

Goffman assumes that his theory could be applied to all social activities, but it is especially visible in certain commercial settings. This will be illustrated in the four examples we have chosen to employ. The first is Arlie Hochschild's *The Managed Heart* (1983), in which she looks at the world of airline flight attendants. She describes the types of social interaction found among flight attendants, contending that the entire flight crew must form a coherent, unified team intent on conveying to passengers a sense of competence and friendliness. If any attendant started behaving rudely or, worse, incompetently, the entire project would fail. Similarly, employees in the Disney Store, the focus of Kelly Kraft's ethnographic study, must all foster a sense of adventure and wonder for customers; if one employee looks sullen and bored, the atmosphere will be lost, and the team's attempt to convey a particular understanding of reality will be deemed a failure. The final examples we use come from Guy Oakes's study of insurance salespeople and Stephen Miller's study of car salesmen, who, as we shall see, must expend considerable energy to establish a particular impression of who they are and what they can do for a customer if they are to be successful.

How do people convince other people—specifically consumers—to adopt a particular understanding of various social scenes? Goffman says that this is accomplished by using the tools of the theater. It takes collaborative effort to stage a convincing performance, complete with roles, scripts, costumes, and a stage. Only when all these are employed to create a coherent picture of reality can a team be successful.

Roles

A crucial part of Goffman's dramaturgical metaphor is the role. Generally, the role is the particular image that a single actor wants to convey. It is the essence, the contrived sense of self, that the individual wants to project to the world. Just as an actor may adopt the role of a troubled Danish prince or a blues-loving ex-con, individuals in social settings must adopt the traits necessary to the understanding of reality they want to project. For instance, Guy Oakes argues that to effectively sell insurance, one must adopt the role of the dedicated and knowledgeable professional.

Of course, most people in white-collar careers must put on a display of professionalism. However, Oakes suggests that, in many ways, the insurance agent has a more difficult task than other professionals. For various reasons, there is a widespread public perception that insurance agents are sleazy and underhanded. As one of the insurance agents Oakes (1990) interviewed stated, "You really get shit on in this business" (p. 102).

The more insurance agents in general are believed to be sleazy, the harder particular insurance agents must work to avoid demonstrating such qualities. Being perceived as a "professional" is an ideal way to provide agents with the credibility they so desperately need to close sales. The aspiring agent must figure out precisely what is required to successfully convey a professional role, which, Oakes (1990) states in the following passage, involves an emphasis on expertise and advice rather than a single-minded emphasis on selling a product:

> Like . . . other professionals, the agent claims to be an expert in the solution of certain problems in which the public has a substantial interest. The agent places this expertise at the disposal of a client, who receives confidential advice. . . . This is why training manuals describe the agent as a "financial doctor." The buyer/seller conception of salesmanship is relegated to the pioneer days of personal selling. It is replaced by the professional/client relationship, in which the function of the agent is to assist clients in solving their problems by applying specialized skills and offering expert advice. (p. 102)

Insurance agents must understand not only that they are to present themselves as experts who want to help, but also that they must have enough knowledge of the life insurance industry to actually be of assistance. Most insurance agencies provide comprehensive training to prospective agents. This training process serves a dual purpose. First, of course, is to make sure that agents have all the information they will eventually need. It is difficult to look like a credible professional if one does not understand what one is selling. Second, although the training process itself has value to the industry, if there is a public perception that agents require specialized education, agents will instantly get a certain credibility—they will look like professionals—when they obtain some kind of educational credential. Goffman (1959) explains this as follows:

> Labor unions, universities, trade associations, and other licensing bodies require practitioners to absorb a mystical range and period of training . . . in part to foster the impression that the licensed practitioner is someone who has been reconstituted by his learning experience and is now set apart from other men. (p. 46)

Airline flight attendants must adopt a role that imposes rather different demands and expectations from that of insurance agents. Flight attendants have more direct contact with the public than anyone else in an airline and therefore have many responsibilities associated with the comfort and safety of passengers. Ultimately, when customers remember a particular flight, they will almost certainly remember the flight attendants more than any other airline employee. Flight attendants represent the public face of the entire company. The most basic role of the flight attendant is to be pleasant and reassuring. This is emphasized in airline advertisements:

> Through the 1950s and 1960s the flight attendant became a main subject of airline advertising, the spearhead of market expansion. The image they chose, among many possible ones, was that of a beautiful and smartly dressed Southern white woman, the supposed epitome of gracious manners and warm personal service. (Hochschild, 1983, pp. 92–93; reprinted with permission of The Regents of California and University of California Press)

The stewardess[2] is supposed to represent all the things passengers would like to see in servants—stewardesses are graceful, elegant, friendly, and, above all, constantly smiling. This is such a crucial component of the flight attendant's job that it is emphasized even before the interview. Hochschild (1983) notes,

> Applicants are urged to read a preinterview pamphlet before coming in. In the 1979–1980 *Airline Guide to Stewardess and Steward Careers*, there is a section called "The Interview." Under the subheading "Appearance," the manual suggests that facial expressions should be "sincere" and "unaffected." One should have a "modest but friendly smile" and be "generally alert, attentive, not overly aggressive, but not reticent either." Under "Mannerisms," subheading "Friendliness," it is suggested that a successful candidate must be "outgoing but not effusive," "enthusiastic with calm and poise," and "vivacious but not effervescent." (pp. 95–96)

In addition to these components of the role, individual airlines add other requirements. There are relatively few qualitative differences between airlines, but to the extent that airlines want to individuate themselves, to stand out in a crowded market, their flight attendants must be in some way unique. Thus, during the time of her study, Hochschild (1983) found that "United Airlines, the consensus has it, is 'the girl-next-door,' the neighborhood babysitter grown up. Pan Am is upper class, sophisticated, and slightly reserved in its graciousness. PSA is brassy, fun-loving, and sexy" (p. 97).

Some companies have tried to further individuate themselves by making their flight attendants adopt semisexualized roles in an attempt to appeal to certain segments of the market. Hochschild (1983) notes the following:

> The omnipresent smile [in airline advertisements] suggests, first of all, that the flight attendant is friendly, helpful, and open to requests. But when words are added, the smile can be sexualized, as in "We really move our tails for you to make your every wish come true" (Continental) or "Fly me, you'll like it" (National). Such innuendoes lend strength to the conventional fantasy that in the air, anything can happen. . . . The sexualized ad burdens the flight attendant with another task, beyond being unfailingly helpful and open to requests: She must respond to the sexual fantasies of passengers. She must try to feel and act as if flirting and propositioning are "a sign of my attractiveness and your sexiness," and she must work to suppress her feelings that such behavior is intrusive or demeaning. (pp. 93–94)

The role of the flight attendant is very tightly circumscribed. At a minimum, the flight attendant must project an impression of friendliness and pleasantness; usually more requirements are added to the role to fit the desires of the particular airline. Of course, flight attendants have other requirements as well. They must know where safety equipment is located, they must make sure that passengers are complying with safety regulations, and they must be able to efficiently and calmly instruct passengers about what to do in case of various types of emergencies. Airlines do not want to play up these features, however, because to mention them would be to raise questions about the airline's safety.

No matter how well an actor understands his or her role, he or she must be capable of conveying it to an audience. In Goffman's sociology, the common or shared understanding of reality *is* reality. A "friendly" flight attendant who seems surly will not please management; a wealthy insurance agent who dresses shabbily probably will not sell many policies. An actor who cannot manipulate the common understanding successfully will be a failure. Goffman's sociology, then, is the study of how people get other people to see things in a certain way. They do this, he claims, by using a variety of theatrical tools.

Scripts

Perhaps the most important means of getting an audience to understand a role is a script; certainly theater as we know it relies on scripts. Goffman claims that scripts are vital to interpersonal interaction as well. Of course, most interpersonal communication is relatively improvisational—we make it up as we go along. In everyday life, however, some elements of conversation are pretty well scripted. If a person asks a casual acquaintance how he or she is doing, the acquaintance is likely to reply with a simple "Fine, yourself?" rather than a sincere, well-thought-out description of what he or she is really thinking or feeling at the moment. This is a fragment of conversation we are so used to employing that it feels automatic. Thus, scripts can allow us a great deal of convenience; they constitute a taken-for-granted quality in which, rather than creating our lines out of whole cloth, we borrow from a stock of well-worn scripts.

Commercial settings often make use of increasingly formalized scripts, which can provide distinct advantages to all parties. Often, retail store managers write scripts that are passed down to the people who must actually go about making sales. One extreme example of this is provided by the Disney company, which, as Kraft (1994) discovered in her research, gives staffers (or "Cast Members," in their words) a set of rigidly prescribed scripts:

> These scripts offer verbatim responses Disney Store executives would like to hear used by Cast Members. . . . Frequently, a Cast Member becomes dependent on the scripts and mindlessly repeats the same message to every guest he or she encounters. The greeting traditionally offered at the front of the store is an example of how closely the scripts are followed. When a Cast Member was trained in 1991, he or she received a handout [which included the statement] "When you are greeting, the exact script is 'Hi! Welcome to the Disney Store!' There are to be no variations of this script used . . . ever." (p. 8)

In this case, a script is used to control and limit employee autonomy. The management has a particular role that it wants employees to adopt: friendly, cheerful, and helpful, but somewhat aloof, like a cartoon character. Disney corporate officials have concluded that the best way to ensure that employees actually adopt this role is to force it on them. It should also be noted that the scripts sometimes have advantages for the clerks. Kraft noted that Cast Members frequently become reliant on the scripts, using them as convenient crutches. Similarly, many telephone solicitors use obviously scripted messages when they call people; reading scripts is a simple process that requires little training or thought and thus makes the solicitor's job much easier.

Script use in direct sales is in no way limited to controlling employees or providing a convenience in place of more sophisticated kinds of training. Frequently, scripts are used to control customers, to compel them to buy a given product. Car sellers need to have a very comprehensive understanding of their customers, and to gain it, they often employ an almost ritualized conversation. For instance, Stephen Miller learned the following in his study of this much-maligned occupation:

> The salesperson employs the demonstration ride to establish a situation in which the customer will communicate to the salesperson what he values in an automobile and why, information which can be used to stress the merits of the automobile being considered and influence a decision. (Miller, 1964, p. 19)

One salesperson explained this technique, claiming, "I ask him how he likes the way it handles, how about the power and a lot of other things. . . . By the time we finish the ride, I have a good idea of what he wants in a car" (Miller, 1964, p. 19; reprinted with permission).

By using a strictly patterned conversational format, the agent can gain insights into what will make the customer buy a car. To the extent that these conversations follow a predictable form, they are scripted, even though the particulars of the discussion will change from one customer to the next.

Furthermore, there is a sense in which the entire sales transaction follows a loose script. Miller divides the process of selling a car into three stages, the second and third arising as a logical result of the previous stage. First comes the "contact," when a salesperson first interacts with someone who may or may not be interested in buying a car. If the potential customer shows any interest, the transaction moves into the second stage, the "pitch," in which the agent attempts to size up precisely what the customer wants and how much he or she will pay for it. Finally, if the customer does not walk out during the pitch, the transaction proceeds to the final stage, the "close," in which the agent tries to get the customer to agree with the agent's understanding of this particular social reality—that is, tries to convince the customer to pay a certain amount for a particular car.

In a sense, these distinct stages of the transaction look like different scenes in a play; each has its own rules, each follows from the developments of the preceding scenes, and the action (if the agent is successful) rises to a cathartic agreement and ultimate resolution in the final act. Thus, sales transactions seem scripted at the level of both individual lines and the broad outlines of the play. In both cases, the script is used to control the customer, to get him or her to see reality the same way the car seller sees it.

In a play, the script is often the most important aspect of an actor's role—ultimately, we are more likely to remember Hamlet's soliloquies than the stage directions or what kind of jewelry he wore. In social interaction, this is not always the case. First, scripted interaction in real life is rarely mutual; the seller is following a script that the buyer is generally unaware of and therefore may not follow. Also, as noted previously, scripted interaction is rarely formal; although the car seller has a general notion of what kinds of things need to be said and when, the phrasing of individual lines is usually improvisational so that the script is more of a general outline than a specific blueprint. Because the script is not quite as important in social interaction as it is in theater, we can expect other tools of the actor to play a slightly larger part in conveying a person's role in a social interaction than those same tools do in a play. An individual selling a car cannot control with precision what the customer will say, so he or she must focus attention more on those things that *can* be controlled.

Costumes

One element that is crucial to actors is the potential impact of their costumes. This is because what people are wearing is probably the quickest way to form an impression of them and their social status. Before a word is uttered in a play, we can size up characters on stage: The one wearing tattered rags is probably much poorer than the one wearing a fine suit, and so on. In precisely the same way, an individual's wardrobe is vital to presenting to the audience his or her particular role in the drama being played out at the moment.

For instance, as noted previously, insurance sellers have a tremendous incentive to look like professionals. This suggests several aspects about their wardrobe. First, of course, because professionals are supposed to be relatively well-off financially (especially, one would hope, professionals in financial services), agents would be wise to adopt the dress and habits of the financially secure. This might partially explain why companies frequently give prizes such as gold watches and vacations to exotic locales to agents who are especially productive (Oakes, 1990)—flashy watches and nice tans are luxuries that come with relative wealth. Although insurance agents generally do not make enough money to qualify as rich, it is helpful if their costumes suggest that they do qualify.

Second, there is more to the costume of the agent than just a suggestion of wealth. One of the selling points of most insurance policies is that they are relatively secure investments; agents urge potential customers to take a fiscally conservative approach to investing. Obviously, it is easier to take someone dressed in a sober business suit seriously on this point than, for example, someone wearing leather pants and an outrageous jacket.

Not all costumes are intended to say the same things, however. Roles that do not involve notions of professionalism may require different types of clothing. At the Disney Store, for example, employees must conform to a very strict dress code, which includes white shoes, pink shirts, and blue cardigans with an "M" on the lower left-hand side. Men must wear gray polyester pants; women must wear gray polyester skirts (Kraft, 1994). Obviously, these costumes are not designed to suggest that the Cast Members are part of the educated professional class; rather, they tie into a notion of nostalgia that Disney is trying to establish and exploit.

Stages and Sets

The other major tool the actor can employ to control audience reaction is the stage and its setting. If, as the curtain rises, the audience members see what looks like the inside of a mansion, they will assume certain things about what the play will be about—things they would not assume if the curtain rose on a jungle scene. The physical environment of a play, then, can provide a context for the action that is to follow, locating it at a particular point in space and time in the audience's mind. Similarly, the use of the physical environment can establish a context for social interaction; if used skillfully, it can help one team convince the other to adopt the preferred understanding of reality.

Perhaps the most obvious aspect of using stages is the introduction of scenery. Of course, some sellers have very little control over the scenery at their place of work; the door-to-door salesperson, for instance, must work with whatever scenery he or she finds in a particular home. Sometimes, however, sellers have a great deal of control over their environments and use it effectively. The Disney Corporation has spent tremendous amounts of time and money designing the scenery in its retail stores to foster an impression of a fantasy world of some sort, right down to selecting the soundtracks that best evoke this conjured reality. Kraft (1994) notes that

> the music playing in the background is a mixture of classic and new Disney tunes. The songs are designed to remind one of a special childhood memory or a much loved movie. . . . The music is intended to capture the imagination and transport the shopper further into the depths of the Magic Kingdom. It is easy to become captivated by the shelves stuffed with familiar characters. Before too long, the shopper has become completely enveloped by the package. The Disney Store is intended to offer more than the average retail shopping experience. It attempts to bring a piece of the Magic Kingdom to all who "visit." (pp. 1–2)

With this manipulation of the physical surroundings, Disney tries to make the process of shopping less like a banal consumer experience and more like some kind of mild adventure, or at least a nostalgia trip. Manipulation of scenery is part of a conscious effort to replace the mundane with the fantastic—that is, to change people's perceptions of reality.

Another use of stages that is common in many social interactions is the division between front and back stages. The front stage is what confronts the audience— what they see. The back stage, by contrast, is a place where all the support activities necessary for maintaining the performance on the main stage will go on. In theater, the back stage is where actors who are not involved in the scene going on at the moment mill about; where props that will be used at other times are stored; and where the counterbalances, lights, and so on that make the scenery convincing to the audience are hidden. Goffman (1959) points out that the crucial element that allows the back stage to be useful for these purposes is that "the back region will be the place where the performer can reliably expect that no member of the audience will intrude" (p. 113). Thus, most back regions are clearly divided from the public fronts so that only team members have access. Manifestations of region-specific behavior abound in everyday life. Goffman claims that putting locks on bathroom stall doors exhibits a certain region behavior because presumably while one is in the stall, the public front cannot be maintained (p. 121). Houses are divided along these front stage/backstage lines as well: Guests are frequently confined to living and dining rooms and rarely invited to see bedrooms or bathrooms. Similarly, many houses have front doors that are used primarily for more formal situations; family members often use back or side doors for day-to-day admission.

Backstage regions have two major purposes, both related to the maintenance of the proper persona or atmosphere on the front stage. They must serve as a storing ground for physical items that cannot be on the front stage, and they must also provide employees a place to regroup, a place where they take care of their emotional needs. The physical requirements of backstage may not be particularly surprising. Most retail shops, for instance, try not to clutter the stage with too much stuff but want to have enough of certain popular items to ensure that they will not run out. A storeroom, then, is crucial. Shoe stores offer perhaps the best example of this; most of them leave one pair of each style of shoe on display, but because they need several pairs of each size of shoe in each style to satisfy customers, they have a need for a well-organized back stage, where piles of shoe boxes can sit without being observed. Back regions are also helpful for storing things not sold by the business but that are vital to the maintenance of the proper atmosphere on stage. Retail stores are almost uniformly clean; this means that vacuum cleaners, mops, glass cleaners, and so on must be kept where they can be accessed regularly, but because cleanliness usually mandates a lack of visible cleaning supplies, the equipment must be hidden from public scrutiny.

The physical requirements of back regions in commerce are frequently rather mundane, as these examples show. Back stages often have a more interesting purpose as well: They often provide for the emotional needs of employees so that they can continue to give the proper performance on stage. One crucial element is the informality afforded by the back stage. During a performance, people have to be constantly vigilant to ensure that they do not betray their roles; they must stay in character, follow whatever script they are using, and so on. Such rigidity can be exhausting, and the ability to go to a place where the audience will not see or hear anything provides a safety valve for employees. Thus, backstage areas provide employees with an opportunity to take a break. Indeed, this is frequently the chief function of one backstage region, the break room, where employees can sit down, have some coffee, and relax for a few minutes before continuing the show at hand.

Backstage areas are also useful in that they allow team members to discuss with each other what could be changed about the performance if, for example, one member of the team is failing or if the customer is behaving oddly. In retail stores, then, one would expect most discussions that are not directly part of the performance to only occur backstage, and almost all parts of the early training process in almost all vocations occur away from the public arena.

The degree to which region behavior is engraved in the consumer's consciousness can be highlighted by an example that shows how this very awareness of the difference between front and back stages is exploited by some businesses to further the impression they want to foster. Car buyers, according to Miller, are not often given access to information such as the actual cost to a dealership of a car or the average selling price of the car, so they have to negotiate, to a certain extent, blindly. This allows the dealerships to get the best possible deal for themselves while leaving the customer, who presumably has haggled a few thousand dollars off the sticker price by the end of the negotiation, feeling satisfied. One technique many dealers employ to guarantee this satisfaction is "changing sides," in which salespeople seem to come to the conclusion that the customer is getting the better end of the deal but, because they like the customer, they will act as advocates for the customer and get the deal approved by the hostile sales manager. This is where the use of space comes into the picture. At this point in the negotiations, the seller will go into the sales office. This is an office inside the dealership where the sales manager approves contracts. The customers see the seller walk into the office but cannot hear what goes on inside it. Presumably, then, the office is a backstage area. The seller and the sales manager, however, are fully aware that the customer is waiting outside, paying close attention to the office. They frequently use this knowledge to dupe the customer. Miller (1964) quotes one sales manager, describing what goes on in the office as follows: "He [the salesman] comes to me and says, 'Here you are' . . . I OK the deal . . . he ain't going to come to me with a bad one . . . he waits, sits down, smokes a cigarette, then goes back to the customer" (p. 20).

Although the process need only take a few moments, it is prolonged so that the customer will get nervous. Presumably, the customer will think the only reason this could take so long is that the deal is being debated hotly. As time passes, the customer will get increasingly nervous and increasingly confident that he or she has indeed driven a hard bargain—perhaps too hard. This is confirmed when the salesperson, on his return to the customer, says he encountered difficulty in having the deal accepted ("you sure got me in a lot of trouble") but that he managed to convince the sales manager ("I got him to accept your deal"). By further implication, the salesperson manages to communicate to the buyer that he is a unique and shrewd negotiator ("I'm glad I don't get many like you") (Miller, 1964, p. 20).

The office, in this case, serves as a tool for fostering the impression of reality that the dealership hopes to convey to the customer, although only because it is thought of as a backstage region even by the customer. This is especially the case in dealerships in which the sales office has windows through which the customer can peek; one would expect to see wild gesticulations and some red faces, although in all probability the manager and seller would be discussing where to go to lunch because the performers know that aurally they are backstage while visually they are on the front stage.

In this case, the car dealership is participating in a complex interaction; it is a version of what Goffman (1974) called a play within a play, used to make audience members think they are seeing a behind-the-scenes interaction that is, of course, happening on stage:

> In brief, a glimpse behind the scenes can be a device for inducing the belief that you are seeing the backstage of something. Obviously, once you've got the staging area and the backstage you've got the whole thing and can feel secure in your frame anchorage. And the moment you feel secure, of course, is the moment you can be diddled. (p. 475)

The sense of security the customer gets in seeing the supposedly backstage rituals of the salesperson and sales manager allows the final phase of the sales process to be completed successfully and amicably, although a good deal of manipulation and misinformation is engaged in before this conclusion can be reached.

Impression Management and Sincerity

Stages and region behavior provide important tools for the manipulation of public perceptions of reality. Combined with scripts, props, and costumes, they allow teams a great deal of control over the impression of reality they convey to audiences. Goffman's analysis is concerned with more than the process of manipulation, however; he is also concerned with the effects of manipulation on the actor. At the most basic level, all the methods described previously, and indeed the very idea of projecting a particular impression of reality, can lead to a certain insincerity. Goffman is very interested in how this insincerity comes about, what actors do to counteract it, and what happens if they are unsuccessful in the attempt to deal with insincerity. The theater example we have been following becomes less relevant at this point; obviously, actors in a play know that the impression of reality they want to project is not "real"; they know they are not Danish princes or poor Londoners. Rather, Goffman is interested in the problems caused by living life *like* a play—on how that affects a person's psychological state and behavior.

As Goffman (1959) claims in the following, whenever actors adopt a role, they must take a position on their belief in the role—they must decide whether they feel that the impression of reality they will project is "true":

> At one extreme, one finds that the performer can be fully taken in by his own act; he can be sincerely convinced that the impression of reality which he stages is the real reality. . . . At the other extreme, we find that the performer may not be taken in at all by his own routine. This possibility is understandable, since no one is in quite as good an observational position to see through the act as the person who puts it on. . . . When the individual has no belief in his own act and no ultimate concern with the beliefs of his audience, we may call him cynical, reserving the term "sincere" for individuals who believe in the impression fostered by their own performances. (pp. 17–18)

It is important to note that although individuals can be anywhere in between these two extremes of belief in their own performance, they must be somewhere— that is, every performer must, consciously or not, have some level of acceptance of the part he or she is playing.

Obviously, in most cases, it will be much easier to present a convincing performance if one is relatively sincere about one's performance, and consequently, many teams will go to great lengths to convince individual performers of the reality of their presentation. The insurance industry works hard to prevent agents from becoming cynical because buyers find it difficult to trust agents who are not committed to their product and because agents are very likely to "burn out" quickly if they do not believe in what they are doing.[3] Agencies are well aware of this and make great efforts to convince their vendors to believe in the product they are selling. To foster genuine belief in the value of life insurance, they promote what Oakes (1990) calls "the philosophy of financial security" (p. 104). This philosophy claims that, macroeconomic trends and luck notwithstanding, each individual is directly responsible for his or her economic lot in life. Furthermore, the purpose of life is, according to this philosophy, to provide financial security for one's self and loved ones. Because each individual is capable of attaining this goal, it is simple to measure people's goodness by their net worth and, more generally, their ability to provide for their family.

Once the insurance agent begins to believe this simple but compelling picture of his or her role, the agent can often be convinced that the role he or she is about to assume is not one of huckster trying to profit off other people's misfortunes but instead approaches that of hero because, as Oakes (1990) explains,

> Life insurance agents constitute the priesthood of the religion of life insurance, the ministers and guardians of financial security planning. Because life

insurance sales is legitimated as a high calling based on ethical imperatives, conscientious agents do not wait for financial exigencies in the lives of prospects to bring in business. For the prospect whose health and security are at stake, tomorrow may be too late. Because of their obligation to safeguard the financial future of prospects, agents are able to take pride in the fact that they are sales personnel. Agents justify their work by conceiving it not as a commercial transaction, but as an exercise of moral responsibility. (p. 106)

In Goffman's language, the industry has an interest in fostering sincerity on the part of their agents. Insurance, for them, must not be merely another commodity but must be something whose value they deeply believe in. Otherwise, the industry suggests, agents will find it impossible to succeed at selling policies because, as the Prudential company's training manual claims, "if you are insincere, your prospect will sense it" (W. Walsh as cited in Oakes, 1989, p. 247).

At the other end of the spectrum of belief, according to Miller, are some car salespeople. Rather than trying to convince themselves that they are doing unappreciative customers a tremendous favor, they tend to realize that they are exploiting buyers but construct a worldview that uses skill in haggling as the basis for determining worth. As Miller (1964) explains,

A majority of automobile salesmen admit that their customers regard them as "con men," who attempt to "put one over" on the buyer. In informal conversations regarding what makes a "good salesman," salesmen describe their role in much the same way: for example, "Anybody can sell something they [the customers] want but the real bit is to make them think they need exactly what you got to sell, only more of it." The consensus appears to be that the "good" salesman is highly proficient at manipulating the situation and customer in such fashion as to produce a favorable deal for the salesman. The object of the sales transaction, as an experienced older salesman expressed it, is to "make them think they are getting something instead of losing anything." . . . Their behavior appears organized around the premise that monetary and social success are the results of opportunistic dealing. (p. 22)

This highly cynical view treats the impression of reality the salesperson wants to project as a sham; furthermore, everyone but the customer knows that it is a sham.

Depending on how cynical people are, it may be possible for them to operate on a day-to-day basis with this assessment of their role. Most people, however, are uncomfortable with the view that they are actively exploiting suckers; they want to think of themselves as decent people. Car salespeople frequently justify their cynicism by claiming that the customers are just as bad or worse; they project the negative aspects of their own roles onto customers. Thus, as Miller (1964) writes, the salesperson sees customers as

opportunistic, "out to make or save a buck any way they can." By selectively perceiving and, if necessary, by misinterpreting the behavior of the customer to fit his own pattern of expectations, the salesman is able to rationalize the exploitative and manipulative aspects of his role, making his work acceptable to himself and tolerable to others. (p. 20)

Why is it necessary for the salesperson to go to such lengths to justify his or her behavior? The profit motive in deceiving and manipulating customers is quite clear, so it might seem obvious that sellers should do anything possible within the law to rip customers off and not worry about it. The near-universal desire not to do so suggests that people are not comfortable with a tremendous amount of cynicism about their roles. They would prefer not to have to establish and maintain what Goffman calls "role distance,"[4] which means that they dissociate themselves from, rather than wholeheartedly embrace, the role.

The role of salesperson is critical to the sales process. The individual selling the car, however, has more roles than just salesperson to maintain at any given time.

A particular performer, for instance, may want to project the images of "parent," "nice guy or nice person," "music lover," and "good friend" all at once. All these roles, however, are, at least to a certain extent, counteracted by a willingness to glee-fully exploit uninformed customers; the individual probably does not want to think of himself or herself, and certainly does not want to be thought of by others, as a greedy, underhanded jerk. Thus, conflicting roles in an individual's life may cause distinct problems because the demands of one role may be incompatible with the demands of other roles.

There are various ways to attempt to reconcile these roles. The salespeople described previously did it by claiming that they were simply protecting themselves from greedy, exploitative customers; the customers are the bad guys, and the seller unfortunately has to respond in kind to survive. This does not make the seller a "bad guy" or "bad person" because, in normal circumstances, the seller would never resort to manipulating people the way he or she does to sell cars. Other methods of coping that Goffman suggests include joking or including other parts of contradic-tory roles in the situation at hand; the seller may try to prove that he or she is a good friend by acting unnecessarily friendly toward the client, or the seller may take an ironic stance toward one of his or her roles. This is not easy to pull off in car sales, but it could occur if, for instance, a salesperson made subtle jokes about the com-pany's promotional literature, fellow employees, or even the act of selling.

These attempts to reconcile roles all involve, to a certain extent, emotion manage-ment. As noted previously, flight attendants have a somewhat unique job—one that focuses considerable attention on managing their emotions. The most important tool of the flight attendants, they are frequently told in training, is a ready smile (Hochschild, 1983, p. 105). Particular airlines emphasize that flight attendants should enjoy being flirted with or should go out of their way to be friendly to rude, drunk, or unreasonable passengers. In cases of role conflict, however, flight attendants can-not, like many workers, resort to the expression of emotions common to other roles to resolve the tension because their employers specifically stake out the emotional space of the attendant as a vital part of the attendant's role. As Hochschild observes,

Some workers conclude that only one self (usually the nonwork self) is the "real" self. Others, and they are in the majority, will decide that each self is meaningful and real in its own different way and time. . . . Such workers are generally more adept at acting, and the idea of a separation between the two selves is not only acceptable but welcome to them. They speak more matter-of-factly about their emotional labor in clearly defined and sometimes mechanistic ways: "I get in gear, I get revved up, I get plugged in." They talk of their feelings not as spontaneous, natural occurrences but as objects they have learned to govern and control. (p. 133)

In either case, flight attendants must recognize that their roles are fundamentally incompatible and must draw a clear division between them.

As soon as attendants realize that they are operating with contradictory goals, they will be in trouble; they will have increasing difficulty in appreciating their jobs and their passengers. Airlines, not surprisingly, do everything possible to put off this realization because the simplest way to convince passengers that the emotions of their attendants are sincere is for the emotions to actually be sincere. Thus, airlines spend a great deal of time in training suggesting ways that flight attendants may merge the seemingly contradictory emotional roles they are forced to deal with. Early in the education process, and frequently thereafter, flight attendants are trained in methods designed to actively manipulate their emotional states to avoid conflict. Delta hopes that, if flight attendants can connect with passengers on some level, they will be able to put forth a show of genuine emotion. For this reason, Hochschild (1983) notes,

The deepest appeal in the Delta training program was to the trainee's capacity to act as if the airplane cabin (where she works) were her home (where she doesn't work). Trainees were asked to think of a passenger as if he were a "personal guest in your living room." (p. 105)

One graduate elaborated,

You think how the new person resembles someone you know. *You see your sister's eyes in someone sitting at that seat.* That makes you want to put out for them. I like to think of the cabin as the living room of my own home. When someone drops in [at home], you may not know them, but you get something for them. You put that on a grand scale—thirty-six passengers per flight attendant—but *it's the same feeling.* (p. 105)

This approach, if successful, could merge many of the roles that are likely to come into conflict for the flight attendant. The attendant's role demands a display of genuine affection, but for most people, genuine affection is reserved for friends and relatives. By inviting flight attendants to think of passengers as friends or relatives, it may be easier for them to reconcile their emotional needs with their employer's emotional demands.

Of course, most passengers are not relatives, friends, or even acquaintances; therefore, the attempt to see them as such is likely to break down fairly quickly, especially in the case of the troublesome passengers whom flight attendants are likely to be forced to deal with more often than they would like. Training programs anticipate this and attempt to build in safeguards to delay the moment when a flight attendant simply can no longer deal with the stresses of the job. One way is to think of irate, unruly, or otherwise troublesome fliers as children attempting to get attention; this not only helps the attendant connect with the customer, in an emotional way, but also allows flight attendants to rationalize their role distancing by claiming that it is caused only by particularly immature customers and not by a fundamental problem in the constitution of the role.

There is only so much value to this coping strategy, however; at some point, flight attendants will not be able to think of drunken businessmen as children. Training programs tend to stress one last check on role-distancing behavior, this one more social than those mentioned previously. Flight attendants tend to work in teams and generally form a strong sense of group unity while flying particular routes. Companies exploit this by training attendants to recognize morale problems among coworkers and to try to counteract them (Hochschild, 1983, p. 115). This does not really do much to address the problem at hand, however; although friends may be able to cheer each other up, they will not be able to reconcile the conflicting roles that got the flight attendant into trouble in the first place. At the end of the day, the cynical flight attendant still must wrestle with the options of seeing his or her role as "fake" or "real."

Whatever option employees adopt, they must, to a certain extent, be insincere. If employees decide that only their "natural" (i.e., off-job) role is real, each action mandated by their role as flight attendants will come off as "phony" because it does not reflect their nonwork, real self. If employees decide that it is impossible to adopt both roles at once, they will constantly be aware, as flight attendants, that they are in some significant sense not being "true to themselves." Insincerity thus becomes a fundamental component of their daily life. Because of the special emotional demands placed on flight attendants, the ways in which their role by definition forces them to feel some insincerity are quite apparent.

According to Stanford Lyman and Marvin Scott (1974), "Goffman seems to see that a brooding and suspicious sense of inauthenticity is the basic condition of performative human existence" (p. 107). Roles always have a great potential to come into conflict, in countless ways. A working mother, for instance, may feel that, by working long hours, she is not dedicating enough time to her children and simultaneously feel, while spending time with her children, that she is neglecting her work.

Conflicting Role Expectations

Minor conflicts arise in all kinds of work situations. One very common source of trouble is an inability to reconcile the demands of a sales job with perceived ideals of service. Kraft (1994) reports a discrepancy between messages handed down by management as follows:

> [Sales contests] imply that it is the quantity of the product that one sells that determines the quality of the clerk's work performance. The obvious message [is that] what is important becomes how much of any one thing is sold. . . . However, the company would, at other times, lead staff to believe that it is more concerned with the overall quality of service delivered. . . . They appear to contradict the sales contest message by claiming [Disney] is not exclusively "hard sell." In short, they expect and explicitly train the Cast Member to practice two contradictory styles. (pp. 10–11)

For clerks, if this problem exists, it arises only because management forces it. Insurance agents also find this problem inherent in the sales process. Insurance agents must convince others and must themselves believe that they are professionals dedicated to the financial well-being of their customers. What counts most to them and their employment future, however, is the ability to generate sales. Generally, professionals do not have to convince people that their services are valuable; doctors do not call people during dinner, convince them that they are ill, and try to schedule an appointment for surgery as soon as possible. Insurance agents, however, are forced to convince people of the need for coverage and then offer a range of alternatives to fulfill this newfound need. There is, therefore, an obvious and necessary friction for any insurance agent between two conflicting role expectations. To be professionals, they must worry about what their client needs and wants. To be salespeople, however, they must be most concerned with the bottom line.

Another type of conflict arises when it becomes impossible to reconcile demands for service and speed. Retailers, for instance, might be told to be personable to customers, to converse with them, and so on. They might be called to task if the actual application of these instructions leads to delay, however—that is, if in talking to a customer they seem to be neglecting other aspects of their job. A revealing example is again provided by flight attendants, who found in the 1970s that, due to an industrywide speed-up, they were forced to give the same amount of emotional labor in significantly less time (Hochschild, 1983, p. 122). In the 1980s, this got even worse because airlines found that, to stay in business, they had to make fewer flight attendants attend to more customers in less time. Something had to give, as stated in the following:

> Before the speed-up, most workers sustained the cheerful good will that good service requires. They did so for the most part proudly. . . . After the speed-up, when asked to make personal human contact at an inhuman speed, they cut back on their emotion work and grew detached. (Hochschild, 1983, p. 126)

Of course, the ideal of service is not abandoned by either management or the flight attendant. The role demands placed on the employee do not change but must, for better or worse, be negotiated by each individual flight attendant.

The demands of the market, whether for speed or raw sales, sometimes are simply incompatible with the roles it compels individuals to adopt. When role distancing occurs, it might seem logical for people to recognize the conflicting nature of their situation and attempt to reconcile their discrepant roles. It is often very difficult, however, for agents caught up in the action to understand that their problems are caused by fundamental inconsistencies in the roles they are expected to adopt; rather, they tend to blame themselves, assuming that the problem is not that roles or role expectations are incompatible but that they are somehow "not good enough" to live up to their assigned roles, because, as Lyman and Scott (1974) note,

> when people experience a suspension in their own belief in the naturalism or "authenticity" of the performance put on by themselves or others they approach a phenomenological understanding of the dramatic fundament of human existence. These suspensions, however . . . are not usually taken to be a clue to the phenomenology of human existence itself, but rather to be an exposure of the "fraudulence" and "bad faith" of certain [performers]. (pp. 110–111)

"Real" Selves in a Commodified World

For insurance agents who cannot convince themselves of the authenticity of their own performances, instead of blaming the fundamental contradiction implicit in the roles they are asked to adopt, there is a tendency to blame themselves. Thus, they will think something similar to the following: "A *real* professional could manage to reconcile the demand to sell at all costs with the need to make service the utmost priority. I cannot. Therefore, I am flawed." Of course, if the agent wants to keep eating, he or she must continue to pretend to be a professional, and every performance will highlight some way in which professionalism is antithetical to the person's identity.

Similarly, flight attendants caught up in the inauthenticity of their emotional displays will find themselves torn between a desire to continue the job and find some way to fake the emotions they "should" authentically experience, on one hand, and a growing recognition that each painted-on smile is more strained and further suggests that they are not cut out for this job, on the other. Role distancing thus tends to get increasingly worse as time goes on and more and more inauthentic productions are delivered. Due to the very nature of role conflict, it is difficult to resolve distancing without fundamentally changing the definition of either the self or the situation that one wants to project. The alienated actor must either quit the job that is causing the role problems or somehow learn to deal with the conflict, either by becoming highly cynical or somehow changing the personal roles that are thought of as constituting the "real" self.

Of course, it is always much more pleasant to give up a work self than a real self; we should not expect people to abandon their perceptions of themselves. In a tight labor market, however, we also should not expect people to give up their jobs, especially because they have likely received years of training, and to switch careers would make them start at the bottom of the employment ladder again, which for someone approaching midlife can be financially disastrous. Cynicism, it seems, becomes a pretty reasonable option by default. Insurance agents might give up their ideals of service and professionalism and only pretend to offer these to the extent that they help the bottom line. Flight attendants might learn to effectively display friendliness, good cheer, and so on when feeling the absolute opposite. In both cases, the alienated professional will turn to a reliance on acting to reconcile his or her unpleasant circumstances.

Thus, Goffman's dramaturgy comes full circle. Social reality is a performed event, highly dependent on the various components of theater. For particular individuals to effectively communicate the social reality most advantageous to them, they must adopt roles regarding their vocations. At a certain point, however, these work roles will almost inevitably collide with the nonwork roles individuals hold dear, their supposed real selves. When this happens, individuals have a wide variety of options, but ultimately none of them is likely to fully resolve the conflict; the best solution, in many cases, is to gloss over the conflict by acting—by using the tools of the stage. Goffman (1959) emphasizes that he is using theater as a metaphor and claims that ultimately, the world is not a stage, and it should not be difficult for readers to find major differences between the two. Given the complexity and compelling character of his dramaturgical sociology, however, it can be hard for readers to share Goffman's asserted willingness to abandon the metaphor of the theater.

Notes

1. Although this book was central to our analysis, we also relied on the following works by Goffman: *Encounters.* (1961). Indianapolis, IN: Bobbs-Merrill; *Interaction ritual.* (1967). Garden City, NY: Doubleday; *Relations in public.* (1971). New York: Harper & Row. For thoughtful commentaries on Goffman's contribution to sociology, see the following: Burns, T. (1992). *Erving Goffman.* London: Routledge; Denzin, N. (2003). Much ado about Goffman. In A. J. Trevino (Ed.)., *Goffman's legacy* (pp. 127–142). Lanham, MD: Rowman & Littlefield; Drew, P., & Wotton, A. (Eds.). (1988). *Erving Goffman: Exploring the interaction order.* Boston: Northeastern University Press; Fine, G. A., & Manning, P. (2000). Erving Goffman. In G. Ritzer (Ed.), *The Blackwell companion to contemporary social theorists* (pp. 456–485). Oxford, UK: Blackwell; Lemert, C. (1997). Goffman. In *The Goffman reader* (pp. ix–xiii). Oxford, UK: Blackwell; Lyman, S. M. (1973). Civilization: Contents, discontents, and malcontents. *Contemporary Sociology, 2,* 360–366; Manning, P. (2005). Erving Goffman. In G. Ritzer (Ed.), *Encyclopedia of social theory* (pp. 333–339). Thousand Oaks, CA: Sage; Schell, T. J. (2005). Looking-glass self: Goffman as a symbolic interactionist. *Symbolic Interaction, 28,* 147–166.

2. Hochschild tended to use "stewardess" and "flight attendant" interchangeably because, during the time of her study, most were women, and even today the vast majority of flight attendants are women. In airline advertisements, most images of flight attendants depict females. We generally prefer the more gender-neutral "flight attendant," although the subjects of Hochschild's study were overwhelmingly women.

3. At this point, Kraft's analysis of Disney stores becomes less relevant because sales jobs with Disney are conceived of not as careers but, for the most part, as short-term work. Certainly, all the features of alienation and role distancing discussed here would apply to someone who tried to model his or her professional role around that advocated by the Disney corporation.

4. Although Goffman hints at role distance briefly in *The Presentation of Self in Everyday Life* (1959), he offers a much more thorough exposition of the phenomenon in a later essay

titled simply "Role Distance." For an analysis of this essay, see Burns (1992), *Erving Goffman.* As an antidote to role distance, see Schweingruber, D. (2006). Success through a positive mental attitude? The role of positive thinking in door-to-door sales. *The Sociological Quarterly, 47,* 41–68.

References

Goffman, E. (1959). *The presentation of self in everyday life.* Garden City, NY: Doubleday.

Goffman, E. (1974). *Frame analysis.* New York: Harper & Row.

Hochschild, A. (1983). *The managed heart.* Berkeley: University of California Press.

Kraft, K. (1994). *The rationalization of fantasy.* Unpublished paper, Augustana College, Rock Island, Illinois.

Lyman, S., & Scott, M. (1974). *The drama of social reality.* New York: Oxford University Press.

Miller, S. (1964). The social base of sales behavior. *Social Problems, 12*(1), 15–24.

Oakes, G. (1989, Winter). Sales as a vocation: The moral ethos of personal sales. *International Journal of Politics, Culture, and Society, 3*(2), 237–253.

Oakes, G. (1990, Fall). The American life insurance salesman: A secular theodicy. *International Journal of Politics, Culture, and Society, 4*(1), 95–112.

DISCUSSION QUESTIONS

1. Enter the same store in a local shopping mall on three or four different occasions and determine the operative sales script. Describe it. What does this corporate-written script say about the kinds of customers the store is catering to and the image of the store's products that is being conveyed?

2. When people interview for a job, they frequently define the process as amounting to an attempt to "sell themselves" to a would-be employer. Use your own experience to describe the techniques you have used in job interviews to accomplish the presentation of self that you thought would make you as attractive an applicant as possible (think about both backstage and front stage aspects of your performance).

3. Door-to-door salespersons and those involved in telemarketing must contend with frequent rejection by would-be customers. Using the ideas of impression management and sincerity, discuss the sorts of techniques that people in such occupations might use to continue to be motivated and to make the occasional sale in spite of many rejections.

4. Discuss the role of costumes and the background props and sets used in consumer culture today. Identify two different chain businesses that sell the same goods (e.g., two restaurant chains such as Applebee's and Hooters). Describe how the costumes and stage settings of both institutions serve to create distinctive identities. Do you think customers view these places as authentic? Are there different or similar clienteles for these different businesses?

5. The idea that we are all actors playing various roles has been interpreted by some critics of Goffman to mean that we are all basically presenting ourselves out of a manipulative self-interest, and therefore we cannot speak about an authentic self beneath the surface. In other words, these critics think Goffman offers a cynical view of human nature. What do you think?

CHAPTER 12

Contrasts of Carnival

*Mardi Gras Between the
Modern and the Postmodern*

Kevin Fox Gotham

***Kevin Fox Gotham**, PhD, is the Associate Dean of Academic Affairs and Professor of Sociology at Tulane University. He has served as a program director for the National Science Foundation in Washington, DC. His research interests focus on how cities develop, how they change, how they affect people, and what they might look like in the future. Most of his early research has concentrated on the significance of racial discrimination in post–World War II urban planning and on the role of federal housing policy in facilitating residential segregation. His book* Race, Real Estate, and Uneven Development: The Kansas City Experience, 1900–2000 *(2002) explores the interlocking nature of racial discrimination and class factors in the origin and development of racial residential segregation over the course of the 20th century. This chapter reflects his current research, which concentrates on the impact of urban tourism on U.S. cities, with a focus on the transformation of pre-Katrina New Orleans into an entertainment hub. He uses the insights of theorists of modernity and particularly of postmodernity in his analysis of Mardi Gras. A fuller account of this research can be found in his book* Authentic New Orleans: Race, Culture, and Tourism in the Big Easy *(2007).*

Over the past few decades, scholars across a variety of disciplines have focused their attention on describing the emergence of a new and uncertain postmodern era. The term *postmodern* is part of larger lexicon of "post" terms—post-industrialism, post-Marxism, post-metropolis, post-Fordism, post-consumerism, and post-structuralism—that anticipate the development of novel types of social organization, power, culture, and aesthetic practices. Diverse thinkers imply that the rise of a globalized form of capitalism, a restructuring of space and territorial identity, and the ascendency of information technologies and media-saturated society intimate a new epoch of chaos, fragmentation, discontinuity, and ephemerality (Harvey, 1989; Soja, 2000). On one hand, postmodernism is not a new term but has a rich and diverse history as reflected in the writings of historian Bernard Rosenberg; architectural scholar Charles Jencks; and sociologists C. Wright Mills, Amitai Etzioni, and Daniel Bell (for an overview, see Best & Kellner, 1991, Chapter 1). On the other hand, a plethora of contrasting postmodern positions now cut across sociology, cultural studies, aesthetics, literature, philosophy, political science, and psychology, among many other fields. Thus, it is now common to see analyses of postmodern society, postmodern war, postmodern art, postmodern music, postmodern literature, postmodern film, postmodern architecture, and so on (for recent views, see Campbell, 2005; Jones, 2003; Magnusson, 2003). The postmodern readings of contemporary society and culture emphasize difference, plurality, and complexity; reject the idea that our theories and methods can represent a social reality; and embrace nonscientific and anti-scientific forms of theorizing and interpretation.

In this chapter, I analyze the Mardi Gras celebration in New Orleans as an expression of larger trends affecting the modern as well as the postmodern world. As reflected in literary, film, and music sources, New Orleans is probably most often identified with Mardi Gras, a celebration that symbolizes the city's collective consciousness while anchoring a vast tourism industry of hotels, convention facilities, and gambling. Traditionally, the Carnival season in New Orleans consists of a series of balls and parades from January 6 (Twelfth Night, or the Feast of the Epiphany) to Mardi Gras Day, or "Fat Tuesday," the day before Ash Wednesday and the beginning of Lent. Before the Civil War, Carnival and Mardi Gras developed as a relatively spontaneous and indigenous celebration for local residents that included public masking, masquerade balls, rambunctious street parades, and widespread frivolity. The second half of the 19th century witnessed the growth of new Carnival clubs, krewes (organizations that plan and stage parades), and cultural traditions in New Orleans. During this time, city leaders and economic elites began promoting the local festival as a tourist attraction. By the end of the century, American and European travel writers advised readers that Mardi Gras in New Orleans was a lavish festival that expressed civic pride, community identity, and a local attitude of *"Laissez le bon temps rouler"* (let the good times roll). As the 20th century unfolded, the growth of media coverage, international publicity, and promotional campaigns helped create an enduring public image of Mardi Gras as the most extravagant celebration staged in any American city (Kinser, 1990; Mitchell, 1995). Today, although other cities around the world celebrate Mardi Gras, none has the intemperate and licentious reputation, long-standing cultural traditions, spectacular floats and parades, formal balls, and tourism infrastructure to accommodate the thousands of tourists that visit New Orleans each year.

Over the past three decades or so, Mardi Gras has become permeated by new global flows of tourism investment, intensified media coverage and advertising, and enhanced government attempts to commodify and sell the celebration to corporate sponsors. A variety of corporations are increasingly attaching Mardi Gras symbols and motifs to their products to stimulate consumer demand. *Entertainment Tonight,* MTV, and the Playboy Channel telecast live reports from New Orleans every year, and camera crews from the BBC, Japan, and other countries showcase the festivities to a worldwide audience. Across the United States, groups use Mardi Gras as a theme for proms, parties, and meetings; several Las Vegas casinos feature a Mardi Gras motif; and Disney World and Universal Studios regularly schedule New Orleans-style parades. In spite of its extra-local and globalized character, Mardi Gras continues to exhibit features of an indigenous and localized premodern festival marked by rich emotional ties, long-standing and venerable traditions, and a well-defined culture and historical authenticity. Today, many dozens of carnival krewes, parade clubs, and local cultural organizations work to constitute Mardi Gras as a community ceremony and a set of cultural practices that reflect the joie de vivre of New Orleans. In addition, although Mardi Gras has changed over the decades, it has remained an organization of rituals and symbolic patterns that local people use to make sense of their experiences, construct notions of local authenticity, and confront the challenges and problems of modern and postmodern society. In short, Mardi Gras is ubiquitous and multifaceted. While Mardi Gras is a local celebration, it is also a marketing slogan to stimulate consumer demand for corporate products, and an imaging device used by private and public actors to enhance the tourism appeal of the city and its region (Gotham, 2002, 2005a, 2005b). The goal of this chapter is to deploy concepts from both modern and postmodern approaches. I maintain that it is a mistake to argue that the transformations that have affected Mardi Gras over the past several decades are primarily an expression of modernity or postmodernity. As I show, we can conceptualize and explain Mardi Gras using Karl Marx's theory of commodification; Max Weber's notion of rationalization; and the postmodern concepts of simulation, implosion, hyperreality, and sign-value.[1]

Between the Modern and Postmodern

The claim of a new social form, a new historical epoch, and a new mode of social and individual experience lies at the heart of postmodern analyses of contemporary society and culture (Best & Kellner, 1997; Dickens & Fontana, 1994; Seidman & Wagner, 1992). Building on these insights, diverse thinkers imply that the postmodern symbolizes widespread sociocultural change, but they disagree over its form, impact, and periodization. In a comprehensive survey of the literature, Antonio (1998) suggests that "different sides in the postmodernism debate speak past one another. Heated exchanges are complicated by the term's multiple meanings and conflation of fundamental usage" (p. 24). It is not clear in many debates, for example, if scholars are talking about a shift to a so-called new era of "postmodernity," the impact of "postmodernism" as a cultural form, or the merits and limitations of postmodern theory and method. Best and Kellner (1991, 1997) make a distinction between *postmodernity* as the social and political epoch that generally follows the modern era in a historical sense; *postmodernism* as a form of politics, identity, and set of cultural products (in art, movies, architecture, and so on) that are different from modern politics, identities, and culture; and, finally, *postmodern social theory* as a new mode of theorizing that is distinct from modern social theory (see also Dickens & Fontana, 1994). As Ritzer (1997) puts it, "the idea of the postmodern encompasses *a new historical epoch, new cultural products, and a new type of theorizing about the world*" (p. 6, emphasis in original).

Within the mode of theory and method, the postmodern turn emerged during the 1970s and 1980s as a major challenge to both the basic tenets of modern social theory and method, and sociology more generally. Although scholars elaborated a host of different postmodern theories and modes of inquiry, five major assumptions came to unite the postmodern: (a) a celebration of difference, identity, and multiculturalism by emphasizing local narratives and micro theory; (b) a rejection of unifying, totalizing, and universal schemes in favor of an emphasis on plurality, difference, and complexity; (c) an abandonment of closed structures and fixed meanings and an adoption of uncertainty, contingency, ambiguity, and irony; (d) a replacement of pragmatic truth seeking with hermeneutics and cultural and theoretical relativism; and (e) an emphasis on removing boundaries within and between academic and cultural disciplines (Best & Kellner, 1997). Emphasizing epochal rupture and radical discontinuity, proponents of postmodernism argued that modernity was finished and that the Enlightenment's emphasis on individual freedom, rationality, progress, and the power of science to better the human condition was bankrupt (for an overview, see Pescosolido & Rubin, 2000). Postmodernists questioned the viability of objectivity and causal analysis in the social sciences and argued that modern theory in the tradition of Marx, Weber, Durkheim, and others was obsolete (for a critical overview, see Antonio & Kellner, 1994). Since the 1980s, radical postmodernists have continued to assail modern theory for its scientism that views knowledge as cumulative, coherent, and rational; its foundationalism that aims to find a vocabulary that mirrors the social world and articulates a universal condition; and its essentialism that supposedly fails to account for social differences based on gender, ethnicity, or sexual orientation (for overviews, see Best & Kellner, 1997; Dickens & Fontana, 1994; Seidman & Wagner, 1992).

During the 1990s, postmodern orientations began to be incorporated into sociological theorizing and mainstreamed into the larger sociology discipline. Theorists such as Robert Antonio, David Harvey, and Douglas Kellner, among many others, contended that the tendency toward relativism and lack of sociological grounding in postmodernism provided little for the social sciences and contributed to apolitical nihilism and vacuous theorizing. In particular, a past president of the American Sociological Association, Joe Feagin (1998), asserted that "a postmodern analysis that privileges cultural complexity and diffuseness . . . runs the danger of ignoring or playing down the still central structure-process factors of class, race, and gender" (p. 6). By this time, scholars were making distinctions between "strong" and "moderate" postmodern approaches in an effort to come to terms with postmodernism's ambiguity and diversity of contrasting and conflicting positions.[2] During this decade, scholarly debates in sociology journals and a plethora of books and edited volumes critiqued, developed, and applied neo-postmodern perspectives to reconceptualize traditional sociological categories—such as agency, structure, gender, social movements, culture, sexuality—while noting the limitations of postmodern approaches.[3] By 2000, articles in the top two American sociology journals, the *American Journal of Sociology* and the *American Sociological Review,* situated postmodern debates within a broader history of the discipline of sociology while noting the opportunities postmodern discourses provided for a renewal and strengthening of modern social theory (Antonio, 2000; Pescosolido & Rubin, 2000).

Today, as Edgley (2003) points out, postmodernism "is here to stay" and "its central tenets are rapidly becoming part of the basic conceptual apparatus of sociology" (p. 1). Postmodern concepts such as deconstruction, decentering, foundationalism, hyperreality, identity, implosion, logocentric, narrative, performativity, simulacrum, text, and totalizing have entered the vocabulary of sociology and are now routinely used by sociologists in their empirical and theoretical research. Movements are afoot to identify convergences between postmodern and modern theory, reinterpret modern theorists and theories through a postmodern lens (for examples, see Bergey, 2004; Fontana, 2005; Weinstein & Weinstein, 1994), and point out blind spots and discordant features to reconstruct rather than dismiss modern theory (Antonio, 2000; Antonio & Bonanno, 2000; Gotham & Krier, 2008; Mirchandani, 2005). Although there remain stark epistemological, analytical, and theoretical differences between sociology and postmodernism, it is clear that we can use the resources of both modern theories and postmodern approaches to illuminate, critique, and analyze the interactions of social structure, human agency, and societal transformation. At a conceptual level, postmodernism offers a loose set of ideas and sensitizing concepts to understand events and processes going on in the world that are novel though not discontinuous with the past. As sociologists, we must pay attention to new ideas and modes of explanation that challenge conventional ways of understanding as well as build on knowledge developed painstakingly over many generations, granting that such knowledge is always limited. It is not enough to assert that present trends and novelties can be explained with long-standing theoretical orientations, traditional conceptual frameworks, or conventional ways of thinking and understanding. To the extent that theories are developed in response to contemporary problems and societal anomalies, we can view the increasing popularity of postmodern ideas as offering fresh insights and innovative views to help us understand the volatility and ambiguity of the present era.

Against either/or positions that assert we are still within modernity or have entered a new postmodern era, I would argue that we are currently between the modern and the postmodern. I show that there are identifiable features of both the modern and the postmodern in Mardi Gras, and postmodern concepts sensitize us to the new forces that are affecting society and culture. One of the central tenets of postmodernism is that we live in "the age of simulation" to the extent that capitalism has moved into a new stage of development where the production of simulations rather than commodities per se now dominates the world (Baudrillard, 1983c). The term *simulation* implies a play of entertaining images, spectacles, and attractions that obliterate distinctions between real and illusory conditions or events. Once simulations come to define the world, reality becomes "hyperreal" whereby the real is produced according to manufactured models. In this situation, people view the image as more authentic (hyperreal) than reality, and the boundary between images and reality implodes. Many scholars view implosion as akin to the de-differentiation or blurring of boundaries between social institutions, classes, politics, culture, and other social activities (for overviews, see Harvey, 1989; Lash, 1990; Urry, 2002). In a world of simulation and implosion, the power of distinctions collapses and the fantasy worlds of celebrity, entertainment, and spectacle become the standard and code to evaluate real life. The unreal Disneyland becomes the framework for building communities throughout the United States; the mythical town of Mayberry in *The Andy Griffith Show* becomes the model people use to measure the "authenticity" of small-town rural life; and the fictional *CSI* shows provide a code jurors use to evaluate prosecutorial evidence in real-life crime cases. In the realm of simulation, media and consumer society replace lived experience, the passive gaze at images supplants active social participation, and new forms of alienation induce social atomization at a more intense and abstract level than in previous societies. In short, for postmodernists, contemporary life is ruled by the logic of simulation where social reality is not "experienced" by creative and reflexive human agents but is manufactured according to the dictates of bureaucratized entertainment and commodified media culture.

As I point out, using postmodern concepts can illuminate a series of sociocultural changes that has affected New Orleans over the past several decades and suggest a more fundamental set of transformations of U.S. cities and metropolitan areas more generally. My argument is that we need to explain both continuities and discontinuities in current societal transformations and use a both/and logic in our analyses rather than an either/or logic. In other words, we need to theorize both novelties and discontinuities as well as clarify the bases for ongoing trajectories of development that flow from and are contiguous with broad historical trends. If one of the central objectives of social theory is to provide an interpretive understanding of the world, then postmodern concepts and heuristics can help illuminate processes of societal development and pinpoint novelties and continuities with the past. Just as there is no one coherent modern theory or theory of modernity, there is no single postmodern theory or unified set of assumptions to explain the postmodern condition. Like modern social theories, postmodern theories are plural, hybrid, conflictual, and eclectic.

The Production of Simulacra: Mardi Gras as Commodity-Spectacle

The concept of simulation flows out of a long history of intellectual efforts to theorize the spread of commodification to non-commodified realms of society, including religion, politics, art and culture, leisure, and entertainment. Beginning with Karl Marx's penetrating critique of the commodity form and continuing through Georg Lukacs, the Frankfurt School, Henri Lefebvre, and many others, diverse theorists have developed new concepts and heuristic devices to capture the pervasiveness of commodity relations in modern society. The concept of simulation reflects the latest attempts by scholars to explain the accelerating pace of commodification and related processes of rationalization and globalization in everyday life.[4] In the case of New Orleans, simulation draws our attention to the various ways in which powerful economic elites, corporate firms, and tourism boosters use the logic of spectacle and entertainment to transform the Mardi Gras celebration into a major tourist attraction and explicit money-making operation. Over the decades, New Orleans city officials and elites have created several tourism organizations; devised promotional strategies; and built attractions to increase tourist travel, commodify space for tourist consumption, and enhance the economic prosperity of the central city. These tourism organizations include the New Orleans Metropolitan Convention and Visitors Bureau, the New Orleans Tourism Marketing Corporation, the New Orleans Multicultural Tourism Network, and the Mayor's Office of Tourism and Arts. The various tourist attractions include the building of a domed stadium, a festival mall, a massive convention center, a major theme park, and a World War II museum, among others. The city has also staged many mega-events, including the 1984 World's Fair, periodic Super Bowls and (Nokia) Sugar Bowls, the NCAA basketball tournaments, the Jazz and Heritage Festival, the Essence Festival, and so on. The hotel industry has grown considerably over the past few decades as indicated by the skyrocketing number of hotel rooms in the metropolitan area, from 4,750 in 1960 to more than 33,000 by 2004 (Gotham, 2005b). In the 1990s, global entertainment franchises, including Harrah's casino, Hard Rock Cafe, Hooters, Tower Records, House of Blues, and Planet Hollywood, have opened in New Orleans (Gotham, 2002, 2005a, 2005b).

The development of New Orleans as a tourist destination parallels a huge growth in the annual number of parades and Carnival organizations (krewes), the number of visitors who attend Mardi Gras in New Orleans, and the money generated through the annual celebration. From 1857 to the late 1930s, there were approximately 4–6 parades per Carnival season in New Orleans. The number of parades grew to 10 in 1940, to 21 by 1960, and reached 25 by 1970. During the 1970s and 1980s, the number of parades increased dramatically, reaching a peak of 55 in 1986, and remaining between 45 and 53 ever since. In 2002, the New Orleans Metropolitan Convention and Tourism Bureau estimated that there were more than 6.1 million total parade viewers, 2.24 million day trippers or visitors staying with friends, and almost 1 million tourists staying in hotels during Mardi Gras. Local leaders have tracked the estimated economic impact of the celebration since the mid-1980s, and in 2000, overall spending from Mardi Gras hit the $1 billion mark for the first time, according to one economist (McLain, 2000).[5] "Economically, [Mardi Gras is] by far the single-largest special event," said Marc Morial, Mayor of New Orleans from 1994–2002. "It's bigger than Jazzfest, it's bigger than the Sugar Bowl, it's bigger than the Super Bowl" ("For New Orleans," 1999, p. 6). "It's the major annual event for this city," said Michele Moore, spokesperson for the mayor's office. "We build many of our tourism and marketing strategies around Mardi Gras" (Charles, 1995).

Over the past few decades, an array of public and private groups have emerged to "simulate" Mardi Gras using sophisticated advertising techniques aimed at promoting desire and fantasy, art and design directed to the production of commercial spaces, and other highly refined techniques of image production and distribution.

Major corporations such as Bacardi rum, Southern Comfort, Coors beer, Kool cigarettes, and other companies are increasingly attaching Mardi Gras symbols and motifs to their products to stimulate consumer demand. Corporations have long used Mardi Gras imagery and themes to sell their products, but what is new today is the increasing rationalization, homogenization, and standardization of corporate marketing and image-building efforts. Although there is considerable diversity in the type and style of simulation, what is common is that corporations recognize the profit potential that comes from connecting their products to Mardi Gras, an event known throughout the world and rich with easily identifiable images of fun and entertainment. Coors Light and Heineken now produce Mardi Gras commemorative beer cans and T-shirts that they distribute nationally. Playboy.com has now established a regular presence in New Orleans during Mardi Gras, beaming images of elaborate parties and playmates tossing beads and flirting with tourists. Since 2000, Bacardi has been manufacturing and selling "Bacardi Gras" kits of hats, beads, and Hurricane drink recipes to bars around the nation not just during the Carnival season but year-round. In 2001, Captain Morgan's Spiced Rum sponsored its "Bombshells From the Bayou," while *Stuff* magazine presented its "Stuff Girls" entourage on Bourbon Street in the French Quarter. In 2001, Southern Comfort employed a staff of "brand ambassadors" and hired three stars of MTV's *Real World New Orleans* to market the beverage. The company also dispatched members of its marketing team to Buffalo, San Diego, and St. Louis to show consumers how they can use Southern Comfort to make Hurricane drinks and celebrate Fat Tuesday. Southern Comfort has also attempted to market itself as an "authentic" New Orleans tradition by emphasizing that the Southern Comfort secret formula was developed on Bourbon Street.

As the above examples suggest, Mardi Gras stands at the nexus of modernity and postmodernity. Clearly, the processes of commodification and rationalization that define modernity are evident in Mardi Gras. At the same time, Mardi Gras has postmodern ramifications, as the celebration links with larger processes of transformation that are creating a new kind of society and culture dominated by the production and consumption of tourism and entertainment. Tourism is a unique set of global-local relations and practices. As a global industry, tourism is dominated by transnational hotel firms, entertainment corporations, gaming casinos, and professional sports franchises that stamp homogeneity and sameness on otherwise idiosyncratic and heterogeneous places. As a local set of practices, tourism involves efforts by local arts and cultural facilities, museums, and historic preservation groups to construct a sense of cultural distinctiveness as an expedient to attracting consumers and investment. Unlike other commodities that people buy and sell in markets, the tourism commodity and related services are spatially fixed and consumed by tourists at the place of production. Consequently, tourism is an amalgam of both the homogenizing forces of capitalist commodification and bureaucratic rationalization that define modern society *and* the diversifying forces of difference and hybridity that constitute the postmodern condition. On one hand, tourism is a thoroughly modern condition that involves the commodification of local culture and authenticity to entice people to travel to specific locations to consume spaces—spaces of leisure, sport, recreation, nature, amusement, history, exoticism, and otherness. On the other hand, as sociologist John Urry (2002) points out, "Tourism is prefiguratively postmodern because of its particular combination of the visual, the aesthetic, the commercial and the popular" (p. 78). In short, tourism is not about representing or advertising real or authentic representations of a place or culture to attract visitors and investment. Tourism is about simulating local culture to appeal to and satisfy tourists' demands and interests. As a mode of simulation, tourism seeks to expand and enhance the processes of commodification and rationalization and transform places into contrived tourist destinations that annihilate real authenticity and create what sociologist Dean MacCannell (1992) calls "staged" authenticity.

We can also see the interplay of the modern and postmodern in the transformation of the Mardi Gras float-building market into a global industry. Today, the New Orleans–based Kern Company is the largest float builder for Mardi Gras and Carnival celebrations throughout the world, netting $20 million in annual revenues from building and maintaining more than 300 floats for 40 parades. Once a local and seasonal business, Kern Studios is now busy year-round not only with designing floats but also renting its facilities for Mardi Gras theme parties. Kern Studios creates sculptures, themed environments, and visual signage for such clients as Paramount Park, Harrah's Casino, MGM Casino, and Circus Casino, among others. Other projects include parades for Disney World in Orlando, Florida; Euro Disney in Paris; Warner Bros. Movie World theme park in Madrid, Spain; Universal Studios in Barcelona, Spain; Samsung Corp.'s Everland theme park in Seoul, South Korea; Par Que Espana outside Osaka, Japan; and Disneyland, Tokyo. In the United States, Kern Studios has signed deals to produce parades at the Gasparilla Pirate Fest in Tampa, Florida; Fiesta San Antonio; and Mardi Gras in Galveston, Texas ("Going for the Purple, Green, and Gold," 2003). Together, the Kern Companies—Kern Studios, Mardi Gras World, and Blaine Kern Artists—earn about half their annual revenue outside New Orleans. Float building, sculpture, and other art production facilities are now found in Orlando, Florida; Valencia, Spain; and Las Vegas, Nevada (www.kernstudios.com).

Mardi Gras in New Orleans has always been a prime field of spectacle, but in today's global entertainment society, spectacle and simulation combine to enmesh Mardi Gras within an expanding international tourism industry dominated by enhanced spatial flows of people, capital, and commodities. With some exceptions, media coverage, corporate advertising, and tourist modes of presentation frame Mardi Gras as a commodity-spectacle rather than a community-oriented festival that celebrates and symbolizes the cultural identity of New Orleans. Indeed, the appropriation of New Orleans and Mardi Gras imagery and symbols to sell commodities intimates the celebration as a floating signifier that is abstracted and disembedded from local contexts of interaction and meaning creation. This process of simulation is not neutral but reflects the relentless pursuit of corporate profit as ruled by the logic of capitalist competition, commodification, and the rationalization of production and consumption.

Today, a combination of tourism organizations and networks, corporate firms, and government actors are hard at work to transform festivals like Mardi Gras into touristic spectacles. Yet the production of simulacra is constrained by the local uniqueness; place distinctiveness; and the idiosyncratic nature of diverse cultural creations, activities, and relationships. In the realm of tourism, simulation expresses the delocalization of indigenous culture and denotes a situation in which the play of images, signs, and spectacles is the organizing form of postmodern society. An important rationale for creating simulations is that they can be made more spectacular, enticing, and profitable than their authentic counterparts. Today, almost all local festivals are becoming rationalized spectacles and simulations that are organized by the prepackaging and staging of activities and experiences. Thus, the postmodern process of simulation articulates with the modern processes of commodification and rationalization to expand consumption opportunities and legitimate the commodity form.

Implosion of Mardi Gras and Tourism

One of the central tenets of postmodernism is that broad social transformations in society and culture have reversed the modern processes of differentiation and specialization and ushered in a new era of implosion or dedifferentiation of social activities, structures, and institutional boundaries. For modern theorists like Durkheim and Marx, modern society is constituted by a process of structural differentiation by which relatively distinct social institutions and activities—such as work and the economy, education, the political system, religion, family, science, and art and culture—come to specialize in particular tasks and functions to reinforce and maintain society. In contrast, postmodern society dissolves the distinctiveness of different spheres of social activity such that institutional forms and meanings implode into one another. Reality television collapses the distinction between the real and the fake; *Entertainment Tonight* blends celebrity information and entertainment codes with a serious news format to create "infotainment"; the mall-like character of some university student unions blurs the distinction between education and shopping ("edutainment"); and the spread of tourism and amusement-like characteristics to cities erases the differences between authentic and manufactured culture (Disneyification).[6]

The spread of simulation in Mardi Gras draws our attention to the erosion of distinctions between Carnival and other aspects of New Orleans society and culture. Before the 1970s, Mardi Gras was a discrete tourist attraction that the city celebrated for approximately 2 weeks. By the 1970s and 1980s, however, Mardi Gras had become a year-round "industry" with hundreds of local residents employed in float building, museums, and the mass production of souvenirs. It is during these decades that we see the development of a new global network of supply houses and factories to produce and distribute Mardi Gras–themed T-shirts, videos, music, flags, hats, coffee and beer mugs, among many other products displaying the official Mardi Gras colors of purple, green, and gold. The maturation of this industry took place in the 1990s as the Internet opened a burgeoning market for buying and selling Mardi Gras memorabilia, as well as other New Orleans paraphernalia, commemorative souvenirs, and various trinkets. The combination of instantaneous communication with the global reach of the Internet has accelerated the standardization of production of Mardi Gras products and made it possible to purchase and ship Carnival merchandise year-round. Gambinos, one of the larger bakers in the metropolitan area, produces annually up to 165,000 King Cakes—circular green, yellow, and purple cakes—that sell to customers not only in the United States but also in Europe and Latin America (King, 2003). On one hand, the production of Mardi Gras beads, souvenirs, and memorabilia is no longer the province of local craftspeople geared toward local consumption; it has been appropriated, reimagined, and retooled for mass production and mass consumption. On the other hand, the rise of a standardized Mardi Gras industry signifies the dominance of impersonal bureaucratic norms and rational procedures in the production of Mardi Gras. This last point suggests that Mardi Gras continues to be animated with modern modes of production and organization at the same time that the postmodern logic of implosion transforms the celebration.

More important, as Mardi Gras has become a high-profile mega-event for tourist consumption, it has become ever more conflated with tourists' impressions of how New Orleans should look year-round. That is, the spectacular festivities and revelry that used to be confined to a delimited Carnival season and Mardi Gras day (Fat Tuesday) have imploded into the larger everyday life of New Orleans society. Since at least Mardi Gras 2000, more than a dozen Internet cameras have been set up throughout the city to beam images of Mardi Gras (and advertisements for companies) to viewers around the world. Souvenir and trinket shops that specialize in Mardi Gras paraphernalia are open year-round, and they design, package, and sell their commodities primarily to tourists and nonresidents. Conventions now provide Mardi Gras beads for conventioneers, and tourists wander about the French Quarter wearing beads year-round. Carnival songs by Cajun, zydeco, and brass bands pulsate from the many clubs, bars, and souvenir shops, creating a continual climax of carnival festivity. At all times of the year, tourists gather beneath Bourbon Street balconies to beg other tourists to toss beads. These and other Carnivalesque activities suggest that the festive release and transgression that used to distinguish a Carnival and Mardi Gras period of limited duration are now ubiquitous and omnipresent. According to Louis Sahuc, a photographer and French Quarter resident,

Mardi Gras used to be a special day. We waited for it and enjoyed it. Now we have it every day. Any convention or group that can afford it can stage a parade now. They roll all the time, people wander around in beads year round. (Foster, 1998)

This conflation of New Orleans with Mardi Gras is not accidental or coincidental but is an outgrowth of a series of deliberate and methodical campaigns undertaken by local tourism agencies and advertisers for many years. To stimulate consumption and accumulate profit, tourism organizations, chain entertainment firms, and varieties of corporate marketing now embrace a plethora of advertising strategies and promotional campaigns to elide the distinction between residents and tourists, to urge residents to acquire the consumption practices and visual orientation characteristic of tourists. Unlike residents, tourists are in a place but not of a place. A presumption of temporariness and looseness of ties is built into the tourist experience as a consumer of culture and place. Reflecting Zygmunt Bauman (1992), tourists have no ties to a place except that of the "consumption of pleasurable experiences" (quoted in Franklin, 2003, p. 208). Residents, on the other hand, are locked into everyday local struggles and conflicts, shared experiences of the mundane and commonplace, and collective practices to create shared rules and cultural traditions to give meaning to their lives. Such actions are the antithesis of touristic experiences, which are explicitly designed to be worry-free, spectacular, extraordinary, and short term. Although tourism advertising campaigns directed at residents span many decades, what is new since the 1990s is the scale, intensity, and sophistication of the marketing strategies to encourage residents to be tourists in their own hometown. These points and examples suggest that not only does the past distinction between tourism, Carnival, and other aspects of culture implode, but also tourist modes of staging, visualization, and experience become increasingly central to other areas of social life and postmodern society more generally.

In recent years, many cities have hosted Mardi Gras celebrations, attempting to simulate New Orleans-style parades and balls and thereby obliterate distinctions between real and illusory celebrations. Austin, Texas, now celebrates Mardi Gras 4 days past Ash Wednesday, and Nashville, Tennessee, now has a "Mardi Gras in May" that includes several weeks of special jazz and blues performances. The simulated Mardi Gras at Universal Studios park in Florida is a fully commodified experience that is hosted for 44 nights. Adrian LePeltier, the director of the annual Mardi Gras celebration at the Universal Studios park, maintains that people cannot tell the difference between the Mardi Gras parade in the park and the "real" one in New Orleans: "The people on the float and the ones lined up along the streets to watch react exactly the same here as they do in New Orleans. We have captured the excitement and quality of those parades." Universal Studios officials contend that spectators get a lot more Mardi Gras things to do, including live music, nightly parades, and "authentic" food and drink. "Our streets turn into the French Quarter every night," according to LePeltier (quoted in O'Brien, 2000).

Beads, Breasts, and Beyond: Hyperreality and Sign-Value

The process of implosion cuts across the postmodern phenomenon of hyperreality. As developed by Umberto Eco (1986) and Jean Baudrillard (1983a, 1983b, 1983c), hyperreality signifies a world that is realer than real, whereby people come to believe that mythical images and models are more authentic than the real activity, place, or person. Hyperreality implies a proliferation of simulations where the boundary separating the extraordinary and spectacular from the everyday and commonplace implodes, and people lose the ability to distinguish between fantasy and reality. For Baudrillard (1970/1988), the hyperreal describes the model body, home, or relationship as projected in television, magazines, and media culture that are "models of a real without origin or reality: a hyperreal." On one hand, the hyperreal is characterized by intensification or enhancement of reality. On the other hand, the logic of hyperreality is not to imitate the real but to devour the real, whereby everything authentic can be commodified into homogenized and easily exchangeable units that can be bought and sold in markets. In short, for Umberto Eco (1986), simulation and hyperreality combine to not only produce illusion but "stimulate demand for it" (p. 44).

From a postmodern perspective, we can analyze Blaine Kern's Mardi Gras World as an example of a hyperreal realm. Since its opening in 1989, Mardi Gras World has given spending consumers the opportunity to view costumes, shop for gifts, dress up in Carnival costumes, and "experience Mardi Gras year-round." Kern's Mardi Gras World rationalizes the production and consumption of entertainment and simulation to provide a more concentrated and intense Carnival experience than what one could normally experience in New Orleans during a demarcated season. At the same time, Mardi Gras World supplies a code and model to structure people's interpretations of the celebration. As the Web site tells us,

> Blaine Kern's Mardi Gras World is New Orleans' showcase of carnival, with thousands of sensational sculptured props and breath taking giant figures on display all-year round. . . . Colorful Mardi Gras props, like a gigantic jovial jester, fiercely realistic alligators, and a gorgeously exciting Marilyn Monroe with skirt flying greet one and all to this amazing fantasy factory. You will even view the most awesome floats ever built for carnival . . . you can dress up in authentic, ornate carnival costumes. During the self-guided portion of your tour, you'll enter a maze of amazing props of all sizes. In one area, heaps of props await repair, and you'll see artists, painters, and sculptors creating before your very eyes. A 15-foot torso of the lovely and captivating Cleopatra stands nearby. Follow the yellow arrows to the next "den" (float artists' warehouse). It's a big carpentry and paint shop, where workers build and decorate sensational floats. For each "krewe" (club), artists paint each float with brightly-colored themed scenes. . . . The floats appear as colorful and animated as any imaginative Hollywood movie, with strings of lights tracing their outlines to illuminate them at night. (www.mardigrasworld.com)

Mardi Gras World presents a model and ideal version of Mardi Gras, more real than the complex and diverse social reality could ever be. The Kern Company creates a hermetically sealed, completely commodified realm in which one can retreat from the real and consume mythologized history and sanitized culture. Interpreted from a postmodern perspective, we can view Mardi Gras World as a hyperreal world of artificially constructed experience that purifies the banality of Carnival to create an exciting world of mass-mediated, celebrity-inspired, simulated experiences. Interpreted from a modern perspective, we can view Mardi Gras World as an extension of Marx's concept of commodification and Max Weber's notion of rationalization. As a vehicle of commodification, Mardi Gras World restricts access based on ability to pay the admission fee. As a paradigm of bureaucratic rationalization, Mardi Gras World uses the techniques of organizational control and hierarchical administration to reduce uncertainty, achieve goals, and accumulate profit.

Reflecting George Ritzer's concept of McDonaldization, just as the fast-food restaurant helps to rationalize and standardize the ability to purchase and consume food, Mardi Gras World incorporates rational procedures to create a carefully controlled pleasure space to enhance the efficiency, calculability, and predictability of obtaining and consuming a Carnival experience.

Another example of how the modern and postmodern intersect in Mardi Gras is in the practice of commodifying and packaging images of women "baring breasts for beads" on Bourbon Street in the French Quarter. For years, visitors have flocked to Bourbon Street during Mardi Gras to witness people participating in flashing breasts and displaying other forms of nudity and exhibitionism (Shrum & Kilburn, 1996). Yet in recent years, these entertaining and transgressive activities have become marketed to a global audience through sundry videos such as *Girls Gone Wild*. Visual technology combined with the growth of international media coverage of Mardi Gras discloses deviant activities and displays them as an entertaining spectacle (Redmon, 2003). In this situation, profiteering entrepreneurs commodify and circulate on a global scale relatively obscure, infrequent, and fleeting images of women baring breasts, erasing distinctions between the real and the imaginary. Once commodified and transmitted globally, the fantasy images simulate reality, and people conflate Mardi Gras with spectacular nudity and believe that exhibitionism is widespread and *the* defining characteristic of Carnival. As much as possible, companies that sell nude Mardi Gras videos seek to blend images of fun and celebration, using nudity as a marketing device, to persuade consumers that the naked female breast is the master sign and signature motif of Mardi Gras. It is interesting to note that, although some people contend that the practice of "baring breasts for beads" has "always existed" in New Orleans, there is little evidence to suggest that it was a popular practice before the mid-1970s. Signs and displays such as "show your tits" and other sexual slogans have become commodified on T-shirts, buttons, and a variety of Mardi Gras paraphernalia. The increasing ubiquity and commercialization of nudity and exhibitionism at Mardi Gras mirror the telecasting of the celebration worldwide.

From a postmodern perspective, we can view Mardi Gras as organized around the production and consumption of simulations, the implosion of tourism and culture, and the display of commodities through which individuals project status and gain prestige. Here, the phenomena of simulacra and implosion interconnect with the buying, selling, and display of Mardi Gras souvenirs, paraphernalia, and beads to multiply the quantity of Carnival signs, and thereby generating a proliferation of sign-values. Mardi Gras beads are not just commodities characterized by use-value and exchange-value, as in Marx's theory of the commodity; they also radiate with sign-value, which postmodern theorist Jean Baudrillard argues is an expression and mark of honor and cultural distinction. For Baudrillard, the dominance of sign-value signifies a society organized around consumption and the display of commodities as objects of prestige, identity, and standing. In Mardi Gras, the longer and thicker the beads one wears, the higher one's standing in the realm of Carnival sign-value. Thus, just as a commodity's use-value and exchange-value take on meaning according to their positions in a system of economic production, so sign-values take on meaning according to their place in a system of prestige and status. Sign-value reflects a dual process of homogenization-diversification. As Mardi Gras becomes homogenized into simultaneously commodity, spectacle, and simulation, the Mardi Gras sign becomes available in a diversity of consumable forms and images. As Baudrillard (1970/1988) puts it, "In order to become an object of consumption, the object must become a sign" (p. 22).

Theorizing Mardi Gras as between the modern and postmodern sensitizes us to global corporate efforts to increase profit through exploiting labor in the production of Mardi Gras beads and the circulation of sign-values. Indeed, the consumption of beads and the projection of sign-values reflect and are embedded within a global capitalist system of labor exploitation. As depicted in David Redmon's award-winning documentary *Mardi Gras: Made in China,* the vast majority of Carnival beads are produced by a handful of factories in China and imported to the United States (www.mardigrasmadeinchina.com/news.html). Although no official statistics are available, estimates suggest that the bead industry sells $500 million (U.S.) of beads each year worldwide. Workers in China sew the plastic beads for $4.25 a day, or about $85 a month. Local krewes contract with U.S. bead distributors to order customized beads to sell to individuals who toss the beads from the parade floats (LaFrance, 2001; Warren & Fowler, 2004). Mardi Gras beads express the proliferation of sign-values as a constituent of postmodern society, but they also symbolize the thoroughly modern process of routinized factory work and capitalist globalization. According to Redmon,

> The workers in the [Mardi Gras bead factory] are employed based on contractual labor and are disallowed to form unions or strike. In fact, it is illegal, a crime to strike or form a union. Consequently, the owner of the factory can fire, fine, punish, or dismiss workers at any time without legitimate justification. The majority of these workers are teenagers and women who migrate from rural provinces in China to work year round in factories. Instead of gaining autonomy, high wages, and job security . . . the factory workers' labor is commodified into contractual relationships in which they work for minuscule piece-work wages. Their employment is often insecure and the jobs they perform are labor intensive, repetitive, and require them to work between ten and eighteen hours a day to create profit for the factory and foreign owners. (www.mardigrasmadeinchina.com/essay_1.html)

As the above quote intimates, the production of Mardi Gras beads has evolved into a labor-intensive industry governed by rational techniques of labor organization and production for mass consumption. Peasant workers in China produce beads at subsistence wages to survive while revelers in the United States consume them as entertaining sign-values during Mardi Gras celebrations in New Orleans and many other cities. Thus, the entertainment and revelry enjoyed by many during Mardi Gras are built upon the exploitative labor of workers in less-developed countries. Mardi Gras thus encompasses both a postmodern domain of simulation, implosion, and hyper-reality, and a modern world of commodification and rationalization.

Conclusion

In his classic treatise *Capital, Volume I*, Karl Marx described modernity as a volatile and unstable system where "all that is solid melts into air" and everything is "pregnant with its contradictory." Modern life is a life of irony, paradox, and contradiction (Berman, 1982). Marx's melting metaphor sensitizes us to ironies and contradictions of Mardi Gras while directing our attention to the macro processes of rationalization and commodification that are transforming the celebration, generating a condition of chronic instability and ephemerality. Mardi Gras continues to be animated by modern forms of organization while new processes of simulation, spectacle, hyperreality, and implosion increasingly permeate the celebration. As I have pointed out, postmodern concepts call attention to the changes and novelties of the present moment. In addition, by deploying the resources of both modern and postmodern theory, I have eschewed interpretations of the present conjuncture in terms of discontinuity, radical break, or epochal rupture, as was popular among postmodernists during the 1970s and 1980s. Here I have followed the lead of scholars such as Antonio (2000), Berman (1982), Giddens (1991), Harvey (1989), and Jameson (1991), among others, who have viewed postmodernity as an intensification of modernity or a radicalizing moment within a long, uneven, and conflictual historical development of modern society. My goal has been to combine postmodern concepts to identify novel features of Mardi Gras while situating the transformation of the celebration within broader sociocultural transformations that are affecting society. Giving postmodern terms a sociological footing and analytical grounding helps point to a strengthening and fuller development of social theory and sociology more broadly. In addition, proceeding eclectically by merging modern with postmodern concepts not only offers an opportunity to reinvigorate empirical and theoretical sociology, but also helps to update, clarify, and provide nuance to our understandings of the modern process of commodification and rationalization.

Although the modern and postmodern concepts sensitize us to the different processes that are affecting Mardi Gras, viewing Mardi Gras as either modern or postmodern is reductive, one-sided, and limited. Just as New Orleans has changed economically, culturally, and socially over the decades, so too has Mardi Gras changed with the times. Today, Mardi Gras is a many-sided phenomenon that expresses a variety of diverse meanings. In spite of the devastation caused by Hurricane Katrina, more than 50 parades took to the streets of New Orleans during 2006 to celebrate Carnival and Mardi Gras. For local leaders, Mardi Gras 2006 was an important statement of the city's strength and fast-paced rebuilding efforts. More than 300 news outlets from around the world, including every European country, Russia, Taiwan, Australia, and China, visited New Orleans to report and showcase the Carnival festivities to a global audience. Whereas some derided the idea of celebrating Mardi Gras in the context of hardship and devastation, others looked to the celebration as a means of reaffirming local culture and reconstituting a sense of community identity. Today, the devastation of Hurricane Katrina is leading to new calls to commercialize Mardi Gras, expand the advertising of Carnival, and sell the celebration to corporate sponsors as an expedient to rebuilding New Orleans. On the other hand, local residents and Carnival enthusiasts have launched vehement protests and assailed corporate and government efforts to turn the celebration into a contrived tourist attraction that is abstracted from local culture and empty of communal value.

Generally speaking, debates over commercialization and the future of New Orleans and Mardi Gras express disagreements over meanings of authenticity in the city's signature celebration, who owns Carnival, and how people should use and celebrate Carnival to invigorate local culture. Thus, Mardi Gras is multifaceted, and the more theories, concepts, and methods one can bring to its analysis, the better one will be able to enrich sociological understanding of the celebration and broader cultural phenomenon. Moreover, multidimensional theorizing that borrows concepts and heuristics from both modern and postmodern approaches can assist in uncovering the variety of connections between local events and larger processes of modernity and postmodernity that affect our lives.

Notes

1. Drawing upon the work of Karl Marx and other scholars, I define *commodification* as the conversion of local products, cultures, and social relations and identities into saleable products that are sold on markets for profitable exchange. Following Max Weber, *rationalization* refers to a process whereby social actions and interactions become based on considerations of efficiency and calculation rather than on motivations derived from custom, tradition, or emotion (for overviews and applications of these terms, see Antonio & Bonanno, 2000; Berman, 1982; Gotham, 2002; Gotham & Krier, 2008).

2. During the 1970s and 1980s, proponents of "strong" postmodernism such as Jean Baudrillard, Jacques Lyotard, and others proclaimed the death of the "real," rejected the idea of the "social" as a theoretical and empirical category, called for a "war against totality," and championed new postmodern discourses and politics to deal with the striking novelties of the present (Baudrillard, 1983a, 1983b, 1983c; Lyotard, 1984). Others, such as Harvey (1989) and Jameson (1991), dismissed the ideas of "strong" postmodernism and argued that postmodernism was a cultural manifestation of a larger intensification and acceleration of capitalist commodification and global expansion (for an overview of "strong" and "moderate" postmodernism, see Antonio, 1998, pp. 30–31).

3. For scholarly debates on postmodernism in sociology journals, see Antonio (1991); Gottdiener (1993, 1994); Kivisto (1994); and Seidman (1991). For critical and celebratory books on postmodernism, see Best and Kellner (1991, 1997), Denzin (1991), and Lemert (1997); see also contributors to edited volumes by Dickens and Fontana (1994), Nicholson and Seidman (1995), and Seidman and Wagner (1992).

4. Globalization implies the intensification of social and geographical interconnectedness and an accelerated circulation of people, capital, information, and cultural symbols on a worldwide scale. Globalization is an uneven and conflictual historical process that occurs through the interaction of commodification and rationalization processes (for overviews and applications of these terms, see Antonio & Bonanno, 2000; Gotham & Krier, 2008).

5. James McLain also reported that Mardi Gras 2003 generated $20.5 million in direct tax revenues for the city of New Orleans while costing $4.6 million for city services such as police overtime and trash collection (reported in Dart, 2006).

6. Scholars have used the concept of Disneyification to suggest that amusement park characteristics are imploding into virtually every other realm of society. In urban sociology, for example, this city-as-theme-park explanation suggests that urban spaces are being refashioned into places of fun and entertainment to attract consumption-based investment and spending consumers. As discussed by many scholars, *Disneyification* is the use of theming techniques, the promotion of corporate brands, the dominance of security and surveillance, and the blurring of boundaries between consumption and other social activities. Scholars argue that what diverse places such as Disneyland, Las Vegas, Times Square in New York City, heritage sites, and theme parks share is a decontextualization of place that elides the distinction between past and present, and real and staged authenticity (Bryman, 1999; Eeckhout, 2001; Sorkin, 1992).

References

Antonio, R. J. (1991). Postmodern storytelling versus pragmatic truth-seeking: The discursive bases of social theory. *Sociological Theory, 9,* 154–163.

Antonio, R. J. (1998). Mapping postmodern theory. In A. Sica (Ed.), *What is social theory? The philosophical debates* (pp. 22–75). Oxford, UK: Blackwell.

Antonio, R. J. (2000). After postmodernism: Reactionary tribalism. *American Journal of Sociology, 106*(1), 40–87.

Antonio, R. J., & Bonanno, A. (2000). A new global capitalism? From "Americanization and Fordism" to "Americanization-globalization." *American Studies, 41*(2/3), 33–77.

Antonio, R. J., & Kellner, D. (1994). The future of social theory and the limits of postmodern critique. In D. R. Dickens & A. Fontana (Eds.), *Postmodernism and social inquiry* (pp. 127–152). New York: Guilford.

Baudrillard, J. (1983a). *Fatal strategies.* New York: Semiotext(e).

Baudrillard, J. (1983b). *In the shadow of silent majorities.* New York: Semiotext(e).

Baudrillard, J. (1983c). *Simulations.* New York: Semiotext(e).

Baudrillard, J. (1988). Consumer society. In M. Poster (Ed.), *Jean Baudrillard: Selected writings* (pp. 29–56). Palo Alto, CA: Stanford University Press. (Original work published 1970)

Bauman, Z. (1992). *Intimations of postmodernity.* New York: Routledge.

Bergey, J. (2004). Georg Simmel's metropolis: Anticipating the postmodern. *Telos, 129,* 139–150.

Berman, M. (1982). *All that is solid melts into air: The experience of modernity.* New York: Simon & Schuster.

Best, S., & Kellner, D. (1991). *Postmodern theory: Critical interrogations.* New York: Guilford.

Best, S., & Kellner, D. (1997). *The postmodern turn.* New York: Guilford.

Bryman, A. (1999). Disneyization of society. *Sociological Review, 47*(1), 25–47.

Campbell, C. (2005). The craft consumer: Culture, craft, and consumption in a postmodern society. *Journal of Consumer Culture, 5*(1), 23–42.

Charles, A. (1995, January 28). Revelers made 1994 a Carnival to bank on. *The* (New Orleans) *Times-Picayune.*

Dart, R. (2006, February 26). Party pays, dispels qualms about storm. *Atlanta Journal-Constitution,* p. 15A.

Denzin, N. (1991). *Images of postmodern society: Social theory and contemporary cinema.* Newbury Park, CA: Sage.

Dickens, D. R., & Fontana, A. (Eds.). (1994). *Postmodernism and social inquiry.* New York: Guilford.

Eco, U. (1986). *Travels in hyperreality* (W. Weaver, Trans.). San Diego, CA: Harcourt Brace Jovanovich.

Edgley, C. (2003, January). Why postmodernism is here to stay: Or, the mainstreaming of a (semi)radical idea. *Perspectives: The ASA Theory Section Newsletter, 26*(1), 1, 5, 7–8.

Eeckhout, B. (2001). The "Disneyification" of Times Square: Back to the future? In K. F. Gotham (Ed.), *Critical perspectives on urban redevelopment*. New York: Elsevier.

Feagin, J. R. (1998). *The new urban paradigm: Critical perspectives on the city*. New York: Rowman & Littlefield.

Fontana, A. (2005). The postmodern turn in interactionism. *Studies in Symbolic Interaction, 28*, 239–254.

For New Orleans, Mardi Gras is becoming an all-year cash cow. (1999, February 7). *New York Times*, section 3, p. 6.

Foster, M. (1998, February 23). Mardi gross. *Milwaukee Journal Sentinel*. Available online at http://www.findarticles.com/p/articles/mi_qn4196/is_19980223/ai_n10405163

Franklin, A. (2003). The tourist syndrome: An interview with Zygmunt Bauman. *Tourist Studies, 3*(2), 205–217.

Giddens, A. (1991). *Modernity and self-identity: Self and society in the late modern age*. Palo Alto, CA: Stanford University Press.

Going for the purple, green, and gold. (2003, September 7). *The* (New Orleans) *Times-Picayune*.

Gotham, K. F. (2002, September). Marketing Mardi Gras: Commodification, spectacle, and the political economy of tourism in New Orleans. *Urban Studies, 39*(10), 1735–1756.

Gotham, K. F. (2005a). Theorizing urban spectacles: Festivals, tourism, and the transformation of urban space. *City: Analysis of Urban Trends, Culture, Theory, Policy, Action, 9*(2), 225–246.

Gotham, K. F. (2005b). Tourism from above and below: Globalization, localization, and New Orleans's Mardi Gras. *International Journal of Urban and Regional Research, 29*(2), 309–326.

Gotham, K. F., & Krier, D. (2008). From the culture industry to the society of the spectacle: Critical theory and the situationist international. In H. F. Dahms (Ed.), *No social science without critical theory* (pp. 155–192). Bingley, UK: Emerald Group.

Gottdiener, M. (1993). Ideology, foundationalism, and sociological theory. *Sociological Quarterly, 34*(4), 653–671.

Gottdiener, M. (1994). Oh no! Not another dichotomy: Reply to Kivisto. *Sociological Quarterly, 35*(4), 729–732.

Harvey, D. (1989). *The condition of postmodernity*. New York: Free Press.

Jameson, F. (1991). *Postmodernism, or, the cultural logic of late capitalism*. Durham, NC: Duke University Press.

Jones, C. (2003). Theory after the postmodern condition. *Organization, 10*(3), 505–525.

King, R. (2003, January 4). King Cake bakers will roll in the dough: Hundreds of thousands sold here, shipped out. *The* (New Orleans) *Times-Picayune*.

Kinser, S. (1990). *Carnival, American style: Mardi Gras at New Orleans and Mobile*. Chicago: University of Chicago Press.

Kivisto, P. (1994). Toward an anti-foundational yet relevant sociology: Can Gottdiener have it both ways? *Sociological Quarterly, 35*(4), 723–728.

LaFrance, S. (2001, February 21). The Chinese connection. *The* (New Orleans) *Times-Picayune*.

Lash, S. (1990). *The sociology of postmodernism*. London: Routledge.

Lemert, C. (1997). *Postmodernism is not what you think*. Malden, MA: Blackwell.

Lyotard, J.-F. (1984). *The postmodern condition.* Minneapolis: University of Minnesota Press.

MacCannell, D. (1992). *Empty meeting grounds: The tourist papers.* New York: Routledge.

Magnusson, S. G. (2003). The singularization of history: Social history and microhistory within the postmodern state of knowledge. *Journal of Social History, 36*(3), 701–735.

McLain, J. J. (2000). Mardi Gras 2000: Its economic impact. *Louisiana Business Survey, 31*(2), 2–4, 8.

Mirchandani, R. (2005). Reconstructing Zygmunt Bauman's postmodern sociology of morality. *Current Perspectives in Social Theory, 23,* 301–335.

Mitchell, R. (1995). *All on a Mardi Gras day: Episodes in the history of New Orleans Carnival.* Cambridge, MA: Harvard University Press.

Nicholson, L., & Seidman, S. (Eds.). (1995). *Social postmodernism: Beyond identity politics.* Cambridge, UK: Cambridge University Press.

O'Brien, T. (2000, March 6). Universal Studios Florida kicks spring into gear with Mardi Gras. *Amusement Business.* Retrieved from http://www.allbusiness.com/services/amusement-recreation-services/4558961-1.html

Pescosolido, B., & Rubin, B. A. (2000, February). The web of group affiliations revisited: Social life, postmodernism, and sociology. *American Sociological Review, 65,* 52–76.

Redmon, D. (2003). Playful deviance as an urban leisure activity: Secret selves, self-validation, and entertaining performances. *Deviant Behavior, 24,* 27–51.

Ritzer, G. (1997). *Postmodern social theory.* New York: McGraw-Hill.

Seidman, S. (1991). The end of sociological theory: The postmodern hope. *Sociological Theory, 9,* 131–146.

Seidman, S., & Wagner, D. G. (1992). *Postmodernism and social theory.* Oxford, UK: Blackwell.

Shrum, W., & Kilburn, J. (1996). Ritual disrobement at Mardi Gras: Ceremonial exchange and moral order. *Social Forces, 75*(2), 423–458.

Soja, E. (2000). *Postmetropolis: Critical studies of cities and regions.* New York: Blackwell.

Sorkin, M. (Ed.). (1992). *Variations on a theme park: The new American city and the end of public space.* New York: Hill and Wang.

Urry, J. (2002). *The tourist gaze* (2nd ed.). London: Sage.

Warren, A., & Fowler, G. A. (2004, February 24). Mardi Gras bead mania bewilders Chinese. *Wall Street Journal.*

Weinstein, D., & Weinstein, M. A. (1994). *Postmodern(ized) Simmel.* London: Routledge.

DISCUSSION QUESTIONS

1. The word *postmodern* has entered everyday life in the modern world, but people often have rather varied and vague notions of what the word means. Based on what you read in this chapter, how would you define the postmodern? What is its relationship to the modern? To the extent that you think postmodern is a relevant characterization of contemporary social life, has it superseded the modern, or do the two coexist?

2. Gotham describes Mardi Gras as a commodity-spectacle. What is he arguing here? To begin with, what do you understand the word *spectacle* to mean? Do you agree or disagree with his characterization of Mardi Gras as a spectacle?

3. Although in many ways, New Orleans was and is a unique city in America, other cities rely on tourism, and one can find evidence of spectacles in them, too. Choose a city with which you are

familiar and propose the outline of a postmodern analysis of that place similar to the analysis of New Orleans offered in this chapter. What difference does it make that a city has a fairly lengthy history (e.g., New York City, San Francisco) or does not (e.g., Las Vegas)?

4. What do Umberto Eco and Jean Baudrillard mean by hyperreality? How does this concept relate to a culture saturated by the mass media and by consumerism? Discuss the relevance of the term for making sense of Mardi Gras in New Orleans.

5. Should Gotham's postmodern analysis of Mardi Gras be read as a theoretical alternative to a Marxist analysis, with its emphasis on economic exploitation, or can the two positions be mutually reinforcing? Explain.

CHAPTER 13

Negotiating the Social Landscape to Create Social Change

Anne F. Eisenberg

__Anne F. Eisenberg__ is Associate Professor of Sociology at the State University of New York (SUNY) at Geneseo. While working in the area of planning and public policy for public hospitals where she helped them create an identity and vision unique to the organization, she realized that the idea of a vision that shapes an organization is literally a form of theory. She has taught theory at the undergraduate and graduate level since 1992—including classical theory, contemporary theory, and feminist theory— where her goal is to illustrate the relevance of theory for both understanding and changing the social world. Receiving her doctorate in sociology in 2002 from the University of Iowa with expertise in theory and social psychology, she regularly presents and writes about the link between classical and contemporary theory, reinterpreting the historical role of the classical theorists, and what constitutes theory. Her current writing and research are in two areas—neurosociology (examining the role of social interactions in shaping mental, physiological, and neurological health) and the relationship between theory and methods.

Imagine you are driving with a friend on a clear and sunny day when all of a sudden, you crash into another vehicle pulling out of a driveway. You could describe the experience in several different ways—from explaining how you physically felt upon getting out of the damaged car; to describing your range of emotions starting from right before the crash to immediately after the crash; to detailing the situation in terms of the weather, other traffic on the street, and the car you struck. Each description reflects a different perspective you might take in explaining what happened. In the same way, much of American sociological theory reflects a particular perspective held by a theorist, resulting in explanations of the social world that focus on specific issues or points of reference. This approach to theorizing is characterized by two distinct discussions among American sociologists— macro versus micro and agency versus structure. The discussion concerning macro versus micro centers on whether the best way to understand and explain the social world is focusing on social institutions and aggregates of (the macro approach), or focusing on individuals, their interactions, and the groups to which they belong (the micro approach). The second distinct discussion concerns whether theorists view the basis of human society as being rooted in agency or structure. Theories concerned with agency focus on how social action and social change occur, whereas those concerned with structure focus on how social order is maintained through particular social institutions.

European theorists such as Jürgen Habermas and Pierre Bourdieu (who is the focus of this chapter) actively sought to overcome what they saw as the constrained and constricted nature of sociological theory—particularly American sociological theory—which created what they considered to be these artificial distinctions between theoretical ideas. Further, the European theorists argue that theories limited to examining one level of society over another or those focusing on either agency or structure are inadequate for explaining the dynamic and fluid nature of human society. As with other French theorists such as Michel Foucault, Bourdieu not only integrates the macro and micro, agency and structure in his theories, but does so by introducing new ways of expressing such a dynamic view of human society. In this chapter, I first introduce you to Pierre Bourdieu's background and how this is reflected in his approach to theorizing, and I then describe four of his key ideas—habitus, social positions, position-taking, and fields. In describing his key ideas, I illustrate how he works with ideas of the classical theorists and integrates them into a new set of terms (a new language, so to speak) so as to provide a way in which to understand and evocatively explain the dynamic nature of social life. In addition, this part of the chapter includes an overview of the range of ways in which Bourdieu applied his ideas to studying the social world. I then present a case study of how the issues associated with a fringe group—in this case, Parents, Families, and Friends of Lesbians and Gays (PFLAG)—are transformed into acceptable mainstream social issues resulting in significant social change. Using Bourdieu's key ideas as I recount the development of PFLAG, from its origins as a locally focused emotional support group for parents into its current status as an international educational and lobbying organization dedicated to issues affecting the lives of gays and lesbians, aptly illustrates the compelling way that his ideas explain the social world. I also illustrate how Bourdieu's ideas implicitly examine social change itself as part of the dynamic and ever-changing nature of human society. Equally important, this chapter is written in Bourdieu's style by introducing and describing relevant ideas and then illustrating such ideas through detailed case studies.

Bourdieu: Background, Theorizing, and Theory

Theorists' ideas reflect their own personal background, academic training, and the central themes that are found throughout their writings. To understand their ideas, therefore, requires that we understand the theorists as well. In this part of the chapter, I present Bourdieu's background and how it is reflected in his approach to theory as well as his theoretical ideas. I also discuss three key issues concerning sociological theory that Bourdieu finds particularly troublesome, resulting in his unique approach to theorizing. Understanding that Bourdieu is trying to resolve limitations in sociological theory serves as a logical segue to more easily understanding his theoretical ideas. In this part of the discussion, I also examine the central theme in his writings. In the last part of this section of the chapter, I highlight four key ideas of Bourdieu and the range of substantive issues he examines with these ideas.

Background

Pierre Bourdieu's background would not have predicted the prominence he achieved as a sociological theorist and social commentator. Bourdieu was born in 1930 in a rural area of France; his grandparents were peasant farmers, and his father was the village postman. During his primary and secondary education, Bourdieu was known as much for his rugby-playing skills as for his intellect, illustrating the origins of his interest in being an active participant in the social world rather than focusing only on an academic or scholarly examination of human society. He was a top student while boarding at a public high school in the nearby Pau, and he received a state scholarship to attend university. He moved to Paris to attend the École Normale Supérieure, where his classmates included the philosopher Jacques Derrida, and where Bourdieu actively opposed what he considered to be the authoritarian policies of the school. His intellectual opposition to the focus in philosophy at the time led to studies in logic and the history of science. After earning a PhD in philosophy in 1954, Bourdieu taught high school in Moulins in central France for 1 year before being drafted into the French army in 1955. His resistance to military authority led to Bourdieu being "swiftly sent for disciplinary reasons to Algeria to serve in the 'pacification' of the North African colony" (Wacquant, 2002, p. 550).

He served in Algiers for 2 years during his tenure in the army, and after his discharge, Bourdieu stayed in the country until 1960 and lectured at the University of Algiers as well as studied farming and conducted ethnographic research concerning the ethnic Berber culture. This research resulted in his first book, published in 1962 after he returned to France, titled *The Algerians*. He also married Marie-Claire Brisard in 1962 and they had three children together. Bourdieu's academic career, starting as an assistant professor at the University of Algiers and later becoming a professor and chair of sociology at the Collége de France in 1981, included serving as the director of the Centre de Sociologie Européenne and creating and publishing the journal *Actes de la Recherche en Sciences Sociales*.

Throughout his career, Bourdieu actively engaged with important social issues such as publicly supporting striking rail workers, advocating for the homeless, regularly publishing articles in newspapers and appearing on television programs, and founding the publishing company Liber-Raisons d'agir. In summary, Bourdieu's life and academic career reflected engagement in what today is called public sociology—interest in linking the knowledge gained through theory and research to key social issues (Marx called this praxis)—as evidenced by his public presentations, his interest in developing new outlets for information and knowledge, and his own activism on behalf of others. Bourdieu's engagement in public sociology is reflected in his focus on empirically related theory; his interest in linking objective and subjective views in both research and theory; his focus on the interaction between social structures and dynamic actors; and finally, his concern with power relations.

Bourdieu and Theorizing

Pierre Bourdieu, writing from 1953 until his death in 2002, consistently focuses on three key issues concerning the process of creating theory (theorizing) in sociology—empirically linked theory, integrating objectivist and subjectivist views, and discussing structure and agency as interlinked aspects of human society—while building on the classical ideas of Marx, Weber, and Durkheim. It is important to understand these three issues as a way of introducing our discussion of his key ideas. In addition, at the end of this section, I highlight Bourdieu's meta-theoretical focus—the central theme around which all of his research and writing is focused.

Robert K. Merton (1968), an American sociologist, argues that sociologists ought to focus on "middle-range theory" that explains specific empirical situations, which he describes as

> theories that lie between the minor but necessary working hypotheses that evolve in abundance during day-to-day research and the all-inclusive systematic efforts to develop a unified theory that will explain all the observed uniformities of social behavior, social organization and social change. Middle-range theory is principally used in sociology to guide empirical inquiry. It is intermediate to general theories of social systems which are too remote from particular classes of social behavior, organization and change to account for what is observed and to those detailed orderly descriptions of particulars that are not generalized at all. (p. 39)

> Similarly, Bourdieu (2002a) states in a lecture to a Japanese audience that

> my entire scientific enterprise is indeed based on the belief that the deepest logic of the social world can be grasped only if one plunges into the particularity of an empirical reality, historically located and dated, but with the objective of constructing it as a "special case of what is possible," as Bachelard puts it, that is, as an exemplary case in a finite world of possible configurations. (p. 268)

Both Merton and Bourdieu argue that theory—our explanations about how and why the world works as it does—needs to be directly connected to empirical situations and lived experiences. This approach to theory reflects the writings of classical theorists such as Marx, Weber, and Durkheim—all three writers developed their theories as they worked with particular empirical, real-world situations. For example, Durkheim's use of Marcel Mauss's ethnographic studies were an integral part of his book on religion, while Weber's extensive research comparing the Occident (West) and Orient (East) led to *The Protestant Ethic and the Spirit of Capitalism*. Finally, Marx's long-term analysis of French revolutions was vital to his discussions of the development and power of capitalism in *Das Capital*. Thus, in using Bourdieu's ideas to explain a specific case study of social change, we are fulfilling his goal for sociological theory.

The second key aspect of Bourdieu's theoretical writings centers on *how* to engage in middle-range theory by integrating what he calls objectivist and subjectivist views. He describes the objectivist view as grasping "practices from outside, as a *fait accompli,* instead of constructing their generative principle by situating itself within the very movement of their accomplishment" (1998, p. 3). The objectivist view is epitomized by using surveys and observational research with which the sociologist collects data to either test a specific theory (deductive research) or so as to engage in theory development by working closely with the data to develop conceptual ideas (inductive research, also known as grounded theory). The objectivist view of sociology is the predominant approach taken in American sociology. Bourdieu describes subjectivist knowledge as "the knowledge we shall call *phenomenological* (or, to speak in terms of currently active schools, "ethnomethodological") [that] sets out to make explicit the truth of primary experience of the social world" (1998, p. 3). Subjective knowledge is gained through directly experiencing the situations in which people find themselves and in which we are interested in better understanding. The subjectivist approach is most frequently found in anthropological research with a minority of sociologists engaging in such work. While most scientists (social, physical, behavioral, and even natural scientists) engage in either one or the other type of research and knowledge development, Bourdieu argues that the only way to truly understand the social world is to account for both the objective outsider observations as well as the detailed primary practices through which individuals engage the social world. Bourdieu (1998) states that

> we shall escape from the ritual either/or choice between objectivism and subjectivism in which the social sciences have so far allowed themselves to be trapped only if we are prepared to inquire into the mode of production and functioning of the practical mastery which makes possible both an objectively intelligible practice and also an objectively enchanted experience of that practice. (p. 4)

As we shall shortly see, Bourdieu's ideas of habitus, social positions, position-taking, and fields link together an objective understanding of the social world from an "outsider's" perspective with recognition of the primary practices that allow individuals to interact with one another as well as with groups and social institutions.

The third unique aspect of Bourdieu's writings concerns linking social structures that shape human behavior with the actions taken by individuals. Integrating ideas of American sociologists George Herbert Mead and Erving Goffman with those of phenomenologist Alfred Schutz, and echoing the work of Peter Berger and Hans Luckmann, Bourdieu states that the structural approach to sociology predominant in American and European sociological theory focuses so firmly on social institutions and structures that it overlooks the way in which such institutions and structures are created. As a segue to discussing habitus, he explains the need to "escape the *realism of the structure,* which hypostatizes systems of objective relations by converting them into totalities already constituted outside of individual history and group history" (1998, p. 72). In other words, while social structures can shape human behavior through formal and informal norms, rules, and values (recall Durkheim's discussion of social facts and Weber's discussion of the different types of social action), Bourdieu argues that individuals forget that they created such institutions through their own actions and interactions. As a way of encouraging us to avoid the pitfall of overemphasizing one or the other (structure or agency), Bourdieu literally introduces a new set of terms as part of his general theory of practice—habitus, social positions, position-taking, and fields.

All three aspects of Bourdieu's writing discussed above allow him to effectively focus on a central theme—his meta-theoretical focus—the impact that power has on social relations and how power itself has relational properties. Each of Bourdieu's theoretical ideas discussed in the next section, as well as all of his other discussions, focus on relations between actors. The term *actor,* used by many theorists from a wide range of theoretical perspectives, is useful in that it can refer to individuals and their interactions as well as to groups and organizations. Whether discussing habitus or fields or positions, Bourdieu argues that human society is based on relations between actors. More important, he argues that such relations implicitly as well as explicitly deal with issues of power since actors have differential access to material and nonmaterial resources (or, in his terms, economic capital and cultural capital). This differential access to resources is part of why actors interact with one another in that each needs resources held by others. This meta-theoretical focus is also reflected in the substantive topics or issues Bourdieu studies—ranging from his discussion of taste (as in style) in the book titled *Distinction,* which examines class distinctions in terms of cultural preferences, to his critical examination of French academia in the book titled *Homo Academicus,* to the title subject of one of his last publications, *Masculine Domination.* In each of these publications as well as in his other projects, Bourdieu examines the way that actors are connected to one another and the way in which such relations are mediated by formal and informal norms.

Bourdieu's Theoretical Ideas

The idea of habitus serves as a central theme in his work, whether Bourdieu is discussing how people are distinguished by taste (1984); describing life in the academy as a professor (1988); or examining the role of education (1994, cowritten with Passeron), culture (1993), and male domination (2001) in human society. Bourdieu (2002b) defines *habitus* as

systems of durable, transposable dispositions, structured structures predisposed to function as structuring structures, that is, as principles which generate and organize practices and representations that can be objectively adapted to their outcomes without presupposing a conscious aiming at ends or an express mastery of the operations necessary in order to attain them. Objectively "regulated" and "regular" without being in any way the product of obedience to rules, they can be collectively orchestrated without being the product of the organizing action of a conductor. (p. 277)

More to the point, Bourdieu (2002b) describes habitus as a

product of history, [which] produces individual and collective practices—more history—in accordance with the schemes generated by history. It ensures the active presence of past experiences, which, deposited in each organism in the form of schemes of perception, thought and action, tend to guarantee the "correctness" of practices and their constancy over time, more reliably than all the formal rules and explicit norms. (p. 278)

For Bourdieu, habitus represents the symbolic meanings that are created and found within social interactions representing informal norms, rules, and values. Actors use their experiential and learned knowledge of these meanings to calculate future actions, in terms of guiding principles, to react to specific situations and the other actors involved. It is actors' ability to combine knowledge of symbolic meanings with rational calculation that reflects their dynamic agency—their ability to respond to all situations with a variety of actions. While actors have this set of guiding principles to shape their interactions, these interactions do become habitual, patterned, and then shared with others. The idea of habitus integrates the symbolic interactionist focus on meanings found in Mead's distinction of significant gestures or significant symbols with Durkheim's emphasis on the sui generis and social facts. Both Mead and Durkheim assumed that we are born tabula rasa and the society is imprinted upon us. While we learn the norms, rules, and values in what may seem to be a structured framework, we are capable of changing the meanings associated with them.

These patterned interactions and meanings become institutionalized such that the original meanings, history, and intentions of interactions are lost within what become structured practices. Bourdieu (2002b) argues that to truly understand particular structured practices requires "relating the social conditions in which the *habitus* that generated them was constituted, to the social conditions in which it is implemented" (p. 279). By presenting a new concept with which to explore both the interpretive experiences that create particular practices as well as the social institutions that represent such practices, Bourdieu encourages us to see the dynamic interchange between individual interactions and the social structures within which they are bound. It is important to note that Bourdieu (1998) also argues

that "interpersonal" relations are never, except in appearance, *individual-to-individual* relationships and that the truth of the interaction is never entirely contained in the interaction. . . . In fact it is their present and past positions in the social structure that biological individuals carry with them, at all times and in all places. (p. 82)

In other words, our everyday knowledge is based on historically constructed information as well as our own experiences, which are framed by such information. Additionally, habitus helps to explain why social inequalities are so difficult to overcome. In discussing social class systems, Bourdieu explains how the habitus creates a commonsense world in which the structure of society is taken for granted. We come to accept the structured practices, which lost their original meaning for us a long time ago in history, as the status quo. Essentially, the idea of habitus explains why it is so easy for Marx's bourgeoisie class to maintain false consciousness.

More generally, the above description of habitus illustrates how Bourdieu links structure and agency within one idea. In his substantive discussions, Bourdieu uses habitus to explain how actors engage with, and affect, organizations and social systems. In addition, when examining relations between different tribes through their gift-giving process (Bourdieu, 1998) and discussing it in terms of habitus, he links an empirical study with specific, middle-range theoretical ideas.

The next three ideas—social positions, position-taking, and fields—all provide an alternative method of describing the way that people interact with one another on the individual level as well as in relation to others within a system of actors. Bourdieu (2002a) states that

> at every moment of each society, one has to deal with a set of social positions which is bound by a relation of homology to a set of activities (the practice of golf or piano) or of goods (a second home or an old master painting) that are themselves characterized relationally. (p. 269)

Bourdieu's goal is to highlight that while social interactions occur between actors (individual, group, or institutional level) occupying particular roles, as traditionally defined by sociologists, they are far more dynamic than has been typically discussed. Weber's discussion of social action, the bases of legitimate authority, and the types of legitimate authority all serve as the basis upon which Bourdieu is building. In talking about social action, Weber states that it is our ability to recognize others and react to them that defines human society. However, Weber's discussion of social action did not focus on individual interactions but rather classification for types of actions, especially those associated with particular positions or roles. Examples of typical contemporary discussions of roles include Goffman's dramaturgical perspective, where actors assume particular masks for which there are accompanying scripts defining expected behaviors, as well as expectation states theory, which argues that shared cultural and social norms lead to shared expectations for behavior within task-oriented groups.

The idea of *social positions,* as described by Bourdieu, combines the seemingly fixed characteristics of roles or expectation states with the possibility for a range of actions by actively engaged actors. He states, "Objective structures (spaces of *positions*) [are] the distribution of socially efficient resources that define the external constraints bearing on interactions and representations" (Bourdieu & Wacquant, 1992, p. 11) and that "these positions are objectively defined, in their existence and in the determinations they impose on their occupants, agents or institutions, by their present and potential situation (*situs*) in the structure of the distribution of species of power (or capital)" (p. 97). Moreover, he explains that social positions exist relative to one another and that such relations change from one point in time to another. In addition, while actors occupying social positions face expectations for behavior, they also have a range of possible actions that can be taken depending on the situation, who occupies the other social positions, and the tensions that exist between different social positions. More to the point, actors are aware of the structure of practices inherent in any habitus that accompanies social positions, as well as aware of the way in which such practices shift. The idea of *social positions*, similar to habitus, also illustrates how Bourdieu links the agency of individual actors with the structured situations in which they find themselves.

To focus on individual agency, Bourdieu's theory of practice recognizes the engaged actor through the idea of *position-taking*, which involves "the 'choices' made by the social agents in the most diverse domains of practice" (2002a, p. 269) and which he also calls the "stance" actors take in occupying a position. Bourdieu argues that actors occupying specific social positions then engage in position-taking whereby they make decisions concerning actions to be taken based on their habitus and the different social positions linked to their own. In other words, actors engage in the process of position-taking that allows them to occupy particular positions in relation to other actors. Whether a stranger in a new town (as discussed by Georg Simmel) or playing a game of baseball (as described by George Herbert Mead), while we occupy specific positions that have accompanying expectations associated with them, we must still be cognizant of who occupies other positions and the environment in which we find ourselves. For example, those of us who have siblings engage in position-taking when interacting with one versus another sibling.

These positions are all located in a field, which occurs on a local level reflecting particular situations as well as in broader, social contexts. Similar to a 3-D chess game, actors find themselves embedded within fields that are embedded in larger fields. Bourdieu (1993) describes a *field* as "a separate social universe having its own laws of functioning independent of those of politics and the economy" (p. 163). More specifically, fields are

> a veritable social universe where, in accordance with its particular laws, there accumulates a particular form of capital and where relations of force of a particular type are exerted. This universe is the place of entirely specific struggles, notably concerning the question of knowing who is part of the universe. . . . The social universe functions somewhat like a prism which *refracts* every external determination: demographic, economic or political events are always retranslated according to the specific logic of the field. (Bourdieu, 1993, p. 164)

Fields can literally be mapped in terms of social positions as well as the position-taking possible for any category of endeavors or organized systems, as it is a network of social relations. Marx's unidimensional view of social relations between categories of people (bourgeoisie vs. proletariat) was challenged by Weber's multidimensional matrix of class, status, and party to describe stratification in society. Mead, on the other hand, viewed society as a system in which our patterned interactions led to formal social institutions that could be shaped by shifts in our interactions. Bourdieu combines structure and agency in talking about broader society in terms of fields—he wants us to view society with 3-D glasses rather than the limited two-dimensional view found in focusing on either one or the other. Similar to habitus, social positions, and position-taking, fields represent the intersection of the structured social world with the dynamic agency of actors.

In summary, Bourdieu's four key ideas of habitus, social positions, position-taking, and fields all integrate structural and ordered aspects of social life with the more dynamic nature of human choice. Habitus refers to the formal and informal social norms and values that proscribe human behavior as well as the knowledge that allows actors to make choices about their actions. Social positions are roles actors occupy relative to one another that are structurally determined by the other positions available but also change depending on the situation, time, and who occupies those other positions. Position-taking refers to the specific manner in which actors occupy their social position by drawing upon their habitus. Finally, a field is the entire collection of social positions and position-taking that occurs within one system.

While Bourdieu does not explicitly discuss social change and only references collective action in passing, I argue that his ideas allow us to better understand how social change occurs. By referencing both structure and agency in his definitions of habitus, social positions, position-taking, and fields, Bourdieu encourages us to examine the way in which actors (on any level) work within, between, and against existing systems, as we will see below.

Evoking Social Change: A Case Study

Introducing PFLAG

Today, PFLAG describes itself as

a national non-profit organization with over 200,000 members and supporters and over 500 affiliates in the United States. This vast grassroots network is cultivated, resourced and serviced by the PFLAG national office, located in Washington, DC, the national Board of Directors and 13 Regional Directors.

The organization defines its vision as

We, the parents, families and friends of lesbian, gay, bisexual and transgender persons, celebrate diversity and envision a society that embraces everyone, including those of diverse sexual orientations and gender identities. Only with respect, dignity and equality for all will we reach our full potential as human beings, individually and collectively.

Furthermore, PFLAG goes on to define its mission as promoting

> the health and well-being of gay, lesbian, bisexual and transgender persons, their families and friends through: support, to cope with an adverse society; education, to enlighten an ill-informed public; and advocacy, to end discrimination and to secure equal civil rights. Parents, Families and Friends of Lesbians and Gays provides opportunity for dialogue about sexual orientation and gender identity, and acts to create a society that is healthy and respectful of human diversity. (www.PFLAG.org)

One of the most interesting aspects of PFLAG is that it did not exist four decades ago. Its historical development through three distinct stages illustrates the dynamic nature of human interactions and society, and how such interactions literally evoke social change. Using archival documents, Web site information, and interviews with two of the original leaders (Adele Starr and Amy Ashworth) of PFLAG, we can see how Bourdieu's ideas of habitus, social positions, position-taking, and fields can be used to explain its development.

The First Stage of Development of PFLAG

The first stage in the development of a national PFLAG organization focused on identifying particular ways in which parents of gay men and lesbians could create an environment where they could help one another to accept and love their children. The creation of PFLAG took place because of a series of events occurring separately on the East and West Coasts between 1972 and 1977. On the East Coast in 1972, 2 months after the *New York Post* published a letter from Jeanne Manford complaining about the lack of police protection for her son and his fellow gay rights activists who were beaten during a gay rights protest, she took the unusual step of marching beside her gay son in New York City's annual Gay Pride march carrying a placard requesting that "Parents of Gays: Unite in Support of Our Children." A picture of this appeared in local papers (http://community.pflag.org/Page .aspx?pid=267), and in printed interviews published after the march, Jeanne stated that she decided to march with her son as a way of showing her support for issues that were important to him.

She recounted how her presence deeply affected the other gay and lesbian marchers, who hugged her and cried when telling of their wish for such acceptance from their own families. While the majority of phone calls and letters she received after the march were mostly from gay men and lesbians thanking her for joining the march, she also received letters from parents of some of the marchers expressing their support for her actions. In the months that followed the march, Jeanne attended panel discussions and participated in radio and television interviews, where she encouraged parents to provide love and support to their gay and lesbian children, who were facing horrible discrimination and violence in their everyday lives. Encouraged by the number of parents concerned about their children and with the goal of creating a support group for one another, in March 1973, Jeanne and Jules Manford held a meeting in a Methodist church in Greenwich Village for parents to talk with one another and share their stories. Twenty people attended that first meeting of what they called "Parents of Gays and Lesbians," and the group began to meet regularly, creating the first public emotional support group for parents of gay and lesbian children. It was in 1973 that the oldest son of Amy and Dick Ashworth told his parents that he was gay, and he gave them Jeanne Manford's name and number. They decided to attend the "Parents of Gays and Lesbians" meetings in an effort to better understand their son and to learn how to be more supportive of him. The Ashcrofts and the Manfords, along with the Benovs, who joined for similar reasons, became leaders in the New York area as well as resources for information and guides for parents around the country who learned about the New York group.

In Los Angeles, in 1968, Adele Starr's son announced to his parents that he was gay. They first encouraged him to go to counseling to solve his "problem" and believed that he was cured, but in 1972, they realized otherwise when they discovered that he was still dating men. After the initial shock of learning that their son was "still" gay wore off, the Starrs started reading everything they could about homosexuality and started working as volunteers at the gay community center. They met Jeanne Manford in 1974 after a gay pride march, and she encouraged them to establish a parents' support group similar to the one in New York City.

In March 1976, the Starrs welcomed 30 parents into their house for the first official meeting of a parents' support group in Los Angeles, which they then incorporated as the first nonprofit, tax-exempt "Parents of Gays and Lesbians" group in 1977. The stated purpose of the New York City group and the incorporated Los Angeles group was the same—to provide support, comfort, and information to the parents of gay and lesbian children. The Manfords, Ashworths, Benovs, and Starrs found that when they met with other parents, everyone discovered that their gay and lesbian children were no different from their straight children. They began developing educational and informational materials to share with new parents joining the support group as well as to share with similar support groups developing across the country.

All four sets of parents began appearing at gay pride marches across the country with the goal of encouraging parents and family members to do two things—first, to accept and love their lesbian and gay children, and second, to join with other parents of lesbian and gay children to support one another. From 1973 until 1978, locally based emotional support groups for parents and family members of gay men and lesbians were created throughout the country and in all types of locations—from urban areas to the suburbs to rural areas. While the groups communicated with one another informally and the leaders of some of the groups met in New York City in the mid-1970s with the Manfords as hosts, their main purpose was to provide support and educational resources for parents and family members. The majority of members were parents of gay and lesbian children.

Stepping into Bourdieu's theoretical world, we can see that the habitus in which these parents found themselves consisted of established social mores concerning acceptable social and sexual relationships. Homosexuality was (and in many places still is) considered deviant, and it was considered reasonable to attack gays and lesbians in public, as evidenced when Jeanne Manford's son was beaten during a protest while the police did nothing to stop the attack. The common logic, and structure, of practices discouraged gay men and lesbians from openly or publicly displaying affection or identifying their sexuality.

The structured environment in which the parents and their children found themselves was supported by existing law and social policy. Despite a legally and socially hostile environment, the range of practices available to all actors also included public forums through which alternative opinions could be expressed, such as letters to the editor, legally sanctioned marches, and public meeting places. When Jeanne Manford wrote a letter to the editor, she engaged in an acceptable practice that, along with marching alongside her son in the gay pride march, initiated a shift in the habitus. Creating a shift in the structured practices for those parents interested in supporting their gay and lesbian children affected the social positions available and the type of position-taking occurring.

Specifically, the parents expanded their existing social positions by redefining their roles as parents as well as created new social positions within the already established systems when the interested and concerned parents chose to meet together and met on a regular basis. Also, the type of position-taking possibilities changed in two ways. First, as parents continued to occupy their original social positions but became more outspoken about supporting their gay and lesbian children, they essentially enlarged the possibilities available. In other words, they began to put a more public face on the issue of gay and lesbian lives by talking about their children.

The second way that position-taking changed for the parents involved with "Parents of Gay and Lesbian Children" is the way in which they actively assisted other parent groups interested in establishing local support groups through providing educational information and participating in gay pride marches around the country. For example, the New York and the Los Angeles groups initially used the same strategies to reach other parents of gay and lesbian children—letters to the editor and personal advertisements in mainstream and community papers. The letters to the editor conveyed the same message each time: Parents (the implication is that they are "normal" and straight) of gay and lesbian children are proud of their children's success and stability, especially in the face of adversity and condemnation from society. However, Amy Ashworth and Adele Starr both commented that advertisements in the mainstream newspapers did not result in many parents contacting them. Their next step was to place advertisements in gay newspapers and to post flyers about the meetings in gay bars. It was through publicity in gay venues that parents were reached. According to Amy Ashworth and Adele Starr, gay men and lesbians would read the ads and flyers, contact their parents, and beg them to meet with the group.

Finally, the field in which the social positions were located was defined in terms of family relations and how they were defined socially and politically. More to the point, the field consisted of the parents, their gay and lesbian children, and public venues through which they communicated with one another.

In summary, Bourdieu's ideas of habitus, positions, position-taking, and fields allow us to describe *how* the parents in PFLAG were able to initiate the first stage of social change. This first stage consisted of identifying a specific social issue (the safety of their gay and lesbian children) as well as an accompanying concern (the emotional needs of parents of gay and lesbian children). They then created an informal social organization within which both the social issue and accompanying concern could be addressed. As each idea addresses both structured situations and individual agency to manage such situations, this enables us to better understand the way that actors engage with the social world. We see how once the parents of gay and lesbian children began to identify with one another, they also created a new field with accompanying positions and habitus. This new field led to the second stage of development of PFLAG into its current status as an international educational and lobbying organization.

The Second Stage of Development of PFLAG

The second stage in the development of an international organization dedicated to addressing gay and lesbian issues occurred between 1978 and 1987 and reflected a changing social environment, resulting in the creation of the national organization whose goal was to more actively support and protect gay and lesbian children. The role of the "Parents of Gays and Lesbians" groups as simply emotional support groups and a source of information started to change in 1978 when Anita Bryant appeared on the Phil Donahue show (*Donahue*) condemning homosexuality and advocating the Christian right's agenda of family values and morality.

Outraged, Jeanne Manford contacted the *Donahue* show to protest Bryant's appearance, and she was asked to appear on the show as a counterpoint. Both the Manfords and the Ashworths appeared on the show, where they talked about their children and their support group. Events on the West Coast were also propelling the Starrs into the public eye. Both Amy Ashworth and Adele Starr vividly recall that they received over 3,000 letters after the *Donahue* show and the Starrs' appearance on several California-based talk shows and news segments. It was in 1979 that the Starrs, Ashworths, Manfords, Benovs, and several other sets of parents began to talk about the need to address the social and political environment their children faced.

They all marched, along with hundreds of thousands of gay men, lesbians, and their families and friends, at the first National March for Gay and Lesbian Rights held in Washington, DC. Dick Ashworth and Adele Starr both spoke at the march, advocating for the rights of their gay children. While in Washington, after holding a press conference proclaiming support for their children and demanding rights and protections for them, a group of 25 parents met to talk about the increasingly conservative and vitriolic nature of American society toward gay men and lesbians. The conservative and religious right had begun a smear campaign against homosexuals, highlighted by Anita Bryant's appearance on the *Donahue* show, and gays and lesbians were facing severe and painful discrimination—even the possibility of personal injury—from strangers. The founding members of PFLAG felt that simply educating other parents and family members, and serving as an emotional support group, was no longer enough; there was a need to significantly change the social and political state of affairs in the United States. In 1981, over 30 people met at the Starrs' house in Los Angeles from July 30 through August 1, where they decided that there was a need for a national organization to advocate, and lobby, for the rights of gay men and lesbians. They created a five-member Board of Directors with Adele Starr as the president of the board, wrote the by-laws for the national organization, and drafted the articles of incorporation.

A total of 20 locally created and based groups decided to join together under the name of the Federation of Parents and Friends of Lesbians and Gays, calling themselves Parents FLAG. The mission statement of the national organization contained the familiar local goals of educating and supporting parents and families of lesbian and gay children, but this group of parents broadened the focus to include enlightening "an ill-informed public; and advocacy, to end discrimination and to secure equal civil rights" (www.pflag.org). What had started as a way for parents of gay men and lesbians to support one another as they dealt with their children's "difference" had become a formal social movement organization whose stated and explicit goal was to effect social change by ending discrimination against, and securing equal rights for, homosexuals. With the national office essentially operating out of the Starrs' home, with Adele as president of the board and her husband Larry as the financial advisor, Parents FLAG vastly expanded their efforts beyond what the locally based groups had done by becoming proactive in three distinct ways. First, the group distributed information to "educational institutions and communities of faith nationwide" (www.pflag.org). Rather than waiting for requests for information from individuals or groups, they took seriously the charge to enlighten the ill-informed public through the two communities most directly responsible for affecting people's beliefs and attitudes—educational and religious. Second, Parents FLAG sought to establish itself as the source of information for the general public by writing letters to Dear Abby and to editors of newspapers as well as appearing on talk shows or news segments addressing gay and lesbian issues.

The organization purposely sought to reframe such concerns as family issues, according to Adele Starr and Amy Ashworth. Finally, the organization actively began to advocate for social change by addressing specific issues such as fighting the U.S. military's efforts to discharge lesbians from the service in the 1980s. As the national group's efforts grew, its leaders realized that they needed to more formally organize operations, and in 1987, after extended discussions and study of the key issues, Parents FLAG moved to Denver, Colorado, with Ellinore Lewallen as its president and the first paid staff member of the federation, whose office was located in a local community center. The organization subsequently grew, requiring the hiring of an additional staff member.

From Bourdieu's point of view, the creation of a national organization with two paid staff members and the more activist agenda changed all aspects of PFLAG. The field has changed as Parents FLAG has enlarged from the local level of establishing support groups and providing information to such groups, to include state and national initiatives concerning gay and lesbian issues. The field includes the local parent support groups, the nationally affiliated groups and officers, the two national staff members, and the politicians with whom they communicate. By expanding the efforts of the national organization, the habitus has also changed for those parents and staff members now interacting with social positions such as those of politicians and their staff members.

Some of the parents were now occupying different social positions from those they had as participants in the local support groups. This led to new position-taking with already established social positions in the smaller field of local groups as well as with the new social positions with which they interacted. An important aspect of the new position-taking included reframing gay and lesbian issues as family issues. Such reframing was necessary to ensure that they were able to effectively communicate, and interact, with the greater variety of social positions within the field. Social movement scholars would label the national organization as a social movement organization since it is formally established with specific goals to achieve and particular roles for its members to play. The limitation of focusing only on the organization is that it does not adequately explain how the dynamic interchange between actors in particular positions, engaging in position-taking, create an organizational actor capable of agency on behalf of individual actors. Bourdieu's ideas literally allow us to view this second stage of social change for PFLAG as it grows from being focused on providing emotional support and educational information for parents into an institutional actor in and of itself.

The Third Stage of Development of PFLAG

The organization continued growing as the number of requests for information continued to increase, and it established task forces to study specific issues such as homosexuality and religion, HIV/AIDS, and youth. The third stage in the development of PFLAG started in 1988 when the organization relocated its national offices to Washington, DC, and hired an executive director as well as full-time, paid staff. Paulette Goodman, the new president, stated that "the organization had been mostly a home-spun grassroots federation [and I] wanted to make the organization more visible, to raise funds and really have a national voice" (www.pflag.org). The organization's move to Washington, DC, highlighted the much more public and activist role being taken as well as reflected a more aggressive role in creating a safer social environment for gay men and lesbians by affecting social policy discussions and decisions on a range of issues, from sex education in schools, to gay men and lesbians serving in the military, to the right to marry. This included Goodman's correspondence with then–First Lady Barbara Bush.

As the national organization's efforts grew, the organization restructured again in 1993, resulting in an affiliation process for all local chapters, electing people to board seats rather than simply appointing the more active members of local groups, and changing the name to Parents, Families and Friends of Lesbians and Gays (PFLAG). Nancy McDonald, PFLAG's president in 1996, highlighted this growth in saying that "we've strengthened locally, and we've taken our place at the national table. When I first became involved with PFLAG 10 years ago, we were an afterthought. Now, people call us to testify before Congress" (www.pflag.org). This change in the organization was reflected in the way in which it interacted with its different publics as well as the role of PFLAG. The local chapters continued to serve as emotional support groups for parents of gay and lesbian children, and they continued to reach these parents through their children by placing advertisements in gay and lesbian publications and through flyers posted in gay and lesbian venues. To date, the local groups still conduct monthly meetings and distribute monthly newsletters.

However, on the national level, PFLAG serves a dual purpose. First, it provides informational and educational materials to the local chapters as well as serving as an information clearinghouse for them. Second, it actively seeks to effect local, state, and national legislation through a variety of activities—including the development of educational materials for primary schools and organizations. Finally, the national organization networks of social relations are far more complex than those of the local chapters in that they focus on relations with formal organizations, institutions, and governments as advocates for change. In talking with Adele Starr and Amy Ashworth about the changes they saw the organization undergo over the years, they commented that as the organization grew to become a national voice for gay and lesbian rights, it required new leaders as well as a new focus. The original leaders of the New York and Los Angeles "Parents of Gay and Lesbian Children" are still active on the local level and provide their support to the national leaders.

At this current point in the history of PFLAG, we can now see that there are two fields, each with its associated habitus, social positions, and position-taking within which gay and lesbian issues are being addressed. During the second stage, the original field had expanded as the original leaders extended their habitus to revised social positions and new position-taking when they became actively involved in establishing local groups nationwide. Even in developing educational materials, becoming the public face of gay and lesbian family issues, and advocating particular views concerning social policy such as gays in the military, the original actors were working within the same set of tensions between social positions that marked their origins.

The establishment of a national office in Washington, DC, with leaders who did not work their way through local and regional groups, created a new field represented by more formal political and social systems. For example, the current president and full-time staff have never been affiliated with a local PFLAG group, but their experience, knowledge, and expertise allow them to easily interact with other lobbyists and politicians. The two distinct fields whose maps would reflect very different sets of habitus and social positions are the following: (a) the national PFLAG organization that includes lobbying and education efforts associated with large social institutions, and (b) the local PFLAG groups whose primary function is providing emotional support for parents of gay men and lesbians. The habitus and social positions for the national PFLAG organization consist of political and economic systems in which the actors are more likely to be groups and social institutions. The type of position-taking reflects a different set of tensions between social positions from those in the second field. The second field consists of the locally based PFLAG groups for whom the habitus, social positions, and position-taking are the same as in the first stage of PFLAG's development as discussed above.

PFLAG—Social Change and Changing Fields

It is obvious that over the past three decades, PFLAG has undergone significant changes with regard to the people involved, its organization, and its goals.

Additionally, it is clear that such changes occurred on all levels of society, from the individuals involved to the broader social environment in which they found themselves. Although Bourdieu does not explicitly discuss ideas of social change, as stated previously, his ideas of habitus and fields implicitly reference social change in that people act and react based not only on established norms, rules, and values but also to specific situations and people. Thus, norms, rules, and values can change as the positions we hold and the position-taking in which we engage changes. We have already discussed changes in the habitus and fields for the people associated with PFLAG over time. If we step into Bourdieu's shoes, we would argue that such changes in one part of the social world should be reflected in other parts of the social world. More to the point, we can also discuss whether, and how, the larger social environment (habitus and field) has changed over time for gay men, lesbian women, bisexual people, and transgendered people (hereafter denoted as GLBT). If their habitus and field have changed over time, we can point to PFLAG as one of the stimulants in a dynamic environment leading to such changes.

There are two specific ways that we can examine whether the habitus and field have changed for GLBT people—legally and socially. In other words, do GLBT people have formal civil rights today that they did not have prior to 1972 (the origins of PFLAG), and do the norms and values today differ significantly from those prior to 1972 in regard to GLBT lives? There are three legal issues that serve as markers for GLBT civil rights—sodomy laws (the right for consenting GLBT adults to have sexual relations in the privacy of their own home); the right to serve in the military (President Clinton's infamous "Don't Ask, Don't Tell" policy concerning gays in the military); and the legal right for GLBT people to marry. Prior to 1986, almost every state in the nation had sodomy laws that were used to persecute GLBT and that essentially made being gay illegal. Although the majority of criminal prosecutions for sodomy occurred in the South, the threat that such similar prosecutions could be made kept the majority of GLBT people "in the closet." In 1986, the Supreme Court heard the case of *Bowers v. Harwick,* in which a gay man convicted of sodomy appealed based on his constitutional right to a consenting sexual relationship with another man. As Toobin (2008) states,

> the Court had upheld the conviction of a Georgia man for consensual sodomy with another man. Byron White's opinion for the 5-4 majority was utterly contemptuous of the whole concept of gay rights. "To claim that a right to engage in such conduct is 'deeply rooted in this Nation's history and tradition' or 'implicit in the concept of ordered liberty' is, at best, facetious," White wrote. (p. 218)

However, 17 years later, the Supreme Court heard the case of *Lawrence v. Texas,* in which the facts of the case were like those of the earlier *Bowers v. Hardwick,* and one of the issues to be addressed was whether the Supreme Court's findings in that case should be overturned. Toobin (2008) dramatically shares the Court's opinion when he writes,

> As the tension rose in the courtroom, Kennedy finally announced the holding on the case: "The instant case requires us to address whether *Bowers* itself has

continuing validity. We conclude the rationale of *Bowers* does not withstand careful analysis. *Bowers* was not correct when it was decided, and it is not correct today. It ought not to remain binding precedent. *Bowers versus Hardwick* should be and now is overruled." There was no mistaking the significance of Kennedy's opinion. The point was not that the Court was halting sodomy prosecutions, which scarcely took place anymore. Rather, the Court was announcing that gay people could not be branded as criminals simply because of who they were. They were citizens. (p. 222)

Although it is obvious that the habitus and field had changed with regard to GLBT people's standing as citizens safe from prosecution, President Clinton's attempt to deal with gay civil rights sends a different message with regard to both serving in the military and gay marriage. One of Bill Clinton's campaign issues was gay civil rights, including the right for GLBT people to be allowed to serve in the military without fear of being dishonorably discharged if it was discovered they were gay. It was the first issue he addressed upon winning the presidency, and despite the support of several key legislators in Congress, the overwhelming opposition among the general population led to a compromise bill enacted in 1992—"Don't Ask, Don't Tell." It was no longer legal for military recruiters to ask potential volunteers about their sexual orientation, nor was it legal for military personnel to ask active servicemen and -women about their sexual orientation. However, it was also still illegal for active-duty military personnel to engage in homosexual activity or to talk about their partners. Although this policy is still in place today, many GLBT people and their supporters feel that the 1992 law did significantly change the opportunities and perceptions of GLBT in the military and therefore was a positive change. The field could not have changed without the habitus itself having changed.

The final legal issue concerning GLBT people is whether they can marry. Prior to 1993, GLBT people were not legally allowed to marry anywhere in the United States until Hawaii's Supreme Court stated, in its review of *Baehr v. Lewin,* that the state had to show why same-sex marriages should be prohibited. In response to this ruling, the U.S. Congress fast-tracked legislation titled the Defense of Marriage Act (DOMA), stating that marriage is only between a man and a woman, and it was signed into law by President Bill Clinton in 1996. Since that time, gay marriage has become a state issue with varying results. California courts mandated gay marriage, which was then overturned by a slim margin in a state-wide vote and supported by the California Supreme Court. Interestingly, as predicted by a number of legal and academic scholars, this California state issue is about to become a federal issue. An appeals court judge has overturned the California Supreme Court decision and, in a carefully crafted judgment, stated that refusing marriage to GLBT people denies them basic civil rights as defined by the Constitution. It is expected that the U.S. Supreme Court will consider this case within the next 3 years. A number of other states have had voter referenda banning gay marriage, and currently only five states legally allow and recognize gay marriage (what the National Gay and Lesbian Task Force calls "full marriage equality")—Connecticut, Iowa, Vermont, New Hampshire, and Massachusetts. A total of 16 states have some level of recognition laws (including those providing full marriage equality) (see http://www.thetaskforce .org/downloads/reports/issue_maps/rel_recog_11_4_09_color.pdf). As with sodomy laws and military service, the habitus and field for GLBT people have changed significantly in the United States.

None of the above changes mentioned could have happened without a significant change in social norms and values. As Toobin (2008) points out in explaining the shift in Supreme Court justices' views,

> A new generation of law clerks brought a new attitude toward homosexuality. . . . In major law schools and the big-city firms that employed their graduates (and many former Supreme Court law clerks), the cause of equality for gay people enjoyed close to unanimous support. Schools and firms bragged about their welcoming attitudes toward homosexuals. Significant numbers of gay law students grew up in this environment, accepted it as normal, and went on to clerk at the Supreme Court. The gay clerks changed the Court, not because of the advocacy but because of their existence. They were, of course, pretty much indistinguishable from their straight colleagues, and that was precisely the point. (p. 217)

In other words, as more GLBT people came to share their lives more openly, it significantly changed the environment in which they worked. For GLBT people today, the habitus in which their social positions and position-taking occurs is drastically different from what it was in 1972, when Jeanne Manford's son was unprotected from homophobic violence. The fields in which our social, personal, and work lives take place have shifted over time, and our legal rights as well as nonlegal rights reflect this change. More to the point, it is clear that PFLAG's actions contributed to the social change evident in the United States.

Conclusion

Pierre Bourdieu's theory of practice sought to provide a language with which to evocatively explain the dynamic nature of human society by highlighting how the interactions between actors (of any level of society—the individual, group, and social institution) reflect not only the structures in which they are engaged but also their own capacity to make choices. Habitus acknowledges the way that our understanding of social norms, rules, and values are historically shaped and objectively taught while also recognizing that actors have a choice in responding to each specific situation. The PFLAG case study aptly illustrates this point when the original set of parents first came "out of the closet" as parents of gay and lesbian children, then encouraged others to do the same, and further advocated on their children's behalf. Both Amy Ashworth and Adele Starr spoke with a bit of wonder in their voices as they described how much they felt had been accomplished. Actors who had previously been "just parents" became spokespeople and activists.

In defining social positions in terms of their relational properties, Bourdieu further emphasizes the situational nature of any role we occupy. While you may all be students, it is likely that the way in which you occupy the position of "student" varies from one classroom to another, depending on the teacher with whom you interact. This is also evident in the transformation of the parents involved in fighting for their gay and lesbian children's rights. The situation in which they occupied social positions changed drastically when Anita Bryant appeared on the *Donahue* show. They were still parents and advocates for their children, but now they were in the public eye, and the number of other social positions with which they might interact had increased dramatically.

Their position-taking also changed as the number of social positions with which the parents interacted changed, as did the setting in which such interactions occurred. When it reached the point that their ability to position-take was no longer adequate for the issues being addressed, we see in the third stage of PFLAG's development that a new field was created (or the organization entered another field that already existed), with new actors engaged in the habitus so as to successfully gain a "seat at the national table" in terms of lobbying efforts with social actors in social positions far different from what the local groups addressed.

Finally, the idea of fields allows us to literally map the social world in which we are located. Such a mapping also allows us to understand that our actions are not totally constrained, and that such systems do reflect the dynamic nature of interactions between actors. While there are aspects of such interactions that might be predictable because of the way they are structured and the actors that are involved, Bourdieu's discussion also encourages us to see that actors make choices in such a way as to literally change the world in which we live. In other words, social change is possible, as shown with the PFLAG case study, if we understand that actor agency can change social structures from the micro level of interactions to the macro level of social institutions.

References

Bourdieu, P. (1984). *Distinction: A social critique of the judgment of taste.* Boston: Harvard University Press.

Bourdieu, P. (1988). *Homo academicus.* Palo Alto, CA: Stanford University Press.

Bourdieu, P. (1993). *The field of cultural production* (R. Johnson, Ed. & Trans.). New York: Columbia University Press.

Bourdieu, P. (1998). *Outline of a theory of practice.* New York: Cambridge University Press.

Bourdieu, P. (2001). *Masculine domination.* Palo Alto, CA: Stanford University Press.

Bourdieu, P. (2002a). Social space and symbolic space. In C. Calhoun, J. Gerteis, J. Moody, S. Pfaff, & I. Virk (Eds.), *Contemporary sociological theory.* Oxford, UK: Blackwell.

Bourdieu, P. (2002b). Structures, *habitus,* practices. In C. Calhoun, J. Gerteis, J. Moody, S. Pfaff, & I. Virk (Eds.), *Contemporary sociological theory.* Oxford, UK: Blackwell.

Bourdieu, P., & Passeron, J.-C. (1994). *Reproduction in education, society, and culture* (2nd ed.). London: Sage.

Bourdieu, P., & Wacquant, L. J. D. (1992). *An invitation to reflexive sociology.* Chicago: University of Chicago Press.

Merton, R. K. (1968). *Social theory and social structure* (enlarged ed.). New York: Free Press.

Toobin, J. (2008). *The nine: Inside the secret world of the Supreme Court.* New York: Anchor Books.

Wacquant, L. (2002). The sociological life of Pierre Bourdieu. *International Sociology, 17*(4), 549–556.

Additional Sources

Baert, P. (1998). *Social theory in the twentieth century.* New York: New York University Press.

Bourdieu, P. (2004). *Science of science and reflexivity.* Chicago: University of Chicago Press.

Calhoun, C., LiPuma, E., & Postone, M. (Eds.). (1993). *Bourdieu: Critical perspectives.* Chicago: University of Chicago Press.

Fowler, B. (1997). *Pierre Bourdieu and cultural theory: Critical investigations.* London: Sage.

Münch, R. (1994). *Sociological theory: Development since the 1960's* (Vol. 3). Chicago: Nelson Hall.

Ritzer, G., & Goodman, D. J. (2004). *Modern sociological theory* (6th ed.). Boston: McGraw-Hill.

Sica, A. (Ed.). (2005). *Social thought: From the Enlightenment to the present.* Boston: Allyn & Bacon.

Stones, R. (Ed.). (1998). *Key sociological thinkers.* New York: New York University Press.

Wallace, R. A., & Wolf, A. (1995). *Contemporary sociological theory: Expanding the classical tradition* (5th ed.). Upper Saddle River, NJ: Prentice Hall.

DISCUSSION QUESTIONS

1. The idea of habitus states that while our behaviors are structured by established social institutions, we are also responsible for creating such structures. This implies that social change is possible, as exemplified by the case study presented herein. Select a specific social issue or problem; describe it in detail, including what type of change is needed to address the issue or problem; and then explain how understanding habitus would allow *you* to evoke such a change.

2. Goffman's idea of dramaturgy argues that life is like a stage where we all wear different masks reflecting the different roles we fulfill. Bourdieu's idea of position-taking builds on the idea of masks and adds a dynamic element. Explain what this statement means by doing field research the next time you are out with a group of friends or with family by focusing on the way in which people interact with others. Pay particular attention to specific characteristics of one selected person's interactions with a range of people, and then describe it in terms of masks and in terms of position-taking. Identify how position-taking represents a more dynamic explanation of the way in which people interact with one another.

3. Bourdieu's discussion of field allows him to take key ideas associated with Marx and integrate them with an interactionist perspective. Explain what this statement means by selecting any type of job or career in which you are interested and creating a spatial map to describe the various

people responsible for achieving a particular goal. Describe the map in terms of social positions, position-taking, and how this represents integrating Marx and interactionist ideas.

4. Similar to other European theorists, Bourdieu builds on the ideas of classical theorists such as Marx, Weber, Durkheim, and Mead, as well as integrates a range of ideas to overcome the limitations of using only one perspective. Discuss why this integrative approach, of linking macro with micro theory and agency with structure, creates a more dynamic understanding of human society. Illustrate your discussion by referring to a specific situation from your own personal life as an example.

5. PFLAG appears to have successfully transformed fringe social issues concerning gays and lesbians into the mainstream issue of family values. Identify one social issue that is considered to be a fringe idea today and explain how it could be reframed into a mainstream issue demanding everyone's attention. As part of your explanation, include references to position-taking and its role in the successful reframing of an issue.

CHAPTER 14

Globalization Theory and Religious Fundamentalism

William H. Swatos, Jr.

William H. Swatos, Jr., is Executive Officer of both the Religious Research Association and the Association for the Sociology of Religion as well as the editor of the Interdisciplinary Journal of Research on Religion. *He received his PhD in sociology from the University of Kentucky in 1973 and received the sociology department's distinguished alumni award in 1989. From 1988 to 1994, he was the editor of* Sociology of Religion: A Quarterly Review. *He has edited, coedited, authored, or coauthored more than 20 books, including* Politics and Religion in Central and Eastern Europe *(1994),* Religious Politics in Global and Comparative Perspective *(1989),* The Power of Religious Publics *(1999), and* On the Road to Being There: Studies in Pilgrimage and Tourism in Late Modernity *(2006). He is Editor-in-Chief of the* Encyclopedia of Religion and Society *(1998) and with Kevin Christiano and Peter Kivisto has coauthored* Sociology of Religion: Contemporary Developments, *at the time of its publication in 2002 the first entirely new American sociology of religion text to appear in 20 years, now in its second edition (2008).*

It is difficult to think of an occurrence that caught Western students of religion more by surprise than the worldwide resurgence of religion—political religion, no less!—that happened with increasing visibility as the 1970s progressed. There had been the appearance of so-called "new religious movements," but many of the leading theorists of religion in modernity could accommodate these into the existing secularization paradigm by their very bizarreness. The highly eclectic character of the religious "marketplace" seemed only to confirm the privatization thesis—that religion had become a leisure-time activity, with no social consequences (except for an occasional figure like Charles Manson, who was more flashy news copy than a serious societal-level assault as a "religious leader").

Religious controversies that did reach political proportions were often "explained" (i.e., explained away) by social scientists as mere symbolic expressions of socioeconomic variables (e.g., in Northern Ireland or Israel/Palestine). The idea that there were concerted groups of people taking religion seriously enough to affect the order of global society gained little credence, in fact, until the appearance of Ayatollah Khomeini in revolutionary Iran. He meant business, and the explanation that he was a mere figurehead for those really in power fell into greater and greater disrepute as the heads of one after another of those "really" in power rolled before the ayatollah's revolutionary justice.

Standard social-scientific models of change seemed ill equipped to account for a worldwide religious resurgence. The two primary theories of modernization— functionalism's *development* and Marxism's *exploitation*—both proceed from the assumption that religious "prejudices" hamper "progress" and are disappearing throughout the world. Secular education, secular armies, secular economics, and secular politics combine to create the modern state. The only real differences between these two models of modernization concern whether capitalism is viewed as a friend or foe to nation-state growth and whether capitalism is beneficial or detrimental to the order of the international system of states.

According to either of these theories, religious resurgence represents a deviant occurrence in the broad sweep of history. If, indeed, only an isolated instance of religious resurgence were now to be observed, one could hardly quarrel with such theoretical presuppositions. We have deviants within our own communities, after all, so why not expect the same at the political level in the international system of states? The problem, however, is that the resurgence phenomenon is global in character—so much so that it strains credulity to accept an argument that worldwide religious resurgence represents some form of mass delusion.

Globalization theory provides an approach to the current world situation that addresses these developments. Although rooted in the materialist analyses of Ferdinand Braudel and Immanuel Wallerstein, generally known as world-system theory, globalization has been reshaped by the later work of John Meyer and especially Roland Robertson to include important cultural components, not the least of which is religion.[1] What globalization refers to is most simply conceptualized by Robertson's felicitous phrase that the world is seen as "a single place" (Robertson, 1992; Robertson & Chirico, 1985; Robertson & Lechner, 1985). As Frank Lechner (2004) observes in a recent survey of the field, "Globalization refers to the worldwide diffusion of practices, expansion of relations across continents, organization of social life on a global scale, and growth of a shared global consciousness," but not only this:

[G]lobalization also recasts the agenda of social theory. . . . [W]hereas social theory once focused on the rise of individual, state-organized societies, it now must address the implications of change of scale in supraterritorial social relations. While modernization could once be treated as change within a single civilizational arena, students of globalization must now examine how world order can arise in the face of civilizational differences. (p. 333)

Globality stands over locality (or localism), but because the local is always within the global, the two are in constant relationship (which may be positive or negative). The global is universalistic, whereas the local is particularistic. In practice, however, there can be both particularistic universalism and universalistic particularism, giving rise, among other things, to the phenomenon of religious resurgence often popularly dubbed *fundamentalism.*

Strictly speaking, the word "fundamentalism" refers to a specific theological movement that originated in American Protestantism at the beginning of the 20th century. A group of Protestant leaders, concerned about what they considered to be a process of modernism that was shaking the foundations of the Christian religion, set forth five "fundamentals" that they considered essential to the Christian faith. People who subscribed to these were subsequently termed—first by their detractors and later by themselves—*fundamentalists.*[2]

When the worldwide religious resurgence of the 1970s gained attention, however, the term fundamentalist was used in a more extensive fashion. It was now extended to all contemporary religious movements that display what Eugen Schoenfeld (1987) has demarcated "exclusive militancy." In a definition that rivals Robertson's "seeing the world as a single place" for its simplicity, T. K. Oommen (1994) has similarly defined fundamentalism as "text without context." What this means is that religious texts (or scriptures) that were originally written in a specific historical context—hence, social setting—are decontextualized and held to be applicable without regard to local circumstances. At the same time, however, all other competing texts are rejected as having no corresponding claim to truth.

It is important to recognize that all fundamentalisms as they are advanced around the globe today are specifically modern products and heterodox faith traditions (see Lechner, 1985). This claim is never made, of course, by fundamentalists themselves, but it is easily documented by historical surveys of the faith traditions they claim to represent. The majority of those who claim to be Christians do not belong to fundamentalist churches—and never have. The majority of Muslims do not belong to fundamentalist sects of that faith. The historic creeds that the majority of those who call themselves Christians affirm are not held by most fundamentalists; the central concerns of fundamentalist Muslims are not the essential "Five Pillars" of Islam. Ultraorthodox Jews are more orthodox than the Orthodox. *All religious fundamentalisms as we know them today were constructed during our own time as responses to the modern world system,* which had its beginnings in the 16th century but has come to fruition in the global project that has progressed with increasing certainty since World War II.

Global Culture

If we are to understand the relationship between the seemingly conflicting dynamics of globalization and fundamentalism, we need to reflect on the culture of modernity itself. World-system theorist John Meyer (1980) observes,

> Modern world culture is more than a simple set of ideals or values diffusing and operating separately in individual sentiments in each society. . . . The power of modern culture—like that of medieval Christendom—lies in the fact that it is a shared and binding set of rules exogenous to any given society, and located not only in individual sentiments, but also in many world institutions. (p. 117)

Such institutions not only as the United Nations or the World Court, but also global financial institutions that make a world economy work, involve an element of faith; that is, they rest on a certain belief that what they do is both right and natural (these two conditions are bound together, for example, in the phrase "human rights").

This worldview (in the double sense) has not characterized human history taken as a whole, even into our own day. Consider the following vignette from social theorist Agnes Heller (1995):

> About 30 years ago I became acquainted with the middle-aged owner of a little trattoria in Rome's Campo dei Fiori. After a lively conversation I asked him to advise me about the shortest way to Porta Pia. "I am sorry, but I cannot help you," he answered. "The truth of the matter is I have never ever in my life left the Campo dei Fiori." About one and a half decades later, on board a jumbo jet en route to Australia, I discussed the then current political affairs with my neighbour, a middle-aged woman. It turned out that she was employed by an international trade firm, spoke five languages, and owned three apartments in three different places. Recalling the confession of the trattoria owner, I asked her the obvious question: "Where are you at home?" She was taken aback. After a while she responded: "Perhaps where my cat lives."
>
> These two people seemingly lived worlds apart. For the first, the earth had a center, it was called Campo dei Fiori, the place where he was born and expected to die. He was deeply committed to the geographic monogamy that wedded him to his tradition. His commitment stretched from the remote past, the past of the Campo, up to a future beyond his own, the future of the Campo. For the second, the earth had no center; she was geographically promiscuous, without pathos. Her whereabouts made no difference to her. My question surprised her because the loaded concept "home" seemingly had no significance for her.
>
> This was confirmed by her unwittingly ironical answer. As long as there is something called home, our cat lives in our home. So when my interlocutor said, in reversing the signs, that "My home is where my cat lives," she had deconstructed the concept "home." Her geographic promiscuity symbolized something uncanny (*unheimlich*), namely the abandonment of, perhaps, the oldest tradition of the homo sapiens, privileging one, or certain, places against all the others. (p. 1)

Not surprisingly, commentators on the condition of modernity have spoken of both "the homeless mind" and "the absent center," or have raised the question of whether globalization and attendant glocalization lead from something to nothing (Berger & Kellner, 1974).

The illustration by Heller can help us understand particularly well the potential problems of globalization. To move from the worldview of the man of Campo dei Fiori to the woman on the jet is to move from one way of knowing to another; it is a total shift in *epistemology*, the technical term philosophers apply to systems of knowledge. All ways of knowing, however, rest on systems of beliefs about the universe that are themselves unprovable to observation. One can make logical assertions about evolution, for example, but one can also make logical assertions about the existence of God, as St. Thomas Aquinas did approximately 1,000 years ago. None of us was there to observe either one, however; hence, we ultimately accept one or another account "on faith": The arguments as a whole have a ring of consistency or plausibility that convinces us that they are inherently worthwhile to getting on with life in the present. In short, the worldview of globalization has an essentially religious character in that it requires us to accept beliefs about "the way the world works" that may be in conflict with other beliefs—not only beliefs of the existing formally organized religions, such as Christianity or Islam, but also beliefs of the popular or "implicit" religions on the basis of which people have constructed their lives for centuries.[3]

Globalization particularly flies in the face of the belief in absolute nation-state sovereignty—what Frank Lechner (1989) terms *institutionalized societalism*, which, ironically, reached its apex as the very capstone of the globalization process that now threatens its undoing. On one hand, the globe appears as a union of sovereign states, recognized by world institutions as having transcendent integrity. On the other hand, the sovereignty of these states as political actors is circumscribed by a set of principles—a "higher law"—that in fact rests on beliefs generated by specific world orientations that are themselves metaphysical; that is, the principles of global society are generated by accepting some kinds of faith propositions and not others. In general, these propositions reflect Anglo-American utilitarian-pragmatic philosophy, which lacks absolutes and is thus subject to contradiction as circumstances change.

Before we turn to religious fundamentalism, we might examine another formally nonreligious vignette. Although it recently went technically financially bankrupt, the nation-state of Iceland has been one of the greatest beneficiaries of the principle of institutionalized societalism. Numbering little more than a quarter of a million people, it has virtually all the privileges in world institutions that are accorded to the United States or Japan and perhaps even more privileges than China. Part of the process of the creation of an independent Iceland, however, was the enshrining of the Icelandic language as the keystone of its claim to distinction—so much so that Icelandic sociologist of religion Pétur Pétursson (1988) has described it as characterized by a "language fundamentalism." A manifestation of Icelanders' fascination with Icelandic is a law that all Icelanders must have Icelandic names. One of the by-products of globalization, however, is a world openness that allows the relatively free exchange of peoples and goods across national borders—a relatively fluid view of citizenship (i.e., world citizenship).

Consider the case of "Eternal Peace" Cabrera Hidalgo/Edgarsson. In the late 1980s, Jorge Ricardo Cabrera Hidalgo came to Iceland from Colombia. After he had attended college and worked for some time, he decided to start his own business, upon which he was informed that, bureaucratically speaking, it would be much easier for him if he were an Icelandic citizen. Upon being granted Icelandic citizenship in the mid-1990s, however, he was required to take an Icelandic name, which he considered "a violation of basic human rights." To settle the matter temporarily, he chose from the list of authorized names "Eilífur Friður"—Eternal Peace—to which was then added the patronymic Edgarsson because Edgar was his father's Christian (first) name. This did not solve his problem, however.

To complicate matters even further, Eilífur Friður had met an Icelandic woman prior to the citizenship adaptation of his name, with whom he has a daughter, Freyja María Cabrera. Little Freyja María is permitted to keep her name, but any sisters or brothers she may subsequently receive will have a surname different from hers: namely, Eilífsdóttir (for a girl) or Eilífsson (for a boy), which, as Eilífur Friður points out, is sure to raise questions when the family travels abroad, and will be outright rejected in his native country.

"My purpose in choosing the name [Eternal Peace]," he says, "is to call attention to the laws and make people question whether or not they are just. . . . I do not find it just to be forced to change my name" ("Eternal Peace," 1996, p. 2).[4] In this curious case, we see the strange collisions of globalization and localization, of the world system and institutionalized societalism, that on a larger scale can lead to intrasocietal and intersocietal tensions and even to open hostilities. A single dynamic simultaneously facilitates cooperation and conflict. When violence is sanctioned by the transcendent norms of religious belief, it becomes a far more threatening option than the irony of "eternal peace."

Excursus on the History of Religions

Because this book is intended primarily to enhance the study of *sociology*, it may be helpful to say a few words here about the historical circumstances that surround the three great Western religious traditions that play into today's controversies: Christianity, Judaism, and Islam. These are not the only religions to have produced religious fundamentalisms in our time, but a good case can be made that the other fundamentalisms that have emerged have used these religious traditions as the models for their programs—e.g., Hindu fundamentalism is a reaction to Islamic fundamentalism and would not otherwise have existed (see Pace, 2009). These three great traditions all find their roots in a single place—namely, the call by God to the patriarch Abraham and his response, as detailed in Chapters 12 through 21 of the biblical book of Genesis. Historians of religions thus often call these three the Abrahamic religions.

Students sometimes ask how it is that three religions and their hundreds of subparts that "worship the same God" can have so much conflict. The answer is that it is really quite easy, because each has a different conception of that "same God"; hence, each may perceive the others as perverting the truth. Because each tradition harkens back to a common narrative recorded in written form that it considers to be "the word of God," differences of interpretation (or "hermeneutics" [in Arabic, *ijtihad*]) can become either magnified or reduced through culture contact. This is precisely the problem that globalization highlights in the contrast of universalistic particularism and particularistic universalism. Consider some alternatives that different configurations of religions offer.

Suppose we live in a world in which we think there are many different gods: I have my god, and you have your god. We could fight over whose god is more powerful, and people certainly have done that. Usually, however, when such a conflict occurs, it is relatively localized, and the winners' god displaces the losers' god. We could also, however, agree to disagree, and peace might prevail. I could worship my god; you could worship your god. In many respects, what were once known as the "religions of the Orient" allowed easily for these possibilities, as do many folk religions.[5] We might call them "preglobal," however, in the sense that they do not view the world as a "single place." They are primarily clientelistic as they persist in modernity—from Voodoo to Zen—and represent countermodern tendencies.

The Abrahamic traditions, however, all begin with the assertion of a single, universal God (monotheism). Such is the First Commandment of Judaism, the Summary of the Law given by Jesus of Nazareth, and the first Pillar of Islam. There is only one God over all the universe, including every human being, and every human being should honor Him.[6] We know, however, that there has been considerable variety within and among the Abrahamic traditions in regard to how God is understood and what fidelity to God means. Again, there are two alternatives. The peaceful alternative allows me to state, in effect, "There is only one God over all the world, but each of us (or each community of us) may come to that God in different ways. We should respect this diversity of approaches." A militant alternative might state the following: "There is only one God over all the world, and there is only one way to come to and live correctly under that God. Anyone who does not conform to this standard must be brought to do so; anyone who persists in acting otherwise is an enemy (both to me and to God)." God's honor demands that enemies be eliminated. The first of these alternatives particularizes the universal, whereas the second universalizes the particular. The universalization of the particular at the world level sets the stage for global fundamentalisms.

Until relatively recently, culture contact even within Abrahamic traditions was narrowly circumscribed. Consider, for example, that when the sociologist Émile Durkheim published his famous study on suicide 100 years ago, he was able to compare what he called "racial" differences by using the French and the Germans as two different races—without any real criticisms of his definition of race. Likewise, when Lutherans from various European locales came to North America, they quickly formed congregations for each variation of cultural practice (principally, but not only, language) rather than homogenizing around a common Lutheranism—until the second half of the 20th century. Similarly, the Roman Catholic Church learned at the end of the 19th century that if it did not accommodate ethnic differences by establishing ethnic parishes in North America, the institutional loyalty of its people was not going to hold. These are the parishes the Roman Church is now often being forced to close as specific ethnicities move out of historic neighborhoods and blend into the general Euro-American population. Jews in major urban areas are as likely to refer to synagogues as Russian, German, Sephardic, or Polish as they are to refer to them as Conservative, Reform, or Orthodox.

Globalization and Fundamentalisms

Globalization, however, breaks across cultural barriers through finance, media, and transport. Anglo-America is the preeminent global societal actor. English is the language of air traffic control and the Internet. The dollar, mediated by European bourses, is the measure of world economic value. These technical systems, however, do not speak to the "soul." That is, the human personality seems to have—at some times and for some people more strongly than others, apparently—something we call a "spiritual" dimension. This dynamic is not, however, purely psychological; spirituality involves an element of power. Although each of the Abrahamic traditions contextualizes divine power differently, none fails to assert that the presence of God is the presence of power. In the global setting specifically, the nature of Abrahamic monotheism coupled with the hegemonic position of Anglo-American "know-how" provides a potential source of confrontation both within our own society and between societies.

As we examine several encounters between "the globe" and fundamentalist agendas, we will see that none of these can be separated from the joint issues of messiahship and the state of Israel. Although the specifics are different in each case, note that in every one, there is a significant commonality in the direction of hostilities, whether rhetorical or corporeal, against national political leaders who favor global peace on the basis of a universal value of human worth. Such hostilities originate with people within their own countries who demand acknowledgment of a particularist view of human action based on transcendent realities. In other words, current religiopolitical crises are not so much based on different ideas about God as they are on different claims about how God expects human beings to behave.

The American Religious Right

Mixing politics and religion is not new in the United States or other nations influenced by American thinking. Not only the civil rights and antiwar movements of the recent past but also prohibition and abolitionism mixed heady doses of politics and religion. In all these cases, social stratification mixed with cultural considerations, including religion. This no more means that economics "causes" religion than that religion causes economics; the two can interact, as can other aspects of human experience, and sometimes these interactions have profound civilizational effects—for example, those that occurred during the Reformation in the 16th century.

One of the differences between some earlier religiopolitical alliances in the United States and the contemporary Religious Right is the global dimension of our experience. Exactly when this began may be debated for generations to come by historians, but we might profitably start with the 1950s and the "Communist Menace." Clearly, some Christian Americans were skeptical of socialism in the 19th century, but it was a largely homegrown version of political radicalism that elicited their ire. After McCarthyism at home and Stalinism abroad, however, "godless communism" became a major foe for Christian combat. Although there was certainly a Catholic anticommunism, fundamentalist Protestants specifically attempted to identify Soviet Marxism with biblical prophecy.

At the center of this religious historiography was the newly founded (or refounded) state of Israel. The evils of Marxism were juxtaposed against the restoration of Israel as a nation-state as part of a grand theological plan to herald the end of time (the millennium), the return of Christ, and the judgment of the world. Elaborate explanations, often with increasingly technologically sophisticated visual representations, were constructed to herald a religious end of history. Atomic and hydrogen weaponry only enhanced the cataclysmic drama that would attend Armageddon, the great final battle. Did every Christian American believe this? Certainly not. People did hear enough of the great weapons race of the superpowers, the launching of satellites, and espionage and counterespionage, however, not to dismiss all of it as pure craziness.

The 1967 attack on Israel by a coalition of Muslim Arab states further enhanced the fundamentalist argument. Whether true or not, the Arabs were perceived as working with Soviet backing—both philosophically and materially. The Israeli triumph was enthusiastically received throughout the United States. A sudden alliance of good feeling and mutuality came to prevail among liberals, moderates, and fundamentalists. The victory of Israel was taken as an American victory. It justified American principles and served to give a tentative point of unity to a nation otherwise divided over civil rights issues at home and the Vietnam War abroad. As the years passed, this picture changed. Further military conflict in 1973 as well as Palestinian problems, the inability to achieve a lasting settlement, the rise of militant Islam in Iran, battles in Lebanon, and so on increasingly tried American patience. The fall of the Soviet empire in 1989 without any apparent resolution of the situation in the Holy Land began to make fundamentalist biblical exegesis of prophetic texts less gripping. A new American religious coalition was rebuilding "family values," and a new missionary thrust toward the formerly communist countries had more immediate success.

What today is often called the Religious Right or (New) Christian Right emerged in its present form in response to an appeal made by Richard Nixon during his presidency to America's "silent majority." Amid the protests of the Vietnam era, Nixon was sure that a silent majority of Americans (sometimes called the "silent generation") agreed with him and his handling of the situation. Before too many years had passed, a Virginia Independent Baptist pastor with a simply formatted television worship service, Jerry Falwell, had formed a political action group, the Moral Majority, which attempted to move the silent generation enough to send money to allow him to lead the nation to righteousness. The formation of Falwell's group coincided fairly closely with the election of the nation's first bona fide "born again" or evangelical president, Southern Baptist Jimmy Carter, but in fact Falwell's vision was quite different from Carter's. The Moral Majority would support tangentially Christian Ronald Reagan, not Carter, in the 1980 presidential election.

What were the sins of the Carter administration that irked the Religious Right? Clearly, no single act can be designated as the cause of Carter's rejection, but his years were ill-fated. He followed on, and would not actively work to use his administrative power or legislative influence to alter, the Supreme Court decision in *Roe v. Wade* (1973), which opened the way for legal abortions. The economy fell into deep recession. The Panama Canal was perceived by many to have been given away. When we examine the global situation, however, two other aspects also emerge: First, Carter and many of his advisers on international affairs had been or were part of a global "think tank" known as the Trilateral Commission. For right-wing activists, the Trilateral Commission represented a form of communist appeasement on one hand, while something of a capitulation to Japanese business interests on the other. Carter was labeled as soft on communism while selling out American industry. He was rejected as not really "believing" in America. Second, Carter allowed Americans to be taken hostage by an infidel regime in Iran and proved impotent as commander in chief. Carter was perceived as having betrayed Christian America on virtually all fronts, an apostate to our civil religion. His humanism was demonized both at home and abroad. He was also hindered by the fact that his vice president, Walter Mondale, whom Reagan absolutely trounced in 1984, was the half-brother of a signer of the *Humanist Manifesto.*

Ironically, the Religious Right saw very little of its specifically religious agenda addressed during the administrations of favorite sons Ronald Reagan and the elder George Bush. Although both presidents talked the right language on abortion and school prayer, neither was able to effect any significant changes. The fall of the "evil" Soviet empire may have been hastened by the Reagan-Bush line, but it was so entirely unanticipated in the West that this can hardly have been a major factor. Wise investors used these years to internationalize the American economy even further, rather than the reverse, and China first became a significant economic player in American markets at this time. Reagan and Bush proved virtually powerless to resolve Holy Land crises—indeed, the worst single loss of American lives in the Holy Land, the bombing of the Marine barracks in Lebanon, occurred during the Reagan years. Also, the United States was plunged ever further into debt.

One might think, therefore, that a joint slate of Southern Baptists in the persons of Bill Clinton and Al Gore would have rallied the evangelical-fundamentalist cadre. This was hardly the case, however: Lukewarm Episcopalian George Bush was by far their choice. Indeed, a demonization process can again be said to have operated with respect to Clinton-Gore, who found themselves not only in trouble with the Christian Right but also precariously positioned in relation to the traditionally Democratic Jewish constituency. Rather than embrace such men, the Religious Right first put its hopes in 1996 on populist Catholic Republican Pat Buchanan, only to eke out a weak compromise with Bob Dole.

The idea of a Catholic president would have utterly horrified fundamentalists when that movement was founded, but a look at Buchanan's candidacy helps us to see the interplay between globalization and religion for the American Religious Right. The issues today are not over a "foreign power" (i.e., the pope) having control over the United States; rather, the Religious Right wants to assert authority in contradistinction to negotiation. The Religious Right is looking for leadership that will assert "traditional Judeo-Christian" moral principles as unassailably true. What Pat Buchanan offered was an "America first" agenda that was palpably uncompromising. He was, at least then, not a politician, and that had an appeal among a sector that increasingly came to assert that politics as "the art of compromise" is also an act of betrayal.

Why is this so? Again, no single reason accounts for any sociocultural complex; nevertheless, we cannot ignore in the growth of the Religious Right the operation of status variables in social stratification. James D. Davidson and colleagues have shown that mainline American religious groups are overrepresented among American elites and that among Protestants, there has been very little change in this proportion over time (Davidson, 1994; Davidson, Pyle, & Reyes, 1995; Pyle, 2006). Fundamentalist Christians, for whatever reason, are people who are not getting their fair share of the politicoeconomic pie. Although they may earn a decent living, they are at increasing distance from economic elites, and they perceive themselves to have little political control, even—perhaps especially—in their local communities (e.g., in public schools, housing projects, and so on). Faceless bureaucracies and court jurisdictions far from their communities mandate systems of action (or prohibit countervailing action) contrary to their perceptions of right and wrong. The more globalization advances, the more their sense of "place" in society recedes. At the same time, other religious groups, most notably Reform Jews and the religiously unaffiliated, advance ahead of the Christian fundamentalists into the political-economic elites. Hence, evangelical-fundamentalist Protestants, traditionalist Catholics, and Orthodox Jews form a loose political alliance that attempts to assert citizen control over local issues. The aim of the "stealth" candidates of the Christian Coalition in the early 1990s, for example, was to place religious conservatives on local boards of education, city councils, and county commissions. And it is certainly the case that George W. Bush's embrace of "faith-based" programs and "charitable choice" were especially directed toward this constituency rather than the historical Protestant or Catholic mainstream.

Islamization

Many Muslims would prefer, because of the historically Christian associations of the word fundamentalist, that the movement often termed "Islamic fundamentalism" be termed *Islamization* and its adherents *Islamicists*. The movement's roots are varied, but they can probably be traced to reactions to the British colonial presence in Egypt and in that part of India now known as Pakistan. Until the Six-Day War of 1967, however, this movement had little effect—although for different reasons, Islamic fundamentalists were largely sidelined, as were the United States' Christian fundamentalists. The failure of the Arab alliance to succeed in defeating the Israelis, however, began to give new urgency to Islamic conservatives.

The attack on Israel was the dream of Egyptian (later, United Arab Republic) president Gamal Abdal Nasser, largely a secularist, who enticed other secular Arab leaders to join his plan. When it failed, this began to allow an opening for conservative Muslim preachers to claim that the basis for the defeat was not Jewish military superiority but rather the failure of Muslims to immerse themselves adequately in Islam. Human pride rather than submission to Allah was at the heart of the Arab defeat.

The momentum for Islamization built slowly because most secular Arab leaders were reluctant to allow the mullahs (Islamic clergy) opportunities to promulgate their critiques. Economic pressures often intervened. Again, an increasing disparity between those largely secular Arabs who benefited from the oil trade and the rest of the population sent the disenfranchised looking for alternative explanations for their plight. University students, small-business people, craftspeople, and some members of the old middle class (not least the religious authorities or religious elites) provided fertile soil for the seeds of Islamization. Palestinians who were termed "terrorists" in the West were made heroes in the Muslim world. Nevertheless, such activities remained relatively marginal to the world system until 1978–1979, with the rise of Ayatollah Khomeini in Iran.

Perhaps no more perfect case of both the interaction of and confrontation between globalization and local intransigence could be imagined than Iran; indeed, in some ways, it stretched the imaginations of many social scientists, who gave inadequate weight to the religious dimension when they attempted to predict Iranian outcomes. Mohammad Reza Shah Pahlavi, Iran's ruler for almost four decades prior to the Iranian revolution, who ascended the throne at age 22, was a dedicated modernist. He rejoiced in U.S. political and economic support and enjoyed the Western lifestyle. He saw his vocation as bringing Iran into the forefront of global geopolitics: He claimed that "Iran could be the showcase for all of Asia. America cannot spread its assistance in every country everywhere. Here is the place with the best prospect for a great transformation" (quoted in Kimmel & Tavakol, 1986).

The shah may have been correct in his analysis, but in hindsight, we can see that he made at least three mistakes in its implementation: (a) Economically, he placed too much emphasis on oil and did not demand sufficient diversification of U.S. assistance to share the benefits of Iran's oil resources and geopolitical setting adequately throughout the population; (b) socioculturally, he demanded changes that exceeded the prerequisites of the project of modernization (such as not permitting the wearing of a veil by women attending universities, reducing support for mosques, and implementing policies to displace small shopkeepers); and (c) politically, he created a secret police force (SAVAK) that used extreme cruelty to attack those who disagreed with his policies.

By the late 1970s, spiraling inflation, population pressures in the cities, and a crisis on the world oil market clearly put the shah in trouble. That was not much of a surprise to American social scientists who were savvy in Middle Eastern studies. What was a surprise was the role that came to be played by the Islamicist Ayatollah Ruholla Khomeini in the foundation of the Islamic Republic of Iran. Why? Predominantly because secular social science had totally overlooked the persistence of the religious dimension as a possible trajectory for the demonstration of human resentment against oppression—this despite the fact that practically every foundational social theorist, including Karl Marx, had recognized the religious dimension as integrally connected to deprivation, and not merely a reflection of deprivation. The ayatollah's explanation of his appeal and success was that "we did not want oil, we did not want independence, we wanted Islam" (quoted in Kimmel & Tavakol, 1986).

What did he mean by that? The shah was a professed Muslim; this was not enough. What the ayatollah meant was a lifeworld-level affirmation of stability, a continuation of "things the way they always ought to have been." Note carefully the use of the word *ought*; it is important to understanding the fundamentalist dynamic because what fundamentalism protests against as much as anything in the internationalist vision of globalization is the relativization of cultural values that seems to be part and parcel of impersonal market "forces" that drive high-technology multinational capitalism. Only the most naive fundamentalist would claim that in some past time, "everyone" was religious or moral or both. What the fundamentalist would claim was that in the past there was a religioethical core within sociocultural systems that was generally acknowledged: sin was sin and truth was truth. Ironically, the world of the nation-state, whether in the Arab world or in Christian Europe, provided a buffering device that established cultural prerogatives. The Reformation principle of *cuius regio, eius religio* (whose rule, his religion) in the Christian world and Muslim principles surrounding the caliphate in the Ottoman empire and its sphere of influence had a commonsense reality for everyday activity, particularly when language separated major cultural groups. People who "talked different" *were* different. Every culture knew it was right and others were wrong. Common language and common religion went hand in hand.

Globalization changed this simple worldview; accommodation and compromise became the order of the day. When we look at Islamization efforts, for example, we see that with few exceptions they are directly proportional to involvement by a Muslim leader in the ethic (ethos) of globalization—that is, in that "shared and binding set of rules exogenous to any given society" of which John Meyer (1980, p. 117) speaks. The murder of Egyptian president Anwar Sadat in 1981 is an excellent but not the sole example. These global values were similar to the set of values to which the shah of Iran was at least giving lip service, and they are the basis on which female leader Benazhir Bhutto of Pakistan ultimately attempted (and failed) to sustain her claim to legitimacy. Although Americans often see specific acts of Islamicist terrorism directed against them, the bigger picture clearly shows the primary targets to be Muslim political leaders themselves. It is not "the American way of life" that is under attack by Islamicists but rather attempts to harmonize Islam with that way of life. Unlike the New Christian Right, most Islamicists are quite willing to let America go to hell if it wants to; what they resist are attempts by the global system of states, of which they see the United States as the principal economic and cultural actor, to alter their lifeworld.

Nowhere do the contradictions between the global system of states and the Islamic lifeworld become more pronounced than in the place given to the state of Israel, particularly by the United States. The state of Israel is an "offense" to Muslims, not merely because the Jews are people of a different religion—because Islam has generally been tolerant toward Jews, indeed in many cases far more so than Christianity. Rather, the state of Israel places into juxtaposition irrational and rational political policies, which themselves result from a unique religious configuration in the United States between Jews and the Christian Right. The creation of the state of Israel caused the undermining of the secular ideology of the nation-state in the Muslim world because, in a Western betrayal of its own commitments to the secular state, a religious ideology was used to justify the creation of Israel. The establishment of the state of Israel was clearly a response to the Holocaust, but it was also intimately related to fundamentalist Protestant understandings of the necessity for the reunion of the Jewish people at Jerusalem prior to some form of millennial return and reign of Jesus Christ. Inseparable from this is the demographic fact that from World War II to 2007, the United States had the largest Jewish population in the world, and the fact that U.S. citizens may hold unique joint citizenship in the

United States and Israel, a condition once virtually unknown elsewhere in the entire global system.

Muslims thus see a moral fissure in the ethic of globalization along these lines: The state of Israel has been established in the center of the historic Islamic world as an outpost for a new campaign to blot out the Islamic way of life. Like the crusades of old, this effort seeks to impede the practice of Islam through other standards of behavior, to which Muslims will be forced to conform or else by which they will be excluded from the benefits of global citizenship. From the Muslim point of view, by contrast, Islam itself provides a set of principles for universal world government. Here, then, is the center of the conflict between Islamization and globalization: As predominantly a system of rules, not beliefs, Islam offers an alternative to the dominant model of secular high-technology multinational capitalism that forms the basis for the global system of states in late modernity. Islamization proposes the universalization of the particular and, by contrast, it views the Western system as doing nothing but the same. That is, Islamicists see the Western system of globalization not as the implementation of "universal" human values but rather of specifically Western values. Islamicists might find some support for their position sociologically in Talcott Parsons's (1964) claim that the West has not been secularized but rather has been so permeated by the core values of the "Judeo-Christian ethic" as to render itself sacralized. Consider simply as one example U.S. postage stamps that carry the message "love."

This observation highlights one of the central propositions of globalization theory—particularly as articulated in the work of Roland Robertson and colleagues—namely, the role of ethics (ethoses) in constructing systems of interaction. Derived from the work of both Weber and Parsons, this point of view suggests that systems of valuing, whether or not they originate in material conditions, have an influence—perhaps a determinative influence—on subsequent political and economic relationships. Peoples whose worldview continues to be shaped by Islam, which is founded on a warrior ethic, will be essentially at variance from the core values of globalization.[7] Failure to recognize the depth to which these cultural components structure political organization leads Westerners to think that the assumptions of modern rationalism can provide a basis for "reasonable" compromise, when in fact they cannot. Instead, the warrior ethic sees the stand-off as a transcendent scenario in which different "strong men" contend for power. This view "came home" to Americans most powerfully in the events of September 11, 2001, with the al-Qaeda attacks on the World Trade Center—perhaps no more dramatic symbol of international capitalism could have been chosen for the *Star Wars*-esque scenario wherein the hub of globalization was attacked by the forces of an almost mythical strong man domiciled in one of the most remote parts of the world, governed by the most religiously reactionary regime.

A fascinating Weberian study of religion and political democracy by James Duke and Barry Johnson (1989) takes up a variant of Weber's Protestant ethic thesis to demonstrate that Protestantism has acted causally with respect to the development of political democracy. More to the point, however, is that, using four different indicators of democracy, Islamic nations appear at the bottom of five major religious groups on two of the four indicators and next to the bottom (higher only than tribal religions) on the other two. This is intensified by the fact that, whereas in the poorest nations (per capita gross national product [GNP] of less than $399) democracy is weak across the board, states with tribal religions drop out of the picture at the uppermost end of the GNP spectrum, but Islamic nations do not. In addition, the undemocratic nature of Islamic regimes is unrelated to whether or not a previous colonial regime was of a more or less democratically oriented religion (e.g., French Catholicism or English Protestantism).

We might turn this around and say that, from the Islamicist viewpoint, Muslim leaders who adopt the ethic of globalization as Meyer summarizes it have already betrayed their faith; that is, the warrior ethic mediates between "upstream" doctrine and day-to-day practice. This dynamic runs through the bulk of Islamic history, although the specific terms have differed across time. Ironically for the West, movements toward democratic pluralism on the global level have actually allowed Islamicist activities to grow in their degree of both local and international influence because the same means of communication, transport, and exchange that provide the infrastructure to globalization can be employed for the deployment of Islamicist values (much the same way, for example, that Christian televangelists in the United States use the very media of which they are hypercritical as the means for propagating their own views). Ayatollah Khomeini himself sent audiotape cassettes to Iran while he was a refugee in France, just as bin Laden appears to continue to provoke his adversaries and encourage his followers. Those societies of Muslim heritage that have most intentionally embraced Western democratic models have created the conditions for the growth of Islamicist parties, which in their extremism simply reinforce the tendencies that are already latent in the warrior ethic. This is particularly the case when the fruits of the globalization project are inequitably distributed—as they were, for example, in Iran.

9/11: Globalization and American Civil Religion

The phrase "God bless America" reflects not only the most popular slogan of the responses to the events of 9/11 as they appeared across the United States, but also the diffuse quality of American civil religion, which stands alongside and both complements and is complemented by the specific traditions that compose the American religious milieu. "God Bless America" was simultaneously slogan and song. It gave voice to American emotions. In addition, it has a history of association with national resurgence and the sociological corpus, as evidenced by the research of Robert Merton (1946) and colleagues on the war bond mass radio audience effort stimulated by singer Kate Smith, who had introduced the song to an immediately successful national reception in 1938, on the occasion of the twentieth anniversary of the World War I armistice.[8] Written by Irving Berlin during his own military service in 1918, the song was rejected for publication at that time, but would become in the radio voice of Smith a powerful rallying cry in the midst of World War II—of course, the fact that Berlin was Jewish was not lost in the midst of Nazi anti-Semitism (see www.katesmith.org/gba.html).

When examined in a religious rather than sociopolitical context, however, what is most immediately obvious is that the song actually says almost nothing about God other than a providential personalism. It primarily exults the goodness of the nation even as it affirms the existence of the deity as an ally for her good. Indeed, various commentators, for example, have noted that if the song were theologically authentic, the title would be something along the lines of "America Bless God." This observation underscores the important theoretical distinction between theological and religious use of language. Inasmuch as more than 95 percent of the U.S. population still acknowledges a belief in God (in relatively simplistic surveys), an appeal to God in this undefined way is an appeal to a singularly unifying religious symbol of high generality.

For the interpretation I am proposing, it is significant that this song (and secondarily the "Battle Hymn of the Republic"), rather than the more secular national anthem, became the expressive focus of the American reaction to the events of 9/11.[9] Within hours of the attack on the World Trade Center, and certainly by the time of the memorial observance at the National Cathedral, a case for the essentially religious character of the nation was increasingly articulated. The Puritan "errand into wilderness" to found a "city upon a hill" was reaffirmed. The United States began as a religious project—the product of a search for "freedom." The American Way of religious freedom, in this mythological recreation—which, as Robert Bellah (1999) has pointed out, is actually far more to be associated with Roger Williams than the "Pilgrim fathers"—was contrasted to a "foreign" way of religious tyranny and oppression. Civil religion in America thus is not as entirely diffuse as it seems at first blush, for there is an aura under which it operates, what Catherine Albanese has termed American "public Protestantism"—the characteristic of Americanism that led G. K. Chesterton (and others) to observe that, in the United States, "even the Catholics are Protestants."[10] Today, we could add other groups as well (e.g., "Protestant Buddhism"). Complementing this public Protestantism is the moral code of the Judeo-Christian ethic.

When the moment came for the specifically religious and the civilly religious to intersect in the events of 9/11, a crucial choice had to be made as to who should utter the prophetic word. Neither the liberal female bishop of Washington Episcopalians, nor the one-time leader of the Moral Majority was chosen. Instead, a man was selected who embodied for many Americans the public Protestantism that they had encountered the most through their lives: Billy Graham mounted the steps of Washington's National Cathedral.[11] Though technically a Baptist, Graham has always been noted as a public figure, both in the United States and abroad, associated neither with a specific church nor with an ostensibly commercial enterprise. In his sermon, Graham interfaced doctrinally specific religion and civil religion as he has done throughout his career. His return to the "national pulpit" in what may be this generation's most lasting public religious expression is in fact a rehabilitation of a figure whose once-brilliant reputation as a leading contender for "most admired American" or "most admired world figure" (by Americans) had been tarnished by too close an association with the Nixon White House. In calling America to repentance and renewal, Graham simultaneously renewed his own cultural capital as the living icon of the public Protestantism that forms the specifically religious interface for the diffuse civil religion of America. Did it occur to no one that Billy Graham had spent the bulk of his evangelistic ministry conducting *crusades*?

Public Protestantism and American civil religion particularly coalesced because the attacks of 9/11 constituted moral outrages inasmuch as they failed to conform to the norms of civil societies in regard to the conduct of public conflicts. By acting outside the norms of structured national conflicts, the perpetrators of these actions were seen to represent persons who had overstepped the bounds of toleration that are inherent in American civil religion. They both violated the norm of taking religion "too seriously," and simultaneously provided evidence of what happens when people take religion too seriously. For there is within American civil religion a juxtaposition of freedom *for* and freedom *from* religion; the latter was outrageously breached on 9/11. The breaching of this norm means that American civil religion itself was attacked. The perpetrators of 9/11 did not simply attack America in general; they attacked the American religious principle of laissez faire—which, of course, is also a political-economic worldview, theoretically the American economic worldview. This interplay of laissez faire religion and laissez faire economics allows constant ultimate value reinforcement for practical behavior. The appeal of Billy Graham is always to bring people to make their "own decision" about religious commitment—*Decision* being, in fact, the title of his magazine for supporters. The attacks on the World Trade Center and the Pentagon thus were cast not merely as military offences against internationally recognized "rules of engagement," but as assaults on core American values, including the religious value of freedom for/from. Not surprisingly, American Muslims quickly had to distance themselves from the contrary values enacted by the terrorists.

The renewal of American civil religion thus can be projected to have an ironic consequence—namely, the decline of the influence of right-wing religious extremism in the political sector within the United States, even as there is a more general turn to religious articulation of central values. This became quickly apparent in the days after the events of 9/11, when attempts by Christian Rightists to associate the attacks with such phenomena as gay/lesbian rights and feminism rang hollow and received scant hearing. American civil religion is not the worship of America, but it is an assertion of central values for the separation of religions from politics even as it asserts the religiousness of the core value of the nation as an instrument of divine intent, if not action. Hence, 9/11 served to knit together a stronger conservative Judeo-Christian core while paring away the fringes. Issues that once animated the extreme are being addressed within the core in a spirit of a search for reinvigorated central values, albeit in the context of a specific threat that may, in fact, obscure the root causes of the problems in question. The contradictions of multinational capitalism, for example, continue to be largely off the agenda of American political and religious discourse.

Not as apparent in the experience of 9/11 was the relationship between the attackers' priorities—the destruction of the state of Israel—and American civil religion. Perhaps because the initial military assaults against Israel in the 1960s by the likes of Egypt's Nasser were fully secularist—Nasser being a great foe of Islamicists, as was the Baath Party that brought Saddam Hussein to power in Iraq—American policymakers and military strategists largely missed or misread the buildup of Islamicist politics during the 1970s. The United States backed democratic efforts where they seemed viable while accepting the leadership of "strong men" as long as they did not threaten American "interests," specifically oil resources. Human rights issues were clearly secondary priorities. On the surface of it, for example, one might have thought Jimmy Carter and Ayatollah Khomeini would have been great friends as advocates of moral high ground; instead, they became mortal enemies. Because the state of Israel is intertwined with the Promised Land myth of America, on one hand, and because of the millennial expectations of American Protestants on the other, American leadership failed to understand the extent to which Islamicists view Israel both as an invasion of their sacred space and, more specifically, as an American client state. Americans by and large continue to fail to see that the Israeli presence in Palestine appears to Islamicists as an American "resettlement project," not essentially different from Soviet resettlements in, for example, the Baltic nations after World War II. Though perhaps born of the highest motives, nevertheless the establishment of the State of Israel, the resettlement of Jews in that territory, and the lack of adequate regard for the people already living there represent a Western incursion of unique significance entirely counter to the decolonization that otherwise characterized the post–World War II era. Hence, by its apparent ignorance and arrogance, the United States becomes the final superpower to be undone.

Undergirding these claims and counterclaims are biblical myths of ownership that extend thousands of years into the past, before either Christianity or Islam was ever named. The Promised Land—which is precisely what God is claimed to have given Abraham—was already populated when the children of Israel arrived. Palestinians claim a pre-Israelitic ancestry. The claims of modern Jews, furthermore, are historically corrupted by the fact that, if the term "Semitic" has any genuinely biological concomitants—rather than its fast-and-loose use by anti-Semites—then many, perhaps most, present-day Jews cannot possibly be biological descendants of those who occupied Judea at the time of the Roman destruction of Jerusalem. Hence, the Jewish claim to land rights in historic Israel is a spiritual one, rooted in religious myth—a myth ironically shared in part with the majority of actual occupants at the time of the creation of the modern state of Israel (i.e., Muslims). Jerusalem thus becomes the epicenter of myths of eternal significance with practical consequences. In this context, the specifically Judeo-Christian roots of American public Protestantism become quite clear. The claim to the "right of the Jewish people to a nation-state of their own" is shot through with specifically modern American "public Protestant" thinking about the nature of the world order. Neither Catholics nor Muslims, for example, would think this way. American history as it has been thought and taught in the United States is retrospectively applied as a universal world history of eternal significance. Manifest destiny is extended, as a result of American participation in World War II, from a "doctrine" regarding the development of the Western hemisphere to a universal law based on a specific civil-religious reading, which is also a political-economic reading, of the purpose of the United States as a nation of eternal significance: "In God we trust"—you can read it on all our money.

Because of the public Protestantism that pervades in the United States, the successes of the medieval Crusades are often minimized. The Latin Kingdom of Jerusalem, by contrast, can teach important lessons to those who would too quickly dismiss the persistence of Islamicist forces. Depending on how its boundaries are evaluated, it can be said to have lasted from 45 to 200 years. The modern state of Israel only recently celebrated its 50th anniversary: As Americans fight the current war against Islamicist terrorism, a perspective on what Max Weber termed the "warrior ethic" of Islam needs to be counterposed to the work ethic that is enshrined within American civil religion (see Swatos, 1995). These ethics represent two competing worldviews of "universal historical" significance. The Islamicist worldview presents a challenge to the United States entirely different in kind from that of the Soviet empire, against which the construction of American civil religious defenses were primarily constructed over the past half century. The terrorists who struck on 9/11 could have chosen many different targets. The specific choices they made need to be seen in their symbolic significance, and the importance of the consequences attached to those choices needs to be addressed in a renewed civil religion in America in the era of globalization. President Barack Obama may be moving the United States in this direction; indeed, the fact that someone named Barack Obama could be elected President of the United States constitutes something of a sea change. He has taken several steps in this direction: His break with his prior pastor whose rhetoric was one of social divisions, his decision to kick-off his serious campaigning in Berlin, and his address to the Egyptian parliament supporting a Palestinian homeland while continuing U.S. support for the state of Israel are all indicators of new trajectories that could be said to be "global savvy." These could provide the basis for a reordering of the global system that would have less divisive consequences, ultimately pointing toward a more stable global order. Whether or not this happens remains to be seen.

Conclusion

This final observation brings us to the heart of globalization theory as an explanation and demonstrates its value in understanding the "resurgence of religion" in our time. It is to be found in the simple definition of fundamentalism from T. K. Oommen that I introduced at the outset: "text without context." What happened between Maimonides, the great 12th-century Jewish philosopher, and Yigal Amir, the young Ultraorthodox Jew who assassinated Israeli Prime Minister Yitzhak Rabin in 1995, was that the context changed. I believe that Maimonides said what he said and that he meant what he said, and, in addition, I believe that in the context in which he was writing—namely, that of Jews as a pariah people—he was morally right. I also believe that Rabbi Abraham Hecht, leader of Brooklyn's largest Syrian synagogue, who sought to justify that assassination by reference to a passage from Maimonides, was absolutely wrong in his application of the text. He was wrong because he chose to discount context, which from a sociological standpoint is utterly stupid and, given the availability of sociological knowledge, morally unjustifiable.

In the previous paragraph, I spoke rather forcefully, perhaps, for a social theorist. I have done so quite intentionally, however, because as a move toward concluding this chapter on globalization, I want to make it as clear as I can that I believe that social theory—at least globalization theory, which is my responsibility in this chapter—has clear, practical application, and that by studying sociology, one actually does learn something useful. I will make my point as simply as I can: Sociology teaches us that *all sociocultural products arise out of sociocultural contexts.*

The words of Maimonides are sociocultural products. This does not mean that they are not true. It does mean that all truth is mediated by context. To say this is not the same thing as saying that "everything is relative" but rather to assert that sociocultural context is integral to the truthfulness of any proposition about social relations. This is most succinctly epitomized in sociology in the phrase "definition of the situation," coined by W. I. Thomas. Situations by their very nature have always been historically particular; hence, the universalizing dynamic of globalization creates an inherently perilous setting for misinterpretation when the particular is universalized (i.e., text is taken out of context). This is precisely what led to the death of Yitzhak Rabin. Globalization theory within sociology can make a crucial contribution to human welfare by demonstrating how understanding context is essential to the application of prescriptive texts, religious or otherwise.

The murder of Yitzhak Rabin, set in the context not only of the rise of political ultraorthodoxy in Judaism but also in relation to the other movements in Christianity and Islam that we have examined, lets us address another important theoretical argument in sociology—namely, the secularization controversy, specifically the supposed privatization of religion. Acknowledging that all these terms admit of definitional manipulation, there has nevertheless been a general debate in sociology about whether there has been a process of secularization, or a declining influence of religion, in the world over a period of centuries. This is a complex issue that cannot be solved in a few pages; what I want to indicate, however, is that the process of globalization itself has created a new publicization of religion (the "resurgence" of religion) that is at variance from the dominant chord of secularization theories. At the same time, however, the resurgent forms of at least the Abrahamic traditions that we have examined in this chapter are *new forms* of these religions.

Globalization theory can, in this respect, help us out of the quagmire of secularization. That is, secularization theories themselves are, generally speaking, unsociological in the same way that most fundamentalisms are unsociological, in that they tend to minimize context. Secularization theories generally treat religion as fixed rather than flexible. I have argued, by contrast, using the definition-of-the-situation concept, that if we understand that sociologically religions as forms of worship and ethical orientation are cultural products of infinite variability—precisely because they refer to a transcendent realm and hence are not subject to the same constraints as sociocultural systems rooted in material objects—then as sociologists, we should expect religions to change (see Swatos, 1990). For example, whereas Jesus Christ may be "the same, yesterday, today, and forever," Christianity is going to change. These changes may be dramatic or gradual, great or small, but they will occur as long as humans practice the religion. Indeed, the only religions that will not change are religions that cease to be practiced.

The global resurgence of religious traditions in new forms is evidence for both the truth of the relation of context to religion, which is inherent to the participation of human beings in religion, and the essential error of the secularization concept. Sociology teaches us that *all religion is secular* because all religion exists in relation to both the system and lifeworld; how specific religions orient and reorient themselves to the system and lifeworld will vary as systems and lifeworlds change. At the same time, however, systems and lifeworlds will include religious considerations in the total matrix of experience and interpretation that leads to specific action and hence to changes in patterns of action. The very processes that create the sociocultural contexts in and through which globalization theory becomes good theory also create the contexts for the resurgent religious forms that we tend to characterize as fundamentalisms. This dialectic between material and ideal culture is inherent in all sociocultural processes *in sæcula sæculorem*—forever. A complete globalization theory will predict countersystem tendencies by the very nature of the dynamics that create the system itself. Globalization theory explains both why the systems of religion that are rising are rising and why those that are falling are falling. It also explains why those forms that are rising are probably unlikely to achieve their ultimate goals, and why those that may appear to be falling may not experience the "withering" that either their critics or mourners expect (Beyer, 1994).

Notes

1. The different approaches within globalization are discussed profitably at considerable length in Beyer, P. (1994). *Religion and globalization* (pp. 15–44). London: Sage. Persons who wish to pursue at greater length the discussion initiated in this chapter will find Beyer's book an excellent starting point.

2. The self-profession of fundamentalists as fundamentalists (or, in other traditions, what may be translated into "pious ones" or "holy ones") is important to a consistent social scientific use of the term that can otherwise become a label for anyone who disagrees with us and maintains his or her position. If one looks in phone books or church advertisements in local newspapers (often appearing in Saturday editions), one can usually find Christian churches that openly profess themselves to be "fundamental" or "fundamentalist." An equivalent process occurs among Jews and Muslims, with the necessary changes of term being made for each tradition. Students of sociological theory need to be especially cautious regarding the dangers of using a concept as a label to stigmatize a sector of the population. The self-profession of fundamentalist identity in a positive way (e.g., advertising) legitimates its social scientific employment.

3. Charles Y. Glock, in his Furfey lecture, "The Ways the World Works" (*Sociological Analysis, 49,* 93–103), argues that the essential religious question is always most properly understood as one of how the world works, and different answers to this question account for religious differences, both small and great. On the concept of implicit religion, see Bailey, E. (1990). The implicit religion of contemporary society. *Social Compass, 37,* 483–509. In a variety of essays, I have similarly argued that the phenomenon that sociologists have often termed "secularization" is preeminently a shift in epistemologies rather than a move away from "religion"; see especially the introductory chapter in Swatos, W. H., Jr., & Gissurarson, L. R. (1996). *Icelandic spiritualism.* New Brunswick, NJ: Transaction Books.

4. To complicate matters even further, Icelandic naming laws now also permit children to take or be given their mother's Christian name to form their last name (matrinymic). This is interesting evidence of the ways in which particularisms and universalisms interact: Iceland has traditionally been relatively gender egalitarian, and this has been enhanced as this norm has been given greater positive sanction in world institutions. Hence, the laws are changed to reflect this universalistic norm but correspondingly are even more particularized in regard to naming. (Of course, just as anywhere else in the world, in everyday interaction people may use whatever name ["nickname"] they please; at issue is one's legal or citizenship name—hence the right of the nation-state to exercise authority over citizens.)

5. Vatro Murvar has indeed pointed out in "Some Tentative Modifications of Weber's Typology" (*Social Forces, 44,* 381–389) that in concrete instances, what has been called the

Occidental/Oriental contrast (following Max Weber) among world religions is really a contrast between the Western religious synthesis and the religions of antiquity generally.

6. Although there is now a practice among some contemporary Western Christians that uses a female pronoun for the deity (Her), the universal practice of the Abrahamic traditions, which are formally patriarchal traditions, is to refer to the deity using male forms of address.

7. The warrior ethic concept derives from the work of Max Weber. I discuss it at some length in Swatos, W. H., Jr. (1995). Islam and capitalism. In R. H. Roberts (Ed.), *Religion and the transformations of capitalism* (pp. 47–62). London: Routledge.

8. The Smith radiothon study conducted by Merton and his colleagues thus set the groundwork for all subsequent empirical mass persuasion research in the United States. Though the use of "God Bless America" was at one level purely coincidental, it also by that coincidence created a specific place for the song in mass settings.

9. Use of "God Bless America" in public civil religious contexts continued well beyond the days immediately following 9/11. For example, at the late-January Superbowl of 2002, it was sung prior to the national anthem, and video pans of players and audience saw persons both singing and, on occasion, wiping a tear from their eyes.

10. For example, in 1982, Congress passed and President Reagan signed a bill declaring 1983 the Year of the Bible. That resolution contained the defining phrase "the Bible, the Word of God." While the resolution was purely gratuitous in that it did not require or prohibit doing anything, it is inconceivable that, even before 9/11, a similar Year of the Koran resolution (containing the phrase "the Koran, the Word of God") would even have received a hearing.

11. Technically, the Cathedral of Sts. Peter and Paul, an Episcopalian institution.

References

Bellah, R. N. (1999). Is there a common American culture? In W. H. Swatos, Jr. & J. K. Wellman (Eds.), *The power of religious publics* (pp. 53–67). Westport, CT: Praeger.

Berger, P., & Kellner, H. (1974). *The homeless mind.* Garden City, NY: Doubleday.

Beyer, P. (1994). *Religion and globalization.* London: Sage.

Davidson, J. D. (1994). Religion among America's elite. *Sociology of Religion, 54,* 419–440.

Davidson, J. D., Pyle, R. E., & Reyes, D. V. (1995). Persistence and change in the Protestant establishment. *Social Forces, 74,* 157–175.

Duke, J. T., & Johnson, B. L. (1989). Protestantism and the spirit of democracy. In W. H. Swatos, Jr. (Ed.), *Religious politics in global and comparative perspective* (pp. 131–146). New York: Greenwood.

Eternal peace. (1996). *Iceland Reporter, 243,* 2.

Heller, A. (1995). Where are we at home? *Thesis Eleven, 41,* 1–18.

Kimmel, M. S., & Tavakol, R. (1986). Against Satan. In R. M. Glassman & W. H. Swatos, Jr. (Eds.), *Charisma, history, and social structure* (pp. 101–112). New York: Greenwood.

Lechner, F. J. (1985). Modernity and its discontents. In J. Alexander (Ed.), *Neofunctionalism* (pp. 157–176). Beverly Hills, CA: Sage.

Lechner, F. J. (1989). Cultural aspects of the modern world-system. In W. H. Swatos, Jr. (Ed.), *Religious politics in global and comparative perspective* (pp. 11–27). New York: Greenwood.

Lechner, F. J. (2004). Globalization. In G. Ritzer (Ed.), *Encyclopedia of social theory.* Thousand Oaks, CA: Sage.

Merton, R. K. (1946). *Mass persuasion: The social psychology of a war bond drive.* New York: Harper.

Meyer, J. (1980). The world polity and the authority of the nation-state. In A. Bergesen (Ed.), *Studies of the modern world-system* (pp. 109–137). New York: Academic Press.

Oommen, T. K. (1994). Religious nationalism and democratic polity. *Sociology of Religion, 55,* 455–472.

Pace, E. (2009). Convert, revert, pervert. In G. Giordan (Ed.), *Conversion in the age of pluralism* (pp. 189–212). Leiden: Brill.

Parsons, T. (1964). Christianity and modern industrial society. In L. Schneider (Ed.), *Religion, culture, and society* (pp. 273–298). New York: Wiley.

Pétursson, P. (1988). The relevance of secularization in Iceland. *Social Compass, 35,* 107–124.

Pyle, R. (2006). Trends in religious stratification. *Sociology of Religion, 67,* 61–79.

Robertson, R. (1992). *Globalization.* London: Sage.

Robertson, R., & Chirico, J.-A. (1985). Humanity, globalization, and worldwide religious resurgence. *Sociological Analysis, 46,* 219–242.

Robertson, R., & Lechner, F. (1985). Modernization, globalization, and the problem of culture in world-systems theory. *Theory, Culture and Society, 2,* 103–118.

Schoenfeld, E. (1987). Militant religion. In W. H. Swatos, Jr. (Ed.), *Religious sociology* (pp. 125–137). New York: Greenwood.

Swatos, W. H., Jr. (1990). Renewing "religion" for sociology. *Sociological Focus, 23,* 141–153.

Swatos, W. H., Jr. (1995). Islam and capitalism: A Weberian perspective on resurgence. In R. H. Roberts (Ed.), *Religion and the transformations of capitalism* (pp. 47–62). London: Routledge.

DISCUSSION QUESTIONS

1. When you describe a person as a "fundamentalist," or you hear someone described that way, what kinds of behaviors do you associate with that description? Do you view this description as basically positive or negative? Why?

2. In your own usage of the term "fundamentalist," would you differentiate it from the label "very religious"? For example, does your understanding of the statement "Kim is a fundamentalist" differ from your understanding of the statement "Kim is very religious"? How?

3. If *fundamentalism* may be defined as "text without context," can you think of any examples from your own experience or reading other than the context of the historical religions in which this term might be applied? What are they?

4. Technology—for example, in the form of fax and Internet communications—has played a significant role in a number of world-altering events, such as the pro-democracy demonstrations in Beijing's Tiananmen Square, the ending of the Soviet empire with "the fall of the Wall," as well as the attack on the World Trade Center. While Americans have tended to celebrate the first two, they deplore the latter. What options do you see for ensuring uses of technology that advance global civilization, and who do you think is best situated to determine what constitutes an advance?

5. Religion can be a significant force contributing to globalization, particularly those religions that seek converts to their faith. Based on your understanding of current events in the Middle East, discuss the ways that religions' globalization contributes to conflict. Is such conflict inevitable? If not, what can be done to avert conflict or, once it has occurred, to remedy the situation?

Index

A. E. Staley Company, 8, 17–18, 20, 30, 33, 38n1, 39n10
AA (Alcoholics Anonymous), 130–131
AAMCO Transmissions, 50
Able-bodiedness, 294–296
Abortion, 404
Abrahamic religions, 400–402, 416n6
AC Sparkplug, 231
Actes de la Recherche en Sciences Sociales (Bourdieu, ed.), 373
Activism
  net activism and, 68, 81–84
  social change features of, 260–261
Adorno, Theodor W., 230, 249–250n10, 251n19, 261
Advanced capitalism, 233, 234, 237–241
Advertising
  PFLAG support groups and, 386–387
  simulation and, 355–356
Africa, 74 (table), 137n2
African Americans
  alcohol consumption and, 117, 137n1
  automobile ownership statistics of, 190, 193
  automobile prices paid by, 142, 189–193, 191 (table), 205–208, 218n1
  bargaining power, capital, and dependency of, 191 (table), 193–196, 219nn4–5
  bargaining process and, 186–187, 200–204
  Chicago population statistics regarding, 189
  cosmetic surgeries of, 282
  crime and, 162, 169–170, 175, 176
  HIV/AIDS and, 292
  Internet shopping by, 207
  "John Henry" folk hero and, 291, 298n6

median income of, 189, 190–191
outcome dependency and, 192
price comparison opportunities and, 218–219n2
risk behavior of, 291–292
segregation (Chicago) of, 189
well-being measures and, 143
See also Race-based critical theory
After the Smoke Clears: Struggling to Get by in Rustbelt America (Mellon), 247
Airline flight attendant. *See* Flight attendants
Albanese, Catherine, 410
Alcohol consumption
  African Americans and, 117, 137n1
  Alcoholics Anonymous (AA) and, 130–131
  alcoholism, alcoholics and, 130
  alcoholism treatment and, 130–132
  alcohol-related problems and, 132–134
  among strangers and regulars in taverns, 123–125
  conclusions regarding, 136–137
  conflict over, 115–120
  contemporary drinking problems and, 129
  custom and fashion regarding, 119–120
  drinking places for, 120–125, 137n2
  18th Amendment repeal and, 117–118
  employees, labor unions and, 118–119
  group dynamics and, 128–129, 134–136
  interactions in taverns and, 125–129
  legal drinking age and, 132
  minimal legal drinking age (MLDA) and, 132–134
  Prohibition and, 116, 117–118, 130, 137n1
  risk behavior and, 293

"real" selves in a commodified world
and, 345–346
roles in, 330–332
roles in, conflicting expectations, 343–345
scripts in, 332–334
selfhood and, 329
stages and sets in, 335–338
"teams" and, 329
unmeant gestures concept and, 319
See also Goffman, Erving
Draus, Paul J., 234
Dreger, Alice, 287
Drexel Burnham Lambert, 215
Drunken Comportment: A Social
Explanation (MacAndrew and
Edgerton), 136, 137–138n3
Ducheneaut, Nicolas, 83
Duke, James, 408–409
Duncan, Margaret Carlisle, 290
Dunlop Tire, 18, 33
Dupont, 231
Durant, Bill, 231, 232, 256n76
Durkheim, Émile
on anomie, 89
class analysis of religious systems and, 157
on collective, group life, 86–87
cyborg societies and, 70, 102–105
on division of labor, 3, 99–102, 101 (table)
The Division of Labor written by, 103
on emotional attachment to a society, 94
empirically linked theory of, 375
on "free market," 89
functionalist theory of, 152
Erving Goffman and, 145
on human community, 3
influence of, xii, 1
on mechanical vs. organic societies, 3,
70, 99, 100–102, 101 (table)
organistic thinking and, 99
racial designations of, 401
on regulation and integration, 69,
86–87, 88 (table), 89, 92
on religion of humanity, 87, 169
on rituals, 89
"rush of energy" phrase of, 87
on Georg Simmel, 114
on social rituals, 87–88
on social solidarity, 3, 84–88, 93, 103
on society, 84
structuralism and, 145
on symbolism, 157, 377
See also Electronic gatherings
Eating disorders, 287, 293–294
Eco, Umberto, 360, 361

EcoNet civic network, 82
Economic Policy Institute, 18, 24
Edgerton, Robert, 136
Edgley, Charles, 353
Edsforth, Ronald, 231
Education
in Flint Michigan, 245-246
nonhuman technologies element in, 58
virtual world applications and, 80
Efficiency, 48, 51–53
See also McDonaldization
Egoism, 88–89, 88 (table)
Egypt, 39n3, 68, 405, 407, 411, 413
18th Amendment, 117–118
Eisenberg, Anne F., 146, 371
Electronic gatherings
building communities of memory in,
98–99
celebrating rituals in, 96–97
changing collective consciousness and,
103–104
computer-mediated communications
and, 68
as Durkheimian societies, 84–105
frequently asked questions (FAQs)
element of, 98
gift exchanges in, 97–98
human-computer interaction and, 68
integration in, 94–99
regulation mechanisms in, 89, 90–94
rules of conduct, definition of, 90–92
rules of conduct, communicating and
clarifying rules of, 92–93
rules of conduct, enforcement of, 93–94
social solidarity and, 84–88, 93, 98–99
Usenet newsgroups and, 77
See also Internet
Electronic mail (e-mail), 71
Elementary Forms of the Religious Life, The
(Durkheim), 87
E-mail, 71
Emerson, Richard, 142, 187, 202, 205
Emoticons, 91
Employer Policy Foundation, 25
Encyclopedia Britannica, 21
Enterprise Company, 306, 312, 314–323
Entertainment Tonight, 358
Entrepreneurs
"environments of action" and, 156
neofunctionalism and, 156, 157–158
Environmentalism
civic networks and net activism
and, 81, 82
fast-food industry and, 61